MEDIEVAL CHURCH LAW
AND THE ORIGINS OF THE
WESTERN LEGAL TRADITION

KENNETH PENNINGTON

MEDIEVAL CHURCH LAW AND THE ORIGINS OF THE WESTERN LEGAL TRADITION

A Tribute to Kenneth Pennington

❀

EDITED BY

Wolfgang P. Müller & Mary E. Sommar

The Catholic University of America Press

Washington, D.C.

Library of Congress Cataloging-in-Publication Data
Medieval church law and the origins of the Western legal tradition :
a tribute to Kenneth Pennington / edited by Wolfgang P. Müller &
Mary E. Sommar.
p. cm.
Includes bibliographical references and index.
ISBN-13: 978-0-8132-1462-7 (cloth : alk. paper)
ISBN-13: 978-0-8132-1868-7 (pbk)   1. Canon law—History.
2. Law—Europe—History—Sources.   I. Pennington, Kenneth.
II. Müller, Wolfgang P., 1960–   III. Sommar, Mary E., 1953–   IV. Title.
KBR190.M43 2006
262.9'2—dc22
2005033358

Contents

❉

Contents

Contents

Preface

On October 6, 2006, Kenneth Pennington celebrates his sixty-fifth birthday. The present volume, with contributions from his teachers, colleagues, friends, and former doctoral students, was compiled to honor him on this occasion and as a tribute to his outstanding scholarly and academic achievements.

From his earliest days as an historian, Kenneth Pennington's research interests have focused on questions about *Church Law and the Origins of Western Jurisprudence*, a life-long pursuit that is recalled in the title of this book. Ken's scholarly agenda took shape under the influence of his principal academic advisers, who are themselves among the leaders of the modern study of medieval canon law. Mentored by James Brundage, Ken received his master's degree in history from the University of Wisconsin in 1967; he then moved to Cornell University where he completed his Ph.D. in 1972 under the supervision of Brian Tierney. Ken's post-doctoral years were marked by prolonged visits to Stephen Kuttner's Institute of Medieval Canon Law in Berkeley, California. Kuttner's exacting standards of manuscript study awakened in Ken an enduring fascination, not only with the development of medieval legal doctrine, but also with intricate philological questions related to the authorship, genesis, and transmission of important juristic texts.

While still completing his doctorate, Ken joined the department of history at Syracuse University as assistant professor in 1971 and remained there for the following three decades. In 2001, he transferred to his current academic home and became the Kelly-Quinn Professor of Ecclesiastical and Legal History at The Catholic University of America in Washington, D.C. Through years of successful teaching, writing, and far-flung organizational activities, Ken built for himself an international reputation as one of the foremost experts in the history of medieval jurisprudence. Graduate students worldwide who are exploring this subject cannot help but be aware of his name and of his role as a key figure in the field. Ken is indeed very widely known: he is the author of numerous learned articles and has edited any number of books and journals. He has also produced two major scholarly monographs, one of which analyzes the twelfth and thirteenth-century canonists' teachings concerning the relationship between the *Pope and Bishops* (1984); the other explores late medieval jurists' reflections on the proper balance between the sovereign will of *The Prince and the Law* (1993).[1] Ken conducted much of the research leading up to these two works while on sabbatical in Florence (1980–81) and in Munich (1985–87), time he also used to establish close and enduring professional friendships with German and Italian medievalists, among them several members of the Monumenta Germaniae Historica. Ken has also played a prominent role as host or co-host of the quadriennial International Congress of Medieval Canon Law, first at Syracuse University in 1996 and then, together with Uta-Renate Blumenthal, at The Catholic University of America in 2004. Ken's great charm and tireless work as a promoter of international gatherings have also been in demand in places outside of the United States. In Italy, perhaps his favorite European destination, he has acted (since 1993) as co-director of the International School of the Ius commune, together with Manlio Bellomo conducting annual sesssions at the Ettore Majorana Center in Erice, Sicily.

Ken's impact on the scholarly community is, of course, far too great to be measured within the covers of a single book. Our volume offers but a small selection of potential contributors and topics, in an attempt that barely reflects the range of his interests and of his personal ties. Some of the authors remember him as an undergraduate and as a graduate student at Wisconsin and Cornell, and in Berkeley. Others came to know him later as his own graduate students, or as students from other universities to whom Ken provided advice and support. Still others have been engaged in scholarly exchanges or have been contributors to one or more of Ken's many editorial enterprises. It is in this last capacity that Ken has repeatedly collaborated with David McGonagle, director of Catholic University of America Press. They have long shared responsibility for the publication of two series, the monographs printed as part of the *Studies in Medieval and Early Modern Canon Law* (since 1987) and the *History of Medieval Canon Law*, co-edited by Ken and Wilfried Hartmann (since 1988). When we asked David to lend his support to a *Festschrift* in Ken's honor, he immediately threw his full weight behind the project. Our most heartfelt thanks go to him and to the editorial staff of CUA Press, especially to Susan Needham who helped us resolve difficult problems of copy-editing in endless telephone conversations. We also wish to express our gratitude to Ken's wife, Marlene, and to Grace-Ann Lewis of the Catholic University of America staff. As work on the volume progressed, we have relied on their vigilance as our covert agents, to provide us valuable 'private' data about Ken and his latest whereabouts.

The editors, contributors, and all those active 'behind the scenes' hope that the result of their concerted efforts reaches Ken as a token of their affection and as a sign of their profound professional respect.

WPM & MES

1. For a full list of Kenneth Pennington's published works, see his Bibliography, pp. 389–97.

Abbreviations

Note: For abbreviated references to biblical texts, see *Vulgata;* to Latin and Greek authors of Antiquity, see *Thesaurus Linguae Latinae;* to canonical collections before 1140, see Kéry, *Can. Coll.* and *KanonesJ;* to canonical collections, 1140–1191, see Chodorow-Duggan; to twelfth-century manuscripts of the *Decretum,* see Weigand, *Glossen.*

ACA = Archivo (Arxiu) de la Corona de Aragón, Barcelona
AD = Archives Départmentales
AHP = *Archivum historiae pontificiae* 1– (1963–)
AKKR = *Archiv für katholisches Kirchenrecht* 1– (1857–)
AS = Archivio di Stato
ASV = Archivio Segreto Vaticano, Vatican City
BA = Biblioteca Ambrosiana, Milan
BAV = Biblioteca Apostolica Vaticana, Vatican City
BC = Biblioteca Capitolare / Biblioteca Capitolar
BL = British Library, London
BM = Bibliothèque Municipale
BMCL = *Bulletin of Medieval Canon Law,* n.s. 1– (1971–)
BML = Biblioteca Medicea Laurenziana, Florence
BN = Bibliothèque Nationale / Biblioteca Nazionale / Biblioteca Nacional
BNU = Biblioteca Nazionale Umbertina, Turin
BP = Biblioteca del Palacio
BSB = Bayerische Staatsbibliothek
BU = Biblioteca Universitaria
C. = *Causa,* see *Decretum* (subdivision of part two)
c. = *capitulum* (chapter)
CCL = *Corpus Christianorum. Series Latina* 1– (Turnhout 1953–); with CCL cont. med. 1– (Turnhout 1973–)
CIC = *Corpus iuris civilis,* ed. T. Mommsen, P. Krüger, R. Schöll, and W. Kroll (3 vols.; Berlin 1872–95)
Clm = Codex latinus monacensis (Latin manuscripts at Munich, BSB)
COD[3] = *Conciliorum Oecumenicorum Decreta,* ed. G. Alberigo et al. (Bologna 1973[3])
CSEL = *Corpus scriptorum ecclesiasticorum Latinorum* 1– (Vienna 1866–)

can. = canon

Canones-Sammlungen = *Die Canones-Sammlungen zwischen Gratian und Bernhard von Pavia*, ed. E. Friedberg (Leipzig 1897; reprint Graz 1958)

Chartularium = *Chartularium Studii Bononiensis. Documenti per la storia dell'Università di Bologna dalle origini fino al secolo XV* 1– (Bologna 1909–)

Chodorow-Duggan = *Decretales ineditae saeculi XII*, ed. S. Chodorow and C. Duggan (MIC B.4; 1982)

Clem. = *Clementinae*, ed. E. Friedberg, *Corpus iuris canonici* 2 (Leipzig 1881), part III

Cod. = *Codex*, see CIC (part three)

Coing, *Handbuch* = H. Coing (ed.), *Handbuch der Quellen und Literatur der neueren europäischen Privatrechtsgeschichte* (3 vols.; Munich 1973–88)

1 Comp., 2 Comp.,..., 5 Comp. = *Compilatio prima (-quinta)*, ed. E. Friedberg, *Quinque Compilationes antiquae necnon Collectio canonum Lipsiensis* (Leipzig 1882)

cont. med. = *continuatio medievalis*, see CCL

Councils & Synods = *Councils & Synods with Other Documents Relating to the English Church*, ed. M. Powicke and C. Cheney (2 vols.; Oxford 1964)

D. = *Distinctio*, see *Decretum* (subdivision of parts one, three)

d.a.c. = *dictum ante capitulum* (Gratian's comment before *Decretum* chapter)

d.p.c. = *dictum post capitulum* (Gratian's comment after *Decretum* chapter)

DA = *Deutsches Archiv für Erforschung des Mittelalters* 1– (1943–)

DBI = *Dizionario biografico degli italiani* 1– (1960–)

DDC = *Dictionnaire de droit canonique* (7 vols.; 1935–65)

DThC = *Dictionnaire de théologie catholique* (15 vols.; 1910–50)

De cons. = *De consecratione*, see *Decretum* (title of part three)

De pen. = *De penitentia*, see *Decretum* (title of subdivision, C.33 q.3, of part two)

Decretum = *Decretum Gratiani*, ed. E. Friedberg, *Corpus iuris canonici* 1 (Leipzig 1879)

Dig. = *Digesta*, see CIC (part two)

Donahue, *Records* = C. Donahue, Jr. (ed.), *The Records of the Medieval Ecclesiastical Courts* (2 vols.; Berlin 1989–94)

ED = *Enciclopedia del diritto* 1– (1958)

EHR = *English Historical Review* 1– (1886–)

EOMIA = *Ecclesiae orientalis monumenta iuris antiquissima*, ed. C. Turner (2 vols.; Oxford 1899–1939)

Extrav. Jo. XXII= *Extravagantes Johannis pape XXII*, ed. E. Friedberg, *Corpus iuris canonici* 2 (Leipzig 1881), part IV

FMSt = *Frühmittelalterliche Studien* 1– (1967–)

fol. = *folium (folia)*

Fournier–Le Bras = P. Fournier and G. Le Bras (eds.), *Histoire des collections canoniques en Occident. Depuis les fausses décrétales jusqu'au Décrét de Gratien* (2 vols.; Paris 1931–32)

Germ. Abt. = Germanistische Abteilung; see ZRG

Germania pontificia = *Regesta pontificum Romanorum: Germania pontificia* 1–, ed. P. Kehr et al. (Berlin and Göttingen 1910–)

HJb = *Historisches Jahrbuch* 1– (1880–)

HMCL = History of Medieval Canon Law, ed. W. Hartmann and K. Pennington (Washington, DC 1999–)

HRG = *Handwörterbuch zur deutschen Rechtsgeschichte* (5 vols.; Berlin 1971–98)

HSA = Hauptstaatsarchiv

Hefele-Leclercq = C. Hefele and H. Leclercq, *Histoire des conciles d'après les documents originaux* (19 vols.; Paris 1907–38)

Hinschius, *System* = P. Hinschius, *System des katholischen Kirchenrechts mit besonderer Rücksicht auf Deutschland* (6 vols.; Berlin 1869–97)

Ibid. = *Ibidem* (i.e. 'as above', in the immediately preceding reference)

Inst. = *Institutiones,* see CIC (part one)

Italia pontificia = *Regesta pontificum Romanorum: Italia pontificia,* ed. P. Kehr et al. (10 vols.; Berlin and Zurich 1906–75)

JE = P. Jaffé and P. Ewald (eds.), *Regesta pontificum Romanorum* 1.1 [to 882] (Leipzig 1885)

JK = P. Jaffé and F. Kaltenbrunner (eds.), *Regesta pontificum Romanorum* 1.2 [882–1143] (Leipzig 1885)

JL = P. Jaffé and S. Löwenfeld (eds.), *Regesta pontificum Romanorum* 2 [1143–98] (Leipzig 1888)

Juristen[2] = *Juristen. Ein biographisches Lexikon. Von der Antike bis zum 20. Jahrhundert,* ed. M. Stolleis (Munich 2001[2])

Kan. Abt. = Kanonistische Abteilung; see ZRG

KanonesJ = L. Fowler-Magerl, *A Selection of Canon Law Collections Compiled Between 1000 and 1140. Access With Data Processing* (Piesenkofen 2003)

Kéry, *Can. Coll.* = L. Kéry, *Canonical Collections of the Early Middle Ages (ca. 400–1140). A Bibliographical Guide to the Manuscripts and Literature* (HMCL; Washington, DC 1999).

Kuttner, *Repertorium* = S. Kuttner, *Repertorium der Kanonistik 1140–1234* (Studi e testi 71; Vatican City 1937)

L'âge classique = G. Le Bras, C. Lefebvre, and J. Rambaud, *L'âge classique 1140–1378. Sources et théorie du droit* (Histoire du Droit et des Institutions de l'Eglise en Occident 7; Paris 1965)

LMA = *Lexikon des Mittelalters* (9 vols.; 1980–98)

LThK[3] = *Lexikon für Theologie und Kirche* (11 vols.; 1993–2001[3])

MGH = *Monumenta Germaniae Historica*

MIC A.1–/B.1–/C.1– = *Monumenta iuris canonici,* series A/B/C, vol. 1– (Vatican City 1981–/1973–/1965–)

MIÖG = *Mitteilungen des Instituts für österreichische Geschichtsforschung* 1– (1880–)

Maassen, *Geschichte* = F. Maassen, *Geschichte der Quellen und der Literatur des canonischen Rechts im Abendlande* 1 (Graz 1870)

Mansi = G. Mansi, *Sacrorum conciliorum nova et amplissima collectio* (31 vols.; Florence 1759–98)

NA = *Neues Archiv* 1–50 (1876–1935)

NB = Nationalbibliothek

n.s. = New series / nova series / nouvelle serie / nuova serie

Nov. = *Novellae;* see CIC (part four)

ÖAKR = *Österreichisches Archiv für Kirchenrecht* 1– (1951–)

ÖNB = Österreichische Nationalbibliothek, Vienna

PL = *Patrologia Latina,* ed. J.-P. Migne (221 vols.; Paris 1844–55, 1862–65)

p(p). = page(s), in a manuscript or early print, as opposed to fol.

Pauly-Wissowa = *Paulys Realencyclopaedie der classischen Altertumswissenschaft,* ed. A. Pauly, G. Wissowa et al. (58 vols., 15 supplements, 1 register; Stuttgart 1894–1980)

Po. = A. Potthast, *Regesta pontificum Romanorum* [1198–1304] (2 vols.; Berlin 1874–75)

Proc. = *Proceedings of the Second* (Third, . . . etc.) *International Congress of Medieval Canon Law* (identified by place), ed. MIC C.1– (1965–)

q. = *quaestio,* see *Decretum* (subdivision of part II)

RDC = *Revue de droit canonique* 1– (1951–)

REDC = *Revista española de derecho canonico* 1– (1946–)

RHDFE = *Revue historique de droit français et étranger* 1– (1922–)

RIDC = *Rivista internazionale di diritto comune* 1– (1990–)

RPG = *Repertorium Poenitentiariae Germanicum* 1–, ed. L. Schmugge et al. (Tübingen 1996–)

RSDI = *Rivista di storia del diritto italiano* 1– (1928–)

Rom. Abt. = Romanistische Abteilung; see ZRG

SB = Staatsbibliothek

Sb. = *Sitzungsberichte der* (. . .) *Akademie,* Academy Proceedings, identified by place

SG = *Studia Gratiana* 1– (1953–)

s.v. = *sub verbo,* medieval commentary 'on the words' (specified in italics)

Sarti-Fattorini = M. Sarti and M. Fattorini, *De claris archigymnasii Bononiensis professoribus* (1769), ed. C. Albicini and C. Malagola (2 vols.; Bologna 1888–96)

Schmitz, *Bußbücher* = H. Schmitz, *Die Bußbücher und das kanonische Bußverfahren* (2 vols.; Stuttgart 1883–98)

Schulte, QL = J. F. von Schulte, *Geschichte der Quellen und Literatur des canonischen Rechts von Gratian bis auf die Gegenwart* (3 vols.; Stuttgart 1875–80)

Settimane = *Settimane di studio del Centro Italiano di studi sull'alto medioevo* 1– (1956–)

Stegmüller = F. Stegmüller, *Repertorium biblicum Medii Aevi* (9 vols.; Madrid 1940–77)

TRE = *Theologische Realenzyklopädie* (36 vols.; 1977–2004)

TRG = *Tijdschrift voor Rechtsgeschiedenis* 1– (1918–)

TUI = *Tractatus universi iuris,* ed. G. Ziletti (18 vols.; Venice 1583–86)

Typologie = Typologie des sources du moyen âge occidental 1– (Turnhout 1972–)

UB = Universitätsbibliothek

VI = *Liber sextus,* ed. E. Friedberg, *Corpus iuris canonici* 2 (Leipzig 1881), part II

Vulgata = *Bibliorum sacrorum iuxta Vulgatam Clementinam nova editio,* ed. A. Gramatica (Vatican City 1929, or any subsequent edition)

WH = W. Holtzmann, *Studies in the Collections of Twelfth-Century Decretals,* ed., rev., and trans. C. Cheney and M. Cheney (MIC B.3; 1979)

Wahrmund, *Quellen* = L. Wahrmund, *Quellen zur Geschichte des römisch-kanonischen Processes im Mittelalter* (5 vols.; Innsbruck 1905–31)

Walther = H. Walther, *Proverbia sententiaeque Latinitatis medii aevi. Lateinische Sprichwörter und Sentenzen des Mittelalters in alphabetischer Anordnung* (6 vols.; Göttingen 1963–69)

Wasserschleben = F. Wasserschleben, *Die Bußordnungen der abendländischen Kirche* (Halle/S. 1851)

Weigand, *Glossen* = R. Weigand, *Die Glossen zum Dekret Gratians* (SG 25–26; Rome 1991)

X = *Liber extra (Decretales Gregorii IX)*, ed. E. Friedberg, *Corpus iuris canonici* 2 (Leipzig 1881), part I

ZRG = *Zeitschrift der Savigny-Stiftung für Rechtsgeschichte* (in three divisions: Roman, Canon, and German Law) 1– (1880–)

MEDIEVAL CHURCH LAW
AND THE ORIGINS OF THE
WESTERN LEGAL TRADITION

Introduction

Medieval Church Law as a Field of Historical Inquiry

Wolfgang P. Müller

❋

The Subject

The study of medieval ecclesiastical norms, known among experts as 'medieval canon law' (from the Greek word, *kanōn*, for 'rule'), concerns the period roughly coincid-
ing with the Western Middle Ages, between 500 and 1500 A.D. Its geographical focus
includes all territories of the Latin Church, as opposed to the Eastern European areas
of 'Byzantine Canon Law', which rather followed Greek liturgy and were culturally ori-
ented toward the capital of the former Eastern Roman Empire, Constantinople or Byzantium.[1] The fundamental difference between the two, Greek and Latin, hemispheres,
politically reinforced by the fourth-century division of the Roman Empire and sealed
by the schism (from 1054) between Eastern Orthodox and Western Catholic Christianity, has further prompted modern students to extend their investigations to the Latin
canonical texts of late Antiquity. Regarding the exact chronological boundaries separating medieval canon law from early modernity, on the other hand, the definitive break-
up of religious unity in the West, marked by the establishment of Protestant churches
in the 1520s and 1530s and the Catholic 'Counter'-Reformation set into motion by the
Council of Trent (1545–63), has commonly been accepted as the demise of the medieval
Church, in general as well as in legal and institutional terms.

Within the given spatial and chronological limitations of medieval canon law, scholars have subdivided their subject into two principal phases, one preceding, and the other beginning with, the publication of Gratian's 'Concordance of Discordant Canons', or
Decretum, around the year 1140. The significance of the distinction between canon law
'pre-Gratian' and 'post-Gratian' cannot be overrated. To capture its enormous cultural

---

1. See C. Gallagher, *Church Law and Church Order in Rome and Byzantium. A Comparative Study* (Aldershot
2002); see also *The History of Byzantine and Eastern Canon Law to 1500* (HMCL; Washington, DC; to appear).

connotations, legal historian Manlio Bellomo has succinctly characterized the time from 500 to 1140 as an 'Age Without Jurists'.[2] Conversely, Stephan Kuttner has greeted the contribution of Gratian and his successors as 'The Revival of Jurisprudence', that is, the return of professional lawyers who, upon the demise of Roman Antiquity, had completely disappeared from the Latin West.[3] In the light of Kuttner's and Bellomo's sweeping affirmations, what exactly constituted the essence of Gratian's accomplishment, rendering it, as is widely assumed, an event of truly epochal proportions?

Although difficult to imagine for modern Westerners, the societal conditions permitting continued reliance on professional legal expertise had been wanting prior to the twelfth-century rise of 'Universities', urban centers of higher education that offered students the prototypes of a 'scholastic' study program. Gratian belonged to the generation of intellectual 'Founding Fathers', who managed to place the newly emerging theological, medical, and legal disciplines on sound 'scientific' foundations. As it turned out, he put together a textbook for lectures in canon law that was comprehensive, systematic, and methodically compelling at the same time. In classrooms across Western Europe, the final version of his *Decretum* quickly eclipsed all older canon law collections. While preserving most of the authoritative material compiled and transmitted over the centuries, Gratian chose to display the normative tradition in an unprecedented dialectic arrangement, juxtaposing canons in support of *(pro)* as well as against *(contra)* propositions said to reveal the canonical truth. In addition, Gratian supplied a running commentary *(dicta)* of his own, expressly inviting readers to identify contradictions between 'Discordant Canons'. Through informed reasoning, they were to be reduced to the 'Concordance' of real, that is to say, coherent 'canonistic' doctrine. For many generations, concern about internal inconsistencies between Church norms had been minimal, limited to single-handed corrections or rhetorical exercises in the prefaces of early medieval canon law collections. The greatest 'turning point' in the history of canon law was reached when scholastic teachers like Gratian, swept into the limelight by a rapidly growing intellectual trend, established the elimination of logical 'dissonances' for the sake of overall doctrinal 'harmony' as the principal assignment of academic professionals.[4] The canonists, juristic experts trained in the canons, and the 'science' of canon law were born.

2. M. Bellomo, *The Common Legal Past of Europe 1000–1800,* trans. L. Cochrane (Washington, DC 1995) 22–41 (heading of chapter 2); see also the title of Part One in the present volume.

3. S. Kuttner, 'The Revival of Jurisprudence', in: *Renaissance and Renewal in the Twelfth Century,* ed. R. Benson and G. Constable (Cambridge, MA 1982) 299–323; reprinted in: S. Kuttner, *Studies in the History of Medieval Canon Law* (Aldershot 1990) no. 3, with 'Retractationes III', ibid. 5–7.

4. The quotations allude to important articles by S. Kuttner, *Harmony from Dissonance. An Interpretation of Medieval Canon Law* (Latrobe, PA 1960); reprinted in: idem, *The History of Ideas and Doctrines of Canon Law in the Middle Ages* (Aldershot 1992²) no. 1, with (revised) 'Retractationes I', ibid. 1–2; P. Fournier, 'Un tournant de

Whereas scholars agree on Gratian's position at a fundamental divide in the history of medieval canon law, a second categorization of the subject into two distinct traditions, 'legal' and 'penitential', appears to be chiefly the result of long-standing literary conventions. In Roman Antiquity, collections of ecclesiastical law had treated confession and penance, aiming at the reconciliation with God in Heaven, alongside other juridical norms designed to maintain order within the earthly community of the faithful. Ancient canonical collections transmitted to the Middle Ages a penitential regime of great rigor, insisting, for instance, that purifying acts imposed on sinners be performed publicly before the bishop and no more than once in a lifetime. During the early medieval period, the original, close relationship between penance and church law as part of a unique disciplinary apparatus was gradually obscured by the emergence of so-called Penitentials, books detailing a process of formal reconciliation with the Church that was far more flexible than what the ancient Romans had envisioned. First brought to Western Europe by Anglo-Irish missionaries during the sixth and seventh centuries, Penitentials introduced modes of retribution patently inspired by practices of conflict settlement in contemporary Celtic and Germanic societies. The new type of literature listed sins with fixed tariffs of penance, typically measured in weeks and years of fasting or other feats of mortification. Different degrees of sinfulness depended greatly on considerations of social status and clan solidarity, of who had committed the sin, and of who had suffered from it. However, and most important for the way matters of sin were henceforth perceived, the penances prescribed by Penitentials could be performed as often as Christian conscience deemed it necessary.

Transforming penance from a highly exceptional event into a disciplinary tool of day-to-day relevance, copies and adaptations of the Anglo-Irish Penitentials rapidly proliferated throughout Western Christendom. The older and more severe Roman rules of penance were soon handed down together with norms drawn from the Penitentials, which simultaneously circulated separately in manuals offering advice to monks and clerics who had to tend to priestly and confessional activities rather than serving at a court. The transmission of texts on penance in the form of monographic manuals, geared toward pastoral rather than legal purposes, thus created a formal dichotomy between penitential and canonical types of literature that had not had a precedent in Antiquity. Modern scholarship, moreover, has much accentuated the distinction through

---

l'histoire du droit 1060–1140', *Nouvelle Revue historique de droit français et étranger* 41 (1917) 129–80, reprinted in: idem, *Mélanges de droit canonique*, ed. T. Kölzer (2 vols. Aalen 1983) 2.373–424 (no. 17); and S. Kuttner, 'Urban II and the Doctrine of Interpretation: A Turning Point?', SG 15 (1972) 53–85, reprinted in: idem, *The History* no. 4, with 'Retractationes IV', ibid. 5–6; Fournier, Kuttner, and others, have emphasized the importance of canonical compilers like Bernold of Constance († 1100), Ivo of Chartres († 1115/16), and Alger of Liège († ca. 1145) as precursors and models of Gratian's method of concordance.

the publication of repertories that focus exclusively on either canonical or penitential and pastoral source material, for the pre-Gratian period as well as afterwards.[5]

Some historical interpretations, it is true, have tried to discern differences of substance between Roman canonical and Anglo-Irish penitential forms of confession, including Cyrille Vogel's attempt to distinguish the private injunctions of the Penitentials from a public rite laid down by the ancient Romans. Others have felt that the significance of the Penitentials should depend on whether they had been disseminated officially by the Apostolic See or had originated unofficially elsewhere. As the more recent historiography has emphasized, however, such subtle conceptual distinctions, along with clear-cut opposites between sin and crime, earthly punishment and spiritual penance, are anachronistic and too categorical and technical for an age that conducted all of its affairs without jurists and without an institutionally perpetuated body of jurisprudence.[6] When the establishment of canon law as a scholastic discipline in the wake of Gratian finally created the preconditions for precise definitions, canon lawyers quickly took the lead in forging ancient Roman and Anglo-Irish precepts into a logically coherent, scientific doctrine. Pastoral manuals carried the new scholastic format of penance again into parishes, circles, and places far beyond the legal sphere.[7] The decisive canonistic intervention implied that, for the rest of the Middle Ages, the legal and penitential regulations of the Church formed two aspects of an inseparable normative construct. If the profound and pervasive interdependence between the penitential and legal elements of late medieval canon law has not always found proper recognition among experts, the oversight may have been the result of specific expectations and approaches, to which our attention must now turn.

Established Approaches

It is probably fair to say that, traditionally, the directions of historical research in medieval canon law have been determined by modern lawyers, scholars who received

---

5. C. Vogel, *Les 'Libri Paenitentiales'* (Typology 27; Turnhout 1978), with an update by A. Frantzen (1985); and P. Michaud-Quantin, *Sommes de casuistique et manuels de confession* (Louvain 1962), offer comprehensive surveys of 'penitential' texts pre- and post-Gratian; see also M. Bloomfield, *Incipits of Latin Works on the Virtues and Vices, 1100–1500* (Cambridge, MA 1979), covering 'pastoral' materials more broadly. Kéry, *Can. Coll.*, and Kuttner, *Repertorium*, have concentrated, respectively, on canon law collections (pre-Gratian) and canonistic literature after Gratian.

6. See S. Hamilton, *The Practice of Penance 900–1050* (Woodbridge and Rochester, NY 2001) 1–12, criticizing, among others, the views expressed by Vogel, *Libri Paenitentiales* 34–59; see also the references given below in note 36.

7. See J. Goering, 'The Internal Forum and the Literature of Penance and Confession', *Traditio* 59 (2004) 175–227; P. Biller, 'Confession in the Middle Ages: Introduction', in: *Handling Sin: Confession in the Middle Ages*, ed. idem and A. Minnis (Woodbridge 1998) 3–33.

their professional training in one of the Western law schools. One of their typical study assignments would have been to trace the origins of a current juristic concept, a legal doctrine, or an institution. An alternative query would have explored the life and thought of a renowned jurist. Both types of investigations have tended to focus on historical issues that stress continuity rather than difference, on manifestations that anticipated or at least resemble the ways in which law operates among Westerners today. Departing from notions of current legal culture, legal historians have preferred to examine past 'legislative' texts and 'law codes' in order to obtain authoritative guidance on what 'law' had been. In addition, they have consulted the literature of jurisprudence to determine how individual norms were interpreted and fitted into a legal 'system'. With regard to the church law of the Middle Ages, this meant that scholarship has found the period of the so-called Classical Canon Law particularly congenial, a span of roughly two hundred years (mid-1100s to mid-1300s) confronting them with a seemingly familiar interplay of papal legislation and codification on the one hand, and intense interpretive efforts in the form of juristic glosses and commentaries on the other.

Launched into their activity by the oldest general textbook of scientific canon law, Gratian's *Decretum*, the canonistic commentators of the classical phase saw their authoritative source-base augmented and updated by a quick succession of additional textbooks in the form of decretal collections, which after 1200 started to bear the stamp of Apostolic approval. Among these, the *Decretales* of Pope Gregory IX, also known as the *Liber extra* (1234), the *Liber sextus* of Boniface VIII (1298), the *Clementinae* of Clement V (1317), and the *Extravagantes* of John XXII (1322), achieved permanent status throughout Latin Christianity as reference works for academic teaching alongside Gratian.[8] For the remainder of the Middle Ages and beyond, moreover, Gratian's *Decretum* and the papally sponsored compilations circulated with standard sets of marginal glosses *(Glosse ordinarie)* attached to them. The *Glosse* conveyed to readers the common opinion of the doctors of canon law, which emanated from the uncontested center of late medieval canonistic studies in Bologna.[9]

In his historiographical survey entitled *Medieval Canon Law* (1995), James Brundage has illlustrated the extent to which modern scholarship of the nineteenth and twentieth centuries has identified the subject with the study of classical canonistic texts from the

---

8. See above in the List of Abbreviations, under *'Decretum'*, 'X' (= *Liber Extra*), 'VI' (= *Liber Sextus*), 'Clem.', and 'Extrav. Jo. XXII'. Note also that the periodization of 'Classical Canon Law' recurs thematically in Part Two of this volume, with the three articles by Robert Somerville (pp. 154–58), Peter Landau (pp. 159–69), and Charles Donahue, Jr. (pp. 179–97) treating specific aspects of classical decretal collections.

9. While there is no modern edition of the *Glosse ordinarie*, they can be consulted in one of the sixteenth-century versions of the *Corpus iuris canonici*, first printed in Rome 1582; J. Gordley and A. Thompson, *Gratian. The Treatise on Laws (Decretum DD. 1–20)* (Washington, DC 1993), have provided a partial translation of Gratian's *Decretum* (DD. 1–20), accompanied by the Ordinary Gloss in English.

time of Gratian to the demise of papal legislative intervention after John XXII in 1322. Just one-fifth of Brundage's book is devoted to more than half a millennium of pre-Gratian canon law, which received attention primarily in the role of a preparatory stage for the twelfth-century revival of jurisprudence.[10] The years between 500 and 1140 were found worthy of consideration mainly because they had preserved and transmitted the authoritative canons Gratian would eventually retrieve and assemble in his *Decretum*. In search of the sources and the selective criteria he had adopted, generations of experts have sifted through the complex (and largely manuscript) tradition of early medieval canonical materials. One of their chief objectives has been to produce philological pedigrees showing how the older compilations were affiliated and which individual canons or clusters of texts they had taken or received from one another.[11]

The dual emphasis on, first, the transmission of Gratian's sources and, secondly, the reconstruction of the writings, concepts, and doctrines of classical canonistic jurisprudence and law constitutes a long-standing research agenda that is primarily associated with the name of Stephan Kuttner (1907–1996). When Kuttner arrived in the United States from war-torn Europe in 1940, he had already published two books that were to have a massive impact on the future of the field.[12] In the *Kanonistische Schuldlehre* of 1935, Kuttner had analyzed the development of the canonistic theory of guilt during its 'formative' phase, between Gratian and the appearance of the *Liber extra*, exploring how the earliest glossators of the *Decretum* and the decretals, decretists and decretalists, gradually transformed a previously disparate mass of canonical terms and maxims into a consolidated and harmonious body of canonistic learning. Kuttner had distilled the *Schuldlehre* from a vast array of scarcely known legal and theological writers, whose opinions he encountered for the most part in manuscript format. The experience ultimately convinced him to take a step backward. Two years later, Kuttner published his *Repertorium*, a comprehensive survey of authors and texts from the formative stage of canon law between 1140 and 1234. An adequate examination of canonistic teachings, Kuttner observed, would remain difficult as long as the original sources or at least reliable library tools and catalogues had not been made available in print.

In the following decades, Kuttner continued to dedicate himself to the *Decretum* and the writings of the decretists, to decretal collections and the decretalists of the formative age, while successfully communicating his work plan to students on both

---

10. J. Brundage, *Medieval Canon Law* (London 1995); 38 pages (5–43) cover pre-Gratian canon law; 190 pages (1–4, 44–230) the period from 1140 to 1350 (including appendices).

11. For an exhaustive bibliographical survey, grouped by collections, see Kéry, *Can. Coll.;* the transmission of individual canons through the pre-Gratian period can be tracked in the digital repertory of L. Fowler-Magerl, *KanonesJ*, now available (with revisions) as *Clavis canonum* (MGH Hilfs-mittel 21; Hannover 2005).

12. S. Kuttner, *Kanonistische Schuldlehre von Gratian bis auf die Dekretalen Gregors IX. (1140–1234)* (Studi e testi 64; Vatican City 1935); and Kuttner, *Repertorium.*

sides of the Atlantic. During his tenure as director of The Institute of Medieval Canon Law, founded in 1955, a number of editions and studies in the textual tradition of pre-Gratian canonical collections and canonistic texts after Gratian were published, and regular, quadriennial international congresses were held for the coordination of ongoing projects.[13] The enormous impact of the scholarly interests promoted by Kuttner is still manifest in the above-mentioned comprehensive statement of James Brundage, in works like *The Spirit of Classical Canon Law* by Richard Helmholz (1996), in the already published two of eleven projected volumes on the *History of Medieval Canon Law*, edited by Wilfried Hartmann and Kenneth Pennington, and, finally, in the present volume. It is dedicated to one of Kuttner's most accomplished students, who now teaches at Kuttner's first academic home in the United States, The Catholic University of America in Washington, D.C.[14]

A celebrated feature of Kuttner's study agenda was his insistence on the highest philological standards, which he himself employed to the point of perfection and tried to instill in generations of younger students. Over the years, his Institute accumulated an impressive run of canonistic manuscripts on microfilm and served as headquarters for ambitious editorial projects aiming at the publication of important texts from before and during the classical period. Likewise, the analysis of doctrine was strongly encouraged, as were monographic studies on the leading teachers of medieval canon law. Kuttner personally concentrated on the decretists and early decretalists. The rest of the classical phase he left in large part to others.[15] In line with the overall emphasis on textual criticism and the close examination of contents, interpretive work on classical canon law sponsored by the Institute has typically explored historical aspects pertaining to the immediacy of scholastic classrooms, student life, academic institutions, professional ethics, and various professorial activities in and outside of medieval universities.[16]

Investigations of interdisciplinary character most often extended to doctrines formulated in the neighboring schools of Roman law and theology. The studies were certainly inspired by Gratian's own example, who had included in his *Decretum* 'civilian'

13. The Institute has published annual updates on work in the field of medieval canon law, first in a 'Bulletin' that formed part of *Traditio* 12–26 (1956–70), then separately as BMCL 1– (1971–); upon Kuttner's retirement, the Institute, now carrying his name, moved to the University of Munich; bibliographical updates continue to appear in RIDC 1– (1990–).

14. See Kéry, *Can. Coll.*; D. Jasper and H. Fuhrmann, *Papal Letters in the Early Middle Ages* (HMCL; 2001). R. Helmholz, *The Spirit of Classical Canon Law* (Athens, GA and London 1996).

15. Several critical editions of canonical collections and canonistic commentary have appeared in the Institute's two series, MIC A.1– and B.1–; other publications of fundamental importance for the study of the original source materal are included in the List of Abbreviations, above.

16. See J. Brundage, *The Profession and Practice of Medieval Canon Law* (Aldershot 2004); and, in the present volume, the contributions of James Brundage (pp. 201–10) and Manlio Bellomo (pp. 347–56).

textbook passages from the Roman *Corpus iuris civilis* as well as substantial portions of theological material.[17] At least until 1234, the line of demarcation running between the respective intellectual territories of canonists and theologians remained rather un-defined, especially when it came to discussing the proper distribution of power within the Church hierarchy (ecclesiology), or to penitential and other sacramental matters.[18] In the same vein, medieval civilian thought and canonistic jurisprudence were engaged in efforts to create a single set of 'Romano-canonical' procedures, applicable not only in ecclesiastical courts, but also among laity conducting litigation on the basis of scien-tific legal criteria.[19] In exploring the interdisciplinary discourses of medieval canonists, theologians, and civilians, a number of colleagues and students working with Kuttner, including Kenneth Pennington and his former doctoral advisor at Cornell, Brian Tier-ney, have pursued directions of research that have succeded in appealing to much larger audiences. As they were able to demonstrate, many fundamental ideas of representative government, inalienable rights, and 'due process' had made their first appearance in the glosses and treatises of late medieval canonistic jurisprudence. The results of their works have been integrated into general accounts of late medieval church history and modern handbooks on the history of Western political thought.[20]

At the same time, it is arguable that Kuttner's most cherished investigative at-titudes have barely revealed their full interpretive potential. In 1996, the year of Kuttner's death, Anders Winroth announced the discovery of a first 'recension' of Gratian's *Decretum*. Through painstaking comparison of manuscripts and readings, Winroth offered proof that the composition of the oldest scientific textbook of canon law had gone forward in verifiable stages and with a clear design in the original com-piler's mind. Since then, Winroth's thesis has sparked debates on many fronts, with

17. J. Viejo-Ximénes, 'La ricezione del diritto romano nel diritto canonico', in: *La cultura giuridico-canonica medioevale*, ed. E. de León and N. Álvarez de las Asturias (Milan 2003) 157–209; the principal 'theological' sec-tions in the *Decretum* are 'De pen.' and 'De cons.', see under List of Abbreviations, above.

18. On intellectual exchanges between twelfth-century canonists and theologians, see J. Baldwin, *Masters, Merchants, and Princes. The Social Views of Peter the Chanter and His Circle* (2 vols.; Princeton, NJ 1970); and, in the present volume, the articles by Keith Kendall (pp. 170–78) and Charles de Miramon (pp. 320–46). Regard-ing penance, see J. Goering, *William de Montibus (c. 1140–1213). The Schools and the Literature of Pastoral Care* (Toronto 1992). For modern literature on scholastic ecclesiology, note 20 below.

19. The formative stages of procedural literature have been surveyed by L. Fowler-Magerl, *'Ordines iudicia-rii' and 'Libelli de ordine iudiciorum'* (Typology 63; Turnhout 1994); see also the present articles by Lotte Kéry (pp. 229–51) and Susanne Lepsius (pp. 252–74).

20. See B. Tierney, *Foundations of Conciliar Theory. The Contributions of the Medieval Canonists from Gratian to the Great Schism* (1955; Leiden and New York 1988²); idem, *The Idea of Natural Rights. Studies on Natural Rights, Natural Law and Church Law, 1150–1625* (Atlanta, GA 1997); idem, *Origins of Papal Infallibility, 1150–1350. A Study on the Concepts of Infallibility, Sovereignty, and Tradition in the Middle Ages* (1972; Leiden and New York 1998²); and Tierney's article (pp. 365–74) in the present volume. In addition to K. Pennington, *The Prince and the Law, 1200–1600. Sovereignty and Rights in the Western Legal Tradition* (Berkeley, CA, Los Angeles, and Oxford 1993), see below, 'Bibliography of Kenneth Pennington's Published Works' (pp. 389–97).

some scholars challenging the textual details of his argument and others pondering its wider implications for our understanding of the scholastic turning point.[21] While discussions continue and outcomes remain uncertain, Kuttner's intellectual legacy appears to be as alive as ever.

Recent Approaches

In 1984, American legal historian Charles Donahue, Jr., explained to members of the Selden Society in London why, as he put it, 'the history of medieval canon law is not written'. Upon reviewing scholarly work in some detail, he called attention to a much neglected aspect of medieval Church law, the application of canonistic jurisprudence in the ecclesiastical courts of the post-Gratian period. According to Donahue, there were three principal reasons for the traditional indifference toward judicial practice, which, unless mended, would permanently prevent experts from drawing firm conclusions about the role of canonistic norms and institutions in the societies they were intended to serve. To begin with, Continental (as opposed to Anglo-American) legal historians, misled by their own formative experience as professional lawyers, had shunned sources that illustrated day-to-day court activities in favor of legislative material and works of academic jurisprudence. Secondly, nineteenth-century scholarship, institutionally supported by the nation-state, had formulated study agendas based on an historical outlook that emphasized domestic, vernacular, and lay elements of legal development, at the expense of canonistic contributions regarded as too universalist, clerical, and fundamentally alien to 'national' character. Finally, Donahue pointed out that the judicial records of churches across Western Christendom had largely remained unprinted and poorly catalogued, in what seriously impeded consultation by even the most intrepid of students.[22]

In subsequent years, Donahue showed that he had taken his own criticism to heart. He was instrumental in compiling a preliminary survey of court records surviving in archives throughout Western Europe, with one of two volumes concentrating exclusively on extant materials from England.[23] While lacking the degree of coordination that Stephan Kuttner and his Institute had provided for investigators focusing on the nor-

---

21. A. Winroth, *The Making of Gratian's Decretum* (Cambridge 2000). The present volume contains articles from chief participants in the debate following Winroth's discovery, by Anders Winroth himself (pp. 97–109), Titus Lenherr (pp. 110–22), Mary Sommar (pp. 123–33), and Carlos Larrainzar (pp. 134–52).

22. C. Donahue, Jr., *Why the History of Medieval Canon Law Is Not Written* (Selden Society Lecture, 3 July 1984; London 1986).

23. Donahue, *Records*. It remains to be seen whether the well-inventoried judicial records from England in fact outnumber the insufficiently catalogued materials in Spain or on the Italian peninsula; see the article by Mario Ascheri (pp. 275–88) below.

mative and academic texts of medieval canon law, research in documentary evidence
pertaining to court practice has steadily intensified, typically sparked by the discovery
or analysis of specific runs of archival records. Perhaps the most substantial advance
in our knowledge has involved the various types of papal dispensations granted by the
Apostolic Court of Penance, or *Penitentiaria Apostolica*. As a complement to the long-
known records of the papal Chancery chiefly containing contested grants of clerical
benefices, the surviving archives of the *Penitentiaria* have turned out to be particularly
intriguing because they underscore the great significance of canon law for the daily lives
of late medieval laypeople. As late as 1996, Charles Donahue could write that 'church
courts held relatively few (marriage) cases involving incest', committed by spouses who,
canonically speaking, were too closely related to each other. Since then, thousands of
dispensations from purportedly incestuous unions have been tracked in the archives of
the Apostolic Penitentiary, dating from the second half of the fifteenth century alone.[24]

The second impediment highlighted by Donahue, preventing older scholarship
from recognizing the origins of many regional and 'customary' manifestations of law
in medieval canonistic jurisprudence, has meanwhile lost much of its former relevance.
This is due not only to a deeper appreciation of the historical facts, but also to the
current political need of finding common ground for the accommodation of multiple
national legal systems within a larger normative framework provided by the European Community. Today, no expert would deny that the intended legal unification of
(Western) Europe has had important historical antecedents. From the time of Gratian
until the end of the *Ancient Regime*, there existed a commonality of juristic terminology,
institutions, and principles brought into being largely by the clerical culture of the later
Middle Ages. The general demise of former nationalist and laicist assumptions has
meanwhile reached a point where even the rise of Roman law studies in twelfth-century
Bologna, long considered to be one of the lay contributions to the scholastic renewal,
has begun to appear as inspired by Gratian's example rather than as an anticipation
of it.[25] Italian scholarship has ceased to emphasize the distinction between the two
scientific laws, Roman and canon, papal and imperial, stressing instead their essential
unity in the Romano-canonical *Ius commune*.[26] The legal cultures of the European North,

24. C. Donahue, Jr., 'The Monastic Judge. Social Practice, Formal Rule, and the Medieval Canon Law of Incest', SG 27 (1996) 49–69 at 56. The most comprehensive editorial project regarding the registers of the *Penitentiaria* is the RPG (6 vols. to date, with extant entries referring to German petitioners, 1431–84); see also K. Salonen, *The Penitentiary as a Well of Grace in the Late Middle Ages. The Example of the Province of Uppsala 1448–1527*
(Helsinki 2001); and Ludwig Schmugge's article (pp. 289–98) in this volume. The RPG is a companion series of
the *Repertorium Germanicum* (9 vols. to date; Berlin and Tübingen 1916–), cataloguing German petitions recorded at the Apostolic Chancery, 1378–1471.

25. Brought into focus by Winroth, *The Making of Gratian's Decretum* 146–74.

26. See especially M. Bellomo, *The Common Legal Past of Europe 1000–1800*, trans. L. Cochrane (Washington, DC 1995).

traditionally thought to be 'Germanic' creations, have likewise revealed their pervasive canonistic inspiration, which spawned their development long before the 'full reception' of Bolognese jurisprudence from the fifteenth century onward. Finally, English common law, with its unique forms of adjudication centered on the jury system, has started to look not nearly as lay-driven and insular as earlier generations of historians had believed. It is becoming increasingly clear that the omnipresence of church courts, from England to Sicily and Hungary to Portugal, constantly exposed late medieval legal minds to canonistic ways of thinking, whether they dealt with substantive law, procedures, or the formalities of final sentencing.[27]

In offering a third explanation for the traditional lack of interest among legal historians in late medieval court records, Donahue singled out the formative experience of modern Continental lawyers who, unlike their colleagues across the British Channel, would not have expected doctrinal innovation to occur by way of 'case law', formulated in the courtrooms. He convincingly argued that specific aspects of medieval canon law suggesting particularly close links between academic theory on the one hand, and adjudication in court on the other, had suffered from considerable scholarly neglect. No doubt, practicality had been one of the key reasons for the lasting success of scholastic jurisprudence. From Gratian's time onward, the canonistic curriculum had provided space for disputed *questiones*, soon to be distinguished into issues arising either in the classroom *(iuris)*, or in actual litigation outside of it *(facti)*.[28] Once the formative phase of scientific canon law had ended by outlining the fundamental parameters of juristic learning in the *Glosse ordinarie*, the activities of many academic teachers as judicial consultants, commissioned to express their expert opinion *(consilia)* in thousands of individual suits, civil and criminal, became so prominent that some of the modern observers have defined the 'post-classical' period (after 1350) as the 'Age of the Consiliators'. Still, the possibilities of doctrinal refinement inherent in the case-related literature of *questiones* and *consilia* have been explored only in isolated attempts, attesting perhaps more to the nearly unmanageable mass of extant materials than any

27. See R. Helmholz, *Canon Law and the Law of England* (London and Ronceverte, WV 1987); idem, *The Ius commune in England: Four Studies* (Oxford 2001); and the article by Richard Helmholz (pp. 375–88) in this volume. On the reception of canonistic principles in late medieval German law, W. Trusen, *Die Anfänge des gelehrten Rechts in Deutschland* (Cologne 1962). Also in the present volume, the article by Péter Erdö (pp. 357–64) discusses the use of medieval canon law in Hungarian and Polish courts.

28. Surveyed by G. Fransen, 'Les questions disputées dans les facultés de droit', in: *Les questions disputées et les questions quodlibétiques dans les facultés de théologie, de droit et de médecine* (Typologie 44–45; Turnhout 1985) 223–315; see further M. Bellomo (ed.), *Die Kunst der Disputation. Probleme der Rechtsauslegung und Rechtsanwendung im 13. und 14. Jahrhundert* (Munich 1997); the article by Orazio Condorelli (pp. 209–28) in the present volume discusses the career of a late-thirteenth-century canonist between teaching and work as a judicial consultant.

Continental prejudice.[29] Parallel investigations into the administrative practices of the papal *Curia*, another probable source of doctrinal development in the last centuries of medieval canonistic jurisprudence, also remain in their infancy. 'Stagnation or Ulterior Development?' was the title of a recent conference addressing the subject.[30] Thus far, nothing but rudimentary responses have been provided.

As if to confirm the symptoms of Continental neglect diagnosed by Donahue, the first comprehensive treatment of medieval canonistic theory as well as court practice has meanwhile appeared in the opening volume of *The Oxford History of the Laws of England* (2004).[31] This work from the pen of Richard Helmholz provides an implicit recognition of all of the concerns raised by Donahue two decades earlier. The author systematically extended the scope of his source material to English ecclesiastical court records in either manuscript or printed form. He contrasted his findings with similar or differing modes of operation in late medieval church tribunals across the Channel, constantly comparing local English uses and teachings to general Western canonistic doctrine. He discussed areas of jurisdictional overlap and competition between ecclesiastical judges on the one hand and the common law courts of the English laity on the other and surveyed the various judicial procedures adopted by English church officials, thereby furnishing a wealth of important technical detail not included in any of the previous introductions to medieval canon law. And, as if that were not enough, Helmholz also pursued his subject far beyond the limits of the classical period, to the Reformation and even to the temporary end of the English monarchy in the 1640s. In so doing, he expressly adopted an approach that, according to his own words, was informed by 'the interests and prejudices of a lawyer', again in line with Donahue's original recommendations.[32]

Professed or tacit adherence to a modern lawyer's perspective in handbooks and surveys published by the leading representatives of the field continues to relegate significant portions of what medieval people themselves would have recognized as 'canon law' to relative obscurity. To cite the *Oxford History* one more time, Helmholz, for instance, barely mentioned the workings of the internal courts of penance during the later Middle Ages, and he was content to treat the age without jurists prior to

29. For a summary statement, I. Baumgärtner (ed.), *Consilia im späten Mittelalter. Zum historischen Aussagewert einer Quellengattung* (Sigmaringen 1995).

30. M. Bertram (ed.), *Stagnation oder Fortbildung? Aspekte des allgemeinen Kirchenrechts im 14. und 15. Jahrhundert* (Tübingen 2004).

31. R. Helmholz, *The Oxford History of the Laws of England* I: *The Canon Law and Ecclesiastical Jurisdiction from 597 to the 1640s* (Oxford 2004).

32. Ibid. v, and passim; see Donahue, *Why the History of Medieval Canon Law Is Not Written* 17: 'If the history of canon law, as such, is going to be written, it is probably lawyers, though not necessarily canon lawyers, who, in the end, will have to do it'.

Gratian's *Decretum* as a mere prelude to the twelfth-century juristic revival.[33] This long-standing indifference has had the effect that investigations into medieval penance and, in particular, 'pre-Gratian' canon law have become the uncontested domain of students who received their academic training in fields other than law. It is somewhat ironic that these investigators, although certainly aided by the smaller body of surviving orginal documentation, have managed to advance Kuttner's and Donahue's work agendas to levels unattained by studies in later medieval canon law, except, perhaps, for research exploring the formative phase of canonistic jurisprudence in the years from 1140 to 1234.

Guided by bibliographical tools that survey the entire canonical and penitential traditions, and concordances that chart the presence of individual canons in surviving compilations as well as threads of affiliation running from one compilation to another, early medieval canon law scholarship has begun to undertake what can be termed 'historical' assessments of the evidence in the proper sense of the word. Studies not only continue to track the transmission of canonical concepts and texts toward the scholastic turning point.[34] They have added to their concerns the accurate reconstruction of original premises and purposes prompting early medieval compilers to produce their penitential and canon law collections in the first place. Confronted with an age which, in the absence of jurists, defied clear-cut doctrinal categorizations and conceptual uniformity, the close analysis of each compilation, from the process of composition to the authorial manipulation of texts, has shown that many of the conclusions found in older historiography were overly informed by modern juristic thinking. Previous works were prone to detecting firm standards where, in reality, informal trends, momentary consensus, personal initiative, and an approximate sense of 'canonical authority' had prevailed.[35]

As mentioned earlier, it has become quite clear that the powerful penitential tradition of the early Middle Ages had spread from the Anglo-Irish periphery toward the center of Latin Christendom, short of any Apostolic authorization; that, in Carolingian times, the new penitential and older canonical forms of penance began to coexist in

---

33. Helmholz, *The Oxford History of the Laws* I, esp. 12. The work devotes 65 out of a total of 642 pages to early medieval canon law; penitentials are treated on five pages (30–35), scholastic manuals of confession on two (130–31); confessional practice is described as 'secret' (131) and largely beyond the historians' view (209–10); massive recourse to penance rather than punishment in the court records, especially in the so-called 'defamatory suits' (582–90, 604–8, 617–19), does not elicit much comment. See also note 10, above.

34. The present volume contains two articles by Jörg Müller (pp. 77–94) and Franck Roumy (pp. 301–19) on the transmission of specific canonical concepts and phrases before and since Gratian. Surveys of penitentials and pre-Gratian canon law collections have been listed above, notes 5 and 11.

35. Individual canonical compilations and their interpretive agendas form the focus of the present articles by Wilfried Hartmann (pp. 33–49), Rudolf Schieffer (pp. 50–56), and Gerhard Schmitz (pp. 57–65).

the same canonical collections, without any thoroughgoing distinction concerning their private or public application; that the dividing line between confessional, civil, and criminal canons, between compensation and punishment, grew blurred; and that Germanic notions of status and clan solidarity started to affect canonical sanctioning to the detriment of ancient Roman ideas which had aimed at retribution on the basis of abstract principle rather than social standing. While formerly it was assumed that the postponement of acts of atonement until after priestly absolution had been tied to the Anglo-Irish penitential regime, scholars now think of it as post-Carolingian, if not scholastic in origin, and hence part of a fundamental cultural reorientation that permanently transformed Western ideas of justice among clergy and laity alike.[36] Most importantly, however, the recognition of specific institutional and political interests prompting the composition of early medieval canonical collections has extended the scope of research from the study of texts and literary genres toward larger historiographical issues.

It is especially with regard to the pre-Gratian material, then, that the historians' ultimate objective of restoring canon law to the 'totality' of past medieval experience may have assumed the contours of something more than a distant vision.

---

36. See M. de Jong, 'What Was Public about Public Penance? "Penitentia publica" and Justice in the Carolingian World', in: *La giustizia nell'alto medioevo (secoli ix–xi)* (Settimane 44; Spoleto 1997) 863–902; R. Meens, 'The Frequency and Nature of Early Medieval Penance', in: *Handling Sin* 35–61; G. Austin, 'Jurisprudence in the Service of Pastoral Care: The "Decretum" of Burchard of Worms', *Speculum* 79 (2004) 929–59; and, in this volume, the essays of Ludger Körntgen (pp. 17–32) and Greta Austin (pp. 66–76).

PART ONE

Western Church Law in an Age without Jurists, ca. 500–1140

Kanonisches Recht und Busspraxis

Zu Kontext und Funktion
des *Paenitentiale Excarpsus Cummeani*

Ludger Körntgen

Die Entwicklung der kirchlichen Busspraxis im frühen und hohen Mittelalter bietet ein Beispiel für das differenzierte und wechselseitige Verhältnis von geschriebenem Recht und Rechtspraxis. Obwohl seit der Spätantike klare Normen schriftlich fixiert waren, die ein allgemeines kirchliches Verfahren unter Kontrolle der Bischöfe regelten, entwickelte sich ausgehend von Irland und dem irisch beeinflussten England eine Praxis, die sich weitgehend am Beispiel der monastischen Disziplin orientierte und das Bekenntnis gegenüber dem Priester sowie die Zuteilung bestimmter Bussauflagen durch diesen in den Mittelpunkt stellte.[1] Das monastische Vorbild führte dazu, dass Busse jetzt für kleinste Nachlässigkeiten des täglichen Lebens geleistet werden konnte; weil zugleich aber auch Kapitaldelikte wie Mord, Raub oder Ehebruch nach gleichem Schema gebüsst werden konnten, kam es zu einem Neben-, Mit- und Gegeneinander der neuen und der tradierten Busspraxis, das durch die karolingische Unterscheidung und Zuordnung von 'öffentlicher' und 'geheimer' Busse eher abstrakt-systematisch als in der konkreten Praxis geklärt wurde und das noch bis weit ins 11. Jahrhundert hinein die kirchliche Busspraxis Europas bestimmte.[2] Mit Kanon 21 des vierten Laterankonzils (1215) wurde dann eine Praxis in das universalkirchliche Recht integriert, die sich neben

---

1. Cf. C. Vogel, 'Busse (Liturgisch-Theologisch) D I [2]', LMA 2 (1983) 1131–35; K. Hoheisel, 'Busse I.', LThK³ 2 (1994) 824–25; L. Körntgen, 'Kirchenbusse', *Reallexikon für germanische Altertumskunde²* 16 (2001) 561–64.

2. Cf. R. Kottje, 'Busspraxis und Bussritus', in: *Segni e riti nella chiesa altomedievale occidentale* (Settimane 32; Spoleto 1987) 369–95; S. Hamilton, *The Practice of Penance, 900–1050* (Woodbridge and Rochester, NY 2001); L. Körntgen, 'Fortschreibung frühmittelalterlicher Busspraxis. Burchards Liber corrector und seine Quellen', in: *Bischof Burchard von Worms*, ed. W. Hartmann (Mainz 2000) 199–226.

dem kirchlichen Recht und zum Teil sogar im Widerspruch zu dessen Normen entwickelt und durchgesetzt hatte.[3]

Diese Situation spiegelt sich auch darin, dass die neue Praxis von einem neuen literarischen Genre vermittelt wurde, nämlich von den frühmittelalterlichen Bussbüchern.[4]
Die altkirchliche Busspraxis war dagegen durch Bestimmungen spätantiker Synoden
und päpstliche Entscheidungen geregelt worden, die im frühen Mittelalter weiterhin in
kirchenrechtlichen Sammlungen tradiert wurden. Nur wenige dieser alten Synodalkanones haben freilich in den Bussbüchern Berücksichtigung gefunden; diese entnahmen
ihren Stoff vielmehr zum grössten Teil eigenen Quellen, nämlich den Kompilationen
der irischen Äbte Cummean und Columban oder den Sammlungen von Busssatzungen
des angelsächsischen Erzbischofs griechischer Herkunft, Theodor von Canterbury.[5]
Weniger klar stellt sich die Trennung von tradiertem Kirchenrecht und neuen Busssatzungen allerdings auf der Ebene der konkreten Überlieferungsträger dar. Die einzelnen
Handschriften, denen wir unsere Kenntnis von frühmittelalterlichen Bussbüchern
verdanken, tradieren häufig zugleich Sammlungen des kirchlichen Rechts.[6] Dem
Benützer solcher Handschriften also präsentierten sich Busssatzungen der Bussbücher
und Kanones der kirchlichen Synoden im Zusammenhang: Dieser Befund hat die Frage
aufgeworfen, welche Relevanz solchen Zusammenstellungen in der Praxis zukommen
konnte. Konnte ein grosser, unhandlicher Codex überhaupt in der Busspraxis zu Rate
gezogen werden, wenn der Priester einem Büsser eine bestimmte Bussauflage erteilen
musste? Können wir uns Handschriften, die Bussbücher gemeinsam mit umfangreicheren kanonistischen Sammlungen überliefern, in der Hand von einfachen Priestern vorstellen, die doch nach der neuen Praxis das Bekenntnis entgegennahmen und
die Bussleistungen bemessen mussten?

Damit stellt sich die Frage nach der praktischen Relevanz der auf diese Weise überlieferten Bussbücher. Franz Kerff hat auf den beschriebenen Überlieferungsbefund die
These gegründet, dass viele der im Kontext kirchenrechtlicher Sammlungen überlieferten Bussbücher überhaupt nicht in der Busspraxis benützt worden seien, sondern
wie die Synodalkanones dem Bischof zur Entscheidungsfindung im herkömmlichen

3. Cf. M. Ohst, *Pflichtbeichte. Untersuchungen zum Busswesen im hohen und späten Mittelalter* (Tübingen 1995).

4. Cf. C. Vogel, *Libri paenitentiales* (Typologie 27; Turnhout 1978, Supplement, hg. v. A. Frantzen, 1985); R. Kottje 'Bussbücher', LMA 2 (1982) 1118–22; L. Körntgen, 'Bussbücher', LThK³ 2 (1994) 822–24; idem, 'Buss-bücher', *Lexikon für Kirchen- und Staatskirchenrecht* 1 (2000) 307–9; R. Meens, *Het tripartite boeteboek. Overlevering en betekenis van vroegmiddeleeuwse biechtvoorschriften* (Hilversum 1994) 11–72.

5. Cf. L. Körntgen, *Studien zu den Quellen der frühmittelalterlichen Bussbücher* (Sigmaringen 1993) 1–4; Meens, *Boeteboek* 25–42.

6. Cf. Meens, *Boeteboek* 220–66; idem, 'The Frequency and Nature of Early Medieval Penance', in: *Handling Sin*, ed. P. Biller (Woodbridge 1998) 35–61, 39–47.

kirchlichen Bussverfahren oder im karolingischen Sendgericht gedient hätten.[7] Kerff hat damit bestritten, dass ein wichtiger Teil der uns überlieferten frühmittelalterlichen Bussbücher überhaupt als Zeugnis für die Praktizierung der neuen, frühmittelalterlichen Busse irisch-angelsächsischer Prägung herangezogen werden konnte. In Auseinandersetzung mit dieser These hat Rob Meens den Überlieferungskontext der wichtigsten frühmittelalterlichen Bussbücher genauer differenziert. Demnach lässt sich für viele Bussbuchhandschriften aufgrund ihres Inhalts ein Bezug zur Seelsorge oder zur liturgischen Praxis nachweisen; für eine grosse Gruppe von Zeugnissen lässt sich allerdings der von Kerff angenommene kirchenrechtliche Kontext bestätigen.[8] Solche Handschriften werden nicht unmittelbar für die priesterliche Busserteilung benützt worden sein; bedeutet das aber, dass sie überhaupt keinen Bezug zur frühmittelalterlichen Busspraxis besassen? Warum hat man solche Handschriften zusammengestellt, warum hat man seit dem 8. Jahrhundert Bussbücher und kirchenrechtliche Sammlungen gemeinsam überliefert? Die von Kerff angenommene Funktion im Sendgericht lässt sich nur für die spät- und nachkarolingische Überlieferung diskutieren; die Verbindung mit einer Kanonessammlung prägt aber schon den Überlieferungskontext eines der wichtigsten vor- oder frühkarolingischen Bussbücher, des sogenannten *Excarpsus Cummeani*. Was dieser Überlieferungskontext über Funktion und Bedeutung des Bussbuches und über die Entwicklung der frühmittelalterlichen Busspraxis aussagt, soll im folgenden überlegt werden.

1. Überlieferung und Gestalt des *Excarpsus Cummeani*

Der sogenannte *Excarpsus Cummeani* ist eines der ältesten und eines der am breitesten überlieferten frühmittelalterlichen Bussbücher.[9] Noch 17 Handschriften bezeugen den vollständigen Text, weitere partielle oder fragmentarische Textzeugen belegen eine nicht mehr abschätzbare, aber sicher bedeutende und differenzierte Verbreitung des Bussbuches. Schon am Ende des 8. Jahrhunderts war es in Nordfrankreich, in Burgund, in Südwestdeutschland und Bayern bekannt, während es wohl nur in wenigen

7. F. Kerff, 'Libri paenitentiales und kirchliche Strafgerichtsbarkeit bis zum Decretum Gratiani', ZRG Kan. Abt. 75 (1989) 23–57; idem, 'Mittelalterliche Quellen und mittelalterliche Wirklichkeit: Zu den Konsequenzen einer jüngst erschienenen Edition für unser Bild kirchlicher Reformbemühungen', *Rheinische Vierteljahresblätter* 51 (1987) 275–86.

8. Cf. Meens, *Boeteboek* 220–66; idem, 'The Frequency' 40–47.

9. Cf. L. Körntgen, 'Der Excarpsus Cummeani, ein Bussbuch aus Corbie?', in: *Scientia Veritatis. Festschrift für Hubert Mordek*, ed. O. Münsch und T. Zotz (Sigmaringen 2004) 59–76; Meens, *Boeteboek* 44–46, 311–18; R. Kottje, 'Excarpsus Cummeani', LMA 4 (1987) 155. Editionen: Wasserschleben 460–93; Schmitz, *Bussbücher* 2.597–644; die Neuedition in CCL 156b steht vor dem Abschluss. Grundlegende Analyse von Quellen und Überlieferung: F. Asbach, *Das Poenitentiale Remense und der sogen. Excarpsus Cummeani: Überlieferung, Quellen und Entwicklung zweier kontinentaler Bussbücher aus der 1. Hälfte des 8. Jahrhunderts* (Diss. phil. Regensburg 1975).

Exemplaren nach Italien und Südfrankreich gelangt ist.[10] Noch acht Handschriften des Bussbuches überliefern zugleich die *Collectio Vetus Gallica*, die älteste systematische Kanonessammlung des Frankenreichs.[11] Text- und überlieferungsgeschichtliche Verbindungen lassen erkennen, dass die gesamte noch greifbare Überlieferung des Bussbuches auf die Überlieferung im Kontext der *Vetus Gallica* zurückgeht.[12] Vom nordfranzösischen Kloster Corbie aus, wo die Sammlung vornehmlich gallischer Synodalkanones im zweiten Viertel des 8. Jahrhunderts redigiert worden ist, wurden Bussbuch und Sammlung gemeinsam verbreitet; wie die Sammlung besitzen wir auch das Bussbuch nur in der Gestalt, in der es Corbie verlassen hat. Während sich aber ältere Redaktionsstufen der Sammlung erschliessen lassen, spricht einiges dafür, dass die Kompilation des Bussbuches erstmals in Corbie vorgenommen worden ist.[13] Einzelne kanonistische Stücke wie der Auszug einer Dekretale Leos I. oder mehrere Kanones der Synoden von Ankyra und Epao sind in einer Gestalt in das Bussbuch eingegangen, die in Corbie bezeugt ist.[14] Eine der wichtigsten Quellen des Bussbuches, die unter dem Namen eines *discipulus Umbrensium* firmierende Sammlung von Busssatzungen des Erzbischofs Theodor von Canterbury, war höchstens einige Jahrzehnte alt, als *Excarpsus Cummeani* und *Collectio Vetus Gallica* in Corbie zusammengestellt wurden.[15]

Welchen Zweck hat man in Corbie mit dieser Textkombination, für die das Bussbuch vielleicht überhaupt erst kompiliert worden ist, verfolgt? Unverkennbar ist ein besonderes Interesse am Thema 'Busse'. Die *Collectio Vetus Gallica* ist in Corbie nicht zuletzt um Material zu diesem Thema ergänzt worden.[16] Vor allem ein Zusatztitel am Ende bietet einschlägige Synodalkanones und päpstliche Entscheidungen, die anderen Vorlagen entstammen als die im älteren Kern zusammengestellten Kanones gallischer Synoden.[17] Vom äusseren Befund her wirkt dieser Zusatztitel geradezu wie eine Überleitung zum Bussbuch, das in der ältesten Überlieferung nach einigen Stücken anderer Provenienz auf die Sammlung folgt.[18] Inhaltlich allerdings wird durch diese Abfolge der Gegensatz zwischen der neuen, von den Bussbüchern vermittelten Busspraxis und

---

10. Cf. Kottje, 'Busspraxis und Bussritus' 377–87, mit Ergänzungen zur ausführlichen Zusammenstellung und Analyse der Überlieferung bei Asbach. Die bei Meens, *Boeteboek* 44–47 zusätzlich aufgeführte Handschrift New York, Hispanic Society of America HC 380/819 überliefert nur einen stark bearbeiteten Teil des *Excarpsus Cummeani* und ist deshalb nicht als Überlieferungszeuge, sondern als Rezeption des Bussbuches zu werten.

11. Cf. Körntgen, 'Excarpsus Cummeani' 61–62 Anm. 20; zur *Vetus Gallica* cf. H. Mordek, *Kirchenrecht und Reform im Frankenreich. Die Collectio Vetus Gallica, die älteste systematische Kanonessammlung des fränkischen Galliens. Studien und Edition* (Berlin und New York 1975); Kéry, *Can. Coll.* 50–53.

12. Cf. Asbach, *Das Poenitentiale Remense* 59–64.

13. Cf. Mordek, *Kirchenrecht und Reform* 51–70.

14. Cf. Körntgen, 'Excarpsus' 70–73.

15. Cf. R. Kottje, 'Paenitentiale Theodori', HRG 3 (1984) 1413–16.

16. Cf. Mordek, *Kirchenrecht und Reform* 51–58.

17. *Collectio Vetus Gallica* 64: *De Penetentibus*, ed. Mordek, *Kirchenrecht und Reform* 597–613.

18. Ibid. 217–29.

der alten Praxis der Kanones besonders deutlich erkennbar. Kanon 6 etwa formuliert ausdrücklich, dass die Busserteilung dem Bischof vorbehalten ist.[19] Der offenkundige Gegensatz zur Praxis, die das Bussbuch voraussetzt, konnte einem Redaktor nicht verborgen bleiben, der den Synodalkanon nicht etwa als Teil eines grösseren Materialkomplexes rezipiert, sondern offensichtlich wohlüberlegt neben anderen die Busse betreffenen Kanones aus einer überschaubaren Sammlung exzerpiert und der *Collectio Vetus Gallica* angefügt hat.[20]

Müssen wir aus diesem Befund schliessen, dass der aus dem Kontext der alten Kirchenbusse stammende Kanon hier ganz bewusst dem Bussbuch vorangestellt worden ist, um dessen praktische Funktion zu regeln? War der Textkomplex mit Sammlung und Bussbuch gerade nicht für Priester, sondern ausschliesslich für Bischöfe gedacht, die beim kirchlichen Bussverfahren auf das Bussbuch hätten zurückgreifen sollen? Ging es also um die Einfügung der neuen, von den Bussbüchern vermittelten Busspraxis in die tradierte Kirchenbusse? Eine solche Deutung verbietet sich, wenn wir beachten, dass noch ein viel klarerer Gegensatz zwischen Kanones und Bussbuch wirksam wurde. Die Busserteilung durch den Priester und der Verzicht auf das vom Bischof kontrollierte kirchliche Verfahren bedeuteten nämlich nicht die einzige folgenreiche Neuerung der frühmittelalterlichen Busspraxis. Neu war vielmehr auch, dass jetzt Kleriker auf die gleiche Art Busse leisten konnten wie Mönche und Laien; das kanonische Bussverfahren der Kirche aber stand nur Laien offen, während es für besonders schwere Sünden der Kleriker allein die Strafe der Absetzung gab.[21] Eine kirchliche Busse für Kleriker war demgegenüber ausgeschlossen, und dieses Verbot der Klerikerbusse wurde in verschiedenen Synodalkanones und päpstlichen Schreiben tradiert. Für unsere Fragestellung ist besonders wichtig, dass Kanones, die eine Busse für Kleriker explizit ausschliessen oder dieses Verbot offensichtlich voraussetzen, ebenfalls in den Zusatztitel zur *Vetus Gallica* aufgenommen worden sind.[22] Auch dadurch ergab sich ein

19. *Collectio Vetus Gallica* 64.6, ed. Mordek, *Kirchenrecht und Reform* 599: 'Secundum deferenciam peccatorum episcopi arbitrium penitencie tempora decernantur. Et ut presbiter inconsulto episcopo non reconciliet penitentem nisi absencia episcopi necessitate cogente. Cuiuscumque autem penitentes publicum aut vulgatissimum crimen est, quod universam ecclesiam commoverit, ante absida ei manus inponatur' = *Registri ecclesiae Carthaginensis excerpta* 43 (ed. CCL 149.185).

20. Vorlage war die *Collectio Pithouensis*, die der Corbie-Redaktor 'nur nach einem einzigen Gesichtspunkt, dem der Busse', exzerpiert hat, cf. Mordek, *Kirchenrecht und Reform* 56–57.

21. Cf. R. Kottje, *Die Bussbücher Halitgars von Cambrai und des Hrabanus Maurus. Ihre Überlieferung und ihre Quellen* (Berlin und New York 1980) 216–18.

22. *Collectio Vetus Gallica* 64.23, ed. Mordek, *Kirchenrecht und Reform* 608: 'Item confirmatum est, ut, si quando presbiter vel diaconus in aliqua graviore culpa convicti fuerint, qua eos a ministerio necesse sit removere, non eis manus tamquam penetentibus vel tamquam fidelibus laicis inponatur' = Konzil von Karthago 419, can. 27 (ed. CCL 149.143); 64.27, ed. Mordek 610: 'Penitentia professi ad clericatum penitus non vocentur' = Konzil von Epao 3 (ed. MGH Concilia 1. 20; ed. CCL 148a 25); 64.30, ed. Mordek 611–12: 'Illud quoque nos parum fuit providere, ut, sicut penitentiam agere cuiquam non conciditur clericorum, ita post penitudinem ac

eklatanter, nicht zu übersehender Widerspruch innerhalb des Überlieferungskontextes der Sammlung, und das nicht nur, weil das darin enthaltene Bussbuch die neue Praxis voraussetzte. Bestimmungen zur Busse der Kleriker spielen vielmehr im *Excarpsus* eine besonders wichtige Rolle. Wie wichtig diese Rolle für das Bussbuch war, hat man bisher noch nicht erkannt. Im folgenden sollen zunächst Eigenart, Bedeutung und Herkunft der Satzungen zur Klerikerbusse im *Excarpsus Cummeani* genauer untersucht werden, bevor gefragt werden kann, welche Konsequenzen sich aus diesem Befund für die Beurteilung des Überlieferungskontextes von Bussbuch und Sammlung und vor allem für die Funktion des Bussbuches innerhalb der Überlieferung ergeben.

2. Klerikerbusse im *Excarpsus Cummeani*

Die Differenzierung der Bussleistungen nach Stand und Weihegrad der Büsser gehört zu den allgemein bekannten Merkmalen der frühmittelalterlichen Busspraxis. Nach welchen Kriterien diese Differenzierung vorgenommen wurde, woher die frühmittelalterlichen Bussbücher überhaupt Massstäbe für ihre entsprechend differenzierten Bussbemessungen erhielten, ist bisher nicht untersucht worden. Zwar ist die Quellengeschichte der Bussbücher wenigstens grundsätzlich bekannt. Wir wissen, dass die in den verschiedensten Kompilationen des 8. und 9. Jahrhunderts zusammengestellten Busssatzungen im wesentlichen aus drei Quellengruppen stammen. Aus dem irischen *Paenitentiale Cummeani*,[23] aus verschiedenen Überlieferungen von Busssatzungen des aus Griechenland nach England gekommenen Erzbischofs Theodor[24] sowie aus sogenannten *Iudicia canonica*, die im Frankenreich auf der Grundlage des *Paenitentiale Columbani* entstanden waren.[25] Diesen Quellen konnte der Kompilator des *Excarpsus Cummeani* abgestufte Bussmasse für Laien, Mönche und verschiedene Weihegrade der Kleriker entnehmen. Der *Excarpsus* bietet darüber hinaus aber noch eine Gruppe von neun Bestimmungen, für die bisher keine Quelle nachgewiesen werden konnte. Gemeinsam ist diesen Busssatzungen eine Differenzierung der Bussmasse, die einem einfachen, ganzzahligen Berechnungsschema folgt.[26] Dieses Schema ist uns auch in allgemeiner Formulierung überliefert, und zwar in einem der einfachen

reconciliationem ullum laicum liceat honorem clericatus adepisci, quia, quamvis sint omnium contagionem peccatorum mundati, nulla tamen debent gerendorum sacramentorum instrumenta suscipere, quia dudum fuerint vasa vitiorum' = Papst Siricius an Bischof Himerius von Tarragona (JK 255; ed. PL 13.1145).

23. Cf. Körntgen, *Studien* 7–9; ed. L. Bieler, *The Irish Penitentials* (Dublin 1963) 108–35.

24. Cf. Kottje, 'Paenitentiale Theodori', HRG 3 (1984) 1413–16; idem, 'Busspraxis und Bussritus' 374–77; A. Frantzen, *The Literature of Penance in Anglo-Saxon England* (New Brunswick, NJ 1983) 62–78; Meens, *Boeteboek* 30–36.

25. Cf. Körntgen, *Studien* 227–28; CCL 156, xxii–xxv; Meens, *Boeteboek* 36–42, 79–87. Eine weitere, nur in einer Gruppe von Bussbüchern rezipierte Quelle bildet das *Paenitentiale Oxoniense* II, cf. Körntgen, *Studien* 87–205.

26. *Excarpsus Cummeani* 1.7, 2.2, 3.1, 3.28, 4.3, 5.1, 5.9, 6.16 und 9.11.

fränkischen Bussbücher, dem sogenannten *Paenitentiale Parisiense simplex:* 'Die Todsün-
den betreffend, das heisst bei Totschlag, Ehebruch, Meineid, Unzucht und Unreinheit
(inmundicia) sollen Laien 3 Jahre büssen, Kleriker 4, Subdiakone 6, Diakone 7, Priester
10, Bischöfe 12. Hinsichtlich der geringeren Sünden, dass heisst bei Diebstahl, Lüge
und ähnlichen Sünden sollen Laien 1 Jahr büssen, Kleriker 2, Subdiakone 3, Diakone
4, Priester 5, Bischöfe 6'.[27] Eine andere Überlieferung des gleichen Schemas findet sich
im *Paenitentiale Pseudo-Egberti,* das wohl in der zweiten Hälfte des 8. Jahrhunderts
in einem angelsächsisch geprägten Kloster entstanden ist.[28] Zusätzlich bietet dieses
Bussbuch noch ein Differenzierungsschema für geringfügige Vergehen, das ebenfalls
Parallelen im *Excarpsus Cummeani* hat.[29]

Handschriftlich sind *Excarpsus Cummeani* und *Parisiense simplex* etwa gleich früh in
der Mitte des 8. Jahrhunderts bezeugt. Nach Asbachs ausführlicher Analyse können
wir eine direkte literarische Beziehung zwischen diesen beiden Bussbüchern ausschliessen.[30] Das Schema der Klerikerbusse dürfte deshalb aus einer älteren Vorlage stammen,
auf die beide Bussbücher zurückgehen. Eine solche Quelle wird auch dem Kompilator
des *Paenitentiale Pseudo-Egberti* vorgelegen haben, obgleich er auch die beiden älteren
Kompilationen exzerpiert haben könnte.[31] Dafür gibt es jedoch keine Hinweise aus
dem übrigen Quellenmaterial des Bussbuches.[32]

Auch die Quellenstruktur des *Excarpsus Cummeani* deutet darauf hin, dass die nach
diesem Schema formulierten Busssatzungen wie der übrige Stoff einer bestimmten
Quelle entnommen sind. Dass es eine solche literarische Vorlage gegeben hat, dafür
spricht schliesslich das Zeugnis des *Paenitentiale Remense.*[33] Dabei handelt es sich um
eine etwas jüngere, umfangreichere Bearbeitung des *Excarpsus Cummeani,* die sich nicht
nur in der Anordnung des Stoffes, sondern auch im Umfang von diesem unterscheidet.
Die beiden einzigen vollständigen Zeugen des *Paenitentiale Remense* überliefern auch die
Collectio Vetus Gallica; sie lassen sich eindeutig der französischen Klasse und darin der

27. *Paenitentiale Parisiense simplex* 61–62 (ed. CCL 156.79).

28. *Paenitentiale Pseudo-Egberti* 1.1–2 (ed. Schmitz, *Bussbücher* 2.663); gegenüber dem im *Parisiense simplex*
überlieferten Schema sind die Bussmasse für Bischof und Laien um jeweils ein Jahr variiert. Zu Herkunft und
Entstehungszeit des *Paenitentiale Pseudo-Egberti* cf. R. Haggenmüller, *Die Überlieferung der Beda und Egbert zugeschriebenen Bussbücher* (Frankfurt/M. 1991) 298.

29. *Paenitentiale Pseudo-Egberti* 9.1; ed. Schmitz, *Bussbücher* 2.668: 'De ebrietate uel maledictione uel detrac-
tione causa inuidie uel his similibus laici VII diebus uel IV peniteant, clericus VII diebus uel XIV, subdiaconus II
uel III ebdomadas, diaconus III uel IV ebdomadas, presbyter IV uel V ebdomadas, episcopus V uel VI ebdomadas'; cf. *Excarpsus Cummeani* 1.7, 9.11.

30. Cf. Asbach, *Das Poenitentiale Remense* 131–36; Asbachs Feststellungen zum *Paenitentiale Remense* gelten
entsprechend für den *Excarpsus Cummeani.*

31. Haggenmüller, *Die Überlieferung* 194, setzt eine Abhängigkeit des *Paenitentiale Pseudo-Egberti* vom *Pae-
nitentale Remense* voraus; die Prüfung dieser Möglichkeit muss allerdings einer grundlegenden Quellenanalyse
des *Paenitentiale Pseudo-Egberti* vorbehalten bleiben.

32. Cf. Asbach, *Das Poenitentiale Remense* 330–32.

33. Vorläufige Edition ibid., Anhang 1–77; neue Edition (in CCL 156b) in Vorbereitung.

nordfranzösischen Unterklasse der Sammlung zuordnen, die nach Mordeks Urteil der Corbie-Redaktion am nächsten steht.[34] Trotzdem dürfte nicht das *Remense*, sondern der *Excarpsus* zum ursprünglichen Überlieferungskontext der in Corbie redigierten Sammlung gehört haben, denn nur der *Excarpsus* ist auch zweifelsfrei in der süddeutschen Klasse der Überlieferung vertreten, während eine Handschrift dieser Klasse, die eine Mischform aus beiden Bussbüchern bietet, durch ein Exemplar der anderen Überlieferungsklasse kontaminiert sein dürfte.[35] Die Überlieferung belegt aber auch, dass die Kompilation des *Paenitentiale Remense* in zeitlicher und räumlicher Nähe zur Corbeier Redaktion des gesamten Textkonvolutes erfolgt ist. Schon daher erklärt es sich, dass die Redaktion des *Remense* Zugang zu den ursprünglichen Quellen des *Excarpsus Cummeani* hatte. Dessen Textbestand ist nämlich durch Material aus zusätzlichen, aber auch aus den gleichen Quellen erweitert worden, die schon bei der Kompilation des *Excarpsus* ausgeschrieben worden waren.

Dieser Befund ist auch für die hier interessierende Quelle der Klerikerbussen von Bedeutung. Das *Paenitentiale Remense* unterscheidet sich vom *Excarpsus* nicht zuletzt durch Rubriken, die einen Wechsel der Vorlagen anzeigen. Dabei bezeichnet die Rubrik *De alio penitentiale unde supra* wahrscheinlich nicht ein bestimmtes Bussbuch. Sie findet sich aber mehrfach vor Bestimmungen, die nach dem Schema der gestuften Klerikerbusse formuliert sind.[36] Schon das deutet darauf hin, dass die Redaktion des *Paenitentiale Remense* die entsprechenden Busssatzungen als Material einer bestimmten Quelle identifizieren konnte. Auf diese Quelle hat die *Remense*-Redaktion selbständig zurückgegriffen, denn eine der nach dem fraglichen Schema formulierten Bestimmungen des *Remense* hat keine Parallele im *Excarpsus Cummeani*.[37] Eine andere belegt das Schema vollständiger als die parallele Bestimmung des *Excarpsus*.[38] Rob Meens hat nachgewiesen, dass der Kompilator des *Excarpsus Cummeani* durch Auswahl und

---

34. Cf. Mordek, *Kirchenrecht und Reform* 331–41.

35. Cf. Körntgen, 'Excarpsus Cummeani' 64–65, in Auseinandersetzung mit der entgegengesetzten These von Asbach, oben Anm. 30.

36. Cf. *Paenitentiale Remense* 7.9, ed. Asbach, Anhang 46: 'Item de alio penitentiale unde supra. Si quis periurium fecerit: laici III annos peniteant, clerici V, subdiaconus VI, diaconus VII, presbyter X, episcopus XII'. Ähnliche Rubriken finden sich vor den Bestimmungen 3.13, 5.8, 6.7, 7.9 und 8.14. Asbach, *Das Poenitentiale Remense* 139–42, nimmt an, dass diese Rubriken im *Paenitentiale Remense* grössere Quellenblöcke markieren; es ist jedoch möglich, dass jeweils nur die Herkunft der unmittelbar auf eine Rubrik folgenden Busssatzung auf diese Weise gekennzeichnet werden sollte.

37. *Paenitentiale Remense* 4.34, ed. Asbach, Anhang 29: 'Si quis fornicationem aut inmunditias fecerit: laici III annos, clerici V, subdiaconi VI, diaconi VII, presbyteri X, episcopi XII'.

38. *Excarpsus Cummeani* 1.6 (im folgenden nach dem Manuskript der Neuedition in CCL 156b; cf. ed. Schmitz, *Bussbücher* 2.605): 'Sacerdos si inebriauerit per ignorantiam, VII dies paeniteat in pane et aqua, si per neglegentiam XV, si per contemptu XL dies paeniteat'; ibid. 1.7: 'Diaconi et monachi IIII ebdomadas, subdiaconi III, clerici II, laici I'. Die erste Bestimmung geht zurück auf das britische oder irische *Paenitentiale Ambrosianum* 1.2–4 (ed. Körntgen, *Studien* 258–59); die zweite ist aus unbekannter Quelle übernommen, allerdings ohne das Bussmass für den

Zusammenstellung des Quellenmaterials eigene sachliche Akzente gesetzt hat.[39] An den Bestimmungen zur Klerikerbusse lässt sich eine weitergehende Redaktionsleistung feststellen. Der Kompilator hat nicht nur eine heute nicht mehr erhaltene Vorlage ausgeschrieben, die offensichtlich (ausschliesslich?) Busssatzungen mit entsprechend abgestuften Bussmassen enthielt. Darüber hinaus sind auch Busssatzungen anderer Quellen, die nicht das komplette Schema für alle Weihegrade boten, entsprechend bearbeitet worden. Das lässt sich besonders deutlich an Busssatzungen erkennen, die aus einem einfachen fränkischen Bussbuch ähnlich dem *Paenitentiale Burgundense* stammen. Wir kennen noch acht solcher einfachen Bussbücher, die einen gemeinsamen Grundbestand von Bestimmungen enthalten.[40] Deren wichtigste Quelle, das *Paenitentiale Columbani* B, bot nur für einzelne Delikte Bussmasse, die vom Laien oder einfachen Kleriker bis zum Bischof abgestuft waren.[41] In der gemeinsamen Vorlage der einfachen fränkischen Bussbücher, die uns nicht mehr überliefert ist, sind diese Bussmasse nicht nur übernommen, sondern auch auf weitere Bestimmungen übertragen worden.[42]

Der Kompilator des *Excarpsus* ist noch einen Schritt weiter gegangen. Er hat die

---

Priester, das in 1.6 aus anderer Quelle mitgeteilt wird, und dasjenige für den Bischof, das in 1.1 nach *Iudicia Theodori* U 1.1, ed. P. Finsterwalder, *Die Canones Theodori Cantuarensis und ihre Überlieferungsformen* (Weimar 1929) 288, angegeben wird. Den Wortlaut der unbekannten Quelle bietet wohl *Paenitentiale Remense* 3.13; ed. Asbach, Anhang 17: 'De ebrietate: laici VII dies, clerici II ebdomadas, subdiaconi III, diaconi IIII, presbyteri V, episcopus VI'.

39. Zur redaktionellen Leistung der Kompilatoren des *Excarpsus Cummeani* und anderer *Paenitentialia composita* cf. Meens, *Boeteboek* 267–306, 569–72.

40. Aufgrund von Rubriken im *Paenitentiale Capitula iudiciorum*, das solche Busssatzungen seinen unmittelbaren Vorlagen, *Excarpsus Cummeani* und *Paenitentiale Sangallense tripartitum*, entnommen hat, werden die Bestimmungen dieser Quellengruppe als *Iudicia canonica* bezeichnet. Das ist nur insoweit berechtigt, als man diese Busssatzungen im 8. Jahrhundert wohl als Traditionen der fränkischen Kirche verstanden hat; cf. Kottje, *Halitgar* 186; G. Hägele, *Das Paenitentiale Vallicellianum I. Ein oberitalienischer Zweig der frühmittelalterlichen kontinentalen Bussbücher* (Sigmaringen 1984) 69–70; Körntgen, *Studien* 227–28.

41. *Paenitentiale Columbani* B 4, ed. Bieler, *The Irish Penitentials* 100: 'Si quis uero fornicauerit quidem cum mulieribus sed non filium generauerit et in notitiam hominum non uenerit, si clericus, III annis, si monachus uel diaconus, V annis, si sacerdos, VII, si episcopus, XII annis'. Ibid. B 6: 'Si quis maleficio . . . communionem. Si autem pro amore quis maleficus sit et neminem perdiderit, annum integrum cum pane et aqua clericus ille paeniteat, laicus dimidium, diaconus duo, sacerdos tres; maxime, si per hoc mulieris partum quis[que] deceperit, ideo VI quadragesimas unus quisque insuper augeat, ne homicidii reus sit'. Die beiden Busssatzungen sind rezipiert in *Paenitentiale Burgundense* 11 und 9 (ed. CCL 156.21 und 17). Hier und im folgenden wird jeweils nur auf das *Paenitentiale Burgundense* verwiesen, das ausschliesslich *Iudicia canonica* enthält. Die Parallelen der übrigen einfachen fränkischen Bussbücher, die zusätzlich Material aus anderen Quellen überliefern, sind in CCL 156 synoptisch zum *Paenitentiale Burgundense* ediert.

42. *Paenitentiale Burgundense* 26, ed. CCL 156.37: 'Si quis alium (per iram) percusserit et sanguinem fuderit, XL diebus in pane et aqua peneteat, (diaconus VI mensibus, presbyter annum in pane et aqua peniteat)'. Der eingeklammerte Text ist nur in einer der beiden Handschriften des *Burgundense*, München, BSB Clm 14780, überliefert, wird aber auch von den parallelen Paenitentialia, *Parisiense simplex* 18, *Sletstatense* 24, *Oxoniense* I 20 und *Floriacense* 24 (ed. CCL 156.38–39) belegt. Quelle ist *Paenitentiale Columbani* B 9, ed. Bieler, *The Irish Penitentials* 100: 'Si quis clericus per rixam proximum suum percusserit et sanguinem fuderit, annum integrum paeniteat; si laicus, XL diebus'. In gleicher Weise erweitern *Paenitentiale Burgundense* 12 und 16 (ed. CCL 156.21 und 25) die Busssatzungen *Paenitentiale Columbani* B8 und B11, ed. Bieler 100. Keine Quelle ist bekannt für die

Bestimmungen, die er wahrscheinlich einer uns nicht mehr erhaltenen Überlieferung der *Iudicia canonica* verdankte, weiter ausdifferenziert.[43] Als ein Kennzeichen dieser Bearbeitung können wir die Einfügung des Subdiakons werten; dieser Weihegrad war im *Paenitentiale Columbani* und in den *Iudicia canonica* nicht berücksichtigt worden. Da keines der uns bekannten einfachen fränkischen Bussbücher den Subdiakon anführt, spricht alles dafür, dass der Kompilator des *Excarpsus Cummeani* das Bussmasssschema seiner Vorlage ergänzt hat, und zwar nach dem Vorbild des differenzierten Schemas, das ihm aus einer anderen Quelle bekannt war. Als Beispiel für diese ergänzende Redaktion seien nur zwei Bestimmungen, *Excarpsus Cummeani* 3.1 und 3.28, analysiert.[44]

Das Grundgerüst der Busssatzung in *Excarpsus* 3.1 hat der Kompilator dem *Iudicium canonicum* übernommen, wie es durch *Paenitentiale Burgundense* 8 bezeugt ist.[45] Hinzugefügt hat er die Bussmasse für die Laien, den Subdiakon und den Bischof. Nicht aus einem einfachen fränkischen Bussbuch, sondern unmittelbar aus dem *Paenitentiale Columbani* ist *Excarpsus Cummeani* 3.28 rezipiert. In diesem Fall hat der Kompilator die jeweils separat für Kleriker und Laien formulierten Bestimmungen *Paenitentiale Columbani* 10 und 17 ineinander gearbeitet und die in der Quelle nicht berücksichtigten Weihegrade des Diakons und Priesters ergänzt. Solche Erweiterungen um die Laien oder einzelne Weihegrade finden wir noch in *Excarpsus* 3.3 (cf. *Paenitentiale Burgundense* 16), 7.2 (cf. *Burgundense* 10); nur der *monacus* ist ergänzt in 3.4 (cf. *Burgundense* 30). Unverändert übernommen wurden die Busssatzungen 1.33 (cf. *Burgundense* 32) und 6.18 (cf. *Burgundense* 26).

Auch die beiden wichtigsten Quellen insularer Herkunft, das irische *Paenitentiale Cummeani* und die *Iudicia Theodori* in der Version des *discipulus Umbrensium*, haben spezielle Bussmasse für Kleriker oder abgestufte Bussmasse für verschiedene Weihegrade an den *Excarpsus* vermittelt. Aus dem Bussbuch des Iren Cummean stammen vor allem Bestimmungen zur Trunkenheit und Völlerei sowie zum Verstoss gegen die sexuelle Enthaltsamkeit.[46] Sie sind besonders vom monastischen Kontext der irischen

---

Bestimmungen *Paenitentiale Burgundense* 8, 32–33, ed. CCL 156.13, 17, 49, die ebenfalls abgestufte Bussmasse für Kleriker, Diakon und Priester bieten.

43. Cf. Asbach, *Das Poenitentiale Remense* 131–36.

44. *Excarpsus Cummeani* 3.1; ed. CCL 156b, cf. Schmitz, *Bussbücher* 2.612: 'Si quis adulterium fecerit, id est cum uxore aliena aut sponsa uel uirginem corruperit aut sanctimonialem aut deo sacrata, laici III annos peniteat, unum ex his in pane et aqua, si clericus V annos, II in pane et aqua, subdiaconus VI, II in pane et aqua, diaconus et monachus VII, III in pane et aqua, presbyter X, episcopi XII, V ex his in pane et aqua'; *Excarpsus Cummeani* 3.28; ed. CCL 156b, cf. Schmitz, *Bussbücher* 2.616: 'Si laicus cum iumento fornicauerit, annos II peniteat, si uxorem habet, si non habet, annum I, si clericus II, diaconus III, presbyter V, II ex his in pane et aqua'.

45. *Paenitentiale Burgundense* 8; ed. CCL 156.13 und 17, mit Varianten aus München, BSB Clm 14780: 'Si quis adulterium commiserit, id est cum uxore aliena (alterius) aut sponsa uel uirginitate corruperit, si clericus, III (V) annos peneteat, unum (duos) ex his in pane et aqua, (si diaconus septem, tres ex hiis in pane et aqua), si presbiter VII (XII) annos, III (quinque) ex his in pane et aqua'.

46. Die Abschnitte *Excarpsus Cummeani* 1.7–13, 2.22–26, stammen fortlaufend aus *Paenitentiale Cummeani* 1.2–13, 2.1–5; ed. Bieler, *The Irish Penitentials* 112–14.

Busspraxis geprägt, aber auch durch allgemeinkirchliche Normen der britischen Kirche beeinflusst.[47] Die Sammlung des *discipulus Umbrensium* hat nicht zuletzt solche Satzungen beigesteuert, die entsprechend der griechischen Herkunft und der hierarchischen Stellung des Erzbischofs Theodor Elemente der kirchlichen Disziplin wie die Absetzung und Degradierung der Kleriker mit den Bussleistungen der durch die Iren im angelsächsischen England verbreiteten Busspraxis verband.[48]

Der Kompilator des *Excarpsus* hat also in den verschiedenen Quellen, die er ausgeschrieben hat, Bussbestimmungen für die Klerikerbusse gefunden, die in unterschiedlicher Differenzierung Bussmasse für die einzelnen Weihegrade boten oder zumindest zwischen Klerikern, Mönchen und Laien unterschieden. Er hat diese Bestimmungen nicht mehr oder weniger unkontrolliert übernommen, sondern zumindest einzelne redigiert; bei dieser Redaktion kam es ihm offenbar besonders auf die möglichst differenzierte Bemessung der Busse für die einzelnen Weihegrade an. Die Klerikerbusse kann nicht nur deshalb als ein zentraler Gegenstand des Bussbuches verstanden werden. Dessen drei letzte Titel sind sogar fast ausschliesslich den verschiedenen Aspekten der Liturgie, Sakramentenspendung und Seelsorge gewidmet, die zwar auch im Kloster von Bedeutung waren, ebenso aber den nicht im Kloster lebenden Kleriker, besonders den Priester, betrafen.[49] Der *Excarpsus* ist also als ein Bussbuch kompiliert worden, das gleichermassen für die Busse der Laien wie für die der Mönche und Kleriker zu benutzen war. Der Kompilator dürfte nicht zuletzt deshalb das Material seiner verschiedenen Quellen zusammengestellt haben, weil diese jeweils in verschiedenem Umfang die Busse der drei Gruppen berücksichtigten und sich gerade unter diesem Gesichtspunkt ergänzten.

3. Bussbuch und Überlieferungskontext

Ist es plausibel, dass für eine solche Kompilation die *Vetus-Gallica*-Redaktion in Corbie verantwortlich war? Das Problem erscheint nur ein wenig kleiner, wenn wir annehmen, dass man das Bussbuch in Corbie nicht kompiliert, sondern nur in das Textkonvolut mit der *Vetus Gallica* eingefügt hat. Der Widerspruch zur kanonischen Busse,

47. Auf Reste spätantiker Kirchenstrukturen und wohl auch der kirchlichen Busse verweisen *Sinodus Luci Victorie* und *Excerpta quedam de libro Davidis*, ed. ibid. 68–72; cf. Körntgen, *Studien* 60–72.

48. Cf. etwa *Excarpsus Cummeani* 1.2; ed. CCL 156b, cf. Schmitz, *Bussbücher* 2.604: 'Si quis episcopus aut aliquis ordinatus in consuetudine uitium habuerit ebrietatis, aut desinat aut deponatur'; aus *Iudicia Theodori* U 1.1.1, ed. P. Finsterwalder 288; die Bestimmung geht zurück auf *Canon Apostolorum* 41, ed. EOMIA 1.29: 'Episcopus aut presbiter aut diaconus aleae atque ebrietati deseruiens aut desinat aut certe damnetur'. *Excarpsus Cummeani* 2.1, ed. CCL 156b, cf. Schmitz, *Bussbücher* 2.608: 'Episcopi, presbyteri, diaconi fornicationem facientes degradari debent et paenitere iudicio episcopi, tamen communicent'; aus *Iudicia Theodori* U 1.9.1, ed. Finsterwalder 302; die Bestimmung geht zurück auf *Canon Apostolorum* 25, ed. EOMIA 1.18: 'Episcopus aut presbiter aut diaconus qui in fornicatione aut periurio aut furto captus est deponatur, non tamen communione priuetur'.

49. Quelle dieser Titel sind im wesentlichen *Paenitentiale Cummeani* und *Iudicia Theodori* U.

auf die sich die im Zusatztitel 64 zusammengestellten Kanones beziehen, kann einem Redaktor der Sammlung nicht verborgen geblieben sein; der Überlieferungskontext bietet sogar ein bemerkenswertes Indiz dafür, dass man diesen Widerspruch in Corbie nicht nur wahrgenommen, sondern dass man sich damit auch auseinandergesetzt hat. Unmittelbar auf das Bussbuch folgt nämlich im Überlieferungszusammenhang ein apokrypher Brief unter dem Namen des Papstes Hormisda, der explizit gegen die Klerikerbusse Stellung nimmt und die alte kanonische Tradition bekräftigt.[50] Aber auch ein ebenso entschiedenes Plädoyer für die jüngere Praxis findet sich im Überlieferungskomplex, nämlich ein Brief Isidors von Sevilla an Bischof Massona von Mérida.[51] Die beiden einander widersprechenden Stellungnahmen sind im Überlieferungszusammenhang nur durch zwei Briefe Gregors I. getrennt, die andere Fragen betreffen.[52] Dem Isidor-Schreiben ist Kanon 20 des Konzils von Ankyra angefügt, eine Bussbestimmung zum Ehebruch, auf die im Schreiben verwiesen wird. Im Textzusammenhang liest sich das wie eine Replik auf das Ps.-Hormisda-Schreiben, das sich ebenfalls konkret auf den Ehebruch von Klerikern bezieht. Wahrscheinlich hat die Corbie-Redaktion diesen Bezug hergestellt, denn der Ankyra-Kanon zeigt die charakteristischen Merkmale der *Vetus Gallica*.[53] Die Corbie-Überlieferung bietet neben der nur wenig älteren *Collectio Hibernensis* den frühesten Beleg für das später weit überlieferte Isidor-Schreiben, dessen Authentizität umstritten ist.[54] Das für die kanonische Tradition argumentierende Ps.-Hormisda-Schreiben, wohl in den dreissiger Jahren des 6. Jahrhunderts von Caesarius von Arles verfasst, war in der fränkischen Kirche schon länger bekannt—das älteste erhaltene Zeugnis stammt von etwa 600.[55] Dagegen hat man für den entgegengesetzten Standpunkt einen vielleicht erst seit wenigen Jahren verfügbaren Text herangezogen. Auch das bezeugt, dass die Frage der Klerikerbusse im Kontext der Corbie-Redaktion aktuell war.

In der fränkischen Kirche wurde die Klerikerbusse, wie nicht zuletzt die entschiedene Stellungnahme des Caesarius zeigt, trotz der einhelligen kanonischen Tradition schon seit dem frühen 6. Jahrhundert diskutiert.[56] Das dürfte nicht zuletzt erklären, warum das spätestens am Beginn des 7. Jahrhunderts in seiner heute noch erhaltenen

50. JK †868, ed. W. Gundlach, MGH Epistolae 3.49–54; cf. Mordek, *Kirchenrecht und Reform* 225–26 Anm. 56.

51. *Clavis patrum latinorum*, ed. E. Dekkers (Steenbrugge 1995³) 1209; *Clavis patristica pseudoepigraphorum medii aevi* 2 A, ed. J. Machielsen (Turnhout 1994) 1076; cf. Mordek, *Kirchenrecht und Reform* 221 Anm. 13, 227 Anm. 62.

52. Die Briefe Gregors I. an Bischof Etherius von Lyon und die fränkische Königin Balthilde betreffen kirchliche Probleme wie die Simonie; dazu unten bei Anm. 62.

53. Cf. Mordek, *Kirchenrecht und Reform* 227 Anm. 62.

54. Cf. ibid. 227 Anm. 63; Kottje, *Halitgar* 219.

55. Cf. Mordek, *Kirchenrecht und Reform* 225 Anm. 56.

56. Cf. Kottje, *Halitgar* 218.

Gestalt vorliegende *Paenitentiale Columbani* B, dessen erster Teil explizit Bussen für Kleriker bereitstellt, im Frankenreich rezipiert worden ist und warum gerade dieser erste Teil die Grundlage für die *Iudicia canonica* der einfachen fränkischen Bussbücher geboten hat.[57] Einen weiteren Beleg für die Bedeutung der Klerikerbusse bietet das nicht erhaltene *Paenitentiale*, aus dem das im *Excarpsus Cummeani* und anderen Kompilationen bezeugte differenzierte Schema der Bussmasse für die verschiedenen Weihegrade stammt. Diese Traditionen der fränkischen Kirche sind im *Excarpsus Cummeani* mit der durch das *Paenitentiale Cummeani* vermittelten irischen Tradition, in der das kanonische Verbot der Klerikerbusse offensichtlich keine Rolle spielte, und der noch jungen angelsächsischen Überlieferung, die auf Theodor von Canterbury zurückging, verbunden worden. Einiges spricht dafür, dass die Corbie-Redaktion der *Vetus Gallica* auch für diese Zusammenstellung verschiedener Bussbuch-Überlieferungen verantwortlich war. Die grosse Bedeutung der Klerikerbusse in der neuen Kompilation entspricht jedenfalls der Aufmerksamkeit, die man dem Thema in Corbie bei der Zusammenstellung der Begleittexte der *Vetus Gallica* gewidmet hat.

Zur Entstehungszeit der Sammlung war das Thema der Klerikerbusse im Frankenreich alles andere als ein bloss theoretischer Gegenstand kanonistischer Interessen. Mordek hat die *Vetus Gallica* überzeugend in das zweite Viertel des 8. Jahrhunderts datiert, also in die Jahrzehnte, in denen der Angelsachse Bonifatius im Frankenreich wirkte. Ein Thema, das den Erzbischof immer wieder in Konflikt mit wichtigen Amtsträgern der fränkischen Kirche brachte, war der Kampf gegen unwürdige Bischöfe wie Milo von Trier und Gewilib von Mainz, denen auch Kapitaldelikte zur Last gelegt wurden.[58] Abt von Corbie war zu dieser Zeit Grimo, der wohl auf Bitten des Bonifatius im Jahr 744 das Pallium als Erzbischof von Rouen erhielt.[59] Genaueres lässt sich über den Abt und seine möglichen Verbindungen zu Bonifatius nicht ermitteln.[60] Bemerkenswert erscheint allerdings, dass weitere Zusätze und Begleittexte der in Corbie redigierten *Vetus Gallica* Fragen ansprechen, mit denen sich auch Bonifatius konfrontiert sah. Exzerpte aus Schriften Isidors von Sevilla haben allgemeine Anforderungen an das Bischofsamt

---

57. *Paenitentiale Columbani* B 12; ed. Bieler, *The Irish Penitentials* 102: 'Sed haec de clericis et monachis mixtim dicta sunt. Caeterum de laicis'. Aus dem Laien-Teil des *Paenitentiale Columbani* B ist nur c.18 in den gemeinsamen Grundstock der einfachen fränkischen Bussbücher eingegangen; cf. CCL 156.212, Index fontium; Körntgen, *Studien* 230–31.

58. Cf. E. Ewig, 'Milo et eiusmodi similes', in: Idem, *Spätantikes und fränkisches Gallien*, ed. H. Atsma (2 Bde.; München 1979) 2.189–219.

59. Trotz der Bedenken gegen die Identität des Abtes von Corbie und des Erzbischofs von Rouen, die zuletzt T. Zotz, 'Grimo', LMA 4 (1994) 1716–17 geäussert hat, halte ich die Überlegungen bei Mordek, *Kirchenrecht und Reform* 93–94 Anm. 139, für überzeugend; unentschieden bleibt S. Schipperges, *Bonifatius ac socii eius. Eine sozialgeschichtliche Untersuchung des Winfrid-Bonifatius und seines Umfeldes* (Mainz 1996) 85–86.

60. Ein insulares Manuskript mit dem Autographen des Bonifatius (St. Petersburg, Ms. Q v I 1 15) und ein anderes mit seinen Rätseln (Paris, BN lat. 13046) mögen nach dem Tod des Erzbischofs nach Corbie gelangt sein; cf. D. Ganz, *Corbie in the Carolingian Renaissance* (Sigmaringen 1990) 41–42.

und den Lebenswandel der Bischöfe und Kleriker zum Thema.[61] Die beiden Schreiben
Gregors I. an Etherius von Lyon bzw. Königin Brunichild behandeln etwa das Problem
der Bischofspromotionen ohne klerikalen Cursus.[62] Ausserdem fordern sie, zweimal im
Jahr eine Synode abzuhalten.[63] Noch deutlicher verbunden mit konkreten Problemen,
die aus der Korrespondenz des Bonifatius bekannt sind, zeigen sich die Bestimmungen
der beiden römischen Synoden Gregors I. aus dem Jahr 595 und Gregors II. aus dem
Jahr 721. Die ältere Kanonesreihe bietet neben einzelnen Regelungen zur römischen
Liturgie ein Verbot von Gebühren für die Verleihung des Palliums oder die Ausstellung
von Urkunden.[64] Genau diese Praxis hat Bonifatius im Jahr 744 dem Papst Zacharias
vorgehalten, was bei diesem zu deutlicher Verstimmung führte.[65] Die Kanonesreihe der
Synode Gregors II., jüngster Text des Überlieferungskomplexes und damit *terminus post*
für die Corbie-Redaktion der *Vetus Gallica*, bietet den ersten Beleg für das Eheverbot
aufgrund geistlicher Verwandtschaft, mit dem Bonifatius von fränkischen Gegnern
konfrontiert worden ist und nach dessen kanonischer Grundlage er geforscht hat.[66]

Die sachlichen Parallelen besagen noch nicht, dass der Corbeier Überlieferungskomplex für Bonifatius redigiert oder diesem an die Hand gegeben worden wäre. Die
Verbindung der beiden römischen Synoden etwa lag der Corbie-Redaktion schon vor.[67]
Auch ausserhalb des Klosters bestand also Interesse an deren Inhalt. Damit wird aber
eines deutlich: Das Material, das man in Corbie zusammengestellt und gemeinsam mit
der *Vetus Gallica* tradiert hat, entstammte nicht nur zu einem Teil sehr jungen, noch
nicht lange im Frankenreich zugänglichen Quellen wie der *Collectio Hibernensis*, der
römischen Synode von 721 oder der Theodor-Sammlung des *discipulus Umbrensium*.
Es war zugleich höchst aktuell, weil es Probleme betraf, die im zweiten Viertel des
8. Jahrhunderts in der fränkischen Kirche und nicht zuletzt unter Beteiligung des angelsächsischen Reformers Bonifatius diskutiert wurden. Dabei ging es nicht nur um die

61. *Collectio Vetus Gallica* 4.13d–14 und 41.28–30; aus Isidor, *Mysticorum expositiones sacramentorum, Super
Levitico* 12–13 bzw. *De ecclesiasticis officiis*; cf. Mordek, *Kirchenrecht und Reform* 52, 510–11.

62. Gregor I. an Etherius von Lyon, *Caput nostrum* (JE 1747), ed. MGH Epistolae 2.206; Gregor I. an Königin
Brunichild, *Postquam excellentiae* (JE 1742), 1. Teil, ed. MGH Epistolae 2.198–199.18.

63. Zur Bedeutung dieser kanonischen Forderung für Bonifatius und zu seiner Kritik an den Zuständen in
der fränkischen Kirche cf. W. Hartmann, *Die Synoden der Karolingerzeit im Frankenreich und in Italien* (Paderborn 1989) 47–50.

64. 'Antiquam patrum regulam sequens nihil umquam de ordinationibus accipiendum esse constituo
neque ex datione pallii neque ex traditione cartarum neque ex ea quam nova per ambitionem simulatio invenit
appellatione pastelli', ed. P. Ewald und L. Hartmann, MGH Epistolae 1.364.

65. Papst Zacharias an Bonifatius, 744 November 5 (JE 2271); *Germania Pontificia* 4.24 Nr. 58; ed. M. Tangl,
MGH Epistolae selectae 1.107; cf. R. Schieffer, 'Zum Umgang der Karolingerzeit mit Simonie', in: *Scientia Veritatis* 117–26 besonders 120.

66. Bonifatius, Ep. 32–33 aus dem Jahr 735; ed. MGH Epistolae selectae 1.55–58. Cf. Mordek, *Kirchenrecht
und Reform* 86; Hartmann, *Synoden* 39.

67. Cf. Mordek, *Kirchenrecht und Reform* 228–29 Anm. 64.

Verständigung über allgemeine Normen des kirchlichen Rechts oder um die Dignität bestimmter Traditionen, sondern um die aktuelle Praxis. Im Fall der geistlichen Verwandtschaft war das alltägliche Handeln von Bischöfen und Priestern angesprochen, die Frage der Gebühren für Pallien oder Urkunden betraf den zu dieser Zeit intensivierten Kontakt der fränkischen Kirche mit dem Papst. Auch die Frage, ob es für Kleriker, denen Kapitalvergehen vorgeworfen wurden, eine Möglichkeit gab, im Amt zu verbleiben und zugleich wie ein Laie Busse zu leisten, war im Hinblick auf wichtige Amtsträger der fränkischen Kirche von ganz aktueller Bedeutung. Sie musste nicht nur einen entschlossenen Reformer wie Bonifatius beschäftigen, sondern auch Persönlichkeiten der fränkischen Kirche, die an der kirchenrechtlichen Tradition interessiert und für Reformen der Kirche aufgeschlossen waren. Auf Grimo, den Abt von Corbie, dürfte diese Charakterisierung zutreffen.[68] Die während seines Abbatiates, vielleicht auf seine Initiative hin entstandene Zusammenstellung und Redaktion von Texten, die das kirchliche Recht und zugleich Lebensgestaltung und Lebenswandel von Mönchen und Klerikern betrafen, war jedenfalls keine gelehrte Arbeit aus theoretischem Interesse, sondern zielte auf die aktuelle Situation von Mönchtum und Kirche im Frankenreich.

4. Die praktische Bedeutung des *Excarpsus Cummeani*

Was bedeutet das für die Funktion des Bussbuches, das in diesen Kontext gestellt und vielleicht auch dafür kompiliert worden ist? War es vornehmlich für die obersten Ränge der kirchlichen Hierarchie konzipiert, diente es eher der rechtlichen und moraltheologischen Information eines Abtes und eines Bischofs oder Erzbischofs als der Busserteilung durch einen Priester? Die praktische Ausrichtung des Überlieferungszusammenhangs spricht gegen eine solche klare Alternativsetzung. Während etwa die Frage der Palliumsgebühren ausschliesslich Erzbischöfe interessieren musste, war die Kenntnis der Eheverbote aufgrund von geistlicher Verwandtschaft auch für Priester von Bedeutung. In gleicher Weise muss die Relevanz der für das Bussbuch und für den Überlieferungskontext besonders wichtigen Frage der Klerikerbusse differenziert werden. Die Zusammenstellung von Kanones der kirchenrechtlichen Tradition, Busssatzungen, die seit dem 6. Jahrhundert in Irland, England und im Frankenreich entstanden waren, und kontroversen Stellungnahmen wie Ps.-Hormisda und dem Isidor-Brief an Massona konnte in der Praxis beides ermöglichen, die Entscheidung für die Depositur eines Klerikers oder die Erteilung einer Busse. Ein Erzbischof konnte im Überlieferungskontext und im Bussbuch Bestimmungen finden, an denen er sein Verhalten gegenüber einem Bischof oder Priester orientieren konnte, der ein Kapitalde-

---

68. Cf. ibid. 93–94.

likt begangen hatte. Zugleich konnte aber auch ein Priester das Bussbuch heranziehen, wenn er einem Laien Busse für Ehebruch oder eine Körperverletzung auferlegen musste. Ein Priester im Kloster konnte auf das Bussbuch zurückgreifen, wenn nicht nur ein Verstoss gegen die Regel disziplinarisch zu ahnden, sondern Busse für die Sünden der Mönche zu erteilen war. Schliesslich konnten vor allem Priester dem Bussbuch entnehmen, welche Busse sie bei Nachlässigkeiten und Verfehlungen während ihrer liturgischen Handlungen zu leisten hatten.[69] Bei der Lektüre der Begleittexte konnten sie einiges über ihr Amt und dessen Anforderungen lernen.

Das alles setzte einen Bildungsstand voraus, der in der Mitte des 8. Jahrhunderts nur bei wenigen fränkischen Priestern vorzufinden war. Zur Standardausrüstung eines fränkischen Priesters gehörte eine Handschrift mit dem kompletten Überlieferungskontext von *Vetus Gallica* und *Excarpsus Cummeani* sicher nicht. Mit grösserer Wahrscheinlichkeit werden solche Handschriften in nordfranzösischen Klöstern und im Umkreis von Bischofskirchen zu finden gewesen sein, dort allerdings nicht nur zum Gebrauch von Äbten und Bischöfen, sondern wahrscheinlich auch für die Praxis von Mönchspriestern und Priestern aus dem Kathedralklerus bestimmt. Diese Einschränkungen gelten allerdings nur bedingt für das Bussbuch selbst. Dessen früh differenzierte Textgeschichte deutet darauf hin, dass der *Excarpsus Cummeani* schon in der zweiten Hälfte des 8. Jahrhunderts in einer grösseren Zahl von Exemplaren verbreitet war, als es die handschriftliche Überlieferung heute erkennen lässt.[70] Die verschiedenen Überlieferungskontexte der erhaltenen Textzeugen belegen, wie Rob Meens ausführlich dargestellt hat, dass zum ursprünglichen Kontext der Corbie-Redaktion bald auch andere, klarer auf die liturgischen und seelsorgerischen Aufgaben der Priester ausgerichtete Überlieferungskontexte getreten sind, bis hin zur separaten Überlieferung des Bussbuches.[71] Wie die Analyse eines besonderen sachlichen Schwerpunktes, der Klerikerbusse, gezeigt hat, entsprach diese differenzierte Überlieferung der Bandbreite, die das Bussbuch nach der Herkunft seiner Quellen, seinen sachlichen Schwerpunkten und seiner redaktionellen Anpassung auszeichnet.

---

69. Cf. A. Angenendt, 'Missa specialis. Zugleich ein Beitrag zur Entstehung der Privatmessen', FMSt 17 (1983) 153–221, 184–89.

70. Cf. Asbach, *Das Poenitentiale Remense* 64–72.

71. Cf. Meens, *Boeteboek* 231–34; idem 'Frequency' 42–44.

[2]

Zu Effektivität und Aktualität von Reginos Sendhandbuch

Wilfried Hartmann

❖

Eine alte und immer noch ungeklärte Frage ist, ob die Sammlungen des kirchlichen Rechts überhaupt im praktischen Rechtsleben benutzt wurden. Am ehesten scheint dies noch beim Sendhandbuch Reginos von Prüm erwiesen werden zu können, denn dieses Werk wurde für die Praxis des Sendgerichts zusammengestellt. Ob es allerdings dort auch auf dem Tisch des bischöflichen Richters lag, wissen wir nicht.[1] Was wir aber wissen oder ergründen können, ist, in welcher Weise sich der Verfasser des Werks bemühte, ein Buch zusammenzustellen, das den aktuellen Bedürfnissen beim bischöflichen Gericht entsprach.

In einem Brief, mit dem Regino von Prüm sein kirchenrechtliches Handbuch dem Erzbischof Hatto von Mainz widmete, spricht er davon, dass er sein Werk 'über die Rechtsfälle des Sendgerichts und über die kirchliche Zucht' 'auf Befehl und Mahnung des ehrwürdigen Erzbischofs Ratbod' (von Trier) zusammengestellt habe.[2] Das 'handliche Büchlein' *(manualis codicillus)* soll dem Mainzer Erzbischof Hatto als 'Handbuch' *(enkyridion)* dienen, damit er bei seinen Visitationsreisen durch seine Diözese nicht gezwungen ist, 'sehr viele Konzilienbände immer mit sich herumzutragen'.[3] Aus die-

---

1. Einen Beleg dafür aus der 2. Hälfte des 10. Jahrhunderts bietet vielleicht ein Kapitel in der *Vita* des heiligen Bischofs Ulrich von Augsburg, vgl. W. Hartmann, 'Probleme des geistlichen Gerichts im 10. und 11. Jahrhundert: Bischöfe und Synoden als Richter im ostfränkisch-deutschen Reich', in: *La giustizia nell'alto medioevo (secoli IX–XI)* (Settimane 44; Spoleto 1997) 631–72, bes. 637–42, wo c.6 der *Vita Uodalrici* zitiert und eingehend besprochen ist.

2. *Das Sendhandbuch des Regino von Prüm*, hg. und übersetzt von W. Hartmann (Ausgewählte Quellen zur deutschen Geschichte des Mittelalters. Freiherr-vom-Stein-Gedächtnisausgabe 42; Darmstadt 2004, künftig zitiert als: *Regino-Ausgabe*) 21.

3. Ibid.

sem Schreiben geht also ganz klar hervor, dass Regino sein Werk für den praktischen Gebrauch des reisenden Bischofs abgefasst hat.[4]

Noch zu einer anderen Frage nimmt Regino bereits in diesem Widmungsbrief Stellung, nämlich zur Frage der Aktualität seiner Rechtssammlung:[5]

Wenn aber jemanden die Frage umtreibt, warum ich ziemlich häufig Beispiele aus unseren eigenen Konzilien, das heisst aus denen Galliens und Germaniens, benutzt habe, so möge er die Antwort bekommen und wissen, dass ich dafür Sorge getragen habe, besonders die Dinge einzufügen, die nach meiner Erkenntnis in diesen unseren gefährlichen Zeiten von grösserer Notwendigkeit sind und die sich auf die übernommene Aufgabe meines oben angegebenen Anliegens zu beziehen schienen. Auch das muss hinzugefügt werden, dass in dieser sehr schlimmen Zeit in der Kirche viele Arten von Schandtaten begangen wurden und begangen werden, von denen man in den alten Zeiten nichts gehört hat—weil sie nicht begangen wurden—und die deshalb nicht aufgeschrieben und durch unabänderliche Urteilssprüche verurteilt wurden, während sie durch die modernen Vorschriften der Väter verurteilt wurden und noch täglich verurteilt werden.

Regino war also der Meinung, dass es in seiner eigenen Zeit eine grosse Anzahl von Neuerungen im Kirchenrecht gegeben hat, und er führte diese Innovationen darauf zurück, dass seine Zeit bis dahin unerhörte Vergehen hervorgebracht habe. Nur in Parenthese sei gesagt, dass diese Vorstellung bei Regino mit der Auffassung zusammenhängen dürfte, dass er seine eigene Gegenwart als *tempus periculosum*, als Endzeit angesehen hat.[6] Wir wollen uns hier aber nicht mit den eschatologischen Anschauungen Reginos befassen, sondern mit der Frage, ob die zweite Hälfte des 9. Jahrhunderts als Zeit kanonistischer Neuerungen anzusehen ist oder nicht. Dazu wollen wir in drei Schritten vorgehen: Erstens soll etwas zum jeweiligen Anteil der in einer bestimmten Zeit entstandenen Quellen gesagt werden, die Regino in sein Sendhandbuch aufgenommen hat. Zweitens sollen die bis ins 9. Jahrhundert hinein unbekannten Verfahren im kirchlichen Gericht benannt und beschrieben werden. Und endlich sollen einige inhaltliche Aspekte näher betrachtet werden, die Neuerungen der Karolingerzeit gegenüber dem älteren Kirchenrecht darstellen.

Was Reginos Quellen und ihre Entstehungszeit angeht, so interessieren dabei vor allem solche Kapitel, die er aus den Synoden seiner eigenen Zeit entnommen hat. Nach den Aufstellungen von Wasserschleben hat er aus folgenden ostfränkischen Synoden der zweiten Hälfte des 9. Jahrhunderts eine grössere Anzahl von Kapiteln bezogen:

---

4. Zur Verbreitung des *Sendhandbuchs*, vgl. ibid. 7. Spuren der Benutzung des Werkes gibt es zuerst auf der Synode von Hohenaltheim im Jahre 916, vgl. MGH Concilia 6.1.36 Anm. 128.

5. *Regino-Ausgabe*, 21, 23.

6. Vgl. zur Bedeutung der Rede von *tempora periculosa* in der Zeit um 800, W. Brandes, 'Tempora periculosa sunt. Eschatologisches im Vorfeld der Kaiserkrönung Karls des Grossen', in: *Das Frankfurter Konzil von 794* I: *Politik und Kirche*, hg. von R. Berndt (Mainz 1997) 49–79, bes. 66–71.

13 Kapitel aus der Synode von Mainz 847, vier Kapitel aus der Synode von Mainz 852, 18 Kapitel aus der Synode von Worms 868 und 40 Kapitel aus den verschiedenen Versionen der Kanones von Tribur 895. Von der westfränkischen Synode von Meaux-Paris 845/46 hat Regino 46 Kapitel rezipiert.[7] Ausserdem stammen 22 von Reginos Kapiteln aus westfränkischen Kapitularien der zweiten Hälfte des 9. Jahrhunderts. Insgesamt ergibt das die stattliche Zahl von 143 Kapiteln, die aus Texten entnommen wurden, die in der zweiten Hälfte des 9. Jahrhunderts entstanden sind; bei einem Gesamtumfang von Reginos Werk von 909 Kapiteln sind das 15,7 %.

Wenn man alle aus karolingischen Konzilien und Kapitularien bezogenen Texte Reginos berücksichtigt, kommt man auf 308 Kapitel; das sind dann 33,88 %, also mehr als ein Drittel der Gesamtzahl. Einen besonders grossen Anteil, nämlich 155 Kapitel, das sind 16,5 %, nehmen dabei Kapitel aus den Kapitularien der karolingischen Könige und Kaiser ein, die Regino zum grössten Teil aus der Kapitulariensammlung des Abtes Ansegis von Fontenelle bezog.[8]

Zu diesen vielen Texten aus Synoden und Kapitularien der Karolingerzeit wären noch die 6 Kapitel aus Briefen Papst Nikolaus I. und die 13 Kapitel aus den falschen Dekretalen Pseudoisidors (gegenüber insgesamt 55 Exzerpten aus echten Papstdekretalen von Siricius bis Gregor dem Grossen) zu zählen sowie diejenigen Texte aus Bussbüchern, die aus karolingerzeitlichen Paenitentialien übernommen sind (vor allem aus dem *Quadripartitus* und aus dem Doppelpaenitentiale Beda-Egberts). Aus dem im dritten Viertel des 9. Jahrhunderts in Reims entstandenen *Quadripartitus* hat Regino 155 Kapitel, das sind 16,5 % seiner Texte, übernommen.[9]

Zum Vergleich: Das systematische Handbuch des Kirchenrechts, das vielleicht Agobard von Lyon am Anfang des 9. Jahrhunderts erstellt hatte, die sogenannte *Collectio Dacheriana*, hatte überhaupt keine zeitgenössischen Texte aufgenommen, und auch die fast gleichzeitig mit Reginos Werk kompilierte *Collectio Anselmo dedicata* konzentrierte sich auf das ältere Kirchenrecht. Allerdings muss man hier sagen, dass in diese Sammlung in grösserem Ausmass pseudoisidorische Texte eingegangen sind: ca. 500 von 1980 Kapiteln, also ziemlich genau ein Viertel (25,25 %), sind aus den Falschen Dekretalen Pseudoisidors übernommen.[10] Diese pseudoisidorischen Texte wurden

---

7. Vgl. Regino abbas Prumiensis, *Libri duo de synodalibus causis et disciplinis ecclesiasticis*, ed. Wasserschleben 519–21 (Quellenverzeichnis).

8. Zur Benutzung der Kapitulariensammlung des Ansegis durch Regino vgl. G. Schmitz (Hg.), *Die Kapitulariensammlung des Ansegis* (MGH Capitularia n.s. 1) 330–35.

9. Vgl. F. Kerff, *Der Quadripartitus. Ein Handbuch der karolingischen Kirchenreform. Überlieferung, Quellen und Rezeption* (Sigmaringen 1982) 71.

10. Zur Pseudoisidor-Rezeption in der *Anselmo dedicata*, vgl. H. Fuhrmann, *Einfluss und Verbreitung der pseudoisidorischen Fälschungen. Von ihrem Auftreten bis in die neuere Zeit* II (Schriften der MGH 24.2; Stuttgart 1973) 425–35.

vom Kompilator dieser Sammlung gerade nicht als Erzeugnisse des 9. Jahrhunderts aufgefasst, sondern als solche aus den Zeiten der Urkirche, also des 1. bis 4. Jahrhunderts.

Was Regino angeht, so ist seine Abhängigkeit von Quellen aus der Karolingerzeit noch grösser als bisher angedeutet: Denn die nicht wenigen Kapitel, die Formulare für Eide oder die Exkommunikation darstellen, dürften ebenfalls aus zeitgenössischen Quellen stammen. Es handelt sich um 14 Kapitel mit Eidformularen (2.2–4; 2.232–236; 2.239–244), sieben Kapitel mit Exkommunikationsformeln (2.412–418) und sechs Kapitel mit Formbriefen (2.413–416 und 2.450–451). Dazu kommen die beiden Fragekataloge (vor 1.1 und in 2.5) sowie der umfangreiche Ordo mit Beichtfragen (1.304). Wahrscheinlich entstammt auch die Mehrheit jener Texte, die aus sonst nicht bekannten Vorlagen entnommen sind, vor allem die Kapitel, die Regino den Synoden von Rouen und von Nantes zugeschrieben hat, aus Rechtsquellen, die in der Karolingerzeit entstanden sind; insgesamt gibt es bei Regino 88 sogenannte *Capita incerta*.[11]

Damit wären wir bei ziemlich genau 600 Kapiteln, die Regino aus zeitgenössischen Quellen entnommen hätte, das sind 66 %, also zwei Drittel des gesamten Bestandes!

Zu den *Capita incerta* soll hier nur noch bemerkt werden, dass es sich bei diesen um Texte handelt, die zum grössten Teil ohne inhaltliche Parallelen im älteren und auch im zeitgenössischen Kirchenrecht sind. Entweder hat Regino hier von der Möglichkeit Gebrauch gemacht, durch gefälschte Texte ihm nötig erscheinende Innovationen 'zu erfinden', oder er hat entlegene Quellen aufgespürt und diese rezipiert, weil er ihren Inhalt für so wichtig hielt, dass er diese Texte in sein Werk aufnahm.

In einem zweiten Abschnitt sollen nun die neuen Verfahren im kirchlichen Gericht kurz vorgestellt werden: Vor allem handelt es sich dabei um das Sendgericht, dann geht es um bis dahin nicht bekannte Formen des Gottesurteils und schliesslich um die Verfahrensweisen bei der Exkommunikation und bei der Gestaltung der Busse.

a. Sendgericht

Die wichtigste Neuerung des 9. Jahrhunderts ist sicher die 'Erfindung' des Sendgerichts.[12] Wann genau diese neue Form des Gerichts von dem seine Diözese bereisenden und visitierenden Bischof zum ersten Mal durchgeführt wurde, können wir nicht sagen. Neben den Texten in der Sammlung Reginos von Prüm (2.1–4 und 2.290), deren

---

11. Zu den von Wasserschleben sogenannten *Capita incerta* vgl. W. Hartmann, 'Die Capita incerta im Sendhandbuch Reginos von Prüm', in: *Scientia veritatis. Festschrift für Hubert Mordek zum 65. Geburtstag*, hg. von O. Münsch und T. Zotz (Ostfildern 2004) 207–26; ibid. 225–26 findet sich eine (vorläufige) Liste der *Capita incerta* bei Regino.

12. Vgl. dazu vor allem A. Koeniger, *Die Sendgerichte in Deutschland* (München 1907).

Entstehungszeit nicht feststeht, gibt es eine kleine Anzahl von Texten, die ausserhalb von Reginos Sendhandbuch überliefert sind und die sich auf diese neue Form des bischöflichen Gerichts beziehen. Allerdings wissen wir auch bei diesen Texten nicht, in welcher Zeit genau sie entstanden sind. Es handelt sich um folgende Texte:

1) Den *Canon extravagans 3* von Meaux-Paris.[13] Nach Koeniger ist das ein echter Kanon der Synode von Meaux-Paris, der Text wäre dann 845 oder 846 entstanden.[14] Das Kapitel ist aber nur in fünf Handschriften des 10. bis 12. Jahrhunderts überliefert, von denen die älteste (Clm 6241) in der 2. Hälfte des 10. Jahrhunderts geschrieben wurde (in dieser Handschrift sind ausser dem *Canon extravagans 3* auch zwei echte Kanones von Meaux-Paris [c.73–74] enthalten).[15] Alle fünf Handschriften stammen übrigens aus Baiern, und zwar aus Freising, Schäftlarn, Salzburg und Benediktbeuern.

2) Die sogenannte *Augsburger Sendordnung* ist nach Koeniger zwischen 860 und 890 entstanden.[16] Überliefert ist sie in den Handschriften Clm 3851 und 3853, die beide ehemals aus Augsburg stammen.[17] Die ältere der beiden Handschriften, Clm 3851, war um und kurz nach 900 in Ellwangen.[18] Ob sie dort entstanden ist, wissen wir nicht; nach Bernhard Bischoff wurde sie im 4. Viertel des 9. Jahrhunderts in 'Lothringen' geschrieben.[19] Vielleicht kann man soviel sagen: Aufgrund der Provenienz der Handschrift kommt die *Sendordnung* mit Sicherheit nicht aus Augsburg; sie ist vielleicht eher nach 'Lothringen' oder genauer nach Langres zu lokalisieren, da es in der 2. Hälfte des 8. und in der 1. Hälfte des 9. Jahrhunderts mit Sicherheit enge Beziehungen zwischen Langres und Ellwangen gab; vielleicht bestand diese Verbindung auch noch am Ende des 9. Jahrhunderts.[20]

3) Zur Frage nach der Entstehungszeit des Sendgerichts gibt es einen weiteren Text, der nicht nur einigermassen präzise datiert werden kann, nämlich ins Jahr 877, sondern

---

13. MGH Concilia 3.130–31.

14. A. M. Koeniger, 'Zu den Beschlüssen der Synoden von Meaux 845 und Koblenz 922', NA 31 (1906) 377–98.

15. Vgl. zu dieser Handschrift MGH Concilia 3.68 und 3.129.

16. Vgl. Koeniger, *Die Sendgerichte* 51. Der Text ist ibid. 191–94 ediert.

17. Vgl. V. Krause, 'Die Münchener Handschriften 3851, 3853 mit einer Compilation von 181 Wormser Schlüssen', NA 19 (1894) 85–139, hier 118–20.

18. Vgl P. Geary, 'Der Münchener Cod. lat. 3851 und Ellwangen im 10. Jahrhundert', DA 33 (1977) 167–70.

19. B. Bischoff, *Katalog der festländischen Handschriften des neunten Jahrhunderts (mit Ausnahme der wisigotischen)* II: *Laon–Paderborn* (Wiesbaden 2004) 226.

20. Vgl. W. Störmer, 'Die Bischöfe von Langres aus Alemannien und Bayern. Beobachtungen zur monastischen und politischen Geschichte im ostrheinischen Raum des 8. und frühen 9. Jahrhunderts', in: *Aux origines d'une seigneurie ecclésiastique. Langres et ses évêques, VIIIe–XIe siècles. Actes du colloque Langres-Ellwangen* (Langres 1986) 43–74, der darauf hinweist, dass nicht nur der Bruder des Gründers von Kloster Ellwangen in der 2. Hälfte des 8. Jahrhunderts Bischof von Langres war, sondern dass es auch im 1. Drittel des 9. Jahrhunderts Beziehungen zwischen den beiden Orten gegeben hat.

der auch etwas anderes ist als eine Norm, nämlich der Bericht über eine 'Sitzung' des bischöflichen Gerichts. In der Formel Nr. 30 des sog. *Formelbuchs Salomos III. von Konstanz* stehen folgende Sätze:[21]

Als ich meine Diözese visitierte, kam ich an den Ort, an dem die erwähnten Leute lebten, und dort lernte ich von den angesehenen Männern dieses Ortes, dass diese Eheleute auf die Weise verwandtschaftlich verbunden waren, dass sie auf der einen Seite in der fünften, auf der andern in der vierten Generation eine gemeinsame Abkunft besassen. Das habe ich als wahr erkannt durch eine Untersuchung *(inquisitio),* die angestellt wurde und deren Richtigkeit durch einen Eid gesichert wurde, bei der nämlich alle, vom geringsten bis zum höchsten darlegten, dass sich die Sache so verhalte.

Im Jahre 877 gab es demnach in der Diözese Konstanz ein vom Bischof geleitetes Sendgericht, das der Bischof während seiner Visitationsreise durchführte und auf dem die Anwesenden durch einen Eid verpflichtet wurden, ihr Wissen über ein mögliches Verwandtschaftsverhältnis von Ehegatten wahrheitsgemäss offen zu legen. Eine wichtige Aufgabe dieser bischöflichen Inquisition war die Aufspürung von sogenannten inzestuösen Ehen. Ausserdem werden in dem Text aus Konstanz auch 'angesehene Männer' *(memorati homines)* genannt, die vom Bischof anscheinend erst befragt wurden und in anderen Texten zum Sendgericht als *homines veraces* oder ähnlich auftauchen.[22]

4) Reginos Werk enthält implizit eine umfassende Darstellung der formalen Regelungen des Sendgerichts: Hier tauchen 96 Sendfragen an Kleriker und 89 Fragen, die an Laien gerichtet werden sollen, auf.[23] Regino zitiert weitere Texte, aus denen wir Einzelheiten über die Durchführung dieses neuartigen Gerichts erfahren. So wird (Regino 2.1) die Visitationsreise eines Bischofs beschrieben: Der Archidiakon oder der Archipresbyter soll einen oder zwei Tage vor der Ankunft des Bischofs die Priester versammeln, um geringfügige Vergehen dieser Personengruppe bereits vor dem Erscheinen des Bischofs zu behandeln.[24] Von einer vorbereitenden Sitzung mit ausgewählten Laien ist nicht die Rede.

Im folgenden Kapitel (Regino 2.2) heisst es dann, dass in jeder Gemeinde einige Laien ausgewählt werden sollen, die als sogenannte Sendzeugen über die eventuell

---

21. Druck: K. Zeumer (MGH Formulae Merowingici et Karolini aevi; Hannover 1886) 415–16, das Zitat auf 416. Auf diesen Text hat bereits Hinschius, *System* 5.428–29 Anm. 5 hingewiesen. Zur zeitlichen Einordnung dieses Textes vgl. E. Dümmler, *Das Formelbuch des Bischofs Salomo III. von Konstanz aus dem 9. Jahrhundert* (Leipzig 1857) 126–27.

22. Bei Regino 2.2, wo es um die Sendgeschworenen geht, heissen sie *viri maturiores, honestiores atque veraciores (Regino-Ausgabe* 236); in der sogenannten *Augsburger Sendordnung* heissen sie *veriores et prudentiores* (Koeniger, *Die Sendgerichte* 191). Vgl. auch *Canon extravagans* 3 des Konzils von Meaux-Paris 845/46 (MGH Concilia 3.130–31).

23. *Regino-Ausgabe* 24–39 (vor Regino 1.1) und 236–51 (Regino 2.5).

24. Ibid. 234–35.

justiziablen Vorkommnisse in ihrer Gemeinde berichten sollen.[25] Dass erst der Bischof selbst sich mit den Vergehen der Laien befasst, geht aus der Formulierung dieses Kapitels klar hervor.

Der Bischof soll also zuerst die Sendgeschworenen benennen und sie auf die Reliquien der Kirche vereidigen lassen. Einen Eid müssen dann aber auch sämtliche Gemeindeglieder schwören, die ja vollzählig auf dem Send erscheinen müssen, wenn sie nicht die Exkommunikation riskieren wollen. In Reginos Kapitel ist in diesem Zusammenhang vom Erzbischof von Trier die Rede.[26] Das dürfte wohl bedeuten, dass dieser Text aus der Praxis des bischöflichen Gerichts in der Trierer Diözese stammt.

Die Überwachung der Lebensführung der Gläubigen, die nach Regino 2.2 den Sendzeugen übertragen ist, wird an einer anderen Stelle von Reginos Handbuch sogenannten Dekanen zugewiesen (2.395). Es geht bei der in diesem Text vorgeschriebenen Überwachung der Gläubigen anscheinend vor allem darum, die Einhaltung der im engsten Sinn kirchlichen Gebote zu kontrollieren, nämlich den Besuch des Gottesdienstes und die Heiligung der kirchlichen Feiertage.[27]

Reginos Kapitel 2.1 bis 2.4 enthalten also zentrale Texte für die praktische Durchführung des Sendgerichts; sie werden—wie auch Regino 2.395—durch ihre Inskription einem Konzil von Rouen zugeschrieben, dessen Beschlüsse ausserhalb von Reginos Sammlung nicht überliefert sind. Müssen wir annehmen, dass Regino hier auf die Beschlüsse eines sonst gänzlich unbekannten Konzils zurückgegriffen hat, die ihm noch zur Verfügung standen, die aber keine weitere Spur hinterlassen haben, oder hat er vielleicht Texte obskurer Herkunft einem von ihm erfundenen Konzil zugeordnet? Immerhin erscheint es möglich, dass Regino Texte aus dem Nordwesten des Westfrankenreichs gekannt hat, denn das Kloster Prüm hatte dort Besitzungen und daher dürfte es auch einen Austausch von Gütern, von Nachrichten und wohl auch von Texten zwischen dieser Region und dem Mutterkloster Prüm gegeben haben.[28]

Andernfalls müssten wir Regino für einen Fälscher halten, und Fälscher und Fälschungen hat es ja im 9. Jahrhundert zahlreich gegeben, nicht nur Pseudoisidor und sein grosses Fälschungsunternehmen waren damals aktiv.

Die von Regino gesammelten Texte lassen jedenfalls erkennen, dass das Sendgericht zu seiner Zeit bereits vollständig entwickelt war. Es gibt genaue Vorschriften über seinen äusseren Ablauf (2.1), über die Art und Weise, wie die Delikte in den einzelnen Pfarreien aufgespürt werden sollen (2.2), und es gibt Eidformulare, nach denen ver-

25. Ibid. 236–37.
26. Ibid. (Regino 2.3).
27. Ibid. 432–33.
28. Vgl. dazu K. F. Werner, 'Zur Arbeitsweise des Regino von Prüm', *Die Welt als Geschichte* 19 (1959) 96–116, hier 106–107, und Hartmann, 'Capita incerta' 218.

schiedene Delinquenten ihre Vergehen offenbaren oder ihr zukünftiges Verhalten festlegen sollen.[29]

b. Gottesurteile

Vor dem bischöflichen Gericht wurden anscheinend auch Gottesurteile durchgeführt, und zwar auch in solchen Formen, die erst in der 2. Hälfte des 9. Jahrhunderts aufgekommen sind. In zwei Kapiteln bei Regino (2.277 und 2.278) ist eine Abendmahlsprobe vorgesehen, wonach die Beschuldigten aufgefordert werden, das Abendmahl zu nehmen mit den Worten: 'Der Leib des Herrn diene dir heute zur Prüfung' (nämlich der Wahrheit deiner Aussage). Beide Texte stammen aus dem Konzil von Worms 868; sie wurden auf diesem Konzil neu formuliert (c.42–43).[30]

Gab es eine Abendmahlsprobe auch schon früher? Peter Browe beantwortete diese Frage schon 1928 mit der Aussage: 'Aus Deutschland ist das Verfahren, die Kommunion allein, getrennt von anderen Ordalien, als Reinigungsmittel zu gebrauchen, seit der Mitte des 9. Jahrhunderts bekannt'.[31] Und Browe meinte auch: 'Vor dieser Zeit wird die Sitte nicht entstanden sein'.[32] Als Beleg für diese Ansicht weist er darauf hin, dass in Mainz 852 (c.8) auch für Priester und Bischöfe noch ein Reinigungseid vorgesehen war, während in Worms 868 bei Diebstahl im Kloster und bei kriminellen Anschuldigungen wie Totschlag, Ehebruch oder Magie gegen hohe Kleriker (Bischöfe und Priester sind genannt) eine Abendmahlsprobe vorgesehen ist. Als Grund für die Einführung dieses neuartigen Ordals machte bereits Browe darauf aufmerksam, dass anscheinend vor allem im Ostfrankenreich eine Eidesleistung von Geistlichen für unzulässig angesehen wurde.[33]

Auch nach Westfranken ist die Abendmahlsprobe noch im 9. Jh. gelangt, wie die Synode von Châlons-sur-Marne (894) zeigt, in der ein des Mordes beschuldigter Mönch einer Abendmahlsprobe unterworfen werden soll.[34]

Bereits Karl der Grosse hatte übrigens beabsichtigt, die blutigen Gottesurteile durch

---

29. So in Regino 2.232–33 über Verwandtenehen, in 2.234 beim Versprechen der Trennung von einer Frau, mit der ein inzestuöses Verhältnis bestanden hat; in 2.235: Reinigungseid im Fall eines vorgeworfenen Ehebruchs; 2.236 beim Verkehrs- und Eheverbot mit der Frau, mit der ein Ehebruch oder Unzucht begangen wurde. 2.239 bietet einen Reinigungseid im Fall des Vorwurfs des Mords am Ehegatten, 2.240 einen Eid zur Abwehr des Vorwurfs des Mordkomplotts, und 2.241 ein Formular für ein Versprechen, die weggeschickte Frau wieder aufzunehmen.

30. MGH Concilia 4.281.

31. P. Browe, 'Die Abendmahlsprobe im Mittelalter', HJb 48 (1928) 193–207, hier 196.

32. Ibid. 196 Anm. 11. Allerdings berichtet bereits Gregor von Tours in seiner Fränkischen Geschichte (10.8) von einer Abendmahlsprobe, die er selbst an einem des Mordes beschuldigten Grafen vorgenommen haben will.

33. Ibid. 199 verweist Browe auf c.21 von Tribur 895 (MGH Capitularia 2.224–25).

34. Vgl. I. Schröder, *Die westfränkischen Synoden von 888 bis 987 und ihre Überlieferung* (MGH Hilfsmittel 3; München 1980) 138.

unblutige zu ersetzen; so sollte die Kreuzprobe, die bereits unter Pippin eine Rolle spielte, an die Stelle des Zweikampfs treten.[35] Von den übrigen Gottesurteilen finden sich in den Synodalkanones der 2. Hälfte des 9. Jahrhunderts nur die Wasser- und die Eisenprobe (aber nur die Probe des kochenden, nicht die des kalten Wassers); der Zweikampf ist nicht erwähnt, er kommt nur vor, weil er von Papst Nikolaus I. abgelehnt wird.[36]

c. Exkommunikation

Die wichtigste Form der Sanktion, die ein Sendgericht ausgesprochen hat, war die Exkommunikation. Diese Ausschliessung aus der kirchlichen Gemeinschaft darf aber nicht als Strafe missverstanden werden; sie sollte vielmehr Druck auf die Delinquenten ausüben, die ihnen auferlegten Busshandlungen und Genugtuungsleistungen tatsächlich zu vollziehen. Wegen der hohen Bedeutung der Exkommunikation im Kontext des Sendgerichts ist es nicht erstaunlich, dass es seit dem ausgehenden 9. Jahrhundert genaue Vorschriften und liturgische Formulare für die Durchführung dieser Massnahme gab, die dann Regino—wieder einmal als erster—in sein Sendhandbuch aufgenommen hat. Es sind dies die Kapitel 412 bis 417 des 2. Buches.[37]

Regino 2.418 bietet dann auch ein Ritual für die Rekonziliation eines Büssers. Die Formulare für die Exkommunikation sind aus Reginos Werk ins *Pontificale Romano-Germanicum* aufgenommen worden.[38] Auch die Bekanntgabe der Exkommunikation wird in einem der bei Regino überlieferten Formulare beschrieben: Zuerst soll die Gemeinde unterrichtet werden, weiterhin sollen alle Pfarrer der Diözese durch den Bischof schriftlich informiert werden.[39]

d. Busse

Am Anfang seines 2. Buches bietet Regino genaue Vorschriften über die einzelnen Schritte der Busse, die ein Büsser zu erfüllen hat (2.6–2.9). Er hat diese Texte aus den Beschlüssen des Konzils von Tribur 895 übernommen. Sie stehen bezeichnenderweise unter der Überschrift 'Die Busse für Totschlag soll nicht auf unterschiedliche Weise wie früher, sondern in allen Diözesen auf dieselbe Weise durchgeführt werden'.[40]

35. Vgl. Kapitular von Herstal 779 c.10 (MGH Capitularia 1.49, linke Spalte).

36. Vgl. H. Nottarp, *Gottesurteilstudien* (München 1956) 320–21.

37. Regino, ed. Wasserschleben 369–75. Weder bei F. Kober, *Der Kirchenbann nach den Grundsätzen des canonischen Rechts dargestellt* (Tübingen 1857), noch bei Hinschius, *System,* oder bei E. Vodola, *Excommunication in the Middle Ages* (Berkeley, Los Angeles, London 1986) findet sich etwas zur Entstehungszeit dieser Formulare.

38. *Pontificale Romano-Germanicum saeculi decimi,* hg. von C. Vogel and R. Elze (Studi e testi 226; Città del Vaticano 1963) 1.308–14.

39. Vgl. Hinkmar von Reims, Brief 17 (PL 126.101); Kober, *Kirchenbann* 177–78.

40. So lautet die Rubrik von Regino 2.6 (*Regino-Ausgabe* 253).

Dieser wichtige Punkt, der Kampf gegen die 'Verschiedenheit und Willkürlichkeit' der Busspraxis wurde bereits in der Zeit Karls des Grossen geführt.[41] So heisst es im Bischofkapitular Haitos von Basel (c.19): 'Bei der Verhängung von Bussleistungen soll man nicht unterschiedlich vorgehen, indem dem einen eine geringe, dem anderen eine höhere Busse auferlegt wird, dem einen geschmeichelt und der andere herabgesetzt wird, sondern nachdem der Stand der jeweiligen Person berücksichtigt wurde, soll nach dem Mass der Schuld die Höhe der Strafe festgelegt werden'.[42]

Und das von Theodulf von Orléans wesentlich mitbestimmte Konzil von Chalon 813 formulierte in c.38: 'Die Form der Busse aber soll denen, die ihre Sünden bekennen, entweder gemäss den Vorschriften der alten Kanones oder nach der Autorität der Heiligen Schrift oder nach der Gewohnheit der Kirche auferlegt werden'. Es folgt dann die bekannte Ablehnung der Bussbücher mit den Worten *quorum sunt certi errores, incerti auctores*.[43]

Besonders interessiert an der Fortführung dieser Reformbemühungen zeigte sich Hrabanus Maurus, der nicht nur in seinen beiden Paenitentialien, sondern auch in den von ihm bestimmten Synoden von Mainz 847 und 852 eine ganze Reihe von Texten aus den Synoden von 813 übernommen hat (so zum Beispiel den oben zitierten Kanon von Chalon 813, der als c.31 in verkürzter Form in Mainz 847 rezipiert wurde).[44] Eine ganze Reihe dieser Texte hat Regino in sein Handbuch aufgenommen.

Nur exemplarisch kann im folgenden Abschnitt belegt werden, dass es eine ganze Reihe von inhaltlichen Neuerungen im Kirchenrecht gab, die am Ende des 9. Jahrhunderts erstmals auftauchen. Von diesen Neuerungen sollen Erweiterungen und Präzisierungen der Inzestgesetze, Bestimmungen über unbeabsichtigten Totschlag, Mord an Verwandten und an Klerikern sowie die Beachtung sozialer Probleme wenigstens vorgestellt werden.

a. Inzestbestimmungen

Die Kapitel über den Inzest nehmen in Reginos Handbuch einen beachtlichen Umfang ein; kein anderes einzelnes Delikt ist mit so vielen Texten vertreten: Kapitel 98 bis 265 des 2. Buches, also insgesamt 168 Kapitel (das sind mehr als ein Drittel des gesamten 2. Buchs!) gelten dem Thema Ehe, Inzest und Sexualdelikten. Besonders eif-

41. Vgl. Hinschius, *System* 5.85–104, besonders 91 mit Anm. 1.

42. 'Nec diversa sentiant in iudiciis poenitentium, cum uni minus, alteri maius, alteri adolando, alteri detrahendo placere velit; sed considerata qualitate personae iuxta modum culpae agatur censura vindictae' (MGH Capit. 1.365); vgl. Hinschius, *System* 5.91 Anm. 3.

43. MGH Concilia 2.1.281. Vgl. dazu W. Hartmann, *Die Synoden der Karolingerzeit im Frankenreich und in Italien* (Paderborn 1989) 136 und 436–37.

44. MGH Concilia 3.176; zur Vorlage dieses Kanons, ibid. 176 Anm. 115.

rig hat Regino auch hier wieder auf Zeugnisse aus der Karolingerzeit zurückgegriffen. 13 Kapitel zum Inzest entnahm Regino dem Konzil von Tribur 895 (2.204–216),[45] sechs Kapitel (2.217–222) der Synode von Compiègne 757.[46]

Seit der Merowingerzeit gab es strenge kirchliche Verbote, nahe Verwandte zu heiraten. Schon das erste Konzil im merowingischen Frankenreich, Orléans 511, hatte in seinem Kanon 18 damit begonnen, einen Katalog von Heiratsverboten zusammenzustellen, in dem die Verwandtschaftsgrade, mit denen eine Ehe verboten war, genannt wurden. Fast alle späteren fränkischen Synoden des 6. Jahrhunderts hatten den Katalog weiter ausgestaltet.[47] Eine weitere wichtige Etappe war dann das Konzil von Rom 721, in dem in den ersten elf Kanones—vor allem in den Kapiteln 4 bis 8—der Verstoss gegen die Eheverbote mit dem Anathem belegt wurde.[48]

Kapitularien und Synoden zur Zeit König Pippins (751–768) erweiterten abermals den Bestand an solchen Eheverboten und brachten Klarstellungen für Spezialfälle sowie Regelungen zur Bestrafung durch das weltliche Gericht, so etwa im c.1 des Kapitulars Pippins, das bei Regino 2.223 rezipiert ist:[49]

Wenn jemand mit seiner Verwandten Inzest begeht, soll er sein Privatvermögen verlieren, wenn er welches hat. Und wenn er sich nicht bessern will, soll keiner ihn in sein Haus aufnehmen noch ihm Speise geben. Wenn einer dies tut, soll er dem König 60 Solidi zahlen. Und wenn er kein Geld hat, soll er, wenn er ein Freier ist, in den Kerker geworfen, wenn er ein Unfreier ist, mit vielen Schlägen geprügelt werden.

In einer ganzen Reihe von Kanones von Tribur (895) wurden die seit den Synoden der Zeit König Pippins (751–768) intensivierten Bemühungen um ein Verbot der Ehe zwischen nahen Verwandten oder mit solchen Personen, die mit nahen Verwandten sexuelle Beziehungen hatten, erweitert und verfeinert. In Tribur wurden auch mehrere Kanones über das Inzestvergehen mit der Bemerkung *Perlatum est ad sanctam synodum*—'es ist der heiligen Synode berichtet worden' oder ähnlich eingeleitet.[50] Das heisst doch, dass die Synode aktiv wurde, weil sie über einen tatsächlich geübten Missbrauch informiert wurde. Man muss sich fragen, ob alle diese neuen Inzestbestimmungen eine Reaktion auf praktische Erfahrungen mit dem kirchlichen Inzestverbot sind oder ob manche der erwähnten Fälle nicht eher 'am grünen Tisch' ausgedacht wurden.

45. Ed. Wasserschleben 295–300.   46. Ibid. 300–02.

47. P. Mikat, *Die Inzestgesetzgebung der merowingisch-fränkischen Konzilien, 511–626/27* (Paderborn 1994).

48. Vgl. Hartmann, *Synoden der Karolingerzeit* 39–40, 469.

49. *Regino-Ausgabe* 355. Die Vorlage für dieses Kapitel ist wohl weniger Pippins Kapitulare von 754–755, c.1 (MGH Capitularia 1.31), sondern Benedictus Levita 1.9 (MGH Leges 2.2.47).

50. Vgl. Tribur 895 c.39a (*Pervenit ad notitiam nostram*, MGH Capitularia 2.235.29), c.40a (*Relatum est auribus sanctorum sacerdotum*, ibid. 236.25–26), c.2 und c.6 der *Canones extravagantes* (*Perlatum est ad sanctam synodum*, ibid. 247.10 und 248.6). In den früheren Konzilien der Karolingerzeit findet sich übrigens eine solche Wortwahl nicht.

Die Widerstände, die diese neuen Bestimmungen bei den betroffenen Personen erregten, lassen sich aus einigen Konzilskanones des ausgehenden 9. Jahrhunderts erschliessen, weil sich diese immer wieder mit konkreten Einzelfällen zu befassen hatten. Eine besonders deutliche Sprache spricht c.10 der Synode von Metz 893, in dem die brutale Reaktion eines Betroffenen unter Nennung von Namen dargestellt ist. Eine Frau namens Ava hatte auf Anraten ihres Bruders Folcrius und ihrer Verwandten ihren Mann verlassen und weigerte sich, zu diesem zurückzukehren. Der Priester namens Folcardus, der die Frau ermahnen wollte, die eheliche Gemeinschaft wieder herzustellen, wurde von ihrem Bruder und dessen Helfern entmannt. Da die Täter nicht vor der Synode erschienen waren, wurden sie exkommuniziert.[51] Bei dem Priester handelte es sich offensichtlich um einen Eigenpriester *(sacerdos illorum);* Frau Ava wird als seine Herrin *(domina)* bezeichnet; das heisst doch, dass die von der Exkommunikation betroffene Familie dem Adel angehörte.

Eine andere Möglichkeit der Erzwingung von Gehorsam als die Verhängung des Ausschlusses aus der Kirche besass die Synode nicht; ob ein Kirchenbann in dem erwähnten Fall die widerspenstigen und wohl auch hochgestellten und mächtigen Täter zum Einlenken gebracht hat, wissen wir nicht—es ist kaum wahrscheinlich.

b. Unbeabsichtigter Totschlag

Hans Hattenhauer hat in einem vor über 20 Jahren erschienenen Aufsatz dargelegt, worin die umwälzende Neuheit bestand, als auf dem Konzil von Worms 868 das Prinzip der 'fahrlässigen Tötung' erfunden wurde. Mit 'einem erstaunlichen Grad der Abstraktion' werde das Problem der Fahrlässigkeit erfasst und dargestellt:[52] Wenn einer—so heisst es in diesem Text—'unerwartet herbeikommt und unvorhergesehen unter den Baum gerät und von diesem erschlagen wird, ohne dass man ihm helfen kann, so darf der Baumfäller ohne Zweifel nicht einem Totschläger gleichgestellt werden'.[53]

In ähnlicher Weise wird dasselbe Thema dann auch in Tribur behandelt; beide Texte hat Regino hintereinander in sein Handbuch aufgenommen (2.17–18).

Zu beachten ist auch, dass Papst Nikolaus I. in einem Brief an Erzbischof Adalwin von Salzburg das Thema des Todes beim Baumfällen behandelt hat. Ein Mann, durch dessen Aktion ein anderer ums Leben kam, sollte als unschuldig gelten und nicht bestraft werden.[54]

51. Mansi 18.80 D.

52. H. Hattenhauer, *'De arbore inciso homineque occiso*—Stationen eines Rechtsproblems', in: *Studien zu den germanischen Volksrechten. Gedächtnisschrift für Wilhelm Ebel,* hg. von G. Landwehr (Frankfurt/M. und Bern 1982) 11–34, hier 25.

53. Ibid. 24. Der lateinische Text ist ediert in MGH Concilia 4.265–66.

54. JE 2846. MGH Epistolae 6.631.12–16; vgl. W. Hartmann, *Das Konzil von Worms 868. Überlieferung und*

Ebenfalls vom Konzil von Tribur stammt das folgende Kapitel (2.19), in dem der Fall eines Kindes behandelt wird, das an Verbrühungen stirbt, die es durch kochendes Wasser erleidet. Bei den Kapiteln 2.60 und 2.61 sind wir ebenfalls bei der fahrlässigen Tötung von Kindern; diesmal geht es darum, dass ein Kind—vielleicht unabsichtlich—im Schlaf erdrückt wird, weil es im Bett der Eltern schläft. Dieses Problem hatte Hrabanus Maurus bereits in den 840er Jahren behandelt und auch ein von G. Schmitz aufgefundener kleiner Traktat aus jener Zeit hatte sich damit befasst.[55]

In all diesen Texten geht es darum, dass nicht einfach die Folge einer Handlung als strafwürdig betrachtet wird, sondern dass die Frage nach der Absicht gestellt wird, die nur dann beantwortet werden kann, wenn eine Gewissenserforschung erfolgt.[56]

c. Verwandtenmord

Über dieses Thema gibt es eine ganze Reihe von Papstbriefen aus der Zeit kurz nach 850. Sowohl Benedikt III. (855–858) als auch sein Nachfolger Nikolaus I. (858–867) haben sich in mehreren Briefen an Empfänger aus dem Osten des Frankenreichs über dieses Thema geäussert und dabei vor allem Aussagen über die Dauer der Busse bei derartigen Vergehen gemacht.[57] Auch schon früher hatten sich Päpste (wohl aufgrund von Anfragen) mit diesem Thema befasst. Der älteste Beleg ist ein Brief Papst Gregors III. an Bonifatius. Dort heisst es:[58]

Was aber diejenigen betrifft, welche Vater, Mutter, Bruder oder Schwester getötet haben, so erklären wir, dass keiner während der ganzen Zeit seines Lebens den Leib des Herrn empfangen darf ausser am Ende seiner Zeit als Wegzehrung. Er soll sich des Essens von Fleisch und des Trinkens von Wein enthalten, so lange er lebt. Er soll am zweiten, vierten und sechsten Tag der Woche fasten und so unter Tränen das begangene Verbrechen sühnen.

Dem Schreiben des Papstes lag eine Anfrage des Bonifatius zugrunde, zu der er vielleicht nicht nur von der praktischen Erfahrung bei der Mission, sondern auch von den angelsächsischen Bussbüchern angeregt wurde; dort ist das Thema zwar sehr selten behandelt; es gibt nämlich nur einen Beleg aus der ersten Hälfte oder der Mitte des 8.

Bedeutung (Abhandlungen der Akademie der Wissenschaften in Göttingen, phil.-hist. Klasse, 3. Folge Nr. 105; Göttingen 1977) 75.

55. Vgl. G. Schmitz, 'Schuld und Strafe. Eine unbekannte Stellungnahme des Rathramnus von Corbie zur Kindestötung', DA 38 (1982) 363–87.

56. Das umstrittene Problem, seit wann im Kirchenrecht nicht nur die Tat und ihre Folge, sondern die Absicht des Täters berücksichtigt wurde, kann hier nicht behandelt werden. Vgl. H. Lutterbach, 'Intentions- oder Tathaftung? Zum Bussverständnis in den frühmittelalterlichen Bussbüchern', FMSt 29 (1995) 120–43, und die Einwände von L. Körntgen, DA 52 (1996) 754.

57. Vgl. Hartmann, *Konzil von Worms* 71–75.

58. JE 2239; *Die Briefe des heiligen Bonifatius und Lullus*, ed. M. Tangl (MGH Epistolae selectae 1.28.51.12–17).

Jahrhunderts im *Paenitentiale Egberti* c.3.[59] Ein zweiter Beleg findet sich im sogenannten *Paenitentiale mixtum Pseudo-Bedae-Egberti* aus der 2. Hälfte des 9. Jahrhunderts (c.16).[60]

In die Zeit Karls des Grossen gehören dann drei Kapitularien aus der Zeit nach 800, die sich mit Morden an Verwandten befassen. Hier wird deutlich, warum der Kaiser solche Vergehen verfolgt sehen will, die in den weltlichen *Leges* gar nicht erwähnt wurden. Bluttaten innerhalb der Familie wurden meistens nicht vor das weltliche Gericht gebracht, weil hier keine Gefahr der Blutrache oder der Fehde bestand. Die früheste Regelung enthält das *Capitulare missorum* (802), das in zwei Kapiteln (c.32 und c.37) auf dieses Thema eingeht.[61]

In den Synoden der Karolingerzeit wird das Thema dann seit der Mitte des 9. Jahrhunderts immer wieder behandelt. In c.20 des Konzils von Mainz 847 ist ein Text übernommen, den Hraban in seinem *Paenitentiale ad Otgarium* c.11 formuliert hatte.[62] Und Worms 868 c.13 (30) stammt aus einem Brief von Papst Nikolaus I.[63] Beide Texte hat Regino in sein Sendhandbuch aufgenommen; Worms c.13 ist Regino 2.27, und Mainz c.20 ist Regino 2.28 und 2.29. Die beiden Kapitel haben über das *Dekret* Burchards von Worms weiter gewirkt.[64]

d. Priestermord

Auch mit dem Thema 'Mord an Klerikern' hat sich das kirchliche Recht anscheinend erst seit der 2. Hälfte des 9. Jahrhunderts beschäftigt.[65] Denn zuerst unter den Kanones des Konzils von Mainz 847 finden sich zwei Kapitel, die diesem Thema gelten: c.24 (= Regino 2.43) und 25 (= Regino 2.44); beide Texte wurden auf dem Konzil neu formuliert.[66] Auch in Worms 868 hat man sich in einem Kapitel diesem Problem gewidmet (c.16 [26] = Regino 2.42); dieser Text ist identisch mit einem Kapitel in einem Brief Papst Nikolaus' I.[67] Auf der Synode von Mainz 888 wurde der Kanon von Worms 868 als c.16 nochmals wiederholt.[68] In Kanon 2 der Synode von Vienne 892 wurden zwar keine

59. Schmitz, *Bussbücher* 1.578. Zur Entstehungszeit dieses Bussbuchs, C. Vogel, *Les Libri Paenitentiales* (Typologie 27; Turnhout 1978) 71.

60. Schmitz, *Bussbücher* 2.691. Nach R. Haggenmüller, *Die Überlieferung der Beda und Egbert zugeschriebenen Bussbücher* (Frankfurt/M. 1991) 293, ist dieses Bussbuch in den 870er oder 880er Jahren in Lotharingien entstanden.

61. MGH Capitularia 1.97–98.

62. MGH Concilia 3.171; zur Vorlage des Mainzer Kapitels, ibid. Anm. 80.

63. MGH Concilia 4.268; zur Vorlage, ibid. Anm. 22.

64. Vgl. zur Nachwirkung von Mainz 847 c.20: MGH Concilia 3.156; zur Nachwirkung von Worms 868 c.13: MGH Concilia 4.254.

65. Vgl. Hinschius, *System* 5.176–77 Anm. 5; ibid. 5.80 mit Anm. 7–9.

66. MGH Concilia 3.173.   67. MGH Concilia 4.270–71.

68. Mansi 18A.68C–E.

Einzelheiten der Bussauflagen für Priestermörder aufgezählt, aber es wurde generell davon gesprochen, dass eine derartige Tat wiedergutgemacht werden müsse bei Gefahr der Exkommunikation.[69] In Tribur 895 hat man in c.5 die in Worms 868 festgelegten Bussauflagen abermals wiederholt.[70] Regino hat diesen Text allerdings nicht rezipiert.

Im weltlichen Recht gab es allerdings schon im 8. Jahrhundert Texte, die den Mord an einem Priester oder Bischof mit—zum Teil ausserordentlich schweren—Strafen belegen: Es sind hier zwei Kapitel aus der *Lex Baiwariorum* I,9 und I,10 und je ein Kapitel aus der *Lex Alamannorum* (c.12) und aus der *Lex Ribvaria* (40,5) zu nennen.[71] Nicht verwunderlich ist unter diesen Umständen, dass auch die Kapitularien mindestens einen sicheren Beleg bieten: *Capitula legibus addenda* (803) c.1.[72]

Nicht älter als die oben genannten Konzilien ist jedoch ein gefälschtes Kapitular, das in die Zeit nach 895 gehört.[73]

In den Bussbüchern wird das Thema Priestermord sehr selten erwähnt. Es gibt nur zwei eindeutige Belege, den einen aus dem *Paenitentiale* Theodors von Canterbury 1.4.5,[74] den andern aus dem *Paenitentiale Vallicellianum III*.[75]

e. Gleichheit von Mann und Frau

Vielleicht der erste Text, der hier einschlägig ist, ist Mainz 852 c.13, 2. Teil, in dem ausdrücklich betont wird, dass ein Tötungsdelikt am Ehegatten in jedem Fall gebüsst werden muss: 'Wenn ein Mann seine Frau oder eine Frau ihren Mann tötet, dann soll das gleiche Urteil über sie verhängt werden'.[76] Damit sind die Bestimmungen des weltlichen Rechts, dass ein Mann seine Frau busslos töten kann, wenn er sie beim Ehebruch ertappt, ausgehebelt.[77]

---

69. Mansi 18A.121D.

70. MGH Capitularia 2.217.

71. LBai I.9–10 (MGH Leges nationum Germanicarum 5.2.279–83); LAlem 12 (ibid. 5.1.77); LRib 40,5 (ibid. 3.2.93). Berühmt ist davon vor allem LBai 1.10, wo der Bischofsmord mit einer exorbitanten Strafe belegt ist.

72. MHG Capitularia 1.113.1.

73. Gedruckt MGH Capitularia 1.359–62; vgl. zu seiner Entstehungszeit H. Mordek, *Bibliotheca capitularium regum Francorum manuscripta. Überlieferung und Traditionszusammenhang der fränkischen Herrschererlasse* (MGH Hilfsmittel 15; München 1995) 133–34.

74. Schmitz, *Bussbücher* 1.528.

75. Ibid. 785.

76. MGH Concilia 3.250. Bei Regino ist das Kapitel 2.73, vgl. *Regino-Ausgabe* 287.

77. So zum Beispiel in den *Leges Visigothorum* 3.4.4 (MGH Leges nationum Germanicarum 1.149); in den *Leges Burgundionum* LXVIII (ibid. 2.1.95); *Lex Romana* 25 (ibid. 2.1.146); in der *Lex Baiwariorum* 8.1 (ibid. 5.2.353); im *Edictus Rothari* 212 (ed. F. Beyerle, *Die Gesetze der Langobarden* [Weimar 1947] 84). Ich kann nicht verstehen, warum angesichts dieser Belege I. Weber, 'Una lex de viris et de feminis. Zur Religions- und Gesellschaftsgeschichte der Ehe im frühen Mittelalter' (Diss. masch. kath. theol. Tübingen 2003) 244–45, behauptet, dass auch schon in den frühmittelalterlichen Leges die Geschlechter gleich behandelt worden seien.

Regino hat (als Kapitel 2.130) noch einen weiteren Text zu diesem Thema, den er angeblich einem Konzil von Nantes entnommen hat:[78]

Wenn eine Frau Ehebruch begeht, und dies wird vom Mann entdeckt und öffentlich bekannt gegeben, darf er die Frau, wenn er will, wegen Unzucht verstossen; sie aber soll sieben Jahre öffentlich büssen. Ihr Mann aber darf auf keinen Fall eine andere nehmen, solange sie lebt. Wenn er nun die Ehebrecherin wieder mit sich versöhnen will, soll er die Erlaubnis (dazu) haben, jedoch so, dass er in gleicher Weise mit ihr zusammen Busse tun soll, und wenn die Busse abgeschlossen ist, sollen beide nach sieben Jahren zur Kommunion kommen. Die gleiche Vorschrift soll auch bei einer Frau beachtet werden, wenn ihr Mann sie durch Ehebruch betrogen hat.

Es geht in diesem Text nicht nur um Gleichheit der Geschlechter, sondern auch darum, dass mit der Bereitschaft zur Verzeihung gerechnet wird. Diese wird aber erschwert durch die Bedingung, dass auch der unschuldige Teil des Paares eine siebenjährige Busse auf sich nehmen muss.

f. Soziale Probleme

Zu diesem Thema soll nur ein einziges Kapitel betrachtet werden, dessen Herkunft nicht bekannt ist; daher kann auch nichts über seine Entstehungszeit gesagt werden (Regino 2.68 inskribiert mit *Ex eodem* und weist den Kanon damit dem Konzil von Rouen zu):[79]

Da auf Anraten des Teufels und weil die Schwachheit des Fleisches Gefallen daran findet und deshalb zustimmt solche Vergehen häufig begangen werden, deshalb wünschen die Ehebrecherinnen, mit dem einen todbringenden Gift das andere Verbrechen irgendwie zu heilen. Daher geben wir den Rat, dass ein jeder Priester—damit das Verbrechen nicht verdoppelt werde, indem nämlich zum Ehebruch noch der Mord kommt—in seiner Gemeinde öffentlich bekannt gibt, dass eine heimlich verführte Frau, wenn sie empfängt und gebiert, ihren Sohn oder ihre Tochter auf keinen Fall entsprechend dem Rat des Teufels töten soll, sondern dass sie ihr Neugeborenes, auf welche Weise sie es auch immer vermag, vor die Tore der Kirche bringen und dort niederlegen lassen soll, damit das ausgesetzte Kind am nächsten Tag in Anwesenheit eines Priesters von einem Gemeindeglied aufgenommen und grossgezogen wird und die Frau so der Schuld des Mordes und, was schwerwiegender ist, des Verwandtenmordes entgeht. Denn wer seinen Sohn oder seine Tochter tötet, der ist auf jeden Fall des Verwandtenmordes schuldig.

---

78. *Regino-Ausgabe* 311.
79. *Regino-Ausgabe* 285.

Der entscheidende Punkt in diesem Text ist, dass eine Frau, die durch einen Ehebruch schwanger geworden ist, die Frucht dieser Verbindung nicht töten, sondern an der Kirchentür aussetzen soll. Ausserdem werden Regeln formuliert, was mit dem ausgesetzten Kind geschehen soll. Heime für Findelkinder gab es anscheinend nicht; daher sollte das Kind in der Familie eines Gemeindeglieds aufgezogen werden.

Um das Aussetzen von Kindern geht es auch in den folgenden Kapiteln bei Regino (2.69–2.71); diese Texte stammen allerdings aus dem *Codex Theodosianus* und sie behandeln vor allem Fragen des Erbrechts und der sozialen Stellung der ausgesetzten Kinder.[80] Die Stossrichtung dieser römisch-rechtlichen Texte ist also eine völlig andere als die in dem apokryphen Kanon, der vielleicht erst im ausgehenden 9. Jahrhundert entstanden ist. Man wird auch an der praktischen Verwendbarkeit der römisch-rechtlichen Bestimmungen in der frühmittelalterlichen Gesellschaft zweifeln können.

Reginos Interesse für das, was wir heute 'soziale Fragen' nennen würden, zeigt sich auch an einigen anderen Stellen seines Werkes, etwa dann, wenn er zum Thema Kindsmord einen Text in seine Sammlung aufnimmt (Regino 2.65), in dem die soziale Stellung der Täterin berücksichtigt wird.[81] Oder in den beiden Kapiteln 2.433–434, in denen die schlechte und ungerechte Behandlung von Flüchtlingen angeprangert und mit Strafen bedroht wird.[82] Bei dem einen dieser beiden Kapitel (2.434) ist die Herkunft wieder einmal unbekannt. Ob man angesichts solcher Texte Regino ohne weiteres als Vertreter der Adelskultur bezeichnen darf, erscheint mir zweifelhaft.[83]

80. Ibid. 284–87. 81. Ibid. 282–83.
82. Ibid. 454–55.
83. Anders sieht das H. Löwe, 'Regino von Prüm und das historische Weltbild der Karolingerzeit', in: Idem, *Von Cassiodor zu Dante. Ausgewählte Aufsätze zur Geschichtsschreibung und politischen Ideenwelt des Mittelalters* (Berlin und New York 1973) 149–79, hier 152–61.

[3]

Zur Entstehung des Sendgerichts im 9. Jahrhundert

Rudolf Schieffer

❀

Das Sendgericht ist charakteristischer Ausdruck der bischöflichen Diözesanhoheit in der mittelalterlichen Kirche.[1] Seine Basis war weniger die seit ältester Zeit bestehende Disziplinargewalt über den Klerus als ein umfassend verstandener Seelsorgeauftrag gegenüber allen Gläubigen, die von sündhaftem Handeln abgehalten werden sollten, vor allem soweit es öffentlich sichtbare Formen wie Totschlag, Raub, Ehebruch, Inzest (Verwandtenehen) oder manifesten Aberglauben annahm. Über die blosse Visitations-praxis hinaus, die ebenfalls bereits spätantike Wurzeln hatte,[2] handelte es sich um ein förmliches Verfahren, bei dem vereidigte Sendzeugen Auskunft über vorgefallene Vergehen zu geben hatten und so eine inquisitorische Untersuchung der erhobenen Beschuldigungen mit dem Ziel einer Bestrafung durch den geistlichen Richter in Gang brachten, offenbar in Analogie zum Rügeverfahren weltlicher Gerichte in fränkischer Zeit.[3] Im Vorsitz der periodisch anzuberaumenden Verhandlungen liessen sich die

---

1. Vgl. Hinschius, *System* 5.425–48; A. Koeniger, *Die Sendgerichte in Deutschland* I (Veröffentlichungen aus dem Kirchenhistorischen Seminar München 3/2; München 1907); W. Hartmann, 'Der Bischof als Richter. Zum geistlichen Gericht über kriminelle Vergehen von Laien im früheren Mittelalter (6.–11. Jahrhundert)', *Römische Historische Mitteilungen* 28 (1986) 103–24; H.-J. Becker, 'Send, Sendgericht', HRG 4 (1990) 1630–31.

2. Vgl. W. Hellinger, 'Die Pfarrvisitation nach Regino von Prüm', ZRG Kan. Abt. 48 (1962) 1–116; ibid. 49 (1963) 76–137; H.-J. Becker, 'Visitation', HRG 5 (1998) 927–28.

3. Vgl. J. Weitzel, *Dinggenossenschaft und Recht. Untersuchungen zum Rechtsverständnis im fränkisch-deutschen Mittelalter* (Quellen und Forschungen zur höchsten Gerichtsbarkeit im Alten Reich 15; Köln, Wien 1985) 1124–39; F. Kerff, 'Die Urteilsfindung im Sendgericht', *Rechtshistorisches Journal* 8 (1989) 397–407; J. Weitzel, 'So scheiden sich die Geister', ibid. 407–13; J. Müller, 'Karl von Amira und das kanonische Recht am Beispiel des Rügeverfahrens', in: *Karl von Amira zum Gedächtnis*, hg. v. P. Landau, H. Nehlsen und M. Schmoeckel (Rechtshistorische Reihe 206; Frankfurt/M. 1999) 273–89.

Bischöfe mit der Zeit immer häufiger durch Beauftragte vertreten, Archidiakone und Landdekane, aber auch einfache Pfarrer, die alle dafür sorgten, dass das Sendgericht bis zum Ende des Mittelalters eine fühlbare Realität beim Kirchenvolk blieb.[4]

Auf der Suche nach den Ursprüngen dieser Form kirchlicher Strafverfolgung fällt selbstverständlich der erste Blick auf das bekannte Sendhandbuch, das der aus seinem Kloster vertriebene Abt Regino von Prüm um 906 in Trier zusammengestellt hat.[5] Dieser *Libellus de synodalibus causis* ist laut Vorrede ausdrücklich für die ambulante Praxis des bischöflichen Richters abgefasst worden.[6] Er enthält zu Beginn des 2. Buches die in alle kanonistischen Handbücher eingegangenen verfahrensrechtlichen Bestimmungen über das Zustandekommen der Gerichtsversammlung, über die Vereidigung der Sendzeugen und über den langen Fragenkatalog zur Aufdeckung aller Missetaten in der Gemeinde.[7] Da das Werk auf Veranlassung des Trierer Erzbischofs Radbod entstand und dem Mainzer Erzbischof Hatto I. gewidmet ist, darf wohl vorausgesetzt werden, dass die von Regino normierten Prozeduren zumindest in den beiden genannten Sprengeln um 900 gebräuchlich waren. Auch die Provenienz der elf erhaltenen Handschriften des Werkes aus Lotharingien, dem Rheinland und Südwestdeutschland sowie die massive Rezeption hundert Jahre später im *Decretum* Bischof Burchards von Worms[8] lassen auf eine Verbreitung des Sendgerichts im Stile Reginos vor allem im Westen des ostfränkisch-ottonischen Reiches schliessen.

Für zeitlich weiter zurückreichende Spuren ist man primär auf das verwiesen, was Regino selbst in seine Quellensammlung aufgenommen hat. Der schon erwähnte Auftakt des 2. Buches führt Regelungen über die Einberufung des Sendgerichts und über die Bestimmung der Sendzeugen an, die auf ein Konzil von Rouen zurückgeführt werden, ebenso wie ein späteres Kapitel über die Pflicht des Klerus zur Aufspürung von Gesetzesbrechern unter ihren Gläubigen.[9] Da diese Synodalbeschlüsse anderweitig nicht überliefert sind, ist ihre Echtheit (also die Provenienzangabe Reginos) wiederholt angezweifelt worden, aber auch wenn man sie für tatsächliche Zitate von synodalen Kanones oder Bischofskapiteln hält, die Regino noch vorlagen, für uns aber verloren

---

4. Vgl. als langfristigen Überblick W. Janssen, *Das Erzbistum Köln im späten Mittelalter 1191–1515* (2 Bde.; Köln 2003) 2.131–45.

5. F. Wasserschleben (Hg.), *Reginonis abbatis Prumiensis Libri duo de synodalibus causis et disciplinis ecclesiasticis* (Leipzig 1840); gekürzter Nachdruck mit deutscher Übersetzung hg. v. W. Hartmann, *Das Sendhandbuch des Regino von Prüm* (Darmstadt 2004).

6. Regino, Praefatio (ed. Wasserschleben, *Regino* 1–2).

7. Regino 2.1–5 (ed. Wasserschleben, *Regino* 206–16).

8. Vgl. H. Hoffmann, R. Pokorny, *Das Dekret des Bischofs Burchard von Worms. Textstufen—Frühe Verbreitung—Vorlagen* (MGH Hilfsmittel 12; München 1991) 173–244; Kéry, *Can. Coll.* 129–30 (Handschriftenübersicht).

9. Regino 2.1 *(Ex concilio Rotomagensi)*, 2.2 *(Unde supra)*, 2.395 *(Ex Concilio Rotomagensi)* (Wasserschleben 206–7, 364).

sind, bleibt die zeitliche Einordnung letztlich offen; nur allgemeine Erwägungen legen
es nahe, sich nicht allzu weit in die Vergangenheit vor 900 vorzutasten.[10] Etwas präziser
zu datieren, doch im Wortlaut nicht so ganz sicher verbürgt, ist der anonym überlieferte Brief eines Bischofs an seinen Erzbischof über den Fall einer von ihm aufgehobenen
unkanonischen Nahehe, die am Wohnort der Beteiligten *inquisitione facta et fide cum
iuramento data* von allen Nachbarn, vom jüngsten bis zum ältesten, ihm gegenüber
eingeräumt worden sei.[11] Die Überlieferung im etwa 890 abgeschlossenen Formelbuch
des Notker Balbulus von St. Gallen erlaubt es, den Text auf Bischof Salomon II. von
Konstanz (875–889) zurückzuführen und seine Abfassung sogar mit einiger Wahrscheinlichkeit auf die Jahre bis 879 einzuengen, schliesst jedoch die Möglichkeit einer
etwas späteren Umformulierung durch Notker ein.[12] Zumindest in dessen Vorstellungs-
welt ergibt sich damit ein klarer Beleg aus dem Bodenseeraum vor 890 für die inquisitorische Praxis des bischöflichen Gerichts in Ehesachen.

Was die unabhängig von Regino überlieferten, durchweg datierten Synoden des 9.
Jahrhunderts angeht, so sind Bezugnahmen auf das Sendgericht ziemlich selten und
wenig deutlich. Der bestimmte Terminus *inquirere* begegnet gleich zweimal im Kanon
12 der 898 von Papst Johannes IX. abgehaltenen Synode von Ravenna, demzufolge *peccata populi . . . ab episcopis sunt inquirenda* und die Bischöfe der einzelnen Städte freie
Hand in ihren Sprengeln haben *adulteria et scelera inquirere, ulcisci et iudicare secundum
quod canones censuerunt.*[13] Von der eidlichen Verpflichtung zur Erhebung von Anklagen
vor dem Bischof war schon Jahrzehnte früher auf der Synode von Mainz 852 die Rede,
wo es um in schlechten Ruf geratene Priester ging, die vom *populus ab episcopo iuramento seu banno christianitatis constrictus* blossgestellt werden sollten, um dann allerdings
nicht im Sendgericht, sondern nach vergeblicher Ermahnung auf einer Diözesansyn-
ode *(in conventu presbiterorum)* abgeurteilt zu werden.[14] Dass hartnäckige Verbrecher
und Todsünder *in synodicis . . . conciliis* anzuklagen und zumal deren Verwandte unter
Eid zur wahrheitsgemässen Aussage zu bewegen seien, ist in einem Kanon enthalten,
der in fünf Handschriften bayerischer Herkunft aus dem 10. bis 12. Jahrhundert der

---

10. Vgl. E. Seckel, 'Die ältesten Canones von Rouen', in: *Historische Aufsätze Karl Zeumer zum sechzigsten
Geburtstag als Festgabe dargebracht* (Weimar 1910) 611–35; zuletzt W. Hartmann, 'Die Capita incerta im Send-
handbuch Reginos von Prüm', in: *Scientia veritatis. Festschrift für Hubert Mordek zum 65. Geburtstag*, hg. v. O.
Münsch et al. (Ostfildern 2004) 207–26, bes. 216 ff.

11. *Collectio Sangallensis* n. 30, ed. MGH Formulae 415–16.

12. Vgl. W. von den Steinen, 'Notkers des Dichters Formelbuch', *Zeitschrift für schweizerische Geschichte* 25
(1945) 449–90, bes. 463 ff.; Nachdruck: W. von den Steinen, *Menschen im Mittelalter* (Bern und München 1967)
88–120, bes. 99 ff.

13. Mansi 18A.226B–D. Vgl. W. Hartmann, *Die Synoden der Karolingerzeit im Frankenreich und in Italien* (Paderborn 1989) 390–95, 467.

14. MGH Concilia 3.245–46 (c. 8). Vgl. Hartmann, *Synoden* 231.

Synode von Meaux (845) zugeschrieben wird, tatsächlich aber in deren vollständiger Überlieferung nicht begegnet.[15] Die Zuschreibung ist daher kaum haltbar, doch weist die mitgelieferte Eidesformel für laikale Zeugen, die *in synodo aut parroechiali conventu* befragt werden, solche Parallelen zu einem Eidestext im Zweiten Bischofskapitular Hinkmars von Reims aus dem Jahr 852[16] auf, dass eine Formulierung des fraglichen Kanons im Laufe des 9. Jahrhunderts durchaus glaubhaft erscheint. Ähnliches gilt von einem bei Burchard auf die Synode von Tribur (895) zurückgeführten, jedoch in deren Textbestand nicht enthaltenen Kanon, der jeden mit dem Kirchenbann bedroht, der sich der Verhandlung seines Falles auf der *synodus* durch Nichterscheinen vor dem Bischof oder vorzeitiges Verschwinden entzieht.[17]

Etwas grösser an Zahl und hier nicht im einzelnen zu erörtern sind allgemein gehaltene Hinweise in der karolingerzeitlichen Synodalüberlieferung auf die gerichtlichen Befugnisse der Bischöfe auch gegenüber Laien und zumal bei kriminellen Delikten.[18] Dabei liegt der Akzent regelmässig auf der Missachtung der geistlichen Autorität durch die Übeltäter, die sich der Vorladung vor ihren Richter verweigerten oder die verhängten Sanktionen, vornehmlich die Exkommunikation, ignorierten.[19] Von mehr als einer Synode beklagt wurde das unzureichende Zusammenwirken von kirchlicher und weltlicher Gerichtsbarkeit, was zur Forderung nach mehr Unterstützung bald der Grafen durch die Bischöfe, bald der Bischöfe durch die Grafen führte.[20] Von der prozessrechtlichen Frage, wie überhaupt Straftaten dem bischöflichen Gericht zur Kenntnis gelangen und mit welchen Mitteln sie untersucht werden sollten, ist indes in solchen Kanones keine Rede, wenn man von gelegentlichen Fällen absieht, in denen schon früh bei Inzestvergehen ein aktives Aufspüren *(investigare)* verlangt wird.[21] Im übrigen kann nur bekräftigt werden, 'dass die für die Praxis gedachten Vorschriften über die Sendzeugen und die von ihnen und den übrigen Gemeindegliedern verlangten Eidesformeln nicht auf einer der bekannten grossen Synoden der zweiten Hälfte des 9. Jahrhunderts erlassen wurden, sondern als etwas zweifelhafte Extravaganten in einigen Handschriften enthalten sind, die noch weitere Synodaltexte enthalten'.[22]

Der geringe Eifer der fränkischen Bischofsversammlungen für die formelle Ausgestaltung jener spezifischen Form geistlicher Strafjustiz, wie sie dann voll entwickelt

---

15. MGH Concilia 3.130–31. Vgl. Hartmann, *Synoden* 216.

16. MGH Capitula episcoporum 2.58.

17. MGH Capitularia 2.249 (c.12). Vgl. Hartmann, 'Bischof als Richter' 112–13.

18. Vgl. Hartmann, *Synoden* 464–67.

19. So schon die Synode von Tours 813, c.41 (MGH Concilia 2.1.292). Vgl. Hartmann, 'Bischof als Richter' 110.

20. Vgl. MGH Concilia 3.289 Anm. 123, mit weiteren Belegen.

21. Synode von Mainz 813, c.53 (MGH Concilia 2.1.272); Synode von Mainz 847, c.28 (MGH Concilia 3.175).

22. So Hartmann, *Synoden* 466.

und zukunftsträchtig um 906 bei Regino von Prüm in Erscheinung tritt, ist eigentlich erstaunlich und legt den Gedanken nahe, dass die Entwicklung von anderer Seite weit mehr forciert worden ist. Tatsächlich wird das Bild nicht unerheblich ergänzt, wenn man neben den Beschlüssen der Synoden auch die Kapitularien der karolingischen Herrscher in Betracht zieht. Schon in Frankfurt 794 hatte Karl der Grosse 'im Einklang mit der Synode' als König angeordnet, *ut episcopi iustitias faciant in suis parroechiis.*[23] Zwar zeigt der weitere Fortgang des zitierten Kapitels 6, dass traditionsgemäss in erster Linie an schuldig gewordene Kleriker gedacht war und deren Appellationsrecht an den Metropoliten geregelt werden sollte, doch es kommen nach Aufzählung aller geistlichen Ränge auch noch *alii in eius parrochia* zur Sprache, womit nur (vornehme?) Laien gemeint sein können.[24] Sehr viel deutlicher liest sich dann die Aussage eines auf 802/03 zu datierenden Kapitulars aus Aachen, in welchem die Bischöfe angehalten werden, ihre Sprengel zu bereisen und dabei *inquirendi studium* zu verwenden auf alle Fälle von Inzest, Verwandtenmord, Ehebruch, Hochmut und weiteren Gott nicht wohlgefälligen Taten, die Christen zu meiden hätten.[25] Bemerkenswert ist die frühe Betonung des Aufspürens, die zeigt, welcher Wert der nunmehrige Kaiser bei seinem umfassenden Bemühen um die sittliche Besserung und innere Verchristlichung seines Reiches auf die Autorität der Bischöfe legte.[26]

Sozusagen im selben Atemzug brachte Karl zugleich eine Reorganisation des Instituts der Königsboten in Gang, die mit ausserordentlichen Vollmachten nun regelmässig zur Kontrolle von regionalen Machthabern ausgesandt wurden *ad iusticias faciendum.*[27] Ihre Rechtsprechung sollte dem normalen Grafengericht übergeordnet sein und gemäss dem *Capitulare missorum generale* von 802 nicht bloss bereits anhängige Klagen aufgreifen, sondern auch auf eigenen Nachforschungen über geschehenes Unrecht beruhen (*diligenter perquirere, ubicumque aliquis homo sibi iniustitiam factam ab aliquo reclamas-*

23. MGH Concilia 2.1.166–67 (c.6). Vgl. Ph. Depreux, 'L'expression "Statutum est a domno rege et sancta synodo" annonçant certaines dispositions du capitulaire de Francfort (794)', in: *Das Frankfurter Konzil von 794. Kristallisationspunkt karolingischer Kultur,* hg. v. R. Berndt (2 Bde.; Mainz 1997) 1.81–101.

24. Vgl. Hartmann, *Synoden* 463.

25. MGH Capitularia 1.170 (c.1). Vgl. zur Datierung F. Ganshof, 'Zur Datierung eines Aachener Kapitulars Karls des Grossen', *Annalen des Historischen Vereins für den Niederrhein* 155/156 (1954) 62–66; zur Sache Hartmann, 'Bischof als Richter' 109. Das im wiedergegebenen Text enthaltene Wort *cenodoxiis* ist gewiss nicht, wie im Register MGH Capitularia 2.702 geschehen, mit *senodochium* (*xenodochium*) in Verbindung zu bringen, sondern leitet sich von *cenodoxia* ab, was mit *vana gloria* glossiert wird (*Mittellateinisches Wörterbuch* 2.448).

26. Vgl. R. McKitterick, *The Frankish Church and the Carolingian Reforms, 789–895* (London 1977) 19–20.

27. *Annales Laureshamenses* ad a. 802 (MGH Scriptores 1.38–39). Vgl. V. Krause, 'Geschichte des Institutes der missi dominici', MIÖG 11 (1890) 193–300, bes. 217 ff.; K. F. Werner, 'Missus—Marchio—Comes. Entre l'administration centrale et l'administration locale de l'Empire carolingien', in: *Histoire comparée de l'administration (IV–XVIII siècles),* hg. v. W. Paravicini und K. F. Werner (München und Zürich 1980) 191–239; J. Hannig, 'Pauperiores vassi de infra palatio? Zur Entstehung der karolingischen Königsbotenorganisation', MIÖG 91 (1983) 309–74, bes. 363 ff.

set).[28] Von den prozeduralen Regeln solcher Sonderjustiz haben wir keine nähere Kenntnis, doch steht fest, dass Erzbischöfe, Bischöfe und Äbte (wie schon zuvor) mit Vorrang
an diesen missatischen Aufträgen beteiligt wurden, also über ihre geistlichen Amtsbe-
fugnisse hinaus eine zusätzliche Legitimation zur aktiven Bekämpfung von Unrecht aller
Art in die Hand bekamen. Tatsächlich sind das ganze 9. Jahrhundert hindurch immer
wieder Bischöfe in konkreter Funktion als *missi dominici* bezeugt, und zwar durchweg an
Schauplätzen, die ohnehin ihrer hierarchischen Verantwortung unterstanden.[29] Schon
Karl der Grosse hatte sich bei der Festlegung der räumlichen Zuständigkeit seiner *missi*
von kirchlichen Sprengelgrenzen leiten lassen und 802 unter anderem die Metropoliten
von Rouen, Sens und Reims zu Königsboten in ihren Provinzen eingesetzt.[30] 825 sind bei
einer neuerlichen Einteilung von *missatica* unter Ludwig dem Frommen auch die Erzbischöfe von Mainz, Trier und Köln—aus dem späteren Umfeld Reginos von Prüm—
neben weiteren Metropoliten, aber auch einfachen Suffraganen wie den Bischöfen von
Soissons, Noyon oder Langres namentlich als kaiserliche Beauftrage bezeichnet.[31] In
einer Liste, die dem *Capitulare missorum* Karls des Kahlen von 853 angehängt ist und
die westfränkischen Gegebenheiten widerspiegelt, dominieren bereits zahlenmässig die
Suffraganbischöfe.[32] Den Schlusspunkt der Entwicklung scheint ein italisches Kapitular
desselben Herrschers von 876 aus Pavia zu bezeichnen, in dem global allen einzelnen
Bischöfen 'in ihrem Bereich' die missatische Gewalt zugesprochen wird *(episcopi singuli
in suo episcopio missatici nostri potestate et auctoritate fungantur).*[33] Hinkmar von Reims
zufolge sind die Paveser *capitula* nur wenige Monate später in Ponthion auch für die
episcopi Cisalpini in Kraft gesetzt worden.[34]

Auch wenn gegen den Befund eingewandt worden ist, dass die urkundlichen Zeugnisse der Folgezeit keinen derart eindeutigen Vorrang der bischöflichen gegenüber der
gräflichen Autorität in italienischen Städten zu erkennen geben,[35] kann die Lösung kaum

28. MGH Capitularia 1.91–92 (c.1).
29. Vgl. Krause, 'Geschichte des Instituts' 235 ff.; zur frühen Gerichtstätigkeit Erzbischof Arns von Salzburg († 821) als *missus,* J. Hannig, 'Zur Funktion der karolingischen "missi dominici" in Bayern und in den
südöstlichen Grenzgebieten', ZRG Germ. Abt. 101 (1984) 256–300, bes. 281 ff.
30. Vgl. W. A. Eckhardt, 'Die Capitularia missorum specialia von 802', DA 12 (1956) 498–516.
31. MGH Capitularia 1.308–09, überliefert bei Ansegis, *Collectio capitularium* 2.25–27 (MGH Capitularia n.s. 1.541–49). Vgl. zur regionalen Situation J. Hannig, 'Zentrale Kontrolle und regionale Machtbalance.
Beobachtungen zum System der karolingischen Königsboten am Beispiel des Mittelrheingebietes', *Archiv für
Kulturgeschichte* 66 (1984) 1–46.
32. MGH Capitularia 2.275–76.
33. MGH Capitularia 2.103 (c.12). Vgl. Krause, 'Geschichte des Instituts' 245–46.
34. *Annales de Saint-Bertin,* ed. F. Grat et al. (Paris 1964) 203 (zu 876); *The Annals of St-Bertin,* transl. and an-
notated by J. L. Nelson (Manchester 1991) 192 (ohne Kommentar).
35. Vgl. E. Dupré Theseider, 'Vescovi e città nell'Italia precomunale', in: *Vescovi e diocesi in Italia nel medioevo (sec. IX–XIII). Atti del II Convegno di storia della chiesa in Italia* (Padova 1964) 55–109, bes. 75–76; Hartmann,
'Bischof als Richter' 123.

darin liegen, unter *episcopium* allein die Domimmunität innerhalb der Städte zu verstehen.[36] Die unbedingte geistliche Hoheit in diesem engsten Umfeld der Kathedrale verstand sich wohl von selbst und bedurfte schwerlich einer ausdrücklichen Vorschrift. Eher wäre, wie ja auch in anderen Fällen nicht selten, damit zu rechnen, dass sich der in Pavia formulierte umfassende Rechtsanspruch der Bischöfe in der Praxis nur unvollkommen durchsetzen liess und auch bei den nachfolgenden Herrschern nicht denselben starken Rückhalt fand.[37] Immerhin aber ist südlich der Alpen bis ins 10. Jahrhundert hinein eine ganze Reihe von Urkunden überliefert, in denen Bischöfe an ihrem Sitz oder doch innerhalb ihres Sprengels zugleich als *missus imperatoris* beziehungsweise *regis* auftraten.[38] Dabei geht es inhaltlich durchweg um die Klärung von Besitzstreitigkeiten oder um Freilassungen, nicht um Kriminalfälle. Deren Untersuchung und Aburteilung wurde allerdings nirgends im Frühmittelalter eigens beurkundet, wie man auch am Fehlen urkundlicher Zeugnisse für das Sendgericht im Sinne Reginos erkennen kann.[39]

Wir müssen uns daher am Ende mit der Feststellung bescheiden, dass diese Form der bischöflichen Strafjustiz in denselben Jahrzehnten des späten 9. Jahrhunderts ihren Anfang nahm, in denen die Übertragung missatischer Vollmacht an Bischöfe des Karolingerreiches ihren Höhepunkt erreichte. Die Erfahrungen mit dem Auftrag des 'weltlichen' Herrschers zur gezielten Aufdeckung und Ahndung von ärgerniserregenden Vergehen der verschiedensten Art dürfte nicht ohne Rückwirkung auf Entwicklung und Erscheinungsformen der traditionellen geistlichen Gerichtsbarkeit geblieben sein.

36. Vgl. C. Mor, *L'età feudale* (2 Bde.; Milano 1953) 2.203, 2.227 Anm. 25; G. Dilcher, 'Bischof und Stadtverfassung in Oberitalien', ZRG Germ. Abt. 81 (1964) 225–66, bes. 234–35.

37. So lautet der entsprechende Passus im Kapitular Kaiser Widos von Spoleto (891): 'Ut episcopi et comites uniti sint in suis paroechiis et comitatibus pro pace et salvatione in omnibus operibus suis habitantibus' (MGH Capitularia 2.107). Vgl. Dupré Theseider, 'Vescovi e città' 75.

38. Vgl. die Übersicht von Krause, 'Geschichte des Instituts' 276 ff.

39. Demgemäss wird die Praxis des geistlichen Gerichts in nachkarolingischer Zeit ganz vorwiegend nach normativen und erzählenden Quellen dargestellt, vgl. W. Hartmann, 'Probleme des geistlichen Gerichts im 10. und 11. Jahrhundert: Bischöfe und Synoden als Richter im ostfränkisch-deutschen Reich', in: *La giustizia nell'alto medioevo (secoli IX–XI)* (Settimane 44; Spoleto 1997) 631–72.

[4]

Ein Kanonist bei der Arbeit

Kleine Rechtstexte aus Codex Barcelona, *Archivo de la Corona de Aragón Ripoll 77*

Gerhard Schmitz

❀

Was macht ein Rechtsgelehrter, wenn er praktisch arbeitet? Er liest, denkt und schreibt. Das war im Mittelalter nicht anders als es heute ist. Praxis kann nicht nur heissen: Anwendung, Exekution des Rechts, Umsetzung von Vorschriften in Verfahren und Urteil. Der Anwendung geht die Bildung von Rechtsauffassungen und das Studium des Überkommenen voraus. Die Formung bestimmter Rechtsanschauungen ist ein aktiver Aneignungsprozess, in dem die Traditionsmasse kritisch gesichtet und interpretiert, kommentiert, komprimiert oder auch neu formuliert wird. Wir können solche Prozesse nicht allzu oft verfolgen. Was sich uns in den Handschriften präsentiert, sind häufig lediglich Exzerpte von Kanones oder Rechtssätzen anderer Provenienzen, deren Zustandekommen und Zusammenstellung uns manchmal willkürlich erscheint—oft genug wahrscheinlich nur deshalb, weil wir das dahinter stehende Erkenntnisinteresse nicht erkennen (können). Selbsterklärender sind in dieser Hinsicht Glossen, sie spiegeln den individuellen Aneignungs- und bisweilen auch Transformationsprozess viel besser. Fast am Ende stehen die Streitschriften, seien es ausformulierte Texte oder eben eher rudimentäre bis pointierte Bemerkungen, wie zum Beispiel die bissigen Kommentare zu 'einigen der sogenannten Sirmond'schen Constitutionen',[1] wie wir sie beispielsweise der spitzen Feder des Florus von Lyon verdanken—jüngst neu und erstmals vollständig herausgegeben von Klaus Zechiel-Eckes.[2] Deren einziger Sinn und Zweck war es, den

---

1. Aus dem Titel von F. Maassen, 'Ein Commentar des Florus von Lyon zu einigen der sogenannten Sirmond'schen Constitutionen', *Sb. Wien* 92.2 (Wien 1878) 301–25.

2. 'Florus' Polemik gegen Modoin. Unbekannte Texte zum Konflikt zwischen dem Bischof von Autun und dem Lyoner Klerus in den dreissiger Jahren des 9. Jahrhunderts', *Francia* 25 (1998) 34–38.

Florus-Kontrahenten Modoin von Autun als inkompetent erscheinen zu lassen und lächerlich zu machen.

Dies alles sind Texte, die sich durchaus auch unter dem Begriff der 'Rechtspraxis' fassen lassen. Aneignung, Verständnis und Neuformulierung von längst gesetztem und oft genug auch gedankenlos tradiertem Recht zwecks Erfassung und Bewältigung rechtlicher Probleme der jeweiligen Gegenwart ist die Aufgabe jedes 'Intellektuellen', der nicht nur stumpfer Exekutor, sondern auch 'Rechtsdenker', 'Rechtsgelehrter' sein will.

Im folgenden möchte ich zu diesem Problemkreis einen kleinen Beitrag leisten. Es geht dabei um kleine Texte, die in einer wenig, besser: fast unbekannten Handschrift stehen, aus der Karolingerzeit stammen, in dieser Form nirgendwo nachgewiesen werden können und die nach meinem Dafürhalten von eben jenem problemorientierten Aneignungsprozess zeugen.

Die Rede ist von der Handschrift Barcelona, ACA Ripoll 77. Dabei handelt es sich um eine von dem Ripoller Bibliothekar Antonio d'Olmera y Desperat 1776 angefertigte Kopie einer 'wohl karolingischen Vorlage'.[3] Nach einem Datierungsvermerk auf dem letzten Blatt hat er sie dem Kloster am 15. Januar 1776 geschenkt.[4] Der Bibliothekar von Ripoll hat bei seiner Abschrift eine vorbildlich-philologische, geradezu moderne Haltung an den Tag gelegt: Denn das Latein seiner Vorlagehandschrift war miserabel. Der Codex strotzte nur so von Fehlern und Versehen, die zu korrigieren dem Abschreiber hätte in den Fingern jucken müssen.[5] Olmera hingegen schrieb sämtliche Fehler mit ab. Denn wenn er korrigierend und bessernd eingegriffen hätte, wäre es, so formulierte er, nicht mehr sein Vorlagecodex gewesen, sondern ein neues Werk und die Verbesserung in Wahrheit eine Verschlechterung.[6] Die Entscheidung, den Codex abzuschreiben, sollte sich als sehr wertvoll erweisen: Die Vorlagehandschrift ist nämlich beim Brand des Klosters 1835 vernichtet worden. Olmera y Desperat schätzte das Alter seiner Vorlage auf wenigstens 800 Jahre, so dass diese auf jeden Fall in das 10. Jahrhundert zu datieren wäre, obgleich sie von García und Ewald in das 10.–11. Jahrhundert gesetzt wurde.[7] Letzteres bezieht sich aber vermutlich auf den dem flüchtigen Leser gleich ins

3. H. Mordek, *Kirchenrecht und Reform im Frankenreich* (Beiträge zur Geschichte und Quellenkunde des Mittelalters 1; Berlin und New York 1975) 261.

4. Barcelona, ACA Ripoll 77, fol. 63r: 'Dabam Rivipulli decimo octavo calendas Februarii Anni 1776; Dom. F. Antonius de Olmera, et de Desprat, Monachus ac Bibliothecarius Rivipulli'.

5. Ibid. fol. 4r, in seiner Vorbemerkung: 'Librarium vero, qui cum scripsit latinae linguae omnino rudem fuisse constat, non ex barbarismis, et soloecismis, quibus scatet; hoc enim vitium, quia commune non tam scriptori, quam aetati illi ferreae est adscribendum; sed ex notabili defectu intelligentiae latinae linguae ex quo innumera vocabula . . . et dictiones, nec latinas, nec barbaras, nec sensum ullum habentes transcripsit Librarius ille'.

6. Ibid.: 'Mihi autem religio, fuit Codicem illum, ita reddere, qualem accepi; quem si castigatum exhiberem, non idem prorsus, sed novus esset Codex, nec ea castigatio, emendatio, sed corruptio merito dicenda foret'. Auch in seinem 'Nachwort' versichert er, er habe die Handschrift *ad litteram* wiedergegeben.

7. So nach der Notiz, ibid. fol. 4r: 'Hujus vero M.S. Codicis antiquatem annorum octingentorum ad min-

Auge fallenden, hervorgehobenen Schlusssatz der *Admonitio Transcriptoris*, wo in der Tat von einem Codex des 11. Jahrhunderts die Rede ist. Damit ist aber gar nicht diese Handschrift gemeint, sondern eine ebenfalls von Desperat abgeschriebene *Dionysiana*.[8]

Die hier behandelte Handschrift tradiert, wie schon länger bekannt, die *Collectio Dacheriana*.[9] Die Tatsache, dass dieser *Dacheriana* zwei *Formulae* des Adventius von Metz vorgeschaltet sind, hatte Ewald zu der Annahme verleitet: 'vielleicht war Adventius der Autor'.[10] Das trifft zwar nicht zu, aber der Blick wird in die richtige Richtung gelenkt. Metz dürfte in der Tat die Heimat des Ursprungscodex gewesen sein. Dies erhellt ganz klar, wenn man die fol. 45ra–62v tradierten *Capitularia regum et imperatorum* in den Blick nimmt, von denen García lediglich vermeldete: 'Die spätesten sind von Karl dem Grossen und Ludwig dem Frommen', und sie mit den in einer Metzer Handschrift überlieferten Exzerpten vergleicht.[11] Emil Seckel hat diese im zweiten Weltkrieg zugrunde gegangene Handschrift unter dem Rubrum 'Exzerptmassen in Kanonessammlungen' in seiner grundlegenden Studie 'Benedictus Levita decurtatus et excerptus' analysiert. Was dort auf die *Dacheriana* folgt, bezeichnete er als 'Appendix Dacherianae Mettensis', den er wie folgt charakterisierte:[12]

Der Appendix geht mittelbar oder unmittelbar auf fünf grössere Quellengruppen zurück: 1. Konzilien der Merowingerzeit (cc.1–7); 2. ein Opusculum Hincmari Remensis (cc.8–12); 3. Dekretalen (cc.21–29); 4. Sirmondische Konstitutionen (cc.46–48) und zwar const. 1.3.17 ohne den Kommentar des Florus von Lyon; endlich Benedictus Levita.

---

ius esse minime dubito, si codicis habitudinem, et Litterarum caracteres, cum aliis illius aetatis conferamus'; vgl. Z. García, *Bibliotheca Patrum Latinorum Hispaniensis* (nach Aufzeichnungen R. Beers, in: *Sb. Wien* 196.2 [1915]) 44; H. Mordek, *Bibliotheca capitularium regum Francorum manuscripta. Überlieferung und Traditionszusammenhang der fränkischen Herrschererlasse* (MGH Hilfsmittel 15; München 1995) 1034: 'Angeblich des 11. Jahrhunderts', mit dem völlig richtigen Zusatz: 'Vielleicht aber noch karolingisch'; Paul Ewald, 'Reise nach Spanien im Winter von 1878 auf 1879', in: NA 6 (1881) 387, 392.

8. In der *Admonitio* ist nach einem deutlichen Absatz die Rede von einem 'Codex Dionysii exigui, quem transcriptum quoque damus' (Barcelona, ACA Ripoll 77, fol. 4r). Dieser Codex, der sich auch im Pergament von dem in Ripoll 77 tradierten unterschied *(licet enim in Dionysiano membrana sit nitidior)*, wird wie folgt datiert, ibid.: 'Codicem vero istum scriptum conjicio saeculo XI. ex compendiariis notis, quibus uti visum fuit Antiquario, et ex litterarum ductu pro more illius temporis'.

9. 'Auszug der Form B'; näheres dazu http://www.uni-tuebingen.de/mittelalter/forsch/benedictus/haupt. htm; vgl. Mordek, *Kirchenrecht und Reform* 261.

10. Ibid. fol. 5r: 'Exemplar veritatis (statt *libertatis*). Authoritas ecclesiastica patenter—propria illam'; ferner: 'Exemplar formatum (? Unsicher; García, *Bibliotheca* 44: *foratarum* statt *formatarum*, aber es könnte am ehesten *foraratarum* heissen) Reverentissimo Almelieque (statt *almifluaeque*) religionis—nobis conservet incolumen', ed. MGH Formulae 544 Nr. 17, ibid. 563 Nr. 20; vgl. NA 6 (1881) 392.

11. García, *Bibliotheca* 44.

12. In: *Festschrift für Heinrich Brunner zum fünfzigjährigen Doktorjubiläum am 8. April 1914 überreicht von der Juristenfakultät der Universität Berlin* (München und Leipzig 1914) 412.

Zu den Nummern 1–4 verkündete er lapidar: 'Von diesen Quellen kann hier nicht ge-handelt werden'.[13] Die präzise Analyse der Benedictus Levita-Kapitel reicht aber völlig aus, um sich über die Parallelität von Cod. Metz, BM †236, und dem hier in Rede steh-enden Ripoller Codex Gewissheit zu verschaffen.[14] Auf eine weitere, ebenfalls verlorene Schwesterhandschrift hat Hubert Mordek hingewiesen: Cod. Merseburg, Bibliothek des Domstifts †100. Diese Handschrift, die im dritten und vierten Viertel des 9. Jahr-hunderts, also wohl noch zur Hinkmar-Zeit, in einheitlichem Reimser Stil entstanden ist, enthielt nicht nur die *Dacheriana,* sondern auch die dieser vorgeschalteten Formeln des Adventius von Metz.[15] Auch dort fanden sich, so hatte schon Waitz mitgeteilt, nach dem Schluss der *Dacheriana* 'Auszüge aus Concilien, Decretalen und kaiserlichen Con-stitutionen', und dank der Beschreibung Walther Holtzmanns wissen wir wenigstens etwas genauer, worum es sich gehandelt hat.[16]

Die Ripoller Abschrift ersetzt also nicht nur ihre eigene verbrannte Vorlage, sondern auch die *Dacheriana Mettensis* sowie den Merseburger Codex. Sie steht für drei in die Karolingerzeit zurückreichende Überlieferungen.[17] Jedoch sind im folgenden nicht die Benedictus Levita-Auszüge Gegenstand unserer Betrachtungen, obgleich sich auch diesen Exzerpten über die von Seckel gewonnenen hinaus noch neue Erkenntnisse abgewinnen lassen, sondern kleine Texte, die sich im Ripoller Codex direkt im An-schluss an die *Dacheriana* finden. Sie wurden in den Metzer und Merseburger Codices anscheinend nicht tradiert, stellen also Eigengut des *Rivipullensis* und seiner Vorlage dar. Jedenfalls ist weder Seckels noch Holtzmanns Beschreibungen ein Hinweis auf diese Texte zu entnehmen.[18] Da ich zudem keine Beziehungen zu irgendeinem anderen kanonistischen Werk—sei es Sammlung, sei es Streitschrift—nachweisen kann, muss

---

13. Ibid. 412 Anm. 4.

14. Detaillierte Nachweise unter http://www.uni-tuebingen.de/mittelalter/forsch/benedictus/haupt.htm.

15. B. Bischoff, *Katalog der festländischen Handschriften des neunten Jahrhunderts* II: *Laon-Paderborn,* hg. v. B. Ebersperger (Bayerische Akademie der Wissenschaften. Veröffentlichungen für die Kommission der mittel-alterlichen Bibliothekskataloge Deutschlands und der Schweiz; Wiesbaden 2004) 182 Nr. 2750. Nach Bischoff wird die Handschrift 'vermisst seit 1957', nach Mordek ist sie seit dem 2. Weltkrieg verschollen; vgl. G. Waitz, 'Handschriften-Verzeichnisse', *Archiv der Gesellschaft für ältere deutsche Geschichtskunde* 8 (1843) 668; Mordek, *Bibliotheca* 1034; und vor allem W. Holtzmann, *Verzeichnis der Handschriften der Domstiftsbibliothek Merseburg* (Hs. C5 der Bibliothek der MGH; digitale Edition [2000] siehe: http://www.mgh-bibliothek.de/bibliothek/ fol. 102).

16. Im Merseburger Codex endete die *Dacheriana* fol. 96v; ab fol. 97v führt Holtzmann, *Verzeichnis,* an: 'Ex conc. Aurelian c.12: Ne cui liceat; Ex eodem conc. c.15: Si quis quolibet; [Ex eodem conc.] c.16: Quisquis etiam; [Ex eodem conc.] c.17: Si metropolitanus; (98) [Ex eodem conc.] c.18: Id etiam miserationis; Huic concilio inter-fuerunt episcopi LXXI. Item ibi: Qui res ecclesiae petunt. Item. Si quis vero ecclesiasticam rem'. Dazu am Rand: hellerer Nachtrag: 'Fol. 98v frei; fol 99 gehen Canonen in der ursprüngl. Hand, Rubrizierung weiter, zwar aus Papstbriefen und Capitularien; ohne Zählung, aber mit Rubriken'. Diese Beschreibung genügt, um die Fest-stellung treffen zu können, dass hier dieselben Stücke überliefert wurden wie im Codex von Ripoll.

17. Seckel, 'Benedictus Levita' 411, datiert die Metzer Handschrift: '10./11. Jahr.'.

18. Nach Holtzmann, 'Verzeichnis', bleibt zwischen der nach Dach. 3.158 befindlichen *Epistola formata* und den 'griech. Buchstaben' und ihren darüber stehenden Zahlenwerten (wie im Ripoller Codex auch) nicht viel Platz, so dass man vermuten muss, dass sie dort nicht gestanden haben. Seckel, 'Benedictus Levita' 411–12, lässt

man daran denken, hier eine aus speziellem Anlass angefertigte Zusammenstellung vor sich zu haben, deren Besonderheit eben darin liegt, dass sie nicht aus blossen Exzerpten, sondern partiell aus offenbar selbst formulierten und kenntnisreich miteinander verknüpften Texten besteht.

Im folgenden drucke ich sie vollständig ab, wenn die Angabe des Incipit und Explicits nebst Inskription und Rubrik (so vorhanden) nicht genügt:

||Fol. 39v|| *EX CONCILIO NICENO. Excommunicatus non accipiatur accusator. Ut omnes episcopi Metropolitanum obaudiant et de majoribus rebus sine ejus consensu non agant.*

Die Inskription ist falsch, die Sätze stammen nicht aus dem Konzil von Nikäa. Die Quelle lässt sich wohl ermitteln: *Epitome Hispana* 57: 'Excommunicatus non recipiatur accusator' *(El Epitome Hispanico. Una colección canonica española del siglo VII*, hg. von Gonzalo Martinez S.J. [Comillas 1961] 153; vgl. auch CCL 149.315 [c.43]). Der zweite Satz scheint ebenfalls von dort (ed. Martinez 99) zu stammen: 'Ex libro bracarense Martini episcopi Galliciae de diversis conciliis c. IIII. Ut omnes episcopi metropolitano oboediant et nihil agant sine ipso nec metropolitanus agat aliquid sine reliquis episcopis'. Dass die Suffragane dem Metropoliten Gehorsam schulden, ist nichts Besonderes, vgl. etwa c.9 des Konzils von Antiochien (ed. EOMIA 2.257–59), wo die Oberhoheit des Metropoliten über die Kirchenprovinz betont wird; wohl dürfe der Bischof die Angelegenheiten seiner eigenen Diözese regeln: 'Amplius autem nihil agere temptet praeter antistitem metropolitanum'. Andererseits werden auch die Metropoliten an das Mithandeln der Suffragane gebunden: 'Nec metropolitanus sine ceterorum gerat consilio sacerdotum'.

EX CONCILIO TOLETANO. Inter quos fuerunt sub Egigane Rege Pontifices quinquaginta novem, Abbates octo comites decem vicarii tredecim. Convenit illis omnibus ut, sicut ||fol. 40r|| antiquitas—ad decem Mancipia veniat.

Conc. Tolet. XVI c.5 (*Concilios visigóticos e hispano-romanos*, ed. José Vives [España cristiana 1; 1963] 501–02) mit geändertem Anfang und ohne den Schluss. Dieser Kanon ist in keiner der grösseren und bekannteren Sammlungen tradiert. In der *Hispana* (PL 84.539) ist er rubriziert mit: 'De reparatione ecclesiarum vel diversis aliis causis'. Sachlich geht es um eine Spezialität der spanischen Kirche, derzufolge die Bischöfe die *tertiae* ihrer Pfarreien bekommen sollten. Ferner solle kein Priester mehrere Kirchen haben. Die Kirchen ihrerseits sollten eine Mindestgrösse von 10 *mancipia* haben, anderenfalls bis zu dieser Mindestgrösse aufgefüllt werden.

Era quadringentessia trigessima quinta ex concilio Cartaginensi tertio habitum ab episcopis decem et octo de Presbiteris, et Diaconibus quanti episcopi audiunt. Si autem Presbiteri vel Diaconus—||fol. 40v|| et finiat.

Conc. Carth. III c.8 (PL 84.190; CCL 149.331). Sachlich geht es um die bei Gerichtsverfahren gegen Priester und Diakone beizuziehenden Bischöfe als Richter: Für Priester sechs, für Diakone drei. Die übrigen Kleriker bleiben dem Urteil des lokalen Bischofsgerichts vorbehalten.

---

den Appendix der *Dacheriana Mettensis* mit dem (rubrizierten) c.13 des *Concilium Aurelianense* von 549 beginnen (in der Hs. als *cap. XII* bezeichnet), berichtet also ebenfalls nichts von den hier behandelten Stücken.

Ex concilio Cartaginensis Africae quinto habitum ab episcopis tribus, era quadringentessima trigessima octava de clericis ad testimonium non pulsandis. In principio studendum—persona pulsetur.

> Conc. Carth. V c.1 (PL 84.209; CCL 149.355). Inhaltlich geht es darum, dass kein Kleriker zur Zeugenaussage gezwungen werden darf.

Canon Sinodus Romanae ecclesiae. Querendum est in juditio, qualis sit conversatio his, qui accusant, et hii, qui accusantur. Ut a gradu ostiarii usque ad culmen episcopalem nullus crimen audeat sibi Praelato inferre. Id est, ne exorcista adversus acolitum nec acolitum (so!) *adversus subdia||fol. 41r||conum nec Subdiaconus adversus Diaconum, nec Diaconus contra Presbiterum, nec Presbiter adversus episcopum crimen audeat inferre, quia altior gradus Prelatus est minori.*

> Dieser Text ist meines Wissens sonst nirgendwo überliefert. Die Inskription könnte vielleicht eine Provenienz aus den *Capitula Angilramni* nahe legen *(Sinodus Romana)*, aber dort steht der Kanon so wenig wie bei Pseudoisidor oder Benedictus Levita. Der erste Satz stammt aus den *Statuta ecclesiae antiqua* (= Conc. Carthag. IV c.96): 'Quaerendum est in iudicio cuius sit conuersationis et fidei is qui accusat et is qui accusatur' (CCL 149.352 Zeile 388–89; Charles Munier, *Les 'Statuta Ecclesiae antiqua'* [Bibliothèque de l'Institut de droit canonique de l'Université de Strasbourg 5; Strassburg 1960] 88 [c.52]). Ansonsten ist der Einfluss des Pseudo-Symmachus unverkennbar, dessen *Constitutum* jedoch in dieser Form nirgendwo überliefert ist.

CAP. 10. De accusatione vero ut ait Paulus ad Thimoteum, non sub duobus aut tribus testibus non poterit comprobari. Alioquin falsus erit accusator. Sed conventus Patrum catholicorum pro insurgentes falsos fratres haec statuta sanccerunt. Ut de criminalibus causis sine septuaginta testes (so!) *non esset episcopus convincendus nec Presbiteri sine quadraginta quatuor aut Diaconus absque triginta, et qui unum crimen non probaverit, ad alterum mitti non debet.*

> Je nachdem, wie man die einzelnen Stücke beginnen lässt, könnte die Kapitelzahl auf die laufenden Kapitel bezogen werden. Eine andere Erklärung gibt es nicht. Verwertet ist am Anfang 1 Tim. 5.19, das als solches häufig, aber nicht in dieser Form zitiert wird: 'Adversus presbyterum accusationem noli recipere nisi sub duobus et tribus testibus'. Der *conventus Patrum catholicorum* leitet ein indirektes Zitat aus Pseudo-Symmachus ein. Zur Überführung eines Bischofs bedarf es 70 Zeugen, der Presbyter benötigt 44 und der Diakon 30; vgl. zur Tradition S. Kuttner, 'Cardinalis: The History of a Canonical Concept', *Traditio* 3 (1945) 129–214, Appendix C ('The Pseudo-Sylvestrian Rule of Seventy-Two Witnesses for a Bishop's Trial', ibid. 202–03), Appendix D ('Notes on the Medieval Transmission of the Constitutum Silvestri', ibid. 203–12). Der Schlusssatz ist wieder afrikanischer Provenienz: Conc. Carth. 130, Rubrik (PL 67.222 [Dionysio-Hadriana]): 'Ut qui unum crimen non probaverit, ad alterum admitti non debeat' (CCL 149.231 Zeile 1607–08).

Ex concilio Cartaginis Africae Septimo decem et octo episcoporum era trecentessima trigessima octava de Personis quibus Clericorum accusatio interdicitur. Item placuit ut omnes—||fol. 41v|| licentiam negandam.

> Conc. Cart. VII c.2 (PL 84.228); Conc. Carth. 30 Maii 419 (CCL 149.231). Inhaltlich wird davon gehandelt, welche Personen als Ankläger nicht zugelassen werden dürfen: Knechte, eigene Freigelassene und alle, die die öffentlichen Gesetze zur Anklage nicht zulassen, ferner solche, die mit *infamiae maculis*

befleckt sind, wie Schauspieler, Haeretiker, Heiden und Juden. In eigener Sache ist ihnen die Klageerhebung jedoch erlaubt.

De episcoporum aut Presbiterorum vel clericorum accusatoribus, quales debeant suscipere in accusatione ex concilio Caldonensi. Clericos sive laicos, qui accusaverint—opinio perscrutata.

Conc. Chalcedon. 21 *(Hispana)*, in: *Acta conciliorum oecumenicorum* 2.2.2, ed. E. Schwartz (Berlin 1936) 91.28–30. Inhalt: Kleriker und Laien, die Bischöfe oder Kleriker anklagen, dürfen nicht leichtfertig zur Anklage zugelassen werden, vorher ist ihr Leumund und ihre Gesinnung zu prüfen.

De accusatoribus ex concilio Niceno et Arelato vel aliorum. Qui accusaverit et multa crimina mala dixerit, si in prima non probaverit, cetera non credantur et familiares testes non credantur et ante quatordecim enim annos non recipiantur.

Wie schon die Inskription nahe legt, kein direktes Zitat und schon gar nicht aus den genannten Konzilien. Die Quelle ist dieselbe wie zu Beginn, die *Epitome Hispana* 58: 'Qui accusaverit et multa crimina dixerit, si in primo non probaverit, altera non credantur. Familiares testes non recipiantur. Ante XIIII annos testes non recipiantur' (ed. Gonzalo Martinez 153).

Ex concilio Spalitano cap. 6. Subsequuto Rege Isidorus cum aliis octo episcopis. Sexta actione comperimus Fragitanum cordovensis ecclesiae Presbiterum—||fol. 42r||de illis praeceperit definiri.

Conc. Hispalense II c.6 (PL 84.595–96). Es geht um einen unrechtmässig abgesetzten und ins Exil verbannten Priester, der wieder zu restituieren ist. Ohne Kontrolle durch ein Konzil dürfe kein Bischof einen Priester oder Diakon absetzen.

Ex concilio cartaginis. Ut qui aliquo crimine implicatis (so!) vel vilis Persona||fol. 42v|| ad accusationem non admittatur, sed prius requiratur persona his, qui accusat, et his, qui accusatur.

Die Quellenverhältnisse sind relativ kompliziert. Der Verweis auf ein afrikanisches Konzil stimmt so jedenfalls nicht. Der erste Teil geht parallel mit einer bei Benedictus Levita 3.85 zu findenden Floskel: 'Ut criminosus vocem accusandi non habeat. Is qui in aliquibus criminibus irretitus est, vocem adversus maiorem natu non habeat accusandi'. Die Quelle dazu ist nach Emil Seckel, 'Studien zu Benedictus Levita', NA 39 (1914) 344: 'Conc. Carth. c. 8 inf' = *Canones in causa Apiarii* 8 (CCL 149.135 Zeile 77–79); dort heisst es allerdings: 'Qui aliquibus sceleribus inretitus est'. Immerhin würde so die Inskription einen gewissen Sinn bekommen. Für den zweiten Teil ist ebenfalls auf Benedictus Levita zu verweisen—2.362: 'Ne viles personae ad accusandum sacerdotes admittantur. Viles personae nullatenus admittantur ad accusationem sacerdotum'; Seckel, NA 35 (1910) 476, hat nachgewiesen, dass hier zwei Quellen zusammengemischt wurden, *Admonitio generalis* 45 (von 789): 'Ut viles personae non habeant potestatem accusandi' (MGH Capitularia 1.56–57); ferner Conc. Carth. 30. Maii 419: 'Ut omnes servi vel proprii liberti ad accusationem non admittantur' (CCL 149.231). Der Schluss ist den bereits oben zitierten *Statuta ecclesiae antiqua* 96 nachgebildet: 'Quaerendum est in iudicio cuius sit conuersationis et fidei is qui accusat et is qui accusatur'. Dieser Text ist auch bei Benedictus Levita zweimal rezipiert, 3.110 und Add. 3.11 (MGH LL 2.2 [1963] 109 Zeile 29–31; ibid. 139 Zeile 48–50). Insoweit stehen wir vor dem Problem, dass sich mit Blick auf die letztlich verweteten Quellen die Inskription rechtfertigen lässt, als direkte Vorlage aber auch an Benedicts Kapitulariensammlung zu denken ist.

Ex concilio cartaginensi. Interdicitur accusatio his, qui infamiae maculas aspersi vel qui excommunicati fuerint. Placuit, ut quotiescumque clericis ab accusatoribus suis multa crimina obiciuntur et unum ex ipsis, de quo prius egerint, provare non valuerint, ad cetera non admittantur. Testes autem ad testimonium non admittantur, qui nec accusationem admitti praecepti sunt vel etiam, quos ipse, quem accusat, de sua domo produxit. Et si quando episcopus dicit aliquem sibi soli crimen fuisset confessum et ille neget, non poterit ad injuriam suam episcopus pertinere, quod illi non creditur. Causae autem, quae commune(s) non sunt, in suiis Provintijs judicentur.

> Das Stück ist ebenfalls kein Zitat aus einem karthagischen Konzil, sondern aus mehreren Teilen zusammengesetzt. Der erste Teil nimmt einen bereits oben zitierten Kanon des Conc. Carthag. 30. Maii 419 wieder auf: Nicht anklagen dürfen 'omnes etiam infamiae maculis aspersi' (CCL 149.231 Zeile 1602). Der Schluss des ersten Satzes verweist auf dasselbe Konzil, c.128, Rubrik: 'Quod excommunicati ad accusationem admitti non debeant' (ibid. 230 Zeile 1588–89). Der nächste Satz ist ebendort nahezu wortgleich zu finden: 'Item placuit: quotiescumque clericis ab accusatoribus multa crimina obiciuntur, et unum ex ipsis, de quo prius egerint, probare non valuerit, ad cetera iam non admittatur' (c.130; ibid. 231 Zeile 1609–11); desgleichen der folgende: 'Testes autem ad testimonium non admittendos, qui nec ad accusationem admitti praecepti sunt, vel etiam quos ipse accusator de sua domo produxerit' (c.131; ibid. 231 Zeile 1613–15). Angefügt ist c.132: 'Item placuit ut si quando episcopus dicit aliquem sibi soli proprium crimen fuisse confessum, atque ille neget, non putet ad iniuriam suam episcopus pertinere, quod illi soli non creditur' (ibid. 232 Zeile 1620–23). Der Schlusssatz schliesslich stammt aus dem Conc. Milevit. c.9: 'Causae autem quae communes non sunt in suis provinciis iudicentur' (ibid. 364 Zeile 124–25).

Jetzt schliesst sich an, lediglich mit *CAP.* inskribiert, c.21 des *Concilium Arelatense* von 314, dem c.13 (inskribiert als *Ex concilio Aureliensi cap. 12*) des Concilium Aurelianense von 549 folgt. Mit ersterem wird ein eindeutiger Themenwechsel eingeleitet, denn der Kanon von Arles beschäftigt sich mit Priestern und Diakonen, die die Orte verlassen möchten, an denen sie ordiniert worden sind, und letzterer behandelt kirchliches Güterrecht: Als *necator pauperum* ist zu qualifizieren, wer kirchlichen Einrichtungen gewidmete Güter anrührt oder entfremdet.[19] Ausserdem beginnen mit diesem Kanon jene Anhänge zur *Dacheriana*, wie sie Seckel für den Metzer und Holtzmann für den Merseburger Codex beschrieben haben. Das Eigengut der aus Ripoll stammenden Handschrift endet hier also.

Es kann deshalb ein kleines Resümee formuliert werden: Die hier vorgestellten Texte sind nicht einfach abgeschrieben, sondern sie sind die Frucht kanonistischen Studiums. Sieht man von dem etwas deplaziert wirkenden c.5 des 16. Toletanums ab, so hat sich hier jemand Klarheit verschaffen wollen über wichtige Fragen, die hauptsächlich den Klerikerprozess betrafen. Wer darf als Zeuge auftreten, wer nicht? Wie müssen die Zeugen beschaffen sein? Wie viele werden benötigt? Wer darf wen anklagen und wer nicht?

---

19. CCL 148.13 Zeile 69–72; CCL 148A.152 Zeile 108–13.

All dies sind keine praxisfernen Themen, ganz im Gegenteil. Hinkmar von Reims hat, vermutlich 876 und womöglich direkt oder indirekt an den Papst gerichtet, eine ganze Denkschrift über dieses Thema verfasst, denn kirchliche Prozesse gab es in beträchtlicher Anzahl.[20] Bevor man einen Prozess anstrengte oder durchführte, musste man sich erst einmal Klarheit darüber verschaffen, wie er 'funktionierte' und welche Aspekte zu beachten waren. Und genau von einem solchen gedanklichen Aneignungsprozess zeugen die kurzen Texte, die im *Codex Rivipullensis* erhalten geblieben sind. Sie sind eben nicht nur Exzerpte und blosse Materialsammlung, davon heben sie sich durch ihre Zusammenstellung wie durch eigene Formulierungen ab. Sie spiegeln, wie mir scheint, wider, wie sich ein Rechtsinteressierter oder Rechtskundiger der ausgehenden Karolingerzeit genauere Vorstellungen über ein ihn direkt oder indirekt betreffendes Problem verschaffte.[21]

20. G. Schmitz, *De presbiteris criminosis. Ein Memorandum Erzbischof Hinkmars von Reims über straffällige Kleriker* (MGH Studien und Texte 34; Hannover 2004), zur Entstehung 41–42.

21. Zur *Appendix Dacherianae Mettensis* siehe jetzt meine ausführliche Studie: 'Die Appendix Dacherianae Mettensis, Benedictus Levita und Hinkmar von Laon', ZRG Kan. Abt. 92 (2006) 147–206.

Vengeance and Law in Eleventh-Century Worms

Burchard and the Canon Law of Feuds

Greta Austin

❋

At the beginning of the eleventh century, Burchard, bishop of Worms, composed the *Decretum*, a massive compilation of canonical materials in twenty books.[1] From the outset, Burchard sought to identify basic concepts that were constants in the canonical tradition. He believed that the existing books of canon law were chaotic and inconsistent.[2] To make the canons agree with one another, he checked them against overarching scriptural principles that he found in the Bible and the canonical tradition.[3]

Yet how did Burchard go about identifying these principles and applying them in the *Decretum?* We can see better how he derived these principles by looking at his changes to a canon concerning feuds.[4] Earlier books of laws and penances had required only a few

1. For general information on the author and his work, R. Kaiser and M. Kerner, 'Burchard I, Bischof von Worms', LMA 2 (1983) 946–51; T. Kölzer, 'Burchard I., Bischof von Worms (1000–1025)', in: *Decretorum Libri XX* (ed. Cologne 1548; repr. Aalen 1992) 7–23. The thousandth anniversary of Burchard's ascension to the see of Worms prompted the publication of two volumes of essays on his life and accomplishments: *Bischof Burchard von Worms 1000–1025*, ed. W. Hartmann (Quellen und Abhandlungen zur Mittelrheinischen Kirchengeschichte 100; Mainz 2000); and *Burchard I. in seiner Zeit*, ed. T. Müller, M. Pinkert, and A. Seeboth (Beiträge aus den Archiven im Landkreis Eichsfeld 1; Heiligenstadt 2001).

2. See Burchard's comments in his preface to the *Decretum*, ed. G. Fransen and T. Kölzer (Cologne 1548, repr. Aalen 1992) 45, trans. Robert Somerville and Bruce Brasington, *Prefaces to Canon Law Collections in Latin Christianity: Selected Translations, 500–1245* (New Haven, CT 1998) 99.

3. G. Austin, 'Jurisprudence in the Service of Pastoral Care: The *Decretum* of Burchard of Worms', *Speculum* 79 (2004) 943–48.

4. In what follows, I will use 'vendetta', 'retribution', and 'feud' interchangeably. For a more differentiated treatment of the terms, applicable particularly during the later Middle Ages, see O. Brunner, *Land and Lordship: Structures of Governance in Medieval Austria*, trans. from German (ed. Graz 1958[4]) by H. Kaminsky and J. Van Horn Melton (Philadelphia 1992) 16.

years' penance for killing someone in a feud. The canons had assumed that private vengeance was an extenuating circumstance that made the action, in essence, more under-
standable. Burchard, however, took no such moderate view of the offense. For murders
committed to avenge a relative, he increased the penance to seven years—the standard
penance for all intentional homicides. He also identified a scriptural reason for refusing
to allow private vengeance. Burchard's alterations to the canon law had a long-term effect
because they, instead of the earlier versions, were absorbed into the canonical tradition.

In the case of feuds, Burchard's interest in changing the canon law was not purely
abstract and based on principle. As bishop, Burchard struggled with the problem of
feuds. The first part of this paper will provide social context—the feud that got out of
control between the *familia* (or dependents) of Worms and that of Lorsch. The second
part of the paper will describe how Burchard discussed and responded to the problem of
feuding within his own *familia* in his *Lex familiae,* the ruler's law governing his *familia.*
Finally, within this context, we will examine his alterations to a canon in the *Decretum*
on feuding.

The Social Context: Feuds in Worms

In a small, 'face-to-face' community like Worms, the feud was probably an accepted
part of the fabric of life. But one feud between the *familia* of Worms and that of Lorsch
spiraled out of control. The two groups had engaged in 'long-standing and regular
conflicts', *inveteratas et frequentes contentiones,* on account of their 'unfading hatred',
inmarcidas inimicitias. Both had carried out 'countless' murders, according to Henry
II's charter of December 1023.[5] The situation had escalated to the point where the king
intervened. Henry II mandated severe punishments—including branding—for those
who killed, carried out ambushes, or entered someone's house and beat him up. Although the charter does not explicitly use the word *vindicta* or even *faida,* it describes a
cycle of revenge and violence—in short, a feud.

That a feud had spiraled out of control does not mean necessarily that the custom of the feud itself was flawed. The threat of a feud could deter violence. Faced with
the prospect of more deaths, people might well choose to negotiate. They would be
more inclined to negotiate when pressured by other people who did not want more
violence. The more the feuding groups were linked to each other through mem-
bership in broader social associations, the more likely they were to compromise.[6]

---

5. Edited in: MGH Diplomata regum et imperatorum Germaniae 3 (Hanover 1900–1903) 640–41, no. 501.
6. M. Gluckman, *Custom and Conflict in Africa* (1956; repr. New York 1964) 23–25. For an overview of feuding, with attention to comparative approaches, see P. Hyams, *Rancor and Reconciliation in Medieval England*
(Ithaca, NY 2003) 6–25. It may be problematic to compare Burchard's medieval Germany to other societies,

This resulted in 'the peace in the feud', as anthropologist Max Gluckman put it.[7]

Once the 'peace in the feud' collapsed, however, it could be very hard to restore. Feuds could turn into a cycle of recurrent, retributive violence. As Paul Hyams has noted, feuds could erupt into chaos if one part of the system failed. One intransigent individual might refuse to negotiate, or one family group might balk, for whatever reason, at paying a fine.[8] Some such disruption in the balance of death and negotiation seems to have taken place in Worms in the early 1020s.

The question for Burchard as bishop, then, was how to intervene and restore a balance. Burchard wore two hats. As landlord of his dependents, his *familia*, he was in charge of administering justice. But he was also a bishop and a man of God. He could respond to the problem of feuding in two different ways. As a ruler and landlord, he had to be pragmatic. Accepting the existence of feuding as a social fact, he took whatever steps he could to eliminate it, or, if that was impossible, to limit its consequences. As a man of God, however, he could be more ambitious and call for a 'zero tolerance' policy towards feuding. In short, as ruler he would have to compromise, but as a compiler of canons he did not.

Feuds and Secular Law

As ruler of Worms, Burchard took legal steps to stop feuding within the *familia* of Worms. He addressed the problem of vengeance directly in his secular law code for the *familia* of Worms, the *Lex familiae Wormatiensis ecclesiae*.[9] Although most of the laws in the *Lex familiae* are impersonal statements of what the law should be, Burchard introduced the second-to-last law by describing the particular situation to which it responded. Thirty-five members of the *familia*, he wrote, had been killed in a year.[10] These murders he condemned severely.[11] The killings took place because of drunken-

---

such as those in twentieth-century Africa; at the same time, anthropologists may be able to provide useful insights, having observed feud first-hand.

7. Gluckman, *Custom and Conflict in Africa* 1–26.   8. See Hyams, *Rancor and Reconciliation* 19–20.

9. *Lex familiae*, ed. MGH Leges 4.1 (1893; repr. Hanover 1963) 639–44, no. 30. Other editions include H. Boos, *Urkundenbuch der Stadt Worms* (Quellen zur Geschichte der Stadt Worms 1; Berlin 1886) no. 48; and L. Weinrich, *Quellen zur deutschen Verfassungs-, Wirtschafts- und Sozialgeschichte* (Darmstadt 1977) 88–105, no. 22 (with accompanying German translation). On the *Lex familiae* also F. Schulz, 'Das Wormser Hofrecht Bischof Burchards', in: *Bischof Burchard von Worms* 251–78; G. Theuerkauf, 'Burchard von Worms und die Rechtskunde seiner Zeit', *Frühmittelalterliche Studien* 12 (1968) 144–61.

10. *Lex familiae*, ed. MGH Leges 4.1, no. 30.

11. The *Lex familiae* seems to represent the custom of the *familia* of St. Peter in Worms, which Burchard ordered to be written down; as Burchard wrote in the Preface, 'Ego Burchardus Wormatiensis ecclesie episcopus . . . cum consilio cleri et militum et totius familiae has iussi scribere leges'; yet the *Lex* also seems to reflect Burchard's (and his advisors') own opinions about what the law should be—particularly when it describes a very specific situation in its introduction: see Schulz, 'Das Wormser Hofrecht Bischof Burchards' 253–54.

ness or pride or for no reason at all. People had acted 'like beasts' *(more beluino)* and like mad persons *(insana mente)*.

In response to this 'terrible harm to our church' *(maximum detrimentum nostre ecclesie)*, Burchard legislated against feuds in the *Lex familiae*. As Dilcher points out, Burchard began by analyzing the nature of homicide and defining what could not be done licitly. This analysis and definition are not found in Henry II's legislation.[12] Burchard defined licit killing by discussing situations that might provide lawful reasons for killing another person, such as self-defense. He did not, however, include acts of killing in order to avenge a relative. One who killed to avenge a relative received a harsh punishment: a whipping, a branding on either side of the jaw, and payment of wergeld. Henry II had mandated these penalties.

In the *Lex familiae*, however, Burchard went beyond Henry II's measures to institute more rules to forestall inter-family violence. According to the *Lex familiae*, the kinsmen of a murdered person had to accept the ruler's peace. They were entitled to ask the murderer's relatives to swear that they had not contributed to the person's death. If the murderer's relatives swore this, they were entitled to 'firm and perpetual peace', *firmam et perpetuam pacem*. If, in contravention of this rule, the kinsmen of the dead person plotted to take vengeance—even if their plans came to naught—they suffered the same whipping and branding.[13] Burchard took seriously the issues of procedure, as Dilcher has pointed out.

Burchard then spent considerable time describing further procedures for averting future violence between kin groups. If the accused disappeared, for instance, his relatives were entitled to a peace if they were innocent. The accused could also clear himself of guilt by fighting a duel. If none of the dead person's relatives wished to fight, the accused could undergo the ordeal and pay the wergeld, and the relatives were then required to accept the peace. The ordeal, the oath, and the duel might have taken place before the bishop and his men. In this the bishop may well have served as a neutral figure who could restore the peace in the feud. For the Nuer in eastern Africa, the 'sanctity of the chief's person and his traditional role of mediator' allowed him to settle disputes. Similarly, perhaps, the bishop's court in Worms may have provided a neutral ground, a

12. G. Dilcher, 'Mord und Totschlag im alten Worms: Zu Fehde, Sühne und Strafe im Hofrecht Bischof Burchards', in: *Überlieferung, Bewahrung und Gestaltung in der rechtsgeschichtlichen Forschung*, ed. S. Buchholz, P. Mikat, and D. Werkmüller (Rechts- und Staatswissenschaftliche Veröffentlichungen der Görres-Gesellschaft 69; Paderborn 1993) 96.

13. Dilcher repeatedly describes Burchard and his time as 'archaic'; by permitting trial by combat, Burchard revealed 'wie tief das Rechtsverfahren noch in dem archaischen Rechtsgang steckte' (ibid. 97); similarly, in allowing a person made in God's image to be branded, Burchard showed himself to be 'Kind einer harten, archaischen Zeit' (ibid. 102). This description presupposes a certain model of legal progress. It could be debated whether such 'archaic' practices have given way to more 'civilized' ones, or whether other legal methods and punishments—sometimes equally harsh—have simply replaced the earlier ones.

place where a man could 'give way to the chief and elders without loss of dignity where he would not have given way to his opponent'.[14]

As ruler of Worms, then, Burchard sought to eliminate feuds in his *Lex familiae*. These laws responded to a pressing social problem within the *familia*, that of 'thirty-five deaths' in one year. The means he took were extremely practical and, at the same time, innovative. Buchard first defined homicide, reiterated the punishments given by Henry II for those who avenge relatives, and then added new procedures to Henry II's charter. Burchard designed these procedures to ensure that a victim's family could be satisfied without blood vengeance, or, if they were not, punished.

Dilcher sees the *Lex familiae* as deeply colored not only by Burchard's experience of feuds in his *familia*, but also by his views as the spiritual leader of his see and as compiler of a canonical collection.[15] In particular, Burchard's legislation on feuding in the *Lex familiae* grew out of his religious conviction that the feud was wrong. According to Dilcher, the Church took the view that 'die Rache Gottes des Herren sei und an seiner Statt nur die Obrigkeit handeln dürfe'.[16] We need, however, to reconsider this assumption. The Church's teaching on feuds was not a settled matter in the year 1000. As I will show below, it seems to have been Burchard who popularized the view that vengeance was God's and that only the ruling body could carry it out on God's behalf.

Feuds in Canon Law

When Burchard put together his book of canon law, the *Decretum*, he altered a canon on feuding so that someone who killed out of vengeance was to be treated like any other murderer.[17] This change should be viewed in light of the social reality, the problem of feuding in Worms. The most immediate objection, of course, is that the timing was wrong. The *Decretum* was almost undoubtedly compiled before 1023, whereas the feud between Lorsch and Worms was addressed in Henry II's charter in 1023, and the *Lex familiae* is dated to 1024/1025.[18] Burchard's changes to the canon on feuding probably did not respond *directly* to the 35 deaths in his diocese, nor to the feud

---

14. E. E. Evans-Pritchard, *The Nuer* (1940; repr. Oxford 1972) 164.

15. Dilcher, 'Mord und Totschlag' 103–4.   16. Ibid. 103.

17. It is worth considering why Burchard might have believed that he could alter this canon; as P. Fournier has demonstrated ('Études critiques sur le Décret de Burchard', *Nouvelle Revue historique de droit français et étranger* 34 [1910] 302–31, 564–84; reprinted in: idem, *Mélanges de droit canonique*, ed. T. Kölzer [Aalen 1983] 341–91), and, as subsequent work has continued to show, Burchard altered canons regularly. What should be said, though, is that Burchard took more liberties generally with canons attributed to penitentials and councils than with those attributed to Church Fathers like Augustine; Burchard may have considered penitentials to represent custom, especially localized custom, and felt even more at liberty than he usually did to alter them. See G. Austin, *Law, Theology and Forgery around the Year 1000: The Decretum of Burchard of Worms* (Ashgate, forthcoming).

18. The Vatican and Frankfurt manuscripts of the *Decretum* were certainly compiled before 1023 because

between Lorsch and Worms. It is likely, however, that 'the handwriting was already on the wall'. As a bishop intimately involved in the work of his see, and one who had spent the vast majority of his time after 1005 in Worms rather than traveling in the imperial retinue, Burchard was probably aware of the existing problems in his *familia* and of the possibilities of violence between his *familia* and another.[19] In the *Decretum*, he anticipated the outbreak of violence as a result of the feuds already broiling in the *familia* and among the *familiae*.

In the early medieval penitential and legal tradition, the Church did not have a clearly articulated position condemning private vengeance. In fact, in many cases, homicides committed in feuds constituted bloodshed, but they did not require nearly as much penance as other murders. The *Paenitentiale Merseburgense*, for instance, assigned seven years of penance for intentional homicide and five years for accidental homicide. But, if a person killed another to avenge a relative, he would be assigned only three years of penance.[20] Similarly, the *Libri duo de synodalibus causis* of Regino of Prüm mandated three years of penance for a death in a vendetta.[21] Generally speaking, the Church accepted the existence of vendettas.

In the *Decretum*, Burchard did not go along with the accepted wisdom that the existence of a feud was a mitigating circumstance. When he compiled his book of canon law, the *Decretum*, he took a canon on feuds from Regino's *Libri duo*, reproduced in the first column of the chart below.[22] Burchard's changes appear in the second column and are given in bold face:[23]

---

the canons of the council of Seligenstadt (1023) appear as later additions in both manuscripts. P. Fournier dated the *Decretum* to 1012, when Burchard's assistant Olbert departed to assume his new position as abbot of Gembloux; see idem, 'Études critiques' 43 (reprinted in: *Mélanges* 1.249). J. Müller has questioned the timing of Olbert's departure in his *Untersuchungen zur Collectio Duodecim Partium* (Abhandlungen zur Rechtswissenschaftlichen Grundlagenforschung 73; Ebelsbach 1989) 358–360. Canon 2.227 of the *Decretum* gives an example of the proper form of a letter, supposedly from Nicaea; Burchard derived this text from Regino, inserted his own name and that of Walter of Speyer, and concluded it with the date 1012.

19. R. Schieffer, 'Burchard von Worms. Ein Reichsbischof und das Königtum', in: *Bischof Burchard von Worms* 42.

20. *Paenitentiale Merseburgense* A (Merseburg, Archiv des Domkapitals MS 103), ed. R. Kottje, *Paenitentialia minora Franciae et Italiae saeculi VIII–IX* (CCL 156; Turnhout 1994) 127 and 158 (no. 3 and 113).

21. Regino of Prüm, *Reginonis abbatis Prumiensis libri duo de synodalibus causis et disciplinis ecclesiasticis* 2.23, ed. F. Wasserschleben (Leipzig 1840; repr. Graz 1964).

22. Burchard probably worked from a Regino-manuscript similar to that of Vienna, ÖNB lat. 694; see M. Kerner, F. Kerff, R. Pokorny, K. Schön, and H. Tills, 'Textidentifikation und Provenienzanalyse im Decretum Burchardi', SG 20 (1976) 45–46; R. Pokorny, 'Regino von Prüm, Libri duo de synodalibus causis', in: *The History of Western Canon Law to 1000*, ed. W. Hartmann (HMCL; Washington, DC, forthcoming); my thanks to Dr. Pokorny for making this article available to me before publication. The text here is taken from the Vienna manuscript, fol. 94v, and has been checked against Wasserschleben's edition.

23. Readings from Burchard's *Decretum* are based on the earliest manuscript, Vatican, BAV Pal. lat. 585 and 586, and checked against Frankfurt/M., Stadt- und Universitätsbibliothek MS Barth. 50, which was also extensively revised and amended; H. Hoffmann and R. Pokorny identified these as the earliest *Decretum*

Regino, *De syodalibus causis* 2.23	Burchard, *Decretum* 6.32
[Rubric:] One who has killed a man in a feud	[Rubric:] **Regarding those who commit homicides to avenge their relatives.**
[Inscription:] From a penitential	[Inscription:] From the penitential **of Theodore**
A person who has killed a man to avenge his brother or other relatives should do one year of penance, and in the next two years should observe three *quadragesimas* and the normal days, that is, Monday, Wednesday and Friday.	A person who has killed a man to avenge his brother or other relatives should do **penance for homicides committed willfully, since the Truth itself says: Vengeance is mine, and I will exact it.**
Qui per faidum hominem occiderit	*De illis qui pro vindicta parentum homicidia committunt*
Ex penitentiali	*Ex penitentiali **Theodori***
Qui pro vindicta fratris aut aliorum parentum occiderit hominem annum poeniteat, et sequentibus duobus tres quadragesimas observet, et legitimas ferias, id est secundum, quartam et sextam feriam.	*Qui pro vindicta fratris aut aliorum parentum occiderit hominem, ita poeniteat **ut homicidia sponte commissa, cum ipsa Veritas dicat: Mihi vindictam, et ego retribuam.***

First, Burchard changed the rubric so that it spoke not of a 'feud' specifically but of 'vengeance' generally. The change shifted the focus of the canon away from particular situations describing cycles of violence and retribution. Instead, it brought attention to the concepts of vengeance and retribution; the canons speak of the 'vengeance' of penance.[24]

Second, Burchard altered the canon in order to increase the penalty for homicides committed in a feud. Now such actions were punished as harshly as any other willful homicides (that is, seven years of penance). Finally, he provided a reason why homicides committed in a vendetta should be punished like any other. To find his justification, he went to the Bible. In Romans 12.19, Paul had quoted Deuteronomy 32.35 to assert that Christians should not avenge themselves, but should allow God to do so, since God had said 'Vengeance is mine, and I will repay'. Burchard took this phrase from Deuteronomy and transplanted it into his canon.

In altering the canon, the bishop of Worms implied that justice resided ultimately

manuscripts. See their *Das Dekret des Bischofs Burchard von Worms: Textstufen—Frühe Verbreitung—Vorlagen* (MGH Hilfsmittel 12; Munich 1991); the *editio princeps* (Cologne 1548; repr. Aalen 1992) of the *Decretum* is very close to the Vatican manuscript.
24. See *Decretum* 19.31, which speaks of *vindictam et censuram canonum*.

with God. Individuals should not take it upon themselves to punish and avenge. This canon, however, also raised questions. Could humans, like kings or judges, still avenge crimes, or should all punishments be left up to God? Was there a distinction between God's justice and human justice carried out by the Church or the secular arm?

As Burchard made clear in another canon, 6.43, rulers and judges could avenge deaths. In fact, the canon's rubric summarizes its content as 'regarding vengeance which is not prohibited', *de vindicta non prohibenda*. The first line of the canon makes clear that this is based on the New Testament: *De vindicta non prohibenda in novo testamento*. Citing 1 Peter 2.13–14, the text asserts that God has delegated secular rulers to punish malefactors. Similarly, canon 6.44 asserts that God allows his 'ministers' to carry out torture or death sentences: 'The sword has been given to wreak vengeance upon evildoers' *(propter vindicta noxiorum gladium fuisse permissum)*.

For Burchard, then, a ruler could carry out vengeance on God's behalf. Wrongdoers should be punished in this world, and not left to God's final justice. But they should be punished by those rulers and judges delegated by God to carry out his justice. What Burchard condemned were individuals taking justice into their own hands in acts of individual, private vengeance.

Burchard's new condemnation of private vengeance was taken up into the subsequent canonical tradition. Later canonical collections included his altered version, rather than Regino's version. Collections such as Anselm of Lucca's *Collectio canonum* (version A), the *Appendix Seguntina*, the *Collectio Sanctae Mariae Novellae*, the *Collectio V librorum* of Vat. lat. 1348, the *Collectio XIII librorum* of Berlin Savigny 3 and that of Vat. lat. 1361, the *Collectio VII librorum*, the *Collection of Paris, Saint Geneviève*, and the *Decretum* attributed to Ivo of Chartres, included Burchard's version.[25]

Burchard's interest in the nature of vengeance was developed and expanded by the compilers of the Ivonian *Decretum* and of the Ivonian *Panormia*. These collections investigated in depth how judges and rulers could avenge wrongs and use force.[26] They set forth a clear definition of homicide, which did not include cases in which a just law ordered someone to be killed, or when God himself, 'the source of justice', ordered a killing.[27] They also stated with new force that to punish wrongdoers was not to spill blood but to carry out the office of the minister of the law.[28] In addition, the Ivonian

---

25. I have identified these by using *KanonesJ*. The *Collectio III librorum* does not include the scriptural verse, although it requires seven years of penance, like Burchard.

26. See especially the Ivonian *Decretum* 10.59–123, which discusses topics pertaining to the use of force and even death by rulers and judges, including just war and the legislative power of kings. The same discussion was presented more clearly and forcefully in the Ivonian *Panormia*, at 8.15–60.

27. See the Ivonian *Decretum* 10.4 and the Ivonian *Panormia* 8.2.

28. See the Ivonian *Decretum* 10.115a and the Ivonian *Panormia* 8.53.

compilers paid fleeting homage to the problems raised by ongoing strife and violence such as that in feuds; Ivo's *Decretum* 10.42 harshly penalizes those who kill someone after making peace.

Yet neither the Ivonian *Panormia* nor Gratian's *Decretum* included Burchard's altered canon, 6.32. What did enter Gratian was a lengthy discussion on the nature of vengeance at C.23 q.4. Gratian took many canons from the Ivonian collections, which had established an entire discourse on the subject. However, it had been Burchard who first drew attention to the nature of vengeance in the abstract, and, perhaps, set into motion a new discourse about the nature of violence and revenge.

In the *Decretum*, Burchard presented a new vision of the blood feud. No longer would the Church accept it as a viable moral 'excuse' for committing homicide. The earlier canon law had implicitly equated those who killed to avenge their relatives with people who accidentally caused another person's death. With Burchard, however, the feud came under new, critical scrutiny. Those who avenged their kin were considered intentional 'murderers' like any other person who deliberately killed another.

We should not conclude that Burchard considered the feud 'primitive', or that the feud gave way to a more sophisticated form of justice. In fact, as Paul Hyams has reminded us, feud and law could and did coexist.[29] Rather, Burchard seems to have found the uncontrolled feud problematic: the feud as a cycle of violence rather than the threat of feud as a means of keeping the peace. Burchard sought to diminish the effects—and perhaps to restore the equilibrium of social relations—by resorting to legal incentives and mechanisms such as obtaining a royal charter, altering a *Decretum* canon regarding deaths committed to avenge a relative, and taking concrete measures to prevent such retributive deaths in the *Lex familiae*. In the *Lex familiae* he also spelled out particular ways in which vengeance might be eliminated and which might ensure that feuds did not break out into open violence. Through these various legal channels, Burchard worked to discourage feuds and to take concrete measures to break the cycle of violence.

Burchard may represent an intermediate stage in the development of criminal law. In 1859 Heinrich Gengler described Burchard's *Lex familiae* as 'eine Übergangsphase vom alten Volks- zum neueren Land- und Stadtrechte'.[30] Dilcher agrees with this assessment. As he points out, Burchard's *Lex familiae* addresses only his *familiae*, and, in the law of feuds, particularly the *fiscalini* who had property to defend.[31] Nor did Burchard

29. Hyams, *Rancor and Reconciliation* 4.

30. Quoted in Dilcher, 'Mord und Totschlag im alten Worms' 98; see also his discussion, 'Der Kanonist als Gesetzgeber. Zur rechtshistorischen Stellung des Hofrechts Bischof Burchards von Worms 1024/25', in: *Grundlagen des Rechts: Festschrift für Peter Landau zum 65. Geburtstag*, ed. R. Helmholz, P. Mikat, J. Müller, and M. Stolleis (Rechts- und Staatswissenschaftliche Veröffentlichungen der Görres-Gesellschaft 91; Paderborn 2000) 106–8.

31. Dilcher, 'Mord und Totschlag' 98–99.

allow private retaliation. Instead, he required payment of a fine and physical punishment. This was not yet a world in which an impersonal state punished wrongdoers. But, it seems, Burchard was an important intermediary figure in the evolution of criminal law.[32]

Furthermore, as Dilcher points out, the shift away from private vengeance was motivated by religious convictions. I have shown that Burchard did not inherit this idea from his religious training or the canonical tradition. In fact, the canonical tradition tended to treat a feud as an extenuating circumstance. Burchard himself apparently helped to popularize the idea that the Bible forbids private acts of vengeance, and that God (and his agents, the rulers) should punish offenses. By altering a canon he took from Regino, Burchard shaped the Church's subsequent teaching on feuds and the nature of violence.

The question is *how* Burchard came to view the feud with such disapproval. What I suggest is that Burchard's own experience of offenses informed his reading of the Bible. He probably responded to a social reality when he altered the canon law. His normative view was shaped by conceptions of utility arising from his experience as ruler in an area where feuds threatened to disturb the peace. As landlord and justice of the peace of Worms, Burchard knew first-hand what feuds looked like and, I would suggest, he anticipated the problems that eventually would erupt.

We should not envision Burchard as a pure theorist deriving biblical principles in some intellectual place at a great remove from social realities. Rather, when he found guiding principles in the Bible, his selections were informed by his own preoccupations, his mindset and his immediate concerns. Burchard read the Bible selectively, through the particular 'lenses' that he, as bishop and ruler, brought to the text. The canonical tradition might have led him to find a very different principle in the Bible—some passages on vengeance and retribution, especially in the Hebrew Scriptures, might indicate that feuds were licit. Instead, however, Burchard read the Bible as prohibiting acts of individual blood vengeance. He did so, I would speculate, because of his practical experience as bishop, and the recurrent problem of feuding in the *familia* of Worms. The social realities of feuding in his diocese colored his reading of the Bible and led him to select a principle in it which prohibited individual acts of vengeance.

In this way, canon law changed in response to very real situations. It did not develop only as an abstract body of law derived through disinterested study of the Bible and the

---

32. See also D. Willoweit, 'Unrechtsfolgen in Hof- und Dienstrechten des 11. und 12. Jahrhunderts: Mit einer Anmerkung zum Verhältnis von geistlicher Busse und weltlicher Sanktion vor der Ausbreitung des peinlichen Strafrechts', in: *Vom mittelalterlichen Recht zur neuzeitlichen Rechtswissenschaft: Bedingungen, Wege und Probleme de europäischen Rechtsgeschichte*, ed. W. Trusen and N. Brieskorn (Rechts- und staatswissenschaftliche Veröffentlichungen der Görres-Gesellschaft 72; Paderborn 1994) 111–16.

canonical tradition. Just as Dilcher shows that Burchard's religious thought influenced the *Lex familiae*, so too Burchard's own experience of feuding within his *familia* and between the *familiae* of Worms and Lorsch may have influenced his reading of the Bible and so his law in the *Decretum*.

Yet we should not say simplistically that early medieval canon law responded primarily to social realities, and that it was based upon utility rather than theory. Peter Landau has already demonstrated how Burchard worked from scriptural principles in changing the canon law of marriage of free and unfree.[33] This concern with identifying biblical principles in the canonical tradition can also be seen in how Burchard selected canons for inclusion in the *Decretum*. What the issue of feuds allows us to see is how utility and principle intersected. Canon law may have reflected, at the most basic level, implicit social and political values. It changed in response to changing social realities—but also, at the same time, in response to increased theoretical speculation about the nature of God's commands for humans. These speculations would lead, eventually, to the remarkable doctrinal achievements of the twelfth- and thirteenth-century canonists, who found new and fresh ways to articulate and discuss the complex problems of judicial authority, rightful punishment, and scriptural justification.

33. P. Landau, 'Die Eheschliessung von Freien mit Unfreien bei Burchard von Worms und Gratian: Ein Beitrag zur Textkritik der Quellen des kanonischen Rechts und zur Geschichte christlicher Umformung des Eherechts', in: *Cristianità ed Europa*, ed. C. Alzati (Rome 1994) 453–62.

[6]

Gedanken zum Institut
der Chorbischöfe

Jörg Müller

❋

1. Einleitung

Als 'episodenhafte Erscheinung der karolingischen Epoche . . . mit angelsächsischem Ursprung', so charakterisiert H. v. Schubert in seiner Geschichte der christlichen Kirche im Frühmittelalter die Chorbischöfe.[1] Der Befund der Belanglosigkeit wird durch den Blick in ältere Lexika gestützt, die häufig das Lemma gar nicht kennen. Die das heutige Verständnis prägenden Monografien oder umfangreicheren Artikel stammen noch aus der Zeit der vorigen Jahrhundertwende.[2] Langsam ändert sich jedoch das Bild, wie sich an neueren Auflagen und Aufsätzen—jüngst im Zusammenhang mit der fortschreitenden Erhellung des pseudo-isidorischen Fälschungskomplexes—ablesen lässt.[3] Eine der Ursachen für das erwachende Interesse dürfte sein, dass die Geschichte der Kirche immer weniger nur unter dem Blickwinkel einer Entstehungsgeschichte der gegenwärtigen (katholischen) Kirche und ihrer Institute wahrgenommen wird. Auch über das unmittelbare auf das Institut bezogene Interesse hinaus können die Chorbischöfe einen Blick wert sein, da sich an ihnen einige Grundmuster der kirchlichen Rechtsentwicklung aufzeigen lassen. Dazu soll im Anschluss an eine kurze Einführung nach den normativen Grundlagen für das Institut in der fränkischen Zeit gefragt werden sowie

---

1. H. v. Schubert, *Geschichte der christlichen Kirche im Frühmittelalter* (Darmstadt 1962) 575.

2. Vgl. 'La législation conciliaire relative aux chorévêques', in: Hefele-Leclercq 2.2.1197–1237; und unten Anm. 5.

3. G. Schmitz, 'Die allmähliche Verfertigung der Gedanken beim Fälschen', in: *Fortschritt durch Fälschungen, Symposion Tübingen 2000*, ed. W. Hartmann und G. Schmitz (MGH Studien und Texte 31; Tübingen 2004) 29–60; K. Zechiel-Eckes, 'Der "unbeugsame" Exterminator', in: *Scientia veritatis. Festschrift für Hubert Mordek*, ed. O. Münsch und T. Zotz (Ostfildern 2004) 173–90.

nach deren Verbreitung in vorgratianischen Kirchenrechtssammlungen. Zuletzt soll
die Frage nach der Aktualität des Instituts und nach Grundstrukturen kirchlicher Verwaltung am Beispiel der Chorbischöfe behandelt werden.

2. Was sind Chorbischöfe in der westlichen Kirche? Versuch einer Definition und kurzer historischer Abriss

Der Ausdruck Chorbischof, das heisst Landbischof, taucht in Diözesen des Ostens
für den Vorsteher, den Bischof, eines Landgebiets auf. Dabei kann er in Bezug auf die
gedachte Diözese *(parrochia/ecclesia)* neben dem Bischof jener Stadt, die den ländlichen Raum rechtlich dominiert, also zusätzlich vorhanden sein, und dies alleine oder
zu mehreren, oder gar ohne dass es den städtischen Bischof gibt. Er hat die bischöfliche
Weihe. Seine Aufgaben sind über weite Teile denen eines Bischofs gleich.[4]

In der antiken Kirche ist der Chorbischof in den Unterschriftslisten der frühen
Konzilien, zum Beispiel Nicaea 325, fassbar. Sein Rang in Bezug auf die anderen Kleriker und seine Aufgaben ändern sich im Zuge der Entwicklung. Ein Wendepunkt wird im
Konzil von Laodicea (ca. 380) can. 57 sichtbar, das ihn durch Visitatoren, Periodeuten,
ersetzen will. Als Ehrentitel bleibt der Chorbischof in mehreren orthodoxen Kirchen
bestehen.[5]

In der westlichen Kirche findet sich das Institut vereinzelt—vermutlich im Zusammenhang mit der allgemeinen Rezeption der griechischen Kanones—, so zum Beispiel,
um in bestimmten Situationen zwei Bischöfe innerhalb einer Gemeinde unterbringen
zu können; ferner in Grabinschriften, ohne dass hier Details des Amtes bekannt wären;
dann erst—wie bereits einleitend angedeutet—in reichem Masse in fränkischer Zeit.
Das Konzil von Metz 888 (can. 8) markiert sein Ende, nachdem bereits ab 829 kräftig
dagegen polemisiert wurde.[6]

Die Gründe für die Ausbreitung dieses Instituts im Frankenreich werden einmal
in Vorteilen gesehen, die das Institut für die dort vorhandenen noch 'unfertigen' Diözesen und die notwendige Missionstätigkeit bietet; bei den 'fertigen' Diözesen in den
Vorteilen, die das Institut den weltlichen Grossen bieten kann; dass nämlich, wenn ein

---

4. Vgl. W. Cramer, 'Chorbischof', LThK³ 2 (1994) 1090–92; O. Bucci, 'Episcopato delle campagne e corepiscopi', in: *Atti dell'Accademia Romanistica Constantiniana* 4 (Studi in onore di Mario Dominicis; Perugia 1981)
97–163.

5. E. Kirsten, 'Chorbischöfe', *Reallexikon für Antike und Christentum* 2 (1954) 1105–14; und ausführlich F. Gillmann, *Das Institut der Chorbischöfe im Orient* (München 1903).

6. Zu 829, siehe *Episcoporum relatio ad pium Hludowicum* c.6 (9), ed. MGH Capitularia 2.32 Nr. 196; ibid.
c.7 (10), wo vor simonistischen Praktiken gewarnt wird, auch das Amt der Chorbischöfe betreffend; zur Quelle
zuletzt V. Lukas, 'Philologische Beobachtungen zur Rezeption der Relatio episcoporum von 829 bei Benedictus
Levita', in: *Fortschritt durch Fälschungen* 61–87; das Konzil von Paris 829, can. 27, ed. MGH Concilia 2.629–30
Nr. 50, wendet sich nicht gegen die Chorbischöfe als solche, stellt jedoch ihre Weihegewalt in Frage.

Bistum wohl über einen Chorbischof, nicht jedoch über einen 'Vollbischof' verfügt, einerseits das gottesdienstliche Gefüge nicht zusammenbricht, andererseits die Einnahmen nicht dem Chorbischof, sondern den die Diözese dominierenden weltlichen Grossen für die Zeit der 'Sedisvakanz' bis zur Weihe eines 'Vollbischofs' zur Verfügung stehen. Das Verschwinden der Chorbischöfe im Westen wird mit den kirchlichen Reformanstrengungen unter Ludwig dem Frommen und mit der Ausbreitung des den Chorbischöfen feindlich gesonnenen pseudo-isidorischen Fälschungskomplexes verbunden.[7] Zumindest der Titel 'Chorbischof' geht jedoch keinesfalls in der Deutlichkeit verloren, wie die Literatur das vorspiegelt. Er findet sich noch sehr lange im Bistum Köln, in Utrecht und ebenso im Trierer Raum.[8]

Sieht man in der fränkischen Periode genauer hin, zeigen sich—wie bereits angedeutet—zwei Bereiche, in denen die Chorbischöfe auftreten. Einerseits vor allem in der Provinz Mainz, aber auch Salzburg, hier möglicherweise auf die besonderen Bedingungen der Mission rückführbar und eventuell von der Angelsachsenmission beeinflusst. Dann findet sich das Institut in der Westfranzia—hier vielleicht gefördert durch die bereits oben angedeuteten Vorteile, die Chorbischöfe den Laien beim 'Einnahmentransfer' bieten, und zwar durchaus in Bistümern, die nicht im Einzugsbereich der angelsächsischen Wandermissionare lagen.[9] Darüber hinaus finden sich einige Chorbischöfe, die Äbte von grossen, alten Klerikergemeinschaften sind, etwa St. Cassius in Bonn oder St. Quirin in Xanten. Dieser letzte Typ des 'Chorbischofsabtes' lässt sich vereinzelt auch in den erstgenannten Gebieten ('unfertige' Diözese, Mission) nachweisen, so im Bistum Freising.[10] Insgesamt gesehen hat das Institut im Frankenreich durchaus eine eigenständige Verankerung, auch wenn der eine oder andere iro-schottische Wanderbischof auf diese Art in die kirchliche Organisation integriert worden sein mag.[11]

Zu den Aufgaben: Dem Chorbischof kommt in den älteren Belegstellen die Sorge

7. So bereits v. Schubert, *Geschichte;* 'das verhasste Institut der Chorbischöfe', bei E. Seckel, 'Pseudoisidor', *Protestantische Realenzyklopädie* 16 (1905) 265–307, hier 301. Metz (888) can. 8, ed. Mansi 18.80, begründet die völlige Ablehnung des Instituts mit Hinweis auf drei bei Pseudo-Isidor verfälschte Dekretalen.

8. In Köln bei St. Aposteln, St. Gereon, St. Maria im Kapitol, St. Georg und weiteren; in Utrecht am Dom; in Trier am Dom und für einen Pfarrer, vgl. *Germania Sacra* (http://vwebtest1.mpg.de/gs4 _drei.pl vom 7.6.2004). Im Trierer Raum findet sich der Titel ferner bei einigen Herren der Burg Ramstein; im Jahr 1110 wird ein Archidiakon und Chorbischof Bruno von Rammerstein erwähnt; 1402 ist Chorbischof Rupprecht von Hoheneck Herr auf Ramstein (vgl. http://www.burgenwelt.de/ramstein/gealt.htm vom 21.10.2004); zum Fortleben in Deutschland weitere Belege bei Hinschius, *System* 2.169.

9. Ibid. 2.164–69, mit weiteren Nachweisen für die Tätigkeit der Chorbischöfe bei Sedisvakanz, Missionstätigkeit, und zur 'Entlastung der Hauptbischöfe'.

10. Vgl. T. Gottlob, *Der abendländische Chorepiskopat* (Bonn 1928) 12–101; zu Freising, ibid. 49; siehe auch die Kritik bei F. Gillmann, AKKR 108 (1928) 712–23; ferner H. Frank, *Die Klosterbischöfe des Frankenreichs* (Münster 1932).

11. Anders v. Schubert, *Geschichte;* zusammenfassend V. Fuchs, *Der Ordinationstitel von seiner Entstehung bis auf Innozenz III.* (Bonn 1930) 226.

um eine *ecclesia*, vorsichtig gesagt, einen Pfarrbezirk zu; ferner die niedere Weihegewalt, zum Teil auch die Firmung. Weiterhin gilt als unstrittig, dass er im Rahmen der
ihm anvertrauten *parrochia/ecclesia* die Jurisdiktions- und Disziplinargewalt hatte,
einschliesslich der Visitation; und dass er im Rahmen der ihm anvertrauten *parro-
chia/ecclesia* am Altar vor den *sacerdotes* 'der Erste' war. Mit Sicherheit war dabei auch
die Verwaltung des Brotes eingeschlossen. Ob jedoch ebenso eine eigene Verwaltung
des Chrisams, Salböls, damit verbunden war, kann nicht mit hinreichender Sicherheit
gesagt werden. Für die spätere Zeit dürfte es dort ausgeschlossen gewesen sein, wo der
Chorbischof neben einem 'Vollbischof' tätig war—von Ausnahmen abgesehen. Der
Chorbischof galt zwar bereits in den lateinischen Übersetzungen der griechischen
Überlieferung als Stellvertreter des Bischofs—*vicarius episcopi*—, nahm aber bei Sedisvakanz nicht den Platz des Bischofs ein und besass nicht dessen Verfügungsgewalt über
die Einkünfte. Von den *episcopi vagantes*, den Wanderbischöfen, und vergleichbaren
Erscheinungen ist er deutlich zu scheiden, da ihm mit der Weihe wohl grundsätzlich
ein bestimmter 'Bezirk', *territorium, ecclesia* zugewiesen wurde.[12]

Trotz dieser grundsätzlich festen Umgrenzung stellt das Amt des Chorbischofs
ein strukturelles Problem für die fränkische Kirche gerade nach ihrer Konsolidierung
dar: Denn sehr früh setzte sich in der Kirche der Monepiskopat durch. Bischof mit
Lehr-, Zucht-, Tauf- und Weihegewalt kann nur einer sein. Das Bistum ist überhaupt
nur denkbar auf eine Stadtgemeinde bezogen. So wird in Nicaea festgehalten, dass das
städtische Territorium, vor allem im Sinn des Gerichtsdistrikts, den Umfang vorgibt.
Die spätantike Bischofskirche ist die Kirche schlechthin. An bestimmten Terminen wird
getauft, werden die Firmlinge geweiht, die Presbyter ordiniert. Die Gemeinde versam-
melt sich dort, um die grossen Kirchenfeste gemeinsam zu begehen. Den Katechumen
wird Unterricht erteilt, Büsser bekennen ihre Verfehlungen, unterwerfen sich der Busse
und werden wieder in die Gemeinde aufgenommen. Der Bischof ist die Kirche. Wo ist
da noch Platz für den Chorbischof?

3. Die normativen Grundlagen im Rahmen
der fränkischen Kirche

Die im Westen übernommen Quellen aus griechischer Tradition bilden auch hier
in übersetzter Fassung den Kern und seien deswegen etwas ausführlicher betrachtet:
Ancyra (314) can.13 und Neocaesarea (314–25) can.13 kennen die Chorbischöfe in der
lateinischen Übersetzung bereits als *vicarii episcopi*. Sie räumen ihnen die Möglichkeit

---

12. Vgl. oben, Anm. 5; ferner J. Leclef, 'Chorévêque', DDC 3 (1942) 686–95.

zu niederen Weihen, zur Lehre und zum Opfer ein, darin dem Bischof gleichgestellt.[13] Nicaea 325 can. 8 eröffnet die Möglichkeit, im Rahmen der Wiederaufnahme eines novatianischen Bischofs in eine katholische *ecclesia* diesem seinen Titel zu lassen *concedere ei etiam episcopalis nominis honorem,* so dass vom Titel, nicht aber von der Funktion her zwei Bischöfe in einer Stadt sind: *Ut in civitate non videantur duo episcopi esse*—wie es zur Klarstellung heisst.[14] Dieser Konzilsbeschluss wurde von etlichen Chorbischöfen unterzeichnet. Von der Restriktion her ähnlich ist Serdica (ca. 343) can. 6 einzuordnen: In einem Ort, der so klein ist *(vicus vel modica civitas),* das ein Priester genügen würde, soll kein Bischof geweiht werden, damit nicht *nomen episcopi et auctoritas* leiden. Diese Bestimmung könnte gegen Chorbischöfe gerichtet sein, sofern sie als Vorsteher von sehr kleinen Landgemeinden begriffen werden.[15]

Die *Magna charta* des Chorbischofsinstituts bilden in gewisser Weise zwei Kanones von Antiochia 341.[16] In can. 8 werden die Chorbischöfe in der lateinischen Fassung als die Stellvertreter der Bischöfe bezeichnet und ihnen wird im Gegensatz zu den Presbytern zugestanden, *litteras formatas* auszustellen. In Fragen der inneren Verwaltung sind sie somit den Bischöfen gleichgestellt. In can. 10 wird ihnen zugestanden, die ihnen übertragenen Kirchen zu lenken, falls sie von einem Bischof geweiht wurden. Weiterhin wird ihnen das bisher schon zugestandene Recht zu den später sogenannten niederen Weihen bestätigt, und ihnen die Weihe von Presbytern und Diakonen zugestanden, falls der jeweilige Ortsbischof, dem sie beigeordnet sind, Kenntnis davon hat. Geweiht werden sie durch den Bischof, dem sie beigeordnet sind. Aus dem Beginn des can. 10 lässt sich schlussfolgern, dass es möglicherweise auch nicht durch einen Bischof geweihte Chorbischöfe gegeben hat; aus dem Ende des Kapitels, dass der Chorbischof seine Bischofsweihe nur einem einzigen Bischof verdankt—wie es auch nach dem Codex der katholischen Kirche von 1917 wieder möglich war. Bei aller Klarstellung wird den Chorbischöfen aber ebenso vorgeschrieben, dass sie nicht ihre Grenzen überschreiten und mit ihrem Status zufrieden sein sollen. Restriktiver ist dagegen, wie bereits oben angesprochen, Laodicea (ca. 380) can. 57 in Wiederaufnahme des Gedankens von Serdica. Für *vicis* und *villis* sollen keine Bischöfe, also auch keine Chorbischöfe, mehr geweiht werden, sondern Visitatoren, Periodeuten. Die Übergangsregelung für die Be-

---

13. Ancyra can. 13, ed. EOMIA 2.84; zum Text, C. Richardson, 'The Riddle of the 13th Canon of Ancyra', *Church History* 16 (1947) 32–36. Neocaesarea can. 13, ed. EOMIA 2.136–39; hier findet sich im zweiten Teil des Kanons, dass 'die Stellvertreter der Bischöfe, die die Griechen Chorbischöfe nennen, nach dem Beispiel der 70 Ältesten geformt sind', so dass in der Analogie die Bischöfe die Stellung der Apostel einnehmen und die Chorbischöfe aus der apostolischen Sukzession herausfallen.

14. Nicaea can. 8 (Prisc.), ed. EOMIA 1.125.

15. Serdica can. 6, ed. EOMIA 1.500. Bemerkenswert erscheint, dass hier nicht auf den Umfang der christlichen, sondern auf die Grösse der weltlichen Gemeinde abgestellt wird.

16. Antiochia can. 8, ed. EOMIA 2.254–57; can. 10, ed. ibid. 2.261–65.

troffenen legt fest: Diejenigen, die bereits zum Inkrafttreten des Kanons im Amt sind, sollen nichts mehr *sine conscientiae episcopi civitatis* unternehmen, Presbyter dagegen, und hier zeigen sich noch Differenzierungen, *sine praecepto et consilio episcopi.*[17]

Dies ist im Wesentlichen der Normbestand, auf den der Westen, und damit später die Ausbildung des Instituts bei den Franken, zurückgreifen kann.[18] Schon der Erstbeleg für den Westen, das Konzil von Riez 439, nimmt Bezug auf Nicaea can. 8 und löst damit in can. 3 den Fall des Armentarius, der, da ohne Einverständnis des Metropoliten geweiht, abgesetzt wird und eine *ecclesia* zugewiesen bekommt, in der er die Firmung spenden und vor den Presbytern opfern kann.[19] Vorerst gibt es keine neuen Normen. Dann meldet sich das Papsttum. Zacharias schreibt 747 an die Bischöfe des Frankenreichs, die in der Anrede hierarchisch gegliedert werden, wobei auch die *ceteris amantissimis chorepiscopis* erwähnt werden. Er kennt das Institut und scheint keine Einwände dagegen zu haben.[20] Ebenfalls auf 747 zu datieren, jedoch erst in der Fassung des *Codex Carolinus* (ca. 791) überliefert ist eine Stellungnahme Papst Zacharias', in der er in 27 Kapiteln den Franken die Kirchenverfassung erklärt und am Ende von c.1 Antiochia can. 10 und in c.4 Neocaesarea can. 13.2 zitiert.[21] Die Reihe der Päpste schliesst mit Nikolaus I., der auf Anfragen aus der Westfranzia 864 eine Wiederweihe, nachdem die Weihe durch Chorbischöfe erfolgt sei, vermeiden möchte, da die Chorbischöfe die bischöfliche *dignitas* besässen. 865 erklärte er dann in Übereinstimmung mit den spätantiken Normen die Weihe von Presbytern und Diakonen durch Chorbischöfe für nicht statthaft.[22] Die Reihe der Päpste schliesst mit Stephan V., der noch 887 für

17. EOMIA 2.386–87, was neben der Interpretation von Antiochia, can. 10 (oben Anm. 16), als weiterer Beleg für zwei Arten von Chorbischöfen, solchen mit und ohne bischöfliche Weihe, dient. Ferner lässt sich aus der Differenzierung *vicus* und *villa* im Gegensatz zu *vicus* und *modica civitas* (vgl. oben, Anm. 15) folgern, dass das Institut der Chorbischöfe inzwischen wohl auch auf die Landgüter, *villae*, vorgedrungen ist. Wie weit sich die Formen von der vermeintlich typisch germanischen Eigenkirche unterscheiden, muss hier offen blieben, darf aber in Frage gestellt werden. Vielleicht ist auch dies ein Beleg, dass bestimmte Rechts- und Sozialstrukturen bestimmte Rechtsformen in der Entstehung begünstigen.

18. Vgl. die Liste bei Leclef, DDC 3.689–91, wo Grossbritannien und Irland nur summarisch genannt werden, ansonsten wie bereits bei Gottlob, *Der abendländische Chorepiskopat*, diözesenweise aufgezählt wird; wenn Chorbischöfe gelegentlich auch *coepiscopi* heissen, ist das vermutlich nicht immer ein Schreibfehler; vielleicht waren jene den heutigen Koadjutoren vergleichbar.

19. Vgl. C. Munier, *Concilia Galliae* (CCL 148.61–75, hier 66–67).

20. Papst Zacharias I. (JE 2287) an die Bischöfe des Frankenreichs (747), ed. MGH Epistolae 3.362–64 Nr. 82, hier 363.

21. JE 2277 (747/91), in: *Codex Carolinus*, ed. MGH Epistolae 3.479–487 Nr. 3, hier 481; nach *Dionysiana II*.

22. Nikolaus I. (JE 2765) an Radulf von Bourges (864); idem (JE 2787) an Arduicus von Besançon (865); im Brief an den Bischof von Bourges heisst es, *forma genuina* c.1: 'In deiner Gegend kommt es häufig zu Weihen von Presbytern und Diakonen durch Chorbischöfe, die dann zum Teil durch Bischöfe abgesetzt, zum Teil neu geweiht werden; wir wollen nicht, dass Unschuldige leiden, und wir wollen keine Wiederweihe, denn aus den *sacri canones* (vgl. Neocaesarea can. 13, oben Anm. 13) geht eindeutig hervor, dass die Bischöfe ihre *dignitas* auf die Chorbischöfe übertragen haben, so dass es keiner *reordinationes* oder *iteratas consecrationes* bedarf'; vgl. MGH Epistolae 6.633–36 Nr. 117, hier 634.

Mainz und damit vorbildhaft für grosse Teile der Ostfranzia eine Ausnahmeregelung zugunsten des Instituts der Chorbischöfe erlässt.[23] Neben den Päpsten meldet sich der fränkische König in der *Admonitio generalis* von 789 und weist in c.9 unter der Rubrik *Sacerdotibus* unter Bezug auf die Bestimmungen von Antiochia can. 10 und Ancyra can. 13 die Chorbischöfe auf die ihnen gesetzten Schranken hin.[24]

Unter Ludwig dem Frommen wird das Thema virulent, was sich in der Normgebung niederschlägt. Komplexer als zuvor ist das Vorgehen auf der Synode von Paris (829) can. 27. Der Kanon wendet sich zwar nicht gegen die Existenz der Chorbischöfe als solche, bezweifelt auch nicht ihren *ordo*, stellt jedoch ihre Weihegewalt grundsätzlich in Frage; er verweist, was den Umfang der Amtsgewalt betrifft, nur darauf, dass die entsprechenden Normen schon bekannt genug seien, und unterwirft die Chorbischöfe somit noch stärker als bisher den Bischöfen, die ihnen jetzt auch im Einzelfall keine Befugnisse jenseits dessen, was in *sacris canonibus praefixum* sei, einräumen sollen.[25] Die nur wenige Monate später zu datierende *episcoporum relatio* kommt auf Grundlage derselben Quellen in c.6 (9) noch einmal zu einem versöhnlicheren Ergebnis, indem sie—neben den Beschränkungen—den bischöflichen Charakter der Weihe für die Chorbischöfe betont, sie aber in c.7 (10) zugleich unter die *ministri* des Bischofs einreiht.[26] Letzteres wiederholt Aachen 836.[27] Als eigenständiges, nicht in Bezug auf einen Bischof gedachtes Amt sind Chorbischöfe nicht mehr denkbar.

In diesen Jahren nimmt auch das grosse pseudo-isidorische Fälschungsunternehmen seinen Ausgang, das, wie bereits erwähnt, dem Institut der Chorbischöfe zunehmend kritisch gegenübersteht.[28] Inwieweit es das Konzil von Meaux-Paris 845/46 tatsächlich beeinflusst hat, oder dieses nur den Zeitgeist aufgreift, kann nicht entschieden werden. Dass nur ein geringer Teil der Bestimmungen dieses Konzils vom König und den Grossen anschliessend mit Gesetzeskraft versehen wurde, ist nicht bemerkenswert. Wichtig

23. Stephan V. (JE 3443) gestattet Luidbert von Mainz, bis zur Abhaltung einer Synode mit Rücksicht auf den bisherigen Gebrauch die Chorbischöfe beizubehalten.

24. MGH Capitularia 1.53–62 Nr. 22, hier 54: 'Corepiscopi cognoscant modum suum et nihil faciant absque licentia episcopi in cuius parrochia habitant'; interessant ist, dass mit 'habitant' und nicht mit 'subiecti sunt' geschlossen wird, wie es der *Codex Carolinus* (oben, Anm. 21) nahe legen würde.

25. MGH Concilia 2.629–30 Nr. 50: 'Ecce aperte demonstratur, quod non septuaginta discipuli, quorum formam tenent chorepiscopi, sed apostoli, quorum successores sunt episcopi, tradebant spiritum sanctum'; die 70 *seniores* aus Neocaesarea can. 13 (oben, Anm. 13) erscheinen demnach als *discipuli*; die fehlende Weihegewalt der Chorbischöfe wird somit zumindest nahe gelegt. Auch Antiochia can. 10 (oben, Anm. 16) wird von Paris 829 verkürzt zitiert; die erlaubten Ordinationsakte der Chorbischöfe werden nicht mehr genannt. Der Kanon endet mit einer Ermahnung an die Bischöfe, den den Chorbischöfen gesetzten Rahmen weder überschreiten zu lassen noch zu überschreiten; Hinschius, *System* 2.166, sieht darin bereits das Recht auf Firmung entzogen.

26. MGH Capitularia 2.32 Nr. 196: 'Ut [die Chorbischöfe] episcopi consecrati sint, tamen . . . ut modum proprium recognoscant'.

27. Ibid. c.7 (10), wird vor *avaritia* bei 'Funktionsträgern' (*ministros*) des Bischofs gewarnt, von der auch die Chorbischöfe betroffen sein könnten; vgl. Aachen (836) can. 28, ed. MGH Concilia 2.704–67 Nr. 56, hier 711.

28. Vgl. Schmitz, 'Die allmähliche Verfertigung'; Zechiel-Eckes, 'Auf Pseudoisidors Spuren' 1–26.

ist jedoch, dass auf diesem Konzil in can. 44 unter der in der späteren Karolingerzeit fast traditionell gewordenen Überschrift *Ut chorepiscopus modum suum iuxta canonicam institutionem teneat* mit neuen Texten argumentiert wird.[29] Vom ursprünglichen Kontext befreit werden diese als Beleg traditioneller Restriktion zu Lasten der Chorbischöfe gedeutet, was dem Stil des pseudo-isidorischen Unternehmens durchaus entspricht.[30] Kurz: Die Chorbischöfe werden jetzt jeglicher bischöflicher Funktion entkleidet. Demselben Thema nimmt sich dann noch einmal ausführlicher Benedictus Levita an.[31] Parallel dazu sprechen ihnen die pseudo-isidorischen Dekretalen jeglichen bischöflichen Status ab, indem sie es als Makel herausstreichen, dass der Chorbischof, falls er überhaupt bischöfliche Weihen hat, nur durch einen Bischof geweiht worden ist. Stattdessen soll die Weihe durch drei Bischöfe als Zugangsvoraussetzung für den bischöflichen Ordo gelten.[32] Chorbischöfe sind keine Bischöfe mehr. Die genannte Regelung Papst Stephans V. bildet eine einmalige Ausnahme, und das bereits erwähnte Konzil von Metz (888) can. 8 ordnet die erneuten Weihen für den Fall an, dass diese von Chorbischöfen vorgenommen wurden.[33]

Die letzte Stimme zugunsten des Instituts der Chorbischöfe im Frankenreich ist zeitgleich mit der gerade angeführten Entwicklung und wird von ihrem Editor Dümmler als Antwort auf diese Entwicklung eingeordnet. Normativer Charakter im technischen Sinn des Wortes kommt ihr jedoch nicht zu. Es ist ein Brief des Mainzer Erzbischofs Hrabanus Maurus, auch als kleine Schrift: *De chorepiscopis* bekannt.[34] *Si liceat chorepiscopis presbyteros et diaconos ordinare cum consensu episcopi sui* wird für den hier interessierenden Textteil als Überschrift gewählt und zeigt schon die Tendenz: Nicht die Einschränkungen, sondern die Möglichkeiten des Instituts werden seitenlang betont. Hrabanus selbst hatte wohl ein stattliche Anzahl von Chorbischöfen in seinem Gefolge,

29. MGH Concilia 3.61–132 Nr. 11, hier 105–06.

30. Vgl. ibid.; so wird ein Brief von Innocenz I. an den Bischof von Gubbio (JK 311), in dem der Papst Presbytern die Firmung und Verwaltung des Salböls untersagt, auf Chorbischöfe bezogen; ähnlich beim Verbot der Kirchweihe, das zuvor nur Priester betraf; ferner sollte die *reconciliatio* fortan nur mit Mandat des Bischofs erfolgen.

31. Vollständige Fundstellenliste bei Schmitz, 'Die allmähliche Verfertigung' 34 Anm. 21; es erstaunt bei einem vermeintlichen Hauptanliegen der pseudo-isidorischen Fälschungen die letztlich geringe Zahl an Fundstellen.

32. Ps.-Leo (JK +551), ed. P. Hinschius, *Decretales Pseudoisidorianae* (Leipzig 1863) 628, untersagt Chorbischöfen alle bischöflichen Handlungen; sie besitzen zwar die bischöfliche Weihe, nicht jedoch den *pontificatus . . . apicem* der Bischöfe; Ps.-Damasus (JK +244), ed. ibid.; vgl. H. Fuhrmann, *Einfluss und Verbreitung der pseudoisidorischen Fälschungen* 1 (Stuttgart 1972) 192 Anm. 123; Schmitz, 'Die allmähliche Verfertigung' 32–33.

33. Vgl. oben, Anm. 23; Metz (888) can. 8, ed. Mansi 18.80, bestimmt, dass an nicht konsekrierten Orten keinesfalls das Opfer gefeiert werden darf und von Chorbischöfen geweihte Basiliken nach den *decreta* der Päpste Damasus, Innocenz und Leo (wie durch Pseudo-Isidor verformt, oben Anm. 32) erneut durch den Bischof zu weihen sind.

34. Hraban an Drogo von Metz, ed. MGH Epistolae 5.431–39 Nr. 25 (PL 110.1195–1206).

wie sich aus den Adressaten verschiedener Briefe erschliessen lässt, die er namentlich anspricht. Selbstverständlich wird im Gang der Argumentation auch die Unterordnung der Chorbischöfe unter die Bischöfe betont.[35] Hraban greift sinngemäss auf die Unterschriftslisten von Nicaea zurück: 'Wenn das Institut so unkanonisch ist, wie manche behaupten, wieso finden sich dann in diesem berühmten Konzil, das von so vielen Bischöfen besucht wurde, so viele Chorbischöfe unter den Unterschreibenden?' Er argumentiert dann in bekannter Weise mit der Übertragung des heiligen Geistes.[36] Der Vollständigkeit halber sei abschliessend erwähnt, dass in zahlreichen chronikalischen und annalistischen Quellen das vermeintliche Wissen, dass selbst der heilige Petrus mit Linus und Anakleth Chorbischöfe geweiht habe, vorhanden ist—also im Sinne Hrabans historisch argumentiert wird. Noch im späten 12. Jahrhundert kennt die *Historia Romanorum Pontificum* aus Zwettl dieses 'Faktum'.[37] Als zu stark erweist sich jedoch letztlich die Wirkung der restriktiven Argumentation in den pseudo-isidorischen Dekretalen.[38]

4. Die Überlieferung in vorgratianischen Kirchenrechtssammlungen

Die antiken griechischen Texte werden im Westen bekannt, seit sie durch die *Hispana* und die *Dionysiana* im 6. Jahrhundert allgemein zugänglich sind.[39] Sie werden weitergetragen durch die *Breviatio Canonum* des Fulgentius Ferrandus und die *Concordia Canonum* des Cresconius, deren letztere die den Chorbischöfen etwas ungünstigeren Formulierungen der *Dionysiana II* aufnimmt.[40] Isidor fasst in *De officiis* 2.6 unter der Rubrik *De chorepiscopis* Neocaesarea can. 13.2 und Antiochia can. 10 zusammen, wenngleich in der günstigeren, die Zu- und nicht die Unterordnung betonenden Formulierung.[41] So ist bei ihm seiner Vorlage entsprechend auch von den 70 *seniores* als Vorbild der Chorbischöfe die Rede. Kurz: Die Kanones als Grundlage des Normen-

35. Ibid. 431.   36. Ibid. 434.
37. PL 213.990.
38. Vgl. Johannes III. (JK +1042), ed. Hinschius, *Decretales* 715–18, gegen Hraban argumentierend.
39. Hierzu zuletzt P. Landau, 'Il ruolo della critica del testo', in: *La cultura giuridico-canonica medioevale. Premesse per un dialogo ecumenico*, ed. E. de León und N. Álvarez de las Asturias (Mailand 2003) 23–43.
40. Fulgentius Ferrandus, ed. EOMIA 2.84 can. 79; Cresconius 96, ed. K. Zechiel-Eckes, *Die Concordia Canonum des Cresconius* (Frankfurt/M. 1992) 603–04, der zu Antiochia can. 10 die Lesart der *Dionysiana II* bietet: der Chorbischof ist dem Ortsbischof *subjectus*.
41. Isidorus Hispalensis, *De officiis* 6.1 (PL 83.786–87): 'Chorepiscopi, id est, vicarii episcoporum, juxta quod canones ipsi testantur, instituti sunt ad exemplum septuaginta seniorum, tanquam consacerdotes propter sollicitudinem pauperum. Hi in villis et vicis constituti gubernant sibi commissas Ecclesias, habentes licentiam constituere lectores, subdiaconos, exorcistas, acolythos; presbyteros autem aut diaconos ordinare non audeant, praeter conscientiam episcopi, in cujus regione praeesse noscuntur; hi autem a solo episcopo civitatis cui adjacent ordinantur'.

bestands bleiben stabil. Das Institut wird weder übersehen, noch wie später durch bearbeitende Eingriffe umgestaltet. Von den Normen der fränkischen Zeit werden der Brief Papsts Nikolaus I. (JE 2765), weniges aus der *relatio episcoporum* von 829 und dann vor allem pseudo-isidorisches Material rezipiert.[42]

Fragt man nach der Rolle der Chorbischöfe in den relevanten vorgratianischen Kanonessammlungen und orientiert sich an den von Fowler-Magerl in der Datenbank *KanonesJ* (Stand 2003) bereitgestellten ca. 85.000 Kanones, so taucht der Ausdruck Chorbischof 57 mal an exponierter Stelle in Rubrik oder Incipit auf.[43]

Die quantitative Erfassung der rezipierten Vorlagen ergibt, dass die negative Bewertung durch Pseudo-Isidor das Bild dominiert.[44] Blickt man dagegen auf die rezipierenden Sammlungen, so fällt auf, dass sich keinerlei Belege aus der *Hibernensis* finden—was möglicherweise als Argument gegen einen iro-schottischen Ursprung des Instituts auf dem Kontinent herangezogen werden könnte.[45] Von den in der Datenbank enthaltenen Sammlungen, die vor dem Wendpunkt von 829 liegen, tauchen einschlägige Stellen nur bei der *Sangermanensis*, der *Collectio Anselmo dedicata* (CAD) und der Sammlung in 9 Büchern (Coll 9Libr. 1349) in Form spätantiker Kanones auf.

Das argumentative Hin und Her des 9. Jahrhunderts findet keinen Niederschlag in den nachfolgenden Sammlungen. Der bereits bekannte Befund, dass eine der bedeutendsten vorgratianischen Sammlungen, nämlich das Dekret des Wormser Bischofs Burchard (ca. 1020), dieses Institut nicht kennt, wird zunächst bestätigt. Bei der genaueren Analyse wird die Annahme Königers, dass Burchard es scheinbar bewusst eliminierte, eventuell dahingehend zu korrigieren sein, dass Burchard es nicht aufnimmt.[46] Anders dagegen die zweite grosse überregionale Sammlung des beginnenden

---

42. Der Bescheid von Papst Nikolaus I. findet sich in Ivos Sammlungen, der *Caesaraugustana*, vgl. MGH Epistolae 6.633; Pseudo-Isidor/Benedictus Levita 3.402, 3.423, wurde durch das Bischofskapitular des Isaak von Langres 11.30–31, ed. MGH Capitula Episcoporum 2.240, übernommen; weitere Beispiele im Folgenden.

43. Siehe *KanonesJ*.

44. Vgl. dazu die Auswertung unten, Anhang: Ps.-Damasus (JK +244) = 20 Zitate; Ps.-Leo (JK +551) = 15 Zitate; Antiochia can. 10, je nach Rubrik einschränkend oder bestätigend = 10 Zitate; Ancyra can. 13 = 5; *Relatio episcoporum* 829 = 4; Johannes III. (JK +1042) = 2; Neocaesarea can. 13 = 1.

45. Der Titel der zweiten Auflage von *KanonesJ* wurde nicht dem erweiterten Inhalt angepasst; der ursprüngliche zeitliche Rahmen wird unter anderem von der *Collectio Anselmo dedicata* (CAD) und der *Hibernensis* gesprengt; vgl. jetzt *Clavis Canonum*, hg. v. L. Fowler-Magerl (MGH Hilfsmittel 21; Hannover 2005).

46. A. Koeniger, *Burchard von Worms und die deutsche Kirche seiner Zeit* (München 1905) 86 mit Anm. 2; Koenigers Behauptung, Burchards *Decretum* 5.44–45 habe das Institut jeweils 'eliminiert', erweist sich als irrig, da bereits die in CAD 4.72–73 befindliche Variante den auf die Chorbischöfe entfallenen Teil der Quelle (Neocaesarea can. 13) nicht überlieferte, vgl. CAD in der Burchard besonders nahestehenden Form des Ms. Vatikan, BAV Vat. lat. 580, fol. 123rb. Parallelstellen finden sich auch in der *Collectio duodecim partium* (CDP) 124–25, vgl. J. Müller, *Untersuchungen zur Collectio duodecim partium* (Ebelsbach 1989) 262 Anm. 1161. In *Decretum* 3.58 (= JK +878), habe Burchard—so Koeniger—das Auftauchen der Chorbischöfe in seiner Vorlage übersehen. Dass also Burchard die Chorbischöfe bewusst herausgestrichen hat, darf bezweifelt werden. Der Kanon findet sich in derselben, die Chorbischöfe jedoch nennenden Form, in CDP 4.86/5.112.

11. Jahrhunderts: Die aus Freising stammende Sammlung in 12 Teilen (CDP). Sie steht in enger Beziehung zu Burchards Dekret, ist umfangreicher, von der Wirkung her dagegen geringer einzuschätzen. Zugleich ist sie die einzige Sammlung, die negative Stellungnahmen zum Institut der Chorbischöfe jenseits von Pseudo-Isidor, nämlich in Passagen aus der *relatio episcoporum* von 829 aufgenommen hat.[47] Die Sammler der Reformzeit fühlen sich genötigt, im wesentlichen mit Belegstellen aus Pseudo-Isidor gegen die Chorbischöfe Stellung zu nehmen.

Bemerkenswert im Zusammenhang mit der Weiterverwendung der angesprochenen Texte ist, dass die negativen Aussagen zum Institut der Chorbischöfe des Konzils von Meaux-Paris 845/46 can. 44 gar nicht rezipiert wurden, obwohl es sich wegen der Deutlichkeit, mit der es Chorbischöfen viele Amtshandlungen untersagt, geradezu angeboten hätte. Einerseits gehört can. 44 nicht zu jenen Kapiteln, die von der Reichsversammlung in Èpernay bestätigt wurden.[48] Dagegen ist die Rezeption von Meaux-Paris gerade in den Kanonessammlungen häufig, so dass mangelnde königliche Bestätigung meiner Meinung nach für die fehlende Resonanz kein Argument ist.[49] Die Ansicht, das Institut sei obsolet geworden, vermag ebensowenig zu überzeugen, da allein der Blick in den Anhang (unten) zeigt, dass das Institut der Chorbischöfe auch spätere Sammler noch beschäftigte.

Der Ausblick sei mit Gratians Dekret abgeschlossen, der in D.68 im Wesentlichen die einschlägigen Stellen präsentiert und durch entsprechende Rubrizierung das grundsätzlich negative Urteil bestätigt, in D.68 d.a.c.4 jedoch noch einmal sorgfältig zwischen Bischof und Chorbischof distinguiert.[50] Diese Beobachtungen lenken aber bereits zum nächsten Aspekt.

5. Die Aktualität der Kanonessammlungen in Bezug auf die Chorbischöfe

Wenn nun das Institut als solches durch die historische Entwicklung negativ konnotiert wird, durch die pseudo-isidorischen Dekretalen zum Teil sogar als *superstitio* dargestellt wird, und Akte der Chorbischöfe seit der zweiten Hälfte des 9. Jahrhunderts

---

47. Es wurden von der CDP nicht die negativen Stellen aus *Benedictus Levita*, ihr durchaus bekannt, rezipiert, sondern die aus den pseudo-isidorischen Dekretalen; vgl. Zechiel-Eckes, 'Exterminator'.

48. Vgl. C. de Clercq, *La législation religieuse franque* 2 (Antwerpen 1958) 302.

49. Zur Rezeption, vgl. auch die Tabellen in: MGH Concilia 3.73–76.

50. Im *Decretum Gratiani* gibt es 17 Verweise, vgl. *Wortkonkordanz zum Decretum Gratiani*, hg. v. T. Reuter und G. Silagi (MGH Hilfsmittel 10; München 1990) 1.602, davon 9 allein bei D.68 c.4–5; Gratian stellt bereits in der sogenannten Ersten Redaktion mit Hilfe von Pseudo-Isidor die Chorbischöfe auf die Stufe von Presbytern, indem er in D.68 c.4 aus Ps.-Leo (JK +551) zitiert, in c.5 aus Ps.-Damasus (JK +244); dazu kommt das Rubrum: 'Ordo chorepiscoporum a sacra sede reprobatur'.

zunehmend als nichtig angesehen werden, wieso reagierten zeitgenössische oder spätere Sammler des Kirchenrechts unverändert darauf? Kurz, warum sollte in den Kanonessammlungen ein Institut behandelt werden, das es nicht mehr gab? Abgesehen von der Sammlung in zwölf Teilen (CDP) findet sich unter den im Anhang (unten) genannten Sammlungen keine, der man antiquarisches Interesse, oder gar ein Interesse an Vollständigkeit bei der Normsammlung unterstellen könnte.[51]

Für die Zeit des späten 9. Jahrhunderts, also jene Phase, in der man dem Institut des Chorbischofs ablehnend gegenüberstand, und auch noch kurz danach wäre vorab zu fragen: Wie bekämpft man ein Institut? Vielleicht, indem man der zugehörigen Personengruppe die Dinge verbietet, die für das Institut typisch sind, so dass die Personen *de facto* in einen anderen Status hineingedrängt werden? Das wäre der Weg, den Pseudo-Isidor und Benedictus Levita beschritten. Der Chorbischof blieb zunächst weiter bestehen, wurde aber durch Einschränkungen den Presbytern gleichgestellt und im Zweifelsfall eliminiert. Zugleich stehen die 'Chorbischöfe' Linus und Anakleth und damit die Tradition nicht zur Debatte.

Eine andere Möglichkeit wäre, das Institut zu verschweigen, wie bei Burchard von Worms in seinem Dekret geschehen. Burchards Schweigen ist insoweit bemerkenswert, als auch für das Bistum Worms Chorbischöfe aus Subskriptionslisten oder erzählenden Quellen bekannt sind, ferner Burchard aus den Werken Hrabans zitiert, der immerhin an Chorbischöfe und über Chorbischöfe positiv schreibt. Ist Burchards Schweigen vielleicht in dem Sinn zu interpretieren, dass er die Chorbischöfe nicht mehr als ein Problem des geltenden Rechts betrachtet und deswegen übergeht?

Dem Problem zeitlich näher als Burchard steht Regino von Prüm mit seinen einflussreichen *Libri duo de synodalibus causis* (ca. 906). Auch er kennt den Chorbischof nur als Teil einer Anrede aus einem Brief Bischof Hrabans an Reginbald und schweigt ansonsten. In diesem Fall mag das mit der Ausrichtung seines Handbuchs zusammenhängen, das der bischöflichen Visitation dienen soll. Ob der Visitierende Ortsbischof oder vielleicht ein anderer befugter Amtsträger ist, berührt dabei nicht. Zudem kennt Regino bereits den Archidiakon als Helfer des Bischofs beim Sendgericht, einen der funktionalen Nachfolger des Instituts der Chorbischöfe, so dass sich möglicherweise eine Stellungnahme erübrigte.[52]

Wenn in der nächsten Phase der Entwicklung des Kirchenrechts, den Sammlungen

---

51. Vgl. J. Müller, 'Die Collectio duodecim partium und ihr Freisinger Umfeld' (1995), als PDF-Datei unter: http://www.kuttner-institute.jura.uni-muenchen.de (vom 8.11.2004). Die Tatsache, dass sich in der Provinz Salzburg bis 945 Chorbischöfe halten konnten und an den Synoden von Regensburg und Dingolfing 932 teilnahmen, vgl. MGH Concilia 6.1.120–21 mit Anm. 18–19, somit das Institut zur vermutlichen Abfassungszeit der CDP in Bayern erst seit zwei Generationen obsolet geworden war, erscheint gegenüber dem antiquarischen Interesse an Vollständigkeit als Grund für die Behandlung des Instituts nebensächlich.

52. Gerade im Raum Trier, also in Reginos Diözese, hielt sich der Titel Chorbischof besonders lange, vgl.

der Reformzeit, wieder regelmässig gegen die Chorbischöfe Stellung bezogen wird, kann das vielleicht so interpretiert werden, dass mittlerweile der Blick für die klerikale Hierarchie deutlich geschärft wurde, so dass deren Grenzen und Bedingungen stets grössere Aufmerksamkeit fanden, unabhängig davon, ob *chorepiscopi* und ähnliches noch einen Sitz im Leben hatten. Sie fanden jedoch einen Platz in der Sorge um das heilsnotwendig korrekte Verhalten, vielleicht in einer Verunsicherung der Redaktoren—und das rechtfertigte ihre Erwähnung in den nun entstehenden Sammlungen—unabhängig davon, ob sie noch existierten.

Die kirchliche Hierarchie—um diesen Gedanken wieder aufzugreifen—äussert sich in Jurisdiktions- und Ordinationskompetenzen. Während im Rahmen der ersteren für die Chorbischöfe 'funktionale Nachfolger' entwickelt werden, etwa die Archidiakone, die in einer die Hierarchie nicht mehr gefährdenden Weise eingebunden sind, wird im Rahmen der letzteren das Problem der Ordination und nicht nur die Ordinationsgewalt der Chorbischöfe selbst virulent: Könnte doch die Ordination von Chorbischöfen in vielen Fällen als absolute Ordination begriffen werden—und das darf, vorerst zumindest, nicht sein.[53] Auch dies war ein Grund, das Institut trotz nicht mehr bestehender praktischer Bedeutung in den Sammlungen negativ zu erwähnen.

Zur Aktualität lassen sich also keine generellen Aussagen ableiten; zu unterschiedlich sind die Interessen der jeweiligen Redaktoren der einzelnen Sammlungen. Einschränken, mit Schweigen übergehen, oder vielleicht doch noch Erwähnen, das sind einige Reaktionen. Einen direkten Rückschluss auf die aktuelle Geltung des Instituts lassen sie kaum zu.

6. Die sogenannte 'Natur der Sache' oder: Kann das Institut untergehen?

Zu einer ersten Antwort auf die soeben gestellte Frage bietet sich der Blick auf die Weiterentwicklung der Visitation im Rahmen des oben angesprochenen bischöflichen Send an. Es zeigt sich hier, dass das Institut der Chorbischöfe durchaus untergehen kann—wie ja ohnehin nicht jeder Bischof über einen oder mehrere Chorbischöfe verfügte. Einzelne Funktionen des Chorbischofsamtes sind jedoch so vital für das Leben

---

oben, Anm. 8; Regino von Prüm, *Libri duo de synodalibus causis et disciplinis ecclesiasticis*, ed. H. Wasserschleben (Leipzig 1840). Allgemein zur Ausbreitung des Archidiakons, P. Landau, *Officium und Libertas christiana* (München 1991) 14–15, mit weiterer Literatur.

53. Vgl. die oben, Anm. 32, wiedergegebene Argumentation aus Ps.-Damasus (JK +244); ferner Fuchs, *Der Ordinationstitel* bes. 235: 'Den Chorbischöfen mangelte, um Bischöfe im Rechtssinn zu sein, der legitime Titel. Entweder waren sie überhaupt absolut ordiniert oder auf einen ungenügenden Titel. . . . Trotzdem werden sie als wirkliche Bischöfe im Hinblick auf ihre Konsekration anerkannt, sie können bischöfliche Weihehandlungen vollziehen'.

der Kirche, dass sie unverzichtbar bleiben und in anderer institutioneller Einbindung ausgeübt werden müssen. Entsprechend der hierarchischen Durchbildung der Kirche sind sie fortan aber zweifelsfrei dem jeweiligen Bischof untergeordnet.

Zunächst die Stellvertretung bei Ausübung der dem Bischof zustehenden Jurisdiktion, ein Bereich, in dem zunächst Chorbischöfe vereinzelt in den Grenzen des ihnen anvertrauten Sprengels tätig waren.[54] Hier tritt zunehmend der Archidiakon oder, soweit im ländlichen Bereich vorhanden, der Erzdekan, Landdekan und eben nicht mehr der Chorbischof als *vicarius episcopi* auf. Dasselbe gilt für den Bereich der Administration und Disziplin. Die Funktion des Visitators, die für den spätantiken Chorbischof noch so wesentlich war, dass sie zu seiner Entmachtung auf dem Konzil von Laodicea eigens den Periodeuten übertragen wurde, findet sich also beim Archidiakon wieder.[55] Dieses Wissen mag vielleicht noch zwei Jahrhunderte nach dem 'Ende' der Chorbischöfe präsent gewesen sein. Ein Ekbert, *maior decanus, qui tunc chorepiscopatus curam administrabat*, taucht noch 1124 in einer Urkunde Erzbischof Friedrichs I. von Köln auf. Dafür war nun auch keine bischöfliche Weihe mehr erforderlich, nicht einmal, in Übereinstimmung mit Antiochia can. 10, durch den Ortsbischof.[56]

Die Übernahme der Firmung und anderer Pontifikalien auf Anweisung des Bischofs durch den später so genannten Weihbischof—eine Entwicklung, die in Deutschland im 16. Jahrhundert einen Abschluss erreicht—kennzeichnet einen weiteren Aufgabenbereich, in dem wohl ursprünglich dem Institut der Chorbischöfe übertragene Funktionen nach deren Eliminierung durch andere Funktionsträger wahrgenommen werden mussten.[57] Heute treten neben die Ausübung der Pontifikalien auch begrenzte administrative Befugnisse, so dass in diesen Funktionen in Verbindung mit der bischöflichen Weihe der heutige Weihbischof dem Chorbischof der fränkischen Zeit wohl am nächsten steht. Durch die Weihe auf einen ausserhalb der *parrochia* liegenden Titel ist jedoch die potentielle Konkurrenzsituation zugunsten der Auxiliarfunktion bereinigt.

Die Betrachtungen seien mit dem Blick auf die Errichtung des sogenannten Eigenbistums Gurk abgeschlossen: Die Salzburger *parrochia* ist sehr ausgedehnt und die Gegend um Gurk vom Bischofsitz in Salzburg aus schwer erreichbar. Dementsprechend finden sich schon früh und bis weit in die fränkische Zeit Chorbischöfe mit festem Sitz. Dieses Modell wurde nun 1072 nicht erneuert, sondern ein (Eigen)bistum

---

54. Zu den Anfängen des Chorbischofs beim Send, A. Schröder, *Die Entwicklung des Archidiakonats bis zum 11. Jahrhundert* (Augsburg 1890) 45–46, mit Hinweis auf eine entsprechende Praxis bereits zur Zeit des Hrabanus Maurus.

55. Vgl. Schröder, *Entwicklung* bes. 45; ferner oben, bei Anm. 17.

56. T. Lacomblet, *Urkundenbuch für die Geschichte des Niederrheins* 1.196 Nr. 299; ferner Schröder, *Entwicklung* bes. 43–44.

57. Vgl. Hinschius, *System* 2.171–76.

gegründet. Es stand unter der Leitung eines Bischofs, der in Bezug auf Wahl und Ordination völlig vom Salzburger Metropoliten abhing—wie seinerzeit in Antiochia can. 10 in Bezug auf die Chorbischöfe bestimmt.[58] Kurz: In der Gründungsphase des Gurker Bistums sind alle Kriterien eines klassischen Chorbischofs gegeben—nur die Bezeichnung wird vermieden. Und kurze Zeit später beginnen—auch hier in der Natur der Sache liegend—die Verselbständigungsbestrebungen des Gurker Kapitels, der Gurker Bischöfe.[59]

7. Fazit

Im Rahmen des Fazits soll anhand des Instituts der Chorbischöfe auf ein Grundmuster kirchenrechtlicher Entwicklung aufmerksam gemacht werden: Die Ausbildung des Instituts in der Spätantike 'zur Versorgung des ländlichen Raums' durch zum Teil selbständige Presbyter, zum Teil (Chor)bischöfe, zeigt, wie stark das Denken in Bezug auf öffentlichen Raum, 'öffentliches Recht', auch im Bereich der Kirche durch das Denken in städtischen, munizipalen Grenzen bestimmt war. Einerseits lag die Notwendigkeit vor, die kirchliche Sorge dort stattfinden zu lassen, wo die Christen lebten, andererseits war Gemeinde nur vorstellbar in den städtischen Grenzen und—seit Ignatius von Antiochia—auch nur geleitet und belehrt durch einen Einzigen, den Bischof. Was in dieser Weise auf dem Konzil von Nicaea erneut betont wird, wird dort andererseits aus pragmatischen Überlegungen sofort unterlaufen. Um die Aufnahme ehemals novatianischer Bischöfe zu erleichtern, wird ihnen der Bischofstitel belassen und dadurch der Übertritt zur katholischen Partei erleichtert. Als Resultat finden sich nun zwei Titelträger in einer Stadt, in einer *parrochia*. Erscheint dieser Pragmatismus und die daraus entsprungene Flexibilität typisch, so ist ebenso typisch, dass das in der gefundenen Lösung enthaltenen negative Potential erst in der weiteren Entwicklung erfasst wird, und typischerweise im Osten deutlich schneller als im Westen.

Auf den sich anschliessenden Konzilien des 4. Jahrhunderts wird die rechtliche Ausbildung des Instituts abgeschlossen und für den Osten zugleich seine Überwindung eingeleitet. Dies war möglich, da die ursprünglich auf die Unterstützung des Bischofs, auf die Förderung des christlichen Glaubens und auf die Festigung von Gemeinden ausserhalb der weltlichen Gemeindestrukturen abzielenden Zwecke des Instituts der Chorbischöfe in dieser Phase der Entwicklung in der östlichen Kirche bereits obsolet geworden waren.

---

58. MGH Diplomata Heinrici IV 322–23 Nr. 253 (1072 II 4).

59. Aufgrund dieser Erfahrungen wurde wohl bei der nächsten Salzburger (Eigen)bistumsgründung, Chiemsee (1215), zuerst kein Archidiakonat eingerichtet.

Ebenso typisch ist, dass das spätantike Normgefüge beim Institut der Chorbischöfe über die Karolingerzeit hinaus die Grundlage bildet. Päpste und Könige nehmen zu ihm nur Stellung, passen es nicht grundlegend den veränderten Zeitumständen an. Die 'widmungsgerechte Nutzung' des Instituts vollzieht sich dabei im Rahmen der Missionsbistümer, in gewissen Grenzen auch beim chorbischöflichen Abt einer Klerikergemeinschaft. Das Gegenteil einer 'widmungsgerechten Nutzung' ist die Benutzung des chorbischöflichen Instituts, um weltlichen Grossen einige Bistümer der Westfranzia in der Schwächephase des merowingisch-fränkischen Königtums zur wirtschaftlichen Nutzung öffnen zu können.

Warum es unter diesen Umständen nicht zu einer Ausbildung des Instituts im langobardischen Italien kam, erscheint meiner Meinung nach hinreichend durch die grosse Dichte und kleinräumigen Strukturen der italienischen Diözesen, deren hohes Mass an 'Verstädterung' und im Zusammenhang mit der politisch wechselvollen Geschichte erklärt.[60] Das Fehlen von Belegen im westgotischen Spanien erklärt sich vielleicht aus der intensiven Lenkung und Leitung der Kirche durch die Verbindung von Königtum und 'Nationalkonzil' nach dem Übertritt der Westgoten zum Katholizismus; zumindest kannte Isidor von Sevilla in seiner Ämterhierarchie den für *vicis* und *villis* ordinierten 'Eigenbischof'.[61] Vielleicht hat für die Zurückhaltung bei der Übernahme dieses Instituts in beiden Kirchen weiterhin eine Rolle gespielt, dass im Vergleich zum Frankenreich die zusätzliche Existenz einer arianischen Kirche und arianischer Bischöfe länger andauerte—somit vielfach ein 'Zweibischofsproblem' gegeben war.

Erst nach Aufschwung der karolingischen Renaissance ist die Entwicklung so weit fortgeschritten, dass auch in der westlichen Kirche die Problematik des Instituts voll erfasst wird. Das bleibt in diesem Fall dem Klerus unter Ludwig dem Frommen, besonders der pseudo-isidorischen Werkstatt vorbehalten. Die restriktive Haltung beginnt sich bereits im *Codex Carolinus* (791) abzuzeichnen. Zunächst wird nur generell die Gefahr für die kirchliche Hierarchie durch unterstellte oder echte Amtsanmassungen der Chorbischöfe gesehen. Die wieder zunehmende Theologisierung der Kirche führt jedoch bald zur Sensibilisierung gegenüber den Gefahren, die für die Sakramente und das Heil durch die echten oder unterstellten Grenzüberschreitungen der Chorbischöfe gegeben sind. In den Kanonessammlungen schlägt sich diese Entwicklung so nieder, dass die klassischen Traditionskerne durchgeschleust werden und die dem Institut kritisch ge-

---

60. Das Institut als solches war den Kompilatoren 'italienischer' Kanonessammlungen durchaus bekannt, vgl. CAD, wo Buch 2 die Überschrift trägt: 'De honere . . . et . . . diuerso negotio . . . episcoporum et chorepiscoporum', Bamberg, SB Can. 5, fol. 22v; ferner die unten im Anhang gegebenen Belege. Zu Italien, Landau, *Officium* 31–33, der die Entstehung der *Collectio de ecclesiasticis officiis*, die zuerst das neue Bild des Archidiakons als Stellvertreter des Bischofs formt, als wahrscheinlich im urbanen Milieu Oberitaliens entstanden ansieht.

61. Vgl. oben, Anm. 41.

genüberstehenden Texte zunehmend in den Vordergrund rücken. Nach Überarbeitung durch die pseudo-isidorische Werkstatt dominieren sie die Sammlungen der Reformzeit eindeutig. Dass im weiteren Verlauf der Entwicklung das Verbot der absoluten Ordination aufgeweicht wird und damit eines der jüngeren Argumente gegen die Chorbischöfe fällt, vermag am Untergang des Instituts als Ganzem nichts mehr zu ändern. Einzelne Teile sind jedoch unverzichtbar und werden anderen Instituten übertragen, etwa die Visitatorenfunktion den Archidiakonen, ebenso wie die weitere Unterstützung des Bischofs bei administrativen und jurisdiktionellen Aufgaben. Auch Weihbischof und Koadjutor sind—meiner Meinung nach—unterschiedliche, späte Abkömmlinge der Chorbischöfe, wie neuerdings ebenso der Regionalbischof—jedenfalls dort, wo er disziplinäre und jurisdiktionelle Kompetenzen hat. Gerade mit letzterem, so mein Eindruck, kehrt eine Entwicklung wieder zu ihren Anfängen zurück. Wo als historische Ausnahmesituation, etwa bei der Errichtung des Eigenbistums Gurk, das Institut des Chorbischofs im Hochmittelalter vollständig wieder auftaucht, wird es keinesfalls so bezeichnet. Auch dies ist eine Entwicklung, die sich bei anderen Instituten mit ähnlich langer Geschichte feststellen lässt. Hält sich umgekehrt die Bezeichnung, so kennzeichnet sie jetzt eine Würde in einem Kapitel, wobei besonders in den rheinischen Bistümern die Übertragung vielleicht durch das Wissen um die chorbischöflichen Äbte erleichtert wurde. Am Ende der Belege steht vereinzelt der Chorbischof als Chor-Bischof, als seltene Bezeichnung für den Chorleiter; eine zunächst ahistorische Übertragung, die jedoch viel stärker auf die Wurzel zurückweist als *prima facie* deutlich.

Anhang

Die folgende Liste enthält Verweise in vorgratianischen Kanonessammlungen auf Chorbischöfe nach der Datenbank *KanonesJ* (vgl. oben, Anm. 43), sofern diese in Rubriken oder Incipits erscheinen; Angaben zur Entstehungszeit stammen aus *KanonesJ*, mit Ausnahme von Polykarp I, vgl. D. Jasper, 'Burchards Dekret', in: *Bischof Burchard von Worms 1000–1025*, hg. v. W. Hartmann (Mainz 2000) 195. Die Tabelle nennt zitierte Kanones und Dekretalen, ohne dass der Umfang des Auszugs berücksichtigt wird.

Coll. Sangermanensis (saec. 8)
1.32 Antiochia can. 10

CAD (ca. 875)
2.230 Ancyra can. 13
2.231 Neocaesarea can. 13.2

Coll. 9 Libr. (VatLat 1349) (ca. 920)
2.137 Antiochia can. 10

CDP (ca. 1020)
1.193/1.214 *Relatio episcoporum* 829 c.7 (10)
1.323/1.309 Ps.-Leo
1.324/1.310 *Relatio episcoporum* 829 c.6 (9)
2.37/2.98 Antiochia can. 10

Coll. 74Tit. (1050/1077)
197//27.1 Ps.-Damasus
198//27.2 Ps.-Leo

Coll. Lanfranci (nach 1059)
2.3.12 Ancyra can. 13
2.7.10 Antiochia can. 10

Coll. 183 Tit./Santa Maria Novella
  (ca.1063–83)
57.1 Ps.-Damasus
57.1a Ps.-Damasus
57.4 Antiochia can. 10

Atto von San Marco, *Breviarium*
(ca. 1075–1084)
29.2 Ps.-Damasus

Coll. Burdegalensis (nach 1078)
1.81 Ps.-Damasus
1.82 Ps.-Leo

Anselm von Lucca 'A' (ca.1085)
7.110c Ps.-Damasus
7.108 Ps.-Damasus
7.107 Ps.-Leo

Coll. 4Libr. (ca. 1085)
3.2.3 Ps.-Damasus
3.2.7 Ps.-Johannes
3.2.6 Ps.-Leo

Coll. Tarraconensis I (nach 1085)
195 Ps.-Damasus
196 Ps.-Leo

Coll. Paris n.a. 326 (nach 1085)
39 Ps.-Damasus
38 Ps.-Leo

Ivo, Dekret (nach 1093)
6.72 Ps.-Leo

Coll. Tarraconensis II (1093/5)
3.79 Ps.-Damasus
3.80 Ps.-Leo
7.6.13 Ancyra can. 13
7.10.10 Antiochia can. 10

1.Smlg von Paris 3853C (saec. 11^2)
1.94 Ps.-Damasus
1.95 Ps.-Leo

Coll. Madrid BN lat. 11548 (saec. 11 ex.)
35 Antiochia can. 10

Coll. Brugensis (saec. 11 ex. ?)
2.6.4 Antiochia can. 10
2.2.3 Ancyra can. 13

Coll. Atrebatensis (ca. 1100)
141 Antiochia can. 10

Coll. 7Libr. Turin 4.33 (ca.1100)
3.212 Ps.-Damasus
3.213 Ps.-Leo

Coll. Paris BN 13658 (saec. 12)
223 Ps.-Johannes
166 Ancyra can. 13

Coll. 2/8Libr. (nach 1100)
1.345 Ps.-Damasus
1.346.1 Ps.-Leo

Polycarp I (1111–13)
4.27.1 Ps.-Damasus
4.27.2 Ps.-Leo

Coll. 3Libr. (1112)
2.22.16 Ps.-Damasus

Coll. 7Libr. (ÖNB 2186) (1112–20)
1.99.1 Ps.-Damasus

Coll. VatLat 3829 Teil II (ca.1120)
41.10 Ps.-Damasus
47.62 Ps.-Leo

Coll. 9Libr. (San Pietro 118) (nach 1123)
4.9.16 Ps.-Damasus

Coll. 13Libr. (VatLat 1361) (ca. 1135)
7.61c Ps.-Damasus

PART TWO

The Formation of Canonistic Theory

Authors and Texts, ca. 1140–1350

[7]

Neither Slave nor Free

Theology and Law in Gratian's Thoughts on the Definition of Marriage and Unfree Persons

Anders Winroth

In *Causa* 29, Gratian discusses the case of a bride who by mistake married the wrong man. To make things worse, the imposter was not a free man, but a slave. In a meandering discussion, Gratian treats the legal ramifications of this situation.[1] C.29 is among the shortest in the first recension of the *Decretum*. It contains three canons and five *dicta*, and its first question is unusual for not containing any canons at all. It is an interesting *causa* for what it reveals about Gratian's background, outlook, and attitudes.

On the evidence of C.29, Gratian was a legal scholar with a strong theological bent, some radical opinions, and a firm belief in the primacy of eternal natural law over the whims of human legislation.

In his introductory case statement, Gratian tells of an aristocratic woman who has agreed to marry the son of a nobleman. A different man, however, turns up for the wedding, one who is a *servus* and certainly not noble, but she marries him, thinking he is her fiancé. When the latter eventually shows up, she discovers that she has been tricked. She complains and wants to marry the man she originally agreed to marry. Gratian poses two questions. First, whether she in fact is married to the imposter. Sec-

I wish to thank Paul Freedman and, especially, John Dillon for their kind comments and suggestions.

1. J. T. Noonan, 'Catholic Law School—A.D. 1150', *Catholic University Law Review* 47 (1998) 1189–1205, examined the argument of C.29. An analysis of the *Causa* and the decretist commentary on it appears in A. N. Sahaydachny, 'De coniugio seruorum: A Study of the Legal Debate about the Marriage of Unfree Persons among Decretists and Decretalists from A.D. 1140–1215' (Ph.D. diss.; Columbia University 1994). The Gratian that I discuss is the author of the first recension, 'Gratian 1', see A. Winroth, *The Making of Gratian's Decretum* (Cambridge 2000).

ond, whether the servile status of her husband gives her the right to divorce him, if she
did not know of it when they got married.

In the first question, Gratian begins by pointing out that marriage, according to its
definition, comes about through the consent of the two parties. Since in the example
both consented, there is a valid marriage between them. Gratian then objects that the
woman did not in fact consent, since she made an error. He then explains that there
are four kinds of errors and that only two of them invalidate the marriage. Those are
error of person (Plato or Virgil) and error of condition (free or unfree), while error of
fortune (rich or poor) and error of quality (chaste or unchaste) do not nullify consent.
Gratian provides several examples of these errors, both in the context of marriage and
otherwise.

The second question addresses error of condition *(error condicionis)*. The woman of
the case statement made an error not only about the identity of the person she married
but also in thinking him a free man when he in fact was unfree. Gratian explains first,
with reference to scriptural passages from the Pauline letters and a single canon (c.1),
that unfree persons are capable of marriage. He then explains, with the support of two
canons (c.4 and c.5), that a free person who marries an unfree person believed to be free
may get a divorce.

Gratian begins his discussion in question 1 by quoting, without identifying it, the
Roman law definition of marriage from Justinian's *Institutes* (Inst. 1.9.1): 'Wedlock or
marriage is the union of man and woman entailing that they live inseparably together'.
This introduction to the subject led many of Gratian's readers to expect that the rest of
the discussion of marriage law in this *questio* would be based on romanistic principles.
In the *Glossa ordinaria*, Johannes Teutonicus noted several parallels between Gratian's
discussion and Roman law, which has led modern scholars to assume, mistakenly, that
Gratian was inspired by these romanistic passages when he wrote C.29.[2]

In fact, the similarities between Gratian's discussion and the relevant paragraphs
in Justinian's *Corpus* are due either to a coincidental use of similar language or simply
to literary commonplaces. An example of the former is Gratian's definition of consent
(C.29 q.1 c.1 §1): 'Consensus est duorum vel plurium sensus in idem [consent is the
(shared) opinion of two or more persons concerning the same thing]'.[3] This is superfi-
cially reminiscent of the Roman jurist Ulpian's definition of *pactio* (agreement) in Dig.

2. J. Gaudemet, 'Droit canonique et droit romain: A propos de l'erreur sur la personne en matière de mariage (C. XXIX, qu. 1)', SG 9 (1966) 45–64; J. M. Viejo-Ximénez, 'La redacción original de C. 29 del Decreto de
Graciano', *Ius Ecclesiae* 10 (1998) 149–85.

3. My quotations of Gratian are my own edition on the basis of the three available witnesses to the first recension: Admont, Stiftsbibliothek 43 *(Aa)*; Florence, BN Centrale Conventi Soppressi A 1.402 *(Fd)*; and Sankt
Gallen, Stiftsbibliothek 673 *(Sg)*. For the first two manuscripts, see Winroth, *The Making* 23–26, 28–32. For *Sg*
(an abbreviation of the first recension), see A. Winroth, 'Recent Work on the Making of Gratian's *Decretum*', in:

2.14.1.2: 'Est pactio duorum pluriumve in idem placitum et consensus [agreement is the accord and consent of two or more persons about the same thing]'.[4]

Two jurists give definitions for two synonymous words meaning 'agreement, concord', which imply that two or more persons agree to one thing. It should not be surprising, then, that both use the normal Latin way of saying 'two or more' *(duorum vel plurium/pluriumve)* and include the idea that there is an agreement about the same thing *(in idem)*. Gratian and Ulpian use similar terms in their definitions, because they are writing in the same language about synonyms, not because one copied the other.

Gratian uses a cliché when in C.29 q.1 §2 he gives the example of a putative buyer of gold who actually is given orichalcum (an alloy of copper which, when polished, resembles gold):[5]

Si quis promitteret, se venditurum michi aurum, et pro auro offeret michi auricalcum, et ita me deciperet, numquid dicerer consensisse in auricalcum?

[If someone promised to sell me gold and instead of gold gave me orichalcum and thus deceived me, might I be said to have consented to orichalcum?]

Ulpian uses a similar cliché (with bronze instead of orichalcum) in a passage excerpted in Justinian's *Digest* (Dig. 18.1.14):[6]

Quid tamen dicemus, si in materia et qualitate ambo errarent? Ut puta si et ego me vendere aurum putarem et tu emere, cum aes esset.

[Now what are we to say when both parties are in error over both the material and its quality? Suppose that I think that I am selling and you think that you are buying gold, when it is bronze].

The idea of mistaking some cheaper metal (especially orichalcum) for gold is a widespread topos which appears almost everywhere in Latin literature, for example in the Bible (Ies. Syr. 47.20) and in the writings of Cicero, Suetonius, Lactantius, and Isidore of Seville.[7] That two jurists use the same commonplace is a simple coincidence and cannot be used to argue for intertextual influence.

Proc. Washington (MIC C.12; in press), provisionally available on the Internet at: http://pantheon.yale.edu/~haw6/gratian.html; also see C. Larrainzar, 'El borrador de la *Concordia* de Graciano: Sankt Gallen, Stiftsbibliothek MS 673 (=Sg)', *Ius Ecclesiae* 11 (1999) 593–666. An edition of the first recension of C.29 is available in J. M. Viejo-Ximénez, 'La redacción original de C. 29' 181–85. His edition is based on *Aa* and *Fd*. I cite the editions of Viejo-Ximénez and the *Decretum* only when they differ from mine.

4. Viejo-Ximénez, 'La redacción original' 160, gives the impossible reference 'Inst. 2.13.1.1' which might be wrong for Inst. 3.13.2: 'Aut enim re contrahuntur aut verbis aut litteris aut consensu'. My translation of Dig. 2.14.1.2 is adapted from: *The Digest of Justinian*, ed. A. Watson (Philadelphia 1985).

5. This passage is lacking in *Sg*.

6. Translation adapted from *The Digest of Justinian*; see also Dig. 18.1.45.

7. Cicero, *De officiis* 3.23, ed. C. Atzert, *De officiis, De virtutibus* (Leipzig 1963) 113; Suetonius, *Vitellius* 5, ed.

There are no traces of the influence of Roman law in C.29 beyond the introductory definition of marriage. It is clear, however, that Gratian did not take that definition directly from Justinian's *Institutes:* it circulated widely in the early twelfth century. Linda Fowler-Magerl lists its appearance in no fewer than fifteen collections of canon law.[8] The definition is, appropriately, the first canon in the sixth book *(de nuptiis)* of the *Panormia* by Ivo of Chartres, which was one of Gratian's main sources.[9] It also appears in several theological treatises from the early twelfth century (see below).

The exact wording of Gratian's quotation differs somewhat from the phrasing in the *Institutes* (even though there is no significant difference in meaning). Gratian writes (C.29 q.1 pr.: changed words in bold face):

Coniugium sive matrimonium est viri mulierisque[a] coniunctio, individuam vitae consuetudinem **retinens**[b].[10]

a. mulierisque *Aa Fd:* et mulieris *Sg Friedberg*[11]   b. retinens *corr. ex* retinenda *Fd:* servans *Aa:* c. *Sg*

Justinian's formulation is (Inst. 1.9.1):

Nuptiae autem sive matrimonium est viri et mulieris coniunctio, individuam consuetudinem vitae **continens**.

While the *Panormia* 6.1 includes Justinian's formulation verbatim, several French theological treatises contain slightly different formulations. One such treatise, the *Cum omnia sacramenta* displays interesting parallels with Gratian's work. The manuscripts ascribe this text to Anselm of Laon but it was more likely put together by others who were influenced by his teaching. The treatise defines marriage so:[12]

M. Ihm, *De vita caesarum libri VIII* (Stuttgart and Leipzig 1993) 284; Lactantius, *Libri divinarum institutionum* 5.17 (ed. PL 6.602); Isidore of Seville *Etymologiae* 16.20, ed. W. M. Lindsay, *Isidori Hispalensis episcopi Etymologiarum sive Originum libri XX* (Oxford 1911). About *orichalcum,* see Pauly-Wissowa 35.938–41.

8. *Clavis Canonum,* ed. L. Fowler-Magerl (MGH Hilfsmittel 21; Hannover 2005).

9. P. Landau, 'Neue Forschungen zu vorgratianischen Kanonessammlungen und den Quellen des gratianischen Dekrets', *Ius commune* 11 (1984) 1–29. Viejo-Ximénez, 'La redacción original' 173, argues that the *Panormia* was Gratian's source for the three canons in the first recension of C.29 q.2. He also points out some interesting differences between Gratian's text and that of the *Panormia* that might suggest otherwise. For the *Panormia,* I use the provisional edition by M. Brett and B. Brasington, which is available on the internet at http://wtfaculty.wtamu.edu/~bbrasington/panormia.html; the definition also appears in Ivo's *Decretum* 8.1.

10. The scribe of *Sg* only suggested the wording of most of this passage by indicating the initial letters: *Coniugium vel matrimonium vero e. vi. et m. c. in. v. c. c.* Note that the final c. suggests *continens,* as in the *Institutes,* and not *retinens,* as in Gratian.

11. Viejo-Ximénez, 'La redacción original' 179, observes that *Aa* and *Fd* read *mulierque* instead of *et mulier,* which he has found in 32 manuscripts of the second recension and in Justinian's *Institutes.* He emphasizes that one should not exaggerate the importance of this difference.

12. F. P. Bliemetzrieder, *Anselms von Laon systematische Sentenzen* (Beiträge zur Geschichte der Philosophie des Mittelalters: Texte und Untersuchungen 18.2–3; Münster/W. 1919) 139.

Isidorus ita describit: **Coniugium** est consensus masculi et femine, indiuidualem uite consuetudinem **retinens,** et nota hic describi coniugium per efficientem causam suam. Consensus enim facit coniugium, non coitus.

[Isidore defines thus: Wedlock is the consent of male and female entailing that they live inseparably together, and note that wedlock here is defined by its efficient cause. For consent makes wedlock, not coitus].

Gratian's formulation would be easiest to explain if one supposes that he first noted the wording (including *coniugium* and *retinens*) of the *Cum omnia sacramenta* (or a related work), then added the words *sive matrimonium* and changed *masculi et femine* into *viri mulierisque* when he encountered the same text in the *Panormia.*

The inference that Gratian used *Cum omnia sacramenta* (or a related work) as a source is strengthened by an examination of the one other passage in which he defines marriage, in C.27 q.2 d.a.c.1:

Sunt enim nuptie sive matrimonium[a] viri et mulieris coniunctio, individuam vite consuetudinem[b] retinens[c]. Inter hos autem[d] fuit coniunctio que individuam vite consuetudinem exigebat. Fuit enim inter eos consensus, qui est efficiens causa matrimonii[e], iuxta illud Isidori: 'Consensus facit matrimonium.'[f]

> a. sive matrimonium *om. Sg*   b. consuetudinem vite *Aa*   c. consuetudinem retinens *Aa Fd:* c(onsuetudinem) c(ontinens) *Sg*   d. igitur *Sg*   e. Fuit inter—matrimonii *Aa Fd:* Nam consensus ille fuit inter eos, quam causa matrimonii esse intelligi *Sg*   f. Consensus matrimonium facit *Aa Sg*

[For wedlock or marriage is the union of man and woman entailing that they live inseparably together. There was a union between them[13] which required that they live inseparably together. For there was consent between them, which is the efficient cause of marriage according to the following by Isidore: 'Consent makes marriage'].

Again, the formulation is most easily explained if one assumes that Gratian had in front of him a text like the passage in *Cum omnia sacramenta* quoted above, which also contains the attribution to Isidore.[14] The concise formula at the end of the quotation *(Consensus facit matrimonium)* does not appear in any work by Isidore of Seville (or Pseudo-Isidore). Its pedigree is to be found among the *regulae iuris* of Justinian's *Digest,* in the *Opus imperfectum in Mattheum* wrongly ascribed to John Chrysostom, and in the response of Pope Nicholas I to the Bulgarians.[15] The relevant excerpts from the latter two works are richly represented in the canonical tradition and appear, indeed, as canons 1 and 2 in C.27 q.2.

---

13. I.e., the couple in Gratian's C.27.

14. H. Ziementz, *Die Ehelehre der Schule des Anselm von Laon: Eine theologie- und kirchenrechtsgeschichtliche Untersuchung zu den Ehetexten der frühen Pariser Schule des 12. Jahrhunderts* (Münster 1974) 125.

15. Dig. 50.17.30; PG 56.802; JE 2812.

There are further parallels between Gratian and the *Cum omnia sacramenta*. Using the terminology of dialectics, the treatise points out that consent is the efficient cause of marriage, as does Gratian in C.27 q.2 d.a.c.1. The theological text continues by citing a text by Ambrose of Milan, which Gratian also cites as C.27 q.2 c.5, and a text by Augustine, which clearly inspired Gratian's argument in C.27 q.2 d.p.c.2.[16]

I do not think there can be much doubt that, in defining marriage, Gratian's closest inspiration came from the thought of French theologians. Many peculiarities in his text are most plausibly explained thus: *retinens* instead of *continens* in the marriage definition, his characterization of consent as the *causa efficiens* of marriage, the attribution of the phrase *consensus facit matrimonium* to Isidore, as well as the organization of the beginning of C.27 q.2. It is inadvisable and probably impossible to attempt to pinpoint exactly which treatise he might have used. The texts of these treatises are even more fluid than those of canonical collections. The same thoughts and quotations as in *Cum omnia sacramenta* recur in more or less changed form in treatises such as *Decretum dei fuit* and *Cum omnia . . . coniugium*, and much of this matter is subsumed into Hugh of St. Victor's *De sacramentis* and into other works.[17] Gratian probably did not have any one of these in front of him. He might even have worked on the basis of his own notes and memories from the actual teaching of a French master in this tradition. Gratian's thoughts on defining marriage begin with what he learned from French theologians.

Gratian's reworking of that material in composing the *Decretum* reveals him to be a canonist in his great regard for the exact wording of the authorities. Theologians could be bolder and more independent in their readings.[18] Gratian looked up the authorities of his theological sources in the various canonical collections available to him and often preferred the more complete quotations he found there. While the theological treatises quoted only one sentence from Ambrose, Gratian reproduces (in C.27 q.2 c.5) three of the four sentences that he found in (most likely) the *Panormia* 6.14. He also added the words *sive matrimonium* to the definition of marriage in accordance with the authentic wording, which he (almost certainly) found in *Panormia* 6.1.

---

16. Augustine, *De nuptiis et concupiscientia* 1.12: 'Cur ergo non coniuges maneant, qui ex consensu concumbere desinunt, si manserunt coniuges Ioseph et Maria, qui concumbere nec coeperunt (CSEL 42.226; PL 44.422)'; see C.27 q.2 d.p.c.2: '[Si facit matrimonium consensus] carnalis copulae (carnaliter copulandi *Sg*), inter Mariam et Ioseph non fuit coniugium'. The chaste marriage between Mary and Joseph was a much-discussed problem for proponents of the coital theory of marriage formation: see J. A. Brundage, *Law, Sex, and Christian Society in Medieval Europe* (Chicago 1987) 274.

17. *Decretum dei fuit*, ed. H. Weisweiler, *Das Schrifttum der Schule Anselms von Laon und Wilhelms von Champeaux in deutschen Bibliotheken* (Beiträge zur Geschichte der Philosophie und Theologie des Mittelalters: Texte und Untersuchungen 33:1/2; Münster 1936); *Cum omnia . . . coniugium*, ed. F. Bliemetzrieder, 'Théologie et théologiens de l'école épiscopale de Paris avant Pierre Lombard', *Recherches de théologie ancienne et médiévale* 3 (1931) 273–91; Hugo de Sancto Victore, *De sacramentis* (PL 176.173–618).

18. M. L. Colish, *Peter Lombard* (Leiden 1994) 44–45.

After citing the romanistic definition of marriage, much of Gratian's continued discussion in C.29 is firmly rooted in the Bible.[19] For mistaken identity, he refers first to Jacob's unknowingly marrying Leah instead of Rachel (Gen. 29). Then he continues with two examples from Paul's second Letter to the Corinthians: Satan transforming himself into an angel of light (2 Cor. 11.14) and heretics (or pseudo-apostles) claiming to be fathers of the church (or apostles; 2 Cor. 11.13). Gratian was a canon lawyer who knew his Bible. He was, as Titus Lenherr has shown, familiar with the most up-to-date scriptural interpretations, the *Glossa ordinaria*.[20] When Gratian was compiling his *Decretum*, this work was taking shape among a group of French theologians centering on Anselm of Laon and his students. Where a modern lawyer would cite examples from contemporary practice, Gratian goes to the Bible for his casuistry. In many cases, as in C.29 q.1, it is easy to imagine that the original impetus for many of Gratian's questions sprang from a discussion of biblical passages. If marriage comes about through consent and subsequent consummation, was Jacob really married when he consented to Rachel but consummated with Leah? Such questions must have arisen in the teaching of theological masters like Anselm of Laon and his successors in their efforts to interpret the Bible. Another canonist, Ivo of Chartres, was a member of the circle around Anselm, as evinced by the theological sentences which are transmitted under his name in the sentence collections from this circle.[21] Giuseppe Mazzanti interprets a late and problematic chronicle entry that mentions Gratian as a *conscolaris* to Pope Alexander III as evidence suggesting that they had studied together at the famous theological school of St. Victor in Paris.[22] This might very well be accurate, for there are close parallels between Gratian's reasoning and that of Hugh of Saint Victor, as Stephan Kuttner pointed out for instances

19. Two obviously non-biblical names are Plato and Virgil, who are used as stock characters in an example of *error personae*. It is likely that Gratian was harking back to his early schooling in the trivium, and particularly in dialectics. The basic schoolbooks in this field were Aristotle's *Categories* and *De interpretatione*, and the *Isagoge* of Porphyrius. They were all read in the Latin translations of Boethius together with the translator's commentaries. Aristotle used Plato as one of his stock characters and Boethius occasionally added Virgil, see L. Minio-Palulello, ed., *Aristoteles Latinus* 1–2 (Bruges 1961–66); C. Meiser, ed., *Anicii Manlii Severini Boetii Commentarii in librum Aristotelis ΠΕΡΙ ΕΡΜΗΝΕΙΑΣ* (Leipzig 1877); Boethius' commentaries on the *Isagoge* and the *Categories* are reprinted in PL 64.9–294.

20. T. Lenherr, 'Die *Glossa Ordinaria* zur Bibel als Quelle von Gratians Dekret: Ein (neuer) Anfang', BMCL 24 (2000) 97–129. For the theologians inspired by Anselm, see V. Flint, 'The "School of Laon": A Reconsideration', *Recherches de théologie ancienne et médiévale* 43 (1976) 89–110, reprinted in: Flint, *Ideas in the Medieval West: Texts and Their Contexts* (London 1988) no. 1.

21. F. Bliemetzrieder, 'Zu den Schriften Ivos von Chartres († 1216): Ein literaturgeschichtlicher Beitrag', in: *Sb. Wien* 182:6 (1917). I thank Charles de Miramon for generously sharing with me his work in progress, '*Spiritualia et temporalia*: Naissance d'un couple', in which he, *inter alia*, questions the authenticity of the sentences attributed to Ivo.

22. G. Mazzanti, 'Graziano e Rolando Bandinelli', in: *Studi di storia del diritto* 2 (Università degli studi di Milano: Facoltà di giurisprudenza: Pubblicazioni dell'Istituto di storia del diritto italiano 23; Milan 1999) 79–103. I thank the author for kindly referring me to this article.

in *De penitentia*.[23] Parallels are also evident in marriage law. Gratian's discussion in C.29 of possible errors in contracting marriages parallels Hugh's discussion of the same topic:

Hugh of St. Victor, *De sacramentis* 1.11.19[24]	Gratian, C.29 d. init. et q.1
Quaeritur etiam utrum si qua mulier servo nupserit liberum eum existimans . . . coniugium dissolvi debeat . . .	Queritur . . . secundo, si prius[a] putabat[b] hunc esse liberum, et postea deprehendit, illum esse servum[c], an liceat ei[d] statim[e] ab illo discedere[f].
Nam quia hic non **in persona**, sed **in qualitate personae** solum **erratur**, idcirco sanctitatem matrimonii praejudicare debere censent.	sed[g] **error** alius est **persone**, alius fortune, alius conditionis, alius **qualitatis**

a. cum *Sg*   b. putaret *Sg*   c. et postea— servum *Aa Fd:* quem mox deprehensum habet servum esse *Sg*   d. liceat ei *om. Sg*   e. statim *supra lineam add. Fd*   f. possit *post* discedere *Sg*   g. sed *Aa Fd:* Unde sciendum est *Sg*

[It is also asked whether the marriage should be dissolved if a woman has married an unfree person believing him to be free . . .

For since in this case, the error is not in the person, but in the quality of the person, they therefore judge that the sanctity of marriage ought to prevail].

[The second question is whether she is allowed to divorce him immediately, if she first thought he was free and later found out that he was unfree.

But error of person, of fortune, of condition, of quality are different].

Both authors go on to characterize the actions of the *servus* as *dolus* (fraud). It is not immediately obvious whether Hugh influenced Gratian or vice versa (or neither). Hugh most likely finished *De sacramentis* in around 1137.[25] If influence could be proven in either direction, this would be valuable evidence for deciding the much debated question of the date of the first recension of Gratian's work, which different scholars put after 1139 or in the 1120s.[26]

Both Gratian and Hugh drew on the theological works of the early twelfth cen-

23. S. Kuttner, 'Zur Frage der theologischen Vorlagen Gratians', ZRG Kan. Abt. 23 (1934) 243–68; reprinted in: idem, *Gratian and the Schools of Law, 1140–1234* (London 1983) no. III. See also F. Bliemetzrieder, 'Gratian und die Schule Anselms von Laon', AKKR 112 (1932) 37–63.

24. PL 176.520.

25. D. Van den Eynde, *Essai sur la succession et la date des écrits de Hugues de Saint-Victor* (Rome 1960) 207.

26. Winroth, 'Recent work'.

tury, so it is possible that the similarities are to be explained by reference to a common source. I have not been able to find any such work that discusses *error personae* and *error qualitatis.*

A complete examination of the similarities between the *Decretum* and the *De sacramentis* needs to be made. A preliminary analysis of this single passage would focus on the error of quality, by which Gratian and Hugh mean different things. For Hugh, the *qualitas personae* is a person's free or servile status. The bride in his example makes an error in this respect. For the lawyer Gratian, the proper term to use in respect to a person's civil status is *condicio.* Still, he awkwardly introduces in his distinction the *error qualitatis,* which he then explains as misjudging whether something is good or bad. When he returns to the category towards the end of the question, he exemplifies it with a man who thinks he is marrying a chaste woman while she in reality is a prostitute. Gratian's reasoning is weak. It is hard to explain why he introduces *error qualitatis* at all, unless he is following a source. This passage, for what it is worth, suggests that Gratian was familiar with Hugh's thought and perhaps his work.

The second question in C.29 deals with the marriage of unfree persons. The Latin terms that Gratian and his sources use are *servus* and *ancilla,* and there might be doubt whether this is to be translated 'slave' or 'serf'. Since there were still slaves in Northern Italy in the twelfth century, Gratian might have thought of either slaves or serfs or both.[27] In general, I prefer the neutral term 'unfree person'.

When Gratian discusses the marriage of unfree persons his thought is firmly rooted in his reading of the Bible, and his reading is generous to the unfree. The biblical passages that he chooses to discuss emphasize the equality of all people in the eyes of God: 'In Christ Jesus there is neither Jew nor Greek, there is neither slave nor free' (Gal. 3.28) and 'She is free to be married to whom she wishes [i.e., even a slave], only in the Lord' (1 Cor. 7.39; both quoted in C.29 q.2 d.a.c.1). These were radical statements in the time of the Apostle Paul, and they were still radical in the twelfth century. Gratian took them seriously. If he had wanted to, he could have cited passages like 'Slaves, be obedient to those who are your earthly masters' (Eph. 6.5), but he chose not to.

Gratian includes three canons in C.29 q.2. He almost certainly took them from the *Panormia.* With the first, canon 1, he establishes that unfree persons are able to marry, while the other two (canons 4 and 5) confirm that in a mixed marriage, the free partner has the right to divorce an unfree partner whom she or he had believed to be free when they married.

Causa 29 q.2 c.1 was excerpted from the *Panormia* 6.37–38, which in the manuscripts

---

27. P. Landau, 'Hadrians IV. Dekretale "Dignum est" (X.4.9.1) und die Eheschliessung Unfreier in der Diskussion von Kanonisten und Theologen des 12. und 13. Jahrhunderts', SG 12 (1967) 518.

appears as a single canon. The first half of the text (corresponding to 6.37) is an excerpt from Justinian's *Code* (Cod. 5.4.26). It was not excerpted in the first recension of the *Decretum*, but the author of the second recension added it later as C.29 q.2 c.3. Gratian included the second half (6.38) in the first recension. It appears to be an interpretation of or comment on the first part. The composite appears first in the *Decretum* of Burchard of Worms (9.18), where it is already attributed to Pope Julius.[28] This error was due to a simple misunderstanding of the inscription in the *Code*, which indicates that this was a rescript from Emperor Justinian to the praetorian prefect Julianus: 'Idem A. [= Iustinianus] Iuliano pp.'. The abbreviation for *praefectus praetorii* is practically identical to the abbreviation for *papa* (normally *pp.*).

In the first recension, Gratian chooses not to quote the first half of this canon, probably because it concerns the specific situation of a master freeing a slave and then marrying her. The second half of the text gives a general rationale for the equality of free and unfree persons, especially in respect to marriage. Its sentiment fits well with the Pauline statements of equality in C.29 q.2 d.a.c.1:

Omnibus nobis unus pater[a] est in celis, et unusquisque, dives et pauper, liber et servus, equaliter pro se et pro animabus eorum rationem daturi[b] sunt. Quapropter omnes, cuiuscumque condicionis sint, unam legem quantum ad Deum[c] habere non dubitamus. Si autem omnes unam legem habent, ergo sicut ingenuus dimitti non potest, sic nec servus semel coniugio copulatus ulterius dimitti poterit[d].

> a. unus pater *Fd Sg:* pater unus *Aa*   b. daturi *Fd*[ante corr.] *Sg:* reddituri *Aa Friedberg Viejo-Ximénez*
> c. Deum *Aa Fd Sg:* Dominum *Friedberg Viejo-Ximénez*   d. poterit *Aa Fd:* potest *Sg*

[There is one father in heaven for all of us, and each person, rich and poor, free and slave, alike will give account for themselves and their souls. Therefore, we do not doubt that all people, whatever their condition, are under one law before God. If, however, all are under one law, then, just as a free man cannot be divorced, so too an unfree man can no longer be divorced once he has been joined in marriage].

The last sentence does not appear in any source before Gratian's *Decretum*. It is likely that Gratian added it to drive home the conclusion that an unfree person has the same rights as a free person.

The master of the *Decretum* harbored no doubts that *servi* were capable of marriage. He omits any citations of the many discordant authorities available, despite his stated purpose to harmonize discordant canons.

---

28. H. Hoffmann and R. Pokorny, *Das Dekret des Bischofs Burchard von Worms: Textstufen—Frühe Verbreitung—Vorlagen* (MGH Hilfsmittel 12; Munich 1991) 213. M. Sheehan, 'Theory and Practice: Marriage of the Unfree and the Poor in Medieval Society', *Mediaeval Studies* 50 (1988); reprinted in: idem, *Marriage, Family, and Law in Medieval Europe: Collected Studies* (Toronto 1996) 231.

In Roman law, there could be no question of a slave entering into marriage. If two slaves or a master and his slave lived in a permanent marriage-like union, this was called a *contubernium*, not *nuptiae* or *conubium*.[29] Such relationships between a slave and a free woman (a situation Gratian discussed in C.29 q.2) were taboo; a law of Constantine stipulates that both parties be punished with death, the slave by burning.[30]

The early church had similar reservations about servile marriages. Early medieval church leaders eventually accepted that marriage is possible between unfree persons, just as between any other Christians.[31] A turning-point was a resolution of the Council of Chalon sur Saône in 813, which states that *servi* may marry with the permission of their masters. This canon was transmitted in canon law collections as well as received into Lombard law. Its influence was great, while at the same time the romanistic position circulated within canon, Lombard, and Roman law.

Ivo of Chartres summarizes the conflicting views in a letter (Ep. 121) to Bishop John of Orleans, who had asked for advice about a free man having married an unfree woman whom he believed to be free:[32]

> If we wish to consult the decrees of the Fathers and secular law, we will find that legitimate marriage can occur only between free persons of equal condition, and when the contrary occurs out of ignorance, divorce is lawful. But if we consult divine ordinance and natural law, where 'there is neither slave nor free' (Gal. 3.28), I cannot easily be convinced . . . that human law . . . can invalidate the sacrament of marriage, which undoubtedly is confirmed by the Old and the Evangelic Law.

While all are equal and have equal access to the sacraments (including marriage) according to natural law, human law does not allow unfree persons to marry. Like Ivo, Gratian sided firmly with natural law. Unlike Ivo, he omitted mention of the fact that there existed an opposing view.

It is notable that Gratian also chose not to mention that it was generally agreed in his time that unfree persons needed their master's permission to marry. This restriction would have been inconsistent with natural law or the Pauline statements quoted by Gratian in d.a.c.1. This may be the reason why, in the first recension, Gratian chose

---

29. A. Berger, *Encyclopedic Dictionary of Roman Law* (Transactions of the American Philosophical Society, n.s. 43:2; Philadelphia 1953) 415 s.v. *contubernium*.

30. Cod. 9.11.1; see J. E. Grubbs, *Law and Family in Late Antiquity: The Emperor Constantine's Marriage Legislation* (Oxford 1995) esp. 273–74; and J. E. Grubbs, '"Marriage More Shameful than Adultery": Slave-Mistress Relationships, "Mixed Marriages", and Late Roman Law', *Phoenix* 47 (1993) 125–54.

31. Useful surveys of this material are available in Landau, 'Hadrians IV. Dekretale'; J. Gilchrist, 'The Medieval Canon Law of Unfree Persons: Gratian and the Decretist Doctrines c. 1141–1234', SG 19 (1976) 271–301; and Sheehan, 'Theory and Practice'.

32. From the Latin version in PL 162.226.

not to quote the canon from Chalon that is so important for the history of the marriage of unfree persons. This canon requires the permission of the master(s). The canon
was easily available to Gratian, as it appears as 6.40 in his main source, the *Panormia*,
where it immediately precedes the canon that he included in the first recension of the
Decretum as C.29 q.2 c.4.

The theological treatise *Cum omnia sacramenta*, which Gratian might have used as a
source for C.29 q.1, also specifies that *servi* must obtain the permission of their masters
to marry:[33]

> Also, servitude does not prevent marriage, unless it happens against the will of the masters
> or through fraud. It should not happen against the will of the masters, since the apostle
> says: 'Slaves, be submissive to your masters, not only to the good and mild, but also to the ill-
> tempered' (1 Peter 2.18).

The theologian Walter of Mortagne, who from c. 1120 taught in Laon, was the only
theologian who had a somewhat different view. He discussed it in his *De coniugio*, which
he composed at the latest in 1140.[34] Walter thought it was reasonable that unfree persons could marry if their master(s) did not know about it (and thus could not give permission). He gives the example of a young man and a young woman being captured and
enslaved by Saracens; they should unite in marriage, if they so wished, without asking
their master for permission. The argument seems, however, to imply that, normally,
the permission of the master is required.

It was only in the 1150s that a decretal by Pope Adrian IV determined that *servi* could
marry without the permission of their masters (*Dignum est;* JL 10445 = X 4.9.1); it took
time for this decretal to become generally accepted.[35]

While it may be ill-advised to impute too much significance to Gratian's silence
about the role of the masters in the marriage of unfree persons, he certainly differs from
his sources in omitting it. His strong insistence on the equality of all humans before
God, free or unfree, supports the interpretation that Gratian did not think such permission necessary, just as he did not think the agreement of a bride's father absolutely
necessary for a valid marriage.[36] He insists that it was the consent of the marriage part-

---

33. Bliemetzrieder, *Anselms von Laon systematische Sentenzen* 145: 'Seruitus etiam, nisi fiat contra uoluntatem dominorum uel dolo, non impedit coniugium. Contra uoluntatem dominorum non debet fieri, cum dicat
apostolus: "Subditi estote dominis serui, non tantum bonis et modestis, sed etiam dyscolis".'

34. PL 176.165–66. Walter of Mortagne's *De coniugio* is found in most manuscripts and all editions as the
seventh book of the *Summa sententiarum* by an anonymous author; it is often but erroneously ascribed to Hugh
of St. Victor. For the date of *De coniugio*, see L. Ott, 'Walter von Mortagne und Petrus Lombardus in ihrem Verhältnis zueinander', in: *Mélanges Joseph de Ghellinck S.J.* (2 vols.; Gembloux 1951) 2.654.

35. See also *Germania pontificia* 1.26 n. 83.

36. Brundage, *Law, Sex, and Christian Society* 238.

ners that constitutes the marriage, which requires no further consent from fathers or masters.

If my reading is correct, Gratian's point of view was radical, and the times were not yet ready for it. As in so many other instances, the author of the second recension changes the import of the *Decretum*. He adds the Chalon canon (C.29 q.2 c.8) with its requirement for the master's permission. This determined the position of the early decretists until Pope Adrian's decretal *Dignum est* began to influence their views from the late 1170s. Canonists then became ever more favorably disposed to unfree persons.[37] In the first recension of the *Decretum*, Gratian had anticipated this more humane stance on the rights of slaves and serfs by several decades. His stance was the result of the consistent application of his definition of marriage with its strong emphasis on the consent of the marriage partners. To reach his desired conclusions, Gratian did not hesitate to read his sources selectively and out of context, or even to pass off his own words as those of a pope. He must have felt strongly about the marriages of the unfree.

37. Landau, 'Hadrians IV. Dekretale'.

Reos sanguinis [non] *defendat ecclesia*

Gratian, mit einem kurzen Blick erhascht?

Titus Lenherr

❋

War der Anfang so leise, dass der 'Anfänger' nicht bemerkt wurde? War das Neue so aufregend, dass der, der darauf kam, übersehen wurde? Wie ist es passiert, dass uns von Gratian 'nur' der Name und das, was er geschaffen hat, überliefert ist, die *Concordia discordantium canonum?*[1] Wir wissen es (noch) nicht. Gratian gehört so zu den grossen 'Anonymen', die ganz hinter ihr Werk zurücktreten, reine Diener einer Botschaft sind.[2] Vielleicht hält gerade das die Frage nach ihrer Person wach, danach, wer sie sind und was sie auszeichnet.

Das Neue ist nur wahrnehmbar auf der Folie des Alten. Wir müssen wissen, was Gratian vorfand, was ihm vorgegeben war, um erkennen zu können, was er hinzugefügt oder verändert hat. Das Neue kann sich zeigen an der thematischen Ordnung des Stoffes, an der Auswahl der Texte aus dem überlieferten Material, am Umgang mit überkommenen Fragestellungen, an der Einführung von neuen Problemfeldern, an der Formulierung von Unterscheidungen und der eigenständigen, 'rationalen' Argumentation (in den *dicta*), an der Formulierung der Summarien, und auch an den Veränderungen der überlieferten Texte selbst.

Der Vergleich des Vorgefundenen mit dem Neuen fördert 'Gesichtszüge' Gratians zu Tage, bringt uns auf seine Spuren, ermöglicht uns, seine Gestalt nachzuzeichnen. Dazu ist Kleinarbeit nötig. Und besonders wenn es um die Eingriffe in die überlieferten

---

1. Vgl. J. T. Noonan, 'Gratian Slept Here: The Changing Identity of the Father of the Systematic Study of Canon Law', *Traditio* 35 (1979) 145–72; vgl. jetzt auch E. De León, 'La biografia di Graziano', in: *La cultura giuridico-canonica medioevale: Premesse per un dialogo ecumenico*, ed. E. De León and N. Álvarez de las Asturias (Milan 2003) 89–107, wo mit neuen Daten und Argumenten die Überlieferung verteidigt wird, dass Gratian Bischof war.

2. Vgl. unter anderem *Deuterojesaja, Der Verfasser des Hebräerbriefes, 'Dionysius Areopagita'*.

Texte geht, sind die Fälle eher selten, in denen Gewissheit zu erzielen ist, dass wir der *ipsissima manus Gratiani,* der 'ureigenen Hand Gratians' begegnen. Ein Beispiel, das über eine blosse Hypothese hinausführt, könnte die *auctoritas* sein, die Gratian in C.23 q.5 c.7 zitiert. Sie ist Gegenstand dieser Studie.

1. Das Problem von C.23 q.5 c.7

Gratian behandelt in C.23 q.5 die Frage, ob die Todesstrafe erlaubt sei. Seine Anfangsthese lautet: 'Es ist niemandem erlaubt, einen anderen zu töten'.[3] Sie wird begründet mit der Heiligen Schrift, Gesetz und Evangelium (Ex. 20.13 und Mt. 26.52), und (in der '1. Rezension') bekräftigt durch fünf *auctoritates* (cc. 1–3 und 6–7), bevor im d.p.c.7 der Einwand gegen die Anfangsthese formuliert wird.[4]

Der letzte Text dieser Reihe von Bekräftigungen, die alle aus Schriften der Kirchenväter genommen sind, ist C.23 q.5 c.7:[5]

> Item Gregorius.
> *Qui rei sunt sanguinis ab ecclesia debent defendi.*
> Reos sanguinis defendat ecclesia, ne effusione sanguinis particeps fiat.

[Ebenso Gregor. *Die einer Bluttat schuldig sind, müssen von der Kirche verteidigt werden.* Die einer Bluttat Schuldigen soll die Kirche verteidigen, damit sie nicht am Blutvergiessen teilnimmt].

Die Zuschreibung dieses Textes an Gregor teilt Gratian mit der *3-Bücher-Sammlung* (3L 3.17.29), der *9-Bücher-Sammlung* (9L 9.3.20) und der *Collectio Sancte Marie Novelle* (121.16).[6] Das legt die Vermutung nahe, dass Gratian diesen Text der *3-Bücher-Sammlung* entnommen hat, die zur Gruppe der Sammlungen gehört, die er regelmässig benützt hat. Diese Annahme wird dadurch bestätigt, dass Gratian den in der *3-Bücher-Sammlung* unmittelbar folgenden Text (3.17.30) wenig später, in C.23 q.5 c.49, mit Sicherheit dieser Sammlung entnommen hat. Es liessen sich allerdings auch zwei Einwände gegen eine solche Übernahme von c.7 aus der *3-Bücher-Sammlung* formulieren, deren zweiter zum Problem dieser Studie führt:

---

3. Vgl. C.23 q.5 pr.: 'Quod autem nulli liceat aliquem occidere . . .'.

4. Mit '1. Rezension' ist die frühere, kürzere Fassung der *Concordia discordantium canonum* gemeint, die uns unter anderem (und für C.23 ausschliesslich) in den Handschriften Admont, Stiftsbibliothek 43 *(Aa),* und Florenz, BN Centrale, Conv. Soppr. A. 1.402 *(Fd),* erhalten ist. Vgl. A. Winroth, *The Making of Gratian's Decretum* (Cambridge 2000); und C. Larrainzar, 'La ricerca attuale sul *Decretum Gratiani',* in: *La cultura giuridico-canonica* 109–22, mit weiteren Literaturangaben. Zu C.23 q.5, vgl. T. Lenherr, 'Zur Redaktionsgeschichte von C.23 q.5 in der "1. Redaktion" von Gratians Dekret', in: Proc. Washington (MIC C.12; in press).

5. *Decretum,* col. 932; *Aa* fol. 46r; *Fd* fol. 66vb.

6. Zu diesen drei Sammlungen (die Sammlung *Sancte Marie Novelle* heisst auch: *Liber canonum diversorum sanctorum patrum* oder *Collectio 183 titulorum),* vgl. Kéry, *Can. Coll.* 269–72, 216–17; *KanonesJ* 174, 175, 44–45.

a) In 3L (und 9L) hat der Text die Inskription: *Ex dictis Greg(orii)*. Da Gratian in der Regel dem Wortlaut seiner Quellen treu folgt, ist es nicht ganz unbedeutend, dass *ex dictis* in Gratians Inskription fehlt.

b) In 3L (und 9L) ist der (Haupt-)Satz verneint: *Reos sanguinis* non *defendat ecclesia, ne effusione sanguinis particeps fiat*. Gratian sagt also im Hauptsatz direkt das Gegenteil von seiner angenommenen Vorlage:

> *Gratian:* Die Kirche *soll* den einer Bluttat Schuldigen *verteidigen*,
> vs.
> *3L:* Die Kirche *soll* den einer Bluttat Schuldigen *nicht verteidigen*.

Hat Gratian das *non* gestrichen? Bewusst? Und was hätte das zu bedeuten? Oder hat er den Text doch aus einer anderen Sammlung (die den Satz ohne Verneinung überliefert hätte) übernommen? Das führt uns zur Frage nach der Überlieferungsgeschichte dieses Textes.

2. Überlieferung und Ursprung von 'Reos sanguinis [non] defendat ecclesia'

Der Text *Reos sanguinis [non] defendat ecclesia* kommt vor Gratian in 19 Sammlungen vor, und zwar in einer längeren und einer kürzeren Fassung und mit drei verschiedenen Zuschreibungen.[7]

a. Die längere Fassung: Die *Collectio Hibernensis* aus der ersten Hälfte des 8. Jahrhunderts ist die früheste Sammlung, in der *Reos sanguinis* überliefert ist, und zwar in der längeren Fassung mit der Zuschreibung an Augustinus:[8]

> *De ecclesia reos obstinanter non defendente.*

A[u]gustinus ait: Reos sanguinis non defendat ecclesia, ne effusi sanguinis particeps fiat; si enim Dominus eos ergastulo retinuit, noli solvere eos, quos Dominus non solvit.[9]

In dieser Fragmentierung und mit der gleichen Zuschreibung an Augustinus kommt der Text noch in zwei weiteren Sammlungen vor, die von der *Collectio Hibernensis* abhängig sind, nämlich in der um das Jahr 920 entstandenen *Collectio IX librorum* (Vat. lat. 1349) (7.17a) und in der um 1120 entstandenen *Collectio V librorum* (Vat. lat. 1339) (4.86a).[10]

7. Vgl. dazu die Übersicht in der Tabelle am Ende.
8. *Collectio Hibernensis* A 28.12a; *Collectio Hibernensis* B 29.14a; vgl. *Die irische Kanonessammlung*, ed. H. von Wasserschleben (Giessen 1874) 115; Kéry, *Can. Coll.* 73–80; *KanonesJ* 10–12.
9. '*Darüber, dass die Kirche hartnäckig Schuldige nicht verteidigt. Augustinus sagt:* Blutschuldige soll die Kirche nicht verteidigen, damit sie nicht des vergossenen Blutes teilhaftig wird; wenn nämlich der Herr sie im Gefängnis zurückhielt, löse die nicht, die der Herr nicht gelöst hat'.
10. Zu diesen Sammlungen, vgl. Kéry, *Can. Coll.* 196–97 und 157–60; *KanonesJ* 22–24 und 25–27.

b. Die kürzere Fassung: Die früheste Überlieferung der kürzeren Fassung findet sich im *Dekret* des Burchard von Worms (19.109), entstanden um 1008–1012, ebenfalls mit der Zuschreibung an Augustinus:[11]

> De illis qui alios in culpa sua defendere nituntur.[12]
> Ex dictis eiusdem.[13]
> Reos sanguinis non defendat Ecclesia: ne effusione sanguinis particeps fiat.

In dieser Fassung ist der Text noch in 15 weiteren Sammlungen vor Gratian enthalten, die alle nach dem *Dekret* des Burchard von Worms im Zeitraum zwischen 1020 und 1100 entstanden sind. Der Text ist in der Regel Augustinus zugeschrieben, mit den folgenden Ausnahmen: In der *Collectio XII partium* wird der Text Papst Clemens zugeschrieben (CDP1: 11.59; CDP 2: 12.89).[14] In der *Sammlung des Stiftes St-Hilaire-le-Grand* (15.39) fehlt eine *Inscriptio*.[15] In der *Collectio Sancte Marie Novelle* (121.16), der *Collectio III librorum* (3.17.29) und in der *Collectio IX librorum* (Arch. S. Pietro C.118) (9.3.20) wird Gregor als Verfasser genannt.[16] Schliesslich wird in der *Collectio VII librorum*, Turin BNU D.IV.33 (7.127), der Text als von Papst Eusebius stammend bezeichnet.[17]

Bemerkenswert ist, dass der Text—im Gegensatz zu seiner Fassung bei Gratian—in allen Sammlungen, sei es mit der längeren oder kürzeren Fassung, sei es mit der Zuschreibung an wen immer, ausnahmslos mit der Verneinung 'non' überliefert ist.

Die materiale Quelle, stamme der Text von Augustinus oder jemand anderem, ist (bisher) nicht zu finden, weder in einer wörtlichen noch in einer inhaltlichen Entsprechung, von der die *auctoritas* eine Zusammenfassung sein könnte.[18] In der *Collectio Hibernensis* tritt dieser Text für uns also auch materiell zum ersten Mal in die Geschichte ein.

---

11. *Burchard von Worms: Decretorum libri XX*, ed. G. Fransen und T. Kölzer (Köln 1548, Nachdruck: Aalen 1992) 215. Nach den Angaben in *KanonesJ* 28–32 scheint es noch zwei weitere Fassungen zu geben, und zwar a) eine mit dem Explicit: *pro anima eius*, in der *Collectio Sangermanensis* (7.79), und b) eine mit dem Explicit: *excusare nititur excommunicetur*, in der *Collectio Burdegalensis* (12.37). Das trifft aber nicht zu, vielmehr haben beide Sammlungen die kürzere Fassung (wie Burchard von Worms), an die eine andere *auctoritas* angefügt ist. In der *Collectio Sangermanensis* besteht die Anfügung aus dem Satz: 'Lex dicit: Si dimiseris uirum dignum morte, erit anima tua pro anima eius' (Handschrift Wolfenbüttel, Herzog-August-Bibliothek Gud. lat. 212, fol. 43r). Das entspricht dem Text von *Collectio Hibernensis* A 27.19a (*Die irische Kanonessammlung* 109), *Collectio Hibernensis* B 28.25a (*KanonesJ*). In der *Collectio Burdegalensis* folgt: 'et iterum sanctus Eusebius precepit, ut qui alium in culpa sua deffendere uel excusare nititur excommunicetur' (Handschrift Würzburg, UB M.p.j.q.2, fol. 68v). Das entspricht dem Text *Ut qui alium in culpa sua*, wie er bei Burchard von Worms in 19.110, also ebenfalls direkt nach *Reos sanguinis*, und in mehreren anderen Sammlungen, die davon abhängig sind, überliefert ist.

12. 'Über jene, welche darauf hinwirken, andere in ihrer Schuld zu verteidigen'.

13. Das *eiusdem* bezieht sich auf die Angabe von 19.107: *Ex dictis Augustini*, vgl. *Burchard von Worms* 215.

14. Dazu vgl. Kéry, *Can. Coll.* 155–57; *KanonesJ* 33–35.

15. Dazu vgl. Kéry, *Can. Coll.* 213–14; *KanonesJ* 67–69.

16. Zu diesen Sammlungen, vgl. oben Anm. 6.

17. Zur letztgenannten Sammlung, vgl. Kéry, *Can. Coll.* 265; *KanonesJ* 102–04.

18. Als Bezugsstelle käme vielleicht in Betracht: Augustinus, *Ennarratio in Ps. 145* (CCL 40.2118 Z. 23–26): 'Optime per hanc sententiam exposuit nobis omnes superiores; ne forte cum dixisset: Dominus solvit compeditos, ad illos compeditos referremus, qui forte propter aliquam noxam ligantur ferro a dominis suis'.

Mit Hilfe der Fragmentierungen, der Rubriken und der Zuschreibungen kann die Überlieferung bis zu Gratian in folgender Weise nachgezeichnet werden:[19]

(1) Collectio Hibernensis (A / B)

(2) Coll. IX librorum (Vat. lat. 1349)

(3) Burchard von Worms

(4) Coll. V librorum (Vat. lat. 1339)

[von (3) abhängig]
(5) Coll. XII partium (CDP 1)
(6) Coll. XII partium (CDP 2)
[(7) Coll. S. Marie Novelle]
(8) Coll. Burdegalensis
(9) Coll. II libr. / VIII partium
[(10) Sammlung v. St.-Hilaire-le-Grand]
(11) Coll. XIII librorum (Berl. Sav.)
[(12) Coll. Tarraconensis II]
(13) Dekret des Ivo von Chartres

[von (2) abhängig]

(14) Coll. Sangermanensis

[(15) Celle Oberlandesgericht]
[(16) Coll. S. Genoveve]
(17) Coll. VII librorum, Turin

[von (7) abhängig]
(18) Coll. III librorum
(19) Coll. IX. librorum (Arch.S.Pietro C.118)

[von (18) abhängig]
Gratian

Die Überlieferung vom ersten Auftreten des Textes bis zu Gratian verläuft also über die Stufen: *Collectio Hibernensis*—Burchard von Worms—*Collectio III librorum*—Gratian.

3. Zusammenhang und Bedeutung von 'Reos sanguinis' vor Gratian[20]

a. In der *Collectio Hibernensis:* Der Text *Reos sanguinis* gehört zu einer von vierzehn Einheiten im *Liber XXVIII. De civitatibus refugii* der *Collectio Hibernensis*. In diesem 'Buch' sind, wie der Titel 'Von den Städten der Zuflucht' besagt, Texte, vor allem auch

---

19. Vgl. die Tabelle am Ende.

20. Ich beschränke mich dabei auf die ('direkte') Traditionslinie, welche von der *Collectio Hibernensis* über

alttestamentliche Stellen, zum Asylrecht, zu dessen Voraussetzungen und Beschränkungen gesammelt. Das Verb *defendere,* das in *Reos sanguinis* gebraucht wird, kommt
mehrfach in Rubriken und Texten so vor, dass man es direkt mit 'Asyl gewähren' übersetzen könnte, besonders weil es immer (oder fast immer) in Verbindung mit einem
Ort oder einem Gebäude gebraucht ist.[21] Beispiele dafür sind:

a) die Rubrik von Cap. 2: De his, quos civitas refugii defendit;

b) die Rubrik von Cap. 3: De eo, quod debent rei civitatibus refugii defensi ('die
Schuldigen, die in den Asylstädten Asyl gefunden haben') satisfacere his, quibus rei
sunt;

c) der Ausdruck *in sinu defendentis ecclesiae* mit der Bedeutung 'im Schoss der Asyl
gewährenden Kirche' in Cap. 5 (Teil 2), wobei mit 'Kirche' eindeutig das Kirchengebäude gemeint ist;

d) die Rubrik von Cap. 7: De his, quos non defendit civitas refugii;

e) eine Hieronymus zugeschriebene Stelle innerhalb von Cap. 13, die lautet: Quicumque maculaverit sanctum, sancta non defendant eum, wo mit *sanctum* und *sancta*
die heiligen Gebäude bezeichnet werden.

Auch im Text von *Reos sanguinis* ist das *non defendat* auf die *ecclesia* als Subjekt bezogen.
Es liegt nahe, dass auch hier mit 'Kirche' das Kirchengebäude, der Asylort, gemeint ist,
so dass zu übersetzen wäre: 'Blutschuldigen gewährt die Kirche kein Asyl', oder noch
eindeutiger: 'Blutschuldige finden in der Kirche kein Asyl'. Über den Wortlaut des zitierten Textes hinaus begrenzt die Rubrik diesen Verlust des Asylrechtes allerdings auf
die unbussfertigen Schuldigen *(reos obstinanter).*

In der längeren Fassung, wie sie durch die *Collectio Hibernensis* bezeugt ist, folgt auf
die Feststellung, dass die Kirche Blutschuldigen kein Asyl gewährt, eine Begründung:
'Denn wenn der Herr sie im Gefängnis liess, löse die nicht, die der Herr nicht gelöst
hat'. Worauf sich diese offensichtlich auf die Heilige Schrift gründende Argumentation
bezieht, ist nicht auszumachen. Sie scheint auf die Binde- und Lösegewalt anzuspielen
und hängt vielleicht mit Augustins Auslegung zu Psalm 145 zusammen.[22] Die Begründung, welche den 'Rechtssatz' in einen biblischen Zusammenhang stellt und einen
weiteren Horizont von Binden und Lösen andeutet, macht es wahrscheinlich, dass der
Text tatsächlich auf eine Augustinuspassage zurückgeht und deren Zusammenfassung
ist.

Burchard und die *3–Bücher-Sammlung* zu *Gratian* führt, ohne also den Zusammenhang und die Bedeutung dieser *auctoritas* in anderen Sammlungen, etwa im *Dekret* des Ivo von Chartres einzubeziehen.

21. Nicht ganz eindeutig ist das in Cap. 14 (Teil d): *'Sinodus Romanorum:* Non ad reorum defensionem facta
est ecclesia, sed judicibus persuadendum, ut spiritali morte occidant eos, qui ad sinum ecclesiae transfugerint
(*Die irische Kanonessammlung* 116)'. Zum Buch 28 und den folgenden Zitaten, vgl. ibid. 111–16.

22. Vgl. oben Anm. 18.

b. Bei Burchard von Worms: Burchard von Worms hat den Text *Reos sanguinis* in das Buch 19 mit dem Titel *De poenitentia* eingefügt (19.109) und die (biblische) Begründung weggelassen.[23] Er steht thematisch mit einem Text zusammen, der ihm direkt folgt und die Einordnung in den Bussteil verständlich macht, weil in ihm die Exkommunikation dafür angedroht wird, dass jemand einen anderen in seiner Schuld verteidigt oder entschuldigt (19.110).[24] Im Blick ist also hier nicht mehr ein Problem des Asylrechtes (oder seines Verlustes), sondern Schuld und Strafe dessen, der jemanden 'in seiner Schuld verteidigt', wie es auch deutlich Burchards Rubrik besagt: *De illis qui alios in culpa sua defendere nituntur.*

c. In der *3-Bücher-Sammlung:* In der *Sammlung in 3 Büchern* ist der Text *Reos sanguinis* eingefügt unter dem Titel *De tolerandis et fugiendis vel impugnandis malis.* Diese Thematik entspricht jener von Gratians C.23 im ganzen. Daher ist es nicht verwunderlich, dass sich die *auctoritates,* die sich in 3L um *Reos sanguinis* herum gruppieren (die letzten dieses Titels), auch in Gratians C.23 wiederfinden: 3L 3.17.26 = C.23 q.1 c.3; 3L 3.17.28 = C.23 q.2 c.2; 3L 3.17.29 = C.23 q.5 c.7; 3L 3.17.30 = C.23 q.5 c.49.

Der Text ist nicht mehr Augustinus, sondern Gregor zugeschrieben. Das ist ein 'Fehler', der nicht 3L zuzurechnen ist, sondern auf die formale Quelle von 3L, die *Collectio Sancte Marie Novelle* zurückgeht, welche die Stelle bereits im gleichen thematischen Zusammenhang wie 3L (und dann auch Gratian) angesiedelt hat.[25]

Reos sanguinis non defendat ecclesia hat in dieser Überlieferungsgeschichte vor Gratian somit drei verschiedene 'Orte', an denen und entsprechend denen es eine je verschiedene Bedeutung hat: das Asylrecht in der *Collectio Hibernensis,* das Recht oder die Praxis der Busse bei Burchard und das Strafrecht in 3L.

4. Die Bedeutung von 'Reos sanguinis defendat ecclesia' bei Gratian

Schon vor Gratian stand also *Reos sanguinis* im Zusammenhang des Strafrechts. Das ist nichts Neues bei ihm. Aber die Hauptaussage war bisher verneint und der Zusammenhang war die Frage nach dem Strafrecht allgemein. Gratian hat, das lässt sich nach allem wohl mit Sicherheit sagen, den Satz in seiner Quelle verneint vorgefunden und

---

23. Vielleicht auch schon deshalb, weil nicht auszumachen ist, an welcher Bibelstelle die Begründung festgemacht ist?

24. '*Ex decretis Eusebii papae, c. 15. De eadem re.* Vt qui alium in sua culpa defendere, vel excusare nititur, excommunicetur'; vgl. *Burchard von Worms* 215b.

25. Vgl. *Collectio Sancte Marie Novelle* 121.16. Titel 121 lautet: 'Quomodo vindicta sit facienda et si quid mali acciderit de eo quod fit propter bonum'; vgl. *KanonesJ.* Wie es zur Änderung der Zuschreibung von Augustinus auf Gregor gekommen ist, muss hier dahingestellt bleiben.

die Negation selbst bewusst gestrichen. Er hat so den Text erst verwendbar gemacht für seinen speziellen Zusammenhang der Frage nach der Erlaubtheit der Todesstrafe.

Denn der verneinte Satz: 'Die Kirche soll Blutschuldige *nicht* verteidigen, damit sie nicht des Blutvergiessens teilhaftig wird', besagt, die Kirche solle durch die 'Verteidigung' nicht an jenem vergangenen, schon geschehenen Blutvergiessen teilnehmen, das der Blutschuldige begangen hat. Der Satz ohne *non:* 'Die Kirche *soll* Blutschuldige verteidigen, damit sie nicht des Blutvergiessens teilhaftig wird', besagt dagegen, die Kirche solle nicht dadurch des Blutvergiessens schuldig werden, dass sie zulässt, dass die Todesstrafe (in der Zukunft) am Schuldigen vollstreckt wird. Bei der Fassung mit *non* soll die Kirche nicht schuldig werden durch Verteidigung, gedeutet als Zustimmung zu einem Verbrechen, zur Bluttat des Verbrechers, bei der Fassung ohne *non* soll sie nicht schuldig werden durch die 'Zustimmung' zu einem Strafakt, durch die stillschweigende Zulassung der Vollstreckung der Todesstrafe. Einmal soll sie nicht schuldig werden durch nachträgliche 'Teilnahme' an einer bereits geschehenen fremden Tat, das andere Mal soll sie nicht schuldig werden durch Unterlassen einer eigenen Intervention gegen ein bevorstehendes Geschehen, indem sie den Schuldigen nicht vor der Todesstrafe bewahrt oder nicht versucht, ihn davor zu bewahren.

Der Unterschied ist gross. Dort eine Kirche, die davor gewarnt wird, an einer bereits begangenen Tat teilzunehmen, indem sie den Schuldigen (der einen Menschen getötet hat) verteidigt. Hier eine Kirche, die für den Schuldigen (der einen Menschen getötet hat) eintritt, um nicht durch Unterlassen teilzunehmen an seiner bevorstehenden Hinrichtung.

5. Die Streichung des 'non' durch Gratian

Die Veränderung eines überlieferten Textes, durch die nicht einfach der Text verständlicher gemacht, sondern sein Sinn tangiert wird, befremdet uns. Erst recht, wenn der so veränderte Text als 'Autorität' für eine bestimmte Argumentation benützt wird. Wir denken an 'Fälschung'. (Auch) Gratian also ein Fälscher?

Wer die *Concordia discordantium canonum* Gratians im Detail studiert, kann sich nicht der beeindruckenden Sorgfalt und der grossen Treue verschliessen, die Gratian in der Regel gegenüber seinen Vorlagen wahrt. Er erscheint als alles andere als ein 'Fälscher'. Und ist diese Haltung nicht sogar notwendige Folge seines Programms, das im Titel seines Werkes aufscheint? Tritt er mit seinem Programm, die 'Übereinstimmung' aufzuzeigen zwischen *Canones,* 'die von einander abweichen', nicht gerade dafür ein, die *Canones* so zu nehmen, wie sie sind, in ihrer ganzen Schwierigkeit, sie gerade nicht zu verändern (und so akzeptabel zu machen), sondern sie in ihrer (vielleicht die Schwierigkeit gerade begründenden) Originalität zu bewahren und als solche mit anderen, scheinbar widersprechenden zu 'versöhnen'? Gratians Vorhaben lebt von der Treue zur Überlieferung.

Wie stellt sich in diesem Licht die Streichung des *non* in *Reos sanguinis* dar? Darf man sagen, dass Gratian bei dieser 'Untreue' zum Wortlaut der überlieferten *auctoritas* eine tiefere 'Treue' zur Überlieferung (als solcher, zur Überlieferung im ganzen) durchhält, die Treue zur 'Sache' der Kirche, die, in der Nachahmung Gottes, in der Nachfolge Jesu, im Gefolge von Gottes Geist, vor allem anderen dazu berufen und bestellt ist, 'Hilfe' zu sein, 'Anwalt' zu sein, 'Beistand' zu sein? Jedenfalls muss die aussergewöhnliche Änderung dieses Textes durch Gratian mit seinem Bild von Kirche zusammenhängen, dem Bild einer Kirche, die keine Angst hat vor der Befleckung durch schon geschehene Schuld, zu deren Vergebung sie vielmehr ermächtigt ist, dem Bild einer Kirche, die sich als 'orante' sieht, berufen zur Fürbitte für alle Menschen.

6. Zur Wirkungsgeschichte von C.23 q.5 c.7

Soweit ersichtlich, hat niemand bemerkt (oder wenigstens beachten wollen), dass Gratian in *Reos sanguinis non defendat ecclesia* das verneinende *non* gestrichen und dem Satz eine neue Bedeutung gegeben hat.[26]

In den frühesten Werken der Dekretisten der Bologneser Schule stellt sich die Sachlage so dar: Paucapalea geht auf C.23 q.5 c.7 nicht ein und erwähnt das *Caput* auch nicht.[27] Magister Rolandus führt die *auctoritas* im Sinne Gratians an, ohne sie zu kommentieren.[28] Auch in der *Summa* des Rufinus, um 1164 entstanden, findet sich zu C.23 q.5 c.7 kein direkter Kommentar, aber bei der Auslegung von c.45 wird c.7 als Begründung für die Kommentierung s.v. *Auferte tales ab ista provincia* angeführt.[29]

Der Befund für die *Summa* des Rufinus ist insofern von besonderem Interesse, als Rufin das *Decretum Burchardi* kennt und mehrfach zitiert.[30] Die Änderung Gratians konnte nur von jemandem bemerkt werden, der Zugang zur vorgratianischen Überlieferung

26. Die *Correctores Romani* stellen zu *defendat* dann (lediglich) fest: 'Apud Burchardum et Ivonem, qui hoc citant ex dictis Augustini, legitur: *non defendat*', ed. *Decretum*, col. 931.

27. Vgl. Paucapalea, *Summa über das Decretum Gratiani*, ed. J. F. von Schulte (Giessen 1890, Neudruck: Aalen 1965) 101–02.

28. Vgl. *Summa Magistri Rolandi*, ed. F. Thaner (Innsbruck 1874, Neudruck: Aalen 1962) 91: 'Qu. V. Quinto quaeritur, an sit peccatum iudici vel ministro reos occidere. Quod non liceat aliquem occidere, probatur . . . item Gregorius: Reos sanguinis etc.'.

29. Vgl. *Die Summa Decretorum des Magister Rufinus*, ed. H. Singer (Paderborn 1902, Nachdruck: Aalen 1963) 411: 'Non occidendo, sed exilio damnando; non enim esset conveniens ecclesiastice pietati pro illis occidendis supplicare, cum reos sanguinis iubeatur defendere, ut supra ead. q. c. Reos'; zur Datierung, vgl. R. Weigand, 'Frühe Kanonisten und ihre Karriere in der Kirche', ZRG Kan. Abt. 76 (1990) 135–55.

30. Vgl. die Bemerkungen H. Singers in der Einleitung zur Edition: 'Von vorgratianischen Sammlungen wird bei Rufin regelmässig jene des Burchard von Worms . . . citiert . . . Aus Burchard, dessen *Decretum* Ru-

dieses Textes und Umgang mit ihr hatte. Unter den Sammlungen, in denen *Reos sanguinis* enthalten ist, hat, von der *Collectio Hibernensis* abgesehen, einzig das *Dekret* Burchards eine weite Verbreitung gehabt. Und es war wohl die wichtigste Sammlung, die neben der *Concordia discordantium canonum* noch benützt und zu deren Vervollständigung verwendet wurde.[31] Deshalb ist es im Hinblick auf C.23 q.5 c.7 von Bedeutung zu wissen, dass Rufin in seiner *Summa* ausdrücklich Texte aus der Umgebung von *Reos sanguinis* bei Burchard (das heisst aus der Umgebung von 19.109) zitiert, nämlich 19.63, 19.69, 19.76, 19.85, 19.94, 19.101, 19.102, 19.118, 19.121, 19.138, 19.141, 19.143, 19.151, 19.155.[32]

In der *Summa* des Stephan von Tournai, kurz nach Rufin in den 60er Jahren, wird C.23 q.5 c.7 schliesslich (erstmals) selbst kommentiert, allerdings ohne dass die Vorgeschichte dieses Kapitels und somit Gratians Eingriff erwähnt würde: *Reos, idest destinatos morti iniuste, qui sine iudicii examine ducuntur ad mortem. Set et pro iuste condempnatis, si oret ecclesia ne moriantur, non peccat.*[33]

Auch in den frühen Werken der französischen Schule gibt es keinen Hinweis darauf, dass die Streichung des *non* durch Gratian bemerkt worden wäre: Die *Summa Parisiensis* übergeht C.23 q.5 c.7 stillschweigend.[34] In der *Summa Coloniensis*, um 1169 entstanden, wird diese *auctoritas* nicht kommentiert oder auch nur genannt.[35] Im übrigen kennt auch dieses Werk das *Decretum* des Burchard von Worms.[36]

---

fin wohl stets zur Hand hatte, werden dreiundachtzig Stellen in der bei den Glossatoren üblichen Weise zitiert (*Die Summa Decretorum* ciii)'. Vgl. auch P. Landau, 'Vorgratianische Kanonessammlungen bei den Dekretisten und in frühen Dekretalensammlungen', in: Proc. San Diego (MIC C.9; 1992) 93–116; und insbesondere R. Weigand, 'Burchardauszüge in Dekrethandschriften und ihre Verwendung bei Rufin und als Paleae im Dekret Gratians', AKKR 158 (1989) 429–51.

31. Vgl. Landau, 'Vorgratianische Kanonessammlungen' 96–99; R. Weigand, 'Burchardauszüge'.

32. Vgl. die Nachweise bei R. Weigand, 'Burchardauszüge' 440–42. Leider konnte ich nicht untersuchen, ob jene Handschriften von Gratians *Dekret*, deren Burchardanhänge von Rudolf Weigand in diesem Zusammenhang analysiert wurden, eventuell bei C.23 q.5 c.7 eine Bemerkung zum *non* bei Burchard enthalten.

33. Vgl. MS Brüssel, Bibl. Royale 1410, fol. 115rb; ebenso die *Summa* des Johannes Faventinus zu C.23 q.5 c.7: '*Reos* idest destinatos morti <in>iuste, quia sine iuditii examine ducuntur ad mortem; set pro iuste condempnatis si oret ecclesia ne moriantur non peccat (MS Zürich, Zentralbibliothek Rh. 43 p. 259vb)'.

34. Vgl. *The Summa Parisiensis on the Decretum Gratiani*, ed. T. P. McLaughlin (Toronto 1952) 218–19. In seiner Einleitung bemerkt McLaughlin im Hinblick auf die Kenntnis von Burchard: 'Unlike many other canonists of the second half of the 12th century who supplement the text of Gratian by quoting canons contained in the collection of Burchard of Worms, the author of the SP. never mentions him by name and does not appear to have made use of his work (xxi)'. Von den anderen Sammlungen, in denen *Reos sanguinis* überliefert ist, waren dem Autor der *Summa Pariensis* wohl keine zur Hand, auch Ivos *Dekret* braucht ihm, anders als McLaughlin meint (xxi–xxii), nicht vorgelegen zu haben, denn die Rubrik *De rapacitate monachorum* findet sich in der *Panormia* 2.29 tatsächlich so, wie der Autor der *Summa Pariensis* behauptet (vgl. provisorisches Editionsmanuskript der *Panormia* von B. Brasington und M. Brett; im gleichen Sinne Landau, 'Vorgratianische Kanonessammlungen' 111–12).

35. Vgl. *Summa 'Elegantius in iure diuino' seu Coloniensis*, 1, ed. G. Fransen und S. Kuttner (4 vols; MIC A.1.1–4; 1969–90) 1.xi.

36. Vgl. etwa in der *Summa 'Elegantius in iure diuino' seu Coloniensis* 3.324, wo aus Burchard 12.36 zitiert wird.

Es kann sein, dass der Text von C.23 q.5 c.7 mit dem gegenüber der Überlieferung fehlenden *non* deshalb nicht als eine Änderung durch Gratian selbst erkannt wurde, weil der Text bei Gratian als eine Äusserung Gregors, bei Burchard jedoch als eine solche Augustins bezeichnet wird.[37] Erstaunen könnte dann allenfalls, dass niemand zu Gratians Gregortext den konträren Augustinustext aus Burchard als *set contra* allegiert hat.

Aus der weiteren Wirkungsgeschichte von *Reos sanguinis defendat ecclesia* seien, um das Bild abzurunden, noch zwei Stationen erwähnt: der 'Ertrag' der Auslegung dieses Textes durch die Dekretisten, wie er sich in der *Glossa ordinaria* des Johannes Teutonicus findet, und ein Zeugnis dafür, dass diese *auctoritas* in der Fassung Gratians (also ohne das ursprüngliche *non*) über die Lehrtradition hinaus auch eine amtliche, päpstliche Rezeption erfuhr.

In der *Glossa ordinaria* des Johannes Teutonicus zu C.23 q.5 c.7 wird *Reos sanguinis* zunächst im Zusammenhang des Asylrechts gesehen (also wie schon bei seinem ersten Auftreten in der *Collectio Hibernensis*). Denn die 'Verteidigung' wird in erster Linie auf Personen bezogen, die bei der Kirche Zuflucht gesucht haben, seien sie schuldig oder nicht, und es wird auf Ausnahmen vom Asylrecht hingewiesen. Dann wird aber auch eine mögliche oder notwendige 'Verteidigung' durch die Kirche über das Asylrecht hinaus erwähnt: Die Kirche muss helfen, wenn es beim Schuldigen die Hoffnung auf Besserung gibt, und sie muss sogar auf alle möglichen Weisen helfen, wenn jemand unschuldig verurteilt ist. In den Fällen einer gerechten Verurteilung darf die Kirche ihnen in massvoller Weise helfen, wenn es nicht inopportun ist, und zwar nur durch 'Fürsprache'. Schliesslich wird für die Fälle der 'Verteidigung', zu der sie verpflichtet ist, noch festgestellt, dass sie dabei nie gehalten ist, kriegerisch zu intervenieren.[38]

Papst Innozenz III. zitiert *Reos sanguinis defendat Ecclesia* in seinem Schreiben *Cum inaestimabile* vom 14. Juni 1210 zum Verhalten gegenüber bekehrten Waldensern, adressiert an 'alle Erzbischöfe und Bischöfe, zu welchen dieses Schreiben gelangt'.[39]

37. Zudem dürfte die Überlieferung mit dem *non* und zugleich mit der Zuschreibung an Gregor in *Collectio Sancte Marie Novelle*, 3L und 9L, wegen der geringen und nur lokalen Verbreitung dieser Sammlungen für einen Vergleich für kaum jemanden in Betracht gekommen sein.

38. *Glossa ordinaria* zu C.23 q.5 c.7 (ed. *Decretum Gratiani* [Basel 1512]): '*Reos* infra q. viii. si vobis (C.23 q.8 c.28). *Defendat* Omnes fugientes ad ecclesiam tenetur defendere: vt xvii. q. iiii. reum (C.17 q.4 c.9). et hoc verum est siue rei sunt siue non: nisi in casibus extra de immu(nitate) eccle(siarum). inter (X 3.49.6) et c. vl(timum) (X 3.49.10). Set illos qui non fugerint ad ecclesiam quandoque iuuabit, quandoque non si enim est spes correctionis, debet eos iuuare: vt. supra. q. proxi(ma). est iniusta (C.23 q.4 c.33). Item si iniuste sint condemnati aliqui omnibus modis iuuabit eos: si autem iuste, tunc temperate et non importune iuuabit eos: sed tantum intercedendo pro eis ne ex indiscreta defensione incidat ecclesia in malam opinionem: vt xiiii. q. vl(tima). hii qui (C.14 q.6 c.3). et supra q. iii. non inferenda (C.23 q.3 c.7). Et licet teneatur aliquos defendere, non tamen tenetur pro eis bellum mouere, ut C. de epi(scopali) audien(tia). addictos supplicio (Cod. 1.4.6). Jo(hannes)'.

39. Innozenz III. (Po.4014): 'Universis archiepiscopis et episcopis ad quos litterae istae pervenerint. De negotio Valdensium conversorum' (PL 216.298); ibid.: 'Cum inaestimabile pretium sanguinis Christi' (298B).

Es dient ihm bei der Darlegung der differenzierten Haltung der Kirche im Hinblick auf die Strafpraxis des Staates: Der Papst verurteilt die weltliche Gewalt nicht, wenn sie den Gesetzen entsprechend im Vorgehen gegen Übeltäter ihres Amtes waltet, aber 'als Sohn der Kirche' verteidigt er durch religiös motivierte Interventionen die Blutschuldigen, 'weil geschrieben steht: Die Kirche verteidigt die Blutschuldigen'.[40] Damit rezipiert Papst Innozenz III. die Fassung, welche Gratian dem Text *Reos sanguinis* gegeben hat, und ebenso den Zusammenhang, in den Gratian ihn gestellt hat, die Frage nach der Einstellung der Kirche zur Todesstrafe.

7. Ergebnis

Gratians Fassung von *Reos sanguinis defendat ecclesia* in C.23 q.5 c.7 unterscheidet sich von der gesamten Überlieferung vor ihm durch das Fehlen des *non* in *Reos sanguinis non defendat ecclesia*. Es kann keinen begründeten Zweifel daran geben, dass er selbst bewusst das *non* gestrichen hat und so dem Satz eine neue Bedeutung geben wollte. Dieser Eingriff steht in spürbarem Gegensatz zur Treue, die Gratian sonst im Umgang mit der Überlieferung erkennen lässt. Umso mehr vermag sie etwas über ihn selbst und das Bild von Kirche, das er in sich trägt, zu sagen.

Gratian, bei der Streichung des *non* also wirklich mit einem kurzen Blick erhascht? Ein Gratian, der für eine Kirche steht, die, ihrer Grundberufung gemäss, *ecclesia orans*, Fürbitterin ist, für alle, für die ganze Menschheit, nicht zuletzt, sondern sogar vor allem und wesentlich für solche, die in Schuld gefallen sind. Könnte nicht gerade die Treue zur Berufung der Kirche selbst jene 'Untreue' gegenüber der Überlieferung des *non* in *Reos sanguinis* motiviert haben? Wir dürfen es annehmen. Und könnte es nicht gerade auch diese tiefe Übereinstimmung von *Reos sanguinis defendat ecclesia* mit dem Wesen der Kirche sein, die alle Kritik an der Streichung des *non* von vornherein unmöglich gemacht hätte?

---

40. 'Et quamvis ista nos praedicemus, tamen potestatem saecularem secundum leges officium suum in malefactores peragentem non judicamus, neque ob hoc damnandam esse dicimus vel credimus. Verumtamen, sicut filii Ecclesiae, reos sanguinis defendimus piis interventionibus, quia scriptum est: Reos sanguinis defendat Ecclesia' (ibid. 292A).

TABELLE. Übersicht über das Vorkommen von *Reos sanguinis* in den vorgratianischen Sammlungen (in zeitlicher Reihenfolge)

	Entstehungszeit	Sammlung	Zuschreibung	Rubrik	Fragmentierung
1	1. H. 8. Jh.	Coll. Hibernensis A 28.12.a / B 29.14a	Aug	A	Reos—fiat—resolvit
2	920	Coll. IX librorum (Vat. Lat. 1349) 7.17a	Aug	B	Reos—fiat—resoluit
3	1008–1012	Burchard von Worms 19.109	Aug	C	Reos—fiat
4	1020	Coll. V librorum (Vat. lat. 1339)	Aug	D	Reos—fiat—resoluit
5	1020–1050	Coll. XII partium (CDP 1) 11.59	Clem	C	Reos—fiat
6	1020–1050	Coll. XII partium (CDP 2) 12.89	Clem	C	Reos—fiat
7	1063–1083/85	Coll. Sancte Marie Novelle 121.16	Greg	E	Reos—fiat
8	1078	Coll. Burdegalensis 12.37	Aug	F	Reos—fiat
9	um 1085	Coll. II libr. / VIII partium 8.1.2	Aug	C	Reos—fiat
10	1075–1100	Samml. Stift St-Hilaire-le-Grand 15.39			Reos—fiat
11	1090–1100	Coll. XIII libr., Berlin Savigny 3, 12.122	Aug	C	Reos—fiat
12	1093–1095	Coll. Tarraconensis, Fassung II, 1.256	Aug		Reos—fiat
13	nach 1093/95/99	Dekret Ivos von Chartres 15.121	Aug	C	Reos—fiat
14	1096–1100	Coll. Sangermanensis 7.79	Aug	B	Reos—fiat
15	spätes 11. Jh.	Celle Oberlandesgericht C. 8, 2.49.2	Aug		Reos—fiat
16	um 1100	Coll. Sancte Genoveve 4.3.103	Aug		Reos—fiat
17	1100	Coll. VII libr., Turin BNU D.IV.33. 7.127	Eus		Reos—fiat
18	um 1112–?	Coll. III librorum 3.17.29	Greg		Reos—fiat
19	um 1123	Coll. IX libr. (Arch.S.Pietro C.118) 9.3.20	Greg		Reos—fiat

Rubriken:

A = De ecclesia reos obstinanter non defendente.
B = De reis sanguinis.
C = De illis qui alios in culpa sua defendere nituntur.
D = De eo quod ecclesia reos non defendat.
E = Quod reos sanguinis non defendit ecclesia.
F = Ne ecclesia reos sanguinis defendat.

Sammlungen, in denen nach *Reos* unmittelbar *Eusebius: Utqui alium in culpa sua* folgt: 3, 5, 6, 9, [10 umgekehrte Reihenfolge], 13, 15, 16, 17, [14 als 3].

An Nr. 14 ist angefügt: *Lex dicit: Si dimiseris—pro anima eius*, das in Nr. 1, 2, 4 in der Nähe von *Reos* vorkommt (und überhaupt nur in diesen 4 Sammlungen).

[9]

Twelfth-Century Scholarly Exchanges

Mary E. Sommar

In recent years, the debate about the genesis of the most influential legal text of the twelfth century, Gratian's *Decretum,* has grown more complicated and more fascinating.[1] As I write this, it is generally agreed that the version of the *Decretum* that has been familiar since at least the beginning of the thirteenth century is the end product of a long series of stages of composition and refinement. There may well have been multiple authors or compilers; the process may have begun as early as 1120; and a number of manuscripts that were thought, before 1990, to be later abbreviations of the work seem to provide evidence instead of earlier stages of the text, or as Tatsushi Genka has recently described it, of Gratian's *Gedankengänge.*[2]

These earlier versions give us a glimpse of how our twelfth-century colleagues worked in a practical sense. They were often professors who undoubtedly combined research interests and teaching priorities as best they could, constantly refining and updating their teaching and research notes, and occasionally allowing a finished version of a particular project to circulate more publicly. Or they were pastors whose research was often driven by the needs of the souls entrusted to their care. Despite a frustrating lack of detailed data about the lives of these men, one thing has become abundantly

1. I want to express my gratitude to Prof. Harald Siems (University of Munich) and the members of his seminar who graciously asked me to present them an earlier version of this study and who provided a number of helpful suggestions.

2. During a plenary session discussion of new developments in Gratian research at the XII International Congress of Medieval Canon Law, August 6, 2004. For a more detailed overview of the past twenty-five years of Gratian studies, see A. Winroth, 'Recent Work on the Making of Gratian's Decretum', in: Proc. Washington (MIC C.12; in press), available online at http://pantheon.yale.edu/~haw6/gratian.html. Major collections of articles on this issue include: Proc. Washington (MIC C.12; in press); *La cultura giuridico-canonica medioevale: premesse per un dialogo ecumenico,* ed. E. De Léon and N. Álvarez de las Asturias (Pontificia Università della Santa Croce. Monografie giuridiche 22; Milano 2003); RDC 48 (1998); and ibid. 51 (2001).

clear through the past decade of Gratian research: the twelfth-century canonists were engaged in decades-long projects, and occasionally an intermediate version has preserved the process, allowing modern scholars to see—or at least to speculate—how the end product was achieved.[3]

This paper will first summarize a few of the recent insights into the composition of Gratian's *Decretum* and then, through an examination of several decretists' treatments of one of Gratian's case studies, Causa 7, showing the give-and-take among these twelfth-century scholars, suggest that the classical canon law that has been handed down over the generations may well be less the product of a few men of genius working on their own than the fruit of decades of interaction and synergy among the men who lived and taught, especially in Bologna, but also in Rome and Paris and the other centers of learning and inspiration that produced what has often been referred to as the twelfth-century renaissance.

Much of the work that has resulted in the new understanding of the composition of Gratian's *Decretum* has focused on a single *causa*, or case, or even a single *quaestio* within a *causa*, rather than on a broad overview of the entire work. Lenherr's groundbreaking 1987 work on the three stages of composition of C.24 q.1 was followed by Winroth's celebrated study of the same case that led to the realization of the existence of at least two recensions of the *Decretum*.[4] Larrainzar has suggested that the version of the *Decretum* found in one manuscript (St. Gall 673) was an even earlier step in the composition, a draft that preceded the more widely distributed 'Recension I'.[5] Although his idea has not yet received universal acceptance, Larrainzar's work, along with Winroth's discovery, has opened the way for a whole new way of thinking about the way this pivotal text came to be.

It is generally accepted that the so-called Recension I is an earlier, more tightly argued text of Gratian's work that was emended over the years to result in the vulgate text, the version found in most manuscripts and in Friedberg's printed edition, now referred to as 'Recension II'.[6] And there have been a number of studies of various *causae* to test Winroth's and Larrainzar's hypotheses. Many of these more recent studies have

3. More than a half-century ago, S. Kuttner, the founder of modern studies in the history of canon law, cautioned us against too-eager systematization of the work of our predecessors in 'Quelques observations sur l'autorité des collections canoniques dans le droit classique de l'Église', in: *Actes du Congrès de droit canonique, Paris 22–26 Avril 1947* (Paris 1950) 305–12; repr. idem, *Medieval Councils, Decretals, and Collections of Canon Law* (London 1980) no. I.

4. T. Lenherr, *Die Exkommunikations- und Depositionsgewalt der Häretiker bei Gratian und den Dekretisten bis zur 'Glossa Ordinaria' des Johannes Teutonicus* (Münchener theologische Studien 3: Kanonistische Abteilung 42; Munich 1987); A. Winroth, *The Making of Gratian's Decretum* (Cambridge 2000).

5. C. Larrainzar, 'El borrador de la *Concordia* de Graciano: Sankt Gallen, Stiftsbibliothek MS 673 (= Sg)', *Ius Ecclesiae* 11 (1999) 593–666.

6. *Corpus iuris canonici* I, ed. E. Friedberg (Leipzig 1879).

uncovered complications in the structure of Recension I and of the St. Gall manuscript version. These include Paxton's work on C.13, which found that the composition involved multiple steps and that this process had been somewhat different for different *causae*, as well as Lenherr's parallel investigations of C.19, C.3, and D.31–32.[7] Landau has concentrated on the earlier collections that Gratian plumbed in assembling his work, discovering that the master depended on relatively few sources.[8] My own work from 2001 suggested that Gratian's C.7 began with a core of texts taken from Anselm of Lucca's collection but grew to the point where it suffered from several logical difficulties in the arrangement of canons by the time it appeared as the version known as Recension I.[9] Dillon also has found evidence of the use of Anselm of Lucca at an early stage in the development of the *Decretum*, showing that this collection provided the center of C.3, too.[10] Larrainzar's and Viejo-Ximénez's recent work has emphasized the many stages of development in the *Decretum* as well, showing how this process was both 'complex and irregular'.[11] Tarín has even gone so far as to propose a preliminary stemma of the various early versions of the *Decretum*.[12]

Weigand's posthumously published study of C.25 suggested that Gratian may well have begun with several independent tracts on various pressing issues before he combined them into one large casebook.[13] His most persuasive evidence is from C. 25 q.2 d.p.c.25 where Gratian writes: *Sicut sup. in tit. de mutationibus episcoporum*, clearly referring to a no longer extant title that was at one time found in the same work as the material that made its way into C.25 q.2. Weigand also listed a number of similar occurrences elsewhere in the *Decretum* that give hints about the topics of other earlier tracts. Perhaps, before compiling his notes into the *Concordia discordantia canonum*, the master composed a number of individual treatises that were presented in the form of

7. F. Paxton, 'Le cause 13 de Gratien et la composition du Décret', RDC 51 (2001) 233–49, available in English at: http://camel2.conncoll.edu/academics/web_profiles/paxton.html; T. Lenherr, 'Zur Überlieferung des Kapitels "Duae sunt, inquit, leges" (Decretum Gratiani C.19 q.2 c.2)', AKKR 168 (1999) 359–84; idem, 'Die vier Fassungen von C.3 q.1 d.p.c.6 im *Decretum Gratiani*. Zugleich ein Einblick in die neueste Diskussion um das Werden von Gratians Dekret', AKKR 169 (2000) 353–81; idem, 'Ist die Handschrift 673 der St. Galler Stiftsbibliothek (Sg) der Entwurf zu Gratians Dekret? Versuch einer Antwort aus Beobachtungen an D.31 und D.32', available at: http://home.vr-web.de/titus_lenherr/Sg-Entw.PDF.

8. See especially P. Landau, 'Das Register Papst Gregors I. im Decretum Gratiani', in: *Mittelalterliche Texte: Überlieferung—Befunde—Deutungen* (MGH Schriften 42; Hannover 1996) 125–40; idem, 'Burchard de Worms et Gratien: à propos des sources immédiates de Gratien', RDC 48 (1998) 233–45.

9. M. E. Sommar, 'Gratian's Causa VII and the Multiple Recension Theories', BMCL 24 (1999) 78–96.

10. J. Dillon, 'The Construction of Gratian's Cases', in: Proc. Washington (MIC C.12; in press).

11. C. Larrainzar, 'La ricerca attuale sul *Decretum Gratiani*', in: *La cultura giuridico-canonica* 109–22; J. M. Viejo-Ximénes, 'Les étapes de l'incorporation des textes romains au Décret de Gratien', RDC 51 (2001) 251–60.

12. L. P. Tarín, 'An secularibus litteris oporteat eos esse eruditos? El texto de D.37 en las etapas antiguas del Decreto de Graciano', in: *La cultura giuridico-canonica* 469–511.

13. R. Weigand, 'Causa 25 des Dekrets und die Arbeitsweise Gratians', in: *Grundlagen des Rechts. Festschrift für Peter Landau zum 65. Geburtstag*, ed. R. H. Helmholz et al. (Paderborn and Munich 2000) 277–90.

a collection of tracts on various critical topics. The reference to 'the title found above on the translation of bishops' certainly leads one to surmise that these earlier treatises were assembled into one volume.

Our honorand, Kenneth Pennington, has also joined the discussion, providing a fascinating glimpse of the composition process of C.19.[14] He believes that the shorter version of Urban II's decretal text, *Duae sunt,* found in Recension I and in the St. Gall manuscript, is most likely the original version of Urban's letter (C.19 q.2 c.2). The longer version found in Recension II includes canonistic commentary referring to other sections of the *Decretum,* and indeed, to sections found only in Recension II, as well as to biblical material. Pennington suggests that the later 'Gratian' found a longer, altered version of the letter in canonical collections and adapted it to fit his later argument.

Bolstered by all of this corroborating evidence, it is time to have another look at the composition of Causa 7. As I have discussed elsewhere, the argument of the case has a few logical difficulties.[15] The question in C.7 q.1 is whether or not a bishop can be replaced in his see while he is still living. This includes bishops who are incapacitated, those who enter a monastery, and those who transfer to another diocese. After consideration of the ancient canons, Gratian did not really come to any clear or concise conclusion other than to say that when a bishop left his diocese he relinquished all claims to authority there, thus eliminating the possibility that the diocese would be governed by two bishops.[16] Gratian also pointed out that there were a number of mitigating circumstances to the ancient prohibition of leaving one's diocese.

The greatest logical difficulty in the argument of C.7 q.1 as presented in the first recension lies with d.p.c.18. The first part of it is a summary inserted by Gratian of chapters 5, 6, and 11, offering no mention at all of the material in the intervening chapters 12, 13, 14, and 17 (see Table I). It seems fairly clear that these four chapters between c.11 and d.p.c.18, canons that all discuss the same issue and were not taken from Anselm of Lucca's collection as was the surrounding text, were not originally in that location. The second part of d.p.c.18 is introductory to c.31, suggesting that c.19 and c.30 had also been moved at some point.

The other major logical problem with the organization of C.7 q.1 illustrates that the material of Recension II was not added all at one time. Although c.20–29 were all from this later stage of composition, they were not inserted as a unit. The rubric of c.23 says: *Item ex eodem,* that is, 'and again from the same source'. But c.23 is a canon from the Council of Nicaea, and the nearest canon from that council is found, not in c.22, but back in c.19. Clearly, c.20–22 were inserted at some later time. It is much more prob-

---

14. K. Pennington, 'Gratian, Causa 19, and the Birth of Canonical Jurisprudence', in: *La cultura giuridico-canonica* 209–32.

15. Sommar, 'Gratian's Causa' 88–90.   16. C.7 q.1 d.p.c.41.

able that the mismatched *eodem* would have happened during a later revision than when that chapter was first included in the collection.

Thus, the process of composition of Causa 7 seems to have been as follows. A core of texts taken from Anselm of Lucca was gathered to support a discussion of the problem of episcopal translation. Along with the addition of new material, the core was reorganized into the version found in Recension I, then subsequently reorganized in two or more later steps that finally resulted in the vulgate text, or Recension II. Further, various textual difficulties, while proving nothing definitive, lend support to the idea that more than one mind was at work in these various stages of revision.

Let us now move from a study of the efforts that resulted in what we know as Causa 7 of Gratian's *Decretum* to a broader look at other twelfth-century canonists' work on this problem. After the emergence of Recension II, the *Decretum* seems to have retained its form. But scholarly interest in the questions discussed by Gratian did not end. The next stage of the dialogue was carried on by those known as the decretists, the first generation of whom, we assume, were mostly teachers of church law at Bologna.[17]

Paucapalea, whose *Summa* was probably the earliest separate response to the *Decretum*, is generally believed to have been the one responsible for the final arrangement of the vulgate text into *quaestiones* and *causae*.[18] His remarks on Causa 7 are relatively brief. Paucapalea begins with Gratian's initial question: 'When may a living bishop be replaced by another?'[19] And Paucapalea's answer begins with a brief summary of Gratian's four principal criteria: when the bishop is too old or too sick; when he is transferred by papal authority to serve the utility or necessity of the Church; when he leaves on his own authority in order to go to another cathedral; and when a bishop wishes to enter a monastery.[20] The remaining discussion consists of a few biblical excursus on references made in C.7 q.1 c.8, 9, 13, and 41 that are not unlike the *Decretum*'s d.p.c.48 (Recension II), and some minor clarification of the terminology in c.47.

Another *Summa*, known by its incipit, *Sicut vetus testamentum*, along with the biblical material, repeats Paucapalea's four possibilities for episcopal translation and adds a fifth: when the bishop is guilty of a crime.[21] It has been suggested, based on a study of the works as a whole, that the same man is the author of both the *Summa* attributed to

17. For a survey of decretist responses to Gratian, see Kuttner, *Repertorium;* R. Weigand, *Glossatoren des Dekrets Gratians* (Bibliotheca eruditorum 18; Goldbach 1997); Weigand, *Glossen;* K. Pennington, 'The Decretists: The Italian School', in: *The History of Medieval Canon Law in the Classical Period, 1140–1234,* ed. K. Pennington (HMCL; Washington, DC, in press); idem, 'Bio-Bibliographical Guide of Canonists 1140–1500', at: http://faculty.cua.edu/pennington.

18. Paucapalea, *Summa über das Decretum Gratiani,* ed. J. F. von Schulte (Giessen 1890; repr. Aalen 1965).

19. C.7 q.1 d.a.c.1: 'Hic primum queritur, utrum vivente episcopo alius possit in ecclesia eadem ordinari?'.

20. Paucapalea, *Summa* ad C.7 q.1, ed. Schulte 73.

21. Summa *Sicut vetus testamentum* (MS Florenz, BML Conv. Soppr. G IV 1736), ad C.7 q.1. The rest essentially follows the text of Paucapalea.

Paucapalea, *Quoniam in omnibus rebus,* and the *Summa, Sicut vetus testamentum,* or that Paucapalea's text was a later abbreviation of *Sicut vetus testamentum.*[22] However, given the details just discussed, for C.7 q.1 at least it seems more probable that the author of *Sicut vetus testamentum,* whoever he was, was familiar with Paucapalea's work and responded to the Summa *Quoniam in omnibus rebus,* with an 'improved version' of the earlier text.

Next we come to Rolandus, a man whose identity is still in question, although it is clear that he was not identical with Rolandus Bandinelli, Pope Alexander III, as was long believed.[23] Rolandus' treatment of C.7 q.1 is extremely short—only thirty words. A living bishop may be replaced, says Rolandus, if he is a criminal, or if he has left 'voluntarily and of his own will'.[24] Rolandus, focusing on the will of the bishop being replaced and supplying the detail that a criminous bishop may be replaced against his will, seems more interested in the rights of the bishop than were the previous two decretists. It is also apparent that Rolandus was familiar with *Sicut vetus testamentum,* where the issue of criminous bishops is raised to the level of a major concern.

Thus far we have seen the original *Decretum* evolve from an early collection of tracts on various questions through a number of developmental stages involving most likely more than one author until it reached the vulgate version. Then, focusing on C.7, we have seen that Paucapalea summarized Gratian's discussion of the occasions when it is permissible for a living bishop to be replaced by another and that the author of *Sicut vetus testamentum* improved upon the summary. Finally, Rolandus changed the focus from the legality of the change to the rights of the bishop who is being replaced.

Another early decretist, a man known only as 'The Earlier Master P.', in an uncharacteristically long gloss, or commentary, on C.7 q.1 c.11 reorganized the summary formula followed by those discussed above.[25] Master P., also changing the focus of the question, said that bishops may depart from their sees in three ways: one, *recedentes,* that is, either leaving on their own (which is punishable), leaving to serve the good of the Church, or leaving to enter a monastery; two, *expulsi,* expelled, for example if fleeing persecution or invasion; and three, *decedentes,* through death. The focus has changed from when a bishop may be replaced, to the questions of when and how a bishop can be separated from his see. The Earlier Master P., whose work may or may not have preceded that of Rolandus, is less interested in the rights of the bishop than in the mechanics of the separation.[26]

22. See J. T. Noonan, 'The True Paucapalea?', in: Proc. Salamanca (MIC C.6; 1980) 157–86; R. Weigand, 'Paucapalea und die frühe Kanonistik', AKKR 150 (1981) 137–57.

23. J. T. Noonan, 'Who was Rolandus?', in: *Law, Church and Society: Essays in Honor of Stephan Kuttner,* ed. K. Pennington and R. Somerville (Philadelphia, PA 1977) 21–48.

24. *Summa Magistri Rolandi,* ad C.7 q.1, ed. F. Thaner (Innsbruck 1894; repr. Aalen 1962) 22.

25. Weigand, *Glossen* 580–81.

26. In a chronological arrangement, Weigand, *Glossen,* placed P. after Rolandus.

Up to this point I have not discussed the dating of the texts, either of the *Decretum* itself, or of the various decretists. There is so much debate about this at present that it seems prudent to leave the question of dating to another investigation.[27] However, it is important to propose some sort of relative timeline in order to evaluate the decretists' reactions to the *Decretum* and to one another. For the purposes of this discussion, if we take the traditional date of circa 1140 for the appearance of Recension II, then we can place the first generation of decretists' works in the late 1140s or early 1150s, probably in the order in which they have been presented here.

The next twelfth-century scholar for our consideration, Omnebene or Omnibonus, prepared a completely different kind of composition in about 1156. This work has traditionally been classified as an *abbreviatio*, a shorter form of the *Decretum*, most probably made for teaching purposes, although recent scholarship has shown how from very early on the canonists saw how different Omnebene's work is from other *abbreviationes*.[28] An analysis of Omnebene's treatment of Gratian's Causa 7 also allows us more insight into the dialogue among the twelfth-century legal scholars. Omnebene the teacher may well have used Gratian's work with his students, but Omnebene the scholar clearly thought that his understanding of the issues was an improvement on Gratian's. One might, indeed, call Omnebene's C.7 his own version of the case, and not an abbreviation of Gratian at all (see Table I). He omitted c.5–10, put c.8 at the very end of the *causa*, and omitted c.20–22 and 30, as well as c.33, 36, 38, 39, and 41, most of which were from Recension II and all of which were unnecessary to the flow of the argument. Besides rearranging and deleting *capitula*, Omnebene reworked d.p.c.11 to better suit the new lineup of canons; he added a d.p.c.13 as a logical connector between c.13 and c.14, and added, as a new d.p.c.32, a summary of c.28–29, which he had deleted. Finally, Omnebene omitted a number of Gratian's *dicta*, including the problematic d.p.c.18, which he replaced with a new short *dictum* of his own to serve as a connector between c.16 and c.19. Omnebene's new, shorter d.p.c.48 included biblical material from Paucapalea or *Sicut vetus testamentum*.

Of course, many of these changes could be viewed as ways of shortening the text to make it suitable for a particular teaching situation. However, the fact that Omnebene

---

27. Estimates range from c. 1120 or even earlier for the 'Ur-Gratian' text to as late as past mid-century for the emergence of the vulgate text.

28. Omnebene (Vatican, BAV Reg. lat. 1039; Paris, BN lat. 3886). See also R. Weigand, 'Die Dekret-Abbreviatio Omnebenes und ihre Glossen', in: *Recht als Heilsdienst. Festschrift für Professor Dr. Matthäus Kaiser*, ed. W. Schulz (Paderborn 1989) 271–87; R. Weigand, 'Die frühen kanonistischen Schulen und die Dekretabbreviatio Omnebenes', AKKR 155 (1986) 72–91; A. Vetulani and W. Uruszczak, 'L'oeuvre d'Omnebene dans le MS 602 de la Bibliothèque municipale de Cambrai', in: Proc. Toronto (MIC C.5; 1976) 11–26; J. Rambaud-Buhot, 'L'Abbreviatio Decreti Omnibene', in: Proc. Berkeley (MIC C.7; 1985) 93–107; and eadem, 'Les divers types d'abrégés du Décret de Gratien', in: *Recueil de travaux offert à M. Clovis Brunel* (Paris 1955) 397–411.

TABLE I

Gratian's Causa 7 (Bold face = Recension I; Italics = Additions of Recension II)	Omnebene's Causa 7 (Numbering of chapters according to Gratian)	Gratian's Causa 7 (Bold face = Recension I; Italics = Additions of Recension II)	Omnebene's Causa 7 (Numbering of chapters according to Gratian)
d. init.			
d.a.c.1		**c.30**	
c.1	c.1	**c.31**	c.31
c.2	c.2	*c.32*	c.32
c.3	c.4	*d.p.c.32*	d.Om
c.4	c.3	*c.33*	c.27
c.5		**d.p.c.33**	d.p.c.33
c.6		**c.34**	c.34
c.7		**c.35**	c.35
c.8		*c.36*	
c.9		*c.37*	c.37
c.10		*c.38*	
c.11	c.11	**c.39**	
d.p.c.11	shortened d. p.c.11/d.Om*	*d.p.c.39*	d.p.c.39
c.12	c.12	*c.40*	c.40
d.p.c.12	d.Om	*c.41*	
c.13	c.13 & d.Om	**d.p.c.41**	d.p.c.41
c.14	c.14	**c.42**	c.42
d.p.c.14	d.p.c.14	**d.p.c.42**	d.p.c.42
c.15	c.15	**c.43**	c.43
c.16	c.16	**d.p.c.43**	d.p.c.43
d.p.c.16	d.Om	**c.44**	c.44
c.17		**d.p.c.44**	d.p.c.44
c.18		**c.45**	c.45
d.p.c.18		*d.p.c.45*	d.p.c.45
c.19	c.19	*c.46*	c.46
c.20		*c.47*	
c.21		*c.48*	
c.22		*d.p.c.48*	shortened d.p.c.48 & d.Om
c.23	c.23	*c.49*	
c.24	c.24	**d.p.c.49**	
c.25	c.25		c.41
c.26	c.26		c.8
c.27			
c.28			
c.29			

* d.Om = *dictum* of Omnebene

'corrected' the most obvious flaw in the flow of the *causa*, the *dictum* p.c.18, and the fact that so much of the material he eliminated came from the later recension of the *Decretum*, suggest that his aim was more than merely to condense the text. While agreeing with Gratian's solution as seen in d.p.c.41, which he preserved, Omnebene seems to have disagreed with the way Gratian constructed his argument to reach that conclusion. Omnebene cut away a lot of the chaff and left a stronger, tighter progression of *capitula*, linked by shorter, more succinct commentary that incorporated the thinking of other decretists as well as Omnebene's own insights.

The last of these 'first-generation' canonists we will discuss is Rufinus. His *Summa* of perhaps 1164 established the format of the analytical summary of Causa 7 that would continue through the succeeding generations. Rufinus, returning to Master P.'s question of how a bishop could leave his see, expands the list of possibilities to seven: if he is a criminal; too sick; or too old; capriciously (on his own authority); for the good of the Church (with papal approval); in necessity; and to enter a monastery.[29]

In his rather long treatment of C.7, Rufinus also added a completely new idea to the discussion of the questions raised in this case. He said that there are three different kinds of transfers, or translations. There are: translations of a person for the sake of the place, that is for the sake of the local situation; translations of a place for the sake of the person, that is relocation of diocesan headquarters for the benefit of the people, as in the case of a cathedral chapter being taken over by a monastic community; and translations of the place for the sake of the place, as in the relocation of the community for their own safety.[30] While this passage is justly remembered for its organizational insight into a pressing twelfth-century problem, for our purposes it is also instructive. Rufinus, like Omnebene, provided a better version of Gratian's central analysis at d.p.c.18. By the time Rufinus was working with Recension II, it was not so easy to see that originally, in Recension I, these remarks had introduced c.31. Instead, it seemed that this passage was supposed to be introductory to c.19 and following. Rufinus, a superb legal mind, realized that it did not fulfill this function very well. His commentary is a very good summary of the major issues treated by the intervening *capitula* from c.19 through c.30, and thus carries the reader from d.p.c.18 through that section of Gratian's argument to c.31, which at one time probably followed immediately.

The decretists after Rufinus were from a new generation. They continued to refine

---

29. Rufinus, *Summa Decretorum*, ad C.7 q.1, ed. H. Singer (Paderborn 1902; repr. Paderborn 1963) 285–95; see R. Deutinger, 'The Decretist Rufinus—A Well-known Person?', BMCL 23 (1999) 10–15; R. Benson, *The Bishop-Elect: A Study in Medieval Ecclesiastical Office* (Princeton, NJ 1968) 56–89; and K. Pennington, *Pope and Bishops: The Papal Monarchy in the Twelfth and Thirteenth Centuries* (Philadelphia, PA 1984) 87.

30. Rufinus, *Summa* ad d.p.c.18 (second part), ed. Singer 290–94; many, including the editor of Rufinus' *Summa*, refer to the passage as d.a.c.19.

and rework their understanding of Gratian and his colleagues. However, from that time on, the text of the *Decretum,* of Recension II, was fixed and no longer treated as a living text. The dialogue continued among the canonists, but they were not so much in dialogue with Gratian, as with one another, with other glossators and commentators.

It should be no surprise to see this back and forth process among the legal scholars of twelfth-century Bologna. It is merely a larger reflection of their individual methodology, the dialectic exchange of scholasticism. And it neither began nor ended with Gratian and his contemporaries. In his analysis of the pre-1120 *Collection in Seven Books* (7L), Landau has found evidence that this dialogue had already begun in the very early years of the twelfth century.[31] He called 7L 'a Gratian without the *dicta*', due to the care and thought that went into the collection and arrangement of the various texts.[32] Regrettably, 7L's very short title on our subject, the translation of bishops, does not provide enough text—only five canons—for much new insight into the dialogue process.[33] But, based on a larger sampling Landau found that different manuscripts of the collection reveal minor differences in organization that are not likely to be the result of scribal error and suggest a developmental process of some sort. At the other end of the century, the ill-fated *Compilatio decretorum* of Cardinal Laborans, which appeared circa 1180 after more than twenty years' effort, was not successful in challenging Gratian's treatment of the various legal problems, most likely because Gratian's work had become so well established as the normative canon law text that even an improved analysis such as Laborans' could not replace it.[34]

An analysis of one *causa* is not sufficient to allow us to draw too many broad conclusions. It is clear, however, that at least on the issue of episcopal translation, Gratian's contemporaries did not immediately canonize his text; indeed, they produced a lively discussion of how best to organize and understand the problem. Even within the various Gratianic versions, there are major changes in the presentation of his argument. And Omnebene's work on Causa 7 offers persuasive evidence of disagreements among the Bolognese law faculty on at least this one question.

31. *Collectio 7 librorum* (Vatican, BAV Vat. Lat. 1346; Vienna, ÖNB lat. 2186). P. Landau, 'Die Quellen der mittelitalienischen Kanonessammlung in sieben Büchern (MS Vat. Lat. 1346)', in: *Text and Law: Studies in Medieval Canon Law and Liturgy Presented to Roger E. Reynolds*, ed. K. G. Cushing and R. F. Gyug (London 2004) 1–14. See also *KanonesJ* 172–73.

32. Landau, 'Die Quellen' 14.

33. 7L (Vatican, BAV Vat. Lat. 1335) 1.40: 'De transmigratione et profectione episcoporum'; in the later MS Vienna, ÖNB lat. 2186, the same five canons are under 1.110: 'De transmigratione episcoporum'.

34. Laborans, *Compilatio decretorum* (Vatican, BAV Arch. S. Pietro C.110), ed. N. Martin, *Die 'Compilatio Decretorum' des Kardinals Laborans: Eine Umarbeitung des gratianischen Dekrets aus dem 12. Jahrhundert* (Phil. diss.; Heidelberg Univ. 1985); see also A. Theiner, *Disquisitiones criticae* (Romae 1836) 399–446; Maassen, *Geschichte* 148–49.

As the analysis of various *causae* of Gratian's work continues, and as new studies of the commentaries on these *causae* appear, we may hope to obtain a much clearer picture of the decretists' interactions with Gratian and with one another. Yet even at this early stage in our investigations, we can see some evidence of their dialogue. And it is remarkable how many similarities there are between the everyday scholarly interactions of twelfth-century professors and the everyday interactions of scholars of our own age who are trying to better understand the lives and works of their medieval predecessors.

10

Notas sobre las introducciones *In prima parte agitur* y *Hoc opus inscribitur*

Carlos Larrainzar

❋

1. Quienes dedicamos nuestros afanes a la investigación de las fuentes canónicas medievales, desde hace ya unos cuantos años, hemos de agradecer al Prof. Kenneth Pennington su impulso al formidable proyecto editorial sobre la *History of Medieval Canon Law*, que ya ha comenzado a dar sus primeros frutos.[1] En la espera de la publicación de los tomos sobre la 'etapa clásica', deseo contribuir al homenaje a nuestro colega, tan querido para tantos, con una colaboración sobre algunas de las 'introducciones' al Decreto de Graciano que muestran los códices más tempranos de su vasta tradición manuscrita: en especial, sobre la denominada por sus palabras iniciales *In prima parte agitur* (= *IPA*), muy distinta de otra menos conocida intitulada *Hoc opus inscribitur* (= *HOI*), de mayor antigüedad quizás y de menor difusión que *IPA*. Ambas tienden a ser consideradas obras de algún autor anónimo, de entre los pioneros de la primera literatura decretista, aunque en verdad faltan datos para afirmar nada con seguridad.

En el contexto de la revisión que se está operando sobre nuestros conocimientos de la obra gracianea, durante esta última década, *IPA* dista mucho de ser una anónima producción literaria 'posterior' al *Decretum* y más parece que su elaboración debe ponerse en relación directa con el proceso literario que, en diversas etapas irregulares, tiene como resultado final la difusión de un *Decretum vulgatum* o Decreto divulgado.[2]

---

1. Cf. HMCL, un proyecto editorial del cual se dió cuenta detallada en las sesiones del *Xth International Congress of Medieval Canon Law* de Syracuse (New York); vid. una crónica detallada de ese congreso en J. Viejo-Ximénez, '*In memoriam* Stephan Kuttner. A propósito del *Xth International Congress of Medieval Canon Law* de 1996 en Syracuse (New York)', *Ius Ecclesiae* 9 (1997) 221–64. De este proyecto vid. ya publicados: Kéry, *Can. Coll.*; D. Jasper y H. Fuhrmann, *Papal Letters in the Early Middle Ages* (2001).

2. Vid. C. Larrainzar, 'La firma boloñesa del Decreto de Graciano', *Initium* 9 (2004) 69–89. He comentado este nuevo enfoque del tema durante mi intervención en el *XIIth International Congress of Medieval Canon Law*

Si esto es así, la mayor antigüedad de *HOI* reclama también ponderar sus singulares características.

No obstante, la brevedad impuesta a esta colaboración por los editores de este volumen obliga a que, en este momento, me limite sólo a presentar unas modestas 'notas', poco más, que ayuden a un mejor conocimiento de ambas 'introducciones' y, por ende, aporten también algunos datos nuevos o los hagan más accesibles para incrementar nuestro saber sobre la *Redaktionsgeschichte* de la obra gracianea.

2. Hace años Adam Vetulani, después de su análisis del manuscrito *Mv* de Montecasino, había intuido la conveniencia de indagar sobre el origen o la cronología de las diversas 'introducciones' al Decreto más conocidas: *De iure scripto et non scripto* o bien *IPA*, para conseguir dataciones más precisas sobre el proceso de formación del texto de Graciano.[3] Pero ya antes Friedrich von Schulte había destacado, por ejemplo, que *IPA* aparecía en algunos pocos manuscritos antiguos, en especial del siglo XII, y relacionada con el trabajo docente sobre los contenidos del *Decretum*.[4] Después Jacqueline Rambaud advirtió que la presencia de *IPA* en los manuscritos era un indicio claro de la antigüedad del texto copiado en tales códices.[5] Incluso intentó una exposición de conjunto sobre la literatura decretista más temprana que en esos comienzos pretendió facilitar el estudio o resumir el contenido de lo compilado por el *magister decretorum*.[6]

---

celebrado en Washington, a comienzos de agosto de 2004, en mi comunicación *La edición crítica del Decreto de Graciano*, que será publicada durante los próximos meses. Ahí desarrollo algunos aspectos de la síntesis ya publicada como C. Larrainzar, 'La investigación actual sobre el Decreto de Graciano', ZRG Kan. Abt. 90 (2004) 27–59, o su versión italiana, 'La ricerca attuale sul *Decretum Gratiani*' en: *La cultura giuridico-canonica medioevale. Premesse per un dialogo ecumenico*, ed. E. de León (Pontificia Università della Santa Croce. Monografie giuridiche 22; Milano 2003) 45–88.

3. A. Vetulani, 'Le Décret de Gratien dans le ms 64 de Montecasino', *Archivium Iuridicum Cracoviense* 5 (1972) 103–12 (= idem, *Sur Gratien et les Décretales. Recueil d'études édité par Waclaw Uruszczak. Préface d'André Gouron* [Aldershot 1990] no. XII; con *Addenda et corrigenda* donde dice [21]: 'On n'a pas jusqu'à présent établi, laquelle de ces introductions anonymes est plus ancienne').

4. Cf. J. F. von Schulte, 'Zur Geschichte der Literatur über das Dekret Gratians: Dritter Beitrag', *Sb. Wien* 65 (1870) 21–76, especialmente 24–25: 'Dass sie ohne Zweifel in die früheste Zeit hinaufreicht. Dies scheint mir anzudeuten, dass man dem Vortrage, was auch an sich leicht begreiflich ist, eine kurze Übersicht des Inhalts vorausschickte. Bedenkt man, dass ziemlich früh die Zahl der Capitel abwich und dadurch die älteste Methode, auch nach Zahlen zu citiren, der ausschliesslichen, mit den Anfangsworten zu citiren, Platz machte: so steigt die Bedeutung einer solchen Eintheilung, weil sie im Ganzen den Anhalt bot zum Aufsuchen der Stellen'.

5. Vid. los estudios de J. Rambaud-Buhot, 'Plan et méthode de travail pour la rédaction d'un catalogue des manuscrits du Décret de Gratien', RHE 48 (1953) 211–23, donde ofrece además una aplicación práctica del método propuesto. Y además sus otros estudios: 'L'étude des manuscrits du Décret de Gratien conservés en France', SG 1 (1953) 120–45; junto con 'L'étude des manuscrits du Décret de Gratien' y 'Exemple de description de manuscrit' en: *Congrès de droit canonique médiéval (Louvain-Bruxelles 22–26 Juillet 1958) = Bibliothèque de la RHE 33* (Louvain 1958) 25–48 y 49–63 respectivamente.

6. J. Rambaud-Buhot, 'Les divers types d'abrégés du Décret de Gratien. De la table au commentaire' en: *Recueil de travaux offert à M. Clovis Brunel* (Paris 1955) 397–411. Ahí presenta el objeto de su trabajo diciendo, 397:

Los más recientes descubrimientos sobre la tradición manuscrita del *Decretum* han venido a revalorizar directamente esa literatura, ya que de su análisis pueden obtenerse luces para reconstruir el proceso literario de formación de sus redacciones. De este modo, poco después de que Anders Winroth y Rudolf Weigand señalaran la existencia de algunos manuscritos con una 'primera redacción' antigua del *Decretum*, mucho más breve que la divulgada, José Miguel Viejo-Ximénez publicó un interesantísimo estudio analítico sobre C.29 desde la nueva perspectiva.[7] Y fue ahí donde *obiter dictum* señaló la particular importancia de *HOI* por su comparación con los contenidos de *IPA:* extraía sus argumentos del contraste entre esos respectivos contenidos y las coincidencias con las dos etapas de redacción distinguidas.[8] Inequívocamente, pues, *HOI* parecía ser una obra compuesta con anterioridad a *IPA*.

Según la vasta información de Rudolf Weigand, esta *HOI* se conserva sólo en dos códices: el manuscrito *Aa* de Admont, *Stiftsbibliothek* 23 y 43, y el manuscrito *Me* de München, BSB Clm 13004.[9] En ambos casos ese texto va acompañado de otros elemen-

---

'Nous allons essayer de dégager, en présentant quelques-uns de ces abréges, les grands traits de ce genre particulier de littérature'; a continuación, con diverso detalle según los casos, examina obras como *De iure scripto et non scripto*, el *Decretum abbreviatum*, la introducción *IPA*, la abreviación *Humanum genus duobus regitur* del códice de Paris, BN lat. 4709 o del códice lat. 3922A, junto con otros manuscritos más, incluida una específica referencia a la abreviación del maestro *Omnibonus*.

7. J. M. Viejo-Ximénez, 'La versión original de C.29 del Decreto de Graciano', *Ius Ecclesiae* 11 (1998) 149–85; cf. A. Winroth, 'The Two Recensions of Gratian's Decretum', ZRG Kan. Abt. 83 (1997) 22–31, y R. Weigand, 'Chancen und Probleme einer baldigen kritischen Edition der ersten Redaktion des Dekrets Gratians', BMCL 22 (1997/98) 53–75, que recoge su intervención en el Congreso Internacional de 1996 y 'Zur künftigen Edition des Dekrets Gratians', ZRG Kan. Abt. 83 (1997) 32–51.

8. Vid. J. M. Viejo-Ximénez, 'La versión original' 177–78, que asume parte de las conclusiones de P. Landau, 'Die Eheschliessung von Freien mit Unfreien bei Burchard von Worms und Gratian. Ein Beitrag zur Textkritik der Quellen des Kanonischen Rechts und zur Geschichte christlicher Umformung des Eherechts' en: *Cristianità ed Europa. Miscellanea di Studi in onore di Luigi Prosdocimi* I (Roma, Freiburg y Wien 1994) 453–61. Según Viejo-Ximénez: 'Si se comparan los contenidos de las dos introducciones al Decreto aquí mencionadas, *In prima parte agitur* y *Hoc opus inscribitur*, salta a la vista que esta segunda parece redactada para una *Concordia* de "primera recensión", mientras que el autor de *In prima parte agitur* conoce y comenta el Decreto de "segunda recensión"; un buen ejemplo viene de la comparación entre los fragmentos que resumen C.29'. Después de transcribir en paralelo esos textos, su comentario es: 'Las sobrias palabras de *Hoc opus inscribitur* son un escueto resumen de C.29, que contrastan con el carácter más técnico y elaborado del texto de *In prima parte agitur*. Pero, sobre todo, en la *In prima parte agitur* existe una referencia explícita a los temas considerados por las *auctoritates* que *faltan* en la versión admonatense de C.29 y, al contrario, la introducción *Hoc opus inscribitur* se ajusta al contenido de lo que venimos considerando como la *redacción original* de C.29; véase, por ejemplo, cómo en aquella introducción se considera el tema *de coniugiis que dolo et fraude contrahuntur* y cómo se añade más adelante *de seruis etiam ibidem generaliter agitur*, comentando los dos "aspectos nuevos" del tema, añadidos en "segunda recensión": si los siervos pueden contraer matrimonio válido y si los siervos pertenecientes a señores distintos pueden contraer matrimonio sin el consentimiento de aquéllos'.

9. Cf. Weigand, *Glossen*. En este estudio uso las siglas que se relacionan en vol. 1 (SG 25.xxi–xxiv), donde Weigand presenta su *Handschriftenliste*, pero con las ampliaciones que señalé en mi estudio C. Larrainzar, 'La investigación' 57 nota 46 (en su versión italiana 85). Ahora añado además la sigla *O* = Oxford, Corpus Christi College 154, pp. 154a–184a; para las redacciones de IPA vid. *infra* nota 22.

tos 'introductorios', como es la conocida obra *IPA*.[10] Esas dos versiones *Aa Me* son sustancialmente coincidentes, pero conviene transcribir el texto de *Me* porque conserva íntegra la redacción sin correcciones ni alteraciones de otras manos, al contrario de lo que sucede en *Aa* 23. En ese códice de Admont una mano ha borrado la referencia al *liber septimus*—corrigiendo también las referencias a los *libros* que siguen—para hacer coincidir la numeración de sus *Libri* con las *Causae* tradicionales.[11] Así pues, utilizando como 'texto-base' *Me*, en el Apéndice I ofrezco una edición de *HOI* con algunas notas que orientan sobre las 'fuentes formales' de su contenido; esta obra hasta ahora nunca había sido publicada.

3. Ciertamente, del manuscrito *Aa* sorprende su organización sistemática en 'libros' al presentar el contenido de su *Decretum*, como hace en efecto *HOI*, aunque esta ordenación contiene luego en sí las divisiones tradicionales. Pero *Me* no muestra ya esa característica. ¿Es esto, pues, una peculiaridad de carácter local, singular, de esos concretos códices del *Scriptorium* de Admont? O, al contrario, ¿esos 'libros' son los 'restos' o las trazas de un antiguo estado de la obra, ya superado en el momento en que se confeccionaron los códices 23 y 43 de la *Stiftsbibliothek* austríaca? Algunos indicios permiten plantear esta segunda hipótesis o, al menos, no la hacen inverosímil ni rechazable *a priori* de modo absoluto.

De un lado, algunos sumarios de las *auctoritates* parecen haber desempeñado el papel de rúbricas a modo de capitulaciones en una sistemática antigua, que presumiblemente ordenaba las materias en 'libros' y 'capítulos', como sucedía en tantas colecciones canónicas pregracianeas. Baste pensar en la titulación más difundida de la obra, conservada en muchos códices, incluidos los más antiguos: 'Concordia discordantium

10. Cf. *Aa 23* fol. 8rv junto con *Aa 43* fols. 11r–12v, y también *Me* fols. 30ra–31ra. Sobre el manuscrito *Me* vid. la bibliografía y la presentación de sus contenidos hecha por Weigand, *Glossen* 848–50, donde dice, 849: 'Diese zwischen 1160 und 1170 in Salzburg oder Umgebung entstandene Prachthandschrift (im 18. Jh. in der Ratsbibliothek Regensburg) hat manche Besonderheiten mit Admont 23 und 43 (Aa) gemeinsam'. Ciertamente su letra recuerda a las usadas en el *Scriptorium* admonatense durante la segunda mitad del siglo XII, pero *Me* no consta catalogado entre los códices procedentes de Austria; cf. C. Keinz, C. Meyer y G. Thomas, *Catalogus Codicum Latinorum Bibliothecae Regiae Monacensis* 2.2 (Wiesbaden 1968) 92, donde se menciona escuetamente: '13004 (Rat. civ. 4) membr. in 22. s. XIII/XIV 343 fol. cum pictis litteris initialibus', y se describe su contenido así: 'Decretum Gratiani sive Concordantia discordantium canonum. Praecedunt f. 1–31 Claves titulorum cum registro capitulorum'.

11. Vid. *infra* Apéndice I. La unidad de los códices 23 y 43 de la *Stiftsbibliothek* de Admont (= *Aa*) es obvia: el texto de la *Concordia* de *Aa 23* se interrumpe en su *liber xv* que contiene C.14 (fol. 199v) y *Aa 43* comienza con su *liber xvi* que contiene C.15 (fol. 13r); ambos códices son consecutivos uno del otro. Y así también *IPA* termina en *Aa 23* con el resumen de C.14 (fol. 8r) y continúa en *Aa 43* con el resumen de C.15 *In quintadecima causa de quodam clerico agitur—copulari ualeant* (fols. 1r–11r). Sobre su composición material vid. A. Scheichl, *Studien zu Handschriften des 12. Jahrhunderts aus der Stiftsbibliothek Admont* (Staatsprüfungsarbeit *[pro manuscripto]* am Institut für Österreichische Geschichtsforschung; Wien 1999).

canonum *ac primum* de iure nature et constitutionis'.[12] O bien es significativa la rúbrica que en *Aa* (23, fol.1ra) *Me* (fol.2ra) precede a *IPA* diciendo 'incipiunt *claves titulorum* de concordia canonum discordantium'. Y, por otra parte, no deben olvidarse las observaciones de Stephan Kuttner sobre el carácter 'antiguo' de las glosas que consisten en *Allegationen*, ni la investigación de Rudolf Weigand sobre las glosas del 'segundo estrato de composición' que citan el Decreto por 'títulos', aun cuando reconozca expresamente que la ordenación de *Aa* en 'libros' no lleva a que sus glosas tomen como referencia tales divisiones sistemáticas.[13]

He aquí, pues, un conjunto de datos relevantes, pero no suficientes—a mi entender—como para elaborar una 'teoría general' sobre un supesto estadio antiguo en la formación del *Decretum*, cuya sistemática continuaría la inercia de las colecciones canónicas antiguas. No obstante, estos datos sí muestran que todavía son demasiados los aspectos que siguen en la penumbra, sobre el proceso literario de formación de la obra, y su aclaración es necesaria para comprender el sentido de los datos mismos y su propia coherencia.

---

12. Cf. el documentado estudio de P. Pinedo, 'En torno al título del Decreto de *Graciano Decretum seu Concordia discordantium canonum*', AHDE 25 (1955) 845–67; igualmente continúan siendo interesantes muchos de los comentarios de su otro estudio *'Decretum Gratiani: Dictum Gratiani', Ius Canonicum* 2 (1962) 149–66. La expresión *ac primum de iure nature et constitutionis* no suele variar en las rúbricas iniciales, salvo la transposición *constitutionis et nature* (*Pf³* 15vb, *Pk* 10ra, *Pq* 12ra, por ejemplo), a pesar de los cambios en la nominación de la obra misma. Entre otras, vid. una muestra en *Fa* (*discordantium canonum concordia ac primum de iure nature et constitutionis incipit*, fol.2rb) *Fs* (fol.1ra igual que *Fa* pero sin la palabra *incipit*), o bien *Bc* (17ra) *Hk* (8vb) *Kb* (11ra) *Se* (fols. 1ra y 5ra) que leen *concordia discordantium canonum ac primum de iure nature et constitutionis*, y también *Fi* (2ra) *Mc* (2ra) pero con la frase *de iure nature et constitutionis* ausente, tal vez eliminada al miniar la 'H' del *dictum* de apertura; también otras variantes como en *Ld* (1ra) que lee *incipit discordantium concordia canonum ac primum de iure nature et constitutionis*, o bien *Mx* (3ra) con la rúbrica *incipit concordia canonum discordantium ac primum de iure nature et constitutionis*. Esto hace todavía más elocuente la expresión de *Aa* 23 ya que escuetamente comienza su *prima pars* con las palabras *primum capitulum de iure nature et constitucionis* (fol.9r).

13. Cf. Kuttner, *Repertorium* 3–4, para quien el 'primer tipo de glosas' suelen ser 'Allegationen, Zitatenglosse, Notabilia, Nota, Rubrikenglossen'; los manuscritos que sólo incorporan este primitivo tipo de glosas, más antiguo, se distinguen por el escaso uso de los márgenes, pero la cantidad de glosas varía: desde su presencia en apenas unas pocas páginas de un códice completo, hasta la existencia de muchas glosas en una única página; no obstante, estas glosas no suelen ser abundantes ni menos forman una masa conjunta, suelen aparecer sólo en los márgenes del códice o bien como la primera de sus escrituras. Por otra parte, cf. R. Weigand, 'Romanisierungstendenzen im frühen kanonischen Recht', ZRG Kan. Abt. 69 (1983) 200–49, donde prueba la existencia de la segunda *Glossenkomposition* que originalmente cita el Decreto por 'títulos'; vid. también el prólogo de su obra, Weigand, *Glossen*, donde afirma que hizo este descubrimiento en la primavera de 1980, cuando estudiaba las glosas a D.21–D.23: menciona entonces los manuscritos que transmiten ese 'estrato de composición' según varios grupos *(Sr Tx2 Pk; Gt Bd Mb Pe Py; Ar Bl Mf Fc; Sf Mn Gn Na Va)*, añadiendo que en muchos códices son siempre glosas interlineales (425). En esa obra también dice sobre *Aa* (663): 'Dass hier wirklich der *Teil* des Dekrets und nicht etwa das *Buch* gemäss der *Introductio Hoc opus* gemeint ist, geht aus Allegationen im 2. Teil hervor, bei denen öfter ein *p.i.* vor der Distinktionenangabe zu finden ist oder mit *p.ult.* auf *de consecratione* verwiesen wird'.

4. Un examen de conjunto de *HOI* pone a la vista otro hecho que debería ser valorado. En efecto, los contenidos de *HOI* son en general una reiteración de las *quaestiones* formuladas tras el enunciado de los *casus*, en los *dicta* iniciales (*pr.* = 'principio') de las *Causae* tradicionales, a veces algo extractada y muchas otras literal. El hecho no deja de ser sorprendente si valoramos el dato de que la elaboración de *HOI* parece preceder a *IPA* por causa de sus contenidos. Y, en efecto, se impone esta reflexión: ¿cómo es que las redacciones del *Decretum* que son 'prologadas' por *IPA* dan contenido a una 'obra introductoria' como *HOI* que usa una sistemática presumiblemente anterior y muy antigua?, ¿cómo es que su contenido sustancial son parte de los 'principios' *(pr.)* de las *Causae* de las otras redacciones más recientes?

A mi entender, el hecho no resulta contradictorio si se entienden rectamente las etapas diacrónicas de composición del *Decretum* y se valoran las características particulares de los distintos códices. El caso del manuscrito *Aa* es singularísimo, y se ha comentado en el *XII Congreso Internacional* de Washington: desde distintas perspectivas, somos varios quienes coincidimos en afirmar que en *Aa* se mezclan 'informaciones' de distintos estadios o momentos temporales de las redacciones.[14] Y, por tanto, puede suceder que *HOI* sea 'antigua' por su estructura sistemática y también 'reciente' por sus contenidos: en cierto modo su composición pudo obedecer a la 'novedad' que supuso una *nueva redacción* de los *casus* de las *Causae*, si efectivamente esto aconteció. Ninguna mejor 'introducción' a la obra podría hacerse entonces que la compilación concentrada de las *quaestiones* formuladas sobre los *casus* en esos 'principios' *(pr.)* de las Causas.

Este aspecto de *novedad* viene ya sugerido por la concreta información sobre los cinco primeros 'libros': su brevedad impone la pespectiva de un estado de análisis (de esas partes de la obra) en cierto modo incipiente por su más reciente composición (?) o ulterior revisión o, si no, en 'estado de desarrollo' porque el texto se hubiera sometido a modificaciones parciales. Y en igual sentido deberían valorarse las omisiones y discrepancias que se advierten comparando *HOI* con los 'principios' de algunas *Causae* según la redacción del Decreto divulgado, o también el hecho de que el códice *Sg* de Sankt Gallen muestre una redacción diversa de los *casus*.[15]

14. Vid. mi relación en el *Congreso Internacional* de Washington del año 2004 (*supra* nota 2), o la presentada por T. Lenherr, 'Zur Redaktionsgeschichte von C.23 q.5 in der "1. Rezension" von Gratians Dekret (The Making of a *Quaestio*)'. En este sentido se había expresado también L. P. Tarin, '*An secularibus litteris oporteat eos esse eruditos?* El texto de D.37 en las etapas antiguas del Decreto de Graciano' en: *La cultura giuridico-canonica* 469–511.

15. Cf. C. Larrainzar, 'El borrador de la *Concordia* de Graciano: Sankt Gallen, *Stiftsbibliothek* MS 673 (= Sg)', *Ius Ecclesiae* 11 (1999) 593–666. Y he valorado ese dato también en mi otro estudio titulado 'Datos sobre la antigüedad del manuscrito *Sg*: su redacción de C.27 q.2' en: *Panta rei. Studi dedicati a Manlio Bellomo* (5 voll. ; Roma 2004) 3.205–37: 'no debe menospreciarse—reitero ahí—el hecho de que los distintos *incipit* de sus Causas (todos con sus mayúsculas miniadas) apenas coincidan con los propios de la *Concordia* más antigua o del *Decretum* divulgado'. Y no son sólo los comienzos de las Causas; a veces se comprueba también una literalidad diversa en la redacción de los *casus* enunciados.

Así pues, distinguiendo materias y materias, bien podría aceptarse la mayor antigüedad de *HOI* respecto de *IPA* en algunos aspectos y también una cierta contemporaneidad de composición entre ambas: sin duda la estructura sistemática de *HOI* sería la más antigua y, según qué materias, nada obstaría a que conservase a veces un esquema de *quaestiones* más próximo a las primeras redacciones: por ejemplo, en C.29. Con todo, es obvio que este juicio no puede ser definitivo sin un previo estudio sobre *IPA* y un examen detallado de sus contenidos.

5. El análisis de *IPA* resulta más complejo de lo que pudiera parecer a primera vista, pues hoy conocemos casi un centenar de manuscritos que nos transmiten la obra íntegra o fragmentada: un número elevadísimo frente al reducido grupo de códices mencionado por Schulte en el siglo XIX, y un número muy superior a los manuscritos con *IPA* estudiados luego por Jacqueline Rambaud.[16] En este momento no es mi intención ni concluir ni cerrar las múltiples cuestiones que suscita la investigación sobre *IPA:* requiere una mayor atención y, sobre todo, su comentario reclama mayor espacio editorial. Nos bastará ahora, pues, con aportar algunos datos que prueban la complejidad del tema y con orientar las observaciones hacia conclusiones prácticas.

De entrada debería considerarse la 'irregular' transmisión codicológica de *IPA* en los diversos manuscritos: en unos introduce y precede al texto del *Decretum,* en otros aparece fragmentada como parte de la compilación gracianea y prologando 'dentro' del texto sus respectivas secciones sistemáticas; en el singular caso de *Fd* ordena, fragmentada, la colección de sus *Adiciones boloñesas,* e incluso existe una reducida tradición manuscrita, pero existe (!), que la transmite como obra autónoma, independiente de la compilación gracianea.

Otro aspecto es su contenido: no son pocos los códices que la amplían con la referencia a una C.37 para extraer ahí el contenido de la *tertia pars* o tratado *de consecratione.* El hecho cierto, interesante por demás, es que parece existir una evolución de la textualidad de *IPA* en paralelo con el proceso de transformación o ampliación del *Decretum:* una buena muestra es la omisión del período *De notitia apocriphorum librorum* en códices antiguos (por ejemplo en *Aa*[add. pc] *Am Bc Fa*[add. pc] *Fd Mk Mv Pf*[1] *Sl,* o también en la versión independiente conservada en el manuscrito de Oxford, Corpus Christi College 154 p.154a), presente en muchos otros códices (por ejemplo en *Ab Bp Br Ch Mc Mz Pk Po Pq Pu Sp*), pues debe ponerse en relación con la ampliación de D.15 c.3;

16. Vid. von Schulte, 'Zur Geschichte' 24–26; y Rambaud-Buhot, 'Les divers types' 399–401. Es innegable que la investigación desarrollada durante la segunda mitad del siglo XX, sobre la tradición manuscrita del *Decretum Gratiani,* ha superado con creces la perspectiva de estos autores. Cf. sus datos con los dos volúmens de Weigand, *Glossen.*

es más, ese período se ampliará después con la frase *Que scripture quibus temporibus sunt legende*, como muestran *Bs Mf* por ejemplo.

Por tanto, esos modos 'codicológicos' diversos de presentación o de transmisión de *IPA* no son casuales y, a mi entender, deberían ponerse en relación con los momentos diacrónicos o etapas que fueron forjando las redacciones del *Decretum:* casi con toda seguridad podría decirse que esa diversa presentación responde a 'concretos momentos' por los que la obra gracianea pasó hasta convertirse en un texto tan estandarizado como *vulgatum.* Y ahí estaría la explicación de por qué *IPA* aparece en los códices más tempranos, unida al texto sustantivo de la *Concordia*, casi a modo de un 'prólogo' propio, y luego desaparece gradualmente en las copias más tardías, una vez consolidado el desarrollo de la doctrina decretista. Más todavía: si la composición de *IPA* en un contexto docente fue instrumento para ir ordenando las ampliaciones o la transformación de la *Concordia* antigua (mediante la adición de nuevas *auctoritates* y algunos nuevos *dicta*, como se desprende de *Fd*), es lógico que en sus comienzos *IPA* se copiara en íntima relación con ese *Decretum* extenso que ayudó a formar.

6. Ya sólo la vista de esta pluralidad compleja de situaciones y redacciones permite descartar hoy como edición de *IPA* la impresa por la *Biblioteca Casinensis* a finales del siglo XIX, en su descripción del manuscrito *Mv.* Ni ese texto es fiable del original que transcribe, pues contiene muchos errores, ni la tradición textual de *IPA* según *Mv* parece responder al modelo más fiable que nos lleve a su *safe text*, aun cuando sea una tradición antigua.[17] En el Apéndice II presento una edición parcial de *IPA:* sólo su resumen del contenido de la *prima pars* del *Decretum*, y provisional porque se funda en algunos pocos códices que trabajaron con modelos antiguos. Ahora nos sirve para entender mejor los comentarios que siguen.

En efecto, tomando como referencia ese resumen de la *prima pars* según *IPA*, se comprueba que *Mv* comparte con *Pf¹* la omisión de la frase *De notitia apocriphorum librorum*, como sería propio del original antiguo. Pero comparte también con *Pf¹* defectos de copia que no existen en otros valiosos códices antiguos; en concreto estas cuatro omisiones: (i) la primera mención *uel non*, (ii) *episcopi consecrentur—quo tempore* por

17. Vid. *Bibliotheca Casinensis seu Codicum Manuscriptorum qui in tabulario Casinensi asservantur* (2 voll.; Montecasino 1875) 2.169–96. En estas páginas se describe el *Codex LXIV signatus numeris exterioribus 64 et 89, interiori vero 343. Pluteo Z*, comenzando por esta presentación: 'Codex membranaceus in folio, longitudinis metri 41/°, latitudinis 27/°, paginarum 538 duplici columna distinctarum, characteribus Latinis Saec. XII, vel sequentis ineuntis. Continet Decretum Gratiani cum paucis marginalibus scholiis'. Así pues, no se hace propiamente una edición autónoma de *IPA*, sino la descripción de los contenidos del códice 64 de Montecasino, señalando por páginas los comienzos de las distintas partes sistemáticas del *Decretum Gratiani* y, con este motivo, se van copiando los distintos fragmentos de *IPA* que las introducen.

homeoteleuton de *quo tempore,* (iii) *et ordinandus,* (iv) la tercera expresión *in ea.* Y a esto se añade la modificación que cambia *archiepiscopus* por *archiepiscopi* concordando este sujeto con el verbo *debeant* en vez del *debeat* antiguo. Estas coincidencias no pueden ser casuales, más todavía valorando el hecho de que *Pf¹* cambia la textualidad de su modelo, cuya redacción sigue mostrando *Mv.* Y, con todo, el modelo inmediato de *Pf¹* no es *Mv* porque éste presenta otras omisiones de texto amplias que no se dan en *Pf¹*: las frases *De his quoque qui in ecclesia non corde set uoce psallere student* y *De clericis ab episcopis non ordinandis.*

Si ahora se comparan *Mv Pf¹* con *Fd,* el contraste entre estos manuscritos muestra aspectos curiosos, todos de gran interés: primero la proximidad de *Fd* al arquetipo original frente a *Mv Pf¹,* segundo la mayor proximidad del modelo directo de *Mv* con *Fd* y, tercero, la conexión entre *Mv Pf¹* desde un modelo intermedio. De un lado, *Fd* posee en efecto lecturas propias de mayor calidad como, por ejemplo, la presencia de un *aut* al redactar el período *sint distribuendi, aut semel ordinatus,* la expresión *ratiociniorum causas uel,* otras en el período *aliquis—suscipiat,* la lectura *discedentibus* (en vez de *dissidentibus*) o bien *non liceat* (en vez de *non licet*) o *conferre debeat* (en vez de *ferre debeat*). De otro, la mano *G* del códice ha procurado sanar los defectos de lecturas que pudieran ser sustanciales.[18] A mi entender, sucede esto claramente en las correcciones de las lecciones *scripturarum, electionem, promoueri, intersticiis, obedientia* o bien *exerceant.* Ese trabajo de revisión no elimina algunos errores, como la omisión *quam prouincialium, decretalium,* cuya corrección parece haber sido advertida primero y luego tal vez olvidada.

En este marco, la proximidad entre *Mv Fd* se hace patente en la coincidencia de algunas lecturas significativas, frente a las variantes de *Pf¹,* como son entre otras las lecciones *quisquis, conuersione* (en vez de *conuersatione*), *aliorsum habuerit, libertate* (en vez de *liberalitate*), *propter timorem Dei* o el correcto uso de la palabra *causa* en distintos lugares; en algunos momentos se advierte incluso una coincidencia en los modos de escritura como *optineat* (pero esto no es uniforme, pues se lee *obtineant* más adelante), *correctione* o *quinque.* Y, a su vez, las correciones de los márgenes de *Pf¹* muestran que pretendieron ajustarse a un modelo que coincide con las lecturas de *Fd,* algo que se con-

18. Cf. C. Larrainzar, 'El Decreto de Graciano del códice *Fd* (= Firenze, Biblioteca Nazionale Centrale, Conventi Soppressi A.I 402)', *Ius Ecclesiae* 10 (1998) 421–89. La identificación de esta mano y el examen diacrónico de sus tareas en contraste con las otras distinguidas es fundamental para comprender el modo de composición de ese códice florentino 402 (= *Fd*) y la singular información que aporta para comprender la 'historia' (diacrónica) de formación del *Decretum.* En este sentido, vid. los análisis hechos por T. Lenherr, 'Die vier Fassungen von C.3 q.1 d.p.c.6 im *Decretum Gratiani.* Zugleich ein Einblick in die neueste Diskussion um das Werden von Gratians Dekret', AKKR 169 (2000) 353–81; Tarin, *An secularibus litteris;* J. M. Viejo-Ximénez, *'An inter uouentes possit esse matrimonium.* El texto de C.27 q.1 en los manuscritos antiguos del Decreto de Graciano', *Initium* 9 (2004) 73–126.

firma luego por la coincidencia de lecturas correctas entre *Pf¹ Fd* frente a las lecciones correlativas de *Mv.*

7. En fin, he aquí un panorama de problemas filológicos que confirman la riqueza de crítica textual que está por hacer y por descubrir sobre el texto íntegro de *IPA*. La ordenación de todos los manuscritos es, pues, una de las primeras tareas para acometer esta empresa; por eso, describiré ahora el estado actual de mi investigación sobre este aspecto, haciendo unas primeras agrupaciones de manuscritos según la información que aportan sobre *IPA* y su forma de presentación.

De momento, distingo tres grupos de códices.

(i) La introducción *IPA* es copiada 'dentro' del Decreto, como parte de su texto y así fragmentada según sus causas o partes sistemáticas, en un total de 10 manuscritos. Ocho de éstos la conservan íntegra: *Bl Ch Fa Fd Mc Mv Pv Sl.* Los otros dos, *He Pd,* sólo conservan algunos fragmentos: *He* contiene la redacción ampliada con el extracto del tratado *de cons.* como C.37 (fol. 230) y *Pd* carece de esa ampliación, como ya señaló Weigand corrigiendo la descripción del manuscrito hecha en su día por Kéjr.

(ii) Aparece como una introducción propia del Decreto, que precede a su texto, en un total de 82 códices, entre los que deben distinguirse dos grupos: un total de 64 manuscritos (56 sin la adición de C.37 y otros 8 códices más con esa adición) que conservan *IPA* íntegra, y 18 códices más (17 sin la adición y uno más con ese resumen de C.37) que sólo conservan fragmentos más o menos extensos de *IPA.* En estos dos grupos, pues, conviene distinguir siempre entre los manuscritos que poseen la ampliación de C.37 y los otros que carecen de ella; la relación de todos estos códices es como sigue:

a) De un lado, *IPA* se conserva completa en los manuscritos de Arras, BM 585 (493) y en los códices *Ad Am Bc Bi Cc Cg Ck Cv Er Es Fb Fc Gb Gd Gg Gt Hk Hl In Iv Ka Kb Kq La Lb Li Lp Mb Me Mg Mh Mk Mm Mq Pe Pf¹ Pk Pl Pn Py Qa Sa Sb Sf So Sq Tx Ty Tz Vd Vo Vp Vz.* Y también está completa en los códices *Aa Si* aunque dividida en dos partes por causa de los dos códices distintos en que se ha copiado el *Decretum;* en este sentido no deja de ser curioso que *Si* haga su partición al final de C.12, que es donde concluyen también los conocidos manuscritos *Bc P.* De otro, los manuscritos *Ab Bs Dh Mf Po Sp Sr Vl* también presentan *IPA* completa, y ampliada además con el resumen de esa C.37 final.[19]

19. Cf. las redacciones completas en estos códices: Arras, BM 585 (493) fols. 1ra–6ra, *Aa* (23 1r–8r, 43 1r–11r), *Ad* (25ra–33va), *Am* (1ra–8vb), *Bc* (1ra–15rb), *Bi* (1ra–10ra), *Cc* (1ra–11rb), *Cg* (1va–9rb con algunas singularidades entre C.29–C.30), *Ck* (3ra–9vb), *Cv* (1ra–9ra), *Er* (1ra–10vb), *Es* (1–7), *Fb* (1ra–8rb), *Fc* (18ra–25rb), *Gb* (1ra–10rb), *Gd* (1ra–8va), *Gg* (1va–8va), *Gt* (3ra–14rb), *Hk* (1v–8vb), *Hl* (1ra–9vb), *In* (1ra–10rb), *Iv* (1ra–11vb), *Ka* (2ra–8vb), *Kb* (1va–10rb), *Kq* (1ra–11va), *La* (1ra–7ra), *Lb* (4ra–12vb), *Li* (1ra–8va), *Lp* (1r–8r), *Mb* (2ra–12rb), *Me* (2ra–9va), *Mg* (1ra–9vb), *Mh* (1ra–6rb), *Mk* (1ra–9vb), *Mm* (1ra–6ra), *Mq* (4ra–17vb), *Pe* (1ra–10vb), *Pf¹* (3ra–15rb), *Pk* (1ra–9vb), *Pl* (1ra–10ra), *Pn* (3ra–11rb), *Py* (1–12), *Qa* (1r–19vb pero con el folio inicial raspado y así se

b) Se conservan sólo partes o fragmentos de *IPA* en los códices *Ar* (desde el final de
C.2 al comienzo de C.7), *Cd* (desde C.10), *Fe* (el fragmento final), *Fi* (el fragmento final),
Lg (desde el final de C.6 a C.32), *Lm* (desde las palabras finales de C.6), *Mo* (desde C.4),
Mt (desde C.1), *Mx Ol* (hasta C.32), *Pq* (faltan C.26 a C.32), *Pz Ro* (los párrafos finales),
Tr (hasta C.33), *Ts Vc* (hasta C.24), *Vr* (hasta C.22). Y también hay fragmentos en *Ca*,
que añade la ampliación de C.37 a diferencia de todos los otros.[20]

(iii) Finalmente, *IPA* aparece como obra 'independiente' del *Decretum:* es decir, copiada como una obra *a se*, autónoma y separada de la compilación gracianea, en un
total de 4 manuscritos: *Bp* (una copia independiente añadida por una tardía mano al
códice del Decreto), *Br Mz* (copiadas ambas al final códice por los mismos copistas que
han transcrito el Decreto, y tras un *explicit* expreso en el caso de *Br*).[21] Y también en otro
códice más: el manuscrito de Oxford, Corpus Christi College 154, que contiene la suma
de *Sicardus* de Cremona y copia el texto de *IPA* en sus pp. 154a–184a.

Examinando la textualidad de *IPA*, los primeros resultados de mi investigación
conducen a distinguir provisionalmente entre unas y otras redacciones: una primera
antiquísima, próxima a lo que podría ser un 'arquetipo' original, en los manuscritos *O
Aa Fd Bc Mk Fa Sl Ch*, por ejemplo; luego otros códices, también antiguos, pero cuya redacción muestra ya concretas 'desviaciones' (por ejemplo *Mv Pf¹*), que a su vez enlazan
con un tercer grupo que presenta un tipo estándar de redacción como 'introducción'
al Decreto, ya algo ampliada (por ejemplo, en los códices *Bp Mc Pq Pv*). Y, aparte todo
esto, existe la transmisión de una redacción de *IPA* como obra independiente, según
muestran los códices *Br Mz Pk*, por ejemplo.[22] En suma, de todos los datos expuestos

conserva sólo *In prima parte <agitur . . . > de reparatione lapsorum—copulari ualeant*), *Sa* (1ra–7va), *Sb* (1ra–10va),
Sf (1ra–6ra), *Si* (1ra–8ra hasta C.12 y 282rb–291vb de C.13 a C.36), *So* (2ra–11rb), *Sq* (1va–10ra), *Tx* (1ra–9vb), *Ty*
(1ra–7ra), *Tz* (3ra–10vb), *Vd* (1ra–8ra), *Vo* (1ra–14rb), *Vp* (xviira–xxivrb), *Vz* (1ra–10vb). Y aparece con la adición
de C.37 en los manuscritos: *Ab* (1ra–12ra), *Bs* (1ra–10rb con la adición de C.37 al comenzar *de cons.* en fols.
267vb–268va), *Dh* (1r–13r con peculiaridades al comienzo de C.3), *Mf* (1ra–6vb), *Po* (4ra–11ra y en fol.3vb su resumen de C.37), *Sp* (1ra–8vb), *Sr* (1ra–12rb), *Vl* (1ra–9vb).

20. Se encuentran fragmentos más o menos extensos de *IPA* en estos códices: *Ar* (173rv), *Cd* (2ra–6ra), *Fe*
(1rab), *Fi* (1ra–2ra), *Lg* (1r–3v), *Lm* (5ra–6ra), *Mo* (1ra–8va), *Mt* (9–20), *Mx* (2r), *Ol* (3ra–9vb), *Pq* (3ra–12ra), *Pz*
(1ra–vb sólo los párrafos finales y en fols.2ra–4va fragmentos de otra copia de *IPA*), *Ro* (2ra–2va), *Tr* (1ra–8vb),
Ts (2ra-b y fols.3ra–9rb), *Vc* (1ra–8vb), *Vr* (5ra–12va). Y los fragmentos conservados en *Ca* (3ra–9vb y 10ra, con
algunas peculiaridades en C.3) muestran también el resumen de C.37.

21. Vid. el texto de *IPA* en *Bp* (294va–295vb), *Br* (227va–233vb) y *Mz* (274rb–281vb), pero las tres son copias
de características muy distintas. Según Rambaud, 'Les divers types' 400: 'Toute la doctrine de Gratien est bien
exposée en ces quelques lignes *[IPA]* et nous n'hésiterons pas à qualifier ce texte d'abrégé si nous avions la certi-
tude qu'il ait jamais eu une existence indépendante. Mais nous ne l'avons jamais rencontré jusqu'à présent que
dans les manuscrits du Décret et faissant corps avec lui: même écriture, même ornementation, même parchemin'. Sin embargo, pienso que la existencia real de esa tradición manuscrita no lleva necesariamente hacia estas
valoraciones: vid. *infra* notas 22 y 23.

22. De un lado, el códice de Oxford (= *O*) es una excelente copia 'independiente' de la redacción más antigua. De otro, claramente *IPA* ha dejado de ser una 'introducción' al *Decretum* en *Br*, al ser transcrita después de

bien puede deducirse que todavía queda por delante una intensa tarea ecdótica para alcanzar un texto crítico de *IPA* que sea filológicamente aceptable.

8. Con este panorama delante, pienso que todo ese trabajo sobre *IPA* o cualquier progreso filológico en esa dirección serán de gran utilidad para una posterior valoración de los códices que nos transmiten las redacciones del *Decretum Gratiani*. En efecto, si el texto de *IPA* se entiende en cierto modo como un *texte vivant* y se sitúa en perspectiva diacrónica, me parece claro que por esta vía podrían obtenerse criterios para ordenar gradualmente la vasta tradición de los códices antiguos del *Decretum*. Esto sería posible si en efecto existiera una correspondencia o un cierto paralelismo entre las 'familias' o agrupaciones de códices formadas a partir de *IPA* y los contenidos de las redacciones del *Decretum* más o menos estandarizadas, transmitidas por esas distintas copias que la utilizan a modo de prólogo en la compilación gracianea.

No obstante, sea cual fuere el resultado de esta línea de trabajo, pienso que el correcto tratamiento de *IPA*—como el estudio sobre *HOI* también—exige ya una muy precisa corrección de los modos en que hasta ahora se venían considerando ambas obras. Según Jacqueline Rambaud, por ejemplo, *IPA* es un formidable ejemplo de la literatura *'post' Decretum* que manifiesta cómo éste fue entendido e interpretado desde sus fechas más tempranas; en su opinión, no hay inconveniente en agrupar esta obra con otras consideradas análogas, porque muestran la primera actividad de enseñanza 'con' el Decreto: por ejemplo, la abreviación *Quoniam egestas* y otras tablas de contenidos o aquellas otras obras agrupadas bajo el rótulo de 'abreviaciones' del Decreto de Graciano.[23] En mi opinión, estos enfoques deben ser corregidos a fin de considerar ya *IPA* como una

---

un *explicit* por quienes han copiado el Decreto y sin que esto sea una defectuosa ubicación de los folios, ya que los ocho primeros folios de ese códice llevan numeración propia como 'cuadernillo I'. Es indudable que *Br* depende de un modelo análogo a *Pk* por la coincidencia entre ambos de sus lecciones más singulares (vid. Apéndice II): *archipresbiteris* en vez del *archiepiscopis* primero, la omisión del segundo *episcopi, si se* en vez de *si sese*, *suscipiant* en vez de *suscipiat, dignitate* en vez de *potestate, audire* en vez de *adire* y *exequantur* en vez de *exequentur*. Por otra parte, *Mz* parece estar en inmediata relación con *Br* por la coincidencia total de sus lecturas, aquí no corregidas, en lo que son corrupciones del modelo antiguo; una muestra entre otras, por ejemplo: *liberare* en vez de *deliberare*, la omisión *de locis* o bien el escribir de igual modo *quia ss.* por *qui a suis, libertate* en vez de *liberalitate, uocibus* en vez de *uocis* o también *archiepiscopis* con el verbo *deferre* en vez de *archiepiscopus* con el verbo *ferre*. A su vez, la propia dependencia de *Mz* del modelo *Pk* se muestra en la lección *ex eis* en vez del *eis* segundo, que es única de ambos códices, aparte el hecho de darse las coincidencias entre *Br Pk* ya comentadas.

23. Cf. Rambaud-Buhot, 'Les divers types' 411, donde expresa esta valoración conclusiva: 'Nous avons ainsi passé en revue les principaux types d'abrégés qu'il nous a été donné de rencontrer. Ils n'ont de commun entre eux que le but qu'ils poursuivent: substituer à l'énorme compilation de Gratien un ouvrage qui, tout en donnant l'essentiel de la doctrine exposée dans le Décret, sera d'un maniement plus facile et d'une consultation plus rapide'. A mi entender, no fue exactamente esto lo que motivó la composición de *IPA* ni tampoco una tal finalidad explica su génesis: más bien, lo contrario. Por otra parte, la tradición manuscrita de *IPA* como obra 'independiente' (vid. *supra* nota 21) no es necesariamente 'tardía', como demuestra la redacción del manuscrito de Oxford, Corpus Christi College 154.

pieza íntimamente unida a los materiales compuestos o usados en el 'taller de Graciano' para la formación de su *Decretum*.

Según he comentado en otras ocasiones, a partir del examen del manuscrito florentino *Fd*, el *Decretum* es el resultado de una fusión de elementos independientes, entre los que aparecen todos esos fragmentos 'introductorios' *(claves titulorum,* dicen *Aa Me)* que, en un determinado momento, se integran luego formando la 'introducción' *IPA*, a su vez copiada en unidad—'material' o de códice, y 'formal' o de texto—para preceder a la *Concordia* de Graciano.[24] En suma, la génesis de *IPA* parece estar íntimamente unida al proceso interno de la formación literaria del *Decretum Gratiani*, al margen de que luego haya servido también para las actividades docentes de la incipiente Escuela de canonistas y, más tarde, quedara totalmente superada por sus desarrollos.

Apéndice I
Edicion de *Hoc opus inscribitur* segun *Me (Aa)*

Esta edición sigue la versión de *Me* fols. 30ra–31ra (= *Aa* 23 fols. 8rv, *Aa* 43 fols. 11r–12v con ligeras variantes). En *Aa* 23 una mano distinta a la del copista enmienda lo transcrito para hacer que coincidan la numeración de los *libri* con la numeración de las *causae* del Decreto divulgado: se ha borrado la referencia al *liber septimus* (= C.6) y se corrige luego la numeración de los libros que siguen, desde *liber viii* hasta *liber xv,* que entonces pasan a ser erróneamente *liber vii* (= C.7) hasta el *liber xiv.* Pero esta corrección no lleva a ninguna duplicación ni confusión en *Aa* 43: de igual modo que *Aa* 23 concluye con C.14 y a pesar de la modificación de su versión de *HOI* en la numeración de libros, *Aa* 43 comienza su texto de la *Concordia* en C.15 y continúa su texto de *HOI* con el resumen del *liber xvi.* Por tanto, la manipulación del texto de *HOI* en *Aa* 23 es posterior y ajena a la composición del códice.

HOC OPVS INSCRIBITVR

DE CONCORDIA DISCORDANTIVM CANONVM

QVOD A QVODAM GRATIANO COMPOSITVM IN LIBROS XXXVII EST DISTINCTVM

<1> PRIMVS LIBER continet diuisiones: <1> diffinitiones necnon et differentias legum tam secularium quam ecclesiasticarum et quomodo uel a quibus uel quando sint institute, <2> de electione quoque seu ordinatione clericorum.[i]

---

24. Vid. Larrainzar, 'El Decreto de Graciano'; y la explicación compendiada que hice idem, 'La firma boloñesa'. La investigación del Profesor Viejo-Ximénez sobre los textos romanos del Decreto usa mis descripciones con método y ha obtenido excelentes resultados, cf. J. M. Viejo-Ximénez, 'El Derecho romano *nuevo* en el Decreto de Graciano', ZRG Kan. Abt. 88 (2002) 1–19; y Idem, 'La recepción del Derecho romano en el Derecho canónico', *Ius Ecclesiae* 14 (2002) 375–414, cuya versión italiana fue publicada en: *La cultura giuridico-canonica* 157–209.

i. Aa 23 fol. 27v *in margine habet glossam ad locum* D.23 pr. *quae notat novae materiae initium sic dicens* tractatus de electione et de clericorum consecratione.

<2> SECVNDVS continet de scienter seu ignoranter a simoniacis ordinatis et de ordinationibus que per pecuniam fiunt.[ii]

<3> TERTIVS docet quibus accusantibus uel testificantibus quilibet sint conuincendi, quo iudice quisque dampnari uel absolui debeat, <q.5> si deficientibus accusatoribus sit accusatus cogendus ad purgationem, <q.8> quomodo accusationes fieri debeant, an in scriptis an sine scripto, et de appellationibus quomodo sint faciende.[iii]

<4–5> De eodem continet QVARTVS ET QVINTVS.

<6> IN SEXTO. Queritur <q.2> quociens sit aliquis uocandus ad causam antequam sententiam dampnationis accipiat, <q.3> an per procuratorem causam suam agere ualeat qui per semetipsum ad diem cause adesse non potest, <q.4> an absque sinodali sententia sit dampnandus, <q.6> qua pena plectendi sint qui quod intulerunt probare ualent.[iv]

<7> SEPTIMVS. Item de modis accusandi continet.

<8> IN OCTAVO. Queritur <q.1> utrum uiuente episcopo alius possit in loco eius succedere, <q.2> et an ille cathedram suam ualeat reposcere quam sua intercessione alter accepit et a quibus de causis transmigrationes liceat fieri de ecclesiis ad alias ecclesias.[v]

<9> IN NONO. De ordinationibus episcoporum agitur quomodo uel quales ordinentur, <q.1> an liceat episcopo successorem sibi constituere.[vi]

<10> IN DECIMO. Queritur <q.1> an ordinatio que ab excommunicatis facta est aliquo modo rata possit haberi, <q.2> an liceat episcopo uel archiepiscopo uel patriarche clericos alterius sine propriis litteris ordinare, <q.3> an archiepiscopus clericos sui suffraganei illo insonsulto dampnare uel dampnatos possit absoluere.[vii]

<11> IN VNDECIMO. Queritur <q.1> an basilice a laicis facte cum omni dote sua ad ordinationem episcopi pertineant, <q.2> an res ecclesiarum episcopis usurpare liceat, <q.3> quid nomine cathedre a sacerdotibus suis exigere ualeant.[viii]

<12> IN DVODECIMO. Queritur <q.1> an clericus ante secularem sit producendus <qq.2–3> et de clericis qui episcopis suis obedire contempserunt, necnon de excommunicationibus que iniuste facte fuerint, de his quoque qui excommunicatis communicant.[ix]

<13> IN TERTIODECIMO. Queritur <q.1> an clericis liceat proprium habere, <q.2> an res ecclesie que date sunt ab eis possint constare aliqua firmitate his qui eas acceperunt, <q.4> si de suis et ecclesie rebus aliqua acquisisse noscuntur an ecclesie uel sibi uel utrisque iure peruenant, <q.5> si testamenta liceat eis conficere et que res ecclesiarum ab eis non sint alienande.[x]

---

ii. *Ex* D.101 d.p.c.1.

iii. *Ex* C.1 q.7 d.p.c.27, C.2 pr., *ex* C.2 q.5 *et amplius* q.8.

iv. *Idem* C.5 pr. *sine mentione seu* q.1 *seu* q.5.   v. *Idem* C.7 pr. *sed alio modo* q.1 *et amplius* q.2.

vi. *Idem* C.8 pr. *sine mentione* qq.2–5.   vii. *Idem* C.9 pr.

viii. *Idem* C.10 pr.   ix. *Idem* C.11 pr. *sed sola* q.1.

x. *Idem* C.12 pr. *sine mentione* q.3 *et alio modo* q.4 *ampliusque* q.5.

<14> IN QVATUORDECIMO. Queritur <q.1> si diocesani baptismalis ecclesie domicilia sua in aliam diocesim transtulerint, utrum apud priorem ecclesiam debeant exequias suas celebrare et persoluere decimas <q.2> et an per sepultura mortuorum aliquid sit exigendum.[xi]

<15> IN QVINTODECIMO. Queritur <q.1> si canonici ualeant sua repetere, <q.2> si per ecclesia sua ualeant testimonium ferre, <q.4> an liceat clericis uel laicis usuras expetere, <q.5> si elemosine de usuris fieri possint, <q.6> an usurarii penitentiam agere ualeant nisi quod male acceperint restituant.[xii]

<16> IN SEXTODECIMO *(add. LIBRO Aa)*. Queritur <q.1> an ea que mente alienata fiunt sint imputanda, <q.2> si pro impensis patrociniis liceat clericis munera exigere, <q.3> an rei confessio aduersus aliquem admitti debeat, <q.4> an die dominico causa cuiusquam sit uentilanda, <q.6> an confessio cruciantibus sit extorquenda, <q.7> si absque sinodali audientia episcopus ualeat sacerdotem dampnare.[xiii]

<17> IN SEPTEMDECIMO. Queritur <q.1> utrum monachis liceat officia papalia celebrare, penitentiam dare et baptizare. <q.2> Si contigerit eos capellas habere episcopali beneficio, an ab eis sint instituende an ab episcopo. <q.4> Si ecclesia aduersus ecclesiam prescribat an etiam monasterium aduersus ecclesiam prescribere possit, <q.7> et de laicis quod ecclesiasticas tradere dignitates uel ordinare non ualeant.[xiv]

<18> IN OCTODECIMO. Queritur <q.1> de clerico qui infirmitate grauatus monachum se fieri dixerit an liceat ei priusquam conualerit a proposito discedere, <q.2> si ecclesia et beneficia ei reddenda sint que prius libera uoluntate refutauit, <q.3> si contigisset eum se et sua monasterio tradidisse an licentia abbatis licet ei ad priora redire.[xv]

<19> IN NONODECIMO. Queritur <q.1> si de monasterio quis ordinatus episcopus, an monasterium possit petere que ab eo sibi acquisita an episcopalis ecclesia possit sibi uendicare que monasterio fuerant contradita, <q.2> an per episcopum abbas sit eligendus et ordinandus an tamen monasterio a propriis fratribus sit instituendus.[xvi]

<20> IN VIGESIMO. Queritur <q.1> si episcopus debeat permittere ut relictis propriis ecclesiis clerici monasterium ingrediantur <q.2> aut si episcopus licentia dare noluerit an eo inuito monasterium possint adire, <q.3> si contigerit ipsos regulares canonicos suos esse, utrum concedendus sit eis monasterii ingressus.[xvii]

<21> IN VIGESIMOPRIMO. Queritur <q.1> si in puericie annis traditi cogantur religionis propositum tenere, <q.2> si propter parentum voluntatem tonsuram uel religionis uestem quis in puericia accipiat an possit sibi detrahi uel non, <q.3> qui propter uoluntatem propriam cuculla induitur si cogatur eam retinere an non, <q.4> si ab uno monasterio in aliud districtius liceat transire.[xviii]

---

xi. *Alio modo* C.13 pr.

xii. *Idem* C.14 pr. *sed alio modo* q.2 *et sine mentione* q.3.

xiii. *Idem* C.15 pr. *sed alio modo* q.3 *et sine mentione seu* q.5 *seu* q.8.

xiv. *Idem* C.16 pr. *sine mentione seu* q.3 *seu* qq.5–6 *et alio modo* q.7.

xv. *Idem* C.17 pr. *sine mentione* q.4.   xvi. *Idem* C.18 pr.

xvii. *Idem* C.19 pr.   xviii. *Idem* C.20 pr.

<22> IN VIGESIMOSECVNDO. Queritur <q.1> an clericus in duabus ecclesiis possit conscribi, <q.2> si unam uoluerit relinquere an liceat ei ad aliam transire, <q.3> an procurationes secularium negotiorum clericis liceat suscipere, <q.4> an claris et fulgidis uestibus eis ornari expediat, <q.5> an ab episcopo correpti suum officium relinquere et ad secularem iudicem confugere ualeant.[xix]

<23> IN VIGESIMOTERTIO. Queritur <q.1> an iuramentum sit prestandum, <q.2> si sit periurus qui iurat falsum quod putat uerum, <q.4> si constiterit illicitum esse quod iuratur an sit seruandum, <q.5> si sit ille reus periurii qui iurantem contra hoc quod iurauit facere compellit.[xx]

<24> IN VIGESIMOQVARTO. Queritur <q.1> an militare sit peccatum, <q.3> an iniuria sociorum armis sit propulsanda, <q.4> an uindicta sit inferenda, <q.5> an sit peccatum iudici uel ministro reos occidere, <q.6> an mali sint cogendi ad bonum, <q.7> an heretici suis rebus sint expoliandi et qui possidet ab hereticis ablata an dicatur possidere aliena, <q.8> an episcopis uel quibuslibet clericis liceat sua auctoritate uel apostolico uel imperatoris precepto arma mouere.[xxi]

<25> IN VIGESIMOQVINTO. Queritur <q.1> an lapsos in heresim possit aliquos officio priuare uel sententia notare uel ordinare, <q.2> an post mortem aliquis possit excommunicari, <q.3> an pro peccato alicuius tota familia excommunicanda sit et de diuersis sectis hereticorum.[xxii]

<26> IN VIGESIMOSEXTO. Queritur si subsequentibus priuilegiis derogetur antiquioribus, ut uerbi gratia Sancta Romana Ecclesia quandam baptismalem ecclesiam suis muniuit priuilegiis decimationes sue diocesis ex integro sibi attribuens. Quoddam similiter monasterium propriis muniuit priuilegiis, decernens ut ex propriis prediis nullas decimas persolueret. Accidit itaque ut inter diocesim prefate ecclesie monasterium illud alia emptione, alia donatione predia sibi inueniret. Queritur ergo an clerici baptismalis ecclesie decimas sue diocesis ex integro ualeant sibi uendicare.[xxiii]

<27> IN SEPTEMVIGESIMO LIBRO *(om. Aa)*. Queritur <q.1> qui sint sortilegi, <q.2> an (si *Aa*) sit peccatum esse sortilegum, <q.3> a quibus diuinatio sumpsit exordium, <q.4> quot sint genera *(add.* diuina *Aa)* diuinationis, <q.5> an diuini uel sortilegi sint excommunicandi si cessare noluerint, <q.6> an excommunicatus ab episcopo possit reconciliari a presbitero illo inconsulto, <q.7> si morientibus est indicenda penitentia sub quantitate temporis.[xxiv]

<28> IN OCTOVIGESIMO. Queritur <q.1> an coniugium possit esse inter uouentes, <q.2> an liceat sponse a sponso recedere et alii nubere et de coniugio quid sit uel inter quos fieri debeat uel qua de causa dissolui possit.[xxv]

<29> IN NONOVIGESIMO. Queritur <q.1> an coniugium sit inter infideles, <q.2> an liceat uiro fideli aliam ducere priori infideli uxore uiuente, <q.3> an sit reputandus bigamus qui ante baptismum habuit unam et post baptismum alteram.[xxvi]

---

xix. *Idem* C.21 pr.

xx. *Idem* C.22 pr. *sine mentione* q.3.

xxi. *Idem* C.23 pr. *sine mentione* q.2.

xxii. *Idem* C.24 pr. *et amplius et accuratius* q.3.

xxiii. *Idem* C.25 pr. *ex litteris casus determinando* q.1.

xxiv. *Idem* C.26 pr.

xxv. *Idem* C.27 pr. *et amplius et accuratius* q.2.

xxvi. *Idem* C.28 pr.

<30>   IN TRIGESIMO LIBRO. Queritur <q.1> si nobilis mulier a filio alicuius nobilis petitur in coniugem illaque consenserit, alius uero seruilis conditionis se obtulerit et eam in coniugem acceperit: si inter eos fit coniugium. <q.2> Et si prius hunc putabat esse liberum et postea deprehendit illum esse seruum, an liceat ei statim ab illo discedere.[xxvii]

<31>   IN TRIGESIMOPRIMO. Queritur <q.1> an uxori sue debitum reddere ualeat qui proprium filium de baptismate suscepit, <q.2> an sponsalia contrahantur inter infantes, <q.3> an spiritales uel adoptiui filii naturalibus copulari ualeant, <q.4> an uxorem compatris uxoris sue alicui ducere liceat, <q.5> an clandestina desponsatio manifeste preiudicet.[xxviii]

<32>   IN TRIGESIMOSECVNDO. Queritur <q.1> an possit duci in coniugium que prius polluta esset per adulterium, <q.2> an filia inuita tradenda sit alicui, <q.3> an post patris sponsionem illa possit alii nubere.[xxix]

<33>   IN TRIGESIMOTERTIO. Queritur <q.1> an meretrix licite ducatur in coniuge, <q.2> an ea que causa incontinentie ducitur sit coniux appellanda, <q.4> si uiuente uxore liceat alicui ex ancilla filios querere, <q.5> si ea que uim patitur pudiciciam amittere comprobetur, <q.6> si adulter adulteram possit dimittere, <q.7> si uiuente dimissa aliam possit accipere, <q.8> si infidelem promissa conditione liceat alicui fidelium ducere in coniugem.[xxx]

<34>   IN TRIGESIMOQVARTO. Queritur <q.1> an propter impossibilitatem coeundi a uiro suo aliqua sit separanda, <q.2> an post separationem ei nubere ualeat cum quo prius esset fornicata, <q.3> si sola confessione cordis crimen possit deleri, <q.4> si tempore orationis quis ualeat debitum reddere coniugi, <q.5> an uir sine consensu uxoris continentiam uouere possit uel si minis et terroribus licentiam uouendi ab ea extorquere ualeat.[xxxi]

<35>   IN TRIGESIMOQVINTO. Queritur <q.1> an sit rea adulterii que in captiuitatem ducta adhuc tamen uiuente uiro suo alteri nupsit <q.2> et an redeunte primo cogenda sit recedere a secundo et redire ad primum.[xxxii]

<36>   IN TRIGESIMOSEXTO. Queritur <q.1> si liceat aliquam ex propria cognatione duci in uxorem, <q.2> si ex consanguinitate uxoris aliqua possit in coniugem duci, <q.3> usque ad quem gradum debeat aliquis abstinere siue a propriis siue ab uxoris sue consanguineis, <q.6> qui iure iurando propinquitatem firmare debeant, <q.7> an illi qui de incestuosis natis sunt filii reputantur, <q.8> si ignoranter de consanguinitate uel affinitate aliqua in uxorem ducta est: an ex dispensatione possit uiro suo adherere, <q.9> si contigerit ecclesiam decipi et causa consanguinitatis aliquam a uiro suo separari, que post quadriennium nuptiis cum alteri comparatis deprehenderit non fuisse consanguineam prioris: an secunda coniugia sint rescindenda et priora sint redintegranda.[xxxiii]

<37>   IN SEPTEMTRIGESIMO. Queritur <q.1> quid sit raptus, <q.2> an rapta raptori nubere possit patre assensum prebente.[xxxiv]

---

xxvii. *Idem* C.29 pr.
xxix. *Idem* C.31 pr.
xxxi. *Idem* C.33 pr.
xxxiii. *Idem* C.35 pr. *sine aperta mentione* qq.4–5.
xxxiv. *Idem* C.36 pr. *exceptione facta* q.1 *quae sumitur ex rubrica* C.36 q.1 c.1.

xxviii. *Idem* C.30 pr.
xxx. *Idem* C.32 pr. *sine aperta mentione* q.3.
xxxii. *Idem* C.34 pr.

Apéndice II

Edicion parcial de *In prima parte agitur* segun *Bc Mk O Aa (Fd)*

En la actualidad he revisado una treintena de códices, seleccionados del grupo de los cincuenta y seis que conservan *IPA* íntegra y carecen del resumen sobre el tratado *de cons.* como C.37. Aquí presento la redacción de *IPA* a partir de las lecturas de *Bc Mk O* contrastadas en detalle con *Aa Fd:* es probablemente la versión más antigua. Dejando aparte *Fd*, debe entenderse que las lecciones de estos códices son concordes siempre salvo donde se constatan algunas 'adiciones' *(add.)* o bien 'omisiones' *(om.)* en particular; por otra parte, transcribo las lecturas singulares de los códices *Aa Bc Mk O* cuando alguno se aparta del texto donde los otros son concordes. En atención a la excepcionalidad del manuscrito *Fd*, he elaborado aparte el *apparatus criticus* de sus variantes, a fin de no complicar la redacción editada y, no obstante, puedan hacerse los cotejos y contrastes de su versión con el texto fijado: son las notas en números arábigos; fácilmente puede advertirse dónde existe unanimidad con los otros códices y las lecciones que comparten unos y otros entre sí.

<1>   In prima parte agitur de iustitia naturali et positiua, tam constituta quam inconstituta, que cui preponatur. De iure ciuili et ecclesiastico quod cui preferatur. De auctoritate etiam canonicarum scripturarum,[a1] conciliorum tam generalium quam prouincialium.[b] Decretalium[2] quoque epistolarum, necnon aliarum[c] scripturarum que autentice[d] uocantur.

<2>   Agitur etiam in ea[e3] de diuersis ordinibus ecclesiasticis: qui sint, unde originem uel nomen acceperint. De auctoritate quoque et statu ecclesiarum: que inter ceteras primum uel secundum uel tertium locum optineat. Qualiter in ecclesia per singulos gradus quisquis promoueri debeat. De conuersatione[4] et professione ordinandorum. De habitu et officio ordinatorum: quemadmodum, quo tempore episcoporum, presbiterorum, et ceterorum examinatio fieri debeat. Quid ad episcopum, quid ad unumquemque inferiorum specialiter pertineat, qui ex quibus ordinibus in quem gradum conscendere possint, qui post lapsum ualeant reparari uel non.

<3>   Agitur etiam in ea de episcopis et archiepiscopis[f] et ceteris a quibus sint eligendi uel ordinandi, usque ad quem terminum episcoporum electionem[5] differri liceat. Quo tempore sacri ordines sint distribuendi,[6] an semel ordinatus in eodem ordine iterum sit ordinandus. De differentia episcoporum et corepiscoporum. De his qui ab episcopis suis promoueri[7] contempnunt, an sint cogendi uel non. An etiam inuitus aliquis teneri debeat in[g] eo loco in quo ordinatus est. Quo tempore episcopi[8] consecrentur. Post eorum electionem, usque ad quem terminum ipsorum[h9] consecratio differri ualeat. Quo tempore presbiteri, diaconi, et

---

a. scripturarum] *add. et Aa*   b. *Hic sequitur* De notitia apocriphorum librorum *in multis codicibus, v. g. Ab Bs Bp Br Mc Mz Pk Pq Pv Sp, sed om. O Aa Am Bc Fa Fd Mk Mv Pf¹ et aliqui sicut Aa Fa orationem habent per add. interl.*   c. aliarum] *om. Bc sed corrig. per add. interl.*   d. autentice uocantur] (et non autentice)*add. interl.* uocatur Bcᵖᶜ   e. in ea] *om. Mkᵃᶜ sed add. interl. corrig.*   f. archiepiscopis] archipresbiteris Aa Bc   g. in] *om. Mkᵃᶜ sed add. interl. corrig.*   h. ipsorum] episcoporum Bc (Fd)

1. scripturarum] *om. Fdᵃᶜ sed Fdᵖᶜ interl. corrig. a manu G*   2. quam prouincialium. Decretalium] *om. et ibi signum habet ad corrig. sed sine add. in margine*   3. ea] eadem   4. conuersatione] conuersione   5. electionem] delectione Fdᵃᶜ et Fdᵖᶜ interl. corrig. a manu G   6. an] aut   7. promoueri] *om. Fdᵃᶜ et habet Fdᵖᶜ in margine*   8. episcopi] episcopis   9. ipsorum] episcoporum

ceteri sint ordinandi, quibus temporibus ieiunia sint celebranda, quibus temporum interstitiis,[10] qua aetate per singulos gradus promoueri debeant. A quibus etiam romane sedis episcopus et ex quibus sit eligendus et[11] ordinandus. De cuius electione predecessorem etiam deliberare oportet, cui reseruetur eorum electio. In quibus locis patriarche, primates, archiepiscopi,[12] episcopi, corepiscopi et reliqui sacerdotes sint ordinandi. Sequitur in ea breuis superiorum recapitulatio: quem electum ad quamlibet preposituram ecclesie iubet esse sine crimine, qui si ante tempus sue ordinationis uel post aliquod mortale admisisse[13] conuincitur, suscepti gradus officio ibidem priuandus[i] docetur.

<4> Agitur etiam in ea[14] de retrusione lapsorum, de munditia clericorum. De indisciplinato accessu et[k] reprehensibili cohabitatione ac famosa familiaritate clericorum et mulierum. De reparatione lapsorum post penitentiam, qui a suis mundus est. Prohibetur etiam alienis consentire peccatis ne aliorum uitia palpet, ne luporum laudibus glorietur, cuius tamen doctrina, si sese[l] aliorsum habuerit, contempni non debet.

<5> Agitur etiam in ea de hospitalitate et doctrina et correctione episcoporum quorum auctoritatem[m] in docendo preferre debeant, circa necessitatem patientes, liberales esse iubentur. In ipsa liberalitate[15] similiter ostenditur quis modus sit obseruandus rerum et personarum. Prohibetur etiam episcopis ne ad uindictam sint faciles, ne[16] sint turpis lucri cupidi, ne aliquo[n] inhonesto negotio[o] sibi necessaria querant, ne minorum tutelas aut curationes nisi forte legitimas et inexcusabiles suscipiant. Ne secularium causas assumant ne ratiociniorum causas[17] usurpent. Quod de omnibus diuino cultui[18] mancipatis generaliter intelligi oportet, nisi forte aliquis eorum episcopo[19] iubente ecclesiasticarum rerum gubernacula suscipiat.[p] Orphanorum et uiduarum que indefense sunt aut earum personarum que maxime[q20] ecclesiastico indigent amminiculo,[21] patrocinia propter timorem Dei[r] assumant. Ostenditur etiam in ea quibus ecclesie patrocinium denegari non debet. Singula quoque ecclesiastici iuris officia singulis quibusque personis, non tamen propinquis uel[22] sibi fauore coniunctis singillatim committi iubentur. Pariter etiam in ea demonstratur[s] quare diuersa officia uni persone non sunt comittenda. Quod sit officium uice domini. Quare secularibus uiris cura ecclesiasticarum rerum non sit iniungenda.

<6> Agitur in ea de discordantibus et dissidentibus[t23] ratione uel episcopali potestate ad concordiam reuocandis uel etiam condempnandis. De his etiam quibus ecclesia non sufficit ut de labore[24] manuum uiuant absque detrimento sui officii. De his etiam qui ecclesiasticis officiis negligunt[25] adesse. De his quoque qui in ecclesia non corde set uoce psallere student. De diaconibus modulationi uocis inseruientibus. De clericis ab episcopis ordinandis. De episcopis qui a sua parrochia non recipiuntur uel qui pro aliqua causa nolunt eas[u] adire. De obedientia[26] quam inferiores ex ordine superioribus debent. De supercilio diaconorum

---

i. ibidem priuandus] *add. interl.* esse *Aa*, idem priuatus *Bc^{ac}*, i(bi)dem *Bc^{pc interl.}*   k. et] ac *O*   l. si sese] si se *Aa*   m. auctoritatem] auctoritate *Bc*   n. ne aliquo] *Bc^{pc} sed* ne in aliquo *Bc^{ac} Mk*   o. inhonesto negotio] *trans. O*   p. suscipiat] suscipiant *Bc O*   q. maxime] maximo *Aa Bc (Fd)*   r. Dei] *om. O*   s. demonstratur] monstratur *O*   t. dissidentibus] discidentibus *Bc* (discedentibus *Fd*)   u. eas] eam *O*

10. intersticiis] interstiis *Fd^{ac} et Fd^{pc} interl. corrig. a manu G*   11. et] *om. Fd*   12. episcopi] *om. Fd*   13. admisisse] ammisisse   14. in ea] *om. Fd^{ac} sed Fd^{pc} interl. corrig. a manu G*   15. liberalitate] libertate   16. ne] *om. Fd*   17. causas] *sequitur add.* uel   18. cultui] cultu   19. episcopo] episcoporum   20. maxime] maximo   21. amminiculo] amminiculos   22. uel] *add.* etiam *Fd*   23. dissidentibus] discedentibus   24. labore] laboribus   25. negligunt] neglegunt   26. obedientia] obedentia *Fd^{ac} et Fd^{pc} interl. corrig. a manu G*

et episcoporum quibus romanus pontifex uices suas committere ualeat. De his qui eius legationem impediunt. De archidiaconis ne super clericos dominationem exerceant[27] uel censum ab eis exigant.[28] In quibus presbiteri exequentur episcopis. De his etiam[v] qui de ordinibus[w] uel ecclesiasticis rebus a principibus decreta inueniuntur, an uim auctoritatis obtineant. De peregrinis et transmarinis hominibus sine cirographis quinque episcoporum non ordinandis. De his qui in peregre baptizantur[x] non promouendis. De officio primatum et patriarcharum. Que reuerentia ab archiepiscopis[y] sit eis exhibenda. Ne aliquis patriarcharum uniuersali[z][29] appelletur uocabulo ante pallium acceptum archiepiscopi. Primati uel patriarche episcopos ordinare non licet.[30] Quibus diebus uel quibus horis archiepiscopus pallium ferre[31] debeat. In concessione pallii antiqua priuilegia sunt innouanda. Et quod in una prouincia duo metropolitani esse non debent.

v. his etiam] *trans. O*   w. ordinibus] *Aa^{ac} Bc Mk O sed* ordinationibus *Aa^{pc}*   x. peregre baptizantur] *Bc Mk O sed* peregrinatione baptizati sunt *Aa*   y. que reuerentia ab archiepiscopis] *Bc Mk O sed* quod . . . archiepiscopis *Aa^{ac} et* que reuerentia ab episcopis *Aa^{pc}*   z. uniuersali] *Bc Mk O sed* uniuersalis *Aa*

27. exerceant] exercant *Fd^{ac} et Fd^{pc} interl. corrig. a manu G*   28. exigant] exigat   29. patriarcharum uniuersali] *trans. Fd^{ac} et Fd^{pc} corrig. a manu G*   30. licet] liceat   31. archiepiscopus pallium ferre] pallium archiepiscopi conferre

11

A Fragment of *Compilatio prima* at Columbia University

Robert Somerville

✿

The general outline of the developments in canon law between c. 1140 and 1234 is well known, even to non-specialists.[1] In the century between the appearance of the *textus receptus* of Gratian's *Decretum*, c. 1140, and the promulgation of the *Decretales* of Pope Gregory IX in 1234 the schools and the papacy took charge of the study and the promulgation of the Church's law. Some of the collections of papal decretals which served as the principal vehicles for the law's diffusion circulated widely. It is a pleasure to dedicate this note about one of those famous compilations to Ken Pennington, whose editions and interpretive studies have elucidated the world of the *ius novum* for historians on both sides of the Atlantic.

The compilation of papal decretals which came to be designated as the *Compilatio prima* was titled by its author, Bernard of Pavia, as *Breviarium extravagantium <decreta-lium>*. Bernard was a native of Pavia, had been a student at Bologna and then taught there, for a time resided at the papal curia, and in 1187 was provost of the church at Pavia.[2] There he assembled his collection (c. 1190), which survives in different versions. Bernard also composed other works, notably a *Summa decretalium* on 1 Comp., and his career led him to the episcopate, first of Faenza, and then back to Pavia where he died in 1213. The importance of 1 Comp. is clear. As one of the so-called *Quinque compilatio-*

---

1. See, for example, C. Morris, *The Papal Monarchy: The Western Church from 1050 to 1234* (Oxford 1989) 575–77. The author is grateful to Prof. J. Rosenthal, of Barnard College and Columbia University, for information about the fragment of 1 Comp. once in her possession.

2. For Bernard in general see the summary in R. Somerville and B. C. Brasington, *Prefaces to Canon Law Books in Latin Christianity: Selected Translations, 500–1245* (New Haven, CT 1998) 216–20; the details in F. Liotta, 'Bernardo da Pavia', DBI 9 (1967) 279–84, and J. Gaudemet, *Les sources du droit canonique, viii–xx* siècle* (Paris 1993) 124–25.

nes antiquae, the work set a pattern for systematic collections of papal decretals with its structure of five books arranged under titles. Moreover, through the *Decretales* of Gregory IX many of the titles and the texts from 1 Comp. were incorporated into the Church's official canon law.

The *Compilatio prima* was edited in the sixteenth century by Antonio Agustín. Work was started on another edition by Joseph Anton Riegger in 1779, but only the first of five planned volumes appeared.[3] The standard work on 1 Comp. by Friedberg has been termed 'in most parts an analytic description, meant to be used in conjunction with his edition of the *Liber extra*. Only chapters suppressed by Gregory IX were given in full in Friedberg's slender companion volume in 1882'.[4] Friedberg used a handful of German manuscripts in his analysis of 1 Comp., and the need for a new study of the manuscripts of the compilation was acknowledged.[5] That work was undertaken by Gérard Fransen in 1961.[6] Fransen used 38 manuscripts and knew others, and readily conceded that his work represented the 'first results', with 'provisional conclusions', of an investigation of the manuscripts of 1 Comp.[7]

Other aspects of 1 Comp. also have claimed scholarly attention, but Fransen's study remains the starting point for research on the manuscripts.[8] Over the years Fransen himself provided supplements, but he never published a new comprehensive list of the compilation's manuscripts.[9] The diffusion of 1 Comp. was extensive, even remarkably so given the fact that the 'useful life' of the compilation extended for only about 40

3. S. Kuttner, 'Antonio Agustín's edition of the Compilationes antiquae', BMCL 7 (1977) 3, discussed the editorial history of 1 Comp. from the sixteenth to the nineteenth century.

4. Ibid. 3; cf. E. Friedberg, *Quinque compilationes antiquae nec non Collectio canonum Lipsiensis* (Leipzig 1882) xxiii.

5. Ibid. xxiii.

6. G. Fransen, 'Les diverses formes de la Compilatio prima', in: *Scrinium Lovaniense: Mélanges historiques Étienne Van Cauwenbergh* (Université de Louvain, Recueil de travaux d'histoire et de philologie 4.24; Louvain 1961) 235–53 (= G. Fransen, *Canones et Quaestiones* [Bibliotheca eruditorum 25; Goldbach 2002] I.2) esp. 236 n. 2, for the hope expressed in 1958 at the Canon Law Congress at Louvain and Brussels for a modern study of 1 Comp.

7. Ibid. 238–39 and 253. Fransen did not use any of Friedberg's manuscripts, which were all in German repositories.

8. See, for example, P. Landau, 'Alttestamentliches Recht in der "Compilatio prima" und sein Einfluss auf das kanonische Recht', SG 20 (= *Mélanges G. Fransen* II) 111–33 (reprinted with supplements in P. Landau, *Kanones und Dekretalen* [Bibliotheca eruditorum 2; Goldbach 1997] 299*–319*, 480*–81*).

9. See G. Fransen, 'La tradition manuscrite de la "Compilatio prima",' in: Proc. Boston (MIC C.4; 1965) 55–63. Cf. Fransen's comments on 1 Comp. in 'Sources et littérature du droit canonique classique', in: Proc. Munich (MIC C.10; 1997) 14–15. Information on manuscripts of 1 Comp. unearthed subsequent to Fransen's two articles can be found in various works, e.g., S. Kuttner and A. García y García, 'A New Eyewitness Account of the Fourth Lateran Council', *Traditio* 20 (1964) 115–16 (reprinted in S. Kuttner, *Medieval Councils, Decretals, and Collections of Canon Law* [Aldershot 1992²] no. IX); M. Bertram, 'Some Additions to the "Repertorium der Kanonistik",' BMCL 4 (1974) 9–10; G. Dolezalek, 'Another Fragment of the Apparatus "Militant siquidem patroni",' BMCL 5 (1975) 130–32. The bifolium of 1 Comp. described by Dolezalek shares certain similarities to the fragment at Columbia University to be described below.

years, i.e., from c. 1190 to 1234 when it was replaced in an official way by the Gregorian *Decretales*.[10] As could be expected, not only is 1 Comp. represented by a large number of complete exemplars but also many fragments survive.[11] The comments to follow will be concerned with the survival of one of these *membra disiecta* which today resides in New York City.

Medieval/Renaissance Fragment 98 in the Rare Book and Manuscript Library of Columbia University is a bifolium comprising two glossed leaves of 1 Comp. It was written in double columns in the first quarter of the thirteenth century in France, and the pages measure approximately 280 x 211 mm. As is not uncommon with legal manuscripts, the fragment survived as binding reinforcement material for another manuscript or a printed book. The margins of fol. 2 contain a brown stain where glue was applied. The pages were trimmed slightly, and this probably accounts for the absence of pricking. New inscriptions follow directly at the end of a decretal, often within a line, and they usually begin with a small red or blue capital although occasionally the rubricator neglected to insert that first letter. The decretals begin at the left-hand margin of the lines with alternating red or blue decorated capitals which are generally two lines high although the tail of letters such as Q can extend further. One such capital, seemingly a D at the beginning of 2.1.1, was cut out on fol. 1rb, but the note *Secundus liber* written in red, designating the beginning of the second book of the compilation, remains on line 9. In the middle of the top of 1r and again at 2r is *II*, composed on fol. 1 of a blue *I* and a red *I*, but the glue on fol. 2 has turned the numeral brown.[12]

Fragment 98 comprises texts from the end of book 1 and the beginning of book 2 of 1 Comp., i.e., on fol. 1, the end of 1 Comp. 1.35.4 *(propter iniuriam . . .)* through the opening words of 1 Comp. 2.2.3 *(. . . clericum ullum/)*, and on fol. 2, 1 Comp. 2.13.10 through the inscription of 1 Comp. 2.13.22. The segment of the compilation found on these two pages reveals one significant textual deviation from Friedberg's tabulation: 1 Comp. 2.1.9 is missing, a lacuna which also occurs elsewhere.[13] By estimating the amount of

10. Fransen, 'La tradition manuscrite de la "Compilation prima",' wrote: 'Y a-t-il un seul texte médiéval pour lequel nous disposons de 127 MSS échelonnés seulement sur quarante-cinq ans?'

11. Notices about fragments of 1 Comp. can be found in both series of the BMCL: see the entry for *Compilatio prima* in the 'Cumulative Index, 1155–1983', BMCL 14 (1984) 25. More recently, see S. Kuttner, 'Manuscripts of Canon Law in Hungary: An Index to Peter Erdö's Article in Apollinaris', BMCL 18 (1988) 64, under Bernard of Pavia.

12. For the well-attested schema of alternating red and blue initials in the headings and rubrics of high medieval manuscripts, see A. Derolez, 'Observations on the Aesthetics of the Gothic Manuscripts', *Scriptorium* 50 (1996) 9–10 (a reference kindly provided by C. Dutschke); cf. C. de Hamel, *A History of Illuminated Manuscripts* (Boston 1986) 111, pl. 106, from book 2 of a late-twelfth-century Parisian copy of the *Sententiae* of Peter Lombard.

13. Friedberg, *Quinque compilationes* 11–12, 16–17. For 1 Comp. 2.1.9, missing in Friedberg's MS Ab of the *Decretales*, see E. Friedberg, *Corpus iuris canonici* 2 (Leipzig 1881) xlvi, 241 n.1 (for X 2.1.7). For Ab = Freiburg, UB

text that is missing between fols. 1 and 2 it appears that the bifolium was the third sheet of a quire. That is to say, Frag. 98, fol. 1, was separated from fol. 2 by two bifolia constituting four missing folios.

Notwithstanding its brevity and the fact that it exhibits little variation in the structure of 1 Comp. as blocked out by Friedberg, this fragment is not without textual interest. The pages carry a layer of glosses which is neatly written, probably by one hand, and which remains to be identified. This apparatus is organized by means of underlined lemmata designating a section of a decretal's text. Twenty years ago Stephan Kuttner wrote two letters pertaining to the matter. The present writer had shown him photographs of the fragment, then the property of Prof. Jane Rosenthal of Barnard College. On August 27, 1981, Prof. Kuttner wrote as follows: 'I am ashamed to say that I have not yet done anything about identifying the glosses—certainly a major apparatus, and these are frequently unsigned'. On October 2 of the same year he returned to the fragment:

On the fragment from Comp. I . . . I have not come to a conclusion as regards its apparatus of glosses. It is certainly non-Bolognese and may be related to the group of French decretalists represented e.g. by the Apparatus 'Militant siquidem patroni' and layers of glosses in MSS Paris lat. 9632, 15398, Epinal 72 etc. More material would be needed for a closer determination.

This letter of October 1981 seems to be Prof. Kuttner's last mention of Frag. 98, although it is possible that his later correspondence would reveal otherwise. His work and the work of others, especially the recent studies of Prof. Lefèbvre-Teillard, have traced the late twelfth-century study of canon law in France. Those investigations have begun to provide a context for Frag. 98.[14] Even so, it has not yet been possible to identify the accompanying apparatus. For the moment what can be reported is a specific negative result, namely that the glosses in question are not part of the early thirteenth-century apparatus *Militant siquidem patroni*. This work probably was composed by someone who taught at Paris. Excerpts from its gloss on *Ceterum* (1 Comp. 2.1.7) were recently printed, thus providing a comparison with the gloss on *Ceterum* found in Frag. 98 (fol. 1vb, at the top of the page).[15]

361a, see W. Hagenmaier, *Die lateinischen mittelalterlichen Handschriften der Universitätsbibliothek (ad Hs. 231)* (Katalog der Universitätsbibliothek Freiburg 1.3; Wiesbaden 1980) 97–99.

14. See, for example, A. Lefèbvre-Teillard, '"Petrus Brito legit . . .". Sur quelques aspects de l'enseignement du droit canonique à Paris au début du xiii siècle', RHDFE 79 (2001) 153–77 ; eadem, 'Magister A. Sur l'école de droit canonique parisienne au début du xiii siècle', ibid. 80 (2002) 401–17; eadem, '"D'oltralpe": Observations sur l'apparat *Militant siquidem patroni*', in: *Amicitiae pignus: Studi in ricordo di Adriano Cavanna* 2 (Università degli studi di Milano, Pubblicazioni dell'Istituto di storia del diritto medievale e moderno 31; Milan 2003) 1311–35.

15. Ibid. 1328–29.

A few words can be said, in conclusion, about the recent history of Frag. 98 and its arrival at Columbia University. The bifolium was once the property of Prof. Marion Lawrence (1901–78), a professor of art history at Barnard College. Professor Lawrence apparently purchased the fragment at a sale conducted by Gimbel's Department Store in Manhattan in February, 1941, of items from the vast collection of William Randolph Hearst. In the face of the country's bleak financial situation in the 1930s and even into the '40s the newspaper magnate liquidated many of the treasures that he had acquired, as H. P. Kraus wrote, 'by the carload, like an antiques wholesaler. . . . Into cellars and storerooms they went, where they remained for years'.[16]

There is no way to trace the bifolium from 1 Comp. backward from Hearst. His collection would have included bundles of detached leaves from manuscripts used in bindings that came from one of the sweeping purchases of the holdings of a collector or a library. The leaves remained in Professor Lawrence's hands until they were bequeathed to Professor Jane Rosenthal, professor of art history at Barnard College and Columbia University, who subsequently donated them to the Rare Book and Manuscript Library at Columbia University in September 2003. At the request of Prof. Rosenthal and Prof. Florentine Mütherich, Bernard Bischoff localized and dated the leaves in the 1970s. The identification of 1 Comp. was made by the present author in 1981, and there the matter rested for more than twenty years. Perhaps this brief set of comments will serve to bring the bifolium to the notice of scholars who will turn their attention to identifying the apparatus.

16. H. P. Kraus, *A Rare Book Saga: The Autobiography of H. P. Kraus* (New York 1978) 86.

12

Die Phi.-Glossen der *Collectio Cassellana*

Peter Landau

❋

I. Einleitung

Die Dekretalensammlung *Collectio Cassellana* wurde von dem grossen Kanonisten Justus Henning Böhmer (1674–1749) anlässlich seiner Edition des *Corpus Iuris Canonici* 1747 in einer Handschrift der Landesbibliothek Kassel (MS Jur. 15) entdeckt und als zweiter Appendix zu seiner umfangreichen Ausgabe vollständig ediert.[1] Die Sammlung gehört daher bis heute zu den wenigen im Volltext edierten Kompilationen aus der Zeit vor Bernhard von Pavia und wurde in der Dekretalenforschung des 19. und 20. Jahrhunderts vielfach berücksichtigt. Nach der Entdeckung der *Collectio Bambergensis* durch Schulte erkannte Emil Friedberg, dass die Cassellana eine 'fast vollständige Reproduktion von Q' (= Bambergensis) sei.[2] Friedberg lieferte in seinem Standardwerk über die 'Canonessammlungen zwischen Gratian und Bernhard von Pavia' 1897 eine vergleichende Analyse der *Cassellana* unter Berücksichtigung der seinerzeit bekannten Sammlungen.[3] Daraus ergab sich, dass die *Cassellana* der sogenannten Bambergensis-gruppe der Dekretalensammlungen zuzuordnen ist, deren Zahl durch die Forschungen Walther Holtzmanns im 20. Jahrhundert wesentlich vergrössert werden konnte.[4]

---

1. *Corpus Iuris Canonici*, ed. J. H. Boehmer (Halae Magdeburgici 1747), 'Appendix II: Decretales Alexandri III', 180–347. Zur Handschrift, cf. M. Kremer, *Die Handschriften der Murrhardschen Bibliothek der Stadt Kassel und Landesbibliothek* (Wiesbaden 1969) 17–19: Datierung des ersten Teils der Handschrift mit der *Cassellana* auf das letzte Jahrzehnt des 12. Jahrhunderts.

2. J. F. v. Schulte, 'Zur Geschichte der Literatur über das Dekret Gratians. Zweiter Beitrag', in: *Sb. Wien* 64 (1870) 93–142, hier 138–40; *Canones-Sammlungen* 135.

3. Ibid. 130–36.

4. Cf. den Überblick bei W. Holtzmann, 'Kanonistische Ergänzungen zur Italia Pontificia', *Quellen und Forschungen aus italienischen Archiven und Bibliotheken* 37 (1957) 61–102.

Holtzmanns Schüler Walter Deeters lieferte 1956 in seiner Bonner Dissertation eine umfassende vergleichende Analyse aller Sammlungen der Bambergensisgruppe. Er wies darauf hin, dass die Kasseler Handschrift im Anschluss an die Dekretalensammlung einen Papst- und Kaiserkatalog bis 1191 bringt, der den Namen von Papst Cölestin III. enthält, aber noch nicht Kaiser Heinrich VI., so dass der Katalog bald nach 1191 datiert werden muss.[5] Da die jüngsten Dekretalen der *Cassellana* von Papst Urban III. (1185–1187) stammen, wird man die Sammlung selbst um 1187 datieren müssen.[6] Nach dem Inhalt der Sammlung und wegen des in Italien verfassten Papst- und Kaiserkatalogs kann man annehmen, dass die *Cassellana* in Italien kompiliert wurde, vielleicht als ein Parallelunternehmen zu der etwa gleichzeitig von Bernhard von Pavia angelegten *Collectio Lipsiensis*.[7]

Anlässlich der Publikation eines Katalogs der kanonistischen Handschriften der Bamberger Bibliothek durch Hans Fischer 1906 wurde von diesem eine zweite Handschrift der *Collectio Cassellana* entdeckt.[8] Dieses wohl zu Anfang des 13. Jahrhunderts geschriebene Manuskript bringt im Anschluss an die *Cassellana* (fol. 25–43v) die um 1202 kompilierte Dekretalensammlung des Gilbert in fragmentarischer Form.[9] Vor der *Cassellana* enthält die Handschrift den Wahlrechtstraktat des Wilhelm von Mandagoto, also ein Werk vom Ende des 13. Jahrhunderts.[10] Vielleicht ist dieses Stück ursprünglich eine selbständige Handschrift gewesen, die später mit den beiden Dekretalensammlungen zusammengebunden wurde. Jedenfalls gehörte MS can.18 zu den Beständen der Bamberger Dombibliothek, die wahrscheinlich über die *Collectio Cassellana* schon zu Anfang des 13. Jahrhunderts verfügt haben muss.

Anders als die Kasseler Handschrift enthält die Bamberger eine umfangreiche Glosse zu den Dekretalen, die weitaus reichste in allen Sammlungen der Bambergensisgruppe. Zahlreiche kürzere Glossen der Bamberger *Cassellana* begegnen auch in

---

5. W. Deeters, *Die Bambergensisgruppe der Dekretalensammlungen des 12. Jahrhunderts* (Phil. Diss.; Bonn 1956) 46.

6. Cf. *Canones-Sammlungen* 132, 135.

7. Zur *Collectio Lipsiensis*, cf. die Analysen in: *Quinque Compilationes antiquae necnon Collectio canonum Lipsiensis*, ed. E. Friedberg (Lipsiae 1882, repr. Graz 1956) 189–208; *Canones-Sammlungen* 115–130. Zu Bernhard von Pavia als Autor, P. Landau, 'Die systematischen Dekretalensammlungen und die europäische Kanonistik des 12. Jahrhunderts', ZRG Kan. Abt. 65 (1979) 120–48, hier 135–36 (= idem, *Kanones und Dekretalen* [Goldbach 1997] 242–43).

8. H. Fischer, *Katalog der Handschriften der Königlichen Bibliothek zu Bamberg* I.1: *Canonistische Handschriften* (Bamberg 1906) 884–88: MS Can. 18 (früher: P III.1), fol. 25v–43v. Die Handschrift stammt aus der Dombibliothek Bamberg. Zu dieser Handschrift auch F. Heyer, 'Rez. von: H. Singer, Neue Beiträge über die Dekretalensammlungen vor und nach Bernhard von Pavia', ZRG Kan. Abt. 3 (1913) 634–35.

9. Cf. Kuttner, *Repertorium* 310–11. Das Fragment der *Collectio Gilberti* (fol. 44r–59v) gehört nach Kuttner vermutlich mit einem weiteren Fragment derselben Sammlung in MS Bamberg, Can. 20 (fol. 55–63) zusammen.

10. Cf. Fischer, *Katalog* 884–85; Schulte, QL 2.183–85 mit Anm. 5.

anderen Dekretalensammlungen dieser Gruppe, so in der *Collectio Erlangensis* und der *Collectio Lipsiensis*.[11] Ein grösserer Komplex von Glossen, der mit der rätselhaften Sigle (Phi.) versehen ist, findet sich jedoch ausschliesslich in der Bamberger Handschrift der *Cassellana*. Mit diesen Glossen beschäftigte sich zuerst Josef Juncker in seinen grundlegenden kanonistischen Studien 1924 und 1926; er stellte sie in eine Parallele zu der Glossierung in der Handschrift MS Leipzig 1242—beide Glossierungen bezeichnete er als 'interessante Apparate'.[12] In seiner zweiten Studie über Simon von Bisignano edierte Juncker 1926 eine Phi.-Glosse, in der auf Johannes Faventinus und Simon von Bisignano Bezug genommen wird. Juncker vermutete, dass sich hinter der Sigle Phi. ein Kanonist Philippus verbergen könne, der auch als Glossator der *Compilatio III* aufgrund von Phi.-Glossen in der Handschrift MS Chartres 296 bezeugt sei, was auf einer Bemerkung von Schulte beruhte.[13] Stephan Kuttner konnte allerdings derartige Glossen in der Handschrift von Chartres nicht finden; hinter den Phi.-Glossen der *Cassellana* vermutete Kuttner einen in einem Gedicht 1198 erwähnten französischen *Magister Philippus iureconsultus*, wies aber auch auf Glossen mit der Sigle f. hin, die man dem in der Dekretale JL 13854 erwähnten *Magister Fidantia* zuschreiben könne.[14] In einer letzten Stellungnahme 1983 zum Problem der Sigle Phi. in der *Cassellana* bemerkte Kuttner, dass man das ϕ. in Ms Bamberg Can. 18 vielleicht als ein grosses M lesen müsse.[15]

Die Zuordnung der Phi.-Glossen beschäftigte zuletzt Rudolf Weigand in seinem monumentalen Werk über die 'Glossen zum Dekret Gratians' von 1991. Weigand widmete dem als Adressat einer Dekretale Alexanders III. 1176 bezeugten Magister Fidantia hier einen eigenen Abschnitt.[16] Fidantia war Kanoniker in Cività Castellana; von ihm verzeichnete und edierte Weigand insgesamt 10 Glossen in Dekrethandschriften mit den Siglen f. oder f.c.[17] Zur Frage der Phi.-Glossen in der *Collectio Cassellana* bemerkte er: 'Ich halte eine Identität des Verfassers dieser Glosse mit unserem Mag. Fidantia durchaus für möglich, ja wahrscheinlich, falls es sich überhaupt um eine Sigle und nicht nur um ein nachgestelltes *Arg.* handelt'.[18]

---

11. Zur *Collectio Erlangensis* (MS UB Erlangen 342, fol. 291–306), cf. Deeters, *Die Bambergensisgruppe* 9–10. Die Handschrift gehörte bis zu Anfang des 16. Jahrhunderts dem Kloster Michelsberg in Bamberg. Die übereinstimmenden Glossen bringen meist Allegationsreihen. Auf Belege hierzu muss in diesem Beitrag aus Raumgründen verzichtet werden.

12. Cf. J. Juncker, 'Die Collectio Berolinensis', ZRG Kan. Abt. 13 (1924) 284–426, hier 338–39 n. 8; idem, 'Die Summa des Simon von Bisignano und seine Glossen', ZRG Kan. Abt. 15 (1926) 326–500, hier 445–69.

13. Ibid. 448–49 n. 8.

14. S. Kuttner, 'Bernardus Compostellanus antiquus', *Traditio* 1 (1943) 205–340, hier 281–82 n. 16 (= idem, *Gratian und the Schools of Law 1140–1234* [London 1983] no. VII).

15. Kuttner, 'Retractationes VII', in: *Gratian and the Schools* 11.

16. Weigand, *Glossen* 645–51.   17. Ibid. 646–51.

18. Ibid. 648.

Angesichts der hier skizzierten Forschungslage kann mit Sicherheit gesagt werden, dass das Problem der Phi.-Glossen in der *Cassellana* ungelöst ist. Will man zu einer Einordnung dieser Glossen in die Geschichte der Kanonistik kommen, ist es zunächst erforderlich, den Text zu kennen. Ich möchte daher durch die Edition der Glossen eine Grundlage für die Kenntnis eines der frühesten Produkte der Dekretalistik liefern, im Bewusstsein der grossen Beiträge, die Kenneth Pennington zur Erforschung des Dekretalenrechts und der dekretalistischen Kanonistik geleistet hat. In einem abschliessenden Teil sollen einige Schlussfolgerungen aus dem Befund der Glossen gezogen werden.

II. Edition der Phi.-Glossen

1.) Cass. 2.1 s.v. 'humanitate foveri' (fol. 25rb): 'Id est non infestari, de communi causa, id est societate, tunc iudeus contra orthodoxum admittendus, ut hic, secus cum orthodoxus, is contra orthodoxum agit, ut ibi. ϕ.'.

2.) Cass. 3.1 (fol. 25rb): 'Mulierem (?) adulteram intelligitur, que cum primo subegisset, gerentes postea sub tributo, calderorum est proposita, spiritualiter de modo intelligitur, que sensibus quasi provinciis preposita per peccatum de moribus fit tributoria. ϕ.'.

3.) Cass. 3.1 s.v. 'anathematis' (fol. 25rb): 'Arg. § quod cum aliquid prohibitur sub hac forma, nota excommunicatur qui prohibitum facit, non iste canon date sentencie, quod patet per id quod sequitur: "et commoniti" etc. Simile est supra LXIII Obeuntibus (= D.63 c.35), contra est supra e. c. sicut et LXIII Salonitane (D.63 c.24). ϕ.'.

4.) Cass. 6.1 s.v. 'presumunt' (fol. 25va): 'In morte, quod consequentia litem apperit, nam invita possunt donare cuilibet. ϕ.'.

5.) Cass. 6.1 s.v. 'pecunie' (fol. 25va): 'Si ergo certa pecunie quantitas non intercesserit, non videtur esse prohibitum. ϕ.'.

6.) Cass. 12.14 s.v. 'crebra' (fol. 26rb): 'Arg. excommunicatos excommunicare posse, arg. supra III q. IIII Engeltrudam (C.3 q.4 c.12), arg. supra XI q. III Excellentissimus (C.11 q.3 c.102); "sepe dampnata", supra LXXVII Illos (D.77 c.1). Arg. ergo si aliquis excommunicatus verberat clericum, iudicatur in canonem date sentencie. ϕ.'.

7.) Cass. 12.14 (fol. 26rb): 'Id est pro pretio ad serviendum conducto. Nota autem prohibet, quia pagani possint christianos servos habere, vel forte christiani possunt esse servi paganorum, set non incipere, ut infra De iudiis, c. ultimo (Cass. 54.5). ϕ.'.

8.) Cass. 12.17 (fol. 26va): 'Nota instantiam illius regule que omnibus fere doctoribus est communis, sc. quod cum quis pro crimine condempnatur, a degradatione est incipiendum, cum pro contumacia, ab excommunicatione. ϕ.'.

9.) Cass. 12.20 s.v. 'rationabiliter fuerit ostensum' (fol. 26va): 'Obiectio ergo criminis non impedit alicuius promotionem, arg. contra supra LXXXI Tantis (D.81 c.3) et supra IIII q. I c. II in fine arg. ϕ.'.

10.) Cass. 40.6 s.v. 'existeret' (fol. 33vb): 'Hec ad litteram in veteri testamento prohibebat. Hodie tamen distingue, dum puto, nam ad deformitatem gravat vel usura ex toto obnubilat aut non. In primo casu repellitur, ut LV Si evangelica (D.55 c.13), in secundo nequaquam; quod hic excommunicatur, quia precise in hoc casu sentenciare. ϕ.'.

11.) Cass. 41.1 s.v. 'Sane licet forte' (fol. 34ra): 'Sive forte est verum, ut supra VIIII q. III c. I, et II Nullus primus (C.9 q.2 c.3), Conquestus (C.9 q.3 c.8). ϕ.'.

12.) Cass. 41.1 (fol. 34ra): 'Solutio. Aliud est subiectos episcoporum compelli ut praeter appellationem iudicio pareant legatorum, quod ibi prohibetur, aliud sponte legatorum iudicium pretermissis etiam episcopis eligere, quod hic conceditur, que solutio colligitur ex illo verbo: "in voluntate"; ergo subiecti est, cuius iudicium malit eligere; set numquid duo iudices ordinati in eodem episcopatu erant ? ф.'.

13.) Cass. 41.4 s.v. 'appellandum' (fol. 34rb oben): 'Arg. plebanum esse ordinatum iudicem sui plebanatus, alioquin sententia a non suo iudice dicta non obligaret aliquem, quod si est cum episcopus sit ordinarius iudex, patet in eodem loco plures iudices esse ordinarios, quod doctores unde omnino inficiantur. ф.'.

14.) Cass. 41.2 s.v. 'debent remitti' (fol. 34rb): 'Subaudi ad hoc ut ab eis iudicentur. Possunt tamen remitti ad hoc ut absolvantur, ut supra e. cap. ф.'.

15.) Cass. 41.5 (fol. 34rb): 'Si ergo esset persona ecclesiastica illa ad quam spectat representatio, non esset necessarium ibi yconomos ponere. Et est arg. quod de eo ipso quod alia ecclesia habet ius patronatus alterius ecclesie, habet et administrationem temporalium in eadem. ф.'.

16.) Cass. 48.10 (fol. 36va): 'Hoc ipso quia pars defensionis copulam adversario suo detrahebat. Ostendebat iniquam a se causam foveri, ut III q. VII § Tria (C.3 q.7 d.p.c.1), II q. III Prevaricator (C.2 q.3 d.p.c.8 § 2). ф.'.

17.) Cass. 48.11 s.v. 'cistrensi' (fol. 36va): 'Nec faciunt contra iuramentum. Nam cum testes pro utraque parte versentur, ut XIIII q. V Versatur (?), contra neutram dicuntur facere testimonium ferendo. ф.'.

18.) Cass. 48.15 (fol. 36vb): 'Arg. potestatibus compellendis. ф.'.

19.) Cass. 48.16 (fol. 36vb): 'Propter longum etiam tempus in ecclesia erat tollerandus, ut supra De ordinatione, Ex tua nobis (Cass. 33.10), infra De matrimonio, Consuluit (Cass. 58.28). ф.'.

20.) Cass. 48.16 s.v. 'miles quidam' (fol. 36vb): 'Nam si papa scivisset eum laicum, non amisisset eius accusationem contra clericum, ut C. I (?) De cetero (C.1 q.1 c.109?). ф.'.

21.) Cass. 48.16 (fol. 36vb): 'Numquid potuit agi per procuratorem, cum ageretur ad exspoliationem ecclesie? Numquid ammitteretur laicus contra clericum? In bigamia probanda vel simplicitate, cum tantum civiliter operatur (?). ф.'.

22.) Cass. 48.17 (fol. 36vb): 'In civilibus hoc locum habet, in criminalibus nequaquam; ф. § Idem in mulieribus est dicendum, cum ipse in iure (?) ad publicum trahi non debeant, ut C. De iureiurando, propter calumniam dando l. II § Sin Autem (Cod.2.58.2.1), et C. De rebus creditis, l. Generaliter § ult. (Cod.4.1.12.6). ф.'.

23.) Cass. 50.5 (fol. 37ra): 'Quid est quod hic dicitur ab Alexandro? Numquid prescriptio tricennalis contra monasterium amittetur, contra illud quod est supra XXVI q. III § ultimus contra. Resp. dicendum non propter prescriptionem set propter donationem apostolicam hoc factum fuisse. Simile supra XVI q. IIII Volumus (C.16 q.4 c.2). ф.'.

24.) Cass. 51.1 (fol. 37ra): 'Supra e. t. c. I. Nam quanta episcopi de communi iure a clerico possideri non potest. ф.'.

25.) Cass. 51.5 (fol. 37rb): 'Collige in potestate iudicis esse abbreviare vel prorogare inducias, ut supra V q. III Si egrotans (C.5 q.3 c.1). ф.'.

26.) Cass. 51.5 (fol. 37rb): 'Si appellationem fuerit prosecutus. Si vero non fuerit prosecutus, habet locum quod est infra eadem Appellationi (Cass. 51.17). ф.'.

27.) Cass. 51.5 (fol. 37rb): 'Tunc quando excommunicavit, requisitum tantum primo. ф.'.

28.) Cass. 51.6 (fol. 37rb): 'Argue excommunicationem post appellationem factam tenere. In hoc casu excipe ergo hunc casum ab eo quod generaliter dici videtur. Supra II q. VI Quotiens episcopi (C.2 q.6 c.16). ɸ.ʹ.

29.) Cass. 51.8 (fol. 37rb): '§ Nisi in crimine manifesto, ut infra e. t. Proposuit (Cass. 51.35). ɸ.ʹ.

30.) Cass. 51.9 (fol. 37rb): 'Hoc dictum verum est. Comparatus est iudex de suggestione falsi audire. Set pars que vult appellare, non vult de falsis (!) suggestione coram eo agere, set tantum appellare. Illud, cum aliquis paratus est de falso coram iudice agere et iudex audire declinat. ɸ.ʹ.

31.) Cass. 51.11 (fol. 37rb): 'Non tantum est istud verum in eo casu, quando est appellatio sublata, set etiam quando est non sublata, alioquin nec appellatio concederetur. ɸ.ʹ.

32.) Cass. 51.4 oder Cass. 49.1 (fol. 37r unten), ed. Juncker, 'Die Summa' 445–48.

33.) Cass. 58.37 (fol. 42rb): 'Solutio: distinguent utrum prohibitionem que sit affirmative et eam que sit negative. Si sit negative, puta prohiberimus ne contrahatis matrimonium, non impedit prohibitio, quominus matrimonium contrahatur. Set si fit affirmative, puta precipimus, ut si coniuncti fueritis nullum fit inter vos matrimonium, si fiat contra hanc prohibitionem, nullum est matrimonium, set contrarium, arg. XXXIII q. IIII Non oportet a (C.33 q.4 c.10). Non multum intelligo, quid superiori solutione dicatur. Ideoque ita puta distinguendum, quia matrimonium aut contrahitur contra prohibitionem hominis, aut contra prohibitionem iuris. Si contra prohibitionem hominis, non minus est stabilis, ad tempus tantum est separandus, ut in illis c. Sollicitudo (Cass. 58.18), Littere (Cass. 58.33) et Ex litteris (Cass. 58.26) supra e. t. Si autem est contra prohibitionem iuris, aut contra perpetuam prohibitionem aut contra temporalem. Si contra perpetuam, nullum est matrimonium, ut in istis capitulis Contradicimus (C.35 q.2–3 c.21), Videtur (C.35 q.6 c.2). Nam si contra temporalem prohibitionem, stabile est matrimonium, ut in illo §. Set obicitur et supra e. t. Consuluit (Cass. 58.34). Ideo ergo potest hic matrimonium irritari quia contra prohibitionem perpetuam vivente sponsa de presenti, alia fuerat ducta. ɸ.ʹ.

34.) Cass. 58.39 s.v. 'siluisse' (fol. 42va): 'Presumitur enim contra eos quod coniunctioni eorum consenserint, et sic fuerunt consentientes incestui, ut LXXXIII Consentire (D.83 c.5), quare criminosi, ergo non in accusatione re255cipiendi, ut VI q. I Qui crimen (C.6 q.1 c.6) et XXXV q. I Notificamus (C.35 q.6 c.3). Set contra e. q. VIIII § Quia ergo (C.35 q.9 d.p.c.2). Alii tamen dicunt vim habere fieri in illo verbo, "qui possunt quidem recipi", set cum difficultate. Plane tantum potest intelligi de iuratis synodalibus, ut XXXV q. VI Episcopus (C.35 q.6 c.7), qui si a principio taceant, sunt periuri. ɸ.ʹ.

35.) Cass. 59.1 s.v. 'uxori sue infra tempore' (fol. 42va): 'Resp. infra tempus penitentie possit exigi debitum ab adultera. ɸ.ʹ.

36.) Cass. 59.2 s.v. 'desponsationes' (fol. 42va): 'Ergo ubicumque non tenet desponsatio, idem erat fatendum igitur frigidi, spadonis, voventis sollempniter. Frater ducet in uxorem similiter et consanguineam desponsatam fratri. Alter frater habebit si similiter non fuerit consanguinea eius. Set contra infra e. t. Iuvenis (Cass. 59.7). Supra XXVII q. II Quidam de con. (?, desponsavit?) (C.27 q.2 c.31). ɸ.ʹ.

37.) Cass. 59.4 s.v. 'dixit quod' (fol. 42va): 'Nota sponsi. Set sponse alioquin. Si scienter cum uxore sui patris iacuisset, sc. perpetuo ob hoc solum privaretur coniugio. ɸ.ʹ.

38.) Cass. 59.4 s.v. 'non posse matrimonium' (fol. 42va): 'Id est sponsione defuerit matrimonium. Si tantum dicatur propter supervenientem affinitatem matrimonium nondum consumatum prorsus rescindi, coadiuvabis quod de sponsa de presenti dictum est, supra t. De sponsis can. c. I (Cass. 57.1). ɸ.ʹ.

39.) Cass. 59.4 s.v. 'accipere' (fol. 42vb): 'Ergo ipsa nondum erat uxor. Et sic loquitur de sponsa de futuro. ɸ.'.

40.) Cass. 59.6 s.v. 'etiam consilium' (fol. 42vb): 'Putativam. In veritate enim non est uxor. ɸ.'.

41.) Cass. 59.8 s.v. 'nedum' (fol. 42vb): 'Nota maiorem distinctionem esse necessariam in causis matrimonialibus quam in aliis negotiis, ut arg. VII q. II Nuper (C.7 q.2 c.2) et XXXV De parentela (C.35 q.6 c.5). ɸ.'.

42.) Cass. 59.9 (fol. 42vb): 'Set hoc de his episcopis dicitur qui potestatem habent a principibus seculi (Siciliae?) habentes, ibi loquitur de illis episcopis, qui nullam habent iurisdictionem temporalem a principibus, vel hic dicitur de vindicanda iniuria aliis illata, ibi vero interdicitur ne in eos qui sunt iniuriosi episcopis, idem episcopi vindicent cum flagellis, ut supra XXVIIII Inter querelas (C.23 q.4 c.27). Vel ibi effusio sanguinis, non castigatio fustis interdicitur. ɸ.'.

43.) Cass. 61.1 s.v. 'diversorum locorum' (fol. 43ra): 'Inde nobis hic male dicit Alexander; intencio bene, nam nec illi due canones sunt contrarii ut hic dicitur. Primo est immo ut ex cironicis (?) patet, et ex se iure (?) huius corporis posterior invenitur. Quod in fine dicit verum est, set quod in calce capituli, statim de consuetudine subditur. Numquid potest esse verum? Numquid adeo efficax erit particularis consuetudo, ut contractum matrimonium dividat nequaquam, etsi contrahendum inpediat. ɸ.'.

44.) Cass. 62.2 s.v. 'eorum persone' (fol. 43ra): 'Nota quod hoc solum sufficit ad legitimationem filiorum, sc. quod parentes eorum in facie ecclesie contrahunt, ut supra t. De matrimonio, Accessit in fine (Cass. 58.5). Quid autem si uterque conscientiam incestus habeat, vel adulter tantum, cum in facie ecclesie contrahant, numquid ob hoc filii minus erant legitimi? Resp. aut de conscientia incestus potest constare aut non. Set potest constare putas monachus monacham in uxorem habuerit vel laicus aliquis monacham. In hoc casu vel prorsus sunt illegitimi filii, vel ad minus illegitimi sunt quantum ad illam personam, que conscia est criminis sibi bene. Nam quod per testes potest probari, istum esse monachum, et sic constabit de conscientia sui criminis. Si vero de conscientia incestus constare non potest per testes, puta si aliquis suam consanguineam ducat, inpossibile enim est aliquem posse pro teste probare se scire hanc quam ducit suam esse consanguineam. In hoc casu sine exceptione filii sunt legitimi, quia etiam si uterque profiteretur sibi conscium fuisse incestus, nullum tamen fieret preiudicium filiis. Ex quo enim in facie ecclesie contrahunt aliqui, semper presumit ecclesia eos ignorare se esse consanguineos, nisi aperte in contrarium probetur, etiam ponetur tamen parentibus penitentia sine preiudicio filiorum, supra t. De eo qui cognovit, Continebatur arg. (Cass. 59.8). ɸ.'.

45.) Cass. 63.2 (fol. 43rb): 'Ex istis doctores colligunt solutionem istius questionis, que consuevit fieri, sc. utrum invita uxore vel volente possit aliquis minores recipere ordines. Si enim ut inquiunt ab ordinibus ut hic dicitur repellentur uxorati, multo fortius non ordinati inpediuntur, ut ordinari non possint nisi voventibus uxoribus. Set quam sophystica sit hec allegatio, satis patet intentivum consideranti. Non enim hic ab ordinibus uxorati repelluntur, set dumtaxat ecclesiis exuuntur, non ergo per hoc probetur aliquem volente uxore et non castimoniam profitente minores non posse recipere ordines. ɸ.'.

46.) Cass. 63.3 s.v. 'dimittere' (fol. 43rb): 'Solutio: Quod hic dicitur et ab universali ecclesia occidentali tenendum est. Quod vero ecclesia solvatur, vel ad angelicos, qui tunc erant non in fide, est referendum, vel de clericis pauperibus est intelligendum, quibus cum sint clerici indigentibus, non tamquam fratribus, set sicut pauperibus primo quam aliis externis beneficia sint ministranda, ut supra I q. II Sacerdos (C.1 q.2 c.9). ɸ.'.

47.) Cass. 63.12 s.v. 'graviori lapsu' (fol. 43va): 'Non permittit minus, set gravius dicit iurandum, ut XXXIII q. II Si quid (C.33 q.2 c.9?). Non ergo est vera promissio set comparativa, vel forte licet apostolico etiam in hoc casu dispensare ex causa, ut sc. liceat subdiacono contrahere matrimonium. Nam sicut a iuramento potest absolvere aliquem, ut supra XV q. VI Iuratos (C.15 q.6 c.5) et in concilio Romano Sicut ait (3 Conc. Lat. can.27), ita et a voto, arg. supra VIIII q. III Per principalem (C.9 q.3 c.21), et XVIII q. I c. I. Unde et quidam dicunt eum posse dare licentiam monacho ut contrahat. φ.'.

48.) Cass. 63.13 s.v. 'inordinate' (fol. 43va): 'Forte nondum baptizatus se fecit in subdiaconum ordinari, ideoque non suscepit ordinem, ut supra XXXII D. § Porro (D.32 d.p.c.6 §4). Et arg. I q. I Cum Paulus (C.1 q.1 c.26). Vel loquitur de eo qui non habens aliquem inferiorum ordinum, reppente a subdiaconatu incepit, quod non potuit, arg. D. XL Sicut (D.40 c.8), vel forte enormis persone erat nec cum ea fuerat dispensatum, set ita propter pontificis negligentiam ad ordinem illum devenit. φ.'.

49.) Cass. 63.14 (fol. 43va): 'Nota ordinem esse inpedimentum matrimonii, quod sine dubio verum est, nam nec orientales in subdiaconatu contrahunt, ut XXXII D. Si quis eorum (D.32 c.7). φ.'.

III. Ergebnisse

Eine dogmengeschichtliche Auswertung der 49 Glossen würde den für diesen Beitrag vorgesehenen Rahmen sprengen. Immerhin seien einige Beobachtungen zum Inhalt der Glossen festgehalten. Sie betreffen den Autor und seine vorläufige Einordnung in die kanonistischen Schulen am Ende des 12. Jahrhunderts.

Zunächst wird man kaum bezweifeln können, dass es sich bei Phi. um eine individuelle Person handelt, da der Glossator mehrfach von sich in der ersten Person spricht—so in den Glossen Nr. 10, 23, 32, 33, 35. Die Glossen sind durchaus in einem persönlichen Stil geschrieben, wobei sich der Autor häufig auf andere Lehrmeinungen beruft, gelegentlich allgemein auf die *doctores*. In einer einzigen Glosse, die von Juncker ediert wurde (Glosse 32), beruft sich der Verfasser auf Johannes Faventinus und Simon von Bisignano.[19] Diese Glosse hat allerdings die Besonderheit, dass in ihr die Zitate der Dekretalen teilweise nicht auf die *Collectio Cassellana* passen, sondern vielmehr auf die *Collectio Lipsiensis*, was bereits von Juncker bemerkt wurde.[20] Juncker erwog deshalb, dass die Phi.-Glossen insgesamt vielleicht ursprünglich für die *Collectio Lipsiensis* geschrieben sein könnten.[21] Da jedoch alle anderen Glossen in ihren Dekretalenzitaten der *Collectio Cassellana* entsprechen und zudem die Glosse 32 an falscher Stelle in der Bamberger Handschrift eingeordnet ist, könnte hier von Phi. die Glosse eines anderen Autors teilweise übernommen worden sein.[22] Auch stimmt diese Glosse weitgehend

---

19. Cf. Juncker, 'Die Summa' 448.   20. Ibid. 453–54, n. 1.

21. Ibid. 454. Nach ihm soll die *Cassellana*-Glosse auch neues Licht auf die Geschichte der *Collectio Lipsiensis* werfen.

22. Die Glosse bezieht sich auf Cass.49.1 (fol. 36vb), ist aber bei Cass.51.4 (fol. 37r unten) eingeordnet.

mit Ausführungen bei Johannes Faventinus und Simon von Bisignano überein, was Juncker durch parallele Editionen der Texte nachweisen konnte.[23] Die Phi.-Glosse 32 ist vielleicht die Erweiterung einer Glosse des Johannes Faventinus, in der bereits bei Johannes Dekretalenzitate nach einer anderen Sammlung als der *Cassellana* enthalten waren. Phi. übernahm die Glosse einschliesslich der Zitate und erweiterte sie durch einen eigenen Text, den er mit *Mihi aliud videtur dicendum* einleitete.[24] Er bezog sich in seiner Erweiterung auch auf zwei in der *Cassellana* nicht selbständig aufgeführte Dekretalen, wobei eine Verweisung ohne Angabe eines Titels erfolgte.[25] Es ist deshalb nicht wahrscheinlich, dass der gesamte Komplex der Phi.-Glossen ursprünglich für eine Sammlung vom Typ der *Collectio Lipsiensis* geschrieben wurde. Jedoch kann man aus Glosse 32 schliessen, dass Phi. mit den Glossen des Johannes Faventinus und des Simon von Bisignano vertraut war. Bekanntschaft mit Simon lässt sich auch aus einer anderen Glosse der *Cassellana* schliessen, die allerdings ohne die Sigle Phi. überliefert ist, aber hier zusätzlich ediert werden soll, da sie im Stil den Phi.-Glossen entspricht und die Sigle vielleicht nur vergessen wurde:[26]

50.) Cass. 58.20 s.v. 'uxo̧rem' (fol. 41rb): 'Nota quosdam doctores et precipue Symonem hec male intellixisse assignantes hec procuracio ei quod est supra t. proximo, Ex publico (Cass. 57.9). In alio enim casu prorsus hoc dicitur, nam non dicitur hic, quod relicto in seculo non liceat ad alia vota transire, set dicitur, quod non ita licet viro aliam ducere antequam illa convertatur, sicut ei licet monasterium eligere'.

Für die Zuweisung dieser Glosse an Phi. spricht vor allem, dass hier wie in den Glossen 9 und 45 allgemein von *doctores* die Rede ist. Es lässt sich daher festhalten, dass der Glossator Phi. wohl mit der Schule von Bologna in Zusammenhang zu bringen ist.

Kann man den rätselhaften Phi. darüber hinausgehend mit dem Magister Fidantia identifizieren? Die Sigle des *Fidantia* in den von Weigand edierten Glossen—f. bzw. f.C.—stimmt nicht mit der in der *Cassellana* verwendeten Sigle überein. Gegen eine Identifizierung spricht zudem ein weiteres wohl entscheidendes Argument. Für die bisher bekannten Glossen des Fidantia ist es charakteristisch, dass in ihnen zahlreiche Zitate aus Quellen des römischen Rechts zu finden sind. Dagegen beziehen sich die Phi.-Glossen nur an einer Stelle auf römisches Recht (Glosse 22). Man wird daher die Vermutung einer Identität von Phi. und Fidantia aufgeben müssen.

23. Juncker, 'Die Summa' 446–52.
24. Cf. die Edition ibid. 448.
25. Es handelt sich um die Dekretalen 'Quemlibet' (JL 14156 = WH 761, Teil e = Lips.45.3 = 1 Comp.2.14.1) und 'Causam' (JL 14332 = WH 109 = Lips.45.4 = 1 Comp.2.14.2 = X 2.21.1). Zum Vorkommen dieser Dekretalen in den Sammlungen, cf. Juncker, 'Die Summa' 453–54 n. 1. Auf die Dekretale 'Causam' wird in der Cass.-Glosse folgendermassen verwiesen: 'Et in verbo c. Causam (cf. ibid. 448)'.
26. Die Glosse wurde bereits ibid. 467 ediert.

Jedoch bleibt zu prüfen, ob nicht eine andere Spur zur Identifizierung der Herkunft von Phi. verfolgt werden sollte. Die Kasseler Handschrift der *Cassellana* wird paläographisch als Produkt eines deutschen Skriptoriums bestimmt und enthält durch die Veränderung der Textstelle *super Divam* in *super Fuldam* in einer Dekretale Alexanders III. einen Hinweis, dass der Schreiber der Handschrift offenbar in der hessischen Region Fulda/Kassel beheimatet war.[27] Der Papst- und Kaiserkatalog der Handschrift reicht bis 1191.[28] Daraus ist zu schliessen, dass die *Cassellana* schon gegen Ende des 12. Jahrhunderts bekannt war. Die Bamberger Handschrift ist keine Abschrift der Kasseler, sondern soll auf einer gemeinsamen Vorlage beruhen.[29] Deshalb dürfte auch die Bamberger Handschrift am ehesten der Zeit um 1200 zuzuordnen sein. Sie wird heute durch ein Fragment der um 1203 entstandenen Dekretalensammlung Gilberts ergänzt, das allerdings ursprünglich wohl mit dem Manuskript Can.20 verbunden war.[30] Es lässt sich deshalb nicht sicher schliessen, ob der 'Bamberger Gilbert' als Supplement zur *Cassellana* angelegt wurde. Jedoch lässt sich vermuten, dass die *Cassellana* bereits um 1200 nach Bamberg gelangte.

Die Herkunft des in Bologna geschulten Glossators Phi. lässt sich vielleicht wegen des Inhalts der Glossen bestimmen. In Glosse 13 tauchen die Begriffe *plebanus* und *plebanatus* für Pfarrer und Pfarrei auf, die in Oberitalien und Süddeutschland im 12. Jahrhundert gebräuchlich waren, jedoch kaum in der Region von Bologna.[31] Noch aufschlussreicher scheint mir die Glosse 34 zu sein. Der hier kommentierte Fall (Cass. 58.39 = 1 Comp.4.19.3 = JL 14214) betraf eine Ehe innerhalb verbotener Verwandtschaftsgrade, deren Trennung später von denjenigen betrieben wurde, die zur Zeit der Eheschliessung die Verwandtschaft gekannt und dazu geschwiegen hatten. Der Papst will solche Ankläger im Eheprozess ausschliessen, was im Widerspruch zu Ausführungen bei Gratian zu stehen scheint (C.35 q.9 d.p.c.2). Der Kommentator Phi. will den Ausschluss solcher Ankläger durch den Papst unter Berufung auf C.35 q.6 c.7 nur auf das Sendverfahren beziehen: *Plane tantum potest intelligi de juratis synodalibus . . . qui si a principio taceant, sunt periuri.* Er verwendet hier den Begriff *jurati synodales* (Sendzeugen), der bei Gratian nicht vorkommt, kennt also offenbar das Verfahren vor den Sendgerichten. Diese Gerichte hatten sich jedoch in Italien niemals durchgesetzt und waren um 1200

27. Hierzu cf. bereits den Hinweis in P. Landau 'Die Anfänge der Verbreitung des klassischen kanonischen Rechts in Deutschland im 12. Jahrhundert und im ersten Drittel des 13. Jahrhunderts', in: *Chiesa, diritto e ordinamento della Societas Christiana nei secoli XI e XII* (Milano 1986) 272–97 (= Landau, *Kanones* 411*–29*).

28. Cf. oben n. 5.

29. Deeters, *Die Bambergensisgruppe* 8–9.

30. Cf. oben n. 9.

31. Cf. etwa H. Feine, *Kirchliche Rechtsgeschichte* (Köln und Graz 1972⁵) 182–83; ausserdem H. Schäfer, *Pfarrkirche und Stift im deutschen Mittelalter* (Stuttgart 1903) 53–56.

hauptsächlich noch in Deutschland verbreitet, so auch in Bamberg.[32] Glosse 34 liefert folglich einen Hinweis, dass der Glossator Phi. deutscher Herkunft sein könnte. Das würde bedeuten, dass die wissenschaftliche Auseinandersetzung mit dem Dekretalenrecht nicht nur in der anglo-normannischen Kanonistik, sondern auch in Deutschland relativ frühzeitig einsetzte.[33] Der bisher nicht identifizierte Glossator Phi. (Philippus?) war vielleicht der erste deutsche dekretalistische Kanonist.

32. Zur geographischen Verbreitung der Sendgerichte cf. A. M. Koeniger, *Die Sendgerichte in Deutschland* (München 1907) 186–90. Die Verbreitung der Sendgerichte in der Diözese Bamberg lässt sich vor allem aus dem Sendrecht der Main- und Rednitzwenden (ed. ibid. 194–98) erschliessen, das von Koeniger auf den Anfang des 10. Jahrhunderts datiert wurde.

33. Zu den Anfängen des Dekretalistik in der anglo-normannischen Schule, cf. P. Landau, 'Studien zur Appendix und den Glossen in frühen systematischen Dekretalensammlungen', BMCL 9 (1979) 1–21 (= Landau, *Kanones* 257–77).

13

'Mute Dogs, Unable to Bark'

Innocent III's Call to Combat Heresy

Keith H. Kendall

❋

Pope Innocent III (1198–1216) issued the decretal *Vergentis* on 25 March 1199, at the beginning of his second year on the papal throne. He wrote it to the clergy, secular officials, and people of Viterbo, a city notorious at the time for harboring heretics. Viterbo was in the patrimony of St. Peter, making the pope the secular overlord of the city as well as its direct ecclesiastical superior. The situation in Viterbo posed an immediate threat to Innocent's secular and spiritual authority. With Innocent demanding that the bishops in Languedoc take action against the Cathars in their midst, moreover, the situation in Viterbo offered the potential for undermining Innocent's credibility.[1] If heretics lived with impunity in his own lands, how could he hold other bishops accountable for extirpating heresy in theirs?

In *Vergentis* Innocent outlined penalties for heretics and their supporters in Viterbo. This decretal—and its penalties—came to be included in canon law collections during Innocent's pontificate. *Vergentis* was reiterated as part of *De haereticis* in the legislation of the Fourth Lateran Council and eventually included in the *Liber extra* of 1234. The penalties, including one that allowed the public authority to confiscate the property of heretics and their supporters, were cited by canon lawyers and secular rulers alike. However, Innocent's justification for his original sanctions, picked up in part in Constitution 3 of Lateran IV, was dropped by the later canonistic tradition.

The original justification in *Vergentis* included striking images, which Innocent also

---

1. Reg. 1.94; letters contained in Innocent III's registers 1–9 (1198–1206/7) are cited according to: *Die Register Innocenz' III:* 1.–(9.) *Pontifikatsjahr* 1198/99 (–1206/7), ed. O. Hageneder et al. (Vienna 1964–2004); for letters included in registers 10–18 (1207/8–1215/16), see ed. PL 215.1103–216.992.

used in several of his sermons and which may have become part of the inquisitorial mindset of the late Middle Ages. Innocent supported his legal actions against heretics and their allies by using vivid theological images, strongly encouraging church leaders to move actively against heretics. The theological orientation of Innocent III has been part of a long-standing scholarly debate. In 1974, Kenneth Pennington brought into clearer focus a trend that had been building in Innocentian scholarship: scholars had been moving away from understanding Innocent III exclusively as a 'lawyer pope' and toward an understanding of him as a theologian as well.[2] Since then, Pennington has repeatedly called into question the assumption that Innocent was a great lawyer pope with deep knowledge of canon law:[3]

Those scholars who simply assume that Innocent was a learned lawyer should pause for a moment before they repeat old platitudes. The point is that we should squeeze as much evidence as possible out of Innocent's works. We should systematically compare his ideas to those of contemporary canonists and theologians (his sermons offer the best evidence). . . . Only then shall we be in a position to judge the depth of his knowledge of law and theology.

Other Innocentian scholars have responded to Pennington's challenge.[4] The present chapter takes up the argument by tracing one of the theological images that Innocent used to justify the severe legal sanctions in *Vergentis:* 'mute dogs, unable to bark'. In the decretal, in other letters, and in several sermons, Innocent used the image to justify his own actions against heretics and to rouse other bishops and leaders to actively combat heresy.

Vergentis provided penalties against the 'defenders, harbourers, supporters and adherents of heretics', penalties 'of self-defence but of a very aggressive kind'.[5] Focusing more on those who aided and abetted heretics than on the heretics themselves, Innocent ruled that such people should suffer the penalty of infamy, which meant a loss of civil liberties and rights as well as degradation from office if they were clergy, and being barred from practice if they were judges, lawyers, or notaries.[6] In addition, one clause in *Vergentis* decreed that the property of heretics and their supporters should

2. K. Pennington, 'The Legal Education of Pope Innocent III', BMCL 4 (1974) 70–77 (= idem, *Popes, Canonists, and Texts 1150–1550* [Aldershot 1993], article I).
3. K. Pennington, 'Review of Wilhelm Imkamp, Das Kirchenbild Innocenz' III.', ZRG Kan. Abt. 72 (1986) 428 (= 'Further Thoughts on Pope Innocent III's Knowledge of Law', in: idem, *Popes, Canonists, and Texts,* article II).
4. For more recent historiography, see the chapters by E. Peters and R. Kay in: *Pope Innocent III and His World,* ed. J. Moore (Aldershot 1999); and my *Sermons of Pope Innocent III: The 'Moral Theology' of a Pastor and Pope* (Ph.D. diss.; Syracuse University 2003) 29–40.
5. *Vergentis,* Reg. 2.1: 'Defensores, receptatores, fautores et credentes hereticorum'; see P. Clarke, 'Innocent III, Canon Law and the Punishment of the Guiltless', in: *Pope Innocent III and His World* 272.
6. *Vergentis,* Reg. 2.1.

be confiscated by the public authority, against which the previous rightful heirs would have no recourse. *Vergentis* thus allowed the public authority to disinherit the heirs of heretics and supporters of heretics and to benefit from the confiscation of the property. Peter Clarke has suggested that these penalties were intended to be 'coercive rather than vindictive', as Innocent's own justification for such action shows.[7] His justification included the 'mute dogs' metaphor and shows Innocent's pastoral concerns for the defense of his flock even as he was imposing 'somewhat severe' penalties:[8]

Indeed, lest we, who—as it were, at about the eleventh hour—were evangelically appointed by God the Father to be among the day-laborers, or rather over the day-laborers, in the vineyard of the Lord of hosts (Mt. 20.1–16), and to whom Christ's sheep were committed on account of our pastoral duty (Jo. 21.15–17), be viewed as neither capturing the foxes who are destroying the vineyard of the Lord (Cant. 2.15) nor keeping the wolves away from the sheep (Jo. 10.12–13)—and for this reason we could be called 'mute dogs, unable to bark' (Is. 56.10)—and be destroyed with the wicked farmers (Mt. 21.33–41), and be compared to the mercenary (Jo. 10.12–13); we have authorized a somewhat severe resolution against defenders, harborers, supporters, and adherents of heretics, so that through it those who are not able to be recalled to the way of righteousness at least may be confounded by the condition of their defenders, harborers, supporters and also adherents, and when they have seen themselves shunned by everyone, they may desire to be reconciled with complete unity.

Innocent's concern to be a faithful pastor can be seen in this justification, which immediately precedes the presentation of the penalties in *Vergentis*. His commission not only as pastor ('day-laborer') but especially as chief pastor ('over the day-laborers') required him to take steps against heretics and their supporters, lest he fail to defend the people who had been committed to him by Christ. To do less would be to act as a 'mercenary'—his views on 'mercenaries' are discussed below—or as a 'wicked farmer', who turns traitor against the landowner. The 'wicked farmer' refers to Matthew 21.33–41, where Jesus told a parable about a landowner who leased his vineyard to tenants. The tenants proceeded not only to deny the landowner what was owed him but also to murder his representatives. This story from the Gospel forms part of the theological context for Innocent's chief innovation in *Vergentis*, taking the penalties for treason, *laesae maiestatis,* from Roman law, including confiscation of property, and applying them to heresy.[9] Innocent justified the new sanctions in terms of his pastoral duty to defend the flock.

Innocent used biblical authorities and images similar to those in *Vergentis* in one of his sermons, *I Am the Good Shepherd,* preached on the Second Sunday after Easter at St.

7. Clarke, 'Innocent' 278.   8. *Vergentis,* Reg. 2.1.
9. Ibid.

Peter's Basilica some time between 1198 and 1204—probably on either 20 April 1203 or 9 May 1204.[10] On the Second Sunday after Easter, commonly called 'Good Shepherd Sunday', during the late Middle Ages it was customary to preach about the behavior of priests.[11] In the *Good Shepherd*, Innocent clearly laid out his expectations for both laity and clergy. He expected the clergy to imitate the Good Shepherd and to be good shepherds, not mercenaries (also translated as 'hired hands'). One of the duties of good shepherds was the pastoral responsibility of preachers to 'bark' at danger so that the flock could be warned. However, Innocent lamented that he saw too many mercenaries and too few pastors behaving like 'barking-dogs':[12]

The mercenary 'sees' any of those wolves 'coming and abandons the sheep and flees' (Jo. 10.12–13), 'not' always 'changing location, but' often 'withdrawing his protection'.[13] Because he is hiding, remaining silent, and holding back when he refuses to see injustice, violence, and treachery against the powerless, orphans, and widows, he is like a mute dog 'unable to bark' (Is. 56.10). Alas that today we see and suffer such mercenaries in the church, because when they have the name of shepherd, and the duty *[officium]*, but not the merit, heretics prevail, tyrants rage, and the faithless follow, because with difficulty is he found who places himself as 'a wall for the house of Israel' or stands 'against the enemy on the day of the Lord' (Ez. 13.5). For 'the harvest is plentiful', [but] in truth there are 'few workers' (Lc. 10.2), seeing that although we see many in name, nevertheless we see few in works. On that account 'the wolf ravishes and scatters the sheep' (Jo. 10.12), seeing that our 'adversary the devil, like a roaring lion prowls around, looking for someone to devour' (1 Pet. 5.8).

The image of mute or silent dogs comes from Isaiah 56.10. This biblical passage calls for righteous living not only from the common people among the returned Exiles but also from their religious and secular leaders. The text accuses the religious leaders—the dogs—of being lazy and gluttonous, which renders them blind to the dangers confronting Israel and, therefore, silent. The image is based on the thoroughly rural,

---

10. For an edition and translation of *I Am the Good Shepherd (Ego sum pastor bonus)*, see Kendall, *Sermons* 394–418.

11. J. Powell, 'Pastor Bonus: Some Evidence of Honorius III's Use of Sermons of Pope Innocent III', *Speculum* 52 (1977) 526.

12. 'Quemlibet istorum luporum mercenarius "videt venientem, et dimittit oves et fugit" (Jo. 13.10–12), "non" semper "mutando locum, sed" saepe "subtrahendo" praesidium. Quia latet, tacet et sustinet, cum minime "videt iniustitiam", violentiam et perfidiam, contra impotentes, orphanos et egenos; quasi canis mutus non valens "latrare". Heu! quot hodie tales videmus et dolemus in ecclesia mercenarios; propter quod cum nomen pastoris habeant, et officium, et non meritum, invalescunt haeretici, tyranni saeviunt, et perfidi persequuntur. Quia vix invenitur, qui ponat se "murum pro domo Israel", aut stet ex "adverso in die Domini". "Messis" enim "multa, operarii" vero "pauci", quoniam etsi multos videamus in nomine, paucos tamen videmus in opere. Propterea "lupus rapit, et dispergit oves", quoniam "adversarius" noster "diabolus, tanquam leo rugiens circuit, quaerens quem devoret",' ed. Kendall, *Sermons* 402–3.

13. Gregory I, *Homilia* 14 (PL 76.1129–30).

pastoral experience of shepherds, herd dogs, and sheep. God's people are like sheep, being guarded, protected, and provided for by the Shepherd and his dogs. Christian exegetes adopted the images, the interpretation, and—when appropriate—the warning to Christian religious leaders, even though the passage was also used by Christian theologians as a weapon to describe the Christian perception of the faithlessness of Jews when such an exegesis suited their purposes.[14]

Christian preachers had been identified with dogs long before Innocent III. The highly influential Pope Gregory I articulated the same image in his *Exposition on the Song of Songs*. As part of his exegesis of Canticles 2.15 ('Catch us the little foxes that destroy the vines: for our vineyard hath flourished'), he linked foxes and dogs to signify heretics and preachers. After Gregory had identified the foxes as heretics, who 'tear down the vineyards, because through heretics the churches are dried up from the greenness of right faith', he explained:[15]

These [foxes], then, are captured by holy preachers when, at the very time of conflict, they are convinced by words of truth. Of course, holy preachers sometimes are described as dogs, because by untiring preaching, as if by incessant barking, they endeavor to protect the flock of sheep from enemies. These dogs capture foxes for Christ, because they love their leader faithfully, laboring for his love, evading heretics [who ask] convoluted questions, as they lead [heretics] from caves of darkness to the light of truth.

In addition, within the context of discussing pastors as either shepherds or mercenaries in his *Pastoral Rule*, Gregory I linked—as Innocent III would later do—the 'mute dogs' metaphor with that from Ezekiel 13.5 of priests being a wall:[16]

For, on this account the Lord rebukes [mercenaries] through the prophet, saying, 'Mute dogs, unable to bark'. Yet, on the other hand, he inquires, 'You have not gone up against the enemy, nor have you placed yourself as a wall for the house of Israel in order to stand in battle on the day of the Lord'. Of course, 'to go up against the enemy' is to counter with a free voice the authorities of the world for the defense of his flock.

Isidore of Seville also used the metaphor, saying that 'problematic priests' are like mute dogs because they do not defend the people entrusted to them by means of the word of doctrine.[17] Gratian picked up the section from Gregory's *Pastoral Rule* as he discussed

14. See Gregory I, *Moralia* 20.30.15 (PL 76.145D): 'Unde Judaeorum tarditas, qui pro Deo loqui noluerunt, increpante propheta, reprehenditur, qui ait: "Canes muti, non valentes latrare".'
15. Gregory I, *Super Cantica Canticorum expositio* 2.17 (PL 79.500B–C); also see Kendall, *Sermons* 188–89.
16. Gregory I, *Pastoral Rule* 4 (PL 77.30B–C).
17. Isidore of Seville, *Sentences* 3.35 ('De indoctis praepositis') §2 (PL 83.707B): 'Sacerdotes indoctos per Isaiam prophetam ita Dominus improbat: "Ipsi", inquit, "pastores ignoraverunt intelligentiam". Et iterum: "Spe-

the damage that silent preachers caused the church by allowing the wolves to attack, rather than benefiting the church through good works and honorable speech.[18]

From authorities such as Gregory I, Isidore of Seville, and Gratian, twelfth-century preachers and theologians incorporated the metaphor of 'mute dogs' into works about clerical faithfulness and unfaithfulness and into calls for clerical reform. Early in the twelfth century, Honorius of Autun emphasized the need for clergy to live faithfully in order to be able to preach effectively; remaining unreformed had rendered them 'mute dogs, unable to bark; conscious of their wicked lives they had become silent with respect to the word of God, and, lest they be rebuked for living perversely, they had done no barking in [their] preaching'.[19] Gaufridus Babion echoed Isidore's exposition in several mid-twelfth-century synodal sermons and included biblical ideas that Innocent would later find attractive. In one of his sermons, Gaufridus warned the clergy that those who preached goodness but lived wickedly were like the priests castigated by Ezekiel (22.6), being unable to distinguish between what was holy and profane, between one kind of uncleanness and another. These clergy, Gaufridus preached, being 'mute dogs, unable to bark', might be circling the flock and thinking that they were defending it, when in reality the wolf was not fleeing at their preaching.[20] Later in the century, other writers also used the metaphor to portray the inability or unwillingness of clergy to speak up when speaking up was necessary to defend against enemies.[21]

As a result, Innocent could have found the 'mute dogs' image in any number of works. In his theological writings, Innocent freely adopted material from works by Pope Gregory I.[22] Innocent's theology also included ideas found in works attributed to Honorius of Autun and Gaufridus Babion. Innocent could have been familiar with Gratian's use of the metaphor as well, although his wording resembles the language

---

culatores caeci omnes", id est, imperiti episcopi, "nescierunt", inquit, universi, "canes muti, non valentes latrare", hoc est, plebes commissas non valentes resistendo malis per verbum doctrinae defendere'.

18. D.43 d.a.c.1, D.43 c.1.

19. Honorius of Autun, *Surge, illuminare, Hierusalem,* for Epiphany (PL 172.846D): 'Unde dicitur: "Canes muti non valentes latrare". Ob conscientiam pravae vitae a verbo Dei obmutescunt, et ne redarguantur contra perverse viventes, latratus praedicationis non edunt'.

20. Gaufridus Babion, *Sermo* 131 'Fecit Deus duo luminaria magna', in synod (PL 171.926A–B): 'Haec tria vobis necessaria sunt: Lux bonae operationis, oculus discretionis, sal praedicationis. Qui bene praedicant et male vivunt, sunt quidem sal, sed non sunt lux. Dominus per Ezechielem ait: "Sacerdotes contempserunt legem meam, et polluerunt sanctuaria mea; inter sanctum et profanum non habuerunt distantiam, et inter pollutum et immundum non intellexerunt". Sunt alii qui nesciunt praedicare, quibus dicitur: "Canes muti, non valentes latrare". Si oculum discretionis non habet, indigne solvit et ligat. Si non est sal, canis est circa gregem Domini, sed lupum latratu praedicationis non fugat. Si non est lux, alios introducit, sed non intrat. Haec ergo tria vobis necessaria sunt'.

21. E.g., Alan of Lille in an Easter sermon to 'the masters of the clerics', *Sermo* 125 'Ista sunt verba Abrahae ad Saram' (PL 210.208C); Eleanor of Aquitaine in a letter of 1192 to Celestine III (PL 206.1271B).

22. Examples discussed in Kendall, *Sermons* 215–21; also see Powell, 'Pastor Bonus' 528.

of the theologians rather than that of the *Decretum*. In any case, the metaphor of 'mute dogs' was ready at hand for Innocent to use in attempting to promote clerical reforms and to prod his clergy into preaching against enemies of the church, secular authorities who were encroaching on the church's freedoms as well as heretics who were attacking Christian beliefs. In each of the nineteen extant letters written by Innocent *before* his sermon collection of 1203 or 1204, the 'mute dogs' metaphor refers to one of these two issues.[23]

In many of these letters Innocent used the 'mute dogs' metaphor to bring to mind the responsibility of priests—including himself—for the salvation of those who looked to them as mediators with God. For example, in his 1198 letter *Quamvis insula vestra*, after citing the 'mute dogs', Innocent appealed to Acts 20.26–27, in which Paul declared that, since he had proclaimed to the people at Ephesus the whole Gospel, he was 'not responsible for the blood of any of' them. Innocent's implication in this letter was that pastors who remained silent instead of preaching the truth would be required to answer for their silence—and for the demise of those to whom they should have preached—at the final judgment.[24] Indeed, he may have had in mind common twelfth-century commentaries such as that of Honorius of Autun, who preached that the very life of a priest depended on preaching. If a priest, Honorius said, 'announces the kingdom of God and his jurisdiction *[iusticia]* to the people, their souls are saved'. If, however, he does not preach and 'the people die in their sin, then their blood will be required at his hand, as

23. The nineteen letters are: *Solitae benignitatis* (before 1203) to Constantinople, reproduced in his *Gesta* (ed. D. Gress-Wright, *The 'Gesta Innocentii III'. Text, Introduction and Commentary* [Ph.D. diss., Bryn Mawr College 1981] 103–9; trans. J. M. Powell, *The Deeds of Pope Innocent II by an Anonymous Author* [Washington, D.C. 2004] 89–94); *Quamvis insula* (30 July 1198), Reg. 1.320, to Iceland regarding righteous living; *Vergente* (5 Jan.1199), Reg. 1.509, to Syracuse regarding heresy; *Vergentis* (25 Mar.1199), Reg. 2.1, to Viterbo regarding heresy; *Anxiatur in nobis* (Oct./Nov.1199), Reg. 2.188, to clergy of France regarding the interdict and the liberty of the church; *Si ad ovile Dominicum* (Oct.1200), Reg. 3.7, to clergy of Navarre; *Cum credamus* (Nov./Dec.1200), Reg. 3.24, to his legate in Narbonne; *Tua nobis fraternitas* (ca. 10 May 1202), Reg. 5.32, to the archbishop of Verona regarding reform of clerics who encourage heresy; *Quoniam impunitas* (10 May 1203), Reg. 6.17, to clergy of Sardinia regarding the interdict; *Tacti sumus* (ca. 16 Apr. 1203), Reg. 6.46, to Lombardy regarding clerics standing up to lay abuse; *Cum regia serenitas* (ca. 20–30 May 1203), Reg. 6.68, to King Philip of France regarding peace with England; *Si notasses melius* (30 May 1203), Reg. 6.81, to the archbishop of Narbonne telling him to care for his church; *Credebamus* (ca. 10–31 May 1203), Reg. 6.150, to Sens regarding excommunication and interdict against Count Peter of Sens; *Ex divina lectione* (31 Oct. 1203), Reg. 6.163, to King Philip regarding peace with England; *Utinam non fuisset* (5 Dec. 1203), Reg. 6.179, to king of Denmark telling him to release a bishop; *Utinam labor improbus* (9 Dec. 1203), Reg. 6.180, to King Philip regarding Ingeborg; *Licet epistola* (14 Feb. 1204), Reg. 6.235, a reply to Sens regarding King Philip; *Quia omne caput* (28 May 1204), Reg. 7.76, to Arnald Amaury regarding the investigation of Archbishop Berengar of Narbonne; *Sicut is* (29 May 1204), Reg. 7.79, to Berengar regarding an abbey in his province. The analysis of the 'mute dogs' metaphor confirms the assertion of Clarke, 'Innocent' 272: 'Most of [the penalties affecting the guiltless that Innocent] adopted [were] in response to what he saw as the two big dangers facing the church of his day, namely the growth of popular heresy and secular infringements of ecclesiastical liberty'.

24. *Quamvis insula vestra* (30 July 1198), Reg. 1.320.

if he himself had killed them'.[25] Innocent, it seems, took seriously his responsibility for the salvation of those entrusted to him, bishops and laity, all of whom fell within his jurisdiction *(iusticia)* as pope and could come to him for justice *(iusticia)*.

Out of Innocent's sense of responsibility may have arisen his willingness to take action. He reproved mute-dog bishops such as those in Languedoc who refused to confront the Cathars. He eagerly tried to reconcile heretics and heterodox Christians to the church, by first sending preachers to try to convert the Cathars in 1198. Eventually, he tried to protect the faithful from those who he believed threatened them by calling on Philip Augustus, king of France—in 1204, 1205, and 1207—to wield the secular sword against the princes protecting Catharism.[26] The end result of his dogged activity was the Albigensian Crusade, which began in 1209.

We can surmise that Innocent's sense of responsibility to bark at those threatening his flock was sharpened by the continuing existence of heretics in Viterbo and other central Italian *civitates* over which Innocent exercised *iusticia*. In fact, charges seem to have been leveled at Innocent that he had remained silent when he should have corrected clergy over whom he had authority. In another sermon that included the 'mute dogs' metaphor, *Hoc est maius*, for Ash Wednesday, he defended himself against such charges. Innocent distinguished three kinds of bonds: those of heretics, which are false dogma; those of sinners, which are wicked deeds; and those of the damned, which are eternal punishments. In the section on wicked deeds, he highlighted concupiscence, avarice, and pride as bonds of sinners. He named covetousness *(cupiditas)* as a root of all evil and then went on to defend himself. 'From this root [of covetousness] proceeds [the claim] that we smooth over the sins of our subordinates (as if we were "mute dogs, unable to bark"), lest they actively withdraw from us oblations, tithes, and first-fruits offerings'.[27]

As is evident in his justification in *Vergentis*, in other letters, and in several sermons, Innocent was well aware of the duty of a pastor to bark when a wolf approached. Therefore, he barked at clergy who either were not barking or were not barking enough to protect their flocks. Furthermore, though Innocent emphasized the importance of preaching to protect the faithful, he also showed himself willing to 'bite' if 'barking' did not accomplish that defense.

---

25. Honorius of Autun, *Speculum ecclesiae*, Sermon for the Second Sunday in Lent, 'Esto consentiens' (PL 172.886D–887A): 'Erat namque praeceptum in lege ut tintinnabula essent intexta in sacerdotali veste, ut ingrediente tabernaculum sonitus audiretur et non moreretur (Exod.39). Vestis tintinnabulis intexta est vita sacerdotum praedicatione subnixa. Si enim populo regnum Dei et justiciam ejus annuntiant, animas suas salvant. Si autem justiciam absconderint, et populus iniquitate mortuus fuerit, sanguis ejus de manu sacerdotum requiritur, quasi eum occiderint (Ez.3)'.

26. See *Ad sponsae suae* (May 1204), Reg. 7.79; *Ne populus Israel* (early Feb. 1205), Reg. 7.212; and *Inveterata pravitatis* (late Nov. 1207), Reg. 10.149.

27. Innocent III, Sermon *Hoc est maius*, for Ash Wednesday (PL 217.369A).

Using the 'somewhat severe' penalties first outlined in *Vergentis*, Innocent bit as he tried to protect the flock entrusted to him. Other defenses he put in place included the legal procedure of Inquisition and the calling of the Albigensian Crusade. Whether the defenses were military or legal, the justifications Innocent provided for such actions were predominantly pastoral, theological, and biblical. Justified by the necessity for 'mute dogs' to bark or even to bite in defending their flocks, the penalties in *Vergentis* and later in Constitution 3 of the Fourth Lateran Council became part of the bite that the late medieval Church implemented in its pastoral defense of the faithful against heretics and others perceived as enemies.

14

Johannes Faventinus on Marriage

(With an Appendix Revisiting the Question of the Dating of Alexander III's Marriage Decretals)

Charles Donahue, Jr.

❊

The *Summa decretorum* of Johannes Faventinus has not received a very good press. It is largely, as the author himself admits, a 'scissors-and-paste job', a compilation of quotations and near quotations from the *summae* of Rufinus and Stephen of Tournai.[1] It is perhaps for this reason that, so far as I am aware, no one has seriously looked at what Johannes has to say about marriage. What he has to say about marriage under the rubric of C.27 q.2 (the *sponsa duorum*) is not what either Rufinus or Stephen said on the topic, although Johannes borrows from both. What Johannes says, we will suggest, is of some importance for the story of the development of the classical canon law on the formation of marriage. More broadly, it may mean that the emphasis that the dedicatee of this piece has placed throughout his career on the role of the schools in the development of the classical canon law is closer to the mark than the emphasis that the author of this piece has placed on the role of the pope, particularly Alexander III.

First, a brief sketch of the background: Gratian's *Decretum* (C.27 q.2) asks whether a woman espoused to one man may leave her espoused and marry another. Gratian's answer to the question, at least as it was reported by his followers, was that she might do so so long as she had not sexual intercourse with the first man.[2] Espousal creates marriage initiate *(coniugium initiatum);* intercourse following espousal creates 'com-

---

1. Kuttner, *Repertorium* 145.

2. C.27 q.2 d.p.c.50 (in the first recension; see A. Winroth, *The Making of Gratian's Decretum* [Cambridge 2000] 222) seems to suggest that the result might be different if the first espousals were solemn, even if not consummated. The decretists, by and large, ignored this suggestion or held that it was not supported by the custom of the church.

plete' marriage *(coniugium ratum)*.[3] Only the second is indissoluble. The arguments that Gratian uses to reach this result are complicated. Suffice it say here that the distinction that he drew explained a number of conflicting rulings in the tradition, among which were those about entry into religion (it could be done without the consent of the spouse before consummation but not after), impotence or frigidity (it was a cause for dissolution of the marriage if it arose before the marriage was consummated but not after), and the prohibition on 'bigamists' taking higher orders (a clerk who married a widow whose marriage had not been consummated was not a 'bigamist', but one who married a widow whose marriage had been consummated was a 'bigamist'). Gratian's resolution did not, however, fit very well with the Roman-law tradition, which seems quite insistent that consummation has nothing to do with the formation of marriage, nor with the doctrine that Mary and Joseph were truly husband and wife, even though they were believed never to have had intercourse.

Although Gratian was unaware of it, at approximately the same time that he was writing or slightly later, Hugh of St. Victor and others in what was to become the theological tradition were also addressing the question of what made a marriage.[4] Hugh made a tripartite division. First, he distinguished between promises to marry and the marriage itself. The promise is a promise, but only a promise. To break it is a sin, but if one promises to marry one person and then marries another, it is the second marriage that is to be held inviolate. In marriage itself, Hugh continued, there are two sacraments. The first arises when the couple presently consent to take each other as husband and wife. This is the sacrament of the yearning of the soul for God and the love of God for the soul. The second arises when the couple has intercourse. This is the sacrament of Christ and the Church, spoken of in the letter to the Ephesians.[5]

Writing after Gratian's first recension, probably in the mid- to late-1150s, Peter Lombard adopted Hugh's ideas (and those of Walter of Mortagne) and explicitly rejected Gratian's. Peter, too, distinguished between present and future consent and attributed to them the same consequences that Hugh of St. Victor had attributed to them. He also held that one who contracted presently could not enter religion without the consent of his or her spouse. Peter treated impotence and frigidity as problems of capacity.

---

3. The meaning of *ratum* was to change, hence the use here of the somewhat less literal 'complete'.

4. Gratian does seem to have known the *Sententiae Magistri A.*, but, quite rightly, did not derive from them the distinction between present and future consent. See P. Landau, 'Gratian und die *Sententiae Magistri A.*', in: *Aus Archiven und Bibliotheken: Festschrift für Raymund Kottje zum 65. Geburtstag*, ed. H. Mordek (Freiburger Beiträge zur mittelalterlichen Geschichte 3; Frankfurt/M. 1992) 311–26. For the origins of the distinction in works of the school of Laon other than the *Sententiae Magistri A.*, see H. Reinhardt, *Die Ehelehre der Schule des Anselm von Laon* (Münster 1974) 78–86.

5. Hugh of St. Victor, *De beatae Mariae virginitate* 1 (PL 176.859; cf. ibid. 864); idem, *De sacramentis* 2.11.4 (PL 176.485). Cf. Eph. 5.32. For the dating of these works, see the Appendix.

Those who are impotent or frigid cannot consent to marriage, even though they may not know of their incapacity until they consent to marriage and attempt intercourse.[6] Peter's distinction is not so good as Gratian's in reconciling the conflicting canonical rulings; it does, however, fit better with the Roman legal tradition and with the doctrine that Mary and Joseph were truly husband and wife.

Rufinus, who was probably writing in the early to mid-1160s, was aware that there were those who were teaching a doctrine contrary to what Gratian had espoused.[7] Although there are those who have expressed doubt as to whether he had Peter Lombard in mind, I am inclined to think that Peter (among others) is indeed the object of the following outburst:[8]

Mighty fickle is the opinion on these questions that those who are not ministers of Christ and dispensers of divine scripture but seekers after empty glory have made two-faced.[9] When they read the works of others, works that are polished in their diction, brought to perfection by moral taste, and consecrated by the reverence of almost the whole world, scarcely having tasted them, they hold them in disdain and with a snap of the fingers produce new sounds,[10] not drawing water from the middle of the mountains, but letting loose an arrow from the quiver of the king of Babylon against the daughter of Jerusalem, so that they might in darkness strike with arrows the

6. Peter Lombard, *Sententiae* 4.27–28, ed. *Sententiae in IV libros distinctae* (2 vols.; Spicilegium Bonaventurianum 5.1–2; Grottaferrata 1981³) 2.421–35.

7. Paucapalea is unaware of the conflict between Gratian's position and that of Peter Lombard, probably because he wrote before Peter wrote or at least before Peter's work was known in Italy. For the date of Rufinus's *Summa*, see A. Gouron, 'Les sources civilistes et la datation des Sommes de Rufin et d'Étienne de Tournai', BMCL 16 (1986) 55–70.

8. Rufinus, *Summa ad* C.27 q.2, ed. H. Singer, *Die Summa Decretorum des Magister Rufinus* (Paderborn 1902, repr. Aalen 1963) 440–41. The doubts are principally those of Singer (ibid. cxxi), whose chronological arguments we can dismiss now that we have dated Rufinus's *Summa* to the 1160s (above, text and note 7), but whose textual arguments still have some bite. Singer found in Rufinus no quotations from or reminiscences of Peter that were not also to be found elsewhere. What he thought was a possible exception (ibid. 431 n.b) is not an exception because the same phrase is found in Gratian, C.27 q.2 d.p.c.3. My conviction that Peter is at least one of the objects of Rufinus's attack is based on the fact that he is attacking someone who expressly disagreed with Gratian. Peter is the only Parisian sentence-writer whose work is known to antedate Rufinus's and who knows Gratian's work and deals with it. None of the Bolognese who ultimately disagreed with Gratian (below, text at nn. 13–15) can be shown to have written before Rufinus, though some of them may have. In the case of the Bolognese, too, we need to consider the possibility that Rufinus was aware of what they were teaching even before they 'published'.

9. The violence of the rhetoric of this passage sometimes leaves the sense unclear. In the Latin it is clear that it is the fickle opinion *(vaga sententia)* that Gratian's opponents have made two-faced *(bifrontem)*, but whether 'two-faced' refers to the distinction between present and future consent (in which case the same argument could be made about the distinction between initiate and consummate marriage), or whether it refers to separating the question of the existence of a marriage from its dissolubility (in which case the argument applies better to Gratian than it does to the opinion being attacked), or whether it refers to accepting some of Gratian but not all of him (a charge that could be leveled against virtually any author of the period, including Rufinus) is not clear. Perhaps 'two-faced' should be understood as a general vituperative, like 'mighty fickle'.

10. *Novas aures*, literally 'new ears'.

righteous of heart.[11] When Gratian of great memory had built an authentic distinction in this matter concerning marriage, saying that between an espoused man and an espoused woman there was marriage initiate not marriage consummate, certain people, envying the drinking water[12] of the simple, in the manner of wild animals on the march, troubled the clear waters, and blowing on this sacred distinction with the high wind of pride, promulgated a new tale, saying that there is not marriage between just any espoused because there is not always among them such consent as makes a marriage. For consent, they say, is of two kinds: of the present tense, as when they say to each other, 'I take you as my [husband] or wife' *(accipio te in meum vel meam)*, 'I will you as my husband or wife' *(volo te in meum vel meam)*, or something similar; or of the future tense, specifically of matrimony to be contracted, as when it is said by both of them 'I promise—or I swear—to take you as my husband', and vice versa, or such like. The former, they say, makes a perfected and complete *(ratum)* marriage, on account of which they cannot join with someone else while the other is living nor can they enter a monastery without the consent of the other; otherwise, there having been an espousal, if either of them, without the consent of the other, goes to a monastery, or joins carnally with another, the former person is to be taken out of the monastery, and the latter person restored to his prior spouse. The second consent they say does not make a matrimony; therefore those among whom such consent intervenes, if they are joined to others, the subsequent coupling *(copula)* is not destroyed; and those who enter a monastery can be bound by a vow [of chastity] without the consent of the other. Indeed, those who allege such things in their writings, [who] make out of some authority of the holy fathers this new creation, how they plot that they should get us to expound [their doctrine] or draw us into imitating it! Therefore holding up to light before all their opinion of the matter, let us see at length what their objections are and how our side is sufficient for them and impugns them.

It is important to emphasize that the Bolognese canonists were not monolithic on this topic. Rolandus in the *Stroma* shows no awareness of the position of the Parisian masters, but his *Sentences* and one of the *quaestiones* reported in his name suggest that he ultimately adopted the distinction between present and future consent as the solution to the problem of the *sponsa duorum*.[13] Gandulphus adopted the Parisian position fully, though it takes a careful reading to see that he did so.[14] Cardinalis, too, adopted the Parisian position.[15] Stephen of Tournai lays out both positions quite clearly, and in

11. A mixed metaphor worthy of the *New Yorker*'s column 'Block that Metaphor!'. The language of the last image is reminiscent of *Lamentations* (Lam. 3.12–13): *tetendit arcum suum et posuit me quasi signum ad sagittam; misit in renibus meis filias faretrae suae* (speaking of God, though He is acting through the king of Babylon).

12. *Potibus*, literally 'drinks'.

13. Rolandus, *Sententiae*, *[De impedimento ligacionis]*, ed. A. Gietl, *Die Sentenzen Rolands nachmals Papstes Alexander III.* (Freiburg 1891) 274; Rolandus, *Quaestiones* 26, ed. F. Thaner, *Die Summa Magistri Rolandi* (Innsbruck 1874) 278.

14. Gandulphus, *Sententiae* 4.235–45, ed. J. de Walter, *Magistri Gandulphi Bononiensis Sententiarum libri quatuor* (Vienna 1924) 520–32.

15. Cardinalis, *ad* C.27 q.2 pr., ed. Weigand, *Glossen* 1.160 no. 777.

a charming aside he leaves it to his reader to decide which is better.[16] So far as we now know, only Rufinus defended Gratian's position to the hilt, and even he adopted the notion of the dual sacramentality of marriage.[17]

The *Summa Parisiensis*, which is roughly contemporary with Rufinus, lacks a treatment of C.27 q.2, but in commenting on the topic of custom the summist reports:[18]

There is found a certain custom which today is observed in one way in the church in *Francia* and in another in the Roman church. For if a man espouses a woman by words of the present tense and receives the blessing of a priest with her, but before he knows her she is espoused by another and carnally known, the French church compels her to return to the first man, but not the Roman church. And it is not yet known which [custom] is better.

Elsewhere, commenting on the question of the ordination of 'bigamists', the *Summa Parisiensis* tells us:[19]

Gratian argues from these [canons] in Causa 27 that there is no marriage between those who are espoused, for if there were marriage, the man who married the espoused of a man who had died would be the husband of a widow. But someone who has married such a woman may be promoted [to higher orders] by the authority of this decree;[20] hence she was not the wife of the first man. But the church of the French *(ecclesia Francorum)* judges that if an espousal is made by words of the present tense, that is, 'I take you as mine', there is thereby complete *(ratum)* matrimony. Whence even if the espoused woman is carnally joined to another, she is compelled to return to the first man who did [not] know her.[21] Thus, therefore, there was a matrimony [by the exchange of present consent].

The summist continues by adopting the argument of Peter Lombard (who is specifically cited) about D.34 c.20, that it concerns a consent of the future tense not of the present.

The *Summa 'Elegantius'*, written probably in the late 1160s, reports the disagreement between the churches in terms similar to those used in the *Summa Parisiensis*.[22]

In this question the Gallican and transalpine churches disagree. The transalpines distinguish between initiate and consummate marriage, teaching *(tradentes)* that marriage is initiated in the

16. Stephen of Tournai, *Summa ad* C.27 q.2, ed. J. F. von Schulte, *Stephan von Doornick. Die Summa über das Decretum Gratiani* (Giessen 1891, repr. Aalen 1965) 235–36.

17. Rufinus, *ad* C.27 q.2, ed. 441–42.

18. *Summa Parisiensis, ad* D.11 c.11, ed. T. P. McLaughlin, *The Summa Parisiensis on the Decretum Gratiani* (Toronto 1952) 11.

19. Ibid. *ad* D.34 c.19, ed. 33–34.

20. D.34 c.20, a decretal ascribed to Pope Pelagius (550–60), which allowed a man who had married a virgin widow to receive higher orders.

21. The 'not' is added by the editor but is required for sense.

22. *Summa 'Elegantius'* 13.31, 33, ed. G. Fransen and S. Kuttner, *Summa 'Elegantius in iure diuino' seu Coloniensis* (MIC A.1.3; Vatican City 1990) 17, 19.

conjugal pact and consummated by carnal coupling, just as a contract of sale or barter is begun by agreement *(conventione)* [but] is perfected by handing over *(traditione)*, because at that point ownership is transferred. . . . To this the Gallican church replies by distinguishing *sponsalia* into legal and canonical. A legal espousal is 'the proposal and promise back of future nuptials',[23] which are called *sponsalia*, and this promises nuptials and marriage; it does not make [them]. From this espousal, they say, which is the promise of contracting marriage, it is permissible to go to a monastery but not to marry another man, because it is a sacrilege to violate the faith which is thus promised to the espoused man.

Canonical *sponsalia*, however, which the summist never defines, are, presumably, *sponsalia* of the present tense. 'Immediately when the conjugal pact intervenes between an espoused man and an espoused woman', the summist reports of the opinion of the Gallican church, 'nothing is lacking from the substance of matrimony; there is therefore immediately full and perfect matrimony among them'.[24] While the summist seems at times to support a resolution based on *traductio* or *deductio,* his most firm statement is that he will not take a position. He concludes:[25]

Indeed, on this question not only individuals *(persone)* but also churches, the Gallican and the Roman, as we have said, are in disagreement. The former begot me in faith; the latter trained me in law; therefore I must be silent, lest I seem to pass judgment either on my mother or on my master.

Let us pause for a moment to consider the evidence that we have of the extent of the controversy. That there was a dispute among the doctors is testified to by many authors. That there was a dispute among the churches is testified to by relatively few; the *Summa Parisiensis* and the *Summa 'Elegantius'* are our principal sources. Neither writer offers much geographical precision. The *Summa Parisiensis* tells us that the view that marriages are made by words of the present tense without any requirement for subsequent intercourse was held by the church in *Francia* or by the church of the French *(ecclesia Francorum)*. In the case of the *sponsa duorum* a contrary view is held by 'the Roman church'. In the case of a clerk who marries a virgin widow, the difference of views is said to be that between Peter Lombard and Gratian. The summist derives the position of the French church from that which it holds in the case of the *sponsa duorum,* and no position of the Roman church is stated or implied. The author of the *Summa 'Elegantius'* ascribes the conflicting views to the 'Gallican church', on the one hand, and the 'Roman church' or the 'transalpine church', on the other. Specific views allied with the general transalpine position are said to be held by 'some of the Bolognese *(aliquos Boloniensium)*'.

23. Dig. 23.1.1; see Stephen of Tournai, *ad* C.27 q.2, ed. 236.
24. *Summa 'Elegantius'* 13.36, ed. 3.20.
25. Ibid. 13.39, ed. 3.24–25.

We should hesitate to accept these statements at face value, and we should certainly hesitate to expand the geographical regions mentioned to all of modern France and Italy. The word *Francia* for the author of the *Summa Parisiensis* need be no broader than the *Île de France*, while the *ecclesia Francorum* is probably broader but needs be no broader than the provinces of Rheims and Sens. The *ecclesia Gallicana* of the *Summa Coloniensis* suggests something broader, and with a slightly different focus. Lyon is the primatial see of the Gauls. The geographical location associated with the alternative view is for both writers, Rome. It is a Rome that apparently includes Bologna, which is in the province of Ravenna, but needs be no broader than the two provinces. Writing in Cologne one might loosely refer to the churches of these two provinces as 'the transalpine church', without committing one's self to (or knowing) what the position was in the numerous other churches of modern Italy.

There are also reasons to doubt how deeply the views of either Gratian or the Parisian sentence-writers had penetrated into the churches in their respective areas. What little we know of the views of the Roman church on the formation of marriage prior to Alexander III would suggest that *sponsalia* were held to be inviolate without regard to the tense in which they were expressed and without regard to whether sexual intercourse had taken place, at least to the extent that those so espoused could not espouse others.[26] There is, so far as I know, no independent evidence of French practice in the case of the *sponsa duorum*.[27] But if we borrow an example from nearby England, the *Anstey* case suggests not that there was a uniform practice but that there was considerable confusion as to what the rules were.[28]

26. Two decretals are sometimes cited for this proposition: Alexander II to the bishop of Arezzo (JL 4617, of 1066/67), ed. PL 146.1403D; Eugenius III to Azo bishop of Florence (WH 415a, JL 8963, of 10 Dec. 1146), cf. *Italia pontificia* 3.10 no. 16 (ed. F. Zacharia [Zaccaria], *Bibliotheca Pistoriensis* [Turin 1752] 18 no. 13). Neither is squarely on point, though the decretal of Eugenius III comes close. The reason that Eugenius's decretal is not squarely on point is that it emphasizes that the second marriage was entered into in defiance of ecclesiastical interdict. Three decretals of Alexander's, all of which could date from the years 1168–73, deal with the problem of impotence. The first two, written to Italian bishops, say that the practice of the Roman church is not to dissolve marriages for impotence, but to have the couple live as brother and sister; the third, written to a French bishop, says that he may dissolve a marriage for impotence if it is the custom of the French church to do so: see JL 14125, WH 183 *Consultationi tue qua nos*, to the bishop of Bisceglie (X 4.15.4); JL 14075, WH 188(b) *Consuluit. Super eo vero*, to the bishop of Andria (1 Comp.4.16.2); JL 11866, WH 822(a) *Quod sedem apostolicam*, to the bishop of Amiens (X 4.15.2). This, of course, does not prove that the Roman church regarded all espousals as indissoluble, but it does show, at a minimum, that it was not following Gratian's doctrine. The one decretal that suggests that prior to Alexander III the Roman church was distinguishing between different kinds of *sponsalia* (JL 8274, WH 1016, Innocent II, *Super eo quod interrogasti*, 1 Comp. 4.1.10) is, in my view, suspect in the wording in which we now have it. See the Appendix.

27. Ivo of Chartres, *Epistola* 99 (PL 162.118D–119D), might be taken as indicating a ruling consistent with those of the early sentence-writers, but the focus of the letter is on nonage and on what a later age would call the impediment of public honesty.

28. See P. M. Barnes, 'The Anstey Case', in: *A Medieval Miscellany for Doris Mary Stenton* (London 1962)

We thus have reason to believe that both summists were exaggerating both the breadth and the depth of the conflict. Both summists nonetheless make an important point. Disagreement about a rule as basic as this is undesirable. The author of the *Summa Parisiensis* suggests this when he says, 'And it is not yet known which [custom] is better'.[29] The implication is that he looks forward to a day when it is known. The author of the *Summa 'Elegantius'* suggests a similar view: 'The controversy which we have described contains great doubt, not so much because of the accompanying reasoning as because of the authority of the contrary opinions on both sides. Those who carry the world are bent under the weight of this burden'.[30] These obscure sentences suggest two points: First, in the view of the summist the problem was not that the doctors had not been clever enough at reconciling the authorities, but that the authorities could not be reconciled. Second, the conflict is undesirable for the unity of the church. Although it is unlikely that Alexander III knew these particular works, they tell us that in the mid-twelfth century informed churchmen sought a unified answer to this question. Some problems that occur relatively infrequently can be left to be worked out by the doctors over time, but the problem of the *sponsa duorum* was too common to be left unresolved if there was an authority that could resolve it. Alexander had a vision of papal authority that permitted him to resolve the problem, and he did so.

This last is, of course, the traditional view, and one to which I have adhered over the course of a number of articles.[31] My reading of Johannes Faventinus leads me to have doubts. The nature of those doubts is best explored after we examine what Johannes has to say.

Johannes begins his discussion of C.27 q.2 by recognizing that there is a diversity of views on the topic. He tells us that he will begin with 'the master's', i.e., Gratian's, opinion and defend it; then he will deal with those of others (with a slight implication that he will try to defend those too).[32] The master, he then tells us, distinguished among

1–24; P. A. Brand, 'New Light on the Anstey Case', *Essex Archaeology and History* 15 (1983) 68–83; C. Brooke, *The Medieval Idea of Marriage* (Oxford 1989) 148–52, all with references to earlier literature.

29. Above, text at n. 18.

30. *Summa 'Elegantius'* 13.39, ed. 3.24. The second sentence is found only in the second recension of the work.

31. E.g., C. Donahue, 'The Policy of Alexander the Third's Consent Theory of Marriage', in: Proc. Toronto (MIC C.5; 1976) 251–81; idem, 'The Dating of Alexander the Third's Marriage Decretals', ZRG Kan. Abt. 68 (1982) 70–124. The idea is at least as old as J. Dauvillier, *Le mariage dans le droit classique de l'Église* (Paris 1933), and is accepted in J. Brundage, *Law, Sex, and Christian Society in Medieval Europe* (Chicago, IL 1987) 332–37.

32. 'Sed quia diversitas est hic sentenciarum, ideo primum magistri sentenciam ponamus ac defendamus, deinde aliorum. Sciendum est itaque ut magister dicit quod matrimonium aliud est initiatum tantum, aliud est initiatum et consummatum tantum, aliud initiatum et consummatum et ratum. Initiatum tantum, ubi est consensus cum pacione coniugali absque comixtione, ut inter sponsum et sponsam. Initiatum et consummatum non etiam ratum, inter infideles vel consanguineos vel voto ligatos ignoranter coniunctos. . . . Initiatum vero et consummatum et ratum dicitur inter personas idoneas et fideles, precedente consensu maritali, carnali-

marriages that were simply initiate, marriages that were simply initiate and consummate, and marriages that were initiate, consummate, and ratified *(ratum)*. This is not, in fact, Gratian's distinction, but that of Rufinus, who introduced the distinction between marriage simply initiate and consummate and marriage intiate, consummate and ratified.

The discussion of Gratian's views goes on for a full page. The most important part of it incorporates Peter Lombard's (and Hugh of St. Victor's) notion of the dual sacramentality of marriage. Like Rufinus, however, Johannes argues that the sacramentality of initiate marriage does not necessarily mean that such marriages are indissoluble. Just as the soul which adheres to God can apostatize, so too initiate espousals can be voided for various reasons.[33]

As Johannes sees it, there are two principal views opposed to Gratian's. One holds that once a couple is married they are truly and perfectly married, for there can never be a half-full or imperfect sacrament of matrimony. This is certainly not Peter Lombard's view nor that of any of the contemporary Paris sentence-writers of whom I am aware, for they all recognized the dual sacramentality of marriage and that sexual intercourse introduced into marriage the sacrament of Christ and the Church.[34] These people, Johannes continues, resolve the contradictions in the authorities by distinguishing between future consent and present consent. Future consent is a promise of marriage, as when a man says 'I promise to take you to wife' or the woman says 'I will receive you as my husband'. Such people are not married, as is shown in the passage from [pseudo-] Augustine, *Duobus modis*.[35] Espousal of the present tense occurs when a man says to a woman 'I take you as mine' and she says 'I grant myself to you as yours'. Such espoused are married, and if they are capable of marrying each other, they cannot be separated. If one of them enters a monastery without the consent of the other, he or she should be removed from the monastery.[36]

---

ter coniunctas (London, BL MS Add. 18369, fol. 132vb [= A]; ibid. MS Royal 9.E.VII, fol. 133vb [= R])'. A is from the first half of the thirteenth century; R is probably late twelfth. In general, R gives readings that make better sense but is harder to read than A. I have preferred R throughout, but I came to the realization that R was the better witness quite late in the only day that I had to do these transcriptions. Hence, not all the readings of R are reflected in my transcriptions, but only those that were found when I had doubts about the reading of A; cf. Rufinus, *ad* C.27 q.2, ed. 441 (close parallel but not exact quotation, with all of the preceding rhetoric omitted).

33. 'Quia vero primum sacramentum est violabile—frequenter enim anima que adheserat deo apostatat—ideo non inmerito eius figura, scilicet desponsatio, etiam inter legitimas personas inita quibusdam causis accidentibus irritatur' (A, fol. 132vb; R 133vb); cf. Rufinus, *ad* C.27 q.2, ed. 442 (virtually a direct quotation).

34. The source of this version of the Parisian view may be Cardinalis. It is he who is said to have said *nec usquam semiplenum aut imperfectum matrimonium sacramentum esse;* see above, n. 15.

35. C.27 q.2 c.51. For a full discussion, see C. Larrainzar, 'La distincción entre "fides pactionis" y "fides consensus" en el "Corpus Iuris Canonici",' *Ius Canonicum* 21 (1981) 31–100.

36. 'Alii non approbant distinctionem illam de initiato et consumato matrimonio. Nam ex quo incipiunt esse coniuges perfecti et veri sunt, nec usquam semiplenum aut imperfectum matrimonium sacramentum esse

There are, however, Johannes continues, those who take the 'middle way'. They say that in espousal marriage is initiate, but if the espousal is *de futuro*, it is not immediately ratified. If, however, it is *de presenti*, as is shown by *Duobus modis*, it is immediately and before carnal mingling made so ratified that it cannot be dissolved except in two cases, entry into religion and impotence.[37]

So far all that Johannes is doing is reporting the views of others. He then goes on at some length to attack the distinction between present and future consent, employing the arguments that Rufinus had used. He even has the obviously forged decretal of Alexander I that Rufinus uses to balance against *Duobus modis*, the latter text being one about which both, quite rightly, express considerable doubt.[38] There is only one important difference. At the very beginning Johannes tells us not—as Rufinus had said—that he intends to refute those who hold that *de presenti* consent makes a marriage consummate and ratified, but that he intends to refute those who hold that *de presenti* consent makes a marriage so consummate and ratified that it cannot be dissolved in any situation.[39]

After all the attacks on the distinction between present and future consent, however, it is something of a surprise to discover that Johannes's own view is that of the 'middle way'. Every espousal is, in his view, an initiate marriage. If the espousal is one

---

dicunt. Hii ut decretorum contrietatem determinent dicunt quod desponsatio alia est de futuro alia est de presenti. Desponsatio de futuro est quando inter virum et mulierem pollicitatio intercedit, scilicet, vel [?] quando iste dicit "promitto quod ducam te in uxorem" et illa dicit "accipiam te in virum meum". Et super hoc dicitur in legibus "desponsatio est mentio et promissio futurarum nuptiarum". Tales sponsi non sunt inter se coniuges, quod plane ostenditur in illo capitulo Augustini "Duobus modis" [ubi] dicitur "fides". Et in hoc casu loquuntur capitula illa quibus probatur non esse matrimonium inter sponsum et sponsam. Desponsatio de presenti dicitur quando vir verbis vel aliis certis signis consensum maritalem mulieri exprimit et econverso mulier viro, cum et ille dicit "accipio te in meam" et illa dicit "concedo me tibi in tuam". Ex tunc tales sponsi coniuges sunt. Et de cetero si persone sunt idonee matrimonium separari non potest nisi alterutrius morte quod etiam de monasterio quod invito sponso intratur abstraheretur' (*A*, fol. 133rb–133va; *R*, fol. 134rb); cf. Stephen, *ad* C.27 q.2, ed. 236 (virtually direct quotation from Stephen except for the last phrase, beginning *quod etiam*).

37. 'Hi autem quasi media via eligentes servata priori distinctione dicunt in desponsatione matrimonium esse initiatum sed si de futuro sit desponsatio non statim est ratum; si vero sit de presenti ut ex predicta auctoritate Augustini monstratur statim ante carnis commixtionem ratum efficitur adeo ut dissolvi nisi in duobus casibus non possit, scilicet causa religionis et maleficiorum impedimento' (*A*, fol. 133rb–va; *R*, fol. 134rb). None of this is found in the printed editions of either Rufinus or Stephen. It is, however, doctrinally quite similar to what is found in Simon of Bisignano, *Summa ad* C.27 q.2 (London, BL MS Royal 10.A.III, fol. 78ra; ibid., MS Add. 24659, fol. 29va); see now the preliminary edition of P. Aimone, available at http://www.unifr.ch/cdc/summa_simonis_de.php (394–95).

38. The decretal is so obviously forged (Singer thought that Rufinus had forged it, ed. cvii–cix) that it may have been included as a joke. This is more likely in the case of Johannes because in Johannes it appears right after Johannes's discussion of *Duobus modis* and right before he offers his own view, which is considerably more nuanced than that of the decretal.

39. '*Nunc autem ad conflictum eorum* veniamus [Rufinus *descendamus*] *qui dicunt consensum de futuro non facere coniugium, consensum vero de presenti facere matrimonium* adeo *consummatum et ratum* ut nullo casu dissolvi possit' (*A*, fol. 133va; *R*, fol. 134rb); words in italics come from Rufinus, *ad* C.27 q.2, ed. 443–44.

of the future tense, the parties ought not to marry others, but if they do they are not to be separated. 'It is otherwise if they consent *de presenti*'. He then goes to argue against those who would say that it is impossible to be espoused of two people. While it is impossible to be the wife of two (living) people, it is possible for a woman to be promised to two people, at least *de facto*. If she is known by one of the men with marital affection, she becomes by the very present consent a *sponsa legitima* and the marriage is consummated indeed without sin, just as in Roman law an object sold to two people for a price becomes in law the property of the one to whom it is first delivered.[40]

Although Johannes does not expressly say here that he adopts 'the middle way' that he described earlier, it would seem that he does. He has just argued extensively that *de presenti* consent does not make a marriage so consummate and ratified that it cannot be dissolved in any situation. He now says that it cannot be dissolved in the case of the *sponsa duorum*. That certainly suggests that he accepted the exceptions to indissolubility espoused by those who took 'the middle way': the dissolubility of an unconsummated *de presenti* marriage on the ground of supervenient entry into religion and the dissolubility of such marriages on the ground of pre-existing or supervenient impotence or frigidity. That he took the latter position is also suggested by the fact that he says that those who consummate a marriage formed by an exchange *de futuro* do so 'without sin'. Apparently, if the couple attempted intercourse without being in some sense married, thay would be committing a sin. Similarly, a couple who have exchanged *de presenti* consent are not sinning if they attempt intercourse. If they prove incapable of intercourse, their marriage may be dissolved. However curious the moral doctrine suggested by this implied argument, it gives further indication that Johannes adopted the exceptions recognized in 'the middle way'[41].

40. 'In hunc ergo articulum nostra sentencia concludatur ut dicamus semper quando legitime et inter legitimas personas desponsatio intercedit esse matrimonium initiatum utique et non consummatum. Et si per verba de futuro initiatum fuerit ad secunda vota transire non debet relicto priori sponso. Si tamen hoc fecerit non separabitur a secundo; secus autem si de presenti consenserint. Si opponatur quia qui desponsatam alteri desponsatam sibi sponsam non fecit, cum prioris sponsa non esse desierit nec duorum sponsa simul esse potuerit quare cognoscendo eam fornicatur cum nec sponsam propriam nec uxorem cognoscat. Ad hoc: duorum uxor nulla esse valet; duorum vero sponsa, i.e. duobus promissa saltim de facto, esse potest, unde cum a secundo maritali affectu cognosceretur ipso consensu presenti fit sponsa legitima et coniugium in opere sine peccato consummatur, sicut secundum leges res duobus vendita precio priori tradita eius iure efficitur' (A, 134vb; R 135ra). I am grateful to Paul Brand for checking this passage for me; any remaining errors are, of course, mine. The statement of the Roman law is substantially accurate. There are reminiscences of the first two sentences in Rufinus, ed. 449; after that it departs completely from both Rufinus and Stephen.

41. The Parisian masters had also held that impotence or frigidity was an impediment to marriage. But they treated it as a problem of capacity rather than as an independent ground for dissolution. See above, text at n. 6. Johannes returns to the problem of impotence and frigidity in A, fol. 135va; R, fol. 135vb. Since I did not transcribe this passage, I am reluctant to say anything about it, other than that it deserves further attention. My notes (once more confirmed through the kindness of Paul Brand) suggest that in this passage, he accepted the general position that impotence that arose after the couple has had intercourse was not a ground for dissolu-

What is striking about Johannes's apparent resolution is that it anticipates, in almost every respect, the doctrine ultimately espoused by Alexander III. The *sponsa* or *sponsus de presenti* is not free to marry another, and if he or she does, the second marriage will be dissolved. An unconsummated *de presenti* marriage may, however, be dissolved for certain causes, supervenient entry into religion being the one most frequently mentioned. The *sponsa* or *sponsus de futuro* ought not to marry another, but if he or she does, the second marriage will not be dissolved. If, however, the *sponsa* and *sponsus de futuro* have sexual intercourse, that creates an absolutely indissoluble marriage between them. We even find in Johannes an anticipation of Huguccio's doctrine that the reason why this intercourse creates an indissoluble marriage is that the couple have thereby presently consented.[42]

But is what Johannes says an 'anticipation' of Alexander? That depends, of course, on when Johannes wrote and when Alexander wrote, indeed, in the latter case on when he wrote what. Certainty about neither case is possible, but the date of Johannes's *summa* can be fixed with a reasonable degree of certainty. Unlike many, perhaps most, Bolognese professors, Johannes wrote his *summa* before he wrote many, if not most, of his glosses. Indeed, he continued his extensive writing of glosses after, in all probability, he left Bologna in 1174 to become a canon of Faenza and even during his probable, though not certain, tenure as bishop of Faenza (1177–90).[43] He would, however, have to have had the *summae* of both Rufinus and Stephen in order to do his work, and the completion dates of those works now seem to be in the mid- or even late-1160s.[44] While it is possible that Johannes was already at work on his *summa* before he became a professor, something that probably happened after Stephen left Bologna in 1167, he probably would not have 'published' the work until after he became a professor, and that gives an approximate publication date for the work of around 1170.[45] There are independent reasons for keeping the date as early as possible. There are no citations of Alexander's decretals in Johannes's *summa*. It is hard to imagine that he would not have cited at least some of them had he known them, and the later that we put the date

---

tion and that impotence that antedated the exchange of consent was a cause for dissolution, probably on the ground of error, and that he stated, but did not fully espouse *(ut dicunt)*, the position that supervenient impotence (presumably after present consent) was not a ground for dissolution.

42. See above, n. 40, last sentence of quotation. The one piece that does not quite fit is Johannes's statement that the couple who consummate an espousal of the future tense do not commit sin. Alexander does not comment on that issue. Later canonists and moralists will have considerable doubt. The issue would seem to have been resolved indirectly by the Fourth Lateran Council, because those who marry without the Lateran IV solemnities are clearly committing sin.

43. See N. Höhl, 'Wer war Johannes Faventinus?', in: Proc. San Diego (MIC C.9; 1992) 189–203.

44. See Gouron, 'Sources civilistes'.

45. Kuttner, *Repertorium* 145, puts the completion of the work after 1171, but he is relying there on older work that has proved to be unreliable.

of the *summa* the more implausible it becomes that Johannes would not have known at least a few of Alexander's decretals. The next *summa* in the Bolognese tradition, that of Simon of Bisignano, probably completed between 1177 and 1179, has numerous citations to Alexander's decretals, and so far as Simon is concerned those decretals solve the problem of the *sponsa duorum*.[46]

The other side of the equation is more difficult. Many of Alexander's decretals on the topic of marriage can be dated only approximately and that by methods that have proven controversial.[47] Suffice it to say here that relatively few of Alexander's decretals on the topic of marriage can be firmly dated to before 1170, and none of the decretals in which he developed what was to become the classical canon law on the formation of marriage can be firmly so dated. While there are a number of marriage decretals that seem to date from the years between 1168 and 1173 and which could be used to infer the pope's general views on the topic of the formation of marriage, only one that subsequently appeared in the decretal collections deals with the problem of the *sponsa duorum*, and that decretal, though it certainly suggests that an unconsummated espousal of the present tense is to prevail over a subsequent consummated one, does not quite say that. It does not use the terms 'present consent' and 'future consent'. It also shows considerable hesitancy.[48] The first clear ruling on the topic (again in a decretal that made it into the collections) does not come until one that is quite firmly dated to 2 June 1173 or 1174, and even this one is not completely clear. It, too, does not use the terms 'present consent' and 'future consent'. It does, however, seem to say, once more, that an unconsummated espousal of the present tense is to prevail over a subsequent consummated one. It also says that one of the partners to an unconsummated espousal of the present tense may enter religion without the consent of the other.[49] It seems, however, almost inconceivable on chronological grounds that Johannes could have known this decretal when he wrote his *summa*.

It thus seems highly unlikely that Johannes says what he says because he knew that that was what the current pope was saying, and it thus seems fair to say that Johannes 'anticipated' the classical canon law that Alexander was to develop on the topic of the formation of marriage. The question is whether we can go further and suggest that Johannes not only anticipated what Alexander was going to say but that he is likely to

---

46. Simon of Bisignano, *ad* C.27 q.2, above, n. 37.

47. See Donahue, 'Dating', criticized in Brooke, *Medieval Marriage* 169–72; I remain of the view that the balance of probabilities favors most of what I said in Donahue, 'Dating'; see the Appendix.

48. JL 14235, WH 991(a) *Sollicitudini*, to Gerard bishop of Padua (1 Comp. 4.4.4[6]).

49. JL 12293, WH 944(f) *Sicut Romana. Porro si*, to William archbishop of Sens (1 Comp. 4.4.5[7]). Whether the partner left in the world could remarry is a difficult question to resolve on the basis of this text. The plain meaning of the text seems to be that he or she could not. That, of course, is not the classical law.

have influenced what Alexander said. If he did, the effect was not direct and immediate. After the decision of 1173 or 1174, Alexander was to go through a period in which he seems to have been holding that for a present consent marriage to impede a subsequent one, the present consent marriage must be accompanied by some form of solemnity or ceremony.[50] That notion is quite foreign to Johannes's scheme. In this period Alexander has two decretals on the topic of future consent followed by intercourse. One of them seems to hold that that makes the parties married, the other that the obligation of the future consent when accompanied by intercourse is so serious that the man should be forced by censure of the church to marry the woman (suggesting that they were not already married).[51]

As I have argued elsewhere it is not until the last four or five years of Alexander's pontificate that we can see the classical scheme at all clearly.[52] It is also in this period that what Alexander's decretals hold most closely resembles Johannes's scheme. There are two major differences. Alexander never uses the term 'marriage initiate', as Johannes does to describe espousals both of the present and of the future tense. This is probably a matter of style. Alexander is not writing in an academic context and sees no reason to preserve as much as possible of Gratian's terminology. Espousals of the present tense and those of the future have radically different effects; it is that fact that must be emphasized. The other difference is that Alexander never suggests that the reason why intercourse following an exchange of future consent becomes an indissoluble marriage is because the parties have thereby presently consented. Such an idea is not inconsistent with what Alexander says, but he does not express it.

These differences, I would suggest, are sufficient to allow us to say that Alexander did not simply adopt Johannes's scheme. He certainly could have been encouraged, however, to adopt a scheme that was the same in terms of its practical effect by the knowledge that the most recent summit at Bologna had adopted a scheme that led to the same results. The fact that Alexander probably did not adopt his scheme until close to the end of his pontificate makes this possibility even more likely, since there would have been enough time for knowledge of what Johannes was teaching to reach Rome.

More generally, Johannes's position on the issue should make us hesitate to view the immediate context of Alexander's decisions as one of a great debate between Paris and Bologna. Gratian was long dead. The only person, so far as I can tell, who espoused his position almost unqualifiedly was Rufinus. Rufinus was very much alive and clearly respected (he gave the opening sermon at the Third Lateran Council in 1179), but by

---

50. Donahue, 'Dating' 105–6.

51. JL 13872, WH 457 *Ex parte C. mulieris*, to the abbots of Bury St. Edmunds and Ramsay (X 4.1.9); JL 13901, WH 723 *Pervenit ad nos quod*, to the bishops of Winchester and Hereford.

52. Donahue, 'Dating' 106–15.

the 1170s he seems to have moved from canon law into pastoral work. Further, we have no idea whether he maintained the position that he had espoused, probably in the mid-1160s. If anyone was going to defend the Rufinian position, it would have been Johannes Faventinus. Much in his discussion of C.27 q.2 is derived from Rufinus. These quotations and paraphrases of Rufinus give the discussion a kind of schizophrenic quality. But when it came to committing himself, Johannes committed against the Rufinian position. A man or woman cannot walk away from an unconsummated present consent marriage and marry another. The soul may apostatize from God, but such apostasy will not be allowed in the visible sign on earth of the union of God and the soul. The views of Parisian masters of sentences will prevail in this critically important area. But there remained some important details about which Johannes was prepared to argue. The sign of the union of God with the soul will be dissolved in the face of a greater union of God with the soul, the espousal of the religious life. The couple who proceed from future consent to intercourse without going through the middle stage of present consent are just as much, indeed, even more, married than those who have just exchanged present consent. The sacrament of the union of Christ and the Church that makes marriage absolutely indissoluble arises when the couple has intercourse. Johannes, as was Rufinus, is very firm about this, but, then again, Hugh of St. Victor and Peter Lombard had also so held.

We have already seen that Rolandus (probably), Cardinalis and Gandulphus (both certainly) had adopted the position that an unconsummated present consent marriage cannot be dissolved in the face of a subsequent marriage to another, even if the latter union is consummated. Granted Johannes's position it would have been difficult for Alexander to have gone back to Gratian's and Rufinus's position on this issue. As it was, the schools accepted Alexander's synthesis quite easily. Simon of Bisignano, Bazianus and, of course, Huguccio all adopted it, admittedly in the case of the latter with some modification.[53] What needed to be worked out was the details. The fact that Johannes Faventinus had at least suggested a resolution of many of those details similar to Alexander's resolutions also made the ultimate acceptance of Alexander's synthesis easier.

53. Sicard of Cremona did too, *Summa ad* C.27 q.2 (London, BL MS Add. 18367, fol. 55ra–55va, especially at the turn of 55rb to 55va), though in his case it is difficult to tell whether that was because he knew what Alexander was doing (he does not cite Alexander, though he does in one sentence refer to a *decretum summi pontificis* [fol. 55va] that orders a *sponsa de presenti* who was taken up by another in a *matrimonium perfectum* to be returned to the first spouse) or because he, like Johannes, anticipated what Alexander was to do (or, in Sicard's case, probably what he had already done). Sicard was, however, so far as we can tell, less influential than those named in the text. For Simon of Bisignano, see the references above, n. 37; for Bazianus, see C. Donahue, 'Bassianus, that Is to Say, Bazianus? Bazianus and Johannes Bassianus on Marriage', RIDC 14 (2004) 46–50; for Huguccio, see J. Roman, 'Summa d'Huguccio sur le Décret de Gratien après le manuscrit 3891 de la Bibliothèque Nationale Causa XXVII, Questio II', *Revue historique de droit* 27 (1903) 745–805.

Hence, while we need not necessarily see any direct influence of Johannes on Alexander, the fact that both moved in the same direction was, I would suggest, a powerful stimulus to the consensus that emerged on these issues shortly after Alexander's death.

Appendix

The Dating of Alexander III's Decretals on Marriage Revisited

As indicated above, Christopher Brooke expresses considerable doubt about the methods that I used to suggest tentative dates for Alexander III's decretals on marriage.[i] This is hardly the place to engage in a full-scale rebuttal, but, briefly, it seems to me that his criticisms are based on a misunderstanding of the nature of the evidence that supports the argument and of the argument itself. Brooke argues that no analysis of the decretals that relies on their language can be undertaken until a critical edition of all the decretals has been completed. Such an edition would, of course, be of great value to students of decretals, but a comparison of the Friedberg editions (and the variants that he reports) with the variants offered in Walther Holzmann's unpublished *Regesta* (WH), which are sometimes quite extensive, and the other printed editions of decretals (especially App., Claustr. and Cass.) suggests that radical changing of language (as opposed to omissions) was not characteristic of the collectors of decretals, until Raymond of Peñafort, with papal authorization, made some fairly radical changes for the *Liber extra*. There are, of course, the usual scribal mistakes, many of which are fairly obvious, and some scribal substitution of one word for its synonym, but most of what we have in the Friedberg editions is genuine Alexander, or to put it more cautiously, can be traced back to the earliest witnesses. Also, Donahue, 'Dating', did not use arguments based on the use of specific words until it had considered all the external evidence for dating.

Brooke then goes on to argue that Dauvillier's argument and that of Donahue, 'Dating', is, to use the colloquial phrase, 'boot-strapping'. Having set out to determine if the decretals can be made consistent by assigning dates to them, we then made them consistent by assigning dates to them based on their content rather than on the external evidence. There is always a danger that once one becomes convinced of the truth of a proposition, one will force the evidence to fit it. The way that Donahue, 'Dating', sought to avoid this danger was by first considering all the external evidence for the date of a decretal, before considering the nature of the ruling contained in it. Only then did it assign undatable or imprecisely dated decretals to periods in which decretals with known dates made similar arguments.

Perhaps more telling is Brooke's objection that the dates of many of the decretals are sufficiently vague that the argument of Donahue, 'Dating', is unfalsifiable. As new evidence for dates appears, one simply juggles the dates of the periods in which a given approach was being taken. There is some validity to this criticism. Donahue, 'Dating', did move the dates of the 'solemnity period' on the basis of new evidence that WH 620 (*Licet praeter solitum* JL 14091) dated from 1176 or 1177, rather than earlier in the 1170s, as had previously been thought. But the external evidence does provide some control. The whole theory would have had to have been abandoned if it had been shown that WH 620 should

i. Above, text and n. 47.

be dated to 1180, and it would have been seriously undermined if the new evidence showed that it should be dated to 1168.

Underlying the difference in Brooke's approach and mine is, I fear, a fundamental difference in methodological assumptions grounded in the two different disciplines in which we were originally trained. The Alexander that Brooke seems to envision was a busy ecclesiastic making rulings in reaction to the circumstances in which he found himself, without too much concern for theoretical consistency. The Alexander that I see was a judge, who tried to do justice to the parties he saw before him, while at the same time trying to maintain some overall consistency at the level of doctrine and theory. I am sure that Brooke would agree that Alexander would have firmly endorsed the principle that like cases should be decided alike. I think where we disagree is about whether we can assume that that commitment to consistency included a commitment to maintaining a consistency in the legal rules that can be abstracted from those cases.

One decretal deserves more attention than it received in Donahue, 'Dating'. It is not a decretal of Alexander III but of Innocent II, *Super eo interrogasti,* Innocent's ruling in the well-known *Anstey* case.[ii] The importance of this decretal for the whole argument is that it seems to anticipate the distinction between present and future consent that Donahue, 'Dating', suggests that Alexander came to only after considerable hesitancy. The text of *Super eo,* as reported in 1 Comp. 4.1.10 reads in full:

> Innocentius II. Vintonien. episcopo. Super eo quod interrogasti de sacramento coniugii breuiter respondeo, illam quam dixisti a patre coniugi traditam et ab eo, cui tradita fuit, patri commendatam, donec statuta die in domum suam traduceret, dico, quod legitimo consensu interueniente ex eo statim coniunx sit, quo spontanea concessione sese coniugem esse asserit. Non enim futurum promittebatur, sed presens firmabatur. Qua propter quidquid cum alia postmodum factum est in coitu siue in generatione prolis tanto reprehensibilius est secundum quanto uerius est primum. Constante enim primo quanto amplius in deo committitur, tanto magis culpa augetur. His igitur cognitis, facile erit discretioni tuae negotium presentium latoris debito fine terminare.

It will be noted that if we remove the second sentence *(Non enim futurum promittebatur, sed presens firmabatur),* the decretal is consistent with what is generally thought to have been the holding of the Roman church prior to Alexander's time: any espousal, at least any solemn espousal, as this one clearly was, is to be preferred to a subsequent espousal, even if the second espousal was followed by intercourse.[iii] That Innocent II, moreover, should have been using language that suggests a distinction between present and future consent (though he does not quite use those terms) is remarkable. That distinction can be derived from writings associated with the school of Anselm of Laon, but not from the *Sententiae Magistri A.,* the only work of the school that we can be reasonably sure Gratian knew.[iv] The distinction does not appear in Alexander III's decretals until, if we have the dating right, well into the 1170s. While there are decretals of Alexander's that antedate the 1170s, including Alexander's letter in the second iteration of the same *Anstey* case, that can be

---

ii. JL 8274, WH 1016. I am grateful to Anne Duggan for reporting to me the contents of WH's notes on this decretal; for the case, see the references above, n. 28.

iii. See above, text and n. 26.

iv. See above, n. 4.

taken as making the distinction, none of them seems to use the terms.[v] While it is possible that Innocent II or those around him had derived the distinction from French sentence-writers unknown to Gratian[vi] or that they independently came to the distinction, it is hard to explain why Alexander and none of the intervening popes (so far as we can tell) made use of it, until Alexander did so, it would seem, quite late in his pontificate. The absence is particularly odd when we consider that Alexander knew the purported text of Innocent II from at least the early 1160s because it was contained in the letter (now in John of Salisbury's letter-collection) that Theobald archbishop of Canterbury wrote to Alexander in connection with the second iteration of the *Anstey* case.[vii] Is it possible that Alexander doubted the text and that we should too?[viii]

The notion that the text of *Super eo interrogasti* is not to be trusted is not new. Palgrave doubted it, on the basis of the caution expressed in Theobald's letter to Alexander.[ix] The letter notes that Theobald has not seen the original but was relying on a letter of Henry of Blois bishop of Winchester who had copied the letter into his.[x] Voss suggested that the reason why Henry had not sent the originals was that he was ashamed that his letter to Innocent had been so favorable to the side of Aubrey de Tresgoz, the first woman in the case.[xi] That is certainly possible. The fact, however, as Brooke long ago pointed out, is that Henry's copy of the letter is the likely source of the copy that we find in the decretal collections.[xii] That Theobald's letter is the source seems to be precluded by the fact that Henry's copy, but not Theobald's copy, contains a final sentence that appears in most of the copies in the decretal collections.[xiii]

The first clear statement of the present/future distinction in a work that circulated widely appears, as we have already noted, in Hugh of St. Victor's *De sacramentis*, a work

v. For the text of Alexander's letter, see L. Voss, *Heinrich von Blois, Bischof von Winchester (1129–1171)* (Berlin 1932) 167–68. A date in December 1162 seems most likely; see Barnes, 'Anstey Case' 13.

vi. Reinhardt, *Ehelehre* 81, prints in parallel three texts, ascribed to Anselm of Laon, Ivo of Chartres, and William of Champeaux, respectively, texts that are clearly the origins of pseudo-Augustine, *Duobus modis*, above, n. 35. The possibility that Innocent knew Hugh of St. Victor is considered below.

vii. *The Letters of John of Salisbury* 1, ed. W. J. Millor, H. E. Butler, and C. N. L. Brooke (London 1955, repr. Oxford 1986) 227–37, at 228–29 no. 131.

viii. Alexander's letter, above n. v, seems clearly to be based on the principle of *res iudicata*. He had delegated the case (ed. Barnes, 'Anstey Case' 24 no. 2) before he rendered his final sentence, apparently in order to have the facts of the case determined. Even if the delegates had examined the original letter of Innocent, they might not have reported a discrepancy in the text that Henry had reported to Theobald unless it affected the underlying facts, which the present/future sentence did not. For other decretals of Alexander's that support the present/future distinction but do not use the terms, see above, text and nn. 48–49.

ix. F. Palgrave, *The Rise and Progress of the English Commonwealth* 1.2 (London 1832) xx n. 25.

x. *The Letters of John of Salisbury* 1.228: 'Scriptum consilii a domino Innocentio decessore uestro, ut aiebant, receperat [dominus Wintoniensis] in haec uerba (nos enim originales numquam, sed domini Wintoniensis litteras super hoc dumtaxat accepimus)'. Palgrave's remark seems warranted: 'it is stated very pointedly that the originals were not adduced; and such precise and guarded terms are employed, as to imply some suspicion of the authenticity of the transcript'.

xi. Voss, *Heinrich von Blois* 142 n. 2; the text of Henry's letter ibid. 166–67.

xii. See *The Letters of John of Salisbury* 1.268–9 n. 2.

xiii. The transmission tradition is extensive: Chelt. 18.22, Cott. 22.6, Pet. 1.6; Tann. 7.5.15; Oriel I 50.28, Erl. 50.28; Flor. 129; Duac. 64; 1 Berol. 55, and Cus. 147; not in Ambr., but in 1 Par. 54. In the systematic collections it appears in App. 6.31, Bamb. 50.28, Lips. 59.41, Cass. 58.29, Brug. 49.5, Sang. 8.44. That the Continental witnesses are derived ultimately from 'primitive' English collections seems virtually certain.

normally dated to the mid- to late-1130s.[xiv] It is thus chronologically possible that Innocent II (1130–43) knew it.[xv] That possibility is enhanced if we accept the testimony of the catalogue of Hugh's works that seems to have been made shortly after his death, which says, with probable reference to the second book of the *De sacramentis:* 'Fecit [Hugo] . . . volumen cum magna diligentia in curia romana iussione pape Innocentii'.[xvi] That Hugh visited Italy is also suggested by a letter that he may have written to the canons of Lucca, but the authenticity of this letter has been questioned.[xvii] The chain of evidence is weak, although it does exist. Even if he did know of Hugh's views, there remain the questions whether Innocent would have incorporated those views into a decretal, and why, if he did, it took, it would seem, more than thirty years for another pope to do the same.

By contrast to the situation in the 1130s and early 1140s, when the *Anstey* case was revived in the early 1160s, Hugh's work was circulating widely, and Peter Lombard's position was beginning to be known. Richard of Anstey obtained from Henry of Blois letters to Theobald explaining what had happened in the first iteration of the *Anstey* case. Henry quoted Innocent's letter. That Henry had supported Aubrey is clear enough; that Innocent had as well is less certain but probable. That Henry, like all judges before his time and since, did not want to be overruled may be assumed. The temptation to add to the pope's letter a brief sentence that supported the ruling the pope had made in terms that were current by the 1160s but had not been current in Innocent's time might have proven irresistible.

xiv. See above, text and n. 5. For the dating, see most fully D. van den Eynde, *Essai sur la succession et la date des écrits de Hugues de Saint-Victor* (Rome 1960) 100–103.

xv. The chronology is tighter than Innocent's pontifical years. William de Sackville, the husband whose second marriage was dissolved, was dead by August 1140, and probably somewhat earlier. Brooke, *Medieval Marriage* 151 and n. 79; *The Letters of John of Salisbury* 1.233 and n. 17. Knowledge of Hugh's position, however, could have come from the *De beatae Mariae virginitate*, above, n. 5, or from oral reports of Hugh's teaching.

xvi. F. E. Croyden, 'Notes on the Life of Hugh of St. Victor', *Journal of Theological Studies* 40 (1939) 250. Even Croyden, who accepted the evidence of the catalogue (ed. J. de Ghellinck, *Recherches de sciences religieuses* 1 [1910] 277–83), did not take its statements literally, but suggested that the *iussio* had been given when Innocent was in France in 1130–32.

xvii. Ed. Croyden, 'Notes', 251. For doubts, see J. Châtillon, 'Hugo von St. Viktor', TRE 15 (1986) 630, with references; R. Goy, *Die Überlieferung der Werke Hugos von St. Victor* (Monographien zur Geschichte des Mittelalters 14; Stuttgart 1976) 483, classifies the letter as *durchaus möglich [echt]*. The question deserves more attention than anyone of whom I am aware has yet given it.

PART THREE

Canonistic Doctrine in Practice

Courts and Procedures, ca. 1140–1500

[15]

The Advocate's Dilemma: What Can You Tell the Client?

A Problem in Legal Ethics

James A. Brundage

❋

When Ken Pennington came to my office in 1965 to tell me that he wanted to do graduate work in medieval history, the possibility that nearly forty years later I would be writing a paper for a *Festschrift* in his honor was certainly the furthest thing from my mind. That I am delighted to be doing so goes without saying. To have watched Ken become a scholar of unrivaled eminence in the field to which I first introduced him has been one of the greatest rewards of my career. I dedicate this brief note to him with heartfelt affection and the most profound esteem.

The oaths that advocates and proctors took when they were admitted to practice in the courts of the medieval church outlined a series of ethical obligations that they solemnly undertook to observe in the practice of their profession.[1] The duties that they thereby assumed fell into two categories: some were obligations toward their clients, while others were obligations toward the court, whose officers (but emphatically not employees) they became at the time of admission.

Advocates and proctors had two principal kinds of obligations toward the court. First, they undertook to be its doorkeepers. They promised that they would screen every case that clients sought to bring before the court, that they would diligently examine the evidence that they hoped to rely on, and that they would agree to advise

1. I have dealt with this in several earlier studies of medieval legal ethics, especially 'The Calumny Oath and Ethical Ideals of Canonical Advocates', in: Proc. Munich (MIC C.10; 1997) 793–805, reprinted in: *The Profession and Practice of Medieval Canon Law* (Aldershot 2004) no. IV; and 'The Lawyer as His Client's Judge: The Medieval Advocate's Duty to the Court', in: *Cristianità ed Europa: Miscellanea di studi in onore di Luigi Prosdocimi*, ed. C. Alzati (2 vols. in 3 parts; Rome 1994–2000) 1.591–607.

and represent only clients who they believed had *bona fide* cases. All others they would reject. When they were admitted to practice, lawyers assured the judge (or judges) of the court in which they were going to practice that they would make a preliminary assessment of the merits of every case and would reject any that they found unworthy of the court's consideration. Should it happen that they accepted a client's case only to discover subsequently that it was frivolous, flawed, or lacked merit, they would forthwith abandon the client, would withdraw from the case, and would inform the judge of their reasons for doing so. They assured the court, in other words, that its judges could rely absolutely on the integrity of its lawyers, who would see to it that judges wasted no time and effort on matters that were silly, inconsequential, or devoid of merit.

Second, lawyers also promised at the time of admission that they would be scrupulously honest in their dealings with the court. They would not knowingly introduce into evidence any witnesses whose testimony they thought might be perjured or any documents that were forged or had been altered. Nor would they rely on any legal texts that they considered irrelevant or whose authenticity they doubted.

In this essay I will examine one small element among these onerous undertakings, yet one that is hardly insignificant and continues to present moral and practical difficulties in the practice of law down to the present day. It represents, however, only one of the numerous difficulties that are apt to arise in communications between advocate and client.

Any advocate, ancient, medieval, or modern, must obviously interview every prospective client before litigation commences in order to discover what the case is about, what the client's version of the affair is, what legal action he is contemplating, and what he hopes to achieve by it. Once the advocate has done that and has determined whether or not he will accept the case, he needs to advise the client about his legal options in dealing with the matter and to suggest whatever opportunities, perils, and pitfalls he foresees in each approach. Together lawyer and client must agree on a method of dealing with the matter that both of them find acceptable.

All of this may seem self-evident, but in practice it is usually neither as simple nor as straightforward as it may appear. Prospective clients are invariably highly selective in what they choose to reveal about the situation that brought them to an advocate in the first place. Lawyers have known this for centuries. Clients regularly try to paint a picture that they think will make them look good. Their reasons for going to law are seldom what they represent them to be. Quintilian was all too familiar with the problem during the first century of the common era and advised intending advocates to deal with prospective clients warily:[2]

---

2. *Institutio oratoria* 12.8.9 and 11. Translations throughout, unless otherwise noted, are my own.

A great many of them lie. They act not as if they were describing the case to their advocate, but as if they were arguing before a judge. As a result it is never enough just to take their word. Instead you have to test them every which way and wring the truth out of them. . . . In short, the best advocate is a skeptical one.

Twelve hundred years later the great proceduralist Bishop William Durand (1231–1296) knew this problem well. He encouraged his thirteenth-century readers to begin their client interviews with a little speech to try to impress would-be clients with the importance of being candid about their situation:[3]

Let [the advocate] say: 'My dear fellow, there are three persons to whom you must tell the whole truth, from whom you conceal nothing. They are your confessor, your doctor, and your lawyer. . . . For even the most experienced counselor may be led astray if he does not know the facts. . . . So tell me absolutely everything, let me have the whole business, and give it to me in writing as well. Then I will be able to give you true and reliable advice and counsel . . . , for rights arise from the facts'.

Durand was realistic enough, however, to warn his readers not to assume that this homily would necessarily have the desired effect. Instead he proceeded to advise them, much as Quintilian had done, to cross-examine their clients vigorously, to reject their evasions and rationalizations, and to demand that they spell out in detail whatever hard evidence they had to support their contentions. Finally he warned the advocate to insist that his clients give him written instructions in which they set down everything that they had told him and directed him specifically about what they wanted him to do for them. The advocate would need these instructions to defend his actions should he be faced with nasty surprises because the client had misrepresented the situation to him in the first place.[4]

Once he had secured the client's account of the situation—or at least as much as the client was prepared to reveal to him—it was the advocate's turn to advise the client. This was as essential as getting the client's version of events in the first place. It was also fraught with at least as much peril. When an advocate was admitted to practice, as we have seen, he assumed a moral and legal obligation not to present false or perjured evidence to the court. This was one of his most basic obligations to the court and judges had to rely upon the advocates who appeared before them to perform it with scrupulous honesty. Failure to do so struck at the foundations of the judicial system itself. The obligation was ancient and appeared in the calumny oath *(iuramentum de calumnia vitanda)* that late ancient Roman imperial law required advocates to take at the beginning of

3. *Speculum iudiciale* 1.4 *De aduocato* § 3.1–2 (Basel 1574; repr. Aalen 1975) 1.265.
4. Ibid. § 3.3–6, ed. 1.265–66.

each trial.[5] When local authorities began in the 1230s to require advocates in civil and ecclesiastical courts that operated under the procedural rules of the medieval *ius commune* to bind themselves by admissions oaths, this undertaking invariably formed part of the oath.[6] Ultimately the constitution *Properandum* of the Second Council of Lyon in 1274 mandated that advocates and proctors in courts throughout the Western church must not only take such an oath when they were first admitted to practice, but also renew it annually so long as they continued in practice.[7]

Admissions oaths forbade advocates to produce spurious evidence during litigation, but they usually did so in broad general terms. These offered only the vaguest glimmerings of guidance to advocates who needed to decide how they ought to behave in the borderline situations that were bound to arise when they came face to face with real clients and real cases.[8] Thus for example an advocate, as we have seen, needed to question his client forcefully in order to learn the details of the case. In the process the client could well refer to facts that might potentially harm his chances of prevailing in court. Could an advocate ethically warn his client that admission of those facts in court would prejudice his case? Having heard about adverse information from his client, could an ethical advocate take steps to suppress it? If he himself were questioned by the judge, was the advocate bound to reveal the unhelpful particulars? Then, too, the client would certainly expect, and might well demand, that the advocate advise him about what he should tell the judge. Could the advocate in good conscience counsel him to suppress relevant information that would harm his chances of prevailing?

Again, the advocate needed to learn from his client the names of any witnesses who he hoped would support his claims. But how could the advocate know what those wit-

5. Cod. 2.58(59).2 and 3.1.14.4.

6. Thus among many others, e.g., Provincial Council of Rouen (1231) can. 48, in: Mansi 23.218–19, and E. Martène and U. Durand, *Thesaurus novus anecdotorum* (5 vols.; Paris 1717, repr. Farnborough 1968–69) 4.181–82; Council of Château-Gontier (1231) can. 35, in: *Les conciles de la province de Tours*, ed. J. Avril (Paris 1987) 154–55, also in: Mansi 23.240–41; *Liber Augustalis* (1231) 1.84, in: *Die Konstitutionen Friedrichs II. für das Königreich Sizilien*, ed. W. Stürner (MGH Constitutiones et acta publica 2, Supplement; Hanover 1996) 258; Legatine Council of London (1237) can. 29, and Statutes of York I (1241 x 1255) can. 36, in: *Councils & Synods* 1.258–59, 1.493; synodal statutes of Guiard de Laon, Bishop of Cambrai (1238 x 1248) can. 187, and Tournai, *Antiqua statuta* 21.3, in: *Les statuts de l'ancienne Province de Reims*, ed. J. Avril (Statuts synodaux français du XIIIᵉ siècle 4; Paris 1995) 63, 349.

7. 2 Lyons (1274) can. 19, in: COD³ 324–25.

8. The synodal statutes of Guiard de Laon, can. 187 (above n. 6) are a striking exception. This oath specified the limits of permissible interaction between advocate and client far more clearly than usual: '[J]urabunt sollemniter quod permittent principales personas recitare factum suum et confiteri nudam veritatem et respondere interrogationibus mutuis factis a partibus vel ab ipso judice, nec intromittent se de facto proponendo vel recitando, nisi de speciali licentia judicis, quam debet judex impertire, habito respectu et consideratione ad simplicitatem partis, nisi forte impeditioris lingue vel etiam idiota vel aliqua alia rationabili causa motus, nec instruent clientes suos subornare vel palliare factum suum. Facta interrogatione autem de hiis que pertinent ad factum, non colloquentur partibus antequam fuerit responsum et, si vellent loqui, judices non permitterent'.

nesses were apt to say? And without knowing that, how could he possibly frame a set of questions to put to them that would adequately bring out the points required to bolster his client's position? During a trial under the rules of Romano-canonical procedure, as every advocate knew, he would not be questioning witnesses himself. Indeed he could not even be present while they were questioned. The judge, or a surrogate whom he appointed, would interrogate each witness individually under oath and in secret.[9] The only other person legally permitted to be present was a notary to record the witness's responses. Under these circumstances, was the advocate permitted to question them privately before trial? How else could any advocate be sure what his witnesses would say, let alone whether they would produce perjured testimony?

Advocates in the courts of the *ius commune* found precious little in the legal texts that they had studied in university law faculties to help them deal with these and a host of similar practical questions. For guidance on these matters they had to turn instead to the burgeoning literature on Romano-canonical procedure, the *ordines iudiciarii* or *ordines iudiciorum*, that began to appear from the mid-twelfth century onward.[10] Law faculties hardly ever made explicit provision in their curricula for instruction on procedure, even though a close knowledge of procedure was absolutely essential for anyone who intended to practice as an advocate in the courts.[11] We can be reasonably certain that law students regularly did in fact study procedure, however, since handbooks on procedure routinely appeared in the lists of books that university booksellers were required to keep in stock.[12] Students apparently did this privately, since it was not a prescribed part of the curriculum in either Roman or canon law. The writers of these manuals, particularly those who worked outside of Bologna, became increasingly concerned during the thirteenth century with the ethics of professional conduct.[13]

---

9. *Glossa ordinaria* to X 2.20.52 s.v. *examinare sigillatim* (ed. Romae 1582 col. 754); Tancred, *Ordo iudiciarius* 3.9.2, in *Pillius, Tancredus, Gratia libri de iudiciorum ordine*, ed. F. Bergmann (Göttingen 1842, repr. Aalen 1965) 237; Hostiensis, *Lectura* to X 2.20.52 s.v. *sigillatim* (Venice 1581, repr. Turin 1965) fol. 105rb; *Speculum iudiciale* 1.4 *De teste* § 7.1–2, ed. 1.324.

10. K. W. Nörr, 'Ordo iudiciorum und ordo iudiciarius', SG 11 (1967) 327–43; L. Fowler-Magerl, *Ordo iudiciorum vel ordo iudiciarius: Begriff und Literaturgattung* (Ius commune 19, Sonderhefte; Frankfurt/M. 1984); eadem, *Ordines iudiciarii and Libelli de ordine iudiciorum (from the Middle of the Twelfth to the End of the Fifteenth Century)* (Typologie 63; Turnhout 1994). I am grateful to Dr. Fowler-Magerl for sharing with me in addition her unpublished monograph, 'Judicial Ordines and Their Circulation'.

11. The University of Orléans was an exception to the general rule.

12. Thus, e.g., *Statuta universitatis scholarium iuristarum Bononiensis* 35, ed. H. Denifle, *Archiv für Litteratur- und Kirchengeschichte* 3 (1887) 254–393 at 298–303; Montpellier, BM sect. Médicine, MS 9, cited by Fowler-Magerl in 'Judicial Ordines'. See also F. Soetermeer, 'Exemplar und Pecia: Zur Herstellung juristischer Bücher in Bologna im 13. und 14. Jahrhundert', in: *Juristische Buchproduktion im Mittelalter*, ed. V. Colli (Frankfurt/M. 2002) 481–516.

13. A. Gouron, 'Le rôle de l'avocat selon la doctrine romaniste du douzième siècle', in: *L'assistance dans la résolution des conflits* (Brussels 1998) 7–19 at 8, 15–16.

In addition, a handful of jurists who had spent significant time as practitioners as well as law professors started to produce books that specifically addressed the needs and problems of advocates who practiced in the courts. It seems unlikely to have been purely a coincidence that these works first commenced to appear at almost precisely the same time that church courts began to require advocates to be formally admitted to practice by swearing oaths that bound them to observe some basic principles of forensic ethics in the practice of their profession.

The earliest of these practitioners' manuals was the *Libellus instructionis advocatorum*, written by a civilian, Jacobus Balduini (d. 1235), who in addition to teaching at Bologna had also served as *podestà* of Genoa.[14] Ubertus de Bobbio (d. after 1245), a legist who had served as a judge, followed quickly with his *Libellus cautele et doctrine*, which he finished in or about 1236.[15] Further handbooks for practitioners appeared during the 1240s. Bagarottus (d. after 1246), who practiced as an advocate and served as a judge of the commune of Bologna during the opening years of the thirteenth century before he began to teach around 1206, compiled a largely unoriginal *Cavillationes advocatorum* that circulated widely in variant recensions.[16] At Orléans, where procedure was studied more formally than it was in other law faculties, Bagarottus' *Cavillationes* was coupled with another popular *Liber cavillationum*, completed in 1246 by Johannes de Deo (d. 1267), a Portuguese canonist, and the merged work was used for teaching.[17] Bonaguida de Arezzo (d. after 1255), a practicing advocate who later became a judge-ordinary and professor of law in his native city, completed his *Summa introductoria super officio advocationis in foro ecclesie* probably in 1249 or 1250.[18]

14. Jacobus' *Libellus*, which remained incomplete at the time of his death, was principally used in Italy and France. It has been edited by N. Sarti, *Un giurista tra Azzone e Accursio: Iacopo di Balduino (1210–1235) e il suo 'Libellus instructionis advocatorum'* (Pubblicazioni del Seminario Giuridico dell'Università di Bologna 137; Milan 1990) 153–92. See also R. Abbondanza, 'Baldovini, Iacopo', DBI 5 (1963) 521–25; Fowler-Magerl, *Ordo iudiciorum* 147–48.

15. Fowler-Magerl, *Ordines iudiciarii* 31; R. Chabanne, 'Ubertus de Bobbio', DDC 7 (1965) 1355.

16. Fowler-Magerl, *Ordo iudiciorum* 196–99; R. Abbondanza, 'Bagarotto', DBI 5 (1963) 170–74; G. Zaccagnini, 'Notizie inedite intorno ad alcuni illustri dottori dello studio bolognese dei secoli XIII e XIV', *Studi e memorie per la storia dell'Università di Bologna* 14 (1938) 171–94 at 173–74. Johannes Andreae noted in his *Additiones* to the *Speculum iudiciale* of William Durand that Bagarottus' *Cavillationes* resembled the *Praeludia causarum* of Uberto di Bonaccorso 'quasi per omnia . . . ad literam . . . de quo sequitur quod aliquis horum fur fuerit'. Johannes added, that 'quis autem fuerit, relinquamus illi cuius est furta punire', *Additiones in proem.*, s.v. *plurimis*, ed. 1.4. One version of the *Cavillationes* appears in: TUI 3.2, fol. 128v–130r.

17. Johannes de Deo's *Liber cavillationum* appeared under the title *Liber qui vocatur doctrina advocatorum* as an appendix to an edition of Durand's *Speculum* at Venice in 1567 and in subsequent editions of the *Speculum* at Lyon 1577 and Turin in 1578; F. von Savigny, *Geschichte des römischen Rechts im Mittelalter* (7 vols.; Heidelberg 1834–52, repr. Aalen 1986) 5.471–74; Schulte, QL 2.104–6; Fowler-Magerl, *Ordo iudiciorum* 196–99; António Domingues de Sousa Costa, *Um mestre Português em Bolonha no século XIII: João de Deus. Vida e obras* (Braga 1957) 109–15.

18. Bonaguida's *Summa* was published in *Anecdota quae processum civilem spectant*, ed. A. Wunderlich (Göttingen 1841) 122–345. Some further material that does not appear in Wunderlich's edition can be found in J.

These writers on professional conduct, together with some later thirteenth-century procedural writers who paid special attention to practitioners' problems—notably William of Drogheda (d. 1245),[19] Aegidius de Fuscarariis (d. 1289),[20] and especially William Durand—are the principal sources for answers to the kinds of questions I have posed above. Bonaguida cautioned advocates that on prudential grounds they must refrain from having any contact with the witnesses whom his client proposed to call. If the advocate spoke to them at all, Bonaguida warned, he ran the risk that people would assume that he was guilty of trying to influence their testimony and might thus consider him a party to subornation of perjury, whether he had actually done so or not. In practical terms there was a danger that the judge (or whoever handled interrogations for him) might ask a witness whether he had spoken to the advocate about matters relevant to the case. Should the witness say that he had, the advocate would, at best, be seriously embarrassed.[21] At worst, he might become liable for prosecution for soliciting perjured testimony.[22]

Hostiensis, writing around 1253, cautioned judges that they must take careful note of whether witnesses gave their evidence as if they had learned it by rote. Likewise when interrogating witnesses they should also be alert to see if two or more witnesses repeated their stories in the same order, using identical words or phrases. It was one thing, Hostiensis declared, for two persons to testify that the same event had taken place, but if they used exactly the same expressions to describe that event, a judge ought to suspect that they had been told what they should say.[23] William Durand, writing a few years later, suggested that a judge should try to confirm that suspicion by varying the order in which he asked questions. He might start, for example, by asking the first question listed in the interrogatories that the advocate had submitted, then skipping

Teige, 'Beiträge zum päpstlichen Kanzleiwesen des XIII. und XIV. Jahrhunderts', MIÖG 17 (1896) 408–40 at 409–14. On Bonaguida see G. Barraclough, 'Bonaguida de Aretinis', DDC 2 (1937) 934–40; S. Caprioli, 'Bonaguida d'Arezzo', DBI 11 (1969) 512–13.

19. William of Drogheda was a practitioner as well as a teacher of civil law at Oxford. He was murdered by his valet at Oxford in 1245, before he was able to complete the ambitious *Summa aurea* on which he had been at work since ca. 1239, A. Emden, *Biographical Register of the University of Oxford* (3 vols.; Oxford 1957–59) 1.594–95; H. Richardson, 'Azo, Drogheda and Bracton', EHR 59 (1944) 22–47; F. Maitland, *Roman Canon Law in the Church of England: Six Essays* (London 1898) 107–15.

20. Aegidius was the earliest layman known to have taught canon law at Bologna. His *Ordo iudiciarius* appears in Wahrmund, *Quellen* 3.1. See also J. Deshusses, 'Gilles de Foscarari', DDC 5 (1953) 967–68; Schulte, QL 2.139–43; P. Landau, 'Die Bedeutung der Kanonistik für die Karriere einer aufsteigenden Bürgerschicht', *Mitteilungen und Forschungsbeiträge des Cusanus-Gesellschaft* 24 (1999) 41–61 at 44–46.

21. Bonaguida, *Summa introductoria* 1.3.12, ed. Wunderlich 158; Aegidius de Fuscarariis reproduced this passage almost verbatim in his *Ordo iudiciarius* § 110, ed. Wahrmund, *Quellen* 185, while Durand closely paraphrased parts of it in *Speculum* 1.4 *De aduocato* § 9.4, ed. 1.280–81.

22. Ibid. 1.4 *De teste* § 1.81; 2.2 *De probationibus* § 4.25; and 2.3 *De sententia* § 9.7, ed. 1.300, 1.627, 1.804.

23. Hostiensis, *Summa*, lib. 2 tit. *De testibus* § 3 and § 10 (Lyon 1537, repr. Aalen 1962), fol. 99vb, 101va; similarly *Speculum* 1.4 *De teste* § 1.81, ed. 1.300.

perhaps to the last question, followed by one from the middle of the document. This tactic, Durand thought, should make it clear whether the advocate or someone else had persuaded the witnesses to memorize a fixed set of replies to the various questions included in the list he had submitted to the judge.[24]

Hostiensis had cited as authority for his statement a rescript of the emperor Hadrian (r. 117–138) reported in Justinian's Digest.[25] But rules calculated to avoid the contamination of testimony, either as a result of collusion among the witnesses themselves or in consequence of instructions given to them by one of the parties to a lawsuit or their legal advisers, were considerably more ancient than that.

Romano-canonical procedure had long required judges to take the testimony of witnesses individually and in secret, precisely so that no witness could overhear the accounts that other witnesses gave.[26] Standard procedural manuals and other authorities[27] found a scriptural basis for this practice in the story of Susanna and the Elders that appears in the Vulgate as part of the thirteenth chapter of the Book of Daniel.[28] The episode concerns two lecherous judges of a certain age who falsely accused a beautiful young woman named Susanna of adultery. The prophet Daniel saved her from a death sentence by questioning each of the old men individually. By inquiring minutely into incidental details in their allegations, Daniel was able to demonstrate discrepancies in their stories, which cast doubt on their accusation and thus saved Susanna from wrongful conviction of a capital crime. Procedural writers advised medieval advocates to follow Daniel's dramatic example by including some questions about details incidental to the matters that they were mainly concerned with—where events took place, who was present, what they were wearing, what the weather was like, and so-forth—in the interrogatories that they submitted to the judges who would actually examine the witnesses.[29] Advocates and judges almost invariably followed this advice in actual practice.[30]

But what about the client? How far could an advocate ethically go in instructing his client about the case? Bonaguida's response was blunt and straightforward: an advocate

24. Ibid. 1.4 *De teste* § 7.3, ed. 1.324.   25. Dig. 22.5.3.1.

26. Cod. 4.20.14.

27. E.g., Tancred, *Ordo iudiciarius* 3.9.1; Gratia of Arezzo, *Summa de ordine iudiciorum* 2.6.1, ed. Bergmann 237–38, 371. See also Bernard of Pavia, *Glossa ordinaria* to X 2.20.2 s.v. *examinare sigillatim*.

28. Dan.13.4–63. The story appears in the Septuagint as the Book of Susanna, immediately following the Book of Daniel, but it was not included in the Masoretic text of the Scriptures and modern scholars have generally relegated it to the Apocrypha.

29. *Speculum* 1.4 *De teste* § 6.9–11, 15, ed. 1.321.

30. See, e.g., *Select Cases from the Ecclesiastical Courts of the Province of Canterbury, c. 1200–1301*, ed. N. Adams and C. Donahue, Jr. (Selden Society Publications 95; London 1981) C.11 at 162–64, C.12 at 192–93, C.14 at 211–13, C.18 at 269–73; *Register of John Morton, Archbishop of Canterbury 1486–1500*, ed. C. Harper-Bill (2 vols.; York 1987) 1.88–92 no. 258.

must not tell a client, either by word or by sign, how he ought to reply to any question that might be put to him. Neither should he do this indirectly, for example by suggesting a hypothetical answer to an imaginary question.[31]

Durand's approach to the problem was more nuanced. He distinguished, to begin with, between law and fact. Clearly an advocate had not merely the right, but a positive duty to instruct his clients about the law relating to the problems they placed before them. He likewise had a duty to warn them about dangers that might arise in litigation. These were professional obligations. Clients expected him to do this and it was part of the service that he undertook to provide when he agreed to accept them as clients.

What an advocate must not do was to coach his client about the facts of a case.[32] Durand noted that an argument could be made that an advocate had the right to tell a client what to say on the basis of a provision in Justinian's Code to the effect that a guardian could instruct his ward about how to reply to questions.[33] But he immediately dismissed that line of reasoning on the grounds that the analogy between an advocate's relationship to his client and that of a guardian to a ward was inappropriate and inadmissible.[34] An advocate was likewise never permitted to encourage a client to lie, by telling him, for example, 'If you admit this, you will lose the case', or 'If you deny that your soul will perish'. After first cautioning the client that he must never deny the truth or tell a falsehood, the advocate could, however, legitimately advise him that the law provided five alternatives that he could choose from in responding to any given question. First he could deny what was put to him. Alternatively he could admit it. A third possibility was to reply that he believed the statement. His fourth alternative was to declare that he did not believe it. Finally he might prefer to say that he doubted it. The client had the right to adopt any of these responses so long as it corresponded to what he knew or believed to be true and accurate.[35]

Prudent advocates needed to be sure that their clients grasped these points clearly, since a misunderstanding on this matter held potentially serious consequences for the advocate. If a judge were to conclude that an advocate's instructions had led his client to give false testimony, the advocate could be held liable to compensate the opposing party for any losses that in the judge's view had resulted from that testimony.[36]

It is impossible to know how often practicing advocates actually contravened the

---

31. Bonaguida, *Summa introductoria* 4.3, ed. Wunderlich 319: '[A]dvocatis remotis procul, ita, quod nec dicto, nec signo clientulo suo a quo quaeritur possint innuere, vel eundem clientulum aliqua verisimili conjectura super responsione docere'.

32. *Speculum* 2.1 *De interrogationibus* § 2.14, ed. 1.546.

33. Cod. 5.39.4.   34. *Speculum* 1.4 *De advocato* § 2.14, ed. 1.546.

35. Ibid. 2.2 *De positionibus* § 9.6, ed. 1.597.

36. Ibid. 2.2 *De positionibus* § 3.7 and 1.4 *De advocato* § 9.6, ed. 1. 582, 1.281.

rules against coaching clients or witnesses on the evidence. Advocates' consultations with their clients were oral and it is unlikely that the details of them were ever set down in writing: certainly I have never encountered such a document or any mention of one. Infringements were thus extremely unlikely to become a matter of record unless or until they were detected in the course of litigation, and that rarely happened.[37] Church authorities, however, complained so often about this type of transgression that one is tempted to assume that offenses of this sort must have occurred much more frequently than court records indicate.[38] Systematic underreporting could well account for this, especially if judges preferred to deal with such matters informally and off the record. At this remove in time, however, that remains nothing more than mere speculation and in all probability the incidence of this sort of professional misconduct can never be reliably established.

37. R. Helmholz, 'Ethical Standards for Advocates and Proctors in Theory and Practice', reports one complaint in a Sede Vacante scrapbook of the Court of Canterbury for 1283 concerning a proctor who coached one of the witnesses for his client, in: Proc. Toronto (MIC C.5; 1976) 283–99 at 298–99, reprinted in his *Canon Law and the Law of England* (London 1987) 41–57 at 56–57.

38. See, e.g., Constitutions of Florence (1310), ed. R. Trexler, *Synodal Law in Florence and Fiesole, 1306–1518* (Studi e testi 268; Vatican City 1971) 239; Oxford, *Statuta antiquiora* (ca. 1300), ed. H. Anstey, *Munimenta academica, or Documents Illustrative of Academical Life and Studies at Oxford* (2 vols.; Rolls Series 50; London 1868) 1.77; Statutes of Salisbury I (1217 x 1219) can. 53, Council of Oxford (1222) can. 3, Statutes of Winchester I (1224) can. 50, Statutes of Coventry (1224 x 1237) can. 14, Legatine Council of London (1237) can. 29, Statutes of Worcester III (1240) can. 73, in: *Councils & Synods* 1.76–77, 1.107, 1.134, 1.213, 1.259, 1.314.

16

L'usuraio, il testamento, e l'Aldilà

Tre *quaestiones* di Marsilio Mantighelli in tema di usura

Orazio Condorelli

1. Marsilio Mantighelli, canonista bolognese della seconda metà del Duecento.

La canonistica bolognese degli ultimi tre decenni del secolo XIII rappresenta un promettente campo di indagine. Si tratta di personaggi ancora poco noti o del tutto oscuri, senz'altro minori rispetto ai giganti della generazione precedente come Sinibaldo dei Fieschi e l'Ostiense, o a più celebri contemporanei come Guglielmo Durante, o a maestri, come Guido da Baisio, le cui fortune si prolungano nel secolo XIV. Siamo di fronte, peraltro, a una generazione il cui lavoro ha posto le basi per le elaborazioni dottrinali dell'epoca successiva. Ignorare o trascurare le figure di questi giuristi minori significherebbe ignorare o trascurare una delle linee di pensiero e di metodo che confluirono nella formazione dell'opera di Giovanni d'Andrea, astro della canonistica bolognese della prima metà del Trecento e autorità influente e prestigiosa per le successive generazioni di giuristi.[1]

Fra i canonisti attivi a Bologna negli ultimi tre decenni del secolo XIII Marsilio Mantighelli è figura di rilievo.[2] Esercitò l'arte del notariato prima di acquisire, in un anno

---

1. Cfr., in questo senso, le mie considerazioni in 'Note su formazione e diffusione delle raccolte di "quaestiones disputatae" in diritto canonico (secoli XII–XIV)', in: *Juristische Buchproduktion im Mittelalter,* ed. V. Colli (Frankfurt/M. 2002) 395–430, in particolare 413–21. L'importanza delle ricerche (condotte e da condurre) sui giuristi della seconda metà del Duecento è dimostrata, soprattutto per il versante civilistico, da numerosi studi di M. Bellomo, fra i quali ricordo il volume su *I fatti e il diritto tra le certezze e i dubbi dei giuristi medievali (secoli XIII–XIV)* (I Libri di Erice 27; Roma 2000), dove si troverà menzione della ulteriore letteratura: si tratta di una esperienza scientifica, durata alcuni decenni, che contribuisce in modo determinante alla maturazione e alla configurazione del sistema del diritto comune e canonico.

2. Siamo debitori agli eruditi settecenteschi della gran parte delle notizie biografiche sull'autore, che nel

incerto, la *licentia docendi* in diritto canonico.[3] Possedeva il titolo di *doctor decretorum* nel 1272, allorché disputava a Bologna la più risalente delle *quaestiones* che le fonti manoscritte tramandano.[4] Era laico e coniugato. La sua attività di docente si estende per circa un trentennio.[5] Fra i suoi allievi fu Giovanni d'Andrea, che più volte definisce Marsilio 'dominus meus'.[6] Nello Studio bolognese acquisì, col tempo, una posizione di rispetto e autorevolezza. Fu arbitro, nel 1281, in una controversia interna all'*universitas* degli ultramontani riguardante l'elezione del rettore. Più volte, in circostanze critiche per la città, fu esentato dal servizio militare insieme con altri colleghi, canonisti e civilisti, *ordinarie legentes*.[7]

La documentazione d'archivio mostra la partecipazione di Marsilio in vari affari ecclesiastici del vescovo di Bologna e di altri prelati, come pure la sua attività di consulente svolta in favore di ordinamenti cittadini.[8] Particolarmente significativa è la sua collaborazione con l'ufficio dell'inquisizione bolognese, attestata da documenti in cui Marsilio compare talvolta come consulente, talaltra come semplice testimone di atti compiuti dall'inquisitore.[9]

___

testo ripropongo sommariamente: Sarti-Fattorini 1.479–81; 2.76 doc. XLVIII; 2.193 doc. XXXVI; 2.220 doc. VIII; G. Fantuzzi, *Notizie degli scrittori bolognesi* (9 voll.; Bologna 1781–1794; rist. anast. Bologna s.d.) 5.203–205. Cfr. poi Schulte, QL 2.166, e il conciso profilo di R. Naz, 'Marsile de Mantighellis', DDC 6 (1957) 830. Varie notizie su Marsilio si ricavano dal *Chartularium* 9 docc. V, IX, XCIII, CLXI, CCXV, CCCXLII, CDI, CDXIII, CDXIV (tutti del 1286); ibid. 11 doc. CCVI (1269); ibid. 12 docc. CXLII (1279), CLIII (1286), CCXXXI; ibid. 14 doc. 155 (1270).

3. In due documenti del 1269 e del 1270 Marsilio è chiamato semplicemente *dominus*, senza che si faccia menzione del titolo di *doctor decretorum* (*Chartularium* 11 doc. CCVI [1269]; ibid. 14 doc. 155 [1270]).

4. Nel ms. Paris, BN lat. 4489, fol. 124rb–va. Cfr. *infra*, § 3.

5. La scuola di Marsilio è ricordata in un documento del 1287 edito da F. Cavazza, *Le scuole dell'antico Studio Bolognese* (Milano 1896) 80–81 e doc. XIV.

6. Sul punto rinvio a quanto da me scritto in 'Dalle "Quaestiones Mercuriales" alla "Novella in titulum de regulis iuris",' RIDC 3 (1992) 125–71, in particolare 153 e nota 71.

7. Oltre al documento edito da Sarti-Fattorini 2.76 doc. XLVIII (21 giugno 1297), v. A. Pini, 'Per una storia sociale dell'Università: i bidelli bolognesi del XIII secolo', *Annali di Storia delle Università Italiane* 1 (1997) 43–75, in particolare 55 e nota 78 (13 aprile 1296).

8. Cfr. *infra*, nota 15.

9. *Acta S. Officii Bononie ab anno 1291 usque ad annum 1310*, ed. L. Paolini e R. Orioli (2 voll.; Roma 1982–84), dal ms. Bologna, Biblioteca Comunale dell'Archiginnasio B 1856, proveniente dall'archivio dell'inquisizione domenicana, che aveva sede nel convento di S. Domenico in Bologna. Marsilio Mantighelli è menzionato nei seguenti documenti: doc. 45 (1.75–76 [1299]; testimone); doc. 115 (1.144–45 [1299]; testimone); doc. 574 (2.326–29 [1299]; testimone); doc. 804 (2.596–97 [1299]; *consilium*); doc. 807 (2.598 [1299]; *consilium*); doc. 813 (2.602 [1299]; *consilium*); doc. 814 (2.602–603 [1299]; *consilium*). Incidentalmente si può notare che negli atti dell'inquisizione bolognese sono presenti vari documenti riguardanti un *magister Iacobus de Mantighellis, medicus, doctor in arte fisice* (*Acta S. Officii*, ad indicem, s.v. Iacobus Manteghellus). Fu inquisito nel 1304 poiché era stato tra coloro che, in buona fede, avevano avuto l'occasione di conoscere e di ospitare Dolcino, con alcuni suoi adepti, allorché egli passò da Bologna nel 1300, doc. 650 (2.437–38 [1304]); fu condannato, doc. 762 (2.551–55 [11 febbraio 1305]); infine assolto dopo aver professato fedeltà alla Chiesa Romana, prestato idonea cauzione, promesso di fare penitenza, doc. 765 (2.558–59 [5 aprile 1305]). Questo Iacopo o Giacomo Mantighelli è probabilmente da identificare con l'omonimo personaggio, figlio di Mantighello Mantighelli (fratello di Marsilio), menzionato da Sarti-Fattorini 1.565. Mantighello fu professore di medicina, e morì nel 1274. Il figlio Jacobus,

Al settembre del 1300 risale il suo testamento.[10] Non era certamente più fra i vivi nel 1301.

2. Notizie sull'opera scientifica di Marsilio Mantighelli.

Non è inverosimile che sui margini dei manoscritti del *Decretum* e delle *Decretales*, utilizzati nelle scuole bolognesi negli ultimi decenni del secolo XIII, si possa rinvenire traccia dell'insegnamento di Marsilio Mantighelli. Si tratta, comunque, di una indagine ancora tutta da compiere, da iscriversi nel contesto di una più ampia ricerca sulle 'tracce d'uso' dei manoscritti canonistici dei secoli XIII e XIV, che di molto arricchirebbe il patrimonio delle nostre conoscenze sulla scienza canonistica di quel tempo.[11]

Allo stato delle conoscenze, la testimonianza dell'insegnamento di Marsilio nello Studio bolognese è affidata a poco più di una ventina di *quaestiones disputatae*, la cui datazione si estende in un arco di anni che va dal 1272 al 1295.[12] Frammiste a quelle di numerosi altri canonisti degli ultimi decenni del secolo XIII, le *quaestiones* di Marsilio sono tramandate in cospicue serie all'interno di collezioni di *quaestiones* contenute in alcuni codici.[13] Negli ultimi anni hanno ripetutamente richiamato l'attenzione degli studiosi.[14]

---

secondo Sarti-Fattorini, seguì le orme del padre, 'non tamen doctoris honores obtinuit'. Nonostante questa precisazione (che però non appare documentata), mi sembra verosimile che possa trattarsi della medesima persona.

10. Noto già a Fantuzzi, *Notizie* 5.204 e nota 9; edito da I. B. Giordani, *Acta franciscana e tabulariis bononiensibus deprompta* (Analecta Franciscana IX; Quaracchi 1927) 1.535 n. 1057, come riferisce C. Mesini, 'De codice iuridico n. 3 Pl. II, l. S. Bibliothecae Malatestianae (Cesenae)', *Antonianum* 26 (1951) 271–94 e 367–85, in particolare 367–68 e nota 1. Su Giovanni, figlio di Marsilio, danno notizie Sarti-Fattorini e Fantuzzi; più recentemente G. Orlandelli, *Il libro a Bologna dal 1300 al 1330. Documenti* (Bologna 1959) 56 doc. 76 (28 febbraio 1302).

11. Per l'impostazione metodologica della ricerca v. M. Bellomo, 'Sulle tracce d'uso dei "libri legales",' in: idem, *Medioevo edito e inedito. I. Scholae, Universitates, Studia* (I Libri di Erice 20.1; Roma 1997) 121–38.

12. Si veda la tavola cronologica compilata, anche per altri autori, da G. Murano, '"Liber quaestionum in petiis". Osservazioni sul ms. Darmstadt 853', *Studi Medievali*, III ser., 33 (1992) 645–94, in particolare 660–61. La tavola comprende *quaestiones* disputate fra il 1275 e il 1295; è da aggiungere la testimonianza del manoscritto parigino citato *supra*, nota 4, relativa alla *quaestio* disputata nel 1272.

13. Serie che nella tradizione manoscritta potevano presentarsi nella forma di piccole sillogi di questioni attribuite a Marsilio; v. la testimonianza di Tommaso Diplovatazio, *Liber de claris iuris consultis. Pars posterior*, ed. F. Schulz, H. Kantorowicz e G. Rabotti (SG 10; Bologna 1968) 204: 'Vidi questiones ipsius, incipiunt: "Questiones domini Marsilii decretorum doctoris. Questio talis est: Utrum compaternitas contrahatur per procuratorem".'

14. A parte il citato manoscritto di Paris, BN lat. 4489, che contiene una sola *quaestio* di Marsilio, gli altri manoscritti che le contengono in serie più o meno ricche sono: Darmstadt, Hessische Landes- und Hochschulbibliothek 853; Bamberg, SB Can. 48 (P.II.23); Modena, Biblioteca Estense Campori App. 1242; London, BL Arundel 493; München, BSB Clm 8011; Cesena, Biblioteca Malatestiana S.II.3. Con riferimento alle *quaestiones* di Marsilio, Mesini, 'De codice iuridico' 367–70; C. Mesini, 'Questioni disputate in diritto canonico nello studio bolognese nel secolo XIII dal cod. Y.Z.1 + Appendice Campori 1242 della Biblioteca Estense di Modena', *Apol-*

Vi sono tracce anche dell'attività consulente svolta da Marsilio. È stato segnalato un suo *consilium* del 1285 rilasciato in favore del Comune di Siena e diretto a negare privilegi fiscali ai 'frati gaudenti'.[15]

Si è fatto cenno, più sopra, della collaborazione di Marsilio con l'ufficio dell'inquisitore a Bologna: sono noti alcuni suoi *consilia* emessi nel quadro di tale attività.[16] Non è da escludere che a tale collaborazione possano essere ricondotti alcuni non meglio precisati scritti in tema di eresia, datati 1291, che una testimonianza cinquecentesca attribuisce a Marsilio.[17] Segno di interesse verso la tematica dell'eresia, se non anche testimonianza della menzionata attività di consulenza, sono i *consilia*, risalenti agli anni 1290 e 1291, che un manoscritto della Biblioteca Casanatense ascrive a Marsilio Mantighelli e a Dino del Mugello, i quali attendono ancora di essere studiati.[18]

---

linaris 50 (1977) 484–520, in particolare 501–18; M. Bertram, 'Kanonistische Quästionensammlungen von Bartholomäus Brixiensis bis Johannes Andreae', in: Proc. Cambridge (MIC C.8; 1988) 265–81, in particolare 270–72; F. Martino, '"Quaestiones" civilistiche disputate a Bologna negli ultimi decenni del secolo XIII. Studio sui manoscritti Leipzig, U.B., 992 e Paris, B.N., Lat. 4489', in: *Studi sulle 'quaestiones' civilistiche disputate nelle università medievali*, ed. G. D'Amelio et al. (Catania 1980) 225–96, in particolare 277 (1272); Murano, '"Liber quaestionum in petiis"' 660–61 (con tavola cronologica delle *quaestiones* datate), 663, 681–90, 691 (la n. 112 vi compare come anonima, ma la paternità è di Marsilio: 'Quidam pater familias fecit testamentum, inter cetera . . .'; cfr. *infra*, § 5.1 e Appendice, *quaestio* n. 1); Condorelli, 'Dalle "Quaestiones Mercuriales"' 130, 134, 153 e nota 71, 157, 160, 162, 170; Condorelli, 'Note su formazione e diffusione' 409–411; 414 nota 64; 416 nota 66; 423–28 (sempre dal ms. monacense, con le corrispondenze con gli altri mss. contenenti raccolte di *quaestiones*); Bellomo, *I fatti e il diritto* 71 note 176–78 (dal ms. londinese).

15. È stato segnalato da M. Ascheri, 'Analecta manoscritta consiliare (1285–1354)', BMCL 15 (1985) 61–94, in particolare 61–62: si tratta della copia notarile del 5 gennaio 1336 (1335 stile senese) dell'originale, datato Bologna, 20 aprile 1285 (Siena, AS Capitoli 2 [Caleffo dell'Assunta] fol. 765v–767v). La questione doveva stare molto a cuore al Comune di Siena, che interrogò ben sette consulenti scelti fra i più noti professori (civilisti e canonisti) bolognesi: oltre a Marsilio compaiono Francesco d'Accursio, Egidio dei Foscarari, Basacomatre de Basacomatribus, Lambertino dei Ramponi, Dino del Mugello, Alberto di Odofredo.

16. Cfr. *supra*, nota 9.

17. Secondo la testimonianza di Camillo Campeggi nelle sue *additiones* a Zanchino di Ugolino Sena, *Tractatus de haereticis* (Roma 1568) 178 (anche in: TUI 12.2 fol. 259vb, *additio* 'fiscus'), ricordata da M. Bellomo, 'Giuristi e inquisitori del Trecento. Ricerca su testi di Iacopo Belvisi, Taddeo Pepoli, Riccardo Malombra e Giovanni Calderini', in: *Per Francesco Calasso. Studi degli allievi* (Roma 1978) 9–57, ora in: idem, *Medioevo edito e inedito*. III. *Profili di giuristi* (I Libri di Erice 20.3; Roma 1998) 129–77 (133 e nota 7).

18. Li ha segnalati Bellomo, 'Giuristi e inquisitori' 133 nota 7: Roma, Bibl. Casanat. ms. 969 (già A.III.34), fol. 78r–80r (1291), 82r–83v (1290), 83v–84v (1290). Nel *Catalogo* della *Mostra del Digesto e della storia dello Studio di Bologna nella Biblioteca dell'Archiginnasio* (Bologna 1933) 11 n. 21, trovo menzione di un non meglio identificato manoscritto della Biblioteca Universitaria (cartaceo, sec. XV), contenente *consilia* (di argomento non precisato) attribuiti congiuntamente a Dino e a Marsilio: 'Consilium dominorum Marsilii de Mantechellis et Dini de Musello' (fol. 126r); 'Consilium dominorum Marsilii de Mantegellis et Dini de Mugello super quibusdam questionibus' (fol. 139r). Il singolare accostamento dei due nomi può far pensare proprio ai *consilia* in tema di eresia di cui si è appena fatto cenno.

3. Le tre 'quaestiones disputatae' in materia di usura.

Nel *corpus* delle *quaestiones* di Marsilio ne ho individuate tre che sviluppano alcuni aspetti problematici relativi al divieto delle usure.

Al 1272 risale la *quaestio 'Quidam usurarius positus in extremis condidit testamentum'*, che a mia conoscenza è tramandata unicamente dal manoscritto Paris, BN lat. 4489 (fol. 124rb–va).[19]

Poco più che un ventennio dopo, nel 1294, Marsilio disputò la *quaestio 'Quidam usurarius mortuus est absque penitentia et satisfactione usurarum'*, che è riportata nei manoscritti Darmstadt, Hessische Landes- und Hochschulbibliothek 853 (fol. 206ra), München, BSB Clm 8011 (fol. 90vb–91ra), Bamberg, SB Can. 48, antea P.II.23 (fol. 288va–b).[20]

Non è datata la *quaestio 'Quidam paterfamilias fecit testamentum'*, che il manoscritto di München (fol. 106ra–b) attribuisce a Marsilio, mentre è priva di attribuzione in quello di Darmstadt (fol. 211rb–vb).[21]

4. Le 'quaestiones' nel contesto normativo: il testamento dell'usuraio, la restituzione delle usure, la sepoltura ecclesiastica.

Le tre *quaestiones* ruotano intorno alla figura dell'usuraio: l'usuraio che redige testamento, col quale dispone la restituzione delle somme ricevute a usura, da un lato; dall'altro, invece, l'usuraio che, morto senza aver fatto penitenza e aver disposto la restituzione del maltolto, riceve fraudolentemente sepoltura ecclesiastica. I testi di Marsilio toccano alcuni aspetti problematici sui quali la legislazione ecclesiastica era stata imponente nell'ultimo secolo. Il *ius novum*, che aveva puntualmente disciplinato i più diversi profili relativi al divieto canonico delle usure, aveva sollecitato le discussioni dei giuristi volte a dirimere gli innumerevoli dubbi emergenti dai casi della vita nella loro relazione con le norme. Ne risulta una copiosa letteratura, nell'ambito della quale ciò che i canonisti scrissero sui margini dei libri di canoni e decretali, o nei vari *apparatus*, *lecturae* e

---

19. È stata segnalata da Martino, '"Quaestiones" civilistiche' 277. Sul gruppetto di *quaestiones* canonistiche contenute nel ms. 4489 (fol. 123ra–126va) v. anche Condorelli, 'Note su formazione e diffusione' 406–407. Sulle *quaestiones* civilistiche del ms. parigino v. ora Bellomo, *I fatti e il diritto* 62–64 e *ad indicem*. V. *infra*, Appendice, *quaestio* n. 2.

20. È datata nei mss. di Darmstadt e Bamberg, non datata in quello di München: Murano, '"Liber quaestionum in petiis"' 690 n. 102 (ringrazio Giovanna Murano per avermi fornito una fotocopia del foglio del ms. bambergense dove è trascritta la *quaestio*); Condorelli, 'Note su formazione e diffusione' 424 n. 21. V. *infra*, Appendice, *quaestio* n. 3.

21. Murano, '"Liber quaestionum in petiis"' 691 n. 112; Condorelli, 'Note su formazione e diffusione' 428 n. 57; da Giovanni d'Andrea è attribuita al 'dominus meus'. V. *infra*, § 5.1 e Appendice, *quaestio* n. 1.

commentaria, costituisce solo la parte più consistente e visibile. Un rilevante numero di *quaestiones* in tema di usura, sparse qua e là nelle varie raccolte e finora sostanzialmente trascurate nelle indagini storiografiche, attende ancora di essere esplorato.[22]

Il divieto dell'usura era tema di assoluta attualità in un'epoca in cui le attività commerciali e l'economia monetaria attraversavano una fase di intenso sviluppo. I molteplici aspetti connessi col divieto tenevano costantemente desta l'attenzione della Chiesa sia dal punto di vista della dottrina morale che sotto il profilo della regolamentazione giuridica. In un'epoca di sentita e condivisa religiosità la pervasività di tale divieto era tale da turbare nel profondo le anime del fedeli.

In poco meno di un secolo—dal 1179 al 1274—la reazione della Chiesa contro la diffusione e l'incremento del *crimen usurarum* fu affidata in due occasioni a solenni decisioni adottate in concili generali. Una medesima prospettiva di azione lega il terzo Concilio Lateranense col secondo di Lione. I loro canoni definiscono alcuni profili repressivi del divieto dell'usura, facendo leva sulla religiosità dei fedeli e sul timore del giudizio divino, che si fa più vivo e acuto in alcuni momenti critici della vita umana. Il c.25 del terzo Concilio Lateranense aveva disposto che gli *usurarii manifesti* non fossero ammessi alla comunione dell'altare e alla sepoltura ecclesiastica.[23] Il secondo Concilio di Lione, ispirandosi dichiaratamente alla politica repressiva del terzo Lateranense, intervenne sul tema con due canoni.[24] In primo luogo si proibì che fossero dati in locazione, o concessi a qualsiasi titolo, immobili a stranieri o a residenti non oriundi del luogo, che esercitassero o intendessero esercitare pubblicamente l'attività feneratizia; le autorità locali avrebbero dovuto disporre prontamente l'espulsione perpetua di tali

22. Ne ho segnalate alcune, risalenti agli ultimi tre decenni del secolo XIII, in 'Note su formazione e diffusione' 416 nota 66. Altre sono state segnalate da Bellomo, *I fatti e il diritto* 109 nota 85, 228 nota 6, 275 nota 36, 488 nota 79.

23. Concilio Lateranense III can. 25, ed. COD[3] 223; poi rifluito nel *Liber Extra* (X 5.19.3). La privazione della sepoltura ecclesiastica per il delitto di usura divenne una sanzione tipica nella legislazione sinodale particolare: cfr. per esempio J. Gaudemet, 'Aspects de la législation conciliaire française au XIIIe siècle', RDC 9 (1959) 319–40, in particolare 337–38, ora in: idem, *La formation du droit canonique médiéval* (Londra 1980) n. VI. Sul concetto di *usurarii manifesti* v. T. P. McLaughlin, 'The Teaching of the Canonists on Usury (XII, XIII and XIV Centuries)', *Medieval Studies* 1 (1939) 81–147; 2 (1940) 1–22, in particolare 2 (1940) 12–13: vi è una tendenza a ritenere l'aggettivo come sinonimo di *notorii* (per esempio l'Ostiense). Ma la volontà di punire l'usura a più largo raggio spinge i giuristi ad enumerare altre circostanze in cui, senza essere *notorii (iuris* o *facti)*, gli usurai sono pur sempre da qualificare *manifesti*. Nella legislazione sinodale si ritrovano anche canoni che definiscono usurai manifesti coloro che ne hanno la reputazione, se vi sono altri indizi concludenti (concilio di Salzburg del 1386, can. 13). Un testo di Federico Petrucci volto ad interpretare il significato del termine *manifestum* nel c. *Quanquam, de usuris*, del *Liber Sextus* (VI 5.5.2) è segnalato da Bellomo, *I fatti e il diritto* 489.

24. I due canoni erano, al momento della promulgazione, riuniti in un singolo testo, successivamente diviso in due parti per la pubblicazione. Sussistono varianti molto significative tra la versione iniziale e quella pubblicata: S. Kuttner, 'Conciliar Law in the Making: The Lyonese Constitutions of Gregory X in a Manuscript at Washington', in: *Miscellanea Pio Paschini* (2 voll.; Roma 1949) 2.39–81, in particolare 69–73, ora in: idem, *Medieval Councils, Decretals, and Collections of Canon Law* (Aldershot 1992) n. XII.

soggetti dalle terre in cui svolgevano i loro commerci illeciti.[25] In un ulteriore canone si stabilì che fosse negata la sepoltura ecclesiastica agli *usurarii manifesti* che, pur avendo disposto la restituzione delle somme ricevute a usura, non avessero, nei limiti delle loro possibilità *(prout patiuntur facultates eorum)*, restituito il maltolto agli aventi diritto; o che non avessero almeno offerto idonea garanzia di restituzione.[26] Il canone lionese si concludeva con una pesantissima sanzione: dichiarava, infatti, invalidi *(irrita)* i testamenti che fossero stati redatti senza l'adozione delle prescritte minuziose formalità.[27]

Il sistema repressivo definito e perfezionato nei due Concili ruota, come è evidente, intorno al cardine della *restitutio*.[28] Il divieto della sepoltura ecclesiastica è lo spettro che si materializza e si agita nelle coscienze degli usurai che non abbiano provveduto a restituire il maltolto in modo conforme alla volontà della Chiesa.[29] La speranza

25. Concilio di Lione II can. 26, ed. COD[3] 328–29; poi rifluito nel *Liber Sextus* (VI 5.5.1).

26. Concilio di Lione II can. 27, in: COD[3] 329–30; poi rifluito nel *Liber Sextus* (VI 5.5.2). Sulla *restitutio* (o almeno *cautio restitutionis*) come premessa per l'imposizione della penitenza e della sepoltura ecclesiastica v. anche, con riferimento ad altre figure delittuose, X 5.17.2.

27. La disposizione diede luogo ad accese discussioni. Secondo Giovanni d'Andrea *(Apparatus in Sextum* [ed. Romae 1584 p. 450a], *in* VI 5.5.2, s.v. *aliter facta)* sarebbe stato sufficiente che l'usuraio avesse comunque prestato cauzione prima di morire: 'Quid si primo testamentum fecit, postea cavit? Dixit hic Garsia quod non firmatur per hoc testamentum, quia ab initio non valuit, ut infra de regulis iuris Non firmatur (VI [5.13].18) . . . Satis videtur sufficere, si ante mortem cavit, cum testamentum morte firmetur . . . Nec obstat regula, Non firmatur, que de solo tractu temporis loquitur'. Ritornando sulla questione nella *Novella in Sextum* (ed. Venetiis 1499 p. 267b–268a), Giovanni d'Andrea ribadisce e difende le parole che 'succincte in scholis soleba(t) dicere'. La costituzione non intende rendere l'usuraio intestabile, ma vuole solo proibire che il testamento privo della cauzione produca effetto. Si tratta dunque di una inefficacia che può essere in seguito sanata mediante la prestazione della cauzione. L'usura è un crimine ecclesiastico: ciò giustifica, secondo Giovanni d'Andrea *(Apparatus in* VI 5.5.2, s.v. *aliter facta)*, l'intervento della Chiesa *in temporalibus*: 'Et quia istud crimen ecclesiasticum est, potuit papa irritare testamenta laicorum per que in alios transferebantur bona et fiebat durior conditio exactorum. Erit ergo quod evincere valebunt et habere, supra ut lite pendente, Ecclesia i. in fine (X 2.16.3). Habet enim ratione huius criminis iurisdictionem in talibus, supra de iudiciis, Novit (X 2.1.13), supra qui filii sint legitimi, Per venerabilem (X 4.17.13), supra de foro competenti, c. ult. (X 2.2.20)'.

28. Sulla dottrina morale e canonica della *restitutio* v. K. Weinzierl, *Die Restitutionslehre der Frühscholastik* (München 1936); N. Iung, 'Restitution', *Dictionnaire de théologie catholique* 13 (1937) 2466–2501; più recentemente J. Kirshner e K. Lo Prete, 'Peter John Olivi's Treatise on Contracts of Sale, Usury and Restitution: Minorite Economics or Minor Works?', *Quaderni Fiorentini* 13 (1984) 233–86, in particolare 277–86, con la letteratura citata. La documentazione d'archivio attesta la pratica della *restitutio* disposta col testamento a partire dal secolo XII: M. Chiaudano, 'Le compagnie bancarie senesi nel Duecento', in: idem, *Studi e documenti per la storia del diritto commerciale italiano nel secolo XIII* (Torino 1930) 1–52, in particolare 14: testamenti con i quali si dispone la restituzione delle usure, dal 1226 al 1259; B. Nelson, 'The Usurer and the Merchant Prince: Italian Businessmen and the Ecclesiastical Law of Restitution, 1100–1550', *The Journal of Economic History* (Supplement 7; 1947) 104–22; B. Nelson, 'Blancardo (the Jew?) of Genoa and the Restitution of Usury in Medieval Italy', in: *Studi in onore di Gino Luzzatto* (2 voll.; Milano 1949) 1.96–116 (un caso risalente al 1178); F. Edler de Roover, 'Restitution in Renaissance Florence', in: *Studi in onore di Armando Sapori* (2 voll.; Milano 1957) 2.773–89; recentemente L. Armstrong, 'Usury, Conscience and Public Debt: Angelo Corbinelli's Testament of 1419', in: *A Renaissance of Conflicts. Visions and Revisions of Law and Society in Italy and Spain*, ed. J. Marino e T. Kuehn (Toronto 2004) 173–240 (con amplissima bibliografia, 203–14).

29. Sulla disciplina della sepoltura ecclesiastica: A. Bernard, *La sépulture en droit canonique, du Décret de Gratien au concile de Trente* (Thèse en droit; Paris 1933); G. Le Bras, *Le istituzioni ecclesiastiche della cristianità*

dell'assoluzione e la fede nell'esistenza di un luogo ultraterreno, dove possano purgare le loro pur gravissime colpe, sono moventi che danno impulso alle estreme determinazioni degli usurai, volte a restaurare, seppure *in articulo mortis*, l'ordine morale e giuridico sconvolto dalle loro malvagie azioni.[30]

Durante i pontificati di Alessandro III e di Innocenzo III furono stabiliti i fondamentali principi canonici che reggono la disciplina della *restitutio*.[31] L'obbligo di restituire le usure incombe primariamente sull'usuraio, secondariamente sui suoi eredi ed aventi causa. La letteratura giuridica e morale attesta come l'applicazione pratica di siffatti principî sollevasse una infinità di dubbi.[32] Quali sono, di fatto, i soggetti tenuti alla restituzione? Nell'obbligo di restituzione sono variamente coinvolti i membri della 'casa' o 'famiglia' dell'usuraio: parenti (a diverso titolo, la moglie e gli eredi), servitori, amministratori; eventuali complici dell'usuraio, o comunque persone che abbiano prestato ausilio all'usuraio nella sua attività (per esempio, il notaio che confeziona l'atto usurario); coloro che, pur non avendo partecipato all'attività usuraria, ne abbiano comunque tratto un beneficio.[33] Si discute ampiamente, inoltre, su quali siano i limiti della responsabilità di questi ulteriori soggetti tenuti alla restituzione: è una responsabilità illimitata, ovvero limitata a quanto dei proventi criminosi fosse loro pervenuto?[34]

È un ambito in cui risulta particolarmente evidente quell'intreccio fra teologia morale e diritto che contribuisce a conformare dall'interno l'ordinamento canonico. La connessione fra *peccatum* e *crimen*, fra teologia e diritto, è resa oltremodo manifesta, fra l'altro, dal modo in cui viene tradizionalmente enunciato il principio intorno al

---

medievale, trad. italiana (2 voll.; Storia della Chiesa 12.1–2; Torino 1973–74) 1.186–89; E. Marantonio Sguerzo, *Evoluzione storico-giuridica dell'istituto della sepoltura ecclesiastica* (Milano 1976); J. Gaudemet, *Eglise et cité. Histoire du droit canonique* (Paris 1994) 556–59; S. Szuromi O.Praem., 'La discipline d'inhumation du XIIᵉ et XIIIᵉ siècle', RIDC 13 (2002) 211–28.

30. L'atteggiamento dell'usuraio di fronte alla morte e alla previsione della punizione eterna è efficacemente rappresentato da J. Le Goff con l'ausilio degli *exempla* dei predicatori: J. Le Goff, *La nascita del Purgatorio*, trad. italiana (Torino 1996) 245–47; idem, *La borsa e la vita. Dall'usuraio al banchiere*, trad. ital. (Roma e Bari 1987) 41–77. L'autore propone la tesi, da lui stesso definita provocatoria, secondo la quale il Purgatorio, permettendo la salvezza dell'usuraio, contribuì alla nascita del capitalismo: J. Le Goff, 'The Usurer and Purgatory', in: *The Dawn of Modern Banking* (New Haven e Londra 1979) 25–52; idem, *La borsa e la vita* 87.

31. X 5.19.5 e X 5.19.9 (Alessandro III); X 5.19.14 e X 5.19.17 (Innocenzo III).

32. Ampia casistica in G. Le Bras, 'Usure. II. La doctrine ecclésiastique de l'usure à l'époque classique (XIIᵉ–XVᵉ siècle)', *Dictionnaire de théologie catholique* 15 (1950) 2336–72, in particolare 2367–71.

33. Si discute su varie ipotesi: il chierico che ha ricevuto elemosina dall'usuraio, il povero soccorso dall'usuraio, il genero dell'usuraio che da costui ha ricevuto la dote, etc.

34. Sul tema della responsabilità degli eredi per il *delictum* del defunto v. X 3.28.14, con la *Glossa ordinaria* s.v. *sed eius heredes* (ed. Romae 1584 p. 854b). Nei commenti a questa decretale viene solitamente rilevata la *differentia* esistente fra *canones* e *leges* nella disciplina di questo aspetto. I civilisti discutevano l'argomento a margine di Cod. 4.17.1. La materia era estremamente controversa. Si può ravvisare la tendenza dei canonisti ad ampliare quanto più possibile le ipotesi di restituzione per l'effetto benefico che questa può avere sul destino ultraterreno dell'anima del defunto.

quale ruota la dottrina canonistica della *restitutio*. Risalente a S. Agostino, esso venne poi riformulato in una *regula iuris* accolta nel *Liber Sextus: Peccatum non dimittitur nisi restituatur ablatum*.[35] L'usuraio, dunque, commette un peccato, ma commette anche un crimine ecclesiastico. All'assoluzione dal peccato e dal crimine si giunge tramite un processo—che è insieme morale e giuridico—che dal *peccatum / crimen* conduce alla penitenza e quindi alla *restitutio* (o *satisfactio cui debetur*).[36] Gli esiti di questo processo sono efficacemente condensati da Alessandro III nella conclusione della decretale *Cum tu* (X 5.19.5): 'Ut sic non solum a pena, sed etiam a peccato possint (quod per usurarum extorsionem incurrerant) liberari'.[37]

5. Descrizione delle tre 'quaestiones'

5.1. Il 'mandatum de restituendis usuris' disposto nel testamento e il vescovo deputato alla sua esecuzione.

Nella *quaestio 'Quidam paterfamilias fecit testamentum'* si dibatte su una particolare fattispecie relativa al tema della restituzione delle usure ordinata mediante una disposizione testamentaria. Un *paterfamilias* fece testamento, nel quale confessò di avere ricevuto a titolo di usura, o comunque indebitamente, trecento lire bolognesi. Diede mandato di restituire la somma a tre persone indicate per nome *(Petrus Sclavinus, Jo-*

---

35. VI [5.13].4: 'Peccatum non dimittitur nisi restituatur ablatum'. Al margine di questa *regula* Giovanni d'Andrea sintetizza rapidamente la disciplina della *restitutio* consolidatasi dal *Decretum* al *Liber Sextus* (*Apparatus in Sextum*, s.v. *peccatum*; ed. Romae 1584 p. 537b): 'Hic ponitur pro regula verbum Augustini quod habet XIV q. VI c. I; supra de usuris, Cum tu (X 5.19.5) . . . Quod autem dicitur in hac regula verum intelligas, si illud ablatum restitui potest . . . Si autem restitui non potest, restituetur eius estimatio, etiam si res illa perierit sine culpa sua, quia in ipso instanti fuit in mora . . . Si autem nec estimationem potest solvere, quia evidenter est inops, tunc bene dimittitur peccatum: remanet tamen obligatio, et si postea ad pinguiorem fortunam perveniret, teneretur'. Ibid. s.v. *restituatur* (p. 537b): 'Restitutio autem ista facienda est ei a quo fuit extortum, vel eius heredibus, si extant . . . His autem non extantibus, solvetur pauperibus . . . Et quod supra dixi, restituendum ei a quo fuit extortum, intellige si fieri potest. Si vero nescitur a quo . . . pauperibus erogabitur providentia episcopi . . . Item dico id verum cum turpitudo versatur ex parte recipientis tantum: si vero ex parte utriusque, et transfertur dominium, nec repetitio competit, nec restituetur danti, sed pauperibus erogabitur'. All'obbligo della *restitutio* è assimilato quello di risarcire il danno ingiusto, ibid. s.v. *ablatum* (p. 538a): 'Pone, nihil abstuli, sed iniuste damnum dedi, ex quo nichil ad me pervenit. Idem, teneor enim damnum passo, alias non remittitur peccatum . . . Tenetur etiam heres meus, licet ad me vel ad ipsum nihil pervenerit ex maleficio, secundum canones, quod dic ut not. XII q.II Episcopus qui filios (c.34), de sepulturis, c. ult. (X 3.28.14). Secundum leges contra, C. ex delictis defunctorum in quantum he. con., l. unica (Cod. 4.17.1)'.

36. L'argomento è accuratamente trattato da P. Bellini, *La coscienza del principe. Prospettazione ideologica e realtà politica delle interposizioni prelatizie nel Governo della cosa pubblica* (2 voll.; Torino 2000) 1.89, 1.163–71. Sulla dialettica fra morale e diritto nell'esperienza occidentale v. lo studio di P. Prodi, *Una storia della giustizia. Dal pluralismo dei fori al moderno dualismo fra coscienza e diritto* (Bologna 2000).

37. Cfr., nello stesso senso ma per altre figure delittuose, X 5.17.5, con la *Glossa ordinaria*, s.v. *heredes* (ed. Romae 1584 p. 1223a). Nella conclusione del capitolo si enuncia il fine a cui mira la restituzione, alla quale devono essere costretti anche gli eredi: 'ut sic (scil. il defunto) a peccato valeat liberari'.

hannes Martini e *Martinus Tencii)* e ad altri non nominati, designando il vescovo del luogo esecutore della propria volontà. I problemi emergenti dal *casus* sono due. Se, anzitutto, il vescovo debba dare esecuzione a un legato che appare sostanzialmente indeterminato, dal momento che la disposizione non dice quante siano le persone aventi diritto alla restituzione e quali le somme di rispettiva pertinenza. Il primo dubbio è risolto affermativamente in ragione del principio del *favor ultimae voluntatis:* l'esecuzione della volontà testamentaria, in questa circostanza particolare, costituisce il presupposto affinché l'usuraio possa ricevere la sepoltura ecclesiastica e i *suffragia Ecclesiae.* Il problema conseguente è relativo alla procedura con la quale debba essere data notizia a tutti gli aventi diritto del legato disposto dal testatore; al modo in cui i creditori debbano provare le proprie pretese; infine alle diverse possibili modalità secondo le quali le trecento lire debbano essere distribuite fra i tre creditori nominati e gli altri che eventualmente si presentino a reclamare la restituzione di qualche somma. Marsilio ipotizza anche il caso che i creditori innominati esauriscano, con le loro richieste, l'intera somma disposta nel legato. In siffatta evenienza egli ritiene che i diritti dei tre creditori nominati possano essere soddisfatti sugli altri beni del testatore, poiché gli eredi sono responsabili per le obbligazioni del defunto nei limiti di quanto sia loro pervenuto dell'asse ereditario.

La *quaestio* era nota a Giovanni d'Andrea: commentando il c. *Quanquam usurarii* del *Liber Sextus,* egli ricorda che essa era stata disputata dal proprio maestro Marsilio, e ne riporta le argomentazioni e la soluzione in modo conciso e fedele.[38] Si può osservare che l'andamento della *quaestio* di Marsilio lascia intravedere, dietro un testo che nella versione a noi nota è stato costruito nella scuola, l'esistenza di una reale controversia che potrebbe avere impegnato Marsilio come consulente. Lo suggeriscono lo svolgimento della *quaestio,* il concatenarsi e lo snodarsi dei dubbi e delle relative soluzioni: il ragionamento di Marsilio sembra quasi costituire una guida per il vescovo relativamente alle modalità di procedere nell'esecuzione del mandato. A ciò si aggiunga che i tre creditori nominati sono indicati con nomi propri che potrebbero non essere di fantasia. E forse non è indifferente la circostanza che Marsilio proponga la sua soluzione 'salvo semper consilio et sententia meliori'—secondo un modulo che, per la verità, si ripete con lievi varianti nelle tre *quaestiones* qui esaminate. Non è inverosimile immaginare che una *quaestio de facto,* sulla quale il canonista aveva dato il suo parere come consulente, abbia poi fornito al Marsilio docente la materia per una disputa scolastica.[39] È, del resto, ben

---

38. Giovanni d'Andrea, *Novella in* VI 5.5.2 (ed. Venetiis 1499 p. 265a): 'Quid si testator in testamento solenniter expressit se pro usuris recepisse ccc <libras ab> a. b. c. et aliis innominatis iubens illas restitui et episcopum executorem fecit, nec de illis tribus nominatis apparere potest quod aliquid solverint. Disputando tenuit dominus meus quod, non obstante quod legatum videatur incertum, favore ultime voluntatis episcopus exequetur'.

39. Sulle espressioni *quaestio de facto, quaestio facti, quaestio ex facto emergens* v. M. Bellomo, '"Factum" e

noto come la scuola 'raccolga' e 'valorizzi' le esperienze del foro, e come questo fenomeno comporti una circolazione di metodi e testi fra le aule dei tribunali e le aule scola-
stiche.[40] Il presupposto di tale circolazione è costituito da un metodo giuridico unitario,
fondato sulle figure giuridiche e sulle tecniche di ragionamento dei *iura communia*, civile e canonico, diritti che vanno coordinandosi e fondendosi nel sistema dell'*utrumque
ius*.[41] Si tratta di un metodo che non conosce cesure fra teoria e prassi, e che pertanto
indica al giurista il modo corretto per operare *in iudiciis et in scholis*.[42]

5.2. 'Fideiussores ad usuras restituendas' e 'procurator generalis in officii causa'.

Nella *quaestio 'Quidam usurarius positus in extremis'*—la più risalente (1272) fra le tre
che ho preso in esame—un usuraio conferisce ad alcune persone di fiducia, qualificate
come *fideicommissari*, l'incarico di dare esecuzione alla propria volontà di restituire le
usure. I *fideicommissari* sono citati di fronte al vicario del vescovo di Bologna su istanza
di un creditore che chiede la restituzione di una certa somma. I convenuti obiettano
che non intendono assumere l'ufficio affidato loro dal testatore, e nominano un *procurator generalis in officii causa*, senza tuttavia sollevarlo dall'onere di fornire la consueta
garanzia *(satisdatio)*. La *quaestio* si articola in due dubbi. In primo luogo ci si chiede
se i *fideicommissarii* possano rinunciare al loro incarico, alla quale domanda Marsilio
risponde che la rinuncia è possibile solo se essi non abbiano già posto in essere attività
attinenti all'*officium fideicommissariae*. Il secondo dubbio riguarda una questione stret-
tamente processuale, cioè se il *procurator generalis* possa essere ammesso in causa senza
prestare idonea garanzia.

Come per la *quaestio* precedente, il lettore non può sottrarsi all'impressione che
dietro la disputa scolastica possa celarsi una controversia sorta nell'esperienza quotidiana e forse effettivamente dibattuta nelle aule di un tribunale. La menzione del vicario
del vescovo di Bologna potrebbe rappresentare un indizio in tal senso.

"ius". Itinerari di ricerca tra le certezze e i dubbi del pensiero giuridico medievale', RIDC 7 (1996) 21–46, in particolare 23–25, anche in: idem, *Medio Evo edito e inedito*. II. *Scienza del diritto e società medievale* (I Libri di Erice
20.2; Roma 1997) 63–89, in particolare 68–69.

40. Secondo la formula usata da Bellomo, *I fatti e il diritto* 457.

41. Con espressione singolarmente efficace un civilista coevo, Iacopo Belvisi, parlava di *iura communia*
come 'iura communicativa omnibus quaestionibus'. La definizione è contenuta in una *quaestio* di Iacopo tramandata dal ms. Vaticano, BAV Archivio S. Pietro A. 29, fol. 77ra, messa in luce e valorizzata da Bellomo, *I fatti
e il diritto* 633–34.

42. Si tratta di temi ampiamente e accuratamente studiati da Manlio Bellomo, alle cui valutazioni mi rifac-
cio sommariamente nel testo: *I fatti e il diritto* 439–70, in particolare 457–64 ('Echi di processi nelle aule universitarie') e 465–70 ('Consilia, prassi, teoria'); l'espressione *(dubitatio incidit in iudiciis et in scholis)*, che dà il titolo a un intero capitolo del libro di Bellomo, è tratta da una *quaestio* di Osberto da Cremona (441 nota 5), della

5.3. I 'fratres' ('Minores vel Praedicatores') e la sepoltura fraudolenta dell' 'usurarius mortuus absque penitentia et satisfactione usurarum'.

Per l'*usurarius manifestus* che fosse morto senza pentirsi e senza disporre—o almeno promettere, con idonea garanzia—la restituzione delle usure, il diritto comune della Chiesa prevedeva il divieto di ricevere la sepoltura ecclesiastica. Il rifiuto della sepoltura ecclesiastica è lo spettro che incombe, con la sua immagine intollerabile, sul morente e sui i suoi congiunti: priva il defunto del conforto di trovare l'ultima dimora in terra benedetta, lo esclude dal suffagio della comunità orante, è per la famiglia ragione di disonore ed infamia.

In questo contesto si iscrive il tema che Marsilio dibatte nella *quaestio 'Quidam usurarius mortuus est absque penitentia et satisfactione usurarum'.* Consapevoli delle scandalose conseguenze di una morte repentina e senza pentimento, i familiari, di nascosto, ma in presenza di tre testimoni, seppelliscono il corpo del defunto in terra sconsacrata. L'inganno si compie. Il cadavere di un uomo probo, spirato con i conforti religiosi, viene posto in una cassa nell'abitazione dell'usuraio defunto, quindi portato nella chiesa di un ordine religioso (dei Frati Minori ovvero dei Predicatori), dove riceve sepoltura ecclesiastica. Data la mancanza di pentimento dell'usurario, nel *casus quaestionis* è ritenuta irrilevante la circostanza che gli eredi abbiano o no prestato garanzia quanto alla restituzione del maltolto. Marsilio si chiede allora se i frati possano essere puniti con le pene canoniche previste *contra recipientes usurarios ad ecclesiasticam sepulturam*, posto che essi siano in grado di provare di avere seppellito nella propria chiesa non l'usuraio, ma un uomo deceduto in grazia di Dio. La soluzione è semplice. Le circostanze del caso sono tali da far presumere che i frati abbiano agito con dolo. Essi pertanto devono essere puniti, se non diano prova di avere ignorato le azioni fraudolente poste in essere dai familiari dal defunto, ovvero non si sottomettano a *purgatio canonica* in quanto siano stati infamati per avere agito con dolo.

L'unico dubbio sollevato nella *quaestio* è risolto con uno svolgimento che si presenta piano e lineare, secondo lo schema scolastico *pro-contra-solutio*.[43] Il caso proposto da Marsilio presenta qualche elemento che l'odierno lettore potrebbe giudicare quanto meno insolito e addirittura bizzarro. E tuttavia i fatti che il nostro testo descrive non erano alieni dalla quotidiana esperienza del pubblico coevo. Solo l'urgenza e la gravità del problema può darci una ragione di come l'ingegno degli uomini medievali potesse

---

quale si può vedere l'edizione in M. Semeraro, *Osberto da Cremona. Un giurista dell'età del diritto comune* (Roma 2000) 123–26.

43. La *quaestio* è ricordata da Giovanni d'Andrea nella *Novella in* VI 5.5.2 (ed. Venetiis 1499 p. 265a–b): 'Disputavit dominus meus quod locus sit huic pene in his qui simulaverunt usurarium sepelire, qui non caverat, cum tamen vere non illum sed alium vel nullum tunc hominem sepellivissent'.

applicarsi, con tanto fraudolenta fantasia, alla ricerca di modi per raggirare una norma-
tiva ecclesiastica rigorosissima, fondata sui canoni di due concili generali (Lateranense
III e Lionese II) e riproposta nell'orbe cristiano anche per il tramite delle molteplici fonti
delle legislazioni particolari. Le preoccupazioni dei familiari dell'usuraio, dirette ad
evitare scandalo e infamia per il defunto e la famiglia, dovevano sovente incontrarsi con
la mancanza di scrupoli e l'avidità di taluni ecclesiastici. Nell'esperienza, e di riflesso
nell'immaginario popolare, non era infrequente che i religiosi si facessero complici dei
familiari nei loro raggiri.[44] Talvolta essi si precostituivano una scusa con l'argomento
che, non essendo direttamente investiti della *cura animarum*, potessero legittimamente
ignorare le circostanze che per diritto comune avrebbero impedito il conferimento
della sepoltura ecclesiastica.[45] Non è, insomma, un caso che il secondo Concilio di Lione ponga in prima fila i *religiosi* tra le figure nei cui confronti viene riproposta la pena
della sospensione sancita dal terzo Concilio Lateranense contro quanti abbiano osato
ammettere alla sepoltura ecclesiastica gli usurai manifesti.[46]

Appendice

Le *quaestiones*

1. 'Quidam paterfamilias fecit testamentum'[i]

Trascrivo il testo dal ms. Darmstadt, Hessische Landes- und Hochschulbibliothek 853
(= *D*), fol. 211rb–vb, nel quale la *quaestio* è priva di attribuzione. La *quaestio* è tramandata
anche dal ms. München, BSB Clm 8011 (= *M*), fol. 106ra–b, nel quale l'iscrizione recita:
'Quaestio domini Marsilii doctoris decretorum'.

[211rb] Quidam paterfamilias fecit testamentum, inter cetera coram sacerdote et
quodam capellano fuit confessus quod ipse habuerat de usuris et male ablatis ccc. libras
bononienses et quod ipse habuerat de istis ccc. libris a Petro Sclavino et Johanne Martini
et Martino Tencii et a quibusdam aliis, quos non nominavit. Quas ccc. libras mandavit re-

---

44. Se ne trova testimonianza in testi letterariamente concepiti, come i sermoni dei predicatori, per esempio la fonte ricordata da Le Goff, *La borsa e la vita* 46–47, come pure in documenti della pratica giudiziaria. In
un processo tenuto di fronte all'inquisizione bolognese nel 1299, un testimone afferma di avere udito un certo
Oddo 'dicentem multa mala de domino papa, de cardinalibus et clericis et de fratribus, dicendo quod sunt mali
homines et quod fratres decipiunt personas et vadunt ad usurarios quando infirmantur et adulantur sibi et se-
peliunt eos in Sancto Dominico et accipiunt usuras pro se, nec faciunt restitui illis personis, que debent habere'
(*Acta S. Officii* 1.232, doc. 359; cfr., nello stesso senso, ibid. docc. 361 e 364).

45. Che il fatto potesse costituire un argomento di difesa è attestato da una argomentazione della nostra
quaestio: 'Quinto, quia cum tales religiosi non habeant curam animarum . . . licitum eis fuit predictum factum
ignorare et in facto alieno tollerabilis ignorancia', cfr. *infra*, Appendice, *quaestio* n. 3.

46. Cfr. *supra*, nota 26.

i. Le note critiche sono poste fra parentesi quadre [. . .]; le fonti fra parentesi tonde (. . .); rare integrazioni
fra parentesi a uncino <. . .>.

stitui, episcopo loci ad predicta per eum executore deputato. Modo queritur, quid habeat facere dictus episcopus, et quantum debeat dare cuilibet de istis tribus nominatis, cum ipsi non possunt probare aliter quod unquam iste testator aliquid ab eis vel eorum altero habuerit.

Et videtur primo quod episcopus se de tali legato non debeat in aliquo intromittere, cum non videatur valere ex eo quod tale legatum [211va] sciri non possit, et legatum quod ex testamento sciri non potest non valet, ff. de iure fisci, Ita fidei (Dig. 49.14.40).

Item, quia census ignorancie nec divinis nec humanis legibus invenitur, extra de censibus, Pervenit (X 3.39.5), arg. ff. de fideiussoribus, Si quis postquam, et l. Si quis pro eo (Dig. 46.137, 56) et ff. quando dies legatorum cedat, l. Huiusmodi legatum (Dig. 36.2.13), et iii. q. v. Quia suspecti (C.3 q.5 c.15) in verbo 'et si manifesta'.

Sed predictis non obstantibus dico quod episcopus debet se intromittere, saltim ultime voluntatis favore, quia nichil est quod magis debeatur heredibus et c., C. de sacrosanctis ecclesiis, l. i (Cod. 1.2.1), et quia ultima voluntas hominis immobilis perseverat, extra de celebratione missarum, Cum Marthe (X 3.41.6). Et, ut omnis fraus curtetur, habet episcopus istos tres nominatos ad se vocare et per iuramentum querere quantum de usuris et male ablatis quilibet eorum huic testatori dedisset, et secreto sigillatim, sicut fit in testibus, C. de testibus, Nullum (Cod. 4.20.14), et extra de testibus, Venerabili (X 2.20.52), et de accusationibus, Inquisitionis (X 5.1.21). Et hoc ne aliquis istorum trium possit ulterius variare, cum hoc possit esse dampnosum, ut infra subiciam, et variatio prohibita sit in alterius preiudicium, extra de rescriptis, Cum in multis (= VI 1.3.2), et C. de prohi<bita> nominis mutatione, l. una (Cod. 9.25.1). Et dicto iuramento recepto habet episcopus preconiçari per terram quod quicunque dedit aliquid testatori pro usuris vel male ablatis infra certum terminum veniat coram ipso et petat et doceat. Simile extra de clandestina desponsatione, Cum inhibicio (X 4.3.3), et extra qui matrimonium accusare possunt, Cum in tua (X 4.18.6), sicut cum inpetitur status alicuius, C. de ingenuis manumissis, Diffamari (Cod. 7.14.5), sicut facit ad accusandum clericum, extra de symonia, Licet Heli (X 5.3.31) et C. qui accusare non possunt, Ea que (Cod. 9.1.7, *Si ea que*) et extra de fide instrumentorum, Accepimus (X 2.22.4), sicut facit ad exceptiones proponendas, extra de exceptionibus, Pastoralis (X 2.25.4), sicut etiam facit iudex ad testes producendos, extra de testibus, In nomine Domini (X 2.20.2). Si vero post terminum aliquis veniat, non audietur, nisi in casibus que ponuntur in preall. decr. qui matrimonium accusare possunt, Cum in tua (X 4.18.6) et xvii. q. ii. Si quis incognitus (C.17 q.2 c.3). Et sic venientes infra terminum audientur, venientes postea non audientur, nisi ut superius est premissum.

Sed ex tunc procedere debet episcopus ad divisionem, unde sequitur videre quantum quilibet istorum habere debeat. Et videtur quod quilibet istorum habere debeat de quadraginta tribus partibus unam, quia usque ad illum numerum dicitur multitudo non effrenata, extra de testibus, Significaverunt (X 2.20.36) et c. Cum causam (X 2.20.37) cum suis similibus, et isti sunt tres. Sed videtur quod quilibet istorum habere debeat de septem partibus unam, quia per illam clausulam in testamento appositam possunt ad plus quatuor comprehendi, ut videtur exemplo clausule generalis 'quidam alii', ut extra de rescriptis, Cum in multis Innocentii iiii. (= VI 1.3.2). Et isti sunt tres, et ita septem. Sed videtur quod quilibet eorum debeat habere quintam partem, per hoc quod dicitur 'quibusdam aliis', quia pluralis elocutio duorum numero est contenta, ff. de testibus, Ubi (Dig. 22.5.12) et iiii. q. iii. § item in criminali, ver. ubi numerus (C.4 q.2–3 d.p.c.2 et c.3). Et isti sunt tres, et ita v., et ita quilibet eorum habebit quintam partem. Sed videtur quod quilibet istorum debeat habere quartam partem per l. ff. de usufructu accrescendo, Si quis Ticio et Sempronio et Mevio sive cum Mevio in tres partes dividitur ususfructus (Dig. 7.2.7 = *Si quis Attio*). Sic videtur in questione presenti a simili et quod quilibet istorum debeat habere quartam partem, cum dicatur in questione 'Petro Johanne et Martino et quibusdam aliis'.

Sed ad veram solutionem huius questionis credo distinguendum, quia, banno posito supradicto, aut veniunt aliqui alii ab istis tribus, aut non.

Si veniunt aliqui, habebunt tantum quantum se testatori dedisse monstrabunt pro usuris et male ablatis, et isti tres nominati habebunt residuum et in ea quantitate in qua iuraverunt. Quod superfuerit pauperibus per episcopum erogetur, postquam nescitur a quibus testator accepit, ut extra de usuris, Cum tu (X 5.19.5) et de homicidio voluntario vel casuali, Sicut dignum (X 5.12.6) cum similibus, et in hoc potest prodesse iuramenti receptio de qua supra premisi, sicut in simili casu dicit Innocentius et consuevit notari per doctores extra de electione, Quia propter (X 1.6.42). Si autem venientes occasione banni et clausule generalis vendicarent totas predictas ccc. libras, istis tribus crederem satisfaciendum de bonis aliis testatoris, vel etiam id quod deesset ei, quod iuraverunt, cum etiam heredes teneantur in tantum satisfacere pro defuncto quantum ad eos pervenit ex bonis defuncti, extra de testamentis, c. ult. (X 3.26.20) et extra de raptoribus, In literis (X 5.17.5) et xvi. q. vi. Si episcopum [episcopus *D*] (C.16 q.6 c.2[3]) et de usuris, Tua nos (X 5.19.9) cum similibus. Et in hoc casu credo sufficere iuramentum predictum, cum in talibus sufficiat probatio semiplena, extra de pignoribus, Illo vos (nos *D*) (X 3.21.4), de iure iurando, c. ult. (X 2.24.36) et de hiis que vi metusve causa fiunt, c. ult. (X 1.40.7) et C. unde vi, l. Si quando (Cod. 8.4.9), habito tamen respectu ad qualitatem persone et rei ut in iuribus preall. et extra de renunciatione, Super hoc (X 1.9.5) cum similibus.

Si autem non veniant aliqui per bannum predictum, credo quod quilibet istorum habebit quartam partem per legem predictam ff. de usufructu accrescendo, Si quis Ticio (Dig. 7.2.7 = *Si quis Attio*), et aliam quartam partem episcopus dabit pauperibus per iura superius allegata in primo membro distinctionis, cum ad ipsum spectet exequi pias voluntates defunctorum, extra de testamentis, Nos quidem, Johannes, et c. Tua nobis (X 3.26.3 et 19 et 17) et C. de episcopis et clericis, l. Nulli (Cod. 1.3.28) et ff. de petitione hereditatis, Hereditas § i. (Dig. 5.3.50). Sed ad hoc non procedet episcopus precipita festinatione sed moratoria contractatione, [211vb] per decretalem extra de sentientia et re iudicata, Cum Bertoldus (X 2.27.18) cum similibus suis. Et si superveniant aliqui post terminum, habentes iustam causam ignorancie banni, audiantur, ut in predicta decretali qui matrimonium accusare possunt, Cum in tua (X 4.18.6), et aliquid habere possunt. Et hoc dico salvo semper consilio et sententia meliori.

2. 'Quidam usurarius positus in extremis condidit testamentum'

Trascrivo il testo dall'unico testimone a me noto: Paris, BN lat. 4489 (= *P*), fol. 124rb–va.

[124rb] Questio disputata per dominum Marsilium doctorem decretorum, anno domini mº.ccº.lxxiiº. indictione xv.

Quidam usurarius positus in extremis condidit testamentum et in eodem testamento iussit usuras restitui et quosdam ad hoc fideicommissarios deputavit. Quidam, cui iste tenebatur ad restitutionem quarundam usurarum, fecit istos fideicommissarios citari coram vicario bononiensis episcopi super usuris. Veniunt fideicommissarii et dicunt quod nolunt uti officio fideicommissarie. Obicitur quod non possunt renunciare tali officio fideicommissarie quia eodem officio uti ceperunt. Fideicommissarii procuratorem [f. *praem. P*] constituerunt generalem in officii causa, quam habent cum illo qui fecit eos citari in causa predicta, non relevatum ab honere satisdationis. Obicitur quod talis procurator non debet admitti nisi satisdet.

Primo queritur si fideicommissarii possunt renunciare tali officio fideicommissarie, et cum in hoc non videatur magna [mag° *aut* magª *P*] questio, secundo queritur utrum talis procurator sit admitendus [!] nisi satisdet.

Quod tales fideicommissarii possunt renunciare videtur probari primo, quia invitus mandatum suscipere nemo cogitur, ff. commodati, In commodato (Dig. 13.6.17). Secundo, quia arbitrium [arbitrum *P*] suscipere nemo cogitur, ff. [*C. P*] de arbi., l. iii § i. (Dig. 4.8.3.1). Tercio, quia videtur esse casus c. extra de testamentis, Nos quidem (X 3.26.3). Quinto, per argumentum a contrario sensu sumptum extra de testamentis, Johannes (X 3.26.19). Et ad hoc possent induci plura alia argumenta, sed ista sufficiant causa brevitatis [ista causa sufficiant brevitatis *P*] ad hunc membrum.

Sed contra videtur posse probari primo, quia ultima voluntas defuncti pro lege servatur, xiii q. ii. [xxxiii q. iii *P*] Ultima voluntas (C.13 q.2 c.4). Secundo, quia nichil est quod magis debeatur hominibus et c., C. de sacrosanctis ecclesiis, l. i. (Cod. 1.2.1). Tertio, quia mandatum suscipere nemo cogitur, susceptum autem cogitur consumare, ff. mandati, Si quis alicui (Dig. 17.1.27), ff. de arbitris, l. iii § i. (Dig. 4.8.3.1) et C. [supra? *P*] de procuratoribus, Invitus (Cod. 2.12[13].17). Quarto, quia videtur esse casus extra [124va] <de> testamentis, Johannes (X 3.26.19).

Super hoc, salvo consilio meliori, credo distinguendum utrum fideicommissarii ceperunt uti officio fideicommissarie necne. Si ceperunt uti, credo omnino eos esse compellendos ut in proximis concordantiis. Si autem nondum uti ceperunt officio fideicommissarie, non credo eosdem compellendos per iura priora. Et ista distinctio videtur posse probari per c. preall. Johannes (X 3.26.19).

In secunda questione videtur posse probari quod talis procurator sit admittendus, quia procurator constituitur sub condicione et in diem et in perpetuum, ff. de procur., l. iii. et iiii. (Dig. 3.3.3 e 4), et ad omnia et ad [ad *add. P marg.*] plura negotia, ff. e. l., Mandato (Dig. 3.3.60). A simili iste procurator sufficiens videtur, ut pote constitutus ad istam causam, utrum potuerunt fideicommissarii renunciare vel non, in qua peccuniarum commodum non vertitur, unde, cum non sit realis huiusmodi causa, videtur quod sit sufficiens procurator, cum omnia iura loquencia quod procurator debeat satisdare loqui videantur in causa reali sive personali, ut videtur posse probari per iura de satisdatione.

Sed contra videtur posse probari primo, quia recte dicitur sufficiens procurator qui est ab honere satisdationis relevatus vel qui satisdat, C. de satisdando, l. una (Cod. 2.57[57].1), ff. de procuratoribus, Qui proprio § qui alium (Dig. 3.3.46.2) et l. Minor (Dig. 3.3.51) et Inst. de satisdationibus, § sin vero (Inst. 4.11.4).

Solutio. Salvo super hoc consilio meliori, credo quod talis non sit sufficiens et quod non est admitendus nisi satisdet, per iura proxime preall., non obstante quod dicitur quod talis causa non videtur realis vel peccuniaria, quia iura de tali satisdatione loquencia sine distinctione loquuntur, et nos hoc sine distinctione tenebimus, ff. qui et a quibus manumissi liberi non fiant, l. Prospexit (Dig. 40.9.12) cum similibus. Item, quia clausula iudicatum solvi tria continet, scil. quod stabit iuri et quod dolum non committet et hoc ipsum quod verbum sonat, ff. iudicatum solvi, l. Iudicatum (Dig. 46.7.6).[ii] Et licet in tali causa, potuerunt renunciare vel non fideicommissarii, in qua iste procurator infuerit, ultima clausula, scil. [si? *P*] de iudicato solvendo non possit committi, tamen quantum ad alias duas committi potest, scil. quod staret [non *praem. P male*] iuri et quod dolum non committit. Item et alia ratione iste sufficiens non dicatur procurator, quia ad hoc ut sit sufficiens procurator debet esse ad omnia sufficienter instructus, extra de postulatione, Bone (X 1.5.4) et c. Postulationem (X 1.5.5) et extra de dolo et contumacia, c. ult. (X 2.14.10). Igitur, cum per allegationem contrariam tantum dicatur dictus procurator intervenisse in causa illa, potuerunt renunciare fideicommissarii vel non, ita per consequens non ad causam principalem [principales *P*], cum non sit constitutus ad omnia, non est sufficiens procurator. Et alia ratione, quia qua ratione non reputaretur sufficiens procuratur ad causam principalem, eadem ratione nec ad accessoriam, scil. si potuerunt renunciare vel non, quia quod iuris est in principali et accessorio, ff. de accept., Per iusiurandum § et fideiussor (Dig. 46.4.13, §§ 7–10), extra de officio delegati, Prudenciam (X 1.29.21) ad finem, et extra de fide instrumentorum, Inter dilectos (X 2.22.6).

3. 'Quidam usurarius mortuus est absque penitentia et satisfactione usurarum'

Trascrivo il testo dal ms. Darmstadt, Hessische Landes- und Hochschulbibliothek 853 (= *D*), fol. 206ra. Altro testimone da me visto è il ms. München, BSB Clm 8011, fol. 90vb–91ra (= *M*); l'iscrizione recita 'Questio domini Marsilii doctor(is) decretorum'. Cfr. Bamberg, SB Can. 48 (= *B*), antea P.II.23, fol. 288va–b; l'iscrizione recita 'Questio disputata per dominum Marsilium de Mantegellis civem Bononie(nsem) decretorum doctorem anno domini m° cc° xcviiii° die viii exeunte aprilis. Talis est'.

Questio disputata per dominum Marsilium sub anno domini m. cc. xciiii. ix.

Quidam usurarius mortuus est absque penitentia et satisfactione usurarum. Eo latenter in fossatis tribus tamen presentibus testibus sepulto, corpus cuiusdam boni hominis in vera penitentia mortui in quadam cassa in domo ipsius usurarii fuit positum, et loco prefati usurarii delatum fuit ad ecclesiam Minorum vel Predicatorum et traditum fuit ecclesiastice sepulture, primo prestita vel non prestita satisdatione de satisfactione usurarum ab heredibus dicti usurarii. Queritur, cum dicti fratres parati [pati *D*; parati *MB*] sunt probare usurarium fuisse sepultum in fossatis, utrum episcopus possit infligere eis penam in canone promulgatam contra recipientes usurarios ad ecclesiasticam sepulturam.

Quod episcopus possit dictam penam imponere dictis fratribus probatur.

Primo, nam fraus et dolus alicui patrocinari non debet. Sed isti fratres videntur esse in fraude et dolo, que non debet eis patrocinari, extra de rescriptis, Sedes (X 1.3.15), xxx. q. i. Dictum (C.30 q.1 c.4) cum vi. capitulis sequentibus, et de eo qui duxit in matrimonium, c. i. (X 4.7.1) et de immunitate ecclesiarum, c. ult. (X 3.49.10) cum suis similibus.

Secundo, fratres sepeliendo corpus predicti hominis loco usurarii ecclesiam gravi scandalo perturbarunt, unde puniendi sunt, extra de renunciatione, Nisi cum pridem (X

---

ii. Cfr. Bernardo da Parma, *Apparatus in* X 1.38.13, s.v. *mandato* (ed. Romae 1584 p. 337a): 'Et sive quis habeat mandatum, sive non, et quantumcunque sit idoneus procurator rei, debet prestare aliquam cautionem, scil. iudicatum solvi . . . que causa scilicet, iudicatum solvi, tria continet, scil. quod defendat reum in causa, et quod dolum non committat, et quod solvat iudicatum: et hoc ipsum quod verbum sonat'.

1.9.10), de eo qui duxit in matrimonium, Cum haberet (X 3.49.5), et de regulis iuris, Qui scandalizaverit (X 5.41.3), de novi operis nunciatione, Cum ex iniuncto (X 5.32.2), de voto et voti redemptione, Magne (X 3.34.7), l. dist., Ut constitueretur (D.50 c.25) cum similibus.

Tercio, quia in istis maleficiis non iuris effectus, sed animi destinacio attenditur, extra de bigamis, Nuper (X 1.21.4), xiii. dist. Nervi (D.13 c.2) cum similibus.

Quarto, quia in talibus communis opinio facit ius, ut dicto c. Nuper (X 1.21.4) cum aliis similibus proxime allegatis, extra de electione, Querelam (X 1.6.24) et de iure patronatus, Consultationibus (X 3.38.19), et ff. de officio pretorum, Barbarius (Dig. 1.14.3).

Quinto, quia non creditur eis si dicant se hoc fecisse bono animo, extra de presumptionibus, Sicut (X 2.23.1).

Sexto, quia probacio per ipsos oblata non sufficit, nisi ignoranciam etiam comprobarent, extra de electione, Innotuit (X 1.6.20) et de postulatione <prelatorum>, c. i. (X 1.5.1).

Septimo, quia fecerunt, ut videtur, rem sibi prohibitam dictum corpus sepeliendo, cum non appareat quod dictus bonus homo apud ipsos religiosos elegit sepeliri, extra de sepulturis, Cum liberum, Ex parte, In nostra (X 3.28.6 et 5 et 10).

Quod episcopus non possit dictis fratribus dictam penam imponere probatur.

Primo, veritas opinioni prefertur, extra de bigamis, Nuper (X 1.21.4), viii. dist. Veritate (D.8 c.4), lxxxi dist. Quicunque (D.81 c.5) et extra qui filii sint legitimi, Per tuas (X 4.17.12), C. plus valere quod agitur, l. iii et iiii (Cod. 4.22.3 et 4).

Secundo, quia cessante causa cessare debet effectus, i. q. vii. [ii. *DMB*] Quod pro remedio (C.1 q.7 c.7), extra de appellationibus, Cum cessante (X 2.28.60), de renunciatione, Post translationem (X 1.9.11), et de voto et voti redemptione, Magne (X 3.34.7).

Tertio, quia presumptio est pro religiosis quod non sint sue salutis obliti, extra de procuratoribus, In nostra (X 1.38.4) et de prebendis, Nisi (X 3.5.21), i. q. vii. Sancimus (C.1 q.7 c.26) cum similibus.

Quarto, quia probabilis error eos excusare videtur, extra de sententia excommunicationis, Inquisitioni (X 5.39.44), de ordinatis ab episcopo qui renunciavit episcopatui, c. i. (X 1.13.1) et de postulatione <prelatorum>, c. i. (X 1.5.1), ff. de iuris et facti ignorantia, l. Error et l. Regula (Dig. 22.6.8, 9).

Quinto, quia cum tales religiosi non habeant curam animarum, ut extra de penitentiis et remissionibus, Omnis utriusque (X 5.38.12), licitum eis fuit predictum factum ignorare et in facto alieno tollerabilis ignorancia, ut in iuribus proxime allegatis.

Sexto, quia in predicto facto nichil episcopo deperit [depit *D*; deperit *MB*], sed in sepeliendo talem opus misericordie videntur egisse, quod religiosis iniungitur, lxxxvi. [xcvi. *DMB*] dist. Pervenit (D.86 c.26?).

Septimo, quia fecerunt, aliis non existentibus qui hoc facerent, id ad quod episcopus eos conpellere debuisset, extra de sepulturis, Ex parte (X 3.28.11), de torneamentis, c. ii. (X 5.13.2) cum similibus.

Ad solutionem questionis premisse, Christi nomine invocato, salvo semper consilio meliori, mihi videtur probabiliter esse dicendum quod si dicti fratres maliciose, ut evitarent opprobrium corporis et heredum defuncti, hoc fecerunt, quod presumitur prima facie nisi probent ignoranciam, vel se purgent si super hoc fuerint infamati, quod episcopus posset eos punire pena predicta, et possunt intelligi iura pro prima parte inducta et extra de purgatione canonica (X 5.34) per totum cum similibus. Alias autem non puniantur pena predicta, et hoc casu possunt intelligi iura pro secunda parte inducta.

17

Ein neues Kapitel in der Geschichte des kirchlichen Strafrechts

Die Systematisierungsbemühungen des Bernhard von Pavia († 1213)

Lotte Kéry

✳

In dem Jahrhundert zwischen der Entstehung des *Decretum Gratiani* (um 1140) und der Publikation der großen Dekretalensammlung Papst Gregors IX., des *Liber Extra* (1234), wurden nicht nur die entscheidenden Weichenstellungen für eine Emanzipation des Kirchenrechts als Wissenschaft vorgenommen, sondern auch für eine systematische Behandlung des kirchlichen Strafrechts als eigenständige und klar abgegrenzte Rechtsmaterie.[1] Wie schon Stephan Kuttner in seiner grundlegenden Untersuchung zur strafrechtlichen Dogmatik dargestellt hat, legten die Dekretisten und frühen Dekretalisten das Fundament für eine autonome Stellung des kirchlichen Strafrechts, indem sie eine Lehre von der strafrechtlichen Schuld entwickelten, zu deren Voraussetzungen auch die Abgrenzung strafrechtlich relevanter Verbrechen zur Sünde gehörte.[2] Um das sehr anschauliche Bild Kuttners aufzugreifen, bedurfte es 'eines praktikablen Rechtsbegriffs, der das rechtlich relevante und fassbare Verbrechen vom grenzenlosen Reich der Sünde schied'.[3]

1. S. Kuttner, *Kanonistische Schuldlehre von Gratian bis auf die Dekretalen Gregors IX. Systematisch auf Grund der handschriftlichen Quellen dargestellt* (Studi e Testi 64; Città del Vaticano 1935) vi.

2. Kuttner, *Schuldlehre* 3–22 (zum 'Verbrechensbegriff der Kanonistik').

3. Kuttner, *Schuldlehre* 4; dazu auch L. Kéry, 'Aspekte des kirchlichen Strafrechts im Liber Extra (1234)', in: *Neue Wege strafrechtsgeschichtlicher Forschung*, ed. H. Schlosser und D. Willoweit (Köln, Weimar und Wien 1999) 241–97, hier 242–45; L. Kéry, 'La culpabilité dans le droit canonique classique de Gratien (vers 1140) à Innocent IV (vers 1250)', in : *La culpabilité. Actes du XXᵉˢ Journées d'Histoire du Droit, 4–6 octobre 2000*, ed. J. Hoareau-Dodineau und P. Texier (Limoges 2001) 429–44, hier 431–35.

Für die in den letzten Jahren wieder vermehrt aufgegriffene Diskussion über die Entstehung des öffentlichen Strafrechts ist die Frage nach dem Anteil des Kirchenrechts, das offenbar auch auf diesem Gebiet eine Vorreiterrolle übernommen hat, aus mehreren Gründen von zentraler Bedeutung.[4] Dazu zählt unter anderem die Feststellung, daß die Kanonistik als Bestandteil des gelehrten Rechts einen wichtigen Beitrag zur Herausbildung der neu aufkommenden Strafrechtslehre geleistet hat, und zwar nicht nur in materieller Hinsicht zur Kriminalisierung abweichender Verhaltensweisen und deren Erfassung durch die Gesetzgebung, sondern auch auf einer allgemeineren Ebene für die Emanzipation des Strafrechts als einheitlicher Rechtsmaterie.[5]

Spätestens seit der umstrittenen Untersuchung von Viktor Achter über die 'Geburt der Strafe' wird eine klare Unterscheidung zwischen Buße und Strafe als einer der deutlichsten Anhaltspunkte für die Existenz eines öffentlichen Strafrechts betrachtet.[6] Während vor diesem Hintergrund und zwecks einer stark vereinfachenden Richtungsbestimmung die Buße im Sinne von *compositio* und Ausgleich zwischen Täter und Opfer als das ältere Modell einer Konfliktregelung zwischen den Parteien anzusprechen ist, hat die Strafe im Gegenzug als Ausdruck für die Verwirklichung eines öffentlichen Anspruches der Gemeinschaft auf die Sanktionierung von Fehlverhalten zu gelten.[7]

Im Hinblick auf eine genauere Bestimmung des Beitrags, den das kirchliche Strafrecht zur Ausbildung eines öffentlichen Strafrechts geleistet hat, ist deshalb die Frage zu stellen, seit wann in diesem Rechtskreis eine solche klare Unterscheidung zur Anwendung gelangt. Eine Antwort darauf wird durch die Beobachtung erschwert, daß der Begriff der Buße im kirchlichen Bereich noch vor der rechtlichen eine umfassendere moraltheologische und pastorale Bedeutung aufweist und gerade die Buße im kirchenrechtlichen Sinne unter bestimmten Voraussetzungen die Funktion einer Strafe übernimmt.[8]

Als ein deutliches Indiz kann in diesem Zusammenhang vor allem die klare begriffliche Unterscheidung von Buße und Strafe betrachtet werden. Es ist also zu fragen, seit wann in den kirchenrechtlichen Quellen eine Systematik geboten wird, die für Buße und Strafe von unterschiedlichen gedanklichen Konzepten ausgeht und dies durch die systematische Anordnung und Behandlung zum Ausdruck bringt.

Eine solche auch äußerlich erkennbare neue Phase in der Geschichte des kirchlichen

---

4. Vgl. das Exposé von D. Willoweit, 'Programm eines Forschungsprojekts', in: *Die Entstehung des öffentlichen Strafrechts. Bestandsaufnahme eines europäischen Forschungsproblems*, ed. idem (Köln, Weimar und Wien 1999) 1–12.

5. Willoweit, 'Forschungsprojekt' 5.

6. V. Achter, *Geburt der Strafe* (Frankfurt/M. 1951).

7. Vgl. E. Kaufmann, 'Buße', HRG 1 (1971) 575–77; zur historischen Entwicklung des Begriffes mit zahlreichen Textnachweisen H. Nehlsen, 'Buße (weltliches Recht) II. Deutsches Recht', LMA 2 (1983) 1144–49.

8. G. A. Benrath, 'Buße V (Historisch)', TRE 7 (1981) 452–73; C. Vogel, 'Buße D [2]', LMA 2 (1983) 1131–36; Kéry, 'Liber Extra' 253–54. Ausführlicher demnächst L. Kéry, *Gottesfurcht und irdische Strafe* (Köln, Weimar und Wien 2006) Kap. I.2–3.

Strafrechts leitete Bernhard von Pavia ein. Mit seiner als *Compilatio prima* bezeichneten Dekretalensammlung vollzog er um 1190 den entscheidenden Schritt zur Systematisierung des kirchlichen Strafrechts, indem er den *crimina et poenae* ein eigenes Buch widmete und damit auf eine eigenständige Stellung des Strafrechts als Disziplin des Kirchenrechts verwies. Die Wirkung dieser Einteilung war erheblich. Zusammen mit der gesamten Gliederung der *Compilatio prima* in fünf Bücher sowie in Titel und Kapitel wurde sie anschließend als Grundmuster von allen anderen privaten wie öffentlichen systematischen Sammlungen und vor allem auch durch den *Liber Extra* Papst Gregors IX. (1234) übernommen.[9] Das *Decretum Gratiani*, die um 1140 entstandene *Concordia discordantium canonum*, mit der die wissenschaftliche Bearbeitung des kirchlichen Rechtsstoffes und damit auch des kanonischen *Strafrechts* in der Schule der Dekretisten begann, hatte dagegen noch keinerlei strafrechtliche Systematik aufgewiesen.[10]

Vor diesem Hintergrund ist im Einzelnen zu untersuchen, in welchem Umfang Bernhard von Pavia zur Herausbildung dieser neuen Entwicklungsstufe des kanonischen Strafrechts beitrug. In welchen Schritten gelangte er zu seiner neuen Systematik? Welche Anregungen griff er auf? An welche Grenzen stieß er bei der Erfüllung seiner eigenen systematischen Vorgaben durch die Texte, die ihm zur Verfügung standen, und zu welchen inhaltlichen Neuerungen gelangte er mit seiner systematischen Vorgehensweise?

Über die Person des Bernhard von Pavia oder Bernardus Balbi, wie er auch genannt wird, ist nur wenig bekannt.[11] Er wurde, wie er selbst berichtet, in Pavia geboren und begann seine Karriere in Bologna als Dekretist.[12] Als seine Lehrer in Bologna werden Gandulphus und Johannes Faventinus genannt.[13] Schon in den 70er Jahren des 12. Jahrhunderts verfaßte er Glossen zum *Decretum Gratiani*.[14] Er nahm wahrscheinlich

---

9. Hinschius, *System* 5.234; J. Hanenburg, 'Decretals and Decretal Collections in the Second Half of the Twelfth Century', TRG 34 (1966) 552–99, hier 589; G. Fransen, *Les décrétales et les collectons de décrétales* (Typologie 2; Turnhout 1972) 24–25; Kéry, 'Liber Extra' 241–42.

10. Ibid. 242.

11. G. Le Bras, 'Bernard de Pavie', DDC 2 (1937) 782–89. F. Liotta, 'Bernardo da Pavia', DBI 9 (1967) 279–84.

12. *Bernardi Papiensis Faventini episcopi Summa Decretalium*, ed. E. Laspeyres (Regensburg 1860; Neudruck Graz 1956) 283: 'Haec ego Bernardus, genuit quem clara Papia / Mitto; sed emendet, socii, rogo vestra sophia. / Qui decretales ad opus commune redigi / Sub titulis, summam nunc Christo dante peregi.'

13. P. Landau, 'Bernardus Papiensis', in: *Juristen*[2] 81–82. Von seiner Theorie, daß Huguccio als mutmaßlicher Lehrer des Bernhard von Pavia in Frage komme, ist Rudolf Weigand später abgerückt; vgl. R. Weigand, *Die bedingte Eheschließung im kanonischen Recht* 1 (München 1963) 242 n. 2; idem, 'Die Durchsetzung des Konsensprinzips im kirchlichen Eherecht', ÖAKR 38 (1989) 301–14, hier 306 n. 32. Mit dem in seinem Frühwerk genannten *doctor meus Hugo* habe Bernhard dem Zusammenhang nach Hugo von Saint-Victor gemeint, obwohl er diesen aus zeitlichen Gründen nur im weiteren Sinne als seinen Lehrer bezeichnen könne; dazu auch F. Cantelar, 'Bernardus Papiensis, *Doctor meus Hugo*. Huguccio de Pisa o Hugo de San Victor', ZRG Kan. Abt. 55 (1969) 448–57. Zu Gandulphus als Lehrer des Bernhard von Pavia, vgl. S. Kuttner, 'Bernardus Compostellanus Antiquus', *Traditio* 1 (1943) 277–340, hier 295 n. 23 (wiederabgedruckt in: Idem, *Gratian and the Schools of Law 1140–1234* [London 1983] no. VII, with 'Retractationes VII').

14. R. Weigand, 'Frühe Glossen zu D.12 cc.1–16 des Dekrets Gratians', BMCL 5 (1975) 35–51, hier 49; idem,

auch Einfluß auf die *Glossa ordinaria* zum Dekret, die Johannes Teutonicus am Anfang des 13. Jahrhunderts verfaßte.[15] Bernhard selbst wirkte ebenfalls als Lehrer an der Rechtsschule von Bologna, bevor er 1187 in Pavia zum Propst ernannt wurde. Wohl 1191 wurde er als Nachfolger des Kanonisten Johannes Faventinus Bischof von Faenza und schließlich am 24. Juni 1198 aufgrund einer *postulatio* der dortigen Kanoniker per Akklamation zum Bischof von Pavia gewählt.[16] Wie er selbst berichtet, hielt er sich während des Pontifikats Alexanders III. (1159–1181) eine Zeitlang an der Kurie in Rom auf.[17] Gestorben ist er am 18. September 1213 in Pavia.

Obwohl Bernhard auch theologische und erbauliche Werke verfaßte, wie zum Beispiel die *Vita* Lanfrancs, seines Vorgängers auf dem Bischofsstuhl von Pavia, beruht sein Nachruhm vor allem auf seinen kanonistischen Werken. Indem er als erster das neue Dekretalenrecht der Päpste, das seit dem Pontifikat Alexanders III. im dritten Viertel des 12. Jahrhunderts einen erheblichen Aufschwung genommen hatte, nach systematischen Gesichtspunkten erfaßte, leitete Bernhard von Pavia das Zeitalter der Dekretalisten ein.[18]

Zwei der frühen systematischen Dekretalensammlungen gehen auf ihn zurück und gehören damit zur unmittelbaren Vorgeschichte des *Breviarium extravagantium*, der später als *Compilatio prima* bezeichneten Dekretalensammlung, die Bernhard als Propst in Pavia und damit wohl zwischen 1188 und 1190 unter seinem Namen veröffentlichte. Es handelt sich um die zwischen 1177 und 1179 zusammengestellte *Collectio Parisiensis secunda* in der Handschrift Paris, BN lat. 1566, fol. 1–54, und die 1185 entstandene *Collectio Lipsiensis* in Leipzig, UB 975, fol. 116–153.[19] Später führte das *Breviarium* als *Compilatio*

'Zur Handschriftenliste des Glossenapparats *Ordinaturus Magister*', BMCL 8 (1978) 41–47, hier 45; idem, 'Bazianus und b.-Glossen zum Dekret Gratians', SG 20 (1976) 453–96, hier 477–90.

15. Landau, 'Bernardus Papiensis' 81–82.

16. Papst Innozenz III. erteilte am 8. August (1198) die Erlaubnis zu dieser Translation, vgl. Reg. 1.326, in: *Die Register Papst Innocenz' III.: 1. Pontifikatsjahr (1198–99)*, ed. A. Haidacher und O. Hageneder (Wien 1964) 472–74; vgl. K. Pennington, *Pope and Bishops: The Papal Monarchy in the Twelfth and Thirteenth Centuries* (Philadelphia 1984) 96–98.

17. *Summa*, ed. Laspeyres 105 § 3: 'Haec autem interpretatio prius Alexandro III. displicuit, ut infra [. . .], verum eam postmodum, ut in eius curia didici, approbavit'. Der Aufenthalt an der Kurie wird auch durch die päpstliche Translationserlaubnis von 1198 bestätigt, Reg. 1.326, ed. *Die Register* 1.474: 'De tua igitur idoneitate securi—utpote cuius scientiam et eloquentiam ac morum honestatem nos et fratres nostri plene cognovimus, dum apud sedem esses apostolicam constitutus'; vgl. Liotta, 'Bernardo' 280.

18. *L'âge classique* 133–45; Fransen, *Décrétales* 12–15; A. Padoa Schioppa, 'Il diritto canonico come scienza nella prospettiva storica: Alcune riflessioni', in: Proc. Munich (MIC C.10; 1997) 419–44, hier 434–35; P. Landau, 'Rechtsfortbildung im Dekretalenrecht. Typen und Funktionen der Dekretalen des 12. Jahrhunderts', ZRG Kan. Abt. 86 (2000) 86, 92, 94–95. Bernhard betont selbst, daß Dekretalen den größeren Teil seiner Sammlung ausmachen: 'Libellus extravagantium a maiori parte decretalium nomen accepit' (*Summa*, ed. Laspeyres 2).

19. E. Richter, *De inedita decretalium collectione Lipsiensi* (Leipzig 1836); *Quinque Compilationes antiquae nec non Collectio canonum Lipsiensis*, ed. E. Friedberg (Graz 1882, Neudruck 1956) 189–208; *Canones-Sammlungen*

prima die Reihe der *Compilationes antiquae* an, jener Dekretalensammlungen aus der Zeit zwischen 1188 und 1226, die als allgemein verbreitete Rechtsbücher für den Rechtsunterricht und die kirchlichen Gerichte besondere Bedeutung erlangten.

Die Originalität seines kanonistischen Werkes wurde bisher allein darin gesehen, daß Bernhard sein *Breviarium extravagantium*—im Unterschied zur bis dahin vorherrschenden chronologischen Abfolge in den Sammlungen—, erstmals 'con geniale intuizione' (Liotta) in fünf Büchern sowie in Titeln und Kapiteln nach Rechtsmaterien anordnete.[20] Das erste Buch enthält Textstücke zu den materiellen Quellen des Rechts, zu den kirchlichen Ämtern und vor allem zur Gerichtsbarkeit, das zweite behandelt im wesentlichen den Prozeß, das dritte das Privatrecht der Kleriker, Mönche und Laien, der kirchlichen Güter und der Verträge, das vierte beschäftigt sich mit dem Eherecht und das fünfte Buch mit dem Straf- und Strafverfahrensrecht.[21] Der Merkvers *iudex, iudicium, clerus, connubia, crimen* sollte helfen, diese Anordnung in fünf Büchern, die für das kanonische Recht definitiv werden sollte, leichter zu behalten.

Bernhard von Pavia lehnte sich mit dieser neuen Einteilung sowohl an die kanonistische als auch an die römische Tradition an. Er folgte jedoch keinem direkten Vorbild, sondern ließ sich offensichtlich von mehreren gleichzeitig zu seiner eigenen Gliederung inspirieren. Man erkennt einen gewissen Einfluß des gratianischen Dekrets, das ebenfalls der Reihe nach die Rechtsquellen, die Weihen, den Prozeß, den Klerus und die Ehe behandelte. Die drei am besten geordneten Bücher beziehen sich zudem auf die drei großen Gattungen der kanonistischen Monographien: Die *ordines iudiciarii*, die *summae de matrimonio* und die Bußbücher. Daneben nahm Bernhard sich wohl auch die innere Anordnung der Digesten und des *Codex Iustiniani* zum Vorbild, indem er seiner eigenen Sammlung die Einteilung des römischen Rechts in *personae, res, actiones* zugrundelegte und die Formulierung der Titel zum Teil übernahm.[22]

Ein weiterer Schritt auf dem Weg zur Systematisierung wurde dadurch vollzogen,

115–130; P. Landau, 'Vorgratianische Kanonessammlungen bei den Dekretisten und in frühen Dekretalensammlungen', in: Proc. San Diego (MIC C.9; 1992) 104. Zur *Parisiensis secunda* siehe *Canones-Sammlungen* 21–45; Kuttner, *Repertorium* 290; Landau, 'Vorgratianische Kanonessammlungen' 93–116, 100. Zur Autorschaft Bernhards an dieser Sammlung schon Le Bras, 'Bernard' 787, der die Übereinstimmungen mit den von Bernhard verfaßten Summen *De matrimonio* und *De electione* anführt sowie die Tatsache, daß alle drei Texte in der Hs. Paris, BN lat. 1566 überliefert sind.

20. Liotta, 'Bernardo' 281. Zum Unterschied zwischen 'primitiven' und systematischen Dekretalensammlungen, vgl. Fransen, *Décrétales* 19–21.

21. So erklärt Bernhard selbst im *Prooemium* zu seiner *Summa*, ed. Laspeyres 2: 'Ordo agendi talis est: Dividetur opus in quinque libros, in quorum primo tractatur de constitutionibus ecclesiasticis, de ordinationibus et officiis clericorum, et de praeparatoriis iudiciorum, in secundo de iudiciis et processu iudiciorum, in tertio de vita clericorum et rebus eorum, de statu monachorum et rebus eorum, in quarto de matrimoniis, in quinto de criminibus et poenis'; vgl. die einzelnen Titel in 1 Comp.; ferner Le Bras, 'Bernard' 784; Liotta, 'Bernardo' 281.

22. Le Bras, 'Bernard' 784; Liotta, 'Bernardo' 281, vgl. Hanenburg, 'Decretals' 592 n. 133.

daß Bernard von Pavia zu den einzelnen Titeln und Kapiteln seiner Sammlung jeweils nur die inhaltlich relevanten Teile und Auszüge der ursprünglichen Texte lieferte. Mit dieser Vorgehensweise steht wohl der Titel des Werkes '*Breviarium* extravagantium' in Zusammenhang. Hier deutet sich schon an, daß Bernhard diese Neuerungen nicht zuletzt aus praktischen Gründen vornahm. Er verfolgte die doppelte Absicht, den Schulen wie den Gerichten eine größere Fülle von Texten zu liefern—*ut uberior allegationum et iudicium copia preparetur*—und diese Texte leichter zugänglich machen. Nicht nur zur größeren Ehre Gottes und der römischen Kirche, sondern auch zum Nutzen der Studierenden wollte er—wie er selbst erklärt—eine Ergänzung zum *Decretum Gratiani* bieten, das als wichtigste Grundlage für die wissenschaftliche Beschäftigung mit dem kanonischen Recht anerkannt war. Dazu griff er sowohl auf alte, von Gratian ausgelassene Texte, als auch auf (neue) Dekretalen zurück.[23] Als Vorlagen für die erste Gruppe hat er, wie er selbst im *Prooemium* seiner *Summa* vermerkt, das Dekret Burchards von Worms, das Register Gregors des Grossen und ein *corpus canonum* benutzt, in dem man die *Collectio Anselmo dedicata* zu erkennen glaubt.[24]

Im Unterschied zu Gratian verzichtete Bernhard weitgehend auf nicht-juristische Texte und trug schon allein damit zu einer klareren Trennung zwischen Theologie und Kanonistik bei 'dont il entendait faire une discipline bien distincte'.[25] Nach Ansicht von Le Bras unternahm Bernhard von Pavia mit seinem *Breviarium* den Versuch, der Kirche einen eigenen Codex zur Verfügung zu stellen, der sich mit dem *Codex Iustiniani* messen konnte. Auf diese Weise habe der Kanonist die 'juristische Unabhängigkeit' der Kirche retten wollen, die von dem wesentlich vollständigeren und harmonischeren 'römischen System' bedroht worden sei, dem das Dekret und seine Ergänzungen nicht das Wasser reichen konnten.[26]

Schließlich verfaßte Bernhard als Bischof von Faenza und damit noch vor dem 24. Juni 1198 neben seinen Dekretalensammlungen eine *Summa titulorum* zur *Compilatio prima*, die sogenannte *Summa decretalium*, die sich in ihrer Gliederung ebenfalls an das Modell der *Compilatio prima* anlehnt und zu jedem Titel eine umfassende systematische Darstellung und Erläuterung der einzelnen Materien liefert, die wiederum in allen Einzelheiten durch Belegstellen aus dem kanonischen und dem römischen Recht abgesichert wird. Bei einer genaueren Betrachtung zeigt sich jedoch, daß die

23. 'Ut autem uberior allegationum uel iudiciorum copia preparetur ad honorem Dei sanctaeque Romanaeque ecclesiae ac studentium utilitatem, ego B. Papiensis prepositus extrauagantia de ueteri nouoque iure sub titulis compilaui super operis imperfectione ueniam postulans a lectore' (ed. 1 Comp., 1).
24. *Summa*, ed. Laspeyres 2: 'Materia sunt decretales quaedam utilia capitula, quae in corpore canonum, registro Gregorii et Brocardo reliquerat Gratianus, poma nova et vetera nobis servans'. Vgl. Le Bras, 'Bernard' 783; Liotta, 'Bernardo' 281.
25. Le Bras, 'Bernard' 784.
26. Ibid.

Bezeichnung dieses Werkes als *Summa decretalium* irreführend ist. Bernhard allegierte in seiner *Summa* wesentlich häufiger Kapitel aus dem *Decretum Gratiani* und Texte des römischen Rechts als Dekretalen.[27]

Schon in ihrer Abfolge und durch die Art, in der sie aufeinander aufbauen und ähnliche Vorlagen verarbeiten, demonstrieren die drei Dekretalensammlungen und die *Summa* des Bernhard von Pavia sein kontinuierliches Ringen um eine Systematisierung des Rechtsstoffes. Mit der noch vor dem 3. Laterankonzil (1179) entstandenen *Collectio Parisiensis secunda* wird der erste Versuch einer systematischen Erfassung des Rechtsstoffes unternommen.[28] Noch ohne Einteilung in Bücher werden die Texte lediglich nach 95 Titeln geordnet präsentiert, deren Reihenfolge dem Aufbau des *Decretum Gratiani* ähnlich ist.[29] Die um 1185 fertiggestellte *Collectio Lipsiensis* stellt eine Kombination der französischen *Collectio Bambergensis* mit der *Parisiensis secunda* dar, die der Kompilator durch weitere Texte des alten und neuen Rechts ergänzte.[30] Ebenso wie die *Parisiensis secunda* bezog die *Lipsiensis* ihre Texte fast ausschließlich aus dem *Decretum Burchardi* und möglicherweise auch römisches Recht aus der *Collectio Anselmo dedicata*. Die Benutzung derselben Vorlagen verstärkt den Eindruck, daß beide von demselben Autor zusammengestellt wurden.[31] Der große Anteil an vorgratianischen Texten in diesen beiden frühen Sammlungen deutet nach Ansicht von Peter Landau darauf hin, daß sie eher für den Unterricht als für die Rechtspraxis gedacht waren.[32] Möglicherweise dienten diese vorgratianischen Texte aber auch einer Vervollständigung im Sinne der Systematik, solange entsprechende Texte aus dem neueren Dekretalenrecht noch nicht zur Verfügung standen.

Wie Peter Landau ebenfalls zeigen konnte, benutzte Bernhard von Pavia bei der Erstellung der *Compilatio prima* nicht, wie man früher annahm, noch weitere Sammlungen der französischen *Bambergensis*-Gruppe, sondern fast ausschließlich die *Parisiensis secunda* und die *Lipsiensis* und kombinierte sie mit Auszügen aus den

---

27. So schon Le Bras, ibid. 785.

28. *Canones-Sammlungen* 21; Kuttner, *Repertorium* 290 ('zwischen dem 11. Mai 1177 und dem 19. März 1179 entstanden'); Landau, 'Vorgratianische Kanonessammlungen' 100. Die Hypothese von Hanenburg, 'Decretals' 596, 598, daß lediglich die Titel der *Collectio Parisiensis secunda* von Bernhard von Pavia stammten, er jedoch nicht der Kompilator der Sammlung sei, hat sich nicht durchgesetzt.

29. *Canones-Sammlungen* 21; Hanenburg, 'Decretals' 592–99; P. Landau, 'Die Entstehung der systematischen Dekretalensammlungen und die europäische Kanonistik des 12. Jahrhunderts', ZRG Kan. Abt. 65 (1979) 120–48, hier 126.

30. Richter, *De inedita decretalium collectione Lipsiensi; Quinque compilationes antiquae* 189–208; *Canones-Sammlungen* 115–30; Landau, 'Vorgratianische Kanonessammlungen' 104.

31. Ibid. 102, 104.

32. Landau, 'Systematische Dekretalensammlungen' 137. Von den 236 Kapiteln der *Parisiensis secunda* beruhen ungefähr ein Viertel auf nachgratianischen Texten; vgl. die Liste der vorgratianischen Quellen in *Canones-Sammlungen* 27–28.

päpstlichen Registern. Auf diese Weise läßt sich leichter erklären, warum Bernhard in vergleichsweise kurzer Zeit zwischen 1188 und 1190 die *Compilatio prima* fertigstellen konnte: 'Er schöpfte nur aus einem bereits geordneten Quellenfundus, der ihm zudem wohlvertraut war'. Eine seiner Hauptquellen, die *Parisiensis secunda*, hatte er selbst zusammengestellt und sie wurde offenbar auch nur von ihm selbst benutzt.[33] Die *Collectio Lipsiensis* als zweite Hauptquelle hatte ihrerseits aus der *Parisiensis* als Material-sammlung geschöpft und wurde jetzt von Bernhard als zweite Quelle für die *Compilatio prima* zugrundegelegt.[34]

Als besonders aufschlußreichen Beitrag zum kirchlichen Strafrecht enthält die *Collectio Parisiensis secunda* unter dem Titel *De pena homicidarum eisque consentientium* einen Ausschnitt aus der Dekretale *Sicut dignum* (JL 12180) Alexanders III. vom 31. Januar 1172.[35] Sie gehört zu den fünfzehn neueren Dekretalen, die dem Sammler möglicherweise im Original vorgelegen haben, denn er hat sie vorher unter dem Titel 46. *De participantibus excommunicatis* als c.3 fast vollständig und in ihrem ursprüngli-chen Zusammenhang wiedergegeben.[36] Schließlich findet sich unter dem Titel 65. *De iniectione manuum in clericum* noch der Schlußteil der Dekretale.[37]

Allein schon die Verweise und Mehrfachverwendungen sowie die in der Handschrift Paris, BN lat. 1566 erkennbare Unterteilung vollständiger Dekretalentexte in einzelne Sinnabschnitte, von denen zum Teil nur die Anfangsworte unter passenden Titeln zitiert werden, belegt einen ersten, noch recht zaghaften Versuch zur Systematisierung. Andererseits deuten solche Mehrfachverwendungen auch darauf hin, daß die Zahl der Texte und vor allem der Dekretalen, die einzelnen (strafrechtlichen) Titeln zugeordnet werden konnten, noch recht überschaubar war.

Dies wird besonders in der *Collectio Lipsiensis* deutlich. Der einzige Titel, der sich hier unmittelbar auf Strafen bezieht, ist zwar allgemeiner formuliert als in der *Collectio Parisiensis secunda*, enthält jedoch keine neuen Rechtstexte, sondern neben der bereits genannten Dekretale *Sicut dignum* lediglich Auszüge aus dem *Decretum Burchardi*, die ausnahmslos auch in Ivos Dekret zu finden sind. Inhaltlich wird der Akzent auf die

---

33. Landau, 'Systematische Dekretalensammlungen' 126, 135–36.

34. Die enge Verknüpfung legt es nach Landau, ibid. 136, nahe, daß Bernhard auch die *Lipsiensis* selbst kompiliert hat. Das Verhältnis Bernhards zu den älteren Dekretalensammlungen ließe sich auf diese Weise am einfachsten erklären. Zur Verwandtschaft der *Collectio Lipsiensis* mit der *Collectio Parisiensis secunda* schon Le Bras, 'Bernard' 787.

35. 1 Comp.5.10.7 (JL 12180; X 5.12.6); Coll. Lips. 10.1, ed. Friedberg, *Compilationes antiquae* 192. Das kor-rekte Datum findet sich in WH 929. In 1 Comp. und X ist die Dekretale jeweils auf fünf Kapitel verteilt: 1 Comp.5.10.7; 1 Comp.5.34.2–5; X 5.12.6; X 5.39.1–4.

36. Dafür spricht auch, daß er bei einer Reihe von ihnen Ort, Tag und Monat ihrer Ausstellung nennt, vgl. *Canones-Sammlungen* 26, 28, 39.

37. Ibid. 42.

Bestrafung von Schwerstverbrechen gelegt: *De poena pro enormi crimine iniungenda*. Der umfassende Rückgriff auf vorgratianische Texte erweckt den Eindruck, daß der Titel, der die Strafen behandelt, mit weiteren Kapiteln angereichert werden sollte, dem Redaktor jedoch noch keine passenden Dekretalen vorlagen.

Sowohl systematisch als inhaltlich betrachtet erzielte Bernhard von Pavia mit dem *Breviarium extravagantium* einen Durchbruch. Es enthielt vor allem Dekretalen und die für die folgenden authentischen Sammlungen einschließlich des *Liber Extra* wegweisende Einteilung in fünf Bücher—*iudex, iudicium, clerus, connubia, crimen*—, von denen das fünfte dem Strafrecht gewidmet war.

Die gleiche Systematik legte Bernhard seiner *Summa decretalium* zugrunde, die bald nach ihrem Erscheinen vor 1198 ähnlich erfolgreich war, wie die große Zahl der Handschriften verrät.[38] Als Vorbild für dieses Werk, das mit seinen Definitionen und systematisch gegliederten Erklärungen eine Gattung darstellt, die Bernhard für die Dekretalistik anscheinend erst entwickelt hat, dienten ihm wohl die Summen der Zivilisten zum *Codex Iustiniani* und einige summenähnliche Schriften zum *Decretum Gratiani*.[39]

Stephan Kuttner bezeichnete Bernhards Summe als Prototyp einer neuen literarischen Gattung, der an Buch- und Titelfolge der Dekretalenkompilationen angelehnten, knapp gefaßten Lehrbücher.[40] Im Vergleich zu anderen Dekretalenkommentaren zeichnen sich die Summen generell dadurch aus, daß sie jeweils eine möglichst systematische und vor allem auch vollständige Erfassung des Rechtsstoffes anstreben, was speziell im strafrechtlichen Teil von Bernhards *Summa decretalium* dadurch zum Ausdruck kommt, daß neben dem kirchlichen auch das römische Strafrecht des *Corpus iuris civilis* berücksichtigt wird.

Mit Bernard von Pavia erreichte das kirchliche Strafrecht gegen Ende des 12. Jahrhunderts auch inhaltlich eine neue Entwicklungsstufe—und zwar zunächst durch die von ihm verankerte klare Unterscheidung zwischen Buße und Strafe. Auch wenn seit Gratian keine inhaltliche Verwechselung zwischen Buße und Strafe mehr möglich war, so ist diese Erkenntnis doch nur indirekt aus den im Dekret zusammengestellten Texten und den entsprechenden *dicta Gratiani* abzuleiten und zwar schwerpunktmäßig in C.23 q.4–6, in denen die Frage nach der Berechtigung der Vindikativstrafe und der Ausübung einer öffentlichen Straf- und Zwangsgewalt nach Art eines dialektischen Straf-

---

38. Vgl. dazu die Zusammenstellung der Handschriften durch Kuttner, *Repertorium* 387–89; mit Korrekturen in 'Retractationes VII', in: idem, *Gratian and the Schools* 16. M. Bertram, 'Some Additions to the *Repertorium der Kanonistik*', BMCL 4 (1974) 10, fügt noch eine weitere Handschrift (Alba Julia, Bibl. Batthyanyana 166) hinzu.

39. Kuttner, *Repertorium* 387.

40. Ibid. 389; zur Gattung der Summen auch ibid. 123–25, 168–70; vgl. Schulte, QL 1.78–82, 1.180–82; Le Bras, 'Bernard' 785: 'C'est donc une sorte de manuel, le premier en date des exposés généraux'.

rechtstraktats behandelt wird.[41] Demzufolge sollte die Buße für das neutestamentliche Konzept der Liebe zum Sünder, der um seines Seelenheils willen gebessert werden soll, die Strafe dagegen für das im Alten Testament dokumentierte Streben nach Rache und Vergeltung stehen.[42] Strafen waren zwar nach Gratians Vorstellung grundsätzlich eher abzulehnen, konnten und sollten jedoch unter bestimmten Voraussetzungen zur Anwendung gelangen, falls andere Besserungsmittel wirkungslos blieben.[43]

Trotz dieser deutlichen inhaltlichen Unterscheidung, die weniger von juristischen als von theologischen Kriterien bestimmt wurde, sucht man im *Decretum Gratiani* eine systematische Gegenüberstellung von Buße und Strafe vergeblich. Auch die Sammlungen, die Bernhard von Pavia noch vor der *Compilatio prima* zusammenstellte, weisen sie nicht auf und verfügen erst recht nicht über unterschiedliche Titel zu Strafe und Buße. Der Titel über die Strafe—*De poena homicidarum eisque consentientium*—, den Bernhard in seine erste systematische Sammlung, die *Collectio Parisiensis secunda*, aufnahm, bezieht sich auf einen Einzelaspekt, der aus dem Inhalt des einzigen Kapitels unter diesem Titel abgeleitet ist. Hierbei handelt es sich um die bereits genannte Dekretale Alexanders III. an Bischof Bartholomäus von Exeter († 1184) mit den Anfangsworten *Sicut dignum* (JL 12180), die als Reaktion auf die Ermordung von Thomas Becket detailliert erläutert, wie nicht nur die eigentlichen Mörder des Erzbischofs von Canterbury, sondern auch deren Helfershelfer und Mitwisser bestraft werden sollten.[44]

Die Tatsache, daß man diesen Text ohne weiteres unter einem anderen Titel hätte unterbringen können,—etwa, wie es dann später in der *Compilatio prima* geschah, unter dem Titel *De homicidio voluntario vel casuali* (1 Comp.5.10.7 = X 5.12.6)—belegt den Wunsch Bernhards von Pavia, einen separaten Titel über die Strafe zu konstituieren und ihn mit Texten aus dem aktuellen Dekretalenrecht zu füllen. Dies wird auch durch die Beobachtung unterstrichen, daß dieselbe Dekretale schon vorher unter einem anderen Titel der Sammlung in voller Länge vorzufinden war. Für die etwas spätere *Col-*

---

41. C.23 q.4–6 passim: 'Quarto, an uindicta sit inferenda? . . . Quinto, an sit peccatum iudici uel ministro reos uccidere? . . . Sexto, an mali sint cogendi ad bonum?'; vgl. Kéry, *Gottesfurcht und irdische Strafe* Kap. II.2.

42. Gratian stellt die körperliche Strafe *(pena corporalis)* als gesetzliche Sanktion des Alten Testamentes der Buße des Neuen Testamentes gegenüber. Während das Gesetz des Alten Testamentes im Schrecken seinen Ausgang nehme und entsprechend die körperliche Strafe gesetzlich vorschreibe, nehme das Neue Testament seinen Ausgang in Duldsamkeit und Erbarmen und ermögliche es jedem Sünder, durch Buße die göttliche Gnade zu erringen, C.23 q.4 d.p.c.15 § 1; vgl. R. Pahud de Mortanges, 'Strafzwecke bei Gratian und den Dekretisten', ZRG Kan. Abt. 78 (1992) 121–58, hier 128, 133.

43. C.23 q.4 d.p.c.54: 'Ex his omnibus colligitur, quod uindicta est inferenda non amore ipsius uindictae, sed zelo iusticiae; non ut odium exerceatur, sed ut prauitas corrigatur'.

44. Vgl. *Materials for the History of Thomas Becket, Archbishop of Canterbury 7*, ed. J. Craigie Robertson und J. Brigstocke Sheppard (London 1885; repr. 1965) 534–36 Nr. DCCLXXX; zur Ermordung des Thomas Becket, D. Knowles, *Thomas Becket* (London 1970); F. Barlow, *Thomas Becket* (London 1986); H. Vollrath, *Thomas Becket. Höfling und Heiliger* (Zürich 2004), mit weiteren Literaturhinweisen.

lectio Lipsiensis konnte Bernhard offensichtlich nur auf vorgratianische Stücke zurückgreifen, um den jetzt schon allgemeiner formulierten Titel *De poena pro enormi crimine
iniungenda* über die Dekretale *Sicut dignum* hinaus mit weiteren Texten zu füllen.

Trotz dieser Einschränkungen spricht Bernhard von Pavia mit den beiden Titeln,
die er für die *Collectio Parisiensis secunda* und die *Lipsiensis* zum Thema Strafe wählte,
zwei grundlegende Themen des kirchlichen Strafrechts an. Zum einen die Frage nach
den verschiedenen Kriterien für die Bemessung der Strafen, die nicht nur die eigentlichen Täter, sondern auch deren Anstifter, Helfer und Mitwisser treffen sollen und zum
andern die Frage, mit welchen Strafen im Kirchenrecht besonders schwere Vergehen zu
ahnden seien.[45]

Die ausführliche Kommentierung, zu der die Dekretalisten durch die Dekretale *Sicut
dignum* (JL 12180) angeregt wurden, führte in mehrere Themenfelder des kirchlichen
Strafrechts ein und verdeutlichte ihre besondere Stellung im Rahmen des kirchlichen
Strafrechts. Ausgehend von *Sicut dignum* wurde nicht nur das Problem der Ermessensstrafen und die Kategorien der Strafbemessung nach den äußeren Umständen der Tat
und der inneren Verfassung des Täters erörtert, sondern auch die Frage angeschnitten,
wie die einzelnen Formen der Teilnahme an einem Vergehen bis hin zum bloßen nach-
träglichen Einverständnis mit der Tat zu bewerten seien.[46]

Damit bewegt sich diese Dekretale in ganz besonderer Weise in jenem Grenzraum
zwischen Buße und Strafe, zwischen Sünde und Verbrechen, zwischen Willens- und
Tatschuld, der für eine Abgrenzung zwischen Bußwesen und Strafrecht von besonderer
Bedeutung ist. Dies wird zusätzlich dadurch unterstrichen, daß im Text der Dekretale
ohne Hinweis auf einen inhaltlichen Unterschied sowohl von Bußen als auch von
Strafen die Rede ist und die einzelnen Handschriften der verschiedenen Sammlungen
mehrfach zwischen den Lesarten *poena* und *poenitentia* schwanken.[47]

Daraus kann man wohl nur den Schluß ziehen, daß die in der Dekretale genannten
Kriterien ohne Unterschied sowohl für Bußen als auch für Strafen gelten sollten. Wie

---

45. Dazu Kéry, *Gottesfurcht und irdische Strafe* Kap. III 2.1–2.

46. Ibid. Kap. III 2.1; Kuttner, der diese Frage nach eigenem Bekunden nur am Rande behandelt, bezeichnet
die Dekretale *Sicut dignum* als zentralen Text für die kanonistische Teilnahmelehre, der kasuistisch 'die möglichen äußeren Formen des Anteils mehrerer an der Deliktverwirklichung' beschreibt, Kuttner, *Schuldlehre* 41–
42; der italienische Jurist Albertus Gandinus zitierte die Dekretale *Sicut dignum* in seinem *Tractatus de maleficiis, De homicidariis* § 6 (um 1300), als einzige kirchenrechtliche Quelle für den Tatbestand der Teilnahme an
einer Tötung im weiteren Sinne, die Beihilfe, Anstiftung und Begünstigung *(auxilium, consilium et favorem)* ein-
schließe, ed. H. Kantorowicz, *Albertus Gandinus und das Strafrecht der Scholastik* 2: *Die Theorie. Kritische Ausgabe
des Tractatus de maleficiis nebst textkritischer Einleitung* (Berlin und Leipzig 1926) 280–82; vgl. ibid. 263 *(De penis*
§ 45). Zu Albertus Gandinus auch L. Kéry, 'Albertus Gandinus und das kirchliche Strafrecht', in: *Inquirens subtilia diversa. Dietrich Lohrmann zum 65. Geburtstag*, ed. H. Kranz und L. Falkenstein (Aachen 2002) 183–200.

47. X 5.12.6; vgl. Kéry, 'Culpabilité' 436–44.

Bernhard es später auch in seiner *Summa* formulieren wird, stellten Bußen, ähnlich wie in den vorgratianischen Texten der *Collectio Lipsiensis,* eine besondere Art kirchlicher Strafe dar. Anders ausgedrückt ist von einer speziellen Art von Strafe, den Ermessensstrafen *(poenae arbitrariae)* die Rede, denen man von ihrem Ursprung her eine besondere Nähe zu den kirchlichen Bußen zuschreibt, da sie ebenso wie diese nach dem Ermessen des jeweiligen Richters verhängt wurden und sich von den Strafen im eigentlichen Sinne als gesetzlich festgelegten Sanktionen *(nulla poena sine lege)* unterschieden. Die Buße diente als eine Form der kirchlichen Strafe für weniger schwere Fälle, die nicht die Verhängung der von den *canones* festgelegten (Höchst-)Strafe erforderten, wie etwa für Kleriker die Deposition oder für Laien die Exkommunikation, sondern eine Abstufung nach dem Ermessen des Richters.

Ermessensstrafen oder *poenae arbitrariae* nahmen in gewisser Weise eine vermittelnde Stellung zwischen Bußen und Strafen ein.[48] Sie waren im kirchlichen Strafrecht auch deshalb so erfolgreich, weil es im kanonischen Recht nur wenige bestimmte Strafen für einzelne Verbrechen gab.[49] Sie erforderten deshalb ebenso wie Bußen eine besonders exakte und differenzierte Festlegung der Kriterien, nach denen sie verhängt werden sollten. Auf der anderen Seite erlaubten sie es dem Richter, die speziellen Umstände des Falles und die Situation des Delinquenten bei der Festsetzung der Strafe zu berücksichtigen und damit auch den seelsorgerischen Aspekt in besonderer Weise einzubeziehen. Sie drängten jedoch über den ihnen ursprünglich zugewiesenen Bereich des Bußwesens hinaus.[50] Die Spannung zwischen einem sorgfältigen, auch das Seelenheil der Übeltäter im Auge behaltenden Vorgehen des Richters, dem mehr an deren Besserung als an einer Vergeltung gelegen sein sollte, und einem scharfen Durchgreifen nach dem Legalitätsprinzip kennzeichnete insgesamt den kirchlichen Strafanspruch.

Diese Deutung wird bestätigt durch den Kommentar des Hostiensis, der sich über unterschiedliche Lesarten der Dekretale *Sicut dignum* irritiert zeigt und auf die Ermessensstrafe als mögliche Erklärung für den undifferenzierten Gebrauch von *poena* und *poenitentia* verweist. Die ungewöhnliche Wortkombination *poenitentia mulctari* erklärt er durch eine Analogie: Hier solle anscheinend zum Ausdruck gebracht werden, daß Bußen nach Ermessen festgelegt werden *(arbitrariae sunt),* weil auch die Geldstrafe

---

48. L. Mayali, 'The Concept of Discretionary Punishment in Medieval Jurisprudence', in: *Studia in honorem eminentissimi Cardinalis Alphonsi M. Stickler,* ed. R. Card. Castillo Lara (Rom 1992) 299–315, hier 303: '[The theory of discretionary punishment] arose as a combination of penitential doctrines and legal ideas expressed in both canon and civil sources'; zur weiteren Entwicklung der Ermessensstrafen im gelehrten Recht und im französischen Gewohnheitsrecht, B. Schnapper, 'Les peines arbitraires du XIIIᵉ au XVIIIᵉ siècles (Doctrines savantes et usages français)', TRG 41 (1973) 237–77, TRG 42 (1974) 81–112.

49. Schnapper, 'Peines arbitraires' 264, mit dem Zitat des Panormitanus, ibid. n. 148: 'Nam de jure canonico modicas habemus poenas expressas pro criminibus. Unde successit arbitrio judicum'.

50. Mayali, 'Discretionary punishment' 303.

(mulcta) nach dem Ermessen des Richters festgelegt werde.[51] Vor allem der Gebrauch von *poenitentia* scheint ihn mehrfach in Erstaunen versetzt zu haben. Er verweist zur Erklärung darauf, daß man bei Bußen einen Ermessensspielraum habe, um sie—so wäre hier zu ergänzen—den unterschiedlich abgestuften Schuld- oder Begehungsformen der Teilnahme anzupassen, während Strafen bereits vorher (gesetzlich) festgelegt sind.[52]

Die *Collectio Lipsiensis* vertritt mit ihren zusätzlich zu *Sicut dignum* angeführten vorgratianischen Kapiteln formal und inhaltlich das ältere kirchliche Strafrecht. Trotz des Titels *De poena* sollen nach Auskunft der dazu zusammengestellten Kapitel schwere Verbrechen wie Körperverletzung und (versuchter) Totschlag vordergründig betrachtet mit Bußen geahndet werden. Wer bei einer tätlichen Auseinandersetzung *(rixa)* einen anderen Menschen zum Krüppel macht oder verunstaltet, soll die Arztkosten übernehmen und darüber hinaus ein halbes Jahr büßen. Wenn er mittellos ist, soll er sogar ein ganzes Jahr büßen. Wenn ein Laie aus Arglist *(per dolum)* Blut vergießt, soll er vollen Schadensersatz leisten; wenn er mittellos ist, kann dies auch in Form von Arbeiten geschehen, die er für den Geschädigten leistet, so lange dieser krank ist. Anschließend soll er 40 Tage bei Wasser und Brot Buße tun.[53] Wer in der Absicht zu töten einen Menschen angreift und schlägt, soll drei Wochen Buße tun, als Kleriker jedoch sechs Monate. Wenn auch der Angegriffene Kleriker ist, soll der Täter ein ganzes Jahr büßen und außerdem eine weltliche Buße *(pecunia)* als Ausgleich und Genugtuung für die Wunde zahlen.[54] Wer seinem Nächsten einen Hieb versetzt, dabei aber keinen Schaden

51. Hostiensis, *Lectura in* X 5.12.6 s.v. *mulctari* (ed. Venetiis 1581 fol. 44–44A): 'Mulcta arbitrio iudicis committitur, ff. de verborum significatio, si qua poena (vgl. Dig. 16.244: "Ex hoc quoque earum rerum dissimilitudo apparere poterit, quia poenae certae singulorum peccatorum sunt, multae contra, quia eius iudicis potestas est, quantam dicat, nisi cum lege est constitutum quantam dicat"); et not. supra de constitu. cognoscentes (vgl. X 1.2.2: "Cognoscentes . . . rem quae culpa caret, in damnum vocari non convenit. Quoties vero novum quid statuitur, ita solet futuris formam imponere, ut dispendiis preterita non commendet; ne detrimentum ante prohibitionem possint ignorantes incurrere, quod eos postmodum dignum est vetitos sustinere"). Ideo ergo hoc verbo usus est, ut det intelligere, quod poenitentiae arbitrarie sunt, ut et not. supra eod. respon. i. super verbo poenitentia'.

52. Vgl. Hostiensis, *Lectura* X 5.12.6 s.v. *poenitentia:* 'Sequitur ergo ipsa vi, quod arbitraria sit, ut patet ex praeced. et sequ. et infra eo. §; illi etiam. respon. i. in fi. ("pari poenitentia uel fere pari existerent puniendi") et § eos insuper ver. i. in fi. ("moderata est poenitentia iniungenda") et § illis praeterea in fi. ("est eis poenitentia indicenda") et infra de poenit. significauit § fi. (X 5.38.3) ubi de hoc' (ed. Venetiis 1581 fol. 44). Da die Formulierung 'pari poenitentia puniendi' die für die Mörder vorgesehene Todesstrafe als Vergleichspunkt voraussetzt, ist erstaunlich, daß es hier *poenitentia* heißt. Friedberg (X 5.12.6) gibt sechs Handschriften an, die dem Ausdruck *poena* den Vorzug geben.

53. Coll. Lips. 10.3; Burch. 19.101, ed. G. Fransen und Th. Kölzer, *Burchard von Worms, Decretorum libri XX, ergänzter Neudruck der Editio princeps Köln 1548* (Aalen 1992) fol. 214r–v (PL 140.1004); vgl. Ivo, *Decretum* 15.113 (PL 161.885).

54. Coll. Lips. 10.5; Burch. 19.120, ed. Fransen und Kölzer, fol. 215v (PL 140.1007): 'Sed et pecuniam pro modo vulneris cui inflixit, tribuat'; siehe auch die Rubrik: 'De illis qui ad feriendum hominem surrexerint, volentes eum occidere, sed non potuerunt'; sowie Ivo, Decr. 15.132 (PL 161.888).

verursacht hat, soll allein schon deshalb drei Tage bei Wasser und Brot büßen, wenn er Kleriker ist jedoch anderthalb Jahre. Wer einen anderen vorsätzlich *(voluntate sua)* verstümmelt hat, soll drei Jahre büßen, eins davon bei Wasser und Brot. Kinder, die sich gegenseitig schlagen, sollen drei Tage, Jugendliche 20 Tage büßen.[55]

Bis auf dieses letzte Kapitel, das aus dem *Paenitentiale* des Beda stammt, sehen alle diese Bestimmungen gleichzeitig materiellen Ausgleich (eine *compositio*) und eine kirchliche Buße vor, so daß die kirchliche Buße den Charakter einer über den unmittelbaren Ausgleich hinausgehenden Strafe annimmt, zumal es sich wegen der Schwere der Vergehen jeweils um eine Zwangsbuße handelt.[56] Die Höhe der Buße richtet sich nach den genaueren Umständen der Tat. So werden nicht nur Vorsatz und Arglist *(dolus)* als 'strafverschärfend' berücksichtigt, sondern auch die Schwere des jeweiligen Vergehens und bestimmte Eigenschaften der Person. Die Buße richtet sich nach dem Alter des Übeltäters, wird aber deutlich erhöht, wenn Täter oder Opfer Kleriker sind.

Durch die Zusammenstellung dieser vorgratianischen Kapitel, von denen kein einziges in die *Compilationes antiquae* oder den *Liber Extra* übernommen wurde, wird noch einmal mit Nachdruck unterstrichen, daß zur Sühnung schwerer Verbrechen, die als Körperverletzungs- und Tötungsdelikte in Erscheinung treten, nach kirchlichem Verständnis die Leistung eines materiellen Ausgleichs nicht ausreicht. In solchen Fällen ist zusätzlich eine kirchliche Buße (als Strafe) zu verhängen, die dem Täter und den anderen Mitgliedern der betreffenden Gemeinschaft vor Augen führen soll, daß nicht nur dem Opfer ein Ausgleich für das ihm zugefügte Unrecht zusteht, sondern darüber hinaus auch eine Versöhnung mit Gott und der kirchlichen Gemeinschaft herbeizuführen ist.

Einen Titel über die Strafen im allgemeinen und eine klare formale Abgrenzung zur Buße findet man erst in der *Compilatio prima*, wo Bernhard von Pavia nicht nur das fünfte Buch den *crimina et poenae* widmet, sondern Strafen und Bußen jeweils eigene Titel zuweist. Im Hinblick auf die äußere Systematik begründete er damit deren begriffliche Unterscheidung in den offiziellen Dekretalensammlungen. Beide Titel gehören zu denjenigen, die im *Liber Extra* eine deutliche Vermehrung der Kapitel gegenüber der *Compilatio prima* aufzuweisen haben.[57]

Das erste Kapitel zu *De poenis* gibt einen kurzen Auszug aus c.7 des 6. Konzils von Toledo (638) wieder und kann mit seiner Aussage, daß jedes Vergehen, gleichgültig wie

---

55. Coll. Lips. 10.7, Burch. 19.102; ed. Fransen und Kölzer, fol. 214v (PL 140.1004); vgl. Ivo, Decr. 15.114 (PL 161.886).

56. Zur Zwangsbuße, Hinschius, *System* 5.100; P. Landau, 'Sakramentalität und Jurisdiktion', in: *Das Recht der Kirche* 2: *Zur Geschichte des Kirchenrechts*, ed. G. Richter, H.-R. Reuter und K. Schlaich (Gütersloh 1995) 58–95, hier 82–83.

57. Vgl. Kéry, 'Liber Extra' 248 (Tabelle).

häufig es begangen wird, mit einer entsprechenden Strafe belegt werden soll, als allgemeines Leitmotiv des Titels angesehen werden.[58] Alle anderen Kapitel beschäftigen sich direkt oder indirekt mit der Verhängung von Geldstrafen.

Das zweite Kapitel schreibt vor, daß die *compositio* für einen getöteten Priester dem Bischof, zu dessen Diözese er gehörte, geleistet werden soll, und zwar in der Weise, daß die eine Hälfte der Kirche, der er vorgestanden hat, zukommen soll und die andere als Almosen für sein Seelenheil gerecht zu verteilen sei.[59] Während dieses Kapitel in der *Compilatio prima* (und anschließend auch im *Liber Extra*) ganz selbstverständlich unter den Titel *De poenis* eingereiht wurde, geben die Kommentare der Dekretalisten eine gewisse Ratlosigkeit wegen dieser Zuordnung zu erkennen, da, wie Bernhard von Parma in der *Glossa ordinaria* zum *Liber Extra* meint, dieser Text gar nicht von Strafe spreche, sondern von einfacher Wiedergutmachung *(simplex satisfactio)* oder zivilrechtlicher Entschädigung *(reparatio civilis)*, die man den Verwandten oder Erben und denen schulde, die einen Schaden erlitten *(damnum passis)* und Anspruch auf Schadenersatz hätten.[60] Man akzeptierte die Zuordnung dieses Kapitels zum Titel *De poenis* offenbar nur unter der Voraussetzung, daß mit der *compositio* zumindest teilweise eine Geldstrafe gemeint war.[61]

Innozenz IV. und Hostiensis lösten das Problem, indem sie die *compositio* als eine Geldstrafe, als eine Privatstrafe im Unterschied zur öffentlichen Strafe identifizierten. Innozenz IV. versteht die *compositio* vor allem als eine Geldstrafe, die das Ziel eines

---

58. 1 Comp.5.32.1 (X 5.37.1): 'Ea que frequenti praevaricatione iterantur, frequenti sententia condemnentur'. Obwohl die Inskription im *Liber Extra* 'Ex concilio Toletano' lautet, konnte Friedberg dieses Kapitel nicht näher identifizieren, wohl weil es sich nur um einen Auszug aus c.7 des VI. Toletanum handelt; vgl. Regino, 1.324; Burch. 19.158, Ivo, Decr. 15.166; H. Hoffmann und R. Pokorny, *Das Dekret des Bischofs Burchard von Worms. Textstufen—Frühe Verbreitung—Vorlagen* (MGH Hilfsmittel 12; München 1991) 59, 238, 285.

59. 1 Comp.5.32.2 (= X 5.37.2) gehört zu den sogenannten *Capitula a Benedicto Levita singillatim tradita*, die im Gegensatz zu den eigentlichen Kapitularien des Benedictus Levita möglicherweise echt sind; Ben. Lev. 1.186 (MGH Leges 2.2) 55.17–24; neu gedruckt bei H. Mordek, *Bibliotheca capitularium regum Francorum manuscripta: Überlieferung und Textzusammenhang der fränkischen Herrschererlasse* (MGH Hilfsmittel 15; München 1995) 1023–24 Nr. 27.3; vgl. auch Kéry, 'Liber Extra' 250 n.28. Ein nahezu gleichlautender Text mit derselben Inskription findet sich im *Decretum Gratiani* (C.17 q.4 c.26 Palea), dessen Fehlen jedoch Friedberg in allen von ihm benutzten Hss. und der Edition Basel 1471 feststellt. Die *compositio* für einen getöteten Priester beträgt, wie Bernhard von Parma vermerkt, 600 *solidi* nach der *Lex Lombardorum;* vgl. *Glossa ordinaria* ad X 5.37.2 s.v. *Compositio* (ed. Venetiis 1572 fol. 1085a); dort auch der Verweis auf C.17 q.4 c.27, wo 600 *solidi* als Wiedergutmachung für die Tötung eines Priesters ausgewiesen sind; ferner Innozenz IV., *Apparatus decretalium* ad X 5.37.2: 'Hoc cap. loquitur secundum Lombardam' (ed. Frankfurt 1570 fol. 541rb).

60. *Glossa ordinaria* ad X 5.37.2 s.v. *Presbyteri:* 'Pro vero intellectu not. quod hic tex. non loquitur de poena sed de simplici satisfactione seu reparatione ciuili, quae personis coniunctis uel haeredibus debetur, et damnum passis' (ed. Venetiis 1572 fol. 1085a).

61. *Glossa ordinaria* ad X 5.37.2 s.v. *Utilitatibus ecclesiae:* 'Et est ar. quod poenas pecuniarias, quas recipit episcopus non lucratur ipse, sed in utilitatem ecclesiae conuerti debet uel diuidet illas ar. i. dis. ius militare (D.1 c.10) et xvi. q. vi. c. (C.16 q.6 c.1)' (ed. fol. 1085a).

zivilrechtlichen Vorgehens gegen ein Verbrechen sei und grenzt sie ausdrücklich von der *vindicta* ab.[62] Hostiensis stellt den 'rechtsgeschichtlichen' Aspekt dieses Kapitels besonders heraus, indem er die *compositio* als eine Strafe bezeichnet, die ursprünglich nach dem lombardischen Strafgesetz für die Tötung eines Menschen verhängt worden sei *(poena ad quam tenetur homicida secundum legem lombardam)* und später vom Kirchenrecht übernommen wurde *(lex lombarda poenalis canonizata)*.[63]

Auch die anderen Kapitel, die Bernhard von Pavia unter dem Titel *De poenis* in sein *Breviarium* einfügte, beschäftigen sich mit der Geldstrafe. Nach dem Wortlaut zweier Dekretalen Alexanders III. mit ähnlichem Inhalt—die eine an den Erzbischof Richard von Canterbury (JL 14315—1 Comp.5.32.3), die andere an den Bischof von Coventry und den Abt von Chester (JL 13857—1 Comp.5.32.4) gerichtet—soll den Archidiakonen der Diözese Coventry die Verhängung von Geldstrafen zur Besserung von Vergehen und zur Bestrafung von Verbrechen, die sie sowohl von Klerikern als auch von Laien erhoben haben, in Zukunft verboten werden. Als Grund wird genannt, daß es dabei—aus Habgier, wie der Papst vermutet,—zu Mißbrauch gekommen sei. Angeblich hätten die Archidiakone mit Hilfe von Gottesurteilen Geld *a quolibet viro vel muliere* erpreßt, oder auch, um sich eine jährliche Einnahme zu sichern *(pro annua exactione)*, Beugestrafen über Personen oder Kirchen verhängt und für die Erlaubnis, in den Kirchen die Messe zu feiern, eine bestimmte Summe Geldes *(denarii)* gefordert.[64] Den Prälaten und speziell den Archidiakonen wurde deshalb fortan untersagt, Geld dafür zu fordern, daß sie über kriminelles Handeln hinwegsähen oder aus Habgier statt einer anderen Strafe, die möglicherweise eher der *correctio* des Übeltäters dienen würde, eine Geldstrafe verhängten.

Unter den Dekretalisten, die sich trotz entsprechender Überlegungen zu einem generellen Verbot der Geldstrafe nicht durchringen konnten, trat deutlich das Dilemma des kirchlichen Strafrechts zutage, Gefahren, die mit der Verhängung von Geldstrafen verbunden waren, so weit wie möglich einzudämmen. Zu den Mißbräuchen gehörte zum einen die Korruption der Gerichtsbarkeit, die sich darin äußerte, daß man sich schwerere Strafen oder Bestrafung generell 'abkaufen' ließ. Dies wurde nach außen hin als Ahndung mit Geldstrafen deklariert, deren Wert im Hinblick auf den von der

---

62. Innozenz IV., *Apparatus decretalium ad* X 5.37.2 s.v. *soluatur:* 'Ubi de crimine agitur ciuiliter ad poenam pecuniariam quia poena pecuniaria non est vindicta' (ed. Frankfurt 1570 fol. 541va).

63. Hostiensis, *Lectura* X 5.37.2 s.v. *compositio:* 'Id est poena ad quam tenetur homicida secundum legem lombardam; et est sexcentorum sol. ubi interficit presbyterum, ut hic, si vero diaconum quadringentorum si subdiaconum trecentorum, si episcopum novemgentorum, si monachum quadrigentorum, et est hec lex canonizata, Qui subdiaconum'; vgl. C.17 q.4 c.27: 'Pro graduum uarietate mulctentur qui clericos occidunt. Qui subdiaconum occiderit, CCC solidos conponat; qui diaconum, CCCC; qui presbiterum, DC; qui episcopum, DCCCC; qui monachum, CCCC'.

64. 1 Comp.5.32.3 (JL 14315; X 5.37.3), 1 Comp.5.32.4 (JL 13857; X 1.23.6).

Kirche propagierten Strafzweck der *correctio* mehr als fragwürdig war. Doch auch der umgekehrte Fall, wonach willkürlich und ohne Grund Beugestrafen verhängt wurden, um anschließend für ihre vollständige oder punktuelle Aufhebung 'Geldstrafen' zu fordern, sollte ausgeschlossen werden. Die Möglichkeit der Umwandlung von andersartigen Strafen in Geldstrafen wurde als Einfallstor für den Mißbrauch zum Zwecke der Bereicherung betrachtet.[65]

Schließlich wurde auch die Verurteilung zu den Kosten des Verfahrens als indirekte Form der Geldstrafe betrachtet. Als letztes Kapitel zum Titel *De poenis* fügte Bernhard von Pavia den angeblichen c.9 des Konzils von Tours, das 1163 unter dem Vorsitz Alexanders III. stattfand, in sein *Breviarium extravagantium* ein.[66] Dieser Kanon leitete auch die Reihe der Kapitel ein, die im *Liber Extra* zum Thema 'Prozeßvergehen' dem Titel noch hinzugefügt wurden, ein Thema das einen wichtigen Schwerpunkt des kirchlichen Strafrechts darstellte.[67] In Anlehnung an eine kaiserliche Strafbestimmung *(sanctio imperialis)*, welche die Erhebung unberechtigter oder auf Verleumdung gründender Klagen unter anderem durch eine Verurteilung zu den Prozeßkosten eingedämmt habe *(condemnando in expensis compescit)* und bekanntlich auch mit den kirchlichen Vorschriften *(sacris institutis)* in Einklang stehe, schreibt dieser Kanon vor, daß auch *in causis pecuniariis*, also in Zivilprozessen, die Prozeßkosten grundsätzlich der unterlegenen Partei aufzubürden seien, außer wenn das Urteil zugunsten eines Abwesenden verhängt werde und diesem keine Kosten entstanden seien.[68]

Diese Bestimmung ist in der *Collectio Lipsiensis* unter dem Titel *De dolo et contumacia alterius partis punienda* zu finden.[69] In der *Compilatio prima* wurde sie unter dem Titel *De poenis* eingeordnet, obwohl der Titel *De dolo et contumacia alterius partis punienda*, der die hinterlistige Täuschung des Prozeßgegners und den Ungehorsam gegenüber dem Richter unter Strafe stellt, im zweiten Buch der *Compilatio prima* vorkommt.[70] Ein Grund dafür ist möglicherweise darin zu sehen, daß nicht nur eine Bestrafung der Verleumdung und anderer Prozeßvergehen vorgesehen ist, sondern ebenso eine Strafe

65. Vgl. Kéry, *Gottesfurcht und irdische Strafe* Kap. III. 3.2.2 b–c.

66. R. Somerville, *Pope Alexander III and the Council of Tours (1163). A Study of Ecclesiastical Politics and Institutions in the Twelfth Century* (Berkeley 1977) 39–40.

67. Siehe Kéry, *Gottesfurcht und irdische Strafe* Kap. IV.2.

68. 1 Comp.5.32.5 (X 5.37.4); vgl. Inst. 4.16 ('De poena temere litigantium'). Im strafrechtlichen Verfahren, dem Akkusationsprozeß, sollte die *inscriptio*, durch die sich der Ankläger verpflichtete, die dem Beschuldigten drohende Strafe zu übernehmen, falls seine Anklage nicht zu dessen Verurteilung führte, eine Versicherung gegen ungerechtfertigte Anklagen bieten; siehe Jacobi, 'Prozeß' 261; L. Kéry, 'Inquisitio-denunciatio-exceptio. Möglichkeiten der Verfahrenseinleitung im Dekretalenrecht', ZRG Kan. Abt. 87 (2001) 226–68, hier 230.

69. Coll. Lips. 40, ed. Friedberg, *Compilationes antiquae* 200; dort mit der Inskription 'Item ex conc. Tollet. III'; vgl. Kéry, *Gottesfurcht und irdische Strafe* Kap. IV.2.

70. 1 Comp.2.10 und 1 Comp.5.32.5 (X 5.37.4); vgl. *Summa decretalium*, ed. Laspeyres 41–42. Im *Liber Extra* wurde ein Titel *De calumniatoribus* (X 5.2.1–2) neu eingefügt.

für die bloße Niederlage im Zivilprozeß angedroht wird. Damit ersparte man sich den Nachweis, daß die unterlegene Partei keineswegs in gutem Glauben die Klage angestrengt hatte, sondern aus Leichtsinn und in der Hoffnung, den Prozeß zu gewinnen, obwohl ihr Anspruch nicht gerechtfertigt war.[71] Nicht zuletzt war mit einer solchen Strafandrohung die Absicht verbunden, eine abschreckende Wirkung gegen das allzu leichtfertige Anzetteln von Prozessen zu erzielen.

Über diese bis zu einem gewissen Grad dem Zufall unterworfene Zusammenstellung von Einzeltexten hinaus kann man Erkenntnisse über die theoretische Begründung seiner neuen Systematik und die Vorstellungen, die Bernhard von Pavia insgesamt zu den Bußen und Strafen vertrat, erst seiner ein knappes Jahrzehnt später entstandenen *Summa decretalium* entnehmen. Dort klärt er nicht über die Unterschiede zwischen kirchlichen Strafen und Bußen auf, sondern verschiebt den Schwerpunkt zu den Strafen, indem er die Bußen lediglich als eine spezielle Erscheinungsform der Strafe darstellt. Der entscheidende Unterschied liegt seinen Worten zufolge im Verfahren begründet: Die Bußen sind diejenigen Strafen, die im geheimen Verfahren *(in iudicio occulto)* auferlegt werden, während die Verhängung von Strafen ein öffentliches Verfahren *(iudicium manifestum)* voraussetzt.[72]

Mit dieser Distinktion greift Bernhard von Pavia die 'karolingische Dichotomie' von *paenitentia publica* und *paenitentia privata* auf.[73] Nachdem letztere bereits das Wesen der öffentlichen Buße zur Strafe hin verlagert hatte, entwickelte sie Bernhard noch um einen entscheidenden Schritt weiter.[74] Bei ihm deutete sich die spätere, erstmals in dem vor 1210 verfaßten Glossenapparat *Animal est substantia* formulierte Gegenüberstellung von *forum penitenitale* und *forum iudiciale* an—und damit auch die allmähliche Verrechtlichung des Bußwesens.[75]

---

71. J. Brundage, 'Taxation of Costs in Medieval Canonical Courts', in: *Forschungen zur Reichs-, Papst- und Landesgeschichte. Peter Herde zum 65. Geburtstag von Freunden, Schülern und Kollegen dargebracht*, ed. K. Borchard und E. Bünz (2 Bde.; Stuttgart 1998) 1.565–74, hier 569; generell zum Problem der Prozesskosten, idem, 'Contingent Fees and the Ius Commune', ZRG Kan. Abt. 118 (2001) 125–37; H. Müller, 'Streitwert und Kosten in Prozessen vor dem päpstlichen Gericht—eine Skizze', ZRG Kan. Abt. 118 (2001) 138–64.

72. *Summa*, zu *De poenitentiis* (5.33), ed. Laspeyres 269: 'Audivimus de poenis, quae inferuntur in iudicio manifesto; nunc de his quae imponuntur occulto iudicio, audiamus, sive de poenitentiis'.

73. Der Begriff wurde geprägt von C. Vogel, *Les 'Libri Paenitentiales'* (Typologie 27; Turnhout 1978) 39–41; Raymund Kottje hat zu Recht darauf hingewiesen, daß unabhängig vom Begriff der 'dichotomie carolingienne' die Zweizügigkeit des kirchlichen Strafverfahrens auch nach der Karolingerzeit weiterbestand, R. Kottje, 'Bußpraxis und Bußritus', in: *Segni e riti nella chiesa altomedievale occidentale* (Settimane 33; Spoleto 1987) 369–95, hier 392 mit n.88; zustimmend F. Kerff, 'Libri paenitentiales und kirchliche Strafgerichtsbarkeit bis zum Decretum Gratiani', ZRG Kan. Abt. 75 (1989) 23–57, hier 34.

74. Vgl. dazu Kéry, *Gottesfurcht und irdische Strafe* Kap. I.1.1 f.

75. P. Landau, *Die Entstehung des kanonischen Infamie-Begriffs von Gratian bis zur Glossa ordinaria* (Köln und Graz 1966) 75 mit n.46; idem, 'Epikletisches und transzendentales Kirchenrecht bei Hans Dombois', ZRG Kan. Abt. 73 (1987) 131–54, hier 148–49; R. Fraher, 'Preventing Crime in the High Middle Ages: The Medieval

Bernhard unterschied seinerseits die Buße im eher technisch-juristischen Sinne als Bußwerk, als Genugtuung, die der Büßende nach dem Urteil und dem Ermessen des Beichtpriesters leistete, von der Buße im theologischen oder wie er selbst sagt 'im eigentlichen' Sinne *(proprie)* in der Bedeutung von Reue und Zerknirschung über eine begangene Tat, einschließlich des Vorsatzes, eine solche Tat nicht wieder zu begehen.[76]

Auch seine Definition der Strafe operiert mit dem Begriff der *satisfactio*, ist jedoch trotz der Bezeichnung des Vergehens als *peccatum* ganz von juristischen Kategorien bestimmt; er unterscheidet sogar den öffentlichen Aspekt der Strafe von ihrer 'privaten' Zielsetzung, wenn er sie gleichzeitig als *iudicialis retributio* und *satisfactio delicti* kennzeichnet, als gerichtliche Vergeltung für eine Missetat und als Wiedergutmachung für ein Vergehen.[77] Anders als im *Decretum Gratiani* ist also nicht von einer *correctio* des Übeltäters oder einer Strafe, die zur Buße bewegen soll, die Rede, sondern von Vergeltung oder Täter-Opfer-Ausgleich und Schadensersatz, wie Bernhard sie vor allem im römischen Recht vorgeprägt fand.

Möglicherweise ging Bernhard mit seiner apodiktischen Begründung für die Einführung eines eigenen Kapitels über die Strafen—*quoniam crimina sunt punienda*—über ähnliche Formulierungen eines öffentlichen Strafanspruches hinaus, wie sie wenige Jahre später Innozenz III. mit dem Satz *et publicae utilitatis intersit, ne crimina remaneant impunita*, oder schon zu Beginn des 11. Jahrhunderts Bischof Fulbert von Chartres (1006–1028) mit der Wendung *sed cum iuris sit ad utilitatem rei publicae cunctos punire maleficos* unternahm.[78] Offenbar hielt Bernhard es nicht für nötig, seine Aussage genauer zu begründen oder zu erläutern.

Lawyers' Search for Deterrence', in: *Popes, Teachers and Canon Law in the Middle Ages*, ed. J. Sweeney und S. Chodorow (Ithaca, NY und London 1989) 212–33, hier 219. Trusen, der die stärkere Verrechtlichung der Bußpraxis seit dem 13. Jahrhundert beschreibt, weist darauf hin, daß die Präzisierung in der Terminologie mit der Abgrenzung des kirchlichen und weltlichen Verfahrensrechts als *lex fori* begonnen habe. Eine Übernahme in die Bußtheologie sei erstmals bei Petrus Cantor († 1197) festzustellen, dessen Schüler Robert von Courçon († 1219) bereits ausdrücklich vom *forum poenitentiale* gesprochen habe, W. Trusen, 'Zur Bedeutung des geistlichen Forum internum und externum für die spätmittelalterliche Gesellschaft', ZRG Kan. Abt. 76 (1990) 254–85, hier 262–63.

76. *Summa*, ed. Laspeyres 269–70.

77. Ibid. ed. 264 § 1: 'Poena est iudicialis retributio pro peccato; vel ita poena est satisfactio delicti'.

78. Vgl. *The Letters and Poems of Fulbert of Chartres*, ed. and trans. F. Behrends (Oxford 1976) 54 Nr.29; die Notwendigkeit, die Bischöfe bei der Durchführung von *paenitentiae publicae* für Kapitalverbrechen zu unterstützen, wurde auch auf dem *Concilium in Francia habitum* (818/9–829) mit den *utilitates rei publicae* begründet, ed. MGH Concilia 2.1.595, c.6; dazu Kéry, *Gottesfurcht und irdische Strafe* Kap. I 1.1.g. Innozenz III., Dekretale *Ut famae* (X 5.39.35; 3 Comp.5.21.8, Po.2038); R. Fraher, 'The Theoretical Justification for the New Criminal Law of the High Middle Ages: "Rei publicae interest, ne crimina remaneant impunita",' *University of Illinois Law Review* 3 (1984) 577–95; K. Pennington, 'Innocent III and the Ius commune', in: *Grundlagen des Rechts. Festschrift für Peter Landau zum 65. Geburtstag*, ed. R. Helmholz et al. (Paderborn 2000) 349–66, hier 352. Außerdem Bernardus, *Summa*, ed. Laspeyres 264: 'Egimus de criminibus. Sed quoniam crimina sunt punienda post tractatum de criminibus agendum est de poenis'.

Im Zuge einer umfassenden Systematik, mit der er sein jeweiliges Thema in der *Summa* möglichst vollständig darzustellen suchte, beschränkte Bernhard sich keinesfalls auf die Darstellung des kirchlichen Strafrechts. Seiner Unterscheidung zwischen kirchlicher und weltlicher Gerichtsbarkeit, zwischen kirchlichem und weltlichem Vergehen entsprechend dehnte er seine Darstellung auch auf die 'weltlichen oder gesetzlichen Strafen' aus.[79] Als kirchliche Strafen kennt er sowohl geistliche Strafen als auch Leibes- und Geldstrafen. Geistliche Strafen sind für ihn Tadel *(increpatio)*, Interdikt, Suspension, Exkommunikation, Infamie und Absetzung, als Leibesstrafen können im kirchlichen Recht Exil, Fasten, Kerkerhaft und Auspeitschung verhängt werden.[80]

Als weltliche oder gesetzliche Strafe *(poena legalis)* nennt er Todesstrafe, Verstümmelung, Auspeitschung, Exil, Deportation, Gefängnis sowie die *aquae et ignis interdictio*, eine alte römische Strafe, welche die Entziehung des zum Leben Notwendigen bedeutet und meist mit der Verbannung gleichgesetzt wird.[81] Weiter erwähnt er die Absetzung, im kanonischen Recht als Suspension bezeichnet, die für immer oder auf Zeit erfolgen könne, sowie Infamie und Geldstrafe, wobei zwischen einer gesetzlich fixierten Summe *(poena pecuniaria determinata)* und einer Vervielfachung des Entwendeten, etwa dem *duplum* bei Diebstahl oder dem Vierfachen bei Raub *(poena pecuniaria indeterminata)*, unterschieden wird. Für zusätzliche weltliche Strafen verweist Bernhard nur noch ganz allgemein auf den *Codex Iustiniani* und die Digesten.[82]

Für eine Reihe von Verbrechen gibt Bernhard in den entsprechenden Titeln seiner *Summa decretalium* die Strafen des weltlichen Rechts *(secundum legem)* an, jedoch nicht etwa aus den Volksrechten, sondern aus dem *Corpus iuris civilis*.[83] Die Gegenüberstellung scheint keinem praktischen Zweck zu dienen, auch wenn aus einer Stelle im Titel

---

79. *Summa,* ed. Laspeyres 196: 'Duo sunt genera causarum, civilis scil. et ecclesiastica; civilis est, cuius examinatio et diffinitio ad civilem iudicem spectat, ecclesiastica, quae est ab ecclesiastico iudice cognoscenda et diffinienda. . . . Et est sciendum, quod crimen aliud ecclesiasticum, aliud civile; ecclesiasticum, quod ab ecclesiastico iudice, civile, quod a civili examinari et puniri debet'.

80. *Summa,* ed. Laspeyres 265–66.

81. Pauly-Wissowa 3.308–09; vgl. Bernardus, *Summa,* ed. Laspeyres 266. Todesstrafe sei vorgesehen für (schwere) Verbrechen wie Majestätsbeleidigung, Tötung und Ehebruch. Die Verstümmelung, so merkt Bernard unter Verweis auf C.6 q.6 c.5, an, wird heute häufiger angewandt als dies aufgrund des Gesetzes berechtigt erscheint. Die Auspeitschung dient als Strafe für Diebstahl, wie nicht nur aus dem *Codex Iustiniani,* sondern auch aus C.12 q.2 c.11 (Gregor I. an Augustinus von Canterbury, JE 1843) hervorgeht; eigentlich handelt es sich bei Gregor I. um Mundraub, da er unterscheidet zwischen einem Diebstahl derjenigen, die genug zum Leben haben und anderen, die aus Mangel stehlen 'qui in hac re ex inopia delinquunt'; nur letztere werden mit der Auspeitschung bestraft, wohl weil sie keinen Schadensersatz leisten können. Unter Deportation versteht Bernhard die Verbannung auf eine Insel ohne Vermögensverlust.

82. *Summa,* ed. Laspeyres 267.

83. Vgl. dazu demnächst L. Kéry, 'Verbrechen und Strafen im kanonischen Recht des Mittelalters', in: *Verbrechen und Strafen. 51. Wolfenbütteler Symposion vom 06.–08.11.2001,* ed. D. Klippel (Wolfenbütteler Forschungen; im Druck).

De raptoribus unter Verweis auf eine Dekretale Alexanders III. über die Möglichkeit der Delegation weltlicher Strafgerichtsbarkeit an Prälaten hervorgeht, daß kirchliche Richter unter bestimmten Umständen weltliche Strafen gegen Laien verhängen könnten.[84]

Bernhard benutzte offensichtlich in Ermangelung einer einschlägigen Kodifikation des geltenden Strafrechts das spätantike römische Strafrecht als Spiegelbild, um Anregungen für den Ausbau und eine bessere juristische Begründung des kirchlichen Strafrechts zu gewinnen. Es ging ihm nicht um eine möglichst zutreffende Schilderung des in seiner Zeit gültigen weltlichen Strafrechts, sondern er benutzte—wie dies auch schon Le Bras angedeutet hat—den *Codex Iustiniani* als Hilfsmittel, um das kirchliche Strafrecht diesem gleichberechtigt gegenüberstellen zu können.

In gewisser Weise wird er damit auch zum Übermittler des römischen Strafrechts unter kirchlichem Vorzeichen, denn er ergreift die Gelegenheit, bestimmte Härten des weltlichen Strafrechts zu verurteilen. Am Ende des Kapitels über Strafen schärft er dem Leser drei Grundregeln ein, deren unmittelbarer Adressat ganz offensichtlich der Gesetzgeber des weltlichen Strafrechts ist, und beruft sich mit einer Ausnahme ausschließlich auf Quellen des römischen Rechts. Er betont, daß niemand im Gesicht gebrandmarkt werden dürfe, und zwar nicht aus humanitären, sondern aus theologischen Gründen, damit, wie Bernhard aus dem *Codex Iustiniani* ableitet, das Bild Gottes im Menschen nicht verunstaltet werde.[85] Die körperliche Strafe sollte zudem nicht unmittelbar vollstreckt werden, sondern erst nach einer Frist von 30 Tagen.[86] Generell sollten Strafen, wie er unter Verweis auf zwei Digestenstellen betont, im Zweifelsfall eher abgemildert als verschärft werden.[87]

Zu besonderer Klarheit gelangt Bernhard von Pavia auch bei seiner wegweisenden Unterscheidung zwischen Schadensersatz und Geldstrafe, die ihm ebenfalls im Wesentlichen mit Hilfe von Anleihen beim römischen Recht gelingt.[88] Die große systematische Bedeutung, die er der Frage beimißt, kann nicht zuletzt daran abgelesen werden, daß er einen eigenen Titel zum Schadensersatz in den strafrechtlichen Teil seines *Breviarium extravagantium* aufgenommen hat, obwohl ihm für diesen Titel

---

84. *Summa*, ed. Laspeyres 231; mit Verweis auf 1 Comp.5.14.3 (= X 5.17.4).

85. *Summa*, ed. Laspeyres 269 § 8, mit Verweis auf Cod. 9.47.17: 'Si quis in metallum fuerit pro criminum deprehensorum qualitate damnatus, minime in eius facie scribatur, cum et in manibus et in suris possit poena damnationis una scriptione comprehendi, quo facies, quae ad similitudinem pulchritudinis caelestis est figurata, minime maculetur'.

86. *Summa*, ed. Laspeyres 269 § 9; mit Verweis auf Cod. 9.47.20; eine gleichzeitig angeführte Dekretstelle, C.11 q.3 c.69, betont, daß die dreißigtägige Frist zwischen Urteil und Exekution Gelegenheit zu Erbarmen und Buße geben soll; im Kapitel *De homicidiis* weist Bernhard darauf hin, daß Amtsträger, die ohne ein Urteil die Todesstrafe verhängen, wegen 'allzugroßer Eile' als Mörder anzuklagen seien, vgl. *Summa*, ed. Laspeyres 221.

87. *Summa*, ed. Laspeyres 269 § 10: 'Sed et illud non omittendum, quod poenae potius sunt molliendae, quam exasperandae, ut Dig. eod. l. penult. (Dig. 48.19.42); et Dig. de reg. iur., Factum § ult. (Dig. 50.17.155.2)'.

88. Vgl. L. Kéry, *Gottesfurcht und irdische Strafe* Kap. III. 3.2.1 a.

lediglich Texte aus dem Alten Testament vorlagen, deren Aussagen er selbst in seiner *Summa* widerspricht.[89] Hier zeigt sich deutlich die bereits angedeutete Diskrepanz zwischen seinen systematischen Ausführungen in der *Summa*, die vor allem durch Anleihen beim römischen Recht dem kirchlichen Strafrecht neue Wege weisen können, und dem eklatanten Mangel an verwertbaren Texten in den Dekretalensammlungen.

Mit Blick auf das weltliche Recht trifft Bernhard von Pavia in seiner *Summa* eine klare Unterscheidung zwischen öffentlicher Geldstrafe und *compositio* und damit zwischen Strafe und (weltlicher) Buße. Er bedient sich dabei des Gegensatzpaares von *poena pecuniaria determinata* und *indeterminata*.[90] Die nicht festgelegte Geldstrafe richtet sich nach dem Wert des Schadens und bietet zivilrechtlich die Möglichkeit, gegen ein Verbrechen, wie etwa Diebstahl, mit einer Klage auf Erstattung des vielfachen Wertes vorzugehen.[91] Für die Begründung der vom Gesetz festgelegten 'absoluten' Geldstrafe hat Bernhard nur Belege aus dem *Corpus iuris civilis* vorzuweisen.[92] Er leitet sie also nicht aus zeitgenössischen Rechtsvorschriften ab, sondern kann diese Form der Strafe nur in Anlehnung an spätantike römische Rechtstexte präsentieren. Er liefert keine Zustandsbeschreibung des bestehenden weltlichen Rechts, sondern literarisch begründetes Entwicklungspotential und einen aus der Vergangenheit in die Zukunft übertragbaren Zielpunkt für die Entwicklung des öffentlichen Strafrechts.

Wie hier an einem kleinen thematischen Ausschnitt, der genaueren Unterscheidung zwischen Buße und Strafe, gezeigt werden konnte, stellt das Werk des großen Kanonisten Bernhard von Pavia einen wichtigen Wendepunkt in der Geschichte des kirchlichen Strafrechts dar. Ihm gelang es, das neue Dekretalenrecht der Päpste systematisch in das kanonische Recht einzugliedern. Außerdem lieferte er als Sammler und innovativer Kommentator entscheidende Anstöße für die Entwicklung des kirchlichen Strafrechts zu einer eigenen wissenschaftlichen Disziplin. Durch die Einbeziehung des römischen Rechts, das ihm nicht nur Anregungen für eine Verbesserung der Systematik bot, sondern auch die inhaltliche Weiterentwicklung des kirchlichen Strafrechts durch eine Gegenüberstellung von weltlichem und kirchlichem Recht ermöglichte, erreichte Bernhard von Pavia eine klarere Abgrenzung und vielfältigere inhaltliche Ausgestaltung des kirchlichen Strafrechts.

---

89. 1 Comp.5.31; abschließend weist Bernhard von Pavia darauf hin, daß bei dieser Art von Wiedergutmachungen, also insgesamt beim Schadensersatz, auch dann die Bestimmungen der *Leges*, des römischen Rechts, vorzuziehen seien, wenn das mosaische Gesetz andere Regelungen vorsehe, *Summa*, ed. Laspeyres 263 § 6; vgl. P. Landau, 'Alttestamentliches Recht in der *Compilatio Prima* und sein Einfluß auf das kanonische Recht', SG 20 (1976) 113–33; H. Lange, *Schadensersatz und Privatstrafe in der mittelalterlichen Rechtstheorie* (Münster und Köln 1955) 69–71.

90. *Summa*, ed. Laspeyres 267.

91. Ibid. 250–51 § 6.

92. Ibid. 267; mit Verweisen auf Dig.2.4.12, Dig. 2.4.25 und Inst. 4.16.3.

Im Zentrum der inhaltlichen Weiterentwicklung des kirchlichen Strafrechts stand vor allem die Geldstrafe, deren Bedeutung und Problematik für das kirchliche Strafrecht schon dadurch belegt wird, daß nahezu alle Texte der *Compilatio prima* zum Titel *De poenis* sich mit diesem Thema beschäftigten. Bernhard gab sich in seiner *Summa* besondere Mühe, die verschiedenen Aspekte der Geldstrafe durch eine klare Unterscheidung vom Schadensersatz sowie durch eine Gegenüberstellung von 'öffentlicher' und 'privater' Geldstrafe genauer zu fassen, was ebenfalls nur mit Hilfe des römischen Rechts möglich war.

Die Schwierigkeit, eine klarere Abgrenzung zwischen Buße und Strafe vorzunehmen, wird insbesondere an der Diskussion um die Dekretale *Sicut dignum* deutlich, die einen hohen Stellenwert in den früheren Sammlungen des Bernhard von Pavia einnahm und mit ihren Hinweisen auf die Ermessensstrafen zum Ausdruck brachte, wie sehr das kirchliche Strafrecht von seiner Nähe zum Bußwesen geprägt war.

18

Summarischer Syndikatsprozeß

Einflüsse des kanonischen Rechts auf die städtische und kirchliche Gerichtspraxis des Spätmittelalters

Susanne Lepsius

❋

Herrscher und Recht: Die Problemstellung

Die Bedeutung des kanonischen Rechts und der Kanonisten für das politische Denken im Mittelalter kann kaum überschätzt werden. Kenneth Pennington hat in wertvollen Untersuchungen gezeigt, wie die Kanonisten seit dem 12. Jahrhundert einerseits dem Herrscher die Kompetenz zusprachen, neues Recht zu setzen und das Recht insgesamt zu gewährleisten—also Herrschaft durch Recht zu legitimieren—, sie aber auch darum bemüht waren, eine allzu unbeschränkte Macht des Fürsten durch Recht einzuhegen.[1] Nach gewichtigen mittelalterlichen Stimmen war der Herrscher sowohl durch naturrechtlich definierte Rechte der Menschen (etwa das Eigentumsrecht), als auch an die rechtssichernde Funktion des *ordo iudiciarius*, also an Verfahrensgrundsätze (bei seinen Handlungen) gebunden.[2] Die höchsten Rechtsprechungsinstanzen, Kaiser und Papst, konnten nicht einmal im summarischen Verfahren, das im Laufe des 13. Jahrhunderts zur Verfahrensbeschleunigung von Legisten und Kanonisten Hand in Hand entwickelt worden war, von den wesentlichen Verfahrensbestandteilen, die die

---

1. K. Pennington, 'Law, Legislative Authority and Theories of Government, 1150–1300', in: *The Cambridge History of Medieval Political Thought c.350–c.1450*, hg. v. J. H. Burns (Cambridge, New York und New Rochelle, NY 1988) 424–53.

2. K. Pennington, 'Due Process, Community and the Prince in the Evolution of the "Ordo iudiciarius",' RIDC 9 (1998) 9–47; K. Pennington, *The Prince and the Law, 1200–1600. Sovereignty and Rights in the Western Legal Tradition* (Berkeley und Los Angeles 1993) 132–64. Zur Frage der Mitwirkungs- und Konsultationspflichten von Körperschaften als Begrenzung von Herrschaft, J. Brundage, *Medieval Canon Law* (London und New York 1995) 99–110.

substantiellen Interessen der gegnerischen Prozeßpartei sicherstellten, abweichen.[3] Die Herrschaftsausübung war vielfach rechtlich gebunden. Was aber sollte geschehen, wenn ein Herrschaftsträger diese Grenzen überschritt? Mittelalterliche Theoretiker richteten ihr Augenmerk vor allem auf die höchsten politischen Amtsinhaber, wobei sie meist die Herrschaftsform der Monarchie als beste Staatsform betrachteten. Folgerichtig diskutierten sie im Falle der Grenzüberschreitung durch den Monarchen, ob er dadurch zum Tyrannen werde, woran man einen tyrannischen Monarchen erkennen könne und ob und durch wen ein solcher Tyrann abzusetzen sei.[4]

Im Bann derartiger theoretischer Schriften hat die moderne Forschungsliteratur die kommunale Rechtspraxis im spätmittelalterlichen Italien häufig vernachlässigt. In den italienischen Kommunen stand der Aspekt der Selbstherrschaft, also unabhängig von den überörtlichen, monarchischen Herrschern zu sein, im Vordergrund. Daneben fanden sich dort bereits zukunftsweisende, bürokratische Merkmale der Herrschaftsorganisation, bei der es auch um Fragen der Umverteilung von Macht ging.[5] In dieser Umgebung entstand der Syndikatsprozeß als ein standardisierter Mechanismus nachträglicher Herrschaftskontrolle durch städtische Institutionen. Der Syndikatsprozeß konnte während oder üblicherweise erst nach Ablauf der turnusmäßigen Amtszeit der gewählten Amtsträger stattfinden, um die Tätigkeit der Amtsträger auf ihre Rechtmäßigkeit hin zu überprüfen und ihre Herrschaft an das Recht zu binden. Er war also ein juristisches Mittel der politischen Praxis. Ob der Syndikatsprozeß auf römische Quellen zurückzuführen ist oder eine originäre Entwicklung der italienischen Kommunen war, soll hier nicht weiter verfolgt werden.[6] Uns interessiert vielmehr

---

3. Pennington, *The Prince and the Law* 187–200.

4. Einen Überblick über die Theoretiker, die sich mit den Fragen von Königsabsetzung und Tyrannenmord auseinandersetzten, also von der Monarchie her argumentierten, bei J. Dunbabin, 'Government', in: *The Cambridge History of Medieval Political Thought* 477–519. Zur berühmten Auseinandersetzung zwischen Kaiser Heinrich VII. und Papst Clemens V., die den Hintergrund für die legistischen Debatten um Mindeststandards für Rechtsverfahren auch im summarischen Prozeß bildete, Pennington, *The Prince and the Law* 165–201; idem, 'Henry VII and Robert of Naples', in: *Das Publikum politischer Theorie im 14. Jahrhundert*, hg. v. J. Miethke und A. Bühler (München 1992) 81–92.

5. J. Quillet, 'Community, Counsel and Representation', in: *The Cambridge History of Medieval Political Thought* 520–72, 525–30. Zur Bedeutung des Syndikatsprozesses für das Herrschaftsverständnis in den mittelalterlichen italienischen Kommunen A. Padoa-Schioppa, *Il diritto nella Storia d'Europa. Il medioevo* (Mailand 1995) 214; K. Nehlsen-von Stryk, 'Entstehung und Entwicklung der italienischen Kommunen (11. bis 14. Jahrhundert)', *Rechtshistorisches Journal* 15 (1996) 349–59, 355.

6. Die römischen Wurzeln betonen W. Engelmann, *Die Wiedergeburt der Rechtskultur in Italien durch die wissenschaftliche Lehre. Eine Darlegung der Entfaltung des gemeinen italienischen Rechts und seiner Justizkultur im Mittelalter unter dem Einfluß der herrschenden Lehre der Gutachtenpraxis der Rechtsgelehrten und der Verantwortung der Richter im Sindikatsprozeß* (Leipzig 1938) 28–40, 344–466; G. Masi, 'Il sindacato delle magistrature comunali nel sec. XIV (con speciale riferimento a Firenze)', *Rivista italiana per le scienze giuridiche* n.s. 5 (1930) 43–115, 331–411. Eigenständige Prägung durch die mittelalterlichen Kommunen sieht dagegen G. Dahm, *Das Strafrecht Italiens im ausgehenden Mittelalter. Untersuchungen über die Beziehungen zwischen Theorie und Praxis des Spätmittelalters,*

erstens, ob und gegebenenfalls welche strukturellen Ähnlichkeiten bei der institutionellen Organisation und bei der Art der verfolgten Amtsvergehen im kirchlichen und
weltlich-städtischen Bereich bestanden und, zweitens, ob der Ablauf der Verfahren zur
Kontrolle von Herrschaft mögliche kanonistische Einflüsse erkennen läßt? Zu denken
wäre vor allem an die Art der Einleitung des Verfahrens (Akkusations-, Denuntiations-
oder Inquisitionsverfahren *ex officio*) oder daran, inwieweit die Durchführung des Verfahrens dem im kanonischen Recht verankerten summarischen Verfahren entsprach.

　　Die genannten Fragestellungen sollen am Beispiel Luccas, mit gelegentlichen Ausblicken auf die Praxis in anderen italienischen Städten, verfolgt werden. Lucca ist nicht
nur deshalb ein besonders lohnendes Beispiel, weil bereits in den ältesten erhaltenen
Stadtstatuten von 1308 für fast alle Amtsträger statuiert war, daß sie ihre Aufgaben
bene et legaliter wahrnehmen und insbesondere alle Statuten und Verfahrensordnungen
einhalten sollten. Zudem konnten ihnen für alle Fälle der absichtlichen oder fahrlässigen Zuwiderhandlung erhebliche Geldstrafen an die Kommune Lucca durch den
Syndikatsrichter auferlegt werden.[7] Bemerkenswert für den Lucchesen Rechtszustand
ist des weiteren folgender Umstand: Während der Pisaner 'Fremdherrschaft' über
Lucca war der *maggior sindaco* zumeist ein Pisaner, der länger als die statutenmäßig
vorgesehenen sechs Monate amtierte. Die Position des *maior sindicus* wurde also von
den Pisanern als politisches Amt verstanden, das es unter Kontrolle zu bringen galt.[8]

---

namentlich im XIV. Jahrhundert (Berlin und Leipzig 1931) 73–78. Zu bio- und historiographischen Hintergründen
der unterschiedlichen Auffassungen Dahms und Engelmanns, S. Lepsius, 'Die mittelalterliche italienische
Stadt als "Utopie". Eine Untersuchung am Beispiel von Hermann U. Kantorowicz, Georg Dahm, Woldemar
Engelmann', in: *Stadt—Gemeinde—Genossenschaft. Festschrift für Gerhard Dilcher zum 70. Geburtstag*, hg. v. A.
Cordes, J. Rückert und R. Schulze (Berlin 2003) 389–455.

　7. So leistete der Podestà, der in den Statuten auch abstrakt als *maius regimen* bezeichnet wurde, den Eid
Buch für Buch auf die Statuten der Kommune und versprach, sich an weiteren Einzelstatuten und Erlassen auszurichten: 'Observabo omnia et singula Statuta Lucani Comunis et Populi, et Constitutum maioris Sindaci et
Iudicis appellationum, et Constitutum et Ordinamenta Societatum armorum Lucani Comunis et Populi, et omnia et singula alia decreta Consiliorum vigentium, que non sint [contra]ria Statutis Lucani Comunis et Populi
et Constitutis domini Maioris Sindici . . . et Societatum Armorum Lucani Populi [. . .] et etiam observare Cartam consulum mercatorum et eorum Constitutiones et Statuta et nominatim quicquid continetur in eis, salvis
supradictis statutis, constitutis et decretis Lucani Comunis', *Statuto del Comune di Lucca dell'anno MCCCVIII*
1.1, ed. S. Bongi (Memorie e Documenti per servire alla storia di Lucca 3.3; Lucca 1867) 7–8. Prägnanter in den
Stadtstatuten von 1372: 'Et observare per me et meam familiam statuta Lucani communis et curiarum civitatis
Lucane facta et facienda et eciam statuta curie mercatorum salvis hiis que in hoc statuto continentur', Lucca,
AS Statuti no. 6, Statuta communis Lucae a. 1372, c. 25 ('De iuramento potestatis'), fol. 10v.

　8. C. Meek, *The Commune of Lucca Under Pisan Rule, 1342–1369* (Cambridge, MA 1980) 17–31, 21–28, betont,
daß die Pisaner wenig in die Institutionen Luccas eingriffen und nur dafür sorgten, daß der Podestà, der *capitaneus*, und die neugeschaffenen Rektoren Pisaner zu sein hatten. Auf das Amt des *maggior sindaco e giudice degli
appelli* geht sie nicht ein. Nach der Aktenüberlieferung dieses Gerichts sind für die Zeit von 1354 bis März 1369
die Syndikatsrichter zumeist Pisaner, die entgegen den Statuten teilweise ganzjährig und ohne die vorgesehenen Sperrfristen einzuhalten wiederholt das Amt ausübten: Bartholomeus Coli Scani (1354, 1355), Johannes
Ranieri (Damiani) Sudinis (1356), Nicolaus Fauglia (Anfang 1357, 1359), Pierus Sciosta (1362), Andreas de Veio

Den Luccheser Bürgern war es nach wiedererlangter Freiheit ein besonderes Anliegen, neben einer umfassenden Statutenrevision im Jahr 1372 auch neue Verfahrensordnungen für verschiedene Gerichte, darunter eine sehr ausführliche Ordnung für die *curia sindici maioris Lucani communis* zu erlassen. An dieser Statutenkommission waren unter anderem drei *doctores legum* beteiligt, die Anhänger eines städtischen Regiments *a popolo* waren und von den Richtern und Notaren der Stadt unterstützt wurden.[9] Wenn im Folgenden die 'Praxis' des Syndikatsprozesses auf mögliche kanonistische Parallelen und Einflüsse hin untersucht wird, sollen darunter diese statutarischen Quellen im Vergleich zu den normativen Anforderungen des römisch-kanonischen Prozeßrechts und der gelehrten Literatur verstanden werden. Eine exemplarische Untersuchung der gerichtlichen Syndikatspraxis anhand der überlieferten Akten aus Lucca muß einer umfangreicheren Studie vorbehalten bleiben.

Institution und Zuständigkeit des Syndikatsrichters

Die Ausgestaltung des Syndikatsprozesses ergibt nach den Quellen des gelehrten Rechts einerseits und den statutarischen oder sonstigen normativen Quellen andererseits ein höchst unterschiedliches Bild. Bereits die Zuständigkeiten waren vielschichtig und kompliziert verteilt.

a) Gelehrtes Recht: Selbständige Schriften zum Syndikatsprozeß sind erst aus dem späten 14. Jahrhundert erhalten, prägen aber zumeist die Vorstellungen vom Ablauf des Verfahrens. Danach war für Syndikatsprozesse stets ein höherer Richter zuständig, nämlich der *praefectus praetorio* des römischen Rechts, der übertragen auf die mittelalterliche Rechtswirklichkeit im weltlichen Bereich der Fürst *(princeps)*, im kirchlichen der Bischof oder ein von ihm delegierter Richter war. Doch schon Baldus de Ubaldis präzisierte: Da es im Italien seiner Zeit keine Prätorianerpräfekten mehr gab, sollte entweder der Nachfolger oder ein nach den jeweiligen Stadtstatuten gewählter Richter die Syndikatsfunktion ausüben.[10]

(1362, 1363), Raynerius de Sampantis (1368), Petrus Dellante (bis 1369). Als Kaiser Karl IV. im April 1369 Lucca endgültig von der Pisaner Herrschaft befreite, wurde der bisherige Pisaner Syndikatsrichter durch einen auswärtigen, Franciscus Remponi de Spadalunga aus Sanminiato, abgelöst. Im Übergangsjahr 1370 war mit Petrus de Dardagnini sogar ein Luccheser Syndikatsrichter und nicht, wie statutenmäßig vorgesehen, ein Richter aus einem mindestens 50 Meilen entfernten Ort.

9. Es handelt sich um die Doktoren Bartholomeus Forteguerra, Symon de Barga und Ludovicus Mercati. Zu ihrer Verankerung innerhalb der Popolarenpartei, C. Meek, *Lucca 1369–1400. Politics and Society in an Early Renaissance City-State* (Oxford 1978) 182 n. 17, 184, 196, 221.

10. Baldus de Ubaldis, 'Tractatus singularis in materia syndicatus extractus e commentariis in l. Observare § Proficisci, ff. de offi. procons.', in: *Tractatus de formatione libelli sindicatus*, hg. v. Sarayna (Venetiis 1586) fol. 2r–5v, fol. 2v n. 1b: 'Item quia istos prefectos pretorio hodie in Italia non habemus debet successor syndicare

b) Praxis kirchlicher Gerichtsbarkeit: Dem hierarchisch geprägten Grundmodell der Herrschaftskontrolle, etwa durch delegierte Richter, entsprach deutlich die kirchliche Disziplinargerichtsbarkeit und die weltliche Verwaltungspraxis im Kirchenstaat. Amtsverfehlungen hochrangiger Kleriker konnten durch delegierte Richter des Papstes verfolgt werden.[11] Für das Gebiet weltlicher Herrschaft der Päpste im *patrimonium Petri* läßt sich für das Herzogtum Spoleto 1333 ein Instrument der Herrschaftskontrolle nachweisen, das dem Syndikatsprozeß sachlich entsprach, auch wenn es nicht als Syndikatsprozeß bezeichnet wurde. Für den Fall, daß ein Podestà oder ein sonstiger Gerichtsbeamter einen Angeklagten zu Unrecht zum Tode, zu einer Leibesstrafe oder zur Arbeit in den Steinbrüchen verurteilte und damit in die Kompetenz des Gerichts des Rektoren eingriff, sollten sowohl der Podestà wie auch die ihn anstellende Stadt zu einer Geldstrafe verurteilt werden.[12] In den Ägidianischen Konstitutionen von 1357, die sich auf ein früheres Mandat Papst Bonifaz VIII. bezogen, ist von einer umfassenderen Syndikatsgerichtbarkeit die Rede. Alle *iudices, potestates, rectores et officiales quicumque* sollten sich nach Ablauf ihrer jeweiligen Amtszeiten im Provinzialgericht des Rektors einem Syndikatsprozeß unterziehen.[13] In allen drei Bereichen ist bei der Zuständigkeit

precessorem suum. Nam finito officio potest coram loci ordinario conveniri. [. . .] Hoc verum, nisi lex municipalis det formam quod syndicetur per alios bonos viros, nam preter illos deputatos nullus potest se intromittere'. Angelus de Ubaldis hielt für Syndikatsprozesse während der Amtszeit eines Amtsträgers grundsätzlich nur den *princeps, episcopus* oder einen von ihnen delegierten Richter für zuständig, nach Ablauf der Amtszeit, also im Regelfall des Syndikatsprozesses, zusätzlich noch *quilibet superior*, vgl. Angelus de Ubaldis, 'Tractatus de syndicatu', in: *Tractatus de formatione libelli sindicatus*, fol. 6r–6v, fol. 6ra n. 1. Von beiden Autoren stammen die frühesten bekannten Spezialuntersuchungen zum Syndikatsprozeß. Im 13. Jahrhundert hatte sich wohl schon Francesco d'Accursio mit diesem Thema in einem Traktat beschäftigt, der allerdings verloren ist und nur aufgrund von Zitaten bei Autoren des späten 15. und 16. Jahrhunderts rekonstruiert werden kann, vgl. A. Era, 'Un trattato disperso di Francesco d'Accursio', *Studi e memorie per la storia dell'università di Bologna* 11 (1933) 1–24.
11. Der exemplarische Fall einer Inquisition gegen den Bischof von Albi wegen angeblicher Amtspflichtverletzungen und sonstigen Verbrechen bei J. Théry, 'Les Albigeois et la procédure inquisitoire: Le procès pontifical contre Bernard de Castanet, évéque d'Albi et inquisiteur (1307–1308)', *Heresis* 33 (2000) 7–48. Ein Mandat Papst Benedikts XII. an den Rektor des Herzogtums Spoleto, eine Generalinquisition über alle denkbaren Verfehlungen von dessen Vorgänger, Petrus de Castaneto durchzuführen, sowie entsprechende Mandate an die Rektoren der Mark Ancona, der Toscana, Kampanien, Marittima, Romandiola und der Stadt Benevent über ihre Vorgänger unter dem vorherigen Papst Johannes XXII. zu inquirieren, in: *Codex diplomaticus dominii temporalis s. Sedis. Recueil de documents pour servir à l'histoire du gouvernement temporel des États du saint-Siège. Extraits des archives du Vatican* 2.12, ed. A. Theiner (2 Bde.; Rom 1861–62) 6b–7a (vom 15.9.1335). Klerikerexzesse und deren Bestrafung sind grundsätzlich in X 5.31, VI 5.6, Clem.5.6 geregelt, vgl. N. München, *Das kanonische Gerichtsverfahren und Strafrecht* (Köln und Neuß 1865) 721–24.
12. *Constitutiones Spoletani Ducatus a Petro de Castaneto edite (a. 1333)* 41–42, ed. T. Schmidt (Fonti per la storia d'Italia 113; Rom 1990) 140.
13. Vgl. das Mandat Papst Bonifaz' VIII. vom 6.9.1303, wonach sich alle Rektoren, Vikare, Marschälle, Richter, Notare und sonstige Beamte zehn Tage nach Ablauf ihrer Amtszeit im Gericht des Rektoren für Amtsverfehlungen verantworten sollten, *Codex diplomaticus dominii temporalis s. Sedis* 1.621, ed. Theiner 395a. Auf dieses Mandat bezieht sich auch die allgemeine Regelung des Syndikatsprozesses, der ausdrücklich so bezeichnet wird, in den Ägidianischen Konstitutionen von 1357. Dort findet sich erstmals eine genauere Regelung zum

eine gewisse Einheitlichkeit erkennbar. Es kann von einem vertikal organisierten Modell der Herrschaftskontrolle, also entlang den jeweiligen Hierarchien, gesprochen werden, das zunächst unregelmäßig und punktuell, in der zweiten Hälfte des 14. Jahrhunderts aber regelmäßig nach Beendigung eines Kirchenamtes durchgeführt werden sollte.

c) Kommunaler Bereich: Demgegenüber könnte man die institutionelle Stellung des Syndikatsrichters, wie sie sich ungefähr ab 1300 in den italienischen Kommunen herausbildete, als ein horizontales Kontrollsystem bezeichnen. Entweder war der für Syndikatsprozesse zuständige Richter ein Richter im Gefolge des neuen Podestà, der über die Amtsführung des vorherigen Podestà samt seiner gesamten Familie zu befinden hatte (so im Fall Bolognas oder Perugias), oder es gab (wie in Parma, Siena, Genua und Lucca) einen eigenen *maggior sindaco*, für dessen Wahl ähnliche Anforderungen wie an die Wahl des Podestà gestellt wurden. Er bildete damit ein institutionelles Gegengewicht zu diesem, war ihm jedoch nicht übergeordnet. In Lucca war der *maior sindicus* zudem der oberste Appellationsrichter. Die rechtliche Kontrolle aller in der Stadt ergangenen Gerichts- und Verwaltungsmaßnahmen lief an seinem Gericht zusammen. Der *maior sindicus* hatte weder institutionell noch rituell gegenüber den anderen wichtigen Institutionen in Lucca, etwa dem *vexillifer iustitie*, den Anzianen oder dem Podestà eine hervorgehobene Position. Nach den Statuten der Kommune von 1308 gab es den *maggior sindaco* zur allgemeinen Kontrolle der Amtsführung aller städtischen Amtsträger, während zur Überprüfung des Podestà ein eigener, auswärtiger Syndikatsrichter durch die Anzianen gewählt wurde. Beide Richter sollten nach einem nicht mehr erhaltenen *Constitutum maioris sindici* urteilen.[14] Schließlich konnten die Anzianen ein Verfahren gegen den für den Ankauf von Pferden zuständigen Beamten veranlassen und dafür eigens gewählte, einheimische Richter einsetzen.[15] Dieser Spezialfall, wie auch der regelmäßig stattfindende Syndikatsprozeß über den Podestà nach Ablauf von dessen Amtszeit, folgte weitgehend dem kirchlichen Modell eines einmaligen, zeitlich klar begrenzten, kurzen Untersuchungsprozesses.

Demgegenüber läßt sich in den allgemeinen Stadtstatuten von 1372 eine deutliche Tendenz zur Professionalisierung des Syndikatsrichters und zur Verstetigung seiner umfassenden Herrschaftskontrolle feststellen. Offensichtlich war es nach wiedererlangter 'republikanischer Freiheit' den Lucchesern besonders wichtig, die Kontroll-

---

Verfahrensablauf, *Costituzioni Egidiane dell'anno MCCCLVII* 2.22 ('De syndicatione officialium curie'), ed. P. Sella (Corpus statutorum italicorum 1; Rom 1912) 96–99, insbes. 96.12–15.

14. *Statuto del Comune di Lucca dell'anno MCCCVIII* 2.9 ('De modo et forma sindicandi Maius Lucanum Regimen et eius familiam et per quem'), ed. Bongi 58–60. So wurde der Syndikatsrichter nur tageweise für den innerhalb von fünf Tagen vorzubereitenden und in den folgenden zehn Tagen durchzuführenden Prozeß bezahlt und mußte auf eigene Kosten und Risiko anreisen. Er sollte pro Tag 3 fior. für sich und einen Notar erhalten.

15. Ibid. 5.25 ('De modo sindicandi officialem, cui commicetur officium de equitatoribus et equis cavallatarum'), ed. Bongi 313–14.

mechanismen von Herrschaft auf allen Ebenen auszubauen und zu präzisieren. Der Syndikatsrichter mußte nun ein *doctor legum* sein. Er war fest besoldet und erhielt samt seinem Gefolge während seiner durchgängigen Amtszeit von sechs Monaten 200£ Gehalt abzüglich Steuern. Er sollte die laufende Kontrolle aller einheimischen wie auswärtigen Beamten und Ratsherren (Anzianen) übernehmen, wie auch diejenige der gewählten Amtsträger nach Ablauf ihrer Amtszeit. Ferner sollte er aus einer mindestens 50 Meilen entfernten Stadt stammen, in den letzten drei Jahren kein Amt in Lucca bekleidet haben und während seiner Tätigkeit in Lucca keinen gesellschaftlichen Umgang mit der einheimischen Bevölkerung suchen.[16] Ähnlich wie für den Podestà war für den Syndikatsrichter somit eine hervorgehobene institutionelle Rolle vorgesehen. Der *maior sindicus* konnte nach Ablauf seiner turnusmäßigen Amtszeit von sechs Monaten durch den neuen Syndikatsrichter zur Rechenschaft gezogen werden, sofern er gegen den Amtseid verstoßen hatte, sein Amt *bene et legaliter* auszuüben.[17]

Ähnliche Bestimmungen finden sich für die ältesten gedruckten speziellen Statuten eines Syndikatsrichters bereits aus dem Jahr 1317 aus Parma.[18] In Parma wie in Lucca wurde der Syndikatsrichter von der gleichen Körperschaft beauftragt wie die Beamten, die er überprüfen sollte. Er war kein unangreifbares, oberstes Kontrollorgan. Insofern unterschied sich der kommunale Syndikatsrichter vom *princeps,* der nach der gelehrten Rechtswissenschaft der grundsätzlich zuständige Syndikatsrichter war, und auch vom päpstlich ernannten Rektor im *patrimonium Petri,* den Kardinal Albornoz in den Ägidianischen Konstitutionen als regelmäßigen Syndikatsrichter vorgesehen hatte.

---

16. Lucca, AS Statuti no. 6, Statuta communis Lucae a. 1372, c.26 ('De eleccione maioris sindici'), fol. 10v–11r.

17. Zum Amtseid des Syndikatsrichters ibid. c.1 ('De iuramento maioris sindici Lucani communis'), fol. 136r: 'Statuimus quod maior sindicus Lucani communis prima die introitus sui officii teneatur iurare in manibus vexilliferi iusticie corporaliter tactis scripturis ad sancta dei evangelia bona fide sine fraude quod ipse toto tempore sui officii sindicatus dictum officium et omnia ad dictum officium quomodolibet spectancia bene et legaliter et cum omni sollicitudine exercebit et toto posse salvare et custodire curabit et salvari et custodiri faciet hec et iura iurisdictiones et quecumque alia bona ad Lucanum commune quomodolibet spectancia vel que inantea ad Lucanum commune quomodolibet pertinere noscentur. Et observabit et observari faciet per quoscumque officiales Lucani communis hoc presens statutum et omnia alia statuta seu ordinamenta facta et fienda ad eius seu dictorum officialium officia spectancia secundum formam presentis statuti. Et contra predicta attemptantes procedet et puniet secundum formam statutorum et iuris'. Der *maior sindicus* samt seiner *familia* (ein Notar und fünf *familiares*) sollte seinerseits bei Amtspflichtverletzungen durch seinen Nachfolger oder durch eigens von den Anzianen zu wählende Richter syndiziert werden, ibid. c.17 ('Qualiter sindicus debeat sindicari et per quem'), fol. 138v.

18. *De officio sindaci generalis civitatis communis et populi Parmae,* ed. U. Benassi (Parma 1898) 9–10, 19 (Syndikatsprozeß gegen Podestà, *capitano del popolo,* Advokaten, *consules iusticie* und deren Notar sowie gegen alle Handwerker), 5–6 (Gehalt, *familia,* isoliertes Leben des Syndikatsrichters), 21 (Syndikatsprozeß gegen den Syndikatsrichter regelmäßig am Ende der Amtszeit durch einheimische Männer, die der große Rat eigens hierfür gewählt hatte).

Zu ahndende Amtsverfehlungen

Weitgehende Übereinstimmung bestand zwischen gelehrten Juristen und der kirchlichen wie städtischen Praxis darüber, welche Amtsverfehlungen und Verbrechen im Syndikatsverfahren verfolgt werden sollten.

a) Frühe gelehrte Autoren, wie Franciscus de Accursiis, dessen Position Angelus de Ubaldis anfangs des 15. Jahrhunderts als veraltet anführte, wollten die *officiales* im Syndikatsprozeß ausschließlich für Bestechlichkeit *(barataria)*, Diebstahl und Unterschlagung *(furtum)* haften lassen.[10] Andere Stimmen, vor allem Baldus de Ubaldis, dehnten die Haftung aus. Baldus hielt daneben vor allem Fehler der Rechtsprechungstätigkeit für überprüfbar. Er erwog ausführlich, ob ein Podestà strafrechtlich oder nur zivilrechtlich für Amtsvergehen der Angehörigen seiner *familia*—also seines Verwaltungs- und Rechtsprechungsstabes—haftete, ferner ob er nur für absichtliche oder auch für fahrlässige Amtsverstöße haftbar gemacht werden konnte. Schließlich grenzte Baldus Amtsdelikte im eigentlichen Sinn von allgemeinen Delikten ab, die während der Amtszeit begangen worden waren, zum Beispiel den Totschlag durch einen *berroarius*.[20]

b) Im kirchlichen Bereich lassen sich schon früh Inquisitionsverfahren gegen hochrangige Kleriker nachweisen, die wegen allgemeiner moralischer Vergehen und spezieller Amtsdelikte, die die Untergebenen belasteten, verfolgt werden konnten.[21] Die Fülle der denkbaren Tatbestände dürfte auf den umfassenden Amtsbegriff der Kirche zurückzuführen sein. Im Kirchenrecht war Bestechung des Richters seit Gratian aufgrund der Verwandtschaft zur Simonie ein streng geahndetes Vergehen. Die Dekretalisten verwendeten große Mühe darauf, die Bestechung von zulässigen Gebührenzahlungen und Aufwandsentschädigungen abzugrenzen, oder danach zu fragen, ob

---

19. Era, 'Un trattato disperso' 20 n. 136; Angelus de Ubaldis, 'Tractatus sindicatus', fol. 6r n. 2, zitiert die ältere Ansicht als Meinung von *quidam*, unter anderem von Ricardus Malumbra. Er selbst vertrat im Gefolge von Azo das Gegenteil: 'Sed veritas est in contrarium quia imo de quolibet commisso potest syndicari'.

20. Baldus de Ubaldis, 'Tractatus sindicatus', fol. 2va n. 2: 'Quaero de quibus rebus syndicetur? Respondeo, de commissis pretextu officii, puta de sententiis male latis et de baratariis et similibus'. Zur Haftung für *dolus* und *culpa* im Syndikatsverfahren, sowie zur Bedeutung der Justizfehler allgemein, Engelmann, *Wiedergeburt der Rechtskultur in Italien* 354–405.

21. Théry, 'Les Albigeois et la procédure inquisitoire' 25–30. Bernard de Castanet wurde beispielsweise angeklagt, ein Rebell gegen den Papst zu sein, sich persönlich bereichert und Kirchengut verschleudert, durch unrechtmäßige Verhaftungen die Albigenser terrorisiert, in seinen Gefängnissen Menschen zu Tode gefoltert, unliebsame Diener vergiftet und die Sexualpraktiken seiner Schäflein unter Bruch des Beichtgeheimnisses ausgeforscht zu haben. Er selbst habe unter Bruch seiner Gelübde verschiedene Beziehungen unterhalten, weibliche Gefangene zum Geschlechtsverkehr gezwungen und keine Gottesdienste abgehalten. Bonifaz VIII. trug 1303 den Provinzialrektoren noch vergleichsweise unspezifisch auf, die Amtsführung der Beamten im Kirchenstaat 'super calumpniis, concussionibus et aliis delictis et contractibus suis' zu untersuchen, *Codex diplomaticus s. Sedis* 1.621, ed. Theiner 395.

jede Bestechung oder nur eine, die zu einem fehlerhaften Urteil führte, strafbar sei.[22] In den normativen kirchlichen Quellen des 14. Jahrhunderts läßt sich demgegenüber eine zunehmende Differenzierung der Amtsvergehen beobachten. Insbesondere verstanden die Päpste nun darunter *venalitas iustitie, extortio* und allgemein *gravari subditos*.[23] Mit den Ägidianischen Konstitutionen von 1357, also für den Bereich der weltlichen Herrschaft im Kirchenstaat, wurden die zentralen Amtsdelikte definiert und eine umfassende Kontrolle der gesamten Amtstätigkeit vorgesehen. So verwundert es nicht, daß erstmals für die Verwaltung des Kirchenstaates auch von einem Syndikatsprozeß gegen kirchliche Funktionsträger gesprochen wird.[24]

c) Im städtischen Bereich, etwa in den Statuten von Lucca aus dem Jahr 1308, wurde als wichtigstes vom *maior sindicus* zu überprüfendes und gegebenenfalls zu bestrafendes Delikt das Fordern oder Empfangen von Geld über das feste Gehalt hinaus definiert. Daneben sollte die genaue Beachtung des Amtseides sowie aller städtischen Statuten durch die Beamten überprüft werden, wie sie allgemein und in zahlreichen Einzelbestimmungen zu den *officia* festgesetzt worden waren. Die wichtigsten Strafandrohungen für Amtspflichtverletzungen des Podestà wurden im dritten Buch der Statuten im Rahmen seiner Rechtsprechungsaufgaben niedergelegt.[25] Vergleichbar findet

---

22. R. Helmholz, 'Money and Judges in the Law of the Medieval Church', in: *The University of Chicago Law School Roundtable—A Journal of Interdisciplinary Legal Studies* 8 (2001) 309–23. Die Glossatoren des römischen Rechts diskutierten die Frage der Richterbezahlung und die Abgrenzung zur Korruption höchst facettenreich, vor allem im Hinblick auf die Strafbarkeit des Bestechenden, vgl. M. Lucchesi, 'Giustizia e corruzione nel pensiero dei glossatori', RSDI 64 (1991) 157–216.

23. Im Mandat Benedikts XII. von 1335 wurden die typischen Amtsvergehen, in der kirchlichen Terminologie als *excessus* bezeichnet, genauer umschrieben als 'gravando subditos indebite, vel extorsiones seu prava et illicita munera recipiendo', *Codex diplomaticus s. Sedis* 2.12, ed. Theiner 6b.

24. Die *Costituzioni Egiziane* 2.22 ('De syndicatione officialium curie'), ed. Sella 98.2–6, ließen die Anklage oder Beschwerde von Privatpersonen zu, 'qui sciverint aliquam baractariam, venalitatem iusticie aut iniquam et illicitam extorsionem seu lucrum factum per talem officialem tempore sui officii', und statuierten erstmals, ibid. 98.25–28, die generelle Überprüfung der Amtsführung im Inquisitionsverfahren 'contra officiales, qui sindicantur, de omnibus et singulis que administrassent, gessissent seu fecissent in eorum officiis et occasione ipsorum officiorum tempore, maxime illicite extorquendo vel illicita percipiendo'.

25. *Statuto del Comune di Lucca dell'anno MCCCVIII* 2.9 ('De modo et forma sindicandi Maius Lucanum Regimen et eius familiam et per quem'), ed. Bongi 59–60: 'Et quod dictum Lucanum Regimen et dicti eius socii, iudices, berroari et familiares possint et debeant sindicari de omni eo quod aliquis eorum receperit, vel alius pro eis vel aliquot eorum, ultra eorum et cuiusque suum salaria, que habere debent, tam ex forma suarum licterarum, quam ex forma alicuius capituli Constituti. [. . .] Et etiam sindicari possint et debeant de omnibus aliis et singulis, de quibus sindicari possunt et debent ex forma alicuius Statui vel iuramenti ipsius'. Einzeln statuierte, syndizierbare Amtspflichten des Podestà waren zum Beispiel, daß er und seine gesamte *familia* guelfisch sein mußten (ibid. 2.1, ed. 53), er kein Pferd auf Kosten der Kommune halten durfte (2.4, ed. 56), alle Anweisungen der Anzianen und Prioren befolgen mußte (2.7, ed. 57–58), nur Notare einsetzen durfte, die fünf Jahre studiert hatten und die übrigen persönlichen Anforderungen erfüllten (2.61, ed. 113), nicht unrechtmäßig zur Folter griff und innerhalb von zwei Monaten in Strafverfahren ein Urteil fällte (3.2, ed. 135), und daß er sich nicht in die Zuständigkeiten des *capitaneus populi* einmischte, ebensowenig wie dieser sich in diejenigen des

sich in den Statuten des Syndikatsrichters in Parma von 1312 der Kernbestand der zu syndizierenden Delikte des Podestà und seines Rechtsstabes, nämlich *barataria* und *extortio*, allgemein ausgeweitet zu 'de omni gesto neglecto vel obmisso eorum'.[26] Parallel zur Entwicklung im kirchlichen Bereich wurde in den Luccheser Statuten von 1372 eine umfassendere, allgemeine Kontrolle rechtmäßiger Amtsführung angeordnet:[27]

Et maior sindicus teneatur et ad eius officium spectet sindicare ancianos et vexilliferum iusticie Lucani communis de hiis omnibus que fecerint contra formam eorum electionis et officii et statutorum deposito officio ancianatus [. . .]. Et omnes singulos alios officiales cives et se pro officialibus se gerentes intus civitatem et extra tam ordinarios quam extraordinarios et eorum familias de omnibus baractariis furtis et illicite ablatis et aliis quibuscumque factis commissis omissis et neglectis contra formam statutorum et aliis quibuscumque commissis tempore dicti sui officii sindicatus et ante per annum si officium talis officialis fuerit annuale vel per sex menses si tale officium fuerit semestre. Et eciam debeat sindicare quoscumque officiales per aliquas communitates Lucani territorii electos de furtis et illicite receptis infra annum a die deposito officii. Et predicta omnia vendicent sibi locum in officialibus forensibus seu per officialibus se gerentibus.

Dazu kamen weitere Vorschriften, durch die sich die Stellung des Syndikatsrichters zu einem allgemeinen Wahrer des öffentlichen Interesses verdichtete. So wurde ihm etwa aufgetragen, das unter der pisanischen Herrschaft verloren gegangene Eigentum der Kommune zurück zu gewinnen, für eine ordnungsgemäße Aktenführung durch die Notare und ihre Aktenablieferungspflichten an die *camera Communis*, also das Archiv der Stadt, zu sorgen, oder Mißbräuche in den Gefängnissen zu unterbinden und regelmäßig die öffentliche Anwesenheit der Beamten an ihrem Tätigkeitsort zu überprüfen.[28]

Podestà einmischen durfte (2.135, ed. 219). *Berroari* waren verpflichtet, gebannte Schuldner und Verbrecher aufzugreifen (ebd.); gewählte Notare und Beamte mußten ihr Amt persönlich ausüben (2.18, ed. 81–82); Vikare, *capitanei*, Richter, Notare und Kämmerer erwartete das Syndikatsverfahren, wenn sie jenseits der engen Voraussetzungen der Statuten gefoltert hatten (2.30, ed. 89–91).

26. *De officio sindaci generalis Parmae*, ed. Benassi 9; einheimische Advokaten, *consules iustitie* und deren Notare sollten daraufhin überprüft werden, 'si in dictis eorum officiis commiserunt vel fecerint aliquid ultra vel aliter quam contineatur in statutis communis [. . .] et maxime de extorsionibus et concussionibus, oppressionibus, illicitis lucris', ibid. 10.

27. Lucca, AS Statuti no. 6, Statuta curie sindici communis Lucani a. 1372, c.3 ('Qualiter maior sindicus debeat sindicare'), fol. 136r. Die allgemeine Verpflichtung aller Beamten, sich mit ihren Gehältern zufrieden zu geben und nichts zusätzlich zu verlangen, also das Verbot von Bestechlichkeit und Erpressung wurde nochmals eigens festgeschrieben, ibid. c.13 ('Qualiter quilibet officialis debeat esse contentus salario sibi statuto et de pena contrafaciencium seu delinquencium in officio'), fol. 134v/138r.

28. Ibid. c.6 ('De avere Lucane communis per maiorem sindicum recuperando'), fol. 136v; c.25 ('De officio sindici circa carceratos'), fol. 139v; c.29 ('Quod quilibet notarius et officialis teneatur consignare et dimittere libros et acta in eius officio descripta custodi camere Lucani communis'), fol. 148r–v; c.18 ('Quod officiales et castellani stare teneantur in eorum officio vel castelanario'), fol. 138v–139r.

Im 15. Jahrhundert scheinen in den italienischen Kommunen zunehmend Policey-funktionen zu den Aufgaben des *maggior sindaco* hinzugekommen zu sein. Sie ließen seine Kontrollfunktion über die Amtsführung aller städtischen Beamten allmählich in den Hintergrund treten. So wurde der *maggior sindaco* in Lucca für die korrekte Landvermessung zuständig. Auch Streitigkeiten von Kommunen und Körperschaften im Luccheser Herrschaftsbereich um die richtige steuerliche Veranschlagung *(estimo)* fielen fortan in seinen Kompetenzbereich.[29]

Einleitung des Syndikatsverfahrens

Der wichtigste Faktor, um den Syndikatsprozeß zu einem effizienten Mittel der Herrschaftskontrolle zu gestalten, war die Zeit. Das Verfahren schnell einzuleiten und abzuwickeln mußte der oberste Grundsatz aller Statutengeber sein. Kirchliche wie auch städtische Verwaltungsexperten sollten und wollten schnellstmöglich neue Aufgaben, meist an anderen Orten, wahrnehmen und nicht durch die Rechtfertigung ihrer Amtsführung festgehalten werden.

a) Fristen zur Einleitung und Durchführung des Verfahrens: Bereits im frühen Mandat Bonifaz' VIII. an die Provinzialrektoren, alle Vikare, Richter, Notare und übrigen Beamten auf ihre Amtsführung hin zu überprüfen, war eine kurze Frist von zehn Tagen unmittelbar nach Beendigung des jeweiligen Amtes vorgesehen.[30] In den italienischen Kommunen des 14. Jahrhunderts schwankten die Fristen zwischen drei (Parma) und fünfzehn Tagen (Florenz), innerhalb derer das gesamte Syndikatsverfahren bis zum Endurteil durchgeführt sein sollte.[31] Nach den Luccheser Statuten von 1308 konnte die zehntägige Syndikatsfrist auf fünf Tage reduziert und der Podestà bereits nach dieser Zeit entlastet werden, soweit keine Klagen von Privatleuten gegen ihn vorgebracht wurden. Andernfalls mußte innerhalb von zehn Tagen ein Urteil ergehen.[32] In den Ägidianischen Konstitutionen von 1357 wurde vermutlich aus Praktikabilitätsgründen

29. *Statuti di Lucca a. 1536* (Lucca 1539) 3.16 ('Dello arbitrio conceduto al signore maggior sindico della citta di Lucca circa le misure delle terre'), fol. 145v; ibid. 5.35 ('Delle questioni che vertissero per cagione delle gravezze, che simpongano dalla Citta di Lucca'), fol. 287v–288r. In Siena hatte der *maggior sindaco* bereits im 15. Jahrhundert die Zuständigkeit, gegen Übertretungen von Luxusvorschriften und Qualitätsanforderungen der Zünfte vorzugehen, vgl. *Un magistrato scomodo: Il Maggior Sindaco nello statuto del 1422*, ed. L. Pagni und S. Vaccara (Siena 1986) 251–336, 268–85.

30. *Codex diplomaticus s. Sedis* 1.571, ed. Theiner 395a.

31. Dahm, *Strafrecht Italiens* 73–75; differenzierter zu einzelnen Fristanforderungen Engelmann, *Wiedergeburt der Rechtskultur in Italien* 567–74. In Parma sollten Bestechlichkeit und Erpressung seitens des Podestà oder des *capitano del populo* sogar innerhalb von drei Tagen, nachdem die Delikte dem Syndikatsrichter bekannt geworden waren, verfolgt werden, alle übrigen Verstöße gegen die Statuten auch durch andere Richter innerhalb von fünf Tagen, *De officio sindaci generalis Parmae*, ed. Benassi 9–10.

32. *Statuto del Comune di Lucca dell'anno MCCCVIII* 2.9 ('De modo et forma sindicandi Maius Lucanum Regimen et eius familiam'), ed. Bongi 59.

bei den Prozeßfristen eine Differenzierung vorgesehen, die sich nach der Amtszeit des überprüften Beamten richtete. War ein Beamter nur sechs Monate im Amt gewesen, sollte der Syndikatsprozeß innerhalb von zehn Tagen abgeschlossen sein. Bei einer sechsmonatigen bis einjährigen Amtszeit sollte er innerhalb von fünfzehn Tagen enden. In Fällen längerer Amtstätigkeit war der immer noch recht kurze Zeitraum von zwanzig Tagen vorgesehen.[33] Eine Differenzierung sahen die späteren speziellen Statuten des Syndikatsrichters in Lucca vor. Für auswärtige Beamte, die entlastet werden mußten, blieb es bei der kurzen Frist von fünf Tagen, innerhalb derer aller Beschwerden gesammelt werden sollten—bei auswärtigen Beamten, die im *contado* von Lucca tätig waren, sogar nur drei Tage—und weiterer zehn Tagen, um das Syndikatsverfahren abzuschließen. Handelte es sich nicht um auswärtige Beamte, waren längere Fristen vorgesehen. Für einheimische *officiales* wie die nur zwei Monate lang tätigen Anzianen, und den *vexillifer iustitie* sollte ein Syndikatsprozeß innerhalb von 15 Tagen eingeleitet und innerhalb von zwei Monaten abgeschlossen sein. Bei den im Territorium von Lucca tätigen einheimischen Amtsträgern, beispielsweise den Vikaren, wurde die Frist für die Durchführung eines Syndikatsprozesses auf ein Jahr verlängert.[34]

Diese statutarischen Fristen scheinen auch Angelus de Ubaldis vor Augen gestanden zu haben, als er überlegte, ob eine Frist von zehn Tagen für Syndikatsverfahren gegen einen Podestà bei einer kürzeren Amtsdauer als sechs Monaten, zum Beispiel von nur drei Monaten, proportional zur abgeleisteten Amtszeit abgekürzt werden könne. Angelus lehnte mit der Begründung ab: 'Dicas quod non, quia esset impossibile syndicatoribus revide[re] omnia acta, cum forte illis tribus mensibus possent evenisse plures quaestiones magni ponderis'.[35]

Demgegenüber ging sein Bruder Baldus de Ubaldis von erheblich längeren Fristen aus, möglicherweise mit dem Ziel, in Prozessen, die gravierende Folgen für die Amtsträger mit sich bringen konnten, die Rechte der angeklagten Beamten besser zu schützen. Gestützt auf antike römische Quellen überging er Effizienzbedürfnisse, die die weltliche wie kirchliche Praxis in der besonderen Verfahrensart des Syndikatsprozesses vorausgesetzt hatte. So ging er davon aus, daß *libelli querimoniarum* von durch rechtswidrige Amtshandlungen betroffenen Bürgern innerhalb von acht Tagen vorgebracht werden konnten, deren Zustellung innerhalb von 25 Tagen erfolgen und der Prozeß innerhalb von 50 Tagen beendet sein sollte, im Bedarfsfall aber auch noch später abgeschlossen werden konnte.[36]

---

33. *Costituzioni Egidiane* 2.22 ('De sindicatione officialium curie'), ed. Sella 96.27–97.2.

34. Lucca, AS Statuti no. 6, Statuta curie sindici communis Lucani a. 1372, c.3 ('Qualiter maior sindicus debeat sindicare'); c.4 ('De modo et forma sindicandi officiales forenses'), fol. 136r–v.

35. Angelus de Ubaldis, 'Tractatus sindicatus' fol. 6vb n. 9.

36. Baldus de Ubaldis, 'Tractatus sindicatus' fol. 2vb n. 3; möglicherweise ging er dabei vom regulären

b) Einleitung durch *accusatio, querela, denunciatio, inquisitio:* Der Inquisitionsprozeß war im Kirchenrecht durch Innozenz III. Anfang des 13. Jahrhunderts eingeführt worden. Dahinter stand das Ziel, Verbrechen hoch stehender Kleriker leichter verfolgen zu können, indem Beweishürden im Akkusationsverfahren, etwa das Erfordernis von 72 Belastungszeugen gegen Bischöfe, entfielen und der Ankläger von den Risiken der Kalumnienstrafe bei scheiternder Anklage freigestellt wurde. Der Ankläger wurde zum bloßen *denunciator*, dessen Aussage der Richter *ex officio* zu berücksichtigen hatte.[37] Während im weltlichen Strafrecht das Akkusationsverfahren weiterhin als Regelfall betrachtet wurde, trat das Inquisitionsverfahren im kirchlichen Bereich seinen Siegeszug an.[38] In der kirchlichen und weltlichen Praxis des hier vorgestellten Verfahrens zur Kontrolle von Herrschaft war das Inquisitionsverfahren das Mittel der Wahl. Benedikt XII., möglicherweise auch schon Bonifaz VIII., stand noch ausschließlich das disziplinierende, durch den Papst angeordnete Moment dieses Verfahrens vor Augen, wenn er eine gründliche Untersuchung der Amtsführung der päpstlichen Provinzialrektoren anordnete. In ihm sollte zunächst erforscht werden, ob es zu Exzessen kirchlicher Amtsträger gekommen war.[39] Anschließend sollte durch Spezialinquisition gegen einzelne bekannt gewordene Vergehen vorgegangen werden.[40] Möglicherweise beeinflußt von der städtischen Praxis des Syndikatsprozesses wurde in den Ägidianischen Konstitutionen erstmals auch die *querela* einzelner Bürger zwecks Verfahrenseinleitung vorgesehen.[41] In den italienischen Kommunen war es dem Syndikatsrichter aufgegeben, sorgfältig alle denkbaren Amtspflichtverletzungen zu inquirieren. Zugleich aber wurde durch aus-

---

kirchlichen Prozeßrecht aus, das eine maximale Verfahrensdauer von zwei Jahren in Straf- und von drei Jahren in Zivilsachen vorsah, ibid. fol. 3ra n. 4.

37. R. Knox, 'Accusing Higher Up', ZRG Kan. Abt. 77 (1991) 1–31; L. Kéry, 'Inquisitio-denunciatio-exceptio. Möglichkeiten der Verfahrenseinleitung im Dekretalenrecht', ZRG Kan. Abt. 87 (2001) 226–68.

38. H. Kantorowicz, *Albertus Gandinus und das Strafrecht der Scholastik* (2 Bde.; Berlin und Leipzig 1907–26) 2.3–6 n. 3–4, listet die Fälle, in denen das Strafverfahren ausnahmsweise durch Inquisition eingeleitet wurde; zum inquisitorischen Strafprozeß überblicksartig S. Lepsius, *Von Zweifeln zur Überzeugung. Der Zeugenbeweis im gelehrten Recht ausgehend von der Abhandlung des Bartolus von Sassoferrato* (Frankfurt/M. 2003) 9–12.

39. Bonifaz VIII. hatte angeordnet, die Vikare, Marschälle, Richter und Notare sollten sich nach Ablauf ihrer Amtszeit im Gericht des Rektors zur Überprüfung ihrer Amtsführung bereithalten; den Verfahrensablauf legte er nicht fest, vgl. *Codex diplomaticus s. Sedis* 1.671, ed. Theiner 395a; Benedikt XII. ordnete ein effizientes, aber nicht genauer bestimmtes Disziplinarverfahren an: 'Ac officialium et aliorum corrigendis excessibus destinandum providimus [. . .] ut facilius et celerius possit ad correctionem predictam, prout rationis suaserit equitas, procedere, studeas fideliter assignare', vgl. *Codex diplomaticus s. Sedis* 2.21, ed. Theiner 7a.

40. Vgl. die Spezialinquisition gegen Bernard de Castanet, Bischof von Albi, oben Anm. 21.

41. 'Sindici in prima medietate temporis sindicatus inquirant de omnibus que habent inquirenda et querelas recipiant ab omnibus volentibus querelare contra officiales, qui sindicantur, de omnibus et singulis que administrassent, gessissent seu fecissent in eorum officiis et occasione ipsorum officiorum tempore', *Constituzioni Egidiane* 22, ed. Sella 98.23–27; Petrus de Castanet hatte in den Statuten für das Herzogtum Spoleto als Vorläufer der Ägidianischen Konstitutionen Strafen für spezifische Amtsdelikte festgelegt, jedoch keine Anordnungen für das Verfahren getroffen, *Constitutiones Spoletani ducatus* 41–42, ed. Schmidt 140.

gefeilte Maßnahmen auch ein eigenes Beschwerderecht der Bürger vorgesehen. Durch öffentliche Ausrufer wurden in der Stadt an fünf aufeinander folgenden Tagen alle Bürger aufgerufen, zu einem bestimmten Termin ihre Beschwerden gegen auswärtige Beamten nach Ablauf von deren Amtszeit vorzubringen. Es ist daher in den Statuten von Parma und Lucca nebeneinander von *inquirere, denunciatio* und *petitio* die Rede.[42]

Die Bürger vor unrechtmäßigen Amtshandlungen des Podestà, seines Verwaltungsstabes und einheimischer Beamten zu schützen, scheint im städtischen Bereich eine wichtigere Motivation für die Statutengeber gewesen zu sein als im kirchlichen. Besonders deutlich wird dies an den einzigartig ausführlichen Bestimmungen des *maior sindicus* in Lucca von 1372 zur *denuncia gravaminis inferendi* und der *querela gravaminis illati*. Bereits während der Amtszeit eines Beamten konnte sich ein Bürger gegen bevorstehende unrechtmäßige Eingriffe schützen, indem er sich an den *maior sindicus* wandte, vortrug, inwieweit der geplante Eingriff des Amtsträgers statutenwidrig war, und ein Mandat *(remissio de observancia iurium et statutorum)* des *maior sindicus* an den Ausgangsbeamten erwirkte, sich recht- und statutenmäßig zu verhalten. In Strafsachen, die einen unumkehrbar belastenden Eingriff erwarten ließen, mußte sich der Ausgangsbeamte an die Verfügung des *maior sindicus* halten, in anderen Fällen konnte er bei seinem Eingriff bleiben. Er mußte allerdings dessen spätere Überprüfung durch den *maior sindicus* ausdrücklich zulassen. Daraufhin konnte der belastete Bürger innerhalb von zwei oder drei Gerichtstagen *(dies utiles)* die eigentliche Klage beim Syndikatsrichter einlegen, über die dieser innerhalb von 25 oder, in Strafsachen, 15 Tagen zu entscheiden hatte. Der *maior sindicus* sollte eine Geldstrafe gegen den Beamten verhängen, wenn sich dieser über die *remissio* hinweggesetzt hatte.[43]

Aufgrund des typologisch horizontalen Verfahrens des Syndikatsrichters im städtischen Bereich scheint es zu einer stärkeren Zweigleisigkeit des Verfahrens gekommen zu sein als im kirchlichen Bereich. Auch in Lucca wurde klargestellt, daß ein Bürger, der Beschwerden gegen einen Beamten vorzubringen hatte, keine Bürgen

---

42. *De officio sindaci generalis Parmae,* ed. Benassi 9 *(inquirere* und *denunciacio); Statuto del Comune di Lucca dell'anno MCCCVIII* c.9 ('De modo et forma sindicandi Maius Lucanum Regimen et eius familiam et per quem'), ed. Bongi 59: *petitio* und *denuncia;* Lucca, AS Statuti no. 6, Statuta curie sindici communis Lucani a. 1372, c.4 ('De modo et forma sindicandi officiales forenses'), fol. 136v: *petitio* und *querela* im Rahmen der *inquisicio; ibid.* c.29 ('Quod quilibet notarius et officialis teneatur consignare et dimittere libros et acta in eius officio descripta custodi camere Lucani communis'), fol. 140r–v: *denuncia* oder *inquisitio* gegen Notare und Beamte, die ihre Akten nicht an das Archiv der Stadt ablieferten. Zu vereinfachten Möglichkeiten, Syndikatsverfahren einzuleiten, mit zahlreichen weiteren Statuten, Engelmann, *Wiedergeburt der Rechtskultur in Italien* 526–34.

43. Lucca, AS Statuti no. 6, Statuta curie sindici communis Lucani a. 1372, c.7 ('De eo quod maior sindicus teneatur mandare quibuscumque officialibus observanciam statutorum et iurium'); c.8 ('De remissione mandati'); c.9 ('De tempore infra quod debet querela exponi coram sindico post gravamen illatum'); c.10 ('De eo quod querela gravaminis illati post denumpciam factam seu remissam seu inferendi debeat certo tempore terminari'); c.11 ('De modo et forma procedendi super denumpciis et querelis'), fol. 136v, 134r–v.

stellen mußte und höchstens zu den Kosten des Verfahrens, nicht jedoch zu einer Kalumnienstrafe verurteilt werden konnte, wenn sich seine Vorwürfe gegen den Beamten
als unrichtig erwiesen.[44] Damit wurde der im Inquisitionsverfahren selbstverständliche
Effekt erneut festgeschrieben, daß der Kläger, also der sich beschwerende Bürger, kein
Risiko bei der Klage tragen sollte.

In der gelehrten Literatur fanden die unterschiedlichen Arten zur Einleitung des
Syndikatsverfahrens kaum Beachtung. Während sich Angelus de Ubaldis gar nicht
äußerte, erörterte Baldus zunächst, ob eine unspezifische Generalinquisition wie sie
im Syndikatsverfahren notwendig erfolge, überhaupt zulässig sei. Er bejahte dies und
fragte anschließend, ob schon im Rahmen der Generalinquisition eine Verurteilung erfolgen könne, soweit die Anschuldigungen erwiesen wurden, also ohne daß zuvor eine
förmliche Spezialinquisition bezüglich eines bestimmten Ortes und einer bestimmten
Tat eingeleitet worden war. Baldus hielt eine Verurteilung zumindest dann für zulässig, wenn es um eine Generalinquisition im Allgemeininteresse ging; soweit aber ein
Beamter einem verletzten Bürger gegenüber zur Strafzahlung verurteilt werden sollte,
war zusätzlich eine Spezialinquisition mit entsprechend sorgfältigeren Verfahrensan-
forderungen angezeigt.[45]

Durchführung des Syndikatsprozesses—
Das summarische Verfahren

Eine weitere Verfahrensbeschleunigung konnte das summarische Verfahren zur
Kontrolle der Amtstätigkeit erbringen. Gegenüber dem normalen *ordo iudiciarius*
handelte es sich um ein Ausnahmeverfahren, in dem auf bestimmte Verfahrensschritte
verzichtet oder zumindest einzelne Termine zusammengefaßt werden konnten.

a) Grundlagen und Entwicklung: Ebenso wie das Inquisitionsverfahren war auch der
summarische Prozeß als einheitlicher Verfahrenstyp maßgeblich durch das kanonische
Recht geprägt. Die Wurzeln des spätmittelalterlichen summarischen Verfahrens lassen
sich bereits im klassischen und spätantiken römischen Recht nachweisen, so etwa,
soweit nur ein vorläufiges Urteil ergehen sollte, in den gesenkten Beweisanforderungen,

---

44. Ibid. c.22 ('De accusacione seu denunpcia recipienda per sindicum non prestita fideiubsione'), fol. 139v.
Der *maior sindicus* konnte hiernach Bürger, die wissentlich falsche Anklagen erhoben, zu einer statutarischen
Strafe verurteilen.

45. Baldus de Ubaldis, 'Tractatus sindicatus' fol. 3vb n. 5: 'Sicut in civilibus est dare generalem actionem
domino contra suum gestorem, sic et reipublicae contra suum rectorem: et sicut ex probatis super generali
actione sequitur specialis condemnatio, ita et super inquisitione generali. Sed adverte, rector civitatis tenetur
generali iudicio domino suo, idest, universitati, seu civitati, particularibus autem, quos laesit, tenetur singulari
iudicio: quo ergo ad publicam penam procedit efficaciter inquisitio generalis, sed quo ad privata commoda non
procedit, nisi incidenter'.

die als *summatim cognoscere* bezeichnet wurden. Zudem konnte auf ein förmliches Klaglibell verzichtet werden und generell war die Schriftlichkeit des Verfahrens nicht so stark ausgebildet.[46] Durch päpstliche Dekretalen und deren Interpretation durch die Dekretalisten kamen weitere Möglichkeiten der Verfahrensbeschleunigung hinzu, beispielsweise daß Verhandlungen auch an Ferien- und Feiertagen stattfinden konnten, zumindest an solchen weniger feierlichen Festtagen, die lediglich zu Ehren der Menschen eingeführt worden waren; zudem konnte der Richter sein Urteil auch ohne feierlich zu Gericht zu sitzen verkünden *(de plano)*.[47] Umfassend geregelt wurden die einzelnen Bestandteile des summarischen Verfahrens in der Konstitution 'Sacpc' (Clem.5.11.2). Sie brachte das summarische Verfahren auf eine zusammenfassende Formel. Johannes Andreae führte in seiner Glossierung aus, es handele sich um ein Verfahren 'simpliciter et de plano ac sine strepitu et figura iudicii'. Zwischen den einzelnen Bestandteilen des summarischen Verfahrens wurde hinfort nicht mehr unterschieden. Die Formel fand fast zeitgleich Eingang in das weltliche Recht durch das Gesetz Kaiser Heinrichs VII. 'Ad reprimendum' von 1313 zur Bekämpfung von Rebellen und Majestätsverbrechern, das seine Standardkommentierung durch Bartolus von Sassoferrato erfuhr. Johannes Andreae und Bartolus beschäftigte hauptsächlich die Frage, welche Anforderungen des *ordo iudiciarius* zu den *substantialia iudicii* gehörten. Die von ihnen herausgearbeiteten *substantialia* waren selbst im summarischen Verfahren unverzichtbar, um die Rechte der beklagten Partei oder Angeklagten nicht unzulässig einzuschränken. Insbesondere mußte auch im summarischen Verfahren der Beklagte ordnungsgemäß geladen werden und Möglichkeiten zur Verteidigung haben.[48] Beide erwähnten in ihren langen Kommentaren das spezielle Verfahren des Syndikatsprozesses nicht. Für das kanonische Recht war dies insofern nachvollziehbar, als nach der Konstitution 'Dispendiosam' (Clem.2.1.2) von 1312 die einheitliche Formel für das summarische Verfahren in päpstlichen *littere missorie* auf Pfründenangelegenheiten, Besetzungen von kirchlichen Ämtern, Ehe-, Wucher- und Zehntfragen, jedoch nicht auf Strafverfahren anwendbar schien. In der Rechtsprechung der römischen *Rota* kam

46. M. v. Bethmann-Hollweg, *Der römische Civilprozess 3: Cognitiones* (Bonn 1866) 342–49; W. Litewski, *Der römisch-kanonische Zivilprozess nach den älteren ordines iudiciarii* (2 Bde.; Krakau 1999) 2.564–66; C. Lefebvre, 'Les origines romaines de la procédure sommaire aux XIIᵉ et XIIIᵉ siècles', *Ephemerides juris canonici* 12 (1956) 149–97.

47. Nach Johannes Fasolus, dem ersten Autoren, der sich monographisch mit dem summarischen Verfahren beschäftigte, sollte dieses *de plano*-Verfahren, in dem auch die Diskussionen der Anwälte möglichst abgekürzt werden sollten, nur in leichten Strafsachen zulässig sein, *De summariis cognitionibus*, ed. Wahrmund, *Quellen* 4.5.9–12. Zur Bedeutung des römischen Rechts für die frühen Dekretalisten, Lefebvre, 'Les origines romaines de la procédure sommaire' 174–77.

48. Die 'rechtsstaatliche' Bedeutung dieser Überlegungen zu den *substantialia iudicii* hebt Pennington, *The Prince and the Law* 187–200, eindrucksvoll hervor; außerdem K. W. Nörr, 'Von der Textrationalität zur Zweckrationalität. Das Beispiel des summarischen Prozesses', ZRG Kan. Abt. 81 (1995) 1–25.

das summarische Verfahren seit dem 14. Jahrhundert in der Tat vor allem bei strittigen Pfründenangelegenheiten zur Anwendung.[49] Im kirchlichen Bereich spielte das summarische Verfahren darüber hinaus in Strafsachen auf dem Gebiet der Ketzer- und Hexeninquisition eine Rolle. Dort konnten ansonsten unzulässige Zeugen, etwa verurteilte Straftäter, zugelassen werden und eine Verurteilung aufgrund eines weniger als vollen Beweises, auf Verdacht hin, erfolgen. Schließlich stand es im Ermessen des Richters, ob einem Angeklagten ein Verteidiger zugestanden wurde.[50]

Welche dieser Merkmale des summarischen Verfahrens fanden in den kirchlichen wie auch städtischen Verfahren zur Kontrolle von Herrschaft Anwendung?

b) Anwendung im Kirchenstaat: Bereits Benedikt XII. hatte in seinem Mandat von 1335 die Rektoren des Kirchenstaates beauftragt, die Exzesse ihrer Vorgänger disziplinarrechtlich zu verfolgen und hierbei 'simpliciter et de plano, sine strepitu et figura iudicii, ac ut secretius commode poteris, solerti tamen adhibita diligencia te informans' vorzugehen.[51] Insbesondere der Zusatz, geheim vorzugehen, könnte darauf hinweisen, daß die üblichen Schritte eines Gerichtsverfahrens nicht eingehalten werden sollten, sondern zunächst nur Informationen im Rahmen einer Generalinquisition beschafft werden sollten, in der keine Verteidigungsmöglichkeiten für die betroffenen Rektoren vorgesehen waren. In den Ägidianischen Konstitutionen wurde ein summarisches Vorgehen durch den Rektor oder delegierten Syndikatsrichter allgemein angeordnet, nunmehr auch im Zusammenhang von Spezialinquisitionen wegen bestimmter Klagen gegen einzelne Beamte.[52] Ein schnelles Durchführen des Syndikatsverfahrens wurde von Albornoz anscheinend für derartig dringend erachtet, daß selbst an Feiertagen *in honorem Dei* verhandelt werden konnte, während nach 'Saepe' das allgemeine summarische Verfahren zwar an Feiertagen, aber lediglich an solchen *in honorem hominum* durchgeführt werden konnte.[53]

---

49. D. Williman, 'Summary Justice in the Avignonese Camera', Proc. Berkeley (MIC C.7; 1985) 437–49; A. Santangelo Cordani, *La giurisprudenza della Rota Romana nel secolo XIV* (Mailand 2001) 357–72. Gleichfalls in Benefizialsachen war es im späten 14. Jahrhundert an der Rota möglich, ein besonders abgekürztes Verfahren durchzuführen, soweit die päpstliche Ermächtigung zu den vier genannten formelmäßigen Bestimmungen auch noch *sola facti veritate inspecta* und *terminis non servatis* enthielt; dieses Verfahren bezeichnet Nörr als 'ultrasummarisch', vgl. K. W. Nörr, 'Über drei Verfahrensordnungen der mittelalterlichen Rota Romana', *Zeitschrift für evangelisches Kirchenrecht* 49 (2004) 89–97, insbesondere 94–97.

50. W. Trusen, 'Vom Inquisitionsverfahren zum Ketzer- und Hexenprozeß. Fragen der Abgrenzung und Beeinflussung', in: *Staat, Kirche, Wissenschaft in einer pluralistischen Gesellschaft. Festschrift zum 65. Geburtstag von Paul Mikat*, hg. v. D. Schwab et al. (Berlin 1989) 435–50, 439–47.

51. *Codex diplomaticus s. Sedis* 2.12, ed. Theiner 6b.

52. 'Et rector seu sindicatores deputati ab eo procedere possunt breviter, summarie et de facto et sine strepitu et figura iudicii, eciam diebus feriatis in honorem Dei vel sanctorum aut alia ratione et omni iure et iudiciorum ordine et sollempnitate obmissa', *Costituzioni Egidiane* 2.22, ed. Sella 98.29–33.

53. *Glossa ordinaria* ad Clem.5.11.2 s.v. *ob necessitates* (ed. Venetiis 1584, col. 335).

c) Die Autoren des gelehrten Rechtes erörterten zwar einzelne Beschleunigungsmöglichkeiten, brachten den Syndikatsprozeß jedoch nicht insgesamt unter die im kanonischen Recht entwickelte Formel für den summarischen Prozeß. Franciscus de Accursiis sprach davon, daß sich das Verfahren *summarie* durchführen ließ, schränkte aber gleich darauf ein, dies sei nur bei einem *civiliter*, nicht *criminaliter* durchgeführten Prozeß zulässig. Außerdem müsse stets ein voller Beweis geführt werden, um nicht die Verteidigungsmöglichkeiten unzulässig einzuschränken.[54] Nicht recht nachvollziehbar erscheint dabei, welche Fälle eines zivil durchgeführten Syndikatsprozesses Franciscus de Accursiis vor Augen hatte. Wie oben gezeigt, wurde im kirchlichen wie im städtisch-weltlichen Bereich das Syndikatsverfahren zumeist von Amts wegen, als Inquisitionsverfahren durchgeführt, und die verhängten Strafen fielen an den Fiskus, nicht vorrangig an den geschädigten Bürger. Es handelte sich also in den meisten Fällen nicht um Akkusationsverfahren, die sich am Beispiel des kontradiktorischen Zivilprozesses orientierten und als *civiliter* durchgeführt bezeichnet werden könnten.

Demgegenüber ging Angelus de Ubaldis von erleichterten Beweismöglichkeiten, also einem summarischen Verfahren aus, wenn ein Beamter wegen Diebstahl oder Korruption vor Gericht stand. Dann sollte nämlich für die Verurteilung ein Eid des Klägers ausreichend sein.[55] Allerdings erörterte Angelus keine weiteren Beweisfragen und Verteidigungsmöglichkeiten für den angeklagten Beamten. Man wird bei ihm daher nicht von einer durchgängigen Vorstellung eines bestimmten Typs von Syndikatsverfahren ausgehen dürfen.

Baldus de Ubaldis wies auf verschiedene, für das summarische Verfahren kennzeichnende Vereinfachungsmöglichkeiten im Syndikatsverfahren hin und wich insofern vom *ordo iudiciarius* ab. Er bezeichnete es jedoch nicht als summarisch. So hielt er keine förmliche Klageschrift *(libellus)* für erforderlich, sondern ließ eine mündliche *narratio* der wichtigsten Beschwerdepunkte durch einen Bürger ausreichen und meinte, daß erforderlichenfalls sogar an Feiertagen in *honorem Dei* verhandelt werden könne. Eine *litis contestatio* aber hielt er für notwendig, obwohl diese im Inquisitionsverfahren als statutenmäßigem Regelfall des Syndikatsverfahrens nicht vorkommen konnte.[56] Auf der Ebene der Beweise war Baldus gleichfalls zögerlich, durch allzu summarisches Vorgehen

---

54. 'Si causa est civilis, licet procedatur summarie, probationes regulariter debent esse plenae . . . non tantum sic litem abbrevient, quin exceptiones et probationes legitimae (non) admittantur', vgl. Era, 'Un trattato disperso' 20 n. 186.

55. Angelus de Ubaldis, 'Tractatus sindicatus' fol. 6rb n. 3.

56. Baldus de Ubaldis, 'Tractatus sindicatus' fol. 4ra n. 7: 'Decimo quaeritur, nunquid accusans officialem, vel de eo conquerens teneatur offerre libellum in scriptis, an sufficiat simplex et verbalis facti narratio? Et dic ut not. C. de sent. ex peri. re. auth. nisi breviores (Cod. 7.44.3); et d. § necessitatem (Dig. 1.16.4.5/6); et facit quod not. 3. q.4 quia praesulatus (C.1 q.4 c.5); et cum causa debeat expediri infra 30 dies, et sic res sit brevissimo tempore peritura, nullae sunt feriae etiam in honorem Dei [. . .] tamen lis debet contestari'.

die Rechte der überprüften Beamten einzuschränken und plädierte in zahlreichen Fall-
varianten für verschiedene Vermutungen zugunsten der Amtsträger. Insgesamt meinte
er, daß selbst in den Fällen, in denen städtische Statuten für das Syndikatsverfahren
zahlreiche Abkürzungen und Vereinfachungen vorsahen, ein Syndikatsrichter nach
dem normalen, nicht abgekürzten *ordo iuris* verfahren könne, ohne daß der Prozeß
deshalb ungültig würde.[57] Vermutlich lagen Baldus die Verteidigungsmöglichkeiten
für einen im Syndikatsprozeß stehenden Beamten besonders am Herzen. Schließlich
stand die Überprüfung von Richtern, Angehörigen der gleichen Profession und möglichen Lesern oder Zuhörern seiner Ausführungen im Zentrum der Überlegungen. Bei
den materiellen Tatbeständen des Syndikatsrechts erörterte er beinahe ausschließlich
Amtspflichtverletzungen *in iudicando* und gestand bei zahlreichen Abgrenzungsfragen
einem syndizierten Richter zahlreiche entlastende Vermutungen zu.[58]

d) Regelungen in den kommunalen Statuten: Sehr viel weniger Hemmungen gegenüber einem summarischen Vorgehen in Syndikatssachen legten die Statutengeber
an den Tag. Soweit sie ausdrücklich ein Vorgehen *summarie* anordneten, verstanden
sie darunter, wie in dieser Paduaner Legaldefinition aus dem Jahr 1302: 'Ubicunque in
aliquo statuto reperitur, quod procedatur summarie vel de plano, vel aliquod simile verbum, debeat procedi breviter et summarie vel de plano, sine strepitu et figura iudicii'.[59]

In den Syndikatsstatuten von Parma aus dem Jahr 1317 fielen zwar nicht die kanonistisch geprägten Bezeichnungen des summarischen Verfahrens, es wurden jedoch
erheblich abgesenkte Beweisanforderungen gegen die Amtsträger formuliert. So
konnten gegen den Kerkermeister, der wegen Erpressung der Inhaftierten beschul-
digt war, die im Kerker Einsitzenden als Belastungszeugen aussagen, eine nach dem
gelehrten Prozeßrecht grundsätzlich ausgeschlossene Personengruppe. Bei Anklagen,
die eine Bestrafung bis höchstens 20 solidi erwarten ließen, sollte der Eid des Klägers
ausreichen, in allen übrigen Fällen 'possit dictus sindicus procedere et condempnare
per indicia et presumptiones que sibi sufficere videbuntur'.[60] In den allgemeinen Statuten Luccas aus dem Jahr 1308 ist lediglich von einem Verfahren *summarie*, noch ohne

57. Baldus de Ubaldis, 'Tractatus sindicatus' fol. 4va n. 8: 'Decimoquarto queritur, statuto cavetur, quod in
syndicatibus ipsis non servetur aliquis ordo, modo servatus est ordo, an valeat processus? Et videtur quod non
quia recessum est a forma statuti. Dic contrarium, quia hoc statutum non praefixit formam, sed recedit a forma, id est non dat formam, sed remittit et relaxat formam communis et servare formam non nocet, dicit Inno.
extra de iud. c. Novit (X 2.1.3)'.

58. Baldus de Ubaldis, 'Tractatus sindicatus' fol. 4va–5va n. 9–14.

59. H. K. Briegleb, *Einleitung in die Theorie der summarischen Processe* (Leipzig 1859) 31 (allerdings ohne spezifischen Zusammenhang mit dem Syndikatsprozeß); inwieweit die zusammenfassenden Normierungen in
den Konstitutionen 'Saepe' und 'Dispendiosam' auf städtische Modelle eines einheitlichen summarischen Verfahrens zurückgreifen konnten, muß an dieser Stelle offen bleiben.

60. *De officio sindaci generalis Parmae*, ed. Benassi 11–12.

Verwendung der kanonistisch geprägten umfassenden Formel im Zusammenhang mit dem Syndikatsverfahren gegen Beamte die Rede, die für den Kauf von städtischen Pferden zuständig waren und als besonders korruptionsanfällig erschienen.[61]

Im Laufe des 14. Jahrhunderts breitete sich die aus dem kanonischen Recht bekannte Prozeßformel des summarischen Verfahrens auch im städtischen Syndikatsverfahren aus. *Querele* einzelner Einwohner aus dem Umland von Lucca gegen ihre Gemeinden und städtischen Beamten sollten durch den Luccheser *maior sindicus* 'summarie et de plano sine strepitu et figura iudicii eciam tempore feriato' behandelt werden.[62] Bei Syndikatsprozessen gegen auswärtige Beamte in Lucca war lediglich davon die Rede, daß der Syndikatsrichter in seinen Untersuchungen die *solemnitates statutorum* nicht zu beachten brauche, während sie in Untersuchungen gegen einheimische Amtsträger durchaus berücksichtigt werden sollten.[63] Bei durch *querela* einzelner Luccheser Bürger eingeleiteten Verfahren gegen Beamte sollte der Syndikatsrichter nach eigenem Gutdünken lediglich Verfahrensverzögerungen eindämmen.[64] Beschleunigungsmöglichkeiten, die sich nach den Luccheser Statuten rekonstruieren lassen, waren vereinfachte Beweisanforderungen im Falle kleinerer Bestechungssummen.[65]

Eine Verfahrensbeschleunigung sollte also angestrebt werden, jedoch nicht um jeden Preis. Insbesondere bei einheimischen Amtsträgern, die weiterhin in der Stadt oder dem *contado* blieben, schien der Zeitdruck keine große Rolle gespielt zu haben. Daß auf die Formel 'summarie et de plano sine strepitu et figura iudicii eciam tempore feriato' in den wichtigsten Fällen der Syndikatsverfahren nicht zurückgegriffen wurde, scheint ein Luccheser Sonderfall zu sein. Möglicherweise läßt er sich dadurch erklären, daß die Verfahrensstatuten des *maior sindicus* in Lucca von drei Legisten, nicht Kanonisten ausgearbeitet wurden. Darüber hinaus sollten die Urteile im Syndikatsprozeß stets öffentlich und feierlich durch den zu Gericht sitzenden Syndikatsrichter erfolgen.[66]

---

61. *Statuto del Comune di Lucca dell'anno MCCCVIII* 5.25 ('De modo sindicandi officialem, cui commictetur officium de equitatoribus et equis cavallatarum'), ed. Bongi 313; hiernach sollte der Syndikatsrichter auch ein besonders weites *arbitrium* haben: 'Et qui syndicus [. . .] habeat et habere debeat et intelligatur plenum et merum arbitrium summarie et de facto illum talem officialem syndicandi et condempnandi pro qualitate facti, negligentie, doli, culpe vel fraudis'.

62. Lucca, AS Statuti no. 6, Statuta curie sindici communis Lucani a. 1372, c.15 ('De conoscendo querelas singularium personarum contra sua communia'), fol. 138v.

63. Ibid. c.4 ('De modo et forma sindicandi officiales forenses'), fol. 136v.

64. Ibid. c.11 ('De modo et forma procedendi super denunpciis et querelis'), fol. 134v.

65. Ibid. c.13 ('Qualiter quilibet officialis debeat esse contentus salario sibi statuto et de pena contrafaciencium seu delinquencium in officio'), fol. 138r; bis zu einer Zahlung von 40 s. reichte der Eid des Anzeigenden aus, soweit er gut beleumdet war, bis 25£ genügte der Eid des Anzeigenden zusammen mit der Aussage eines Zeugen oder andere Indizien; bei größeren Geldzahlungen war zusätzlich zum Eid des Anzeigenden die Aussage zweier Zeugen, also Vollbeweis, erforderlich.

66. Ibid. c.34 ('In quo loco condempnaciones fieri debeant'), fol. 140v: 'Condemnaciones absoluciones et banna in criminalibus faciat ad bancum sue curie prout continetur in statuto Lucani communis libro secundo

Gerade der Bestandteil *de plano* des summarischen Verfahrens blieb unbeachtet. Johannes Andreae in seiner Kommentierung zur Konstitution 'Saepe' und der Kanonist Johannes de Lignano in seiner selbständigen Abhandlung hatten *de plano* folgendermaßen erklärt:[67] 'Et tunc dictio de plano importat: iudice non sedente pro tribunali et sic non in loco alto. Item quod non servatur stilus iudiciorum, sed sine libellis et aliis solempnitatibus cognoscatur'.

Die hohe rituelle Bedeutung des Syndikatsverfahrens, in dem sich die Bindung und Kontrolle von Herrschaft widerspiegelte, für das politische Selbstverständnis der freien Republik Lucca scheint den drei Satzungsgebern bei ihrem Verzicht auf die seit Anfang des 14. Jahrhunderts übliche Formel für das summarische Verfahren deutlich gewesen zu sein.[68] Freisprüche wie Verurteilungen im Syndikatsverfahren sollten daher in feierlicher Form ergehen.

Andere Statuten sahen regelmäßig ein summarisches Vorgehen im vollen Sinne der kanonistisch geprägten Formel durch den Syndikatsrichter vor, darunter die speziellen Syndikatsstatuten des Jahres 1422 aus Siena oder die Statuten von Lucca aus dem Jahr 1536.[69] Die Syndikatsordnung in Bologna aus dem 16. Jahrhundert kannte verschiedene Möglichkeiten einer Verfahrensbeschleunigung, sprach jedoch nicht in der zusammenfassenden Form von einem summarischen Verfahren. Auch in Bologna sollten die Urteile des Syndikatsrichters schriftlich und in feierlicher Gerichtssitzung ergehen.[70]

---

sub rubrica de loco ubi fieri debent condemnaciones et absoluciones et banna. Explicit statutum maioris sindici'.

    67. *Glossa ordinaria* ad Clem.5.11.2 'stans' (ed. Venetiis 1584, col. 340); Johannes de Lignano, *Super Clementina 'Saepe'*, ed. Wahrmund, *Quellen* 4.6.19–20. Johannes Fasolus hatte vor der Konstitution 'Saepe' noch eine gewisse Unsicherheit bezeugt, was man unter *de plano* zu verstehen habe: 'Et intelligunt de plano, id est sine magna disputatione atque summatim [. . .]; vel dic de plano, id est non pro tribunali vel in figura solempnis iudicii', *De summariis cognitionibus*, ed. ibid. 4.4.9, 12.

    68. Korrespondierend zum Syndikatsprozeß nach Ablauf der Amtszeit des Podestà war zu Beginn seiner Amtszeit sein Eid auf die Statuten als zentrales, öffentliches Ritual inszeniert, vgl. C. Dartmann, 'Schrift im Ritual. Der Amtseid des Podestà auf den geschlossenen Statutencodex der italienischen Stadtkommune', *Zeitschrift für historische Forschung* 31 (2004) 169–204.

    69. *Il Maggior Sindaco nello statuto del 1422*, ed. Pagni und Vaccara 258 n. 1. Bei Amtsträgern aus Siena selbst sollte hingegen *ordinarie* verfahren werden, vgl. ibid. 261 n. 6. *Statuti di Lucca a. 1536* 3.16 ('Dello arbitrio conceduto al signore maggior sindico della Citta di Lucca circa le misure delle terre'), fol. 146r: 'Et nelle predite cose tutte et singule possi il ditto Signor Sindico procedere semplicemente, et de plano, senza strepito et figura di giudicio, et non osservata alcuna sollennita di ragione, over di Statuti'; ibid. 5.35 ('Delle Questioni che vertissero per cagione delle gravezze, che simpongano dalla Citta di Lucca'), fol. 287v–88r; ibid. 5.42 ('De dare Copia delle scritture a quelli, che vi hanno interesse'), fol. 289v. Allgemein zu summarischem Vorgehen im Syndikatsverfahren mit weiteren Beispielen aus der gelehrten Literatur und den Statuten, Engelmann, *Wiedergeburt der Rechtskultur in Italien* 542–47.

    70. 'Quae quidem sententia ferratur in scriptis per dictos sindicatores, vel maiorem partem eorum super omnibus, et singulis inquisitionibus querimoniis, seu petitionibus, et processibus supradictis in palatio veteri iuridico communis Bononie ad dischum Ursi in consilio octingentorum publico', *De sindicatu domini potestatis et capitanei Populi et aliorum officialium forensium communis Bononie* (Bologna 1538), fol. 8v.

Zusammenfassung

Syndikatsverfahren sind ein bemerkenswerter Mechanismus zur regelmäßigen Kontrolle von Herrschaft. Unterhalb der Ebene politischer Verfahren zwischen Kaiser und Königen oder Kaiser und Papst angesiedelt, findet man in ihnen Elemente einer Vorstellung von *due process* entwickelt, wie sie Kenneth Pennington für die großen politischen Akteure des späten Mittelalters deutlich akzentuiert hat.[71] Kommunaler Syndikatsprozeß und kirchliche Disziplinargerichtsbarkeit weisen charakteristische institutionelle Unterschiede auf, scheinen sich jedoch im Hinblick auf ihre Durchführung im Laufe des 14. Jahrhunderts aneinander angeglichen zu haben. Zur Einleitung des Verfahrens kannte der städtische Syndikatsprozeß seit seinen frühesten Belegen neben dem kanonistisch geformten Inquisitionsverfahren eine Beschwerde- und Denunziationsmöglichkeit für von unrechtmäßigen Eingriffen betroffene Bürger. Demgegenüber war das vertikal, entlang der Hierarchieebenen angelegte, letztlich auf päpstliches Mandat zurückzuführende kirchliche Disziplinarverfahren ursprünglich ein unregelmäßig durchgeführtes reines Inquisitionsverfahren. Erst in den Ägidianischen Konstitutionen von 1357 läßt sich im Kirchenstaat ein Syndikatsverfahren nach städtischem Vorbild nachweisen. Nunmehr wurde auch dort neben dem Inquisitionsverfahren eine konkrete Denuntiations- und Beschwerdemöglichkeit für die Einwohner des *patrimonium Petri* vorgesehen. Es sollte regelmäßig und zügig durchgeführt werden, und sah außer dem von oben durchgeführten Generalinquisitionsverfahren auch die Verfahrenseinleitung durch *denuncia* und *querela* einzelner Bürger vor. In beiden Fällen sollten die Bürger von den Risiken eines Akkusationsverfahrens freigestellt werden, um ihre Beschwerdemöglichkeiten nicht einzuschränken.

Die erforderliche zügige Durchführung der Verfahren legte es nahe, in den Syndikatsprozessen das kanonistisch geprägte, seit Anfang des 14. Jahrhunderts auch normativ festgeschriebene, einheitliche summarische Verfahren anzuwenden. Bei der kirchlichen Disziplinargerichtsbarkeit läßt sich die klassische Formel des summarischen Verfahrens bereits früher nachweisen. Auch in die kommunalen Syndikatsverfahren ging sie ein, allerdings oft mit der bezeichnenden Ausnahme, daß ein Urteil nicht *de plano*, sondern allen feierlichen Formanforderungen entsprechend ergehen sollte.

Aussagen gelehrter Juristen zum Syndikatsverfahren sind erst aus der zweiten Hälfte des 14. Jahrhunderts erhalten. Bei Baldus und Angelus de Ubaldis fällt auf, daß sie, überwiegend mit Quellen des römischen Rechts argumentierend, entscheidende Merk-

---

71. Pennington, *The Prince and the Law* 40–45, zur Bindung des Podestà an Recht und Statuten, ohne ausdrücklich den regelmäßigen Syndikatsprozess zu erwähnen.

male des Syndikatsprozesses in der städtischen wie kirchlichen Praxis verkennen oder nur ungenau wiedergeben. Vorrangig beschäftigten sie sich mit dem Schutz des im Syndikatsverfahren überprüften Richters, gegebenenfalls durch Anwendung des üblichen *ordo iuris*. Diesen Blickwinkel der spätmittelalterlichen Rechtswissenschaft haben sich die neueren Darstellungen meist zu Eigen gemacht, weshalb der Syndikatsprozeß als praktisches Instrument der Herrschaftskontrolle bislang kaum hinreichend gewürdigt worden ist. Gleichwohl leuchtet an ihm eine weitere Facette der alten Frage auf, wie sich (kanonisches) Recht und Herrschaft im Mittelalter zueinander verhielten.

19

Fonti per la storia della giustizia ecclesiastica medievale a Siena

Mario Ascheri

Da qualche anno attendevo l'occasione di proporre un chiarimento la cui esigenza mi è apparsa subito necessaria nel quadro delle mie ricerche di storia su Siena e il suo territorio.[1] Da quando cioè Charles Donahue introdusse come 'editor' la parte relativa all'Italia nel suo fondamentale *The Records of the Medieval Ecclesiastical Courts* I: *The Continent*.[2] Allora espresse la sua convinzione profonda, e del tutto condivisibile, che 'the history of the medieval ecclesiastical courts will not be fully known until someone can survey the holdings of the Italian archives and come to master their contents'.[3]

Non è certo mio proposito colmare una lacuna del genere ora, ma dato che tra le varie e tante direzioni di ricerca portate avanti da Ken Pennington, quella con la quale mi sono incrociato più spesso probabilmente è la ricerca nel campo della storia processuale, mi piace dedicargli per questa occasione qualche nota sui fondi documentari che a Siena andrebbero studiati per definire concretamente come venne applicato il diritto canonico nel periodo della sua maturità, ossia negli ultimi due secoli del Medioevo. La nota di Giovanni Minnucci che seguiva l'introduzione di Donahue, infatti, per Siena indicava solo sette pezzi d'archivio sulla scorta del ricco inventario analitico da poco pubblicato del fondo notarile conservato presso l'Archivio di Stato di Siena.[4] Di questi solo quattro presentavano alcune carte risalenti ad anni precedenti il 1500.[5] Pochi, ma

---

1. Ora condensate in M. Ascheri, *Siena nella storia* (Cinisello Balsamo 2000); idem, *Lo spazio storico di Siena* (Cinisello Balsamo 2001).

2. Donahue, *Records* 1.   3. Ibid. 1.159.

4. Cf. ibid. 1.159–62; G. Catoni e S. Fineschi, *Archivio di Stato di Siena. Archivio notarile (1221–1862)* (Ministero dei beni culturali e ambientali. Pubbl. degli Archivi di Stato 87; Roma 1975).

5. Gli altri sono 'moderni' (e il registro che copre gli anni 1508–1537 non è al numero 1134 della serie, ma al 1334).

ne prenderemo comunque nota perché contengono carte che sono finite fuori del loro luogo 'naturale', cioè l'istituzione per la quale furono prodotte: la curia vescovile senese. I notai loro redattori, evidentemente, portarono con sé i documenti scritti per quella corte alla conclusione dell'incarico—come del resto è documentato che sia avvenuto anche per notai scrittori di altre corti, a cominciare da quella della Mercanzia.[6]

Andrà però aggiunto che i pezzi archivistici indicati sono stati ricordati in quanto risultanti dall'indice analitico dell'inventario, per cui è ben possibile (se non proprio certo: facile ipotesi) che altri pezzi del fondo notarile riguardino la corte del vescovo di Siena; ovviamente, però, in mancanza di loro segnalazione esplicita negli indici, si tratterà ai nostri fini di fare un paziente lavoro di controllo dei pezzi 'medievali', vedendo quali tra i pezzi traditi per quella via documentaria possano risalire a notai che hanno operato presso la corte ecclesiastica (in parte soltanto risultanti dai registri che verremo indicando tra breve, dato che presentano lacune).

Per ora basterà dire che quei soli quattro pezzi per un verso mi stupirono, data la generale ricchezza di documentazione di cui sempre si parla per Siena.[7] Dall'altro mi confermarono sull'impressione da tempo maturata che la storia della giurisdizione ecclesiastica a Siena fosse ben lontana dall'essere non solo scritta, ma addirittura anche solo impostata per il Medioevo. E in effetti, se è vero che recentemente la ricerca sulla storia della Chiesa senese si è fortemente irrobustita sembra comunque doversi dire che si continua a trascurare il profilo giudiziario—quanto meno per l'età medievale.[8]

Solo per l'età moderna (meglio: post-tridentina) si può dire che siano state effettuate corpose ricognizioni di fonti documentarie e primi sondaggi significativi sull'esercizio della giurisdizione e la tipologia degli interventi attuati nel quadro di una storia del disciplinamento sociale, dei comportamenti devianti e della 'modernizzazione' della nobiltà.[9] Non che non siano stati ricordati documenti giudiziari medievali, naturalmente; ma quasi solo incidentalmente, e non come momento di una pratica giudiziaria

---

6. Ne ho dato notizia nel mio contributo in: *Tribunali giuristi istituzioni dal medioevo all'età moderna* (Bologna 1989, ed. riv. 1996), ma ho aggiunto un'appendice documentaria specifica che è solo nella redazione successiva in: *Sistema di rapporti ed élites economiche in Europa (secoli XII–XVII),* ed. M. Del Treppo (Napoli 1994) 33–61.

7. E per il fatto che lo stesso Minnucci stava curando la pubblicazione di lauree conferite presso lo Studio senese degli anni tra il Quattro e il Cinquecento da registri conservati presso l'archivio arcivescovile: la mancata indicazione di registri del fondo vescovile dalle sue note per Donahue, *The Records* 1.159–62, faceva pensare, per l'argomento *a silentio*, all'assenza di carte in quell'archivio.

8. Una buona testimonianza è offerta dal recente volume: *Chiesa e vita religiosa a Siena dalle origini al grande giubileo,* ed. A. Mirizio e P. Nardi (Siena 2002).

9. Significativo soprattutto il lavoro di O. Di Simplicio, *Peccato penitenza perdono, Siena 1575–1800* (Milano 1994), con indicazioni di fonti e lavori precedenti; nonché il suo 'Confessionalizzazione e identità collettiva—Il caso italiano: Siena 1575–1800', *Archiv für Reformationsgeschichte* 88 (1997) 380–411; lo stesso Autore ha ora pubblicato: *Autunno della stregoneria. Maleficio e magia nell'Italia moderna* (Bologna 2005).

esaminata in modo complessivo anche per periodi brevi ma significativi. Sono stati menzionati momenti di conflitto con le autorità laiche e, cosa che non desta alcuna meraviglia, alcuni momenti di conflitto (tra gli innumerevoli che potrebbero rintracciarsi) tra le singole chiese.[10]

Le pergamene attestanti singoli conflitti fino al secolo XIII sono per lo più le sole fonti a disposizione—salvo le cause che hanno lasciato tracce nella documentazione romana, naturalmente.[11] Sono spesso conservate nei fondi detti 'diplomatici' delle singole istituzioni ecclesiastiche—conventi e monasteri in particolare—, che hanno anche conservato o ricevuto modernamente, di regola, repertori manoscritti antichi che ne agevolano la consultazione. Esse si possono trovare indicate riassuntivamente in preziosi repertori—come quelli notissimi ad ogni ricercatore su Siena del Lisini e dello Schneider—, oppure in edizioni specifiche di fondi documentari.[12]

Ma non è su questi fondi che si intende qui richiamare l'attenzione. Si ritiene piuttosto doveroso richiamare prioritariamente quanto conservato presso l'Archivio arcivescovile di Siena, che ha ricevuto un inventario moderno assai utile per addentrarsi nei suoi (relativamente) ricchi fondi per il periodo indicato—dal secolo XIV appunto al 1500.[13] Ciò perché, se pure è conservato un prezioso codice del diritto locale che, nel 1336, fece il punto della situazione giuridica anche raccogliendo e selezionando l'eredità del passato, e se sono ugualmente conservati molti documenti processuali prodotti dopo questo codice e l'emanazione delle ultime compilazioni di diritto canonico generale, né l'uno né gli altri sembrano aver ricevuto la segnalazione che meritano.

Il quadro normativo locale

Il diritto locale raccolto nel 1336 è presentato come frutto di una elaborazione complessa e fu approvato in modo solenne, che spiega come sia stato ritenuto degno

---

10. Si vedano ad esempio le pergamene relative alla causa tra due parrocchie ricordate in M. Pellegrini, 'Istituzioni ecclesiastiche, vita religiosa e società cittadina nella prima età comunale', in: *Chiesa e vita religiosa* 101–134 (119 nota 59); in quanto ai conflitti fra laici, W. Bowsky, *A Medieval Italian Commune: Siena under the Nine 1287–1355* (Berkeley and Los Angeles 1981; trad. ital. Bologna 1986), *ad indicem*.

11. E per la quale si vedrà in particolare, JL, Po., *Italia pontificia* 3.

12. A. Lisini, *R. Archivio di Stato di Siena. Inventario delle pergamene conservate nel Diplomatico dall'anno 736 all'anno 1250* (Siena 1908); F. Schneider, *Regestum Senense* (Roma 1911). Si vedano singoli atti processuali attestanti momenti diversi della procedura sotto le denominazioni di 'transactio', 'arbitrium', 'iuramentum', 'absolutio', 'attestationes' (testimonianze) e 'sententia' in numeri 43, 46, 50, 56, 57, 58, 60, 73, 74 ecc. in: *Carte dell'Archivio di Stato di Siena. Abbazia di Montecelso (1071–1255)*, ed. A. Ghignoli (Siena 1992); analogamente si veda: *Carte dell'Archivio di Stato di Siena. Opera Metropolitana (1000–1200)*, ed. A. Ghignoli (Siena 1994), ove sotto 'libellus' ci si riferisce alla concessione fondiaria; per una istituzione importante del territorio (ma in diocesi di Chiusi), W. Kurze, *Codex Diplomaticus Amiatinus. Urkundenbuch der Abtei S. Salvatore am Monte Amiata. Von den Anfängen bis zum Regierungsantritt Papst Innocenz III. (736–1198)* (3 voll.; Tübingen 1974–82).

13. *L'archivio arcivescovile di Siena. Inventario*, ed. G. Catoni e S. Fineschi (Roma 1970).

dell'elegante veste con cui ci è pervenuto, ossia un bel codice pergamenaceo fornito
ancora della sua legatura originaria in cuoio con borchie e nel cui interno il testo è stato
copiato con una scrittura libraria molto accurata e arricchita con tanto di belle decorazioni policrome. Credo che sia perciò opportuno riprodurre per esteso il proemio
'dotto' che si legge in apertura del testo (fol. 1r–v):[14]

Infrascripte sunt constitutiones, ordinamenta et decreta episcopatus Senensis et curie episcopalis civitatis et diocesis Senensis quorum si quidem nonnulla noscuntur esse extracta et sumpta
de constitutionibus et decretis veteribus et antiquis repertis ac inventis in libris constitutionum
et decretorum veterum et antiquorum dicti episcopatus et curie episcopalis Senensis et tanquam iuxta honesta et iuri et equitati consona confirmata, emologata et approbata et nonnulla
correcta emendata et in melius reformata ac etiam multa alia decreta et constitutiones de novo
adinvente edita, conposita ac salubriter et utiliter compilata et in unum volumen posita et redacta in scriptis; tempore episcopatus venerabilis in Christo patris et domini domini Donosdei
de Malavoltis de Senis, Dei et apostolice sedis gratia dignissimi Senensis episcopi, videlicet per
venerabiles viros dominum Vannem rectorem ecclesie sancti Salvatoris Senarum, priorem cleri
Senensis, dominum Aççolinum de Malavoltis canonicum Senensem, dominum Guidonem
Bondelmontis priorem canonice Castillionis iuxta Umbronem dyocesis prefate, dominum
Raynuccium de Saracenis rectorem ecclesie sancti Pauli Senensis et per dominum Durellum de
Rossis rectorem ecclesie sancti Vincentii Senensis, constitutarios et officiales habentes plenam
potestatem, baliam et auctoritatem omnimodam ad predicta et infrascripta omnia et singola faciendum; et ad confirmandum, emologandum et adprobandum dictas constitutiones et decreta
vetera et antiqua et ad ea corrigendum, emendandum et reformandum; et ad conponendum et
edendum et conpilandum de novo solemniter electos et assumptos a prefato reverendo patre
et domino domino Donusdeo Dei gratia episcopo Senensi, et ab universo clero Senensi, et ab
universa synodo dominorum clericorum et prelatorum civitatis et diocesis Senensis facientes
omnia// supradicta et infrascripta ex plena potestate et auctoritate et commissione eis facta,
concessa et attributa super predictis et infrascriptis omnibus et singulis a smemorato domino
Senensi episcopo et ab universo clero et generali synodo sepe factis et omni modo, via et iure
quibus melius potuerunt Senis, in episcopali palatio ad predicta et infrascripta specialiter et solemniter convocatis et constitutis; et sic extracta et sumpta, confirmata emologata et approbata,
correcta, emendata et in melius reformata et de novo adinventa edita, composita ac compilata
et in unum volumen infrascriptum redacta.

Ad honorem et laudem omnipotentis Dei et beate Marie virginis gloriose, beatorum quoque Ampsani, Savini, Crescentii atque Victoris, patronorum dicti episcopatus ac defensorum
Comunis et Populi civitatis Senarum et omnium sanctorum Dei ac ad reverentiam smemorati
venerabilis patris domini Senensis episcopi; et ad statum, unionem pacificam et Deo gratam

14. Il prezioso codice è al numero 1 del fondo. Il testo parzialmente edito (v. nota 15) da V. Ricchioni, 'Le
costituzioni del vescovado senese del 1336', *Studi Senesi* 30 (1914) 100–67, l'ho collazionato; mi riprometto di
completare l'edizione con Antonella Cantarella.

civitatis Senensis et ecclesiastice libertatis; et ad bonum et tranquillum statum et bonam conservantiam Comunis et Populi civitatis Senensis et omnium subiectorum.

Lecta et pubblicata fuerunt de mandato prefatorum constitutariorum et officialium (. . .) per me (. . .) notarium (. . .) solempniter in clero et synodo dominorum prelatorum et clericorum civitatis et diocesis Senensis ad hec specialiter convocatis et congregatis (. . .) unanimiter approbata, emologata et confirmata fuerunt per ipsos universum clerum (. . .) in presentia venerabilis et religiosi viri dompni Filippi de Podio Boniçi vicarii generalis prefati domini Senensis episcopi (. . .) sub annis Domini ab incarnatione Mcccxxxvi. indictione iiii. die xxvi. mensis Martii.

Il codice che conserva questo testo è stato solo parzialmente edito.[15] È rimasto in pratica privo di studi particolari, anche se si può immaginarselo come un testo di lunga durata.[16] Una prima direzione di ricerca impone quindi un controllo della parte già edita e un completamento dell'edizione di quella compilazione trecentesca tanto solenne.

Le carte giudiziarie

a) Un primo 'faldone'. Nella serie detta delle cause 'civili' c'è un solo pezzo medievale col numero 4673, ossia il primo 'faldone' della serie, assegnato al 1438–1505.[17] La serie prosegue fino all'anno 1951 con il numero di serie 5239, cui seguono sette volumi di 'repertori' cronologici che aiutano a districarsi in questi oltre cinquecento falconi, cioè cartelle colme di fascicoli. Il numero 4673 reca un foglio dentro la cartella in cui mano ottocentesca (?) ha scritto: '1506 civili'; dentro c'è un foglio ripiegato con indice altrettanto recente degli 'atti riguardanti i privati' (evidentemente contenuti nel faldone): '1—1500—Petizione di Pietro di ser Mariano e compagni contro fra Giovan Battista dell'ordine di S. Agostino; 2—1500 . . .', fino al numero 65 del 1505. Ma dentro la cartella ci sono atti vari: il primo è un foglio pergamenaceo del 1438 con un atto notarile di Pietro *episcopus Calcedonensis* fatto di licenza del vescovo di Siena Carlo, cui segue un fascicolo processuale del 1438 di 36 fogli cartacei rilegati, cui è verosimilmente collegato l'atto precedente, iniziante con la necessaria *petitio* 'coram vobis egregio decretorum doctore domino Georgio de Tholomeis de Senis onorando vicario domini Senensis episcopi et vestra curia'. Seguono i vari atti della causa fino all'elencazione delle spese sostenute, poi fascicoli processuali con date (relativamente) conformi all'indicetto di cui si discorreva: *petitiones, sententiae, appellationes* ecc., di regola con gli atti ulteriori della causa.

---

15. Ricchioni, 'Le costituzioni', ha edito solo la parte iniziale del codice, ossia le cc. 1–21, segnato al numero 1; al 2 c'è una copia, meno formale, che contiene anche altri testi.

16. In Archivio arcivescovile le costituzioni successive sono soltanto del 1564, al numero 3 della serie.

17. *L'archivio arcivescovile di Siena. Inventario* 301.

b) Una serie di 16 registri. Per altri atti medievali nello stesso archivio bisogna 'saltare' al numero 5247, che è un volume cartaceo con copertina pergamenacea. Le 142 carte del registro sono state numerate modernamente e iniziano con:

In nomine Domini amen. Hic est liber memoriarum mei Bartholomei condam Iacobi civis Senensis notarius dominorum Regulatorum factus et scriptus per me Bartholomeum sub annis Domini mccclxxxxv indictione tertia tempore sex mensium inceptorum die kalendis iulii anno dicto et finiendorum ut sequitur, residentibus ad offitium Regulatorum honorandorum civium.

Seguono 5 nomi divisi per i Terzi della città e comincia poi, sempre nella stessa carta, il diario dell'attività che fu solo in un primo tempo svolta presso l'ufficio comunale indicato: 'Die iii iulii. Domini Regulatores concesserunt licteras executorias novis tribus Exactoribus pecunie'. Infatti già a c. 3r ci troviamo, dice l'*inscriptio:* 'In curia episcopali coram domino Francisco de Caponago priore Sancti Martini vicario e(piscopi). Die iii. Ianuarii 1398 indictione 7'.

Di qui diviene diario delle udienze delle cause dinanzi al vicario episcopale, giorno per giorno, ma per ogni causa viene di solito lasciato un foglio, per cui sono poi annotate sempre dalla stessa mano le udienze successive. Quando per qualsiasi motivo gli atti sono altrove, è indicato in margine; a c. 10r ad esempio in margine si legge: 'Require in filça fo. 24', o ci sono segni che vengono poi ripetuti, come a c. 50v: 'Require supra ad simile signum'. L'atto iniziale è indicato in margine come 'ad petitionem et instantiam'. Ma sono registrate anche copie di lettere vescovili a ecclesiastici del territorio (c. 6r) o agli ufficiali di Mercanzia di Siena (c. 8r), sempre di mano dello stesso notaio che cura il registro. Rimane ferma la mano del notaio, ma i fascicoli si riferiscono addirittura al 1401, e non sono solo di contenuto processuale; come a c. 52r, ove al 29 ottobre 1401 figura un provvedimento indicato nel margine come 'contra euntes ad monasteria sine licentia'; infatti per l'affissione 'dominus Florentius vicarius et doctor suprascriptus mandavit per litteras sua patentes et mandatorias omnibus et singulis tam clericis quam religiosis'. Segue il testo per esteso: 'Nos Florentius de Salvis de Placentia decretorum doctor canonicus Pisanus (. . .) Senensis episcopi vicarius generalis'.

Altro provvedimento di Florenzio, ad esempio, a c. 78v, ma sempre frammisto a registrazioni di fatti processuali che corrono fino al 1408 sempre dello stesso notaio. Nell'inventario si dice che questo registro si estende a coprire gli anni fino al 1406 ed è il primo volume dei 'libri delle cause d'immunità', ma il contenuto dei registri è assai più variegato.[18]

I volumi successivi fino al 5262 sono dello stesso genere. Nella stessa serie abbiamo

18. Ibid. 309.

considerato per esempio il volume numerato come 5252, riportato al 1423–1426, cartaceo con rilegatura pergamenacea, che reca questa *inscriptio:*

In nomine Domini amen. Hic est liber seu quaternus mey Antonii olim Pietri Vannuccii de
Monte Sancte Marie notarii et civis Senensis et nunc notarii domini Petri de Sancto Petro
dec<retorum doctoris?>, canonici Pisani et reverendi in Christi patris et . . . domini Antonii
Dei et apostolice Sedis gratia episcopi Senensis vicarii et eius episcopalis curie Senensis in se
continens querimonias petitiones reclamationes citationes relationes et precepta positiones
articulorum et testium et ipsorum responsiones et atestationes instrumentorum et iurium
productorum, sententias pronuntiatas et diffinitas et alias scripturas ad civiles actus et causas
pertinentes et expectantes. Factus et scriptus editus et compositus per me Antonium Pietri notarii prefati (. . .) sub annis Domini mccccxxiii.

Diario processuale, quindi, con note giorno dopo giorno, di 208 carte. Anche il registro successivo (numerato 5253), con una grande 'A' sulla copertina pergamenacea, di
133 carte, è redatto dallo stesso notaio che in un'analoga *inscriptio* dà conto del proprio
lavoro per il 1426–1428.

Un altro dei volumi successivi presenta le stesse caratteristiche. È il numero 5259 (si
veda anche *infra,* Appendice no. 1), relativo al 1430 stando all'annotazione che correda
la copertina pergamenacea che reca una grande 'K' decorata con tiara episcopale e,
sotto, un 'extraordinarius I'; in alto però si precisa: 'Liber causarum civilium editus per
Antonium Gualfredi de Vulterris in anno Domini mccccxxx'. Cioè non si parla di atti
'straordinari', e l'*inscriptio* reca il solito richiamo a commissioni, citazioni, relazioni,
petizioni, querele, eccezioni, repliche e opposizioni, giuramenti di calunnia ecc.; solo,
si parla della *publicatio,* oltreché delle sentenze, *censurarum ecclesiasticarum, dationes et
prolationes et fulminationes.* Prosegue con consueto rinvio alle cause civili ecc.

La ricca serie prosegue per la parte medievale solo fino al 1447 (con il registro 5262,
come si è detto), che è di nuovo un cartaceo con legatura pergamenacea con scritto, in
caratteri grandi, 'civilium causarum. mccccxliii, mccccxliiii' seguito da una grande 'V'
con decorazioni, che richiama il 'III', di nuovo decorato, presente nella copertina del
numero 5255 e relativo agli anni 1438–39 ('hic est liber actorum et rogitorum Senensis
episcopalis curie factus et compositus'), fornito anche di una rubrichetta a sé con indicazione dei fogli in cui compaiono i nomi delle parti coinvolte negli atti riportati successivamente; probabilmente l'elemento comune è dato dalla presenza nei due volumi di
uno stesso notaio: ser Savino di Bartolomeo.

Al primo foglio del 5262, infatti, in basso decorato da un grande *signum tabellionis*
di Filippo notaio di cui nell'*inscriptio* si ricorda il gennaio 1443 (stile dell'incarnazione) e
che è il 'liber actorum civilium curie episcopalis Senensis continens in se omnia singola
acta et actitata in dicta curia episcopali inter quascunque personas pro quibuscunque

agitandis in dicta curia coram egregio decretorum doctore domino Iohanne de Agazaria de Senis', vicario generale in spirituali e temporali del vescovo Carlo; tutto scritto da ser Savino di Bartolomeo e Filippo di ser Giuliano di Casole cittadini senesi e 'scrittori' della curia. Sempre in ordine cronologico.

Sembra quindi di potersi concludere che esistevano due serie ben distinte: una di atti conservati 'in filza', cioè di atti in originale della più diversa provenienza, presentati in corte dalle parti, e poi 'infilzati' per evitarne la dispersione; un'altra di registri, cioè di volumi redatti invece dal notaio ricevente gli atti e addetto a registrare, conservandone memoria, quanto fatto dal giudice, ossia del vicario vescovile. Il falcone ricordato sub a) conserva documenti residui della prima serie, probabilmente a un certo punto dispersi per alleggerire il carico dell'archivio, mentre i registri furono conservati con maggiore continuità perché più sintetici e meno voluminosi: Una parte è nella serie ricordata sub b).

c) Altri cinque pezzi eterogenei. Esiste poi una serie di 'miscellanea'.[19] Il primo volume con numerazione coeva in parte perduta per deperimento per umidità degli angoli superiori dei fogli (si legge ancora '187' cui seguono una decina di fogli non numerati) inizia con un indice (c. 1r–v) che dà conto anche delle carte mancanti e indica il contenuto fino a c. 202: su testamenti, ma frammisti a *inquisitiones* (occasione di usure, testamenti, *contra memoriam, bonorum, ad probandum bona, pro probanda ultima voluntate, pro diritto curie)*, sentenze (ad esempio: *Petri Thomassi contra hospitale*). A c. 2r lo scriptor presenta il volume:

In nomine Domini amen. Hic est liber sive quaternus inquisitionum petitionum querimoniarum libellorum impositionum relationum mandatorum preceptorum et aliorum diversorum processuum et scripturarum factus et compositus tempore vicariatus venerabilis viri domini Philippi Gualterotti de Senis reverendi in Cristo patris et domini domini Donosdei Dei gratia episcopi Senensis vicarii generalis et super executione testamentorum et ultimarum voluntatuum defunctorum ac restitutione usurarum et inlicite acquisitionum fieri faccenda ab ipso domino episcopo specialiter constituti et deputati, et scriptus per me Gerium filium olim ser Nelli notarium curie Senarum et nunc offitialem et scribam curie episcopalis Senensis super officio testamentorum in anno Domini m.cccxlviiii et m.cccl.

Aggiunge 'm.ccli', perché continuato al tempo della vacanza e poi con Azzolino vescovo anche nel 1352–62 (ma con atti fino al 1365 come segnala giustamente l'inventario). Diario giorno per giorno all'interno della singola *inquisitio*.

Il successivo 'miscellaneo' 5434, messo con altri pezzi fino al 5469 (quindi oltre trenta pezzi) tra le 'cause ed atti civili sbandati' dal 1365 al 1906, ha un primo volume che

19. Ibid. 312.

reca solo un foglio molto danneggiato del 1365, mentre il resto è costituito da fascicoli processuali regolarmente introdotti da *petitio* o *protestatio* o *appellatio*, ma del secolo XVI e XVII.[20]

Nel faldone successivo, numerato 5435, ci sono di nuovo carte processuali del Cinquecento, ma con inframezzate molte carte del Quattrocento, specie degli anni ottanta-novanta—gli stessi anni coperti dai pezzi dell'Archivio di Stato di Siena ricordati da Giovanni Minnucci. Tra i pezzi successivi, nel faldone 5440, preso ad esempio, le carte sono invece moderne, per cui possiamo presumere che in questa serie si tratti effettivamente ormai solo di materiale moderno.

Nelle miscellanee c'è però anche un volume, numerato 5470, che reca copia di una settantina di testamenti con lasciti pii, scritti nel corso del Quattrocento, di persone morte negli anni 1434 e seguenti—avverte nota recente. Il volume seguente, al numero 5471, cartaceo con copertina pergamenacea con cappello cardinalizio che sormonta uno stemma dei Piccolomini reca sotto in caratteri grandi: 'Liber actorum testamentorum V'. Nel volume, giorno per giorno, sono annotate le comparse del procuratore dei poveri a partire dal 10 marzo 1473/4.[21] Segue citazione degli eredi negligenti da parte del vicario. A margine c'è indicazione degli eredi coinvolti: 'Contra heredes . . .', fino al 1508.

d) Tre registri 'criminali'. Ci è conservato un volume al numero 5499, ossia un registro cartaceo con legatura pergamenacea con scritto 'criminalium 1408' (mano sec. XVI?):

In eterni Dei nomine amen. Hic est liber inquisitionum accusationum et condemnationum curie episcopali Senensis inceptus factus ac compositus tempore reverendi in Christo patris et domini domini Antonii Dei et apostolice sedis gratia episcopi Senensis currentibus annis Domini ab eodem salutifera incarnatione millesimo quadringentesimo octavo, indictione secunda, mensibus et diebus infrascriptis, Simone Nicolai de Brundutio in iure canonico perito existente vicario generali.

Seguono i nomi di sei notai della curia. Nelle carte del volume ci sono condanne e inquisizioni, ma sembrano riportate in bella copia, e non in ordine giornaliero, di diario; alcune sono state cancellate con tratti di penna; i processi corrono dal 1408 fino al 1411; non mi pare confermato il 1417 indicato dall'inventario.[22] Sono dell'ordine di alcune decine soltanto.

Nel secondo registro conservato del secolo XV, il numero 5500 (si veda anche *infra*, Appendice no. 2), uguale come forma, in copertina si legge 'malefitiorum liber', oltre a

20. Ibid. 312.
21. Le cui entrate e uscite—con atti di laurea del primo Cinquecento—sono nel numero 4405.
22. Ibid. 317.

vari motti tra cui 'pene moliende sunt potiusquam exasperande'. Comincia senza pagina introduttiva, subito con una *inquisitio* fatta dal 'd. Iohannes de Sicilia decretorum doctor vicarius generalis in spiritualibus et temporalibus' grazie ad *auctoritas et balia* data dal vescovo. Gli atti partono dal 1429, ma non sono presentati in ordine cronologico, per cui dovrebbero esser stati riscritti come nel volume precedente; corrono fino al 1440 in poco più di un centinaio di fogli, ma ogni *inquisitio* occupa poche facciate. Sono sintesi di processi con tanto di sentenza finale, di solito.

Questa serie diviene molto ricca dall'anno 1500 in poi, a partire dal numero 5501. Il registro 5612, posto nella serie dei 'precetti' nell'inventario, è certamente collegato a questi precedenti.[23] Per perdita di carta nella parte superiore destra delle carte e la scrittura pessima, non è facile dire molto dei suoi 70 fogli fittamente coperti da annotazioni datate 1419–1423. L'inventario ci presenta il registro come di 'ricordi di ser Giovanni di ser Nello, notaio della curia al tempo del vescovo Antonio Casini con precetti, inquisizioni e condanne pronunciate dal vicario generale Genesio de Campora parmense' (e li riporta al 1418–1421). Ma i 'ricordi' derivano da un cartellino recente apposto nella costola del registro e dal fatto oggettivo che, come i volumi precedenti, anche questo fa la 'storia' delle singole cause trattate dall'inizio alla fine; infatti nell'inscriptio è presentato come *quaternus memorialis* nel quale verranno scritte tutte le 'querimonie, precepta, sequestrationes, inquisitiones, sententie condemnationum, absolutiones et alia quampluria'.

e) Un residuo? Nella serie delle cause delegate, si conserva un faldone che raccoglie qualche decina di fascicoli processuali, soprattutto risalenti al 1500–1502. L'inventario fa datare il faldone dal 1453, ma non sembra ci siano attualmente fascicoli risalenti a quella data. Questa serie è molto ricca dopo il Concilio di Trento, ma i numeri 5622–5625 hanno comunque materiali prodotti secondo regole 'medievali'.

Appendice
15 giorni nella corte in sede 'civile'

Diamo qui una esemplificazione del tipo di registrazioni conservate per la giurisdizione civile, cui—come si vedrà—si rivolgono anche laici contro altri laici; si noterà anche che non è formalizzata l'azione proposta e che per lo più si finisce con la condanna della scomunica per inadempimento. L'impressione è che gli scomunicati in circolazione dovessero essere un numero considerevole!

Le registrazioni sono giornaliere con accanto, sul margine, i nomi delle parti, che venivano poi riportati in rubrichette alfabetiche separate—conservate ancora in alcuni registri—, che facilitavano il reperimento delle varie fasi del procedimento nella stessa causa. Si noterà anche la rapidità nel provvedere alla citazione e la brevità dei termini concessi.

23. Ibid. 318.

Diamo anche una breve esemplificazione da un coevo registro penalistico. Esso risulta redatto con gli stessi criteri; le pene, si noterà, sono assai modeste e seguite anch'esse, in caso di mancato pagamento, dalla scomunica.

Si è scelta documentazione del 1432 perché da poco doveva aver lasciato Siena Niccolò de' Tedeschi (un autore prediletto da Ken Pennington), e la città era allora o era stata luogo di soggiorno dei grandi della Cristianità: l'imperatore Sigismondo e il papa Eugenio IV.

1. Per il nostro esempio si è quindi prescelto il registro già ricordato 5259, che comincia le sue annotazioni di lavoro a c. 2r, in data 1431, 20 marzo dello stile senese, corrispondente quindi al 'nostro' 1432.

Quel giorno il vicario siede *pro tribunali* e 'commette' al nunzio episcopale che notifichi a un tale e ai suoi due figli che per il giorno dopo *(pro tota die crastina)* sotto pena di scomunica *late sententie* restituisca a un ser Mariano rettore della chiesa di San Pietro a Ovile un paio di paramenti *ordinati de colore croceo sive giallo sub pena*. Subito dopo, una nota di stessa mano ma con altro inchiostro riferisce che li ha citati lasciando la cedola con il precetto di cui sopra.

Lo stesso giorno uno *spetiarius* agisce contro le suore di S. Agnese per lire 22, soldi 6, denari 2, *pro mercantia eis vendita et tradita*. Si commette al nunzio ecc. Lo stesso il 22 marzo riferisce di aver citato e il 24 *de mane* compare lo stesso mercante e accusa la contumacia delle monache e chiede che si proceda secondo la *forma iuris*. Il vicario ordina di citarle a contraddire per non scomunicarle.

Sempre il 20 marzo *de mane*, lo stesso speziale agisce contro ser Giovanni di S. Maria a Tressa dal quale vuole una lira, soldi 5, denari 8. Si commette al nunzio. Lui riferisce di aver citato.

Sempre sotto il 20 marzo, *de mane*, il vicario commette a *petitio* della *domina Gemina* di Giovanni che sia fatta ammonizione al priore di S. Martino e la *domina* Bartolomea moglie di Antonio maestro di legname che nei 15 giorni debba ad essa restituire certe sue cose, notificando che passato il termine contro di lei si procederà di diritto, contumacia non ostante.

A c. 3r *mutatur* l'anno del Signore, dice un notabile marginale, per correggere la data del 1431 del registro in cui, al 10 aprile, il vicario commette al nunzio del Comune (di Siena) che, a richiesta di *dominus Bastianus* canonico senese, procuratore delle monache di Casciano, ordini alle monache di s. Paolo di Siena di pagare 35 lire a pena di scomunica entro tre giorni. Il 12 il nunzio riferisce di aver adempiuto; sempre stessa mano ma con inchiostro diverso, come per la nota precedente, il 7 giugno compare Bastiano e accusa la contumacia della badessa chiedendone la condanna. Appunto quello che fa subito il vicario pronunciando la scomunica.

Nello stesso foglio, sotto l'11 aprile, il nunzio riferisce al podestà (del Comune) e al notaio di aver posto il sequestro su una scarsella di cuoio chiusa e altri oggetti beni di Simone *de Alamania* debitore di un Federico di un altro Federico sempre di Germania, e a petizione dello stesso Federico per 40 grossi, e di averli accomodati presso Giovanni di Germania e di avergli intimato come al solito a pena prevista dal diritto ecc.

A c. 4v, sempre all'11 aprile, uno agisce contro un 'ser' per l'affitto di una casa arretrato di sei mesi, oltre alle spese. Si ordina citazione al nunzio. Il 13 si accusa la contumacia e si chiede una nuova citazione per evitare scomunica. Il vicario acconsente.

Dopo mezzo foglio senza scritture, sempre alla stessa data, un ospedaliere di s. Pietro di Siena agisce contro uno di Castel della Pieve dal quale chiede lire 5 soldi 10 per l'affitto di una casa per sei mesi più spese; segue citazione e ordine del vicario di pagare con minaccia di scomunica entro tre giorni; segue contumacia e scomunica 'da pubblicare nelle chiese'.

A c. 5r, il 12 aprile di sera, il vicario commette agli eredi di un senese di produrre entro tre giorni l'ultimo testamento e ogni codicillo in modo che possa disporre l'esecuzione e 'denunciare' il nome del notaio rogante sotto pena di scomunica. Si commette citazione ecc. Il 13 mattina compare uno degli eredi per tutti a chiedere più tempo per adempiere; il vicario accorda otto giorni.

A c. 5v, il 13 aprile di mattina, il fattore delle monache di s. Paolo agisce contro un pizzicaiolo al quale chiede il pagamento di 16 fiorini, salvo il diritto di calcolo come residuo del prezzo di una 'passione' e le spese. Il 16 compare il debitore, ma dice di aver tempo quattro anni a pagare come emergerebbe da scrittura privata del 1430 di mano dello stesso attore presentata. Ma questi dice che non è vera, e che pertanto paghi, anche tenuto conto della *paupertas* delle monache. Il vicario gli dà tempo di pagare entro il mese corrente sotto pena della scomunica e commette al nunzio di comunicarlo. Il convenuto compare nel giorno e ritira il precetto.

Il giorno dopo di mattina, sempre sullo stesso foglio, il vicario intima a ser Nofrio, rettore di s. Salvatore, di terminare entro lunedì la causa che ha tra due e che gli è stata commessa sotto pena di scomunica, mentre alle parti si ordina di produrre i loro diritti entro domenica.

A c. 6r–v siamo al 16 aprile di sera e due agiscono contro tre *sorores* cui chiedono il pagamento di una certa cifra per del panno e le spese; segue come al solito.

Sempre a c. 6v, il 18 aprile di mattina, il vicario a richiesta di ser Mariano procuratore dei poveri ordina a un Piccolomini e una Tommasi di eseguire entro tre giorni i legati disposti da Angelo de Rossi sotto pena di scomunica; segue nunzio che riferisce il 19 facendo *relatio* al notaio il 21.

Il 21 aprile di mattina, a c. 7r, il vicario opera di nuovo su petizione del procuratore dei poveri che chiede l'esibizione del testamento di un Ugurgieri sotto pena di scomunica; nunzio ecc.

Il 28, sempre nello stesso foglio, un ser si fa ordinare a un farsettaio presente e confessante di pagare 18 grossi d'argento entro nove giorni. Segue notazione del 17 maggio mattina, quando si ritenta una nuova citazione per insolvenza e contumacia, ma senza ricavare nulla per cui ha luogo la scomunica 'pubblica'.

A c. 7v, si torna al 30 aprile mattina, quando agisce uno contro un canonico ora defunto e suo debitore di 33 fiorini e 10 soldi per beni lasciatigli per testamento di una signora, ma che gli furono sottratti dal canonico appunto. Allega un suo libro segnato con una croce in cui a foglio 45 c'era il seguente elenco di beni che prosegue a c. 8r: un moggio di vino stimato fiorini 6, 22 staia di grano per 22 lire, due botti di staia 33 stimate dieci lire . . . (seguono lino asciugatoi guanciali ecc.).

A c. 8v, il 30 aprile di mattina, il fedecommissario del testamento di un canonico chiede che si ordini a un 'ser' cantore di pagargli entro tre giorni 16 fiorini sotto pena di scomunica; come al solito segue citazione, contumacia e scomunica.

Il 2 maggio è un 'ser' procuratore di monache (di Ognissanti) che agisce contro una signora e il figlio pizzicagnolo per una loro possessione che tengono e di cui non pagano l'affitto; segue come al solito con scomunica il 9 maggio.

A c. 9r, il 2 maggio di mattina, riprende un processo iniziato a c. 5 come avverte la nota marginale: non c'è stato il pagamento e si va alla scomunica.

Poi un frate sindaco del Carmine chiede al debitore di un legato di due fiorini di pagare; segue come al solito.

A c. 9v, 2 maggio di sera, compare un 'ser' per una *monitio* fattagli dagli ufficiali di Mercanzia (la corte commerciale) in base a una *inibitoria* chiesta da un terzo e dalla quale si sente 'gravato' perché ha ottenuto la sentenza definitiva e si dovrebbe pertanto eseguire; né lui ne aveva declinato la giurisdizione né aveva avanzato l'eccezione di ricusazione. Perciò non doveva essergli concessa la lettera motivata da solo desiderio di dilazione; lui si era rivolto in Mercanzia per seguire il foro del reo; ora essendo andata così chiede al vicario la revoca dell'inibitoria (dell'esecuzione) producendo la sentenza ottenuta. Il vicario fa citare la controparte a comparire venerdì a contraddire.

A c. 10r una signora agisce il 4 maggio contro le monache di s. Abbondio per otto lire per certi mesi: procede come al solito. Poi, compare il citato della posta precedente chiedendo tempo per opporsi.

Compare al verso, lo stesso giorno, un *frater* a testimoniare nella causa introdotta il 30 aprile per il testamento del canonico quanto ai beni lasciati; su quando avvenne non ricorda bene, ma *super generalibus bene respondit*.

A c. 11r lo stesso giorno il vicario ordina a un banchiere di produrre entro il giorno successivo tutti i libri e scritture del fu Angelo di Guido sotto pena di scomunica.

Nello stesso foglio lo stesso giorno si ordina una comparizione a richiesta del procuratore dei poveri.

A c. 11v agisce il 5 maggio un 'ser' rettore della chiesa di s. Donato contro un cappellano della cattedrale per 13 lire per un affitto; si procede come sempre.

Oltre compare un 'ser' procuratore della causa coinvolgente la Mercanzia e chiede termine a opporsi alla petizione contro i suoi clienti. Vicario: va bene fino a lunedì di sera.

Lo stesso giorno, a c. 12r, ricompare il fedecommissario del 30 aprile chiedendo la sentenza e in caso di mancanza di prove il deferimento del giuramento. Il vicario chiede che giuri *de calumpnia* e dopo assegna 33 fiorini dei beni del defunto che vengono pertanto ipotecati. Fu fatto al banco del diritto presenti tre testi rogati.

Lo stesso giorno, a c. 12v, il vicario ordina la produzione di un testamento agli eredi di un defunto; esaurite tutte le formalità, perdurando la contumacia, si va alla sentenza il 10 maggio.

2. Il registro che può essere accostato a questo è quello contemporaneo 'criminalistico', di serie col numero 5550. Comincia al tempo di Giovanni di Sicilia vicario e prosegue con notaio un chierico volterrano (lo stesso del numero 5259) per il nuovo vicario Giovanni *de Ruffaldis* canonico *Maçariensis*—si precisa—al tempo di Eugenio papa con l'imperatore *Senis pro nunc esistens*. Si tratta di un diario delle varie *inquisitiones* promosse dai vicari, giorno per giorno in cui il tribunale era attivo; interi mesi risultano però privi di annotazioni (ad esempio l'aprile 1431).

Ad esempio a c. 54r siamo al 1431, 3 maggio, *causarum hora ad bancum iuris* e si comincia una *inquisitio* che porta alla comparizione di uno dei 5 inquisiti.

A c. 56r la sentenza di condanna di un canonico delinquente a 25 lire e di un suo collaboratore ('suo chierico') a 5 lire da pagare al camerlengo del vescovo il lunedì prossimo sotto pena del doppio, presenti Guglielmo di Catalogna ecc.; il 13 maggio è registrato il pagamento che ha quindi portato alla chiusura del caso.

L'*inquisitio* successiva è del 24 maggio; da c. 77v il 18 marzo 1432 a c. 78r il 22 maggio 1432.

A c. 79 *inquisitio* dell'11 giugno 1432 riguardante *ser Iustinianus* cantore della cattedrale che con la spada voleva ferire, il giorno stesso, Corrado cuoco del S. Maria della Scala nella piazza dell'ospedale delimitata da beni dell'ospedale e dalla chiesa cattedrale. Segue elenco dei testi: un *dominus* ospedaliero, un ser (con accanto l'indicazione: citato il 11 gennaio giurò ecc.); un altro ser *sacrista* della chiesa il 16 di giugno citato giurò ecc. Infine, il 12 giugno compare Giustiniano e nega giurando l'*inquisitio*.

Altra deposizione sempre a c. 80r.

A c. 80v *inquisitio* di due ecclesiastici che hanno litigato all'ospedale; 4 testi, poi a c.81v la sentenza: con condanna a pagare 10 lire al camerlengo.

Poi altra sentenza dell'11 dicembre: di dieci lire, di cui è previsto il raddoppio se non si paga entro dieci giorni con la pena della scomunica e la sospensione *a divinis*.

20

Barbara Zymermanin's Two Husbands

Ludwig Schmugge

※

In the Later Middle Ages, canon law not only regulated the lives and careers of ecclesiastical persons, clerics, monks, and nuns but also had an enormous impact on the daily affairs of the laity. Even marriage, the most intimate relationship between men and women, was not beyond scrutiny, since it was viewed as a holy sacrament of the Church. The degree of supervision and interference is still apparent from the surviving records of thousands of matrimonial cases. These records were produced by the episcopal courts that operated in every diocese of Latin Christendom. According to the matrimonial law defined by late medieval councils and papal legislation, it was the task of the chief judicial officer *(officialis)* or vicar general *(vicarius generalis)* of the local bishoprics to handle all ordinary litigation relating to marriage. The supreme tribunal for spiritual matters at the papal court, the Penitentiary, was responsible for the granting of various marriage dispensations. In a period of less than fifty years, between 1455 and 1503, the scribes of the papal Penitentiary copied into their registers a total of 62,689 petitions involving marriage cases from across Western Europe. The documentation resulting from their efforts is now stored in the Vatican Archives.[1]

In the medieval Church, marriages between Christians, assuming they had been contracted according to proper canonical form, were indissoluble. But at the same time, there were many canonical impediments preventing men and women from contracting fully binding, sacramental marriages.[2] The moral and juridical doctrines of the Church

---

1. E. Göller, *Die päpstliche Pönitentiarie von ihrem Ursprung bis zu ihrer Umgestaltung unter Pius V.* (2 vols. in 4 parts; Bibliothek des Preussischen Historischen Instituts in Rom 3, 4, 7, and 8; Rome 1907–11); L. Schmugge, P. Hersperger, and B. Wiggenhauser, *Die Supplikenregister der päpstlichen Pönitentiarie aus der Zeit Pius' II. (1458–1464).* (Bibliothek des Deutschen Historischen Instituts in Rom 84; Tübingen 1996).

2. For the impediments see J. Freisen, *Geschichte des canonischen Eherechts bis zum Verfall der Glossenlitera-*

also did not condone any form of extra-marital sexual activity. Since medieval people did not always live up to the ecclesiastical standards, church courts were faced with a barrage of litigation between spouses, leading to countless investigations of improper behavior by married and unmarried couples alike. In the present essay, I will examine a single fifteenth-century case from Germany, which seems particularly suited to show the complexities arising from the requirements of church law on the one hand, and the social realities of spousal commitment on the other.

In the past few decades matrimonial litigation has been studied rather intensely on the basis of local diocesan records.[3] However, the pertinent documentation from the registers of the papal Penitentiary has been explored only occasionally.[4] It is often difficult to match up local diocesan sources with the records in the central papal archives. The task has been accomplished by Paolo Ostinelli's study of fifteenth-century cases from the diocese of Como in Northern Italy.[5] But it is also worthwhile to explore those registered petitions of the Penitentiary which—due to loss—do not permit consultation of parallel sources in Rome and in local archives. Here I will examine a case submitted to the Penitentiary archives by a German petitioner from Würzburg, a diocese for which no documentation has survived *in partibus*, that is, in the local church.

The diocese of Würzburg in southern Germany, one of the largest ecclesiastical territories in the Empire, was subdivided into 900 parochial churches.[6] The bishop, simultaneously spiritual leader and political head of the duchy of Franconia, delegated his duties as supreme judge to an officer trained in canon law, the *officialis curiae Herbipolensis*. If we wish to consider the years between 1458 and 1471, based on a comparison with the neighboring diocese of Regensburg we can assume that the Würzburg court

tur (Paderborn 1893, repr. Aalen 1963) 220–768; J. Gaudemet, *Le mariage en occident. Le moeurs et le droit* (Paris 1987) 195–219.

3. The fundamental study is by R. Helmholz, *Marriage Litigation in Medieval England* (Cambridge 1974). For more recent works on Italy, see *Coniugi nemici: La separazione in Italia dal XII al XVIII secolo*, ed. S. Seidel Menchi and D. Quaglioni (Annali dell'Istituto storico italo-germanico in Trento, Quaderni 53; Bologna 2000); *Matrimoni in dubbio. Unioni controverse e nozze clandestine in Italia dal XIV al XVIII secolo*, ed. S. Seidel Menchi and D. Quaglioni (Annali dell'Istituto storico italo-germanico in Trento, Quaderni 57; Bologna 2002). For Germany, C. Deutsch, *Ehegerichtsbarkeit im Bistum Regensburg (1480 bis 1538). Institutionelle Strukturen und jurisdiktionelle Praxis* (Köln 2005).

4. For Germany, see L. Schmugge, 'Deutsche Ehen vor römischem Gericht: Matrimonialdispense der Pönitentiarie aus deutschsprachigen Gegenden Europas (1455–1484)', in: *The Roman Curia, the Apostolic Penitentiary and the Partes in the Later Middle Ages*, ed. K. Salonen and C. Krötzl (Acta Instituti Romani Finlandiae 28; Rome 2003) 115–25.

5. P. Ostinelli, *Penitenzieria Apostolica. Le suppliche alla Sacra Penitenzieria Apostolica provenienti dalla diocesi di Como (1438–1484)* (Milan 2003).

6. *Das Bistum Würzburg* 3: *Die Bischofsreihe von 1455 bis 1617*, ed A. Wendehorst (Germania Sacra, NF 13.3; Berlin 1978); *Die Territorien des Reichs im Zeitalter der Reformation und Konfessionalisierung* 4: *Würzburg*, ed. W. Ziegler (Münster 1992) 99–126. F. Bendel, 'Die Würzburger Diözesanmatrikel aus der Mitte des 15. Jahrhunderts', *Würzburger Diözesangeschichtsblätter* 2 (1944) XXVII.

must have handled several hundred marriage cases during the period in question. Several registers of the *officialis* acting in Regensburg have survived from the second half of the fifteenth century, from which Christina Deutsch has culled references to no fewer than 1,704 marriage cases entered in a span of only seven years. Given this impressive total for Regensburg, it is safe to assume that at least as many marital complaints would have been entered at Würzburg during the much longer period of thirteen years examined in the present essay.[7] From the hundreds of documents that presumably were issued by the Würzburg court at this time, a mere sixty-one entered the records of the Apostolic Penitentiary. Unlike ordinary marriage litigation, dispensations from marriage impediments were reserved to the papacy alone and exceeded the competence of the local court.[8] The supplications recorded at the papal court and preserved in the Penitentiary archives furnish us with the only evidence we have for Würzburg that such litigation ever occurred. Let us now turn to one particular petition and investigate it from the point of view of canon law, while also keeping an eye on matters of local and social interest.

The case I would like to discuss appears in a petition from the beginning of the pontificate of Paul II (1464–71), but relies on legal precedents reaching back into the later years of his predecessor, Pope Pius II (1458–64).[9] The parties involved in our case had been living in the city of Würzburg and in the southwestern part of the diocese, in the small town of Archshofen near Creglingen, located in what today forms part of the German state of Baden-Württemberg. Würzburg is in modern Bavaria.[10]

Interestingly but not all that surprisingly, the petition in question was submitted by a woman, Barbara Zymermanin, who, according to her surname is likely to have been the daughter of a carpenter at Archshofen. It comes as no surprise, given the principle that a supplication would not appear in the registers of the Penitentiary unless it had been answered favorably, that Barbara eventually received a positive response to her request. It was signed by the major penitentiary, Filippo Cardinal Calandrini, who had been in charge of the office since the beginning of Pius II's pontificate.[11] Filippo approved Barbara's petition only after he had consulted his auditor, Antonius de Grassis, the specialist appointed by the office to deal with difficult questions of canon law. The Penitentiary made the following decision: The former sentence of a local ecclesiastical

---

7. Deutsch, *Ehegerichtsbarkeit* 12.

8. For a full translation of Barbara Zymermanin's case, following the version catalogued in RPG 5.222–23 no. 1954, see Appendix below.

9. L. Schmugge, 'Beobachtungen zu deutschen Ehedispensen aus der Zeit Papst Pauls II. (1464–1471)', in: *Festschrift Brigide Schwarz*, ed. M. Matheus et al. (Geschichtliche Landeskunde 59; Stuttgart 2005) 113–28.

10. For Archshofen, see *Handbuch der historischen Stätten* 6: *Baden-Württemberg*, ed. M. Miller and G. Taddey (Stuttgart 1980) 28.

11. For his biography, C. Gennaro, 'Calandrini, Filippo', DBI 16 (1975) 450–52.

tribunal was to be annulled. In addition, Barbara's file was to be sent to the bishop of Bamberg. Should the bishop find Barbara's claims truthful, he would be commissioned to sign a declaration in the name of the pope, stating that Barbara was in fact canonically married to a certain Georg Wildholtz. Her case had to be forwarded to the bishop of Bamberg because Barbara had expressed doubts about the impartiality of her *ordinarius*, the bishop of Würzburg.[12] According to the scholastic *Ius commune*, the *recusatio iudicis*, the rejection of a judge on the grounds of reasonable suspicion, was a fundamental right of any petitioner in the later Middle Ages.[13]

The final papal decision in the controversy about Barbara's marriage was issued in February 1465. It followed a long series of canonical arguments and rebuttals, which Barbara (or the proctor who assisted her in drawing up her petition to the pope) had recounted in full in the body of her letter. The text sheds new light on matrimonial litigation at the bishops' courts in the second half of the fifteenth century. But, unfortunately, the narrative does not allow us to reconstruct the chronology of Barbara's case with certainty, given that exact dates are lacking. It all began when Barbara, still rather young as we shall see, married 'by present consent' *(per verba de presenti)* a certain Georg Wildholtz, layman, from the diocese of Würzburg. The union was arranged with the help of friends and relatives to whom she had been entrusted prior to her father's death, and was announced publicly *(publice)*, in correspondence with the canonical requirements expressed in canons 50 and 51 of the Fourth Lateran Council of 1215.[14] Although Barbara was absent at the time the marriage contract was concluded, she seems to have agreed to it, having confirmed it again later on *(postmodum similiter cum eodem contraxit)*.

What happened next is something that occurred rather often in circumstances similar to Barbara's during the later Middle Ages when the marriage of a prospective heiress general was at stake. Other members of Barbara's family, especially her brothers and relatives from her mother's side, did not agree to her union with Georg. As a result, they forced Barbara, at the time (as her narrative claimed) only 13 years old and fatherless, to contract a marriage with another man, again from the same diocese of Würzburg, by the name of Friedrich Vasner.[15] The indication of her age is revealing. According

12. RPG 5.222–23 no. 1954: 'Cum eius ordinarium in hac parte habeat suspectum'; see also L. Schmugge, 'Kanonistik in der Pönitentiarie', in: *Stagnation oder Fortbildung? Aspekte des allgemeinen Kirchenrechts im 14. und 15. Jahrhundert*, ed. M. Bertram (Bibliothek des Deutschen Historischen Instituts in Rom 108; Tübingen 2004) 105. Regarding the bishop of Bamberg at the time, see E. Greipl, 'Schaumberg, Georg von', in: *Die Bischöfe des Heiligen Römischen Reiches 1448 bis 1648*, ed. E. Gatz (Berlin 1996) 620–21 .

13. See L. Fowler, 'Recusatio Iudicis in Civilian and Canonist Thought', SG 15 (1972) 717–86.

14. Lateran IV can. 50–51, ed. COD³ 257–59; since 1234, both canons have been incorporated into the *Decretales Gregorii IX* (known to medieval canonists as *Liber extra*), X 4.3.3 and X 4.4.8.

15. The printed text in RPG 5 reads *Odasner*, but has to be corrected to *Vasner*.

to canon law, girls were to be considered capable of contracting valid marriages from the age of 12, suggesting that this second marriage might have been valid canonically. Barbara, however, was not prepared to agree to it. Quite the contrary, she refused and protested publicly, claiming that she had already contracted a binding marriage with Georg earlier on. Still, the petition points out, her relatives compelled her to accept the contract with Friedrich Vasner *(sic compulsa similiter cum dicto Friderico contraxit)*, albeit under duress.

Friedrich Vasner, after hearing about Barbara's previous marriage to Georg, took them both to the court of the bishop of Würzburg, Johann von Grumbach.[16] During the pleading, Barbara declared publicly that she had married Georg first, persuading the judge (probably the *officialis*) to indicate to the relatives present that he would be inclined to pass judgment in favor of Barbara's union with Georg. Yet prior to the sentencing, Friedrich protested that he would proceed to prove the contrary, that is, that he had married Barbara first. At this point the parties left the bishop's court and Barbara returned to her brothers' home. The brothers continued to reprimand and bully her, insisting that she must agree to her union with Friedrich. Barbara consequently fled to her, as she put it, legitimate husband, Georg, in order to escape further molestation by her brothers. Georg and Barbara subsequently consummated their marriage by having intercourse and lived together as wife and husband. The carnal consummation of a marriage that previously had existed only through consent, created, according to the teaching of the Church, a valid and full-fledged *matrimonium ratum*. If Barbara had indeed agreed to marry Georg before she contracted with Friedrich, consummation formed the decisive step towards indissolubility, to the detriment of the rival Friedrich's claims.[17]

Alas, Barbara's troubles did not end there. After half a year had passed, her brothers died. Instead of her own family, now Friedrich's relatives took Barbara to court again, in the hope that their favorite would finally 'get hold of her heritage', as Barbara put it in her supplication to the pope. To pursue his claim, Friedrich even seems to have moved (from Archshofen?) to the city of Würzburg, where he approached a secular rather than the ecclesiastical court. Late medieval marriage was not quite the 'worldly thing' Martin Luther later saw it to be.[18] Marriage was heavily regulated by the norms of canon law,

16. *Das Bistum Würzburg* 3–20; E. Greipl, 'Grumbach, Johann von', in: *Die Bischöfe des Heiligen Römischen Reiches* 247–48.

17. See in general J. B. Sägmüller, *Lehrbuch des katholischen Kirchenrechts* (Freiburg 1914) 578–681; J. Gaudemet, *Le mariage en Occident*; P. Toxé, 'La *copula carnalis* chez les canonistes médiévaux', in: *Mariages et sexualité au Moyen Age. Accord ou crise?*, ed. M. Rouche (Paris 2000) 123–33. M. Sheehan, *Marriage, Family and Law in Medieval Europe* (Toronto 1996); R. Weigand, *Liebe und Ehe im Mittelalter* (Bibliotheca Eruditorum 7; Goldbach 1993).

18. *D. Martin Luthers Werke* 30.3 (Weimar 1910) 205.

and Friedrich's move was questionable. The Würzburg lay judges accepted Friedrich's charges against Barbara and finally declared Friedrich and Barbara to be legally married. The court, however, had made a procedural mistake (at least according to canon law) by not hearing either Barbara or Georg. Hence it was easy for Barbara's party to appeal to the episcopal court of Würzburg, where the case rested undecided for more than a year. We don't know exactly when nor do we know why the delay occurred. Perhaps, the military troubles mentioned in Barbara's text prevented ordinary jurisdiction from functioning normally.

Big politics, local sources confirm, affected Barbara's plight at that point. War had broken out *(orte fuerunt guerre capitales)* between the bishop of Würzburg, Johann von Grumberg, and Albrecht Achilles of Brandenburg, a Hohenzollern, who in 1470 would become prince-elector of Brandenburg.[19] Johann and Albrecht had had a long history of conflict about the territory of Würzburg, with the Hohenzollern fighting for sovereignty. In 1459, none other than Pope Pius II had granted Albrecht the title of 'Duke of Franconia', notwithstanding the fact that the bishops of Würzburg had asserted that they had borne the title since the twelfth century. In the ensuing struggle, parts of the Würzburg territory were devastated. In 1462, the castle of Archshofen, the village where Barbara lived, was destroyed.

Barbara and Georg argued that, because of the violent events in the territory of Würzburg, they had been unable, without risking their lives, to travel the thirty kilometers from Archshofen to the city of Würzburg. Their adversary, Friedrich, had taken advantage of the situation and accused Barbara yet again. He received a definitive sentence in his favor from a court that our text does not specify as either lay or ecclesiastical. Again, Barbara had not received any notification or summons, giving rise to her appeal to the Apostolic See in Rome. From Rome and probably at Barbara's own request, her case was eventually delegated *(per rescriptum)* not to the bishop of Würzburg, Johann of Grumbach, but to the *episcopus* of Eichstätt, who in turn sub-delegated the matter to the provost of the cathedral chapter of Eichstätt. This was the usual procedure if one of the parties to a case approached the Apostolic See: the provost was to summon the parties and initiate the hearings. In Barbara's case, though, he never passed definitive judgment *(citra tamen conclusionem)*.

Unfortunately for Barbara, the *iudex apostolicus*, the judge to whom the pope had committed the inquisition of her appeal, the bishop of Eichstätt, died before he could accomplish his task, an event that affords us the first precise chronological indication: From 1445 to 1464, the see of Eichstätt was occupied by Johann von Eych, who died on

---

19. See J. Schultze, *Die Mark Brandenburg 3: Die Mark unter Herrschaft der Hohenzollern (1415–1535)* (Berlin 1963) 107–12.

New Year's Day of 1464.[20] The accuracy of Barbara's report is confirmed by what she tells us about Johann's successor, Wilhelm of Reichenau. Elected on January 16, 1465, Wilhelm had been provost of the Eichstätt chapter since 1463. He held the see of Eichstätt until 1496.[21] As already mentioned, it had been Wilhelm who, while in his office as provost, had been appointed judge sub-delegate by Johann von Eych. As the new bishop, the same Wilhelm was certainly too busy to deal with Barbara's case. He did, however, send Barbara's lawyer and proctor to Rome to have him obtain further information on how to proceed. When the latter had left on his journey to the Roman *curia*, Friedrich's party quickly approached the new bishop's court and again initiated new proceedings against Barbara, eventually securing Wilhelm's wholehearted support. Wilhelm opened a new trial, cited Barbara's party, and eventually confirmed *(per suam sententiam diffinitivam confirmavit)* the sentences formerly passed against Barbara, that is, the one from the city court of Würzburg noted above.

As a result, Barbara felt she had been treated unjustly by the bishop's court which, in her mind, had proceeded against the norms of canon law. Sensing further that her soul was in danger, she declared publicly and in the presence of witnesses and a notary that she would rather enter a monastery than live with Friedrich as an adulteress and dishonor her children. Following up on her promise, she then entered a nearby monastery, the Benedictine observant house (as she called it) of Frauental in the diocese of Würzburg, with the intention of staying there for the rest of her life. The monastery of Frauental, only a few miles away from Archshofen, was founded in 1232 not as a Benedictine but as a Cistercian house.[22] As there are no fifteenth-century records of the nuns available to us today, we cannot verify her statement.[23] After she had been in the monastery for thirteen weeks, Friedrich again intervened, this time with force. Executing orders he had received from the bishop, he and other armed men entered and removed Barbara from Frauental.

Barbara, however, immediately returned to Georg and to her children. We are told that they had several children, implying that at least two or three years must have passed since she and Georg had set up their household. This gives us an approximate date of around 1461/62 for the beginning of their beleaguered cohabitation. After their reunion Barbara again turned to the Apostolic See. All of the historical and canonical

20. A. Schmid, 'Eych, Johann von', in: *Die Bischöfe des Heiligen Römischen Reiches* 173–74.

21. A. Schmid, 'Reichenau, Wilhelm von', in: *Die Bischöfe des Heiligen Römischen Reiches* 575–76. Unfortunately no documents from the Eichstätt *officialatus* have survived, see I. Buchholz-Johanek, *Geistliche Richter und geistliches Gericht im spätmittelalterlichen Bistum Eichstätt* (Eichstätter Studien vol. 23; Regensburg 1988) 28.

22. See *Handbuch der historischen Stätten* 215.

23. M. Wieland, *Das Cistercienserinnenkloster Frauental in Württemberg* (Stuttgart 1905); G. Bossert, 'Urkunden des Klosters Frauental', *Württembergische Vierteljahrshefte für Landesgeschichte* 12 (1889) 218–40.

details I have related thus far appear in her petition as it was recorded in the registers of the Penitentiary.

In the final section of the document, certainly formulated on her behalf by a proctor well-trained in the field of marriage law, Barbara asked the Penitentiary for the issuance of a *littera declaratoria*, a letter of declaration that would state that she and Georg could legally and lawfully remain in their marriage and confirm it, notwithstanding the contrary opinion of their opponents, in church and in solemn form *(ad sollempnizationem ipsius in facie ecclesie procedere)*. The *sollempnizatio* was the official celebration in public of a marriage that had been concluded previously by contract and consummation only. The ceremonies celebrating late medieval marriages varied greatly according to local customs und tradition.[24] For a canonically valid marriage, the exchange of the wedding vows and carnal consummation were the essential elements in creating the sacramental bond between the two spouses. Public announcement in the church *(sollempnizatio)* merely rendered the marital obligation visible to all.

Last but not least, Barbara did not forget in her petition to ask the pope for *legitimatio prolis*, the legitimization of her children. Without this formal act, they would have risked exclusion from inheritance and life-long legal and social stigmatization as bastards.

Considering that there are no pertinent local sources that have survivied from the dioceses of Würzburg and Eichstätt, we would not know anything about Barbara and her two husbands if it were not for the Penitentiary registers.[25] Central to the dispute described in her petition was certainly the question of inheritance. There were many conflicts among clans and families about their property *(substantia)*, the land, castles, and feudal rents they owned, and about the question of who should benefit the most when this was transferred from one generation to the next. These conflicts are to be found not only within the circles of the German nobility, as Karl-Heinz Spiess' recent study shows.[26] They also occurred in small towns such as Archshofen in the diocese of Würzburg, where arguments seem to have been carried out with almost the same intensity as in the higher social strata.

In addition to offering new insights into local Franconian history, Barbara's case allows us to conclude that, even in relatively remote rural areas, there must have been rather detailed knowledge of the canonical regulations regarding marriage controver-

24. See a summary of the different traditions in C. Schott, *Trauung und Jawort. Von der Brautübergabe zur Ziviltrauung* (Frankfurt/M. 1992).

25. I wish to thank Prof. Alfred Wendehorst, Erlangen, and Prof. Karl Borchardt, Rothenburg, for information about the surviving source material from Würzburg, Eichstätt, and Bamberg.

26. K.-H. Spiess, *Familie und Verwandtschaft im deutschen Hochadel des Spätmittelalters (13. bis Anfang des 16. Jahrhunderts)* (Stuttgart 1993).

sies. We find advanced juristic skills in canonical procedure and marriage litigation not only in ecclesiastical centers such as Würzburg, but in small towns like Archshofen as well. Thus, along with regional studies of other areas, for example, Pedersen's work on the English archdiocese of York, Arnòrsdòttir's studies of Iceland, Ingesman's of Denmark, and Maria de Lourdes Rosa's work on Portugal, we can confirm the notion that there existed a veritable 'canon law culture' in the later Middle Ages, in central Europe as well as in more marginal areas of Latin Christendom.[27]

Appendix

Translation of Barbara Zymermanin's Petition to the Apostolic Penitentiary

6 February 1465[i]

Barbara Zymermanin, a woman from Arshofen in the diocese of Würzburg, explains that, aided by relatives and friends to whom she had been entrusted upon her father's death, she once contracted marriage, publicly and by present consent, with a certain Georg Wildholtz, layman of Würzburg diocese, despite the fact that she herself was absent at the time. Because of this, Barbara's brother and other relatives on her mother's side felt aggrieved and induced Barbara with threatening words and by force to contract marriage with a certain Friedrich [V]asner, given that she was about 13 years old and an orphan. She refused and publicly stated before them that she had already contracted marriage with the aforementioned Georg, but eventually submitted and contracted marriage with the said Friedrich as well. Friedrich had heard the words of Barbara and cited her together with Georg before the ordinary court, where she again declared publicly that she had previously contracted with Georg. The same judge wished to adjudicate Barbara in the presence of her relatives to the same Georg as his wife, which Friedrich prevented by saying that he would prove the contrary. Then, he left the court and Barbara returned to the house of her brothers, who harassed her daily to such an extent that she could not suffer their shameful accusations any longer. One day, she left them and went to Georg as her legitimate husband, whereupon the two lived in cohabitation and carnally consummated their union. Half a year later, Barbara's brothers died and Friedrich's relatives persuaded him to proceed against her so as to obtain all of her property. Thus, Friedrich went to Würzburg and presented his case before the judges there, who adjudicated Barbara to the same Friedrich as his legitimate wife, even though neither Barbara nor Georg had been summoned. On

27. See B. Ferme, *Canon Law in Medieval England* (Rome 1996); F. Pedersen, 'Did the Medieval Laity Know the Canon Law Rules on Marriage? Some Evidence from Fourteenth-Century York Cause Papers', *Medieval Studies* 56 (1994) 11–152; A. Arnòrsdòttir, 'Icelandic Marriage Dispensations in the Late Middle Ages', in: *The Roman Curia, the Apostolic Penitentiary and the Partes* 159–69; P. Ingesman, 'Danish Marriage Dispensations: Evidence of an Increasing Lay Use of Papal Letters in the Late Middle Ages', in: *The Roman Curia* 129–57; M. de Lourdes Rosa, 'Mariages et empêchements canoniques de parenté dans la société portugaise (1455–1520)', *Mélanges de l'Ecole Française de Rome. Moyen Age* 108 (1996) 525–608.

i. From the (slightly abbreviated) Latin text in RPG 5.222a–523a (no. 1954); for the (full) registered version, see Vatican, ASV PA 12, fol. 105v–106r.

Barbara's behalf, an appeal against the sentence was lodged at the episcopal court of Würzburg, where the matter was left undecided for more than a year. In the meantime, deadly
wars had erupted between the same ordinary bishop and the noble Margrave Albrecht of
Brandenburg, whence Barbara and Georg could not appear in court without peril; while
these wars continued, the said Friedrich secured for himself another definitive sentence in
his favor, again without summoning Barbara. On Barbara's behalf, another appeal against
the sentence was lodged at the Apostolic See, and the case was commissioned by Apostolic
rescript to the bishop of Eichstätt, who on his part subdelegated it to the dean *(prepositus)*
of Eichstätt, before whom the matter was treated in several judicial sessions without result.
According to God's will, it occurred that the episcopal judge and Apostolic commissioner
of the case went the way of all the flesh before the subdelegate could reach his conclusion;
the said dean was elected bishop and sent both Barbara's advocate and her proctor to the
Roman curia to have the election confirmed. During their absence, the bishop elect, prod-
ded by Barbara's adversaries and upon summoning her, confirmed and approved the two
previous sentences by passing his own definitive sentence in her presence. Barbara, feeling
greatly disadvantaged and aware of the imminent danger for her soul, declared personally,
publicly, and in the presence of notaries and witnesses that she, rather than wishing to co-
habit with the second man in adultery and dishonor her male children, would renounce
the year [of probation] and enter a monastery. She next entered the convent of Benedictine
observants[ii] at Frauental in Würzburg diocese, intending to stay there forever. After a so-
journ of thirteen weeks, however, the said Friedrich and his accomplices expelled Barbara
from the convent by force of arms and ordinary injunction. She returned to her husband
Georg and their children. Since Barbara wishes to remain with the said Georg, but certain
people, perhaps out of envy, assert that she, due to the aforementioned, can neither do so
nor proceed with the solemnization of her marriage in front of the church, she [petitions],
in order to [silence] these rumors, a declaratory letter that includes the legitimization of
her offspring in the usual form.

　　Granted as below, Philip; [the case] be inspected by Antonio de Grassi: Philip; [the
case] be commissioned to the bishop of Bamberg, because [the petitioner] considers her
ordinary suspect in this matter: so be it, Philip; [the case] be committed to the ordinary,
who upon citing those to be cited and upon deciding about the validity of the three previous sentences may declare as petitioned, provided that he determines in accordance with
the law that the supplicant contracted marriage by present consent and legitimately with
Georg before doing so with Friedrich and that the other facts stated in her petition are
truthful as well, the previous sentences and other considerations notwithstanding.

　　ii. The original words *regularis observantie* have not been included in RPG 5.223a.

PART FOUR

Canonists in Conversation with the Wider World

21

L'origine et la diffusion de l'adage canonique
Necessitas non habet legem (VIIIe–XIIIe s.)

Franck Roumy

❀

La maxime *Necessitas non habet legem* est fameuse. Plongeant ses origines dans le
Jus commune, son usage se poursuit jusqu'à aujourd'hui et elle figure encore dans différents dictionnaires d'adages juridiques utilisés tant dans les pays continentaux que
dans ceux de *common law*.[1] En Allemagne, en Angleterre, aux États-Unis, en Italie ou
en France, notamment, la pratique judiciaire y recourt toujours occasionnellement et,
surtout, l'adage a fini par acquérir valeur de proverbe. 'Not kennt kein Gebot', dit-on en
allemand.[2] 'Nécessité n'a point de loi', disent les Français, depuis que le juriste Antoine
Loisel, au début du XVIIe siècle, a popularisé un certain nombre de brocards du *Jus commune*, en les traduisant en langue vernaculaire et en leur donnant ainsi la teinture de
produits nationaux.[3]

La célébrité de l'adage n'exclut cependant pas les controverses quant à sa portée et,
d'une manière générale, les juristes contemporains tendent à n'admettre qu'une application restreinte de la règle. En France, par exemple, celle-ci se réduit pour l'essentiel
à ce que le droit pénal nomme l'état de nécessité.[4] Pendant longtemps, les juristes ont

1. Cf. par ex. D. Liebs, *Lateinische Rechtsregeln und Rechtssprichwörter* (München 1998⁶) N.10; H. Rolland et
L. Boyer, *Adages du droit français* (Paris 1999⁴) n° 238; ou encore B. Garner, *Black's Law Dictionary* (St Paul, MI
1999⁷) 1659.

2. Walther n° 16295a. L. De Mauri (Ernesto Sarasíno), *Flores sententiarum. Raccolta di 5000 sentenze, proverbi
e motti latini di uso quotidiano in ordine per materie con le fonti indicate, schiarimenti e la traduzione italiana* (Milano 1949) 347.

3. Antoine Loisel, *Institutes coutumières* 6.3.13 et 6.6.4 (Paris 1608). L'édition de Dupin et Laboulaye, accom-
pagnée des notes d'Eusèbe de Laurière (Paris 1846) 6.1.14, n° 870, donne également la forme allemande de la
maxime: 'Noth hat kein Gebot'. La forme française ancienne de la maxime paraît plutôt être 'Besoin ne garde
loi', cf. S. Singer, *Sprichwörter des Mittelalters* II (Bern 1946) n° 38, pour qui la forme 'Not kennt kein Gebot' re-
monterait au XVe siècle.

4. Voir Rolland et Boyer, *Adages* 469.

aussi discuté de l'origine de la maxime, hésitant à lui reconnaître des racines romaines ou canoniques. Il est cependant aujourd'hui admis que la sentence est demeurée ignorée du droit romain, tant classique que post-classique. Plus globalement, comme l'a montré, entre autres, Tomasz Giaro, le droit romain n'a pas élaboré de théorie générale de la nécessité.[5] Le concept de *necessitas* est pourtant l'un des *topoi* de la rhétorique latine de l'époque classique et, en particulier, de la rhétorique judiciaire.[6] L'excuse de nécessité, néanmoins, n'intervient en droit que de manière casuistique. La notion de *necessitas* n'est très pragmatiquement avancée que comme argument ultime et les juristes romains n'ont donc pas construit un véritable corps de règles générales s'appliquant au concept.

En réalité, la maxime *Necessitas non habet legem* apparaît dans le droit canonique médiéval. Elle est déjà présente, au milieu du XIIᵉ siècle, à deux reprises, dans le Décret de Gratien. Elle figure en effet dans une pseudo-décrétale attribuée au pape Félix IV, reprise dans le *De consecratione*, et elle est également utilisée dans un *dictum Gratiani*.[7] Il convient en outre de préciser que ces deux textes se trouvent déjà dans la version du Décret, antérieure à sa vulgate, mise à jour par Anders Winroth.[8] Quelques décennies plus tard, l'adage se retrouve dans une décrétale d'Innocent III, adressée le 19 novembre 1199 à Lucius, vicaire apostolique à Constantinople, laquelle passe dans la *Compilatio tertia*, puis dans le *Liber Extra*.[9] Il existe enfin, au titre *De regulis juris* des Décrétales de Grégoire IX, un fragment attribué à Bède le Vénérable, proclamant que ce qui n'est pas permis par la loi, l'est par la nécessité: 'Quod non est licitum lege, necessitas facit licitum'.[10]

L'utilisation de ces textes par les canonistes médiévaux a été étudiée dans le détail par plusieurs historiens, plus spécialement par Stephan Kuttner, dans son monumental ouvrage sur la doctrine canonique de la responsabilité, et par Gilles Couvreur, dans sa thèse sur le vol en cas d'extrême nécessité, à l'époque du droit canonique classique et des débuts de la théologie scolastique.[11] Ce dernier, en particulier, a montré l'extension

5. T. Giaro, *Excusatio necessitatis nel diritto romano* (Studia Antiqua 9; Warsawa 1982). Voir aussi A. Ormanni, 'Necessità (Stato di). Diritto romano', ED 27 (1977) 822–47.

6. B.-J. Schröder, 'Necessitas', *Historisches Wörterbuch der Rhetorik* 6 (2003) 203–06.

7. De cons. D.1 c.11 et C.1 q.1 d.p.c.39.

8. A. Winroth, *The Making of Gratian's Decretum* (Cambridge Studies in Medieval Life and Thought 49; Cambridge 2000) 204, 226.

9. *Quanto de benignitate* (Po. 868 = 3 Comp.1.3.3 = X 1.4.4).

10. 1 Comp.5.37.12 = X 5.41.4.

11. S. Kuttner, *Kanonistische Schuldlehre von Gratian bis auf die Dekretalen Gregors IX., systematisch auf Grund der handschriftlichen Quellen dargestellt* (Studi e Testi 64; Città del Vaticano 1935, réimpr. 1973) spéc. 291–98; G. Couvreur, *Les pauvres ont-ils des droits? Recherches sur le vol en cas d'extrême nécessité depuis la Concordia de Gratien (1140) jusqu'à Guillaume d'Auxerre (†1231)* (Analecta Gregoriana 111; Romae 1962) spéc. 66–70; voir aussi M. Ascheri, 'Note per la storia dello stato di necessità', *Studi Senesi* 87 (1975) 7–74, spéc. 33–34; et J. Pilcher, *Neces-*

prise par l'adage *Necessitas non habet legem*. Dans la pseudo-lettre de Félix IV contenue dans le Décret de Gratien, en effet, le brocard ne s'applique qu'à la permission de célébrer la messe hors des lieux consacrés, en cas de nécessité. Lorsque Gratien l'utilise par ailleurs dans un *dictum*, il s'agit seulement pour lui de justifier l'existence d'une catégorie spécifique de sacrements, qu'il nomme 'nécessaires' car ils ne peuvent être réitérés.[12] Les canonistes médiévaux, cependant, allaient user de l'adage dans bien d'autres contextes, l'exemple le plus significatif étant celui de la discussion relative au vol en cas de nécessité.

Si les circonstances dans lesquelles la doctrine canonique médiévale a utilisé cette maxime et, surtout, les limites qu'elle a posées à son application comme règle de droit ont été minutieusement analysées par Stephan Kuttner et Gilles Couvreur, l'histoire des origines de la sentence reste néanmoins très mal connue. Le contexte dans lequel apparaît cette formule et les débuts de sa diffusion, au moins jusqu'à l'aube du XIIIe siècle, demeurent dans l'ombre. Dans un article paru en 2000, Kenneth Pennington écrivait: 'the history of *necessitas legem non habet*, from its origins in the early Middle Ages to its maturity in the *Ius commune*, remains to be written'.[13] À l'invitation du maître auquel ces lignes sont dédiées, c'est donc à cette histoire que s'attèle la présente contribution, tentant, d'une part, de reconstituer la genèse du proverbe (I) et, de l'autre, d'esquisser un premier aperçu de sa diffusion, d'abord en droit canonique (II), puis, en dehors même de celui-ci, dans les différentes branches du savoir médiéval (III).

I

S'agissant tout d'abord des origines de l'adage, il convient de relever que, bien que celui-ci soit, sans équivoque possible, une création originale du droit canonique médiéval, on rencontre déjà des formules proches, dans la littérature latine de l'Antiquité. L'idée que la nécessité peut fournir, dans des circonstances exceptionnelles, une excuse à l'individu qui se trouve acculé à violer certaines règles est en effet un *topos* très ancien et relativement répandu. Dans les fragments des *Controverses* de Sénèque le Rhéteur—

---

sitas. Ein Element des mittelalterlichen und neuzeitlichen Rechts. Dargestellt am Beispiel österreichischer Rechtsquellen (Schriften zur Rechtsgeschichte 27; Berlin 1983); idem, 'Necessitas non habet legem', dans: *Aus Österreichs Rechtsleben in Geschichte und Gegenwart. Festschrift für Ernst Carl Helbling zum 80. Geburtstag* (Berlin 1981) 659–82, qui analyse plutôt la portée de l'adage à l'Époque moderne.

12. C.1 q.1 d.p.c.39, VI Pars: 'Sed notandum est, quod sacramentorum alia sunt dignitatis, alia necessitatis. Quia enim necessitas non habet legem, sed ipsa sibi facit legem, illa sacramenta, que saluti sunt necessaria, quia iterari non possunt, cum sint vera, auferri vel amitti non debent, sed cum penitentia rata esse permittuntur'.

13. K. Pennington, 'Innocent III and the Ius commune', dans: *Grundlagen des Rechts. Festschrift für Peter Landau zum 65. Geburtstag*, éd. R. Helmholz et al. (Rechts- und Staatswissenschaftliche Veröffentlichungen der Görres-Gesellschaft 91; Paderborn 2000) 351.

dont la transmission est d'ailleurs problématique et qui, peut-être, ne remontent pas au-delà du IVe siècle de notre ère—, on trouve ainsi l'exemple du soldat qui, ayant perdu ses armes au combat, s'empare de celles d'un autre, mort et déjà enseveli. Bien qu'étant vainqueur, celui-ci est ensuite accusé de violation de sépulture. L'auteur des fragments justifie cependant ses agissements, en invoquant, entre autres, la *lex Rhodia de jactu*, et en observant que 'la nécessité fait jeter la charge d'un navire pour l'alléger, la nécessité fait démolir les maisons pour éteindre les incendies; la nécessité est la loi du moment'.[14] La formule *Necessitas est lex temporis* employée par le rhéteur préfigure en partie celle qui proclame que 'Nécessité n'a point de loi', mais en inversant toutefois le propos dans la mesure où la nécessité ne défait pas la loi, mais la fait.

Une autre formule, plus proche de l'adage médiéval, se trouve dans les Sentences de Publilius Syrus, un moraliste aujourd'hui oublié, mais qui connut son heure de gloire en interprétant des mimes devant César.[15] Sa collection de sentences, qui semble avoir été réunie par ses disciples, après sa mort, sous le règne de Néron, contient le brocard: 'Necessitas dat legem, non ipsa accipit'.[16] Il n'est pas impossible que cette formule soit à l'origine indirecte de l'adage *Necessitas non habet legem*, dans la mesure où l'œuvre de Publilius Syrus a connu une certaine diffusion au cours du haut Moyen Âge. Les manuscrits conservés indiquent en effet que plusieurs collections différentes de maximes circulèrent, parfois sous le nom de Sénèque, avant que l'œuvre ne fasse l'objet d'une reconstruction, aux Xe et XIe siècles.[17] Si, compte tenu de cette complexe tradition manuscrite, l'authenticité du fragment en question demeure sujette à caution, proclamer que 'la nécessité fait la loi, mais n'est pas soumise à celle-ci' traduit en tout cas une idée d'inspiration stoïcienne assez répandue à la fin de l'Antiquité.

L'opinion selon laquelle la nécessité est susceptible de modifier l'ordre des règles établies s'est du reste introduite très tôt dans la discipline ecclésiastique. Elle apparaît ainsi avec netteté dans une décrétale du pape Léon Ier, adressée le 11 juin 451 à l'évêque Théodore de Fréjus. Le pontife explique que ceux qui, en cas de nécessité ou de péril imminent, implorent la protection de la pénitence et, peu après, la réconciliation, ne

14. Seneca Rhetoris, *Controversiarum excerpta* 4.4, éd. L. Håkanson (Leipzig 1989) 147.24: 'Necessitas est quae navigia iactu exonerat, necessitas quae ruinis incendia opprimit; necessitas est lex temporis'. Pour la traduction française, voir H. Bornecque, *Sénèque le Père. Sentences, Divisons et Couleurs des orateurs et des rhéteurs*, revue par J.-H. Bornecque (Paris 1992) 201. Sur la *lex Rhodia de jactu*, voir R. Zimmermann, *The Law of Obligations. Roman Foundations of the Civilian Tradition* (Cape Town 1992²) 406–09.

15. M. Schanz et C. Hosius, *Geschichte der römischen Literatur bis zum Gesetzgebungswerk des Kaisers Justinian* I: *Die römische Literatur in der Zeit der Republik* (Handbuch der Altertumswissenschaft 8.1; München 1927⁴, réimpr. 1979) 259.

16. Publilius Syrus, *Sententiae* N 23, éd. W. Meyer (Lipsiae 1880) 45; éd. J. Duff et A. Duff, *Minor Latin Poets* (The Loeb Classical Collection 284; London et Cambridge 1935, réimpr. 1954) 72.

17. L'histoire des différentes compilations a été retracée par W. Meyer, *Die Sammlungen der Spruchverse des Publilius Syrus* (Leipzig 1877).

peuvent se voir refuser cette faveur ni dénier la réconciliation, dans la mesure où il est impossible de poser des bornes à la miséricorde divine et que l'on ne peut non plus imposer des délais, aux termes desquels seulement interviendrait une véritable conversion.[18]

Cette décrétale de Léon le Grand a connu, pendant tout le haut Moyen Âge, un très grand succès. Elle a en effet été recueillie intégralement dans plusieurs collections canoniques, dont certaines ont connu une diffusion importante, comme l'*Hispana*.[19] Par ailleurs, le passage précédemment mentionné est notamment utilisé, à plusieurs reprises, par Hincmar de Reims, dans son traité sur le divorce de Lothaire II, dans sa lettre sur la pénitence de Pépin ou encore dans l'Opuscule en 55 chapitres.[20] Il se trouve encore inclus dans un canon du concile tenu à Metz en mai–juin 859, dont les actes furent également mis en forme par Hincmar.[21] La large diffusion de ce fragment est assurée par les nombreuses collections canoniques dans lesquelles il fut copié.[22] Véhiculé sous une forme longue, le canon *Multiplex misericordia*, ou sous une forme plus brève, le canon *His autem*, celui-ci se trouve présent dans près d'une quarantaine de recueils s'échelonnant de la Réforme carolingienne à la Réforme grégorienne, en particulier dans des collections célèbres qui connurent elles-mêmes une diffusion importante, comme la *Dacheriana* ou, plus tard, les œuvres de Benoît le Lévite, de Réginon de Prüm, de Burchard de Worms ou d'Yves de Chartres.[23]

18. Leo Magnus, *Epistolae* 108.4 (JK 485; ed. PL 54.1012C–1013A): 'His autem qui in tempore necessitatis et in periculi urgentis instantia praesidium poenitentiae et mox reconciliationis implorant, nec satisfactio interdicenda est, nec reconciliatio deneganda: quia misericordiae Dei nec mensuras possumus ponere, nec tempora definire, apud quem nullas patitur veniae moras vera conversio, dicente Spiritu Dei per prophetam: "Cum conversus ingemueris, tunc salvus eris (Is.30.15)".'

19. *Hispana* 2.73 (ed. PL 84.781B–782A). Elle figure aussi dans la *Quesneliana* ou dans des collections de moindre diffusion, mais parfois très anciennes, comme la *Corbeiensis* ou la *Pithouensis*: cf. K. Silva-Tarouca, 'Beiträge zur Überlieferungsgeschichte der Papstbriefe des IV., V. und VI. Jahrhunderts, II.', *Zeitschrift für katholische Theologie* 43 (1919) 690; H. Wurm, *Studien und Texte zur Dekretalensammlung des Dionysius Exiguus* (Kanonistische Studien und Texte 16; Bonn 1939, réimpr. Amsterdam 1964) 168, qui analyse par ailleurs la présentation du texte (protocole, inscription, etc.) dans ces différents recueils (ibid. 186). On la retrouve encore intégralement dans quelques recueils grégoriens, comme la *Collectio Lanfranci* 1.102 (Cambridge, Trinity Coll. B.16.44, p. 152–54) ou la *Coll. VII Lib.* 7.67.39 (Wien, ÖNB 2186, fol. 296r–297r).

20. Hincmarus Remensis, *De divortio Lotharii regis et Theutbergae reginae Responsio* 17, éd. L. Böhringer (MGH Concilia 4, Supplementum 1; Hannover 1992) 216.20–27; *De poenitentia Pippini regis*, éd. E. Caspar (MGH Epistolae 8; Berlin 1939) 164.20–24; *Opusculum LV Capitulorum* 24, éd. R. Schieffer, *Die Streitschriften Hinkmars von Reims und Hinkmars von Laon, 869–871* (MGH Concilia 4, Supplementum 2; Hannover 2003) 244.4–6.

21. Concile de Metz (859) can. 10, éd. W. Hartmann (MGH Concilia 3; Hannover 1984) 442.18–28.

22. Sa diffusion dans les collections canoniques a pu être analysée grâce à l'index réalisé par L. Fowler-Magerl, *Clavis canonum* (MGH Hilfsmittel 21; Hannover 2005).

23. *Dacheriana* 1.14, éd. J.-L. d'Achery et L.-F.-J. de La Barre, *Spicilegium* (Paris 1723²) 520; Benedictus Levita, *Capitularia* 5.119, éd. G. H. Pertz (MGH Leges 2.2; Hannoverae 1837) 52.7–14; Regino Prumiensis, *De synodalibus causis et disciplinis ecclesiasticis* 1.109, éd. F. Wasserschleben (Lipsiae 1840, réimpr. Graz 1964) 72; Burchardus Wormacensis, *Decretum* 18.4 (éd. Köln 1548, réimpr. Aalen 1992) fol. 183; Ivo Carnotensis, *Decretum* 15.29 (PL 161.863CD); *Tripartita* 1.45.38 (Paris, BN lat. 3858B, fol. 29vab) = éd. M. Brett 1.43.38; Deusdedit, *Collectio*

L'idée d'une flexibilité de la règle canonique conditionnée par des circonstances exceptionnelles est donc extrêmement précoce et semble avoir pris forme dès le Ve siècle, au moment même où commençait à émerger un ensemble de dispositions juridiques considérées comme propre à l'Église chrétienne. Cette souplesse de la norme, qui se maintient durant tout le premier millénaire, s'accorde à l'esprit général du droit canonique antérieur au Décret de Gratien, plus empirique que systématique. Le contexte était donc particulièrement propice à la formulation de sentences telles que *Necessitas non habet legem*.

Le premier texte préfigurant directement la confection de la maxime est un passage de l'*expositio* de Bède le Vénérable sur l'évangile de Marc, composée dans les années 725–730. Commentant le verset qui proclame que le Sabbat est fait pour l'Homme et non l'Homme pour le Sabbat (Mc.2.27), Bède se réfère implicitement à l'exemple de David qui, pressé par la faim, avait pénétré dans le Temple et mangé les pains de proposition (Mc.2.26) pour justifier la possibilité, pour un malade, de rompre le jeûne en proclamant que 'ce qui n'était pas permis par la loi, le devient par la nécessité'.[24] L'enseignement de Bède, on le sait, a eu un retentissement important, son commentaire de l'évangile de Marc étant l'ouvrage qui connut le plus de succès.[25] L'œuvre se rattache certes à la littérature exégétique, mais la question abordée est bien de nature

canonum 4.414, éd. V. Wolf von Glanvell (Paderborn 1905) 594.3–15; *Diversorum Patrum Sententiae sive Collectio in LXXIV titulorum distributa* 253, éd. J. Gilchrist (MIC B.1; 1973) 155–56; *Collectio canonum Casinensis* 202a, éd. R. Reynolds (Monumenta Liturgica Beneventana 3, Studies and Texts 137; Toronto 2001) 111–12; *Coll. II Lib./VIII Part.* 2.55, éd. J. Bernhard, RDC 12 (1962) 295; ibid. 7.285.42 (Assisi, BC 222); *Coll. XII Part., Recensio I^a* 11.56 et 171 (Wien, ÖNB lat. 2136, fol. 264vab et 281rb), *Recensio II^a* 12.6 (Troyes, BM 246, fol. 203ra); *Polycarpus, Recensio I^a* 8.1.6 (Madrid, BN 7127, fol. 443v), *Recensio II^a* 8.1.6 (Paris, BN lat. 3882, fol. 142rb–ra); *Caesaraugustana, Recensio I^a* 15.12 (Salamanca, BU 2644, fol. 137rb–va), *Recensio II^a* 15.12 et 25 (Paris, BN lat. 3876, fol. 108rv et 109v), *Recensio III^a* 6.4.3 et VI.14 (Barcelona, ACA 63); *Anselmus Lucensis, Recensio A* 11.11c (BAV, Vat. lat. 1363, fol. 189r); *Coll. Sancte Genoveve* 4.2.4 (Paris, SG 166, fol. 139v); Atto de Sancto Marco, *Breviarium* 35.46 (BAV, Vat. lat. 586, fol. 105v); *Coll. VII Lib.* 7.139 (Turin, BNU D.IV.33, fol. 159v); *Coll. XIII Lib.* (Vat. lat. 1361) 11.11c (fol. 199rb); *Coll. XIII Lib.* (Berlin, SB Savigny 3) 10.11c (fol. 102vb); *Coll. Catalaunensis, Recensio I^a* 18.31 (Châlons-en-Champagne, BM 47, fol. 102v), *Recensio II^a* 12.1.14 (Châlons-en-Champagne, BM 75, fol. 277v); *Coll. Saint-Hilaire-le-Grand* 6.36 (Reims, BM 675, fol. 51v); *Coll. IX Part.* 9.7.25 (Köln, HSA W 199, fol. 162r); *Coll. Ambrosiana III^a* 24 (Milano, BA H 5.inf, fol. 58v); *Coll. Sinemuriensis* 1.119 (Semur-en-Auxois, BM 13, fol. 19v); *Coll. Tarraconensis, Recensio I^a* 257 et 351 (Paris, BN lat. 5517, fol. 89v et 101v) ou 4.48 et 5.31 (Tarragona, BP 26, fol. 93r et 109r), *Recensio II^a* 4.39 et 5.38 (Paris, BN lat. 4281B, fol. 113v–114r et 125r); *Coll. IV Lib.* 3.5.5 (Canterbury, CL B 7, fol. 34v–35r); *Coll. X Part.* 10.25.1 (fol. 198r); *Coll. Florence BML Ashburnham. 1554* 457 (fol. 58v); *Coll. Paris BN lat. 3858C* 1.251 (fol. 23vab); *Coll. Paris BN n.a.l. 326* 166 (fol. 52v–53r); *Coll. IV Lib. (Köln, HSA 124)* 3.2 (fol. 102v–104r); *Coll. IX Lib.* (Vat. lat. 1349) 8.43 (fol. 182rb–vb); *Coll. LXXII cap.* 36 (Roma, Vallicelliana T.XVIII, fol. 54vab); C.26 q.6 c.10.

24. Beda Venerabilis, *In Marci Evangelium Expositio* 2.27, éd. CCL 120.464.1081–85: 'Unde discipulis esurientibus quod licitum non erat in lege necessitate famis factum est licitum. Talis haec causa est qualis hodie in jeiuniis legitimis ubi, si quis aeger jejunium corruperit, nulla ratione reus tenetur'.

25. F. Brunhölzl, *Geschichte der lateinischen Literatur des Mittelalters* 1.1 (München 1975); trad. fr. H. Rochais, *Histoire de la littérature latine du Moyen Âge* 1.1 (Louvain-la-Neuve 1990) 216.

disciplinaire, et l'on ne peut donc s'étonner de trouver presque simultanément des formules proches dans la langue diplomatique ou canonique.

On peut ainsi évoquer une lettre de Charles Martel, adressée en 723 à saint Boniface,
dans laquelle le maire du Palais prend le missionnaire sous sa protection, en précisant
que, s'il survenait, pour ce dernier, 'une indisposition ou un état de nécessité qui ne
puisse être borné par la loi', il n'en demeurerait pas moins sous sa garde.[26] La formule
employée ici, bien entendu, peut très bien n'être qu'une expression de l'art rhétorique
de l'auteur de la lettre. La 'necessitas, que per legem definiri non potuerit' n'en renvoie
pas moins au même *topos* que le fragment de Bède. Il convient du reste de relever que
la lettre en question a été transmise par le biais de la collection renfermant la correspondance de Boniface, laquelle fut mise en forme par son élève Lulle († 786), lui aussi
d'origine anglo-saxonne, l'un et l'autre provenant donc de la même aire culturelle que
Bède.

L'enseignement du maître de Yarrow paraît en tout cas avoir eu un écho direct dans
la littérature exégétique insulaire, comme en témoigne un commentaire sur l'évangile de
Matthieu, longtemps attribué, à tort, à Bède lui-même. Cette *expositio*, que l'érudition
moderne a d'abord cru pouvoir rattacher à Raban Maur, semble en réalité plutôt être
d'origine irlandaise et dater du VIIIe siècle.[27] Se référant, là encore, à l'attitude de David,
l'auteur de ce commentaire écrit qu'on peut considérer que celui-ci a 'par nécessité
rompu les préceptes de la loi'.[28] Une idée proche apparaît encore en filigrane dans le pé-
nitentiel du Pseudo-Bède, qui, après avoir condamné la consommation de la charogne,
conseille de modérer fortement la peine si l'acte a été effectué dans des conditions de
nécessité.[29] Mais la doctrine de Bède a surtout été reçue par son élève, Egbert d'York (†
766), lequel, pour la première fois, a introduit la formule dans le droit canonique.

La maxime apparaît en effet dans un ouvrage juridique, sous une forme plus concise

26. 'Et si aliqua causatio vel necessitas ei advenerit, que per legem definiri non potuerit, usque ante nos quietus vel conservatus esse debeat, quot ipse quam qui per ipsum sperare videntur, ut ei nullus ullam contrari-
etatem vel damnationem adversus eum facere non debeat, nisi ut omni tempore sub nostro mundeburnio vel
defensione quietus vel conservatus residere debeat', éd. M. Tangl, *Die Briefe des Heiligen Bonifacius und Lullus*
(MGH Epistolae selectae 1; Berlin 1916, réimpr. München 1989) 38.2–8. Sur l'importance de cette lettre, voir no-
tam. J. Semmler, 'Bonifacius (Winfrid)', LMA (1983) 2.418.

27. L'attribution à Raban Maur faite par A. E. Schönbach, *Über einige Evangelienkommentare des Mittelalters*
(*Sb.* Wien, Phil.-hist. Classe, 46.4; Wien 1903) 23–34, reprise par Stegmüller n° 1678, a été remise en cause par
R. E. McNally, 'The Three Holy Kings in Early Irish Latin Writings', dans: *Kyriakon. Festschrift Johannes Quasten*,
éd. P. Granfield et J. Jungmann (Münster 1970) 2.676–77, dont l'opinion est reprise par J. Kelly, 'A Catalogue of
Early Medieval Hiberno-Latin Biblical Commentaries', *Traditio* 45 (1989–90) 412 n° 82.

28. Ps. Beda Venerabilis, *In Matthaei Evangelium expositio* 2.12 (PL 92.60BC): 'Si typicus David propter necessitatem legis praecepta fregisse legitur, quanto magis verum David suorum necessitati consulere licebit'.

29. Ps. Beda Venerabilis, *Poenitentiale* 7.1–2: 'Qui manducat carnem inmundam aut morticinam aut di-
laceratam a bestiis, XL dies penitat. Si necessitate famis cogente multo levius est', éd. Wasserschleben 227. La
formule 'necessitate famis' paraît directement empruntée à Bède.

mais aussi plus percutante que chez Bède, avec le *Dialogus ecclesiasticae institutionis* attribué à Egbert. Cette œuvre, dont la paternité a quelquefois été contestée, se présente comme une collection de solutions pratiques de droit canonique, destinée à guider une communauté ecclésiastique dans ses relations avec la société séculière.[30] La treizième question aborde le cas du divorce par consentement mutuel, susceptible d'intervenir en cas d'impuissance de l'un des époux, l'infirme consentant donc à cette séparation et promettant de demeurer dans la continence.[31] La réponse apportée par Egbert est pleine de nuances. Personne ne devant agir contre l'enseignement de l'Évangile ou contre celui de Paul, le consentement à la séparation, qui reviendrait à consentir à l'adultère, ne lui paraît pas possible. Cependant, ajoute-t-il, il est dangereux d'imposer à un individu des charges qu'il ne pourrait supporter. On doit néanmoins tenir compte de celles imposées par Dieu. L'impuissance doit, par conséquent, être appréciée au moyen de l'ordalie, mais, afin de ne pas complaire au Démon, le principe de l'indissolubilité du mariage doit être conservé. Toutefois, il arrive souvent qu'en raison des circonstances du moment, la 'nécessité rompt la loi' et Egbert se réfère aussitôt à l'exemple de David qui, affamé, a mangé les pains de proposition 'sans pour autant commettre de péché' note-t-il. La conclusion, prudente, est qu'il est préférable de ne pas prononcer de sentence dans les cas douteux.[32]

Compte tenu du dernier exemple évoqué, la formule *necessitas frangit legem* paraît bien être ici directement inspirée par Bède, dont Egbert d'York était le disciple. Dans l'œuvre de ce dernier, l'expression vise sans doute d'abord à expliquer la possibilité d'une défaillance humaine, face à la dureté de la règle canonique. Mais elle sert aussi à justifier la transgression de cette norme dont Egbert sous-entend qu'elle peut bien être violée sans qu'un péché soit commis. Il y a donc là l'ébauche d'une théorie canonique de la nécessité qui, en apparence, semble distinguer ce que l'on a nommé beaucoup plus tard le for interne et le for externe.

30. P. Godman, *The Bishops, Kings, and Saints of York* (Oxford 1982) lxiii–liv. Pour l'authenticité de l'attribution, voir en dernier lieu Brunhölzl, *Histoire de la littérature* 292–93.

31. Egbertus Eboracensis, *Dialogus ecclesiasticae institutionis* 13. *Interrogatio:* 'Quod si ex convenientia amborum legitimum dissolvitur conjugium, propter infirmitatem viri vel uxoris, si liceat sano incontinenti secundum inire connubium, infirmo consensum praebente, et promittente sese continentiam in perpetuo servaturum: Vestra Sanctitas quid de hoc judicat?', éd. A. W. Haddan et W. Stubbs, *Councils and Ecclesiastical Documents Relating to Great Britain and Ireland* III (Oxford 1861) 409.

32. Egbertus Eboracensis, *Dialogus* 13. *Responsio:* 'Nemo contra Evangelium, nemo contra Apostolum sine vindicta facit, idcirco consensum minime praebemus adulteris; onera tamen quae sine periculo portari non possunt nemini imponimus, ea vero, quae Dei sunt mandata, confidenter indicimus. Quem autem infirmitas implendi praepedit, uno profecto multum reservamus judicio Dei. Igitur ne forte videamur silentio fovere adulteros, aut diabolus qui decipit adulteros de adulteris exultet, ulterius audi "Quod Deus conjunxit homo non separet (Mt.19.6; Mc.10.9)". Et item: "Qui potest capere capiat (Mt.19.12)". Sepe namque temporum permutatione, necessitas legem frangit. Quid enim fecit David quando esuriit? Et tamen sine peccato est. Ergo in ambiguis non est ferenda sententia'.

Quelle que soit la portée exacte de cette doctrine, celle-ci paraît en tout cas se développer au cours du VIIIe siècle, dans le monde anglo-saxon ou insulaire. Elle est cependant importée sur le Continent au plus tard au milieu du IXe siècle, comme en témoigne l'œuvre de Sedulius Scotus. Parti d'Irlande, celui-ci s'est en effet installé à Liège où il a rédigé, semble-t-il, la plupart de ses écrits, après 850. Dans son commentaire sur l'évangile de Matthieu, Sedulius reprend textuellement la formule employée par Bède qui proclame que 'ce qui n'est pas permis par la loi, le devient par la nécessité'.[33]

La diffusion d'une telle idée dans le droit canonique de l'époque classique allait cependant être assurée par une forme plus concise de l'adage, qui apparaît à la même époque.

II

Au milieu du IXe siècle, en effet, sont élaborées les Fausses Décrétales du Pseudo-Isidore, dans la province ecclésiastique de Reims, sans doute à l'abbaye de Corbie.[34] Parmi celles-ci se trouve la lettre apocryphe de Félix IV, précédemment évoquée, qui pose l'interdiction de célébrer des offices divins hors des lieux consacrés. Une incise précise toutefois que, s'il est bien interdit de chanter ou d'entendre la messe en dehors de ces endroits, cette interdiction peut être levée lorsque survient 'une nécessité du plus haut degré', car *necessitas non habet legem*.[35] Ce texte, dans lequel l'adage se trouve ainsi libellé pour la première fois dans la forme qu'il conserve aujourd'hui, a eu un succès considérable. En effet, l'œuvre du Pseudo-Isidore connaît, dans le courant des Xe et XIe siècles, une diffusion très importante. La collection elle-même, tout d'abord, est copiée, dans son intégralité ou sous forme d'abrégés, à de nombreuses reprises.[36] De multiples extraits, surtout, sont repris dans les recueils canoniques, jusqu'au milieu du XIIe siècle.

---

33. Sedulius Scotus, *In evangelium Matthaei* 12.7: 'Unde discipulis esurientibus, quod licitum non erat in lege, necessitate famis factum est licitum. Talis haec causa est, qualis hodie jejuniis legitimis, ubi si quis aeger jejunium corruperit, nulla ratione reus tenetur', éd. B. Löfstedt, *Kommentar zum Evangelium nach Matthäus* II (Vetus Latina. Aus der Geschichte der lateinischen Bibel 19; Freiburg 1991) 323.20–23.

34. Ainsi que l'ont montré les travaux récents de K. Zechiel-Eckes, en dernier lieu: 'Auf Pseudoisidors Spur, oder: Versuch, einen dichten Schleier zu lüften', dans: *Fortschritt durch Fälschungen? Ursprung, Gestalt und Wirkungen der pseudoisidorischen Fälschungen. Beiträge zum gleichnamigen Symposium an der Universität Tübingen vom 27. und 28 Juli 2001*, éd. W. Hartmann et G. Schmitz (MGH Studien und Texte 31; Hannover 2002) 1–28.

35. JK † 878. Ps. Felix IV: 'Satius ergo est missam non cantare aut non audire quam in his locis ubi fieri non oportet fore, nisi, ut sepe dictum est, pro summa contingat necessitate, quoniam necessitas legem non habet', éd. P. Hinschius, *Decretales Pseudo-Isidorianae et capitula Angilramni* (Lipsiae 1863) 700.

36. Sur la diffusion du Pseudo-Isidore, voir l'ouvrage classique de H. Fuhrmann, *Einfluß und Verbreitung der pseudoisidorischen Fälschungen, von ihrem Auftauchen bis in die neuere Zeit* (MGH Schriften 24.1–3; Stuttgart 1972–74); et la liste des manuscrits établie par Kéry, *Can. Coll.* 100–108.

Trois fragments de la pseudo-décrétale de Félix IV contenant la maxime ont ainsi circulé dans d'innombrables collections canoniques antérieures au Décret de Gratien. Un assez large extrait, tout d'abord, le canon *Judei ergo,* se trouve, entre autres, dans le Décret de Burchard de Worms, dans la Collection en XII Parties, dans le Décret d'Yves de Chartres et dans au moins cinq autres recueils canoniques du XIe ou de la première moitié du XIIe siècle.[37] Un second fragment, beaucoup plus concis, le canon *Satius est,* figure non seulement, lui aussi, dans deux des recueils attribués à Yves de Chartres—le Décret et la Tripartite—, mais encore dans au moins onze collections canoniques se rattachant à la Réforme grégorienne, considérées pour la plupart comme étant d'origine française, parmi lesquelles on compte notamment la fameuse *Collectio Sinemuriensis,* ou, beaucoup plus tard, la *Caesaraugustana* ou bien la Collection de Châlons-en-Champagne.[38] Enfin, un remaniement de la pseudo-décrétale recomposant deux fragments du texte, le canon *Sicut non alii,* est présent dans au moins dix-huit collections réformatrices, principalement italiennes, parmi lesquelles la Collection en 74 Titres, la première recension du recueil d'Anselme de Lucques, ou encore le Polycarpe du cardinal Grégoire de Saint-Grisogone, avant d'être finalement intégré au Décret de Gratien.[39]

À la fin du XIe siècle, commence également à circuler une autre décrétale, dont on conserve plusieurs recensions, l'une d'elles présentant une forme légèrement différente de l'adage. La lettre en question est une missive de Jean VIII, adressée en août 879 aux empereurs de Byzance Basile, Constantin et Alexandre, par laquelle le pontife réintègre

37. Burchardus Wormacensis, *Decretum* 3.58 (éd. Köln 1548, réimpr. Aalen 1992, fol. 62); Ivo Carnotensis, *Decretum* 3.61 (PL 161.211B–212B); *Liber canonum diversorum sanctorum patrum sive collectio in CLXXXIII titulos digesta* [= *Collectio Sancte Marie Novelle*] 27.27, éd. J. Motta (MIC B.7; 1988) 56; *Coll. V Lib.* 1.15.3 (ibid. 306); *Coll. XII Part., Recensio I[a]* 4.86 (Wien, ÖNB lat. 2136, fol. 37vb–38ra), *Recensio II[a]* 5.112 (Troyes, BM 246, fol. 117ra–va); *Coll. de l'Arsenal* 3.141 (Paris, Bibl. Arsenal 721, fol. 206vab); *Coll. Vat. lat. 3829* 2.50.5 (fol. 137r–138r); *Coll. Florence, BML Ashburnham. 1554* 368 (fol. 47v).

38. Ivo Carnotensis, *Decretum* 2.76 (PL 161.176D–177A); *Tripartita* 1.52.1 (Paris, BN lat. 3858B, fol. 41vb) = éd. M. Brett 1.50.1; *Coll. Sinemuriensis* 1.150 (Semur-en-Auxois, BM 13, fol. 24r); *Caesaraugustana, Recensio I[a]* 11.7 (Salamanca, BU 2644, fol. 103va), *Recensio II[a]* 13.33 (Paris, BN lat. 3876, fol. 91r), *Recensio III[a]* 4.27.1 (Barcelona, ACA 63); *Coll. Catalaunensis, Recensio I[a]* 3.22 (Châlons-en-Champagne, BM 47, fol. 16v–17r), *Recensio II[a]* 6.1.26 (Châlons-en-Champagne, BM 75, fol. 143rv); *Coll. IV Lib.* 2.13.8 (Canterbury, CL B.7, fol. 26v); *Coll. IX Part.* 2.12.2 (Köln, HSA W 199, fol. 24r); *Coll. Celle Oberlandesgericht C.8* 2.32 (fol. 42v–43r); *Coll. Paris BN lat. 13658* 218 (fol. 47rb); *Coll. Roma Vallicelliana B.89* 15 (fol. 24) = 142, éd. W. Hartmann, BMCL 17 (1987) 63.

39. *Diversorum Patrum Sententie sive Collectio in LXXIV titulorum distributa* 204, éd. Gilchrist 131; Anselmus Lucensis, *Recensio A* 7.119 (BAV, Vat. lat. 1363, fol. 154v); *Polycarpus, Recensio I[a]* 3.16.3 (Madrid, BN 7127, fol. 345rv), *Recensio II[a]* 3.18.3 (Paris, BN lat. 3882, fol. 53rb); *Coll. Burdegalensis* 3.21 (Würzburg, UB Mp.j.q.2, fol. 35r); *Coll. Ambrosiana III[a]* 51 (Milano, BA H.5.inf, fol. 63r); *Coll. Gadiana* 78 (Firenze, BML Plut. LXXXIX sup. 32, fol. 11rv); *Coll. Tarraconensis, Recensio I[a]* 202 (Paris, BN 5517, fol. 82r) et 3.96 (Tarragona, BP 26, fol. 82v), *Recensio II[a]* 3.86 (Paris, BN lat. 4281B, fol. 107v–108r); *Coll. XIII Lib. (Vat. lat. 1361)* 7.67 (fol. 159rb–va); *Coll. III Lib.* 2.8.9 (BAV, Vat. lat. 3831, fol. 27rab); *Coll. IX Lib. (BAV, Arch. S. Pietro C.118)* 3.1.7 (fol. 25ra); *Coll. VII Lib. (Turin, BNU D.IV.33)* 4.48 (fol. 52r); *Coll. II Lib. (VIII Part.)* 2.2, éd. J. Bernhard, RDC 12 (1962) 250; *Coll. XIII Part. (Berlin, SB Savigny 3)* 10.165 (fol. 118vb); *Coll. Paris BN lat. 3858C* 1.282 (fol. 26rbva); *Coll. Paris BN n.a.l.326* 275 (fol. 70rv); *Coll. Rom. Vallicelliana B.89* 125 (fol. 16r); De cons. D.1 c. 11.

sur son siège le patriarche de Constantinople Photius, auparavant déposé par Nicolas Iᵉʳ, en 863.[40] La déposition et l'excommunication ayant été prononcées au cours d'un synode régulièrement tenu au Latran, Jean VIII justifie la réintégration du schismatique en évoquant une série de textes justifiant, d'une part, la violation éventuelle des 'décrets apostoliques' et des 'constitutions des Pères', en cas de nécessité et, d'autre part, la réintégration dans l'Église de clercs précédemment exclus. S'agissant de la nécessité, le pape se réfère d'abord au canon 2 du concile de Nicée, lequel relevait que les hommes transgressent parfois la règle ecclésiastique par nécessité.[41] Il évoque ensuite une lettre de Gélase aux évêques de Lucanie et de Sicile du 11 mars 493, proclamant que s'il n'y a pas nécessité urgente, on ne doit pas violer les règles posées par les Pères.[42] Dans le même esprit, ajoute-t-il, saint Léon a prescrit 'd'oublier ou de ne pas juger coupable ce qui a été provoqué par la nécessité', citant ainsi, à travers la *Dionysiana*, une missive adressée le 21 mars 456 par Léon Iᵉʳ à l'évêque d'Aquilée.[43]

La décrétale de Jean VIII contenant ces différents fragments, cependant, fut traduite en grec, apparemment par Photius lui-même, et passablement modifiée pour les besoins de sa cause.[44] Cette traduction grecque fut ensuite retraduite en latin et plusieurs versions de ce nouveau texte, qui diffère de manière notable de celui contenu dans le registre de Jean VIII, paraissent avoir circulé au Moyen Âge.[45] Or, l'une d'entre elles se retrouve dans deux œuvres importantes de la période grégorienne. Elle figure ainsi, intégralement, dans la collection du cardinal Deusdedit, achevée vers 1087.[46] Un large extrait est par ailleurs repris dans le Prologue d'Yves de Chartres.[47] Dans celui-ci, le frag-

40. JE 3271. Johannes VIII, *Registrum* 207, éd. E. Caspar (MGH Epistolae 7; Berlin 1928) 166–76. Sur ces événements: F. Dvornik, *Le schisme de Photius. Histoire et légende* (Cambridge 1948; trad. fr. Paris 1950) 230–83, et, plus récemment, G. Dagron, 'L'Église et l'État (milieu IXᵉ–fin Xᵉ siècle)', dans: *Histoire du christianisme* IV (Paris 1993) 169–86.

41. 'Quoniam plura aut per necessitatem aut alias cogentibus hominibus adversus ecclesiasticam facta sunt regulam', ed. MGH Epistolae 7.169.23–25 = Conc. Nicée (325) can. 2, ed. COD³ 6.20–23.

42. JK 636: 'Ubi nulla perurget necessitas, constituta patrum inviolata serventur', ed. MGH Epistolae 7.169.26–28. La citation est en réalité la rubrique d'un fragment de la lettre, empruntée à la *Dionysiana* (PL 67.302D).

43. JK 536: 'Et sanctus Leo eodem spiritu precipit "omittendum esse et inculpabile iudicandum, quod necessitas intulit"', ed. MGH Epistolae 7.169.28–30 = *Dionysiana* (PL 67.297A) = Leo Magnus, *Epistola* 165 (PL 54.1202).

44. L'histoire du texte est retracée par V. Grumel, 'Les lettres de Jean VIII pour le rétablissement de Photius', *Échos d'Orient* 39 (1940) 138–56; et par Dvornik, *Le schisme* 259–60.

45. Deux versions légèrement différentes l'une de l'autre sont données dans: Mansi 16.487–502, ibid. 17.141–146.

46. Deusdedit, *Coll. canonum* 4.434, éd. Glanvell 612–15.

47. Yves de Chartres, *Prologue* 44–48, éd. et trad. J. Werckmeister (Sources canoniques 1; Paris 1997) 117–25. Dans cette édition, l'identification des différents fragments cités par Jean VIII est toutefois erronée et incomplète, l'auteur confondant la lettre précitée de Léon le Grand avec une autre (JK 410; Epistola 12, éd. PL 54.645–63), adressée aux évêques de Césarée de Mauritanie, qui est sans rapport, et n'identifiant pas la citation d'une lettre de Félix III du 15 mars 488 aux évêques de Sicile (JK 609), ni celle du canon 2 du VIᵉ concile de Carthage

ment attribué à Léon le Grand proclame que, s'il y a nécessité, celui qui en a le pouvoir peut dispenser pour l'utilité de l'Église car 'la loi est transformée par la nécessité'.[48] La fortune de cette nouvelle version de la maxime proclamant ainsi *ex necessitate fit mutatio legis* allait être assurée grâce au fantastique succès du Prologue, dont on conserve aujourd'hui encore plus de 170 manuscrits.[49]

À l'aube du XIIᵉ siècle, l'adage 'Nécessité n'a point de loi' connaît donc déjà, sous différentes formes, un succès considérable, au moins chez les canonistes, pour qui il tend à devenir un véritable lieu commun. La législation émise par les réguliers est à ce sujet exemplaire, tant sont nombreuses les règles, monastiques ou canoniales, qui recourent à une formule de ce type pour assouplir certaines de leurs dispositions. Ainsi en est-il des constitutions émises par Lanfranc de Cantorbéry, élaborées, probablement entre 1074 et 1077, afin de réformer le monachisme cathédral propre aux îles britanniques, qui prévoient la possibilité de déroger dans certains cas au respect des heures canoniques 'car la nécessité n'est pas tenue par la loi'.[50] Une disposition très proche se retrouve dans les coutumes des chanoines de Springiersbach-Klosterrath, rédigées vers 1127–1128 dans les diocèses de Trèves et de Liège, dans le sillage du mouvement de réforme des chapitres réguliers, qui interdisent à quiconque de s'abstraire du respect des heures canoniques, 'excepté s'il survient une nécessité, laquelle est exempte de la loi'.[51] La règle de l'ordre de Grandmont, mise en forme par son quatrième prieur Étienne de Liciac (1139–1163), mais attribuée à son fondateur Étienne de Muret († 1124), qui prétend s'inscrire en réaction contre le relâchement des bénédictins, prescrit elle aussi un rigoureux silence qui devra être observé en permanence par les frères 'excepté une grande nécessité, qui n'a pas de loi'.[52] Enfin, la règle de saint François antérieure à la version approuvée par Honorius III en 1223, qui fut sans doute rédigée vers 1210, se

(401), qui suivent, bien que l'identité de ces deux fragments ait pourtant été dûment établie par Caspar, MGH Epistolae 7.169 n. 5–6. Aucune precision n'est donnée dans l'édition critique récente de B. Brasington, *Ways of Mercy. The Prologue of Ivo of Chartres* (Vita regularis: Editionen 2; Münster 2004) 137.

48. *Prologue* 44, éd. Werckmeister 118: 'Ubi vero necessitas fuerit, ad utilitatem Ecclesie, qui potestatem habet ea dispenset. Ex necessitate enim fit mutatio legis'.

49. Cf. B. C. Brasington, 'The Prologue of Ivo of Chartres: A Fresh Consideration From the Manuscripts', dans: Proc. San Diego (MIC C.9; 1992) 1–22; idem, 'Zur Rezeption des Prologs Ivos von Chartres in Süddeutschland', DA 47 (1991) 167–74. Le fragment attribué à Léon le Grand contenant la maxime ne semble pas avoir connu de circulation autonome dans les collections canoniques, quoique qu'il se trouve pourtant dans la *Coll. IX Part.* (Köln, HSA 199) 4.7.3 (fol. 49v): 'Ibi necessitas non est—fit mutatio legis'.

50. Lanfrancus Cantuariensis, *Decreta* 111: 'Porro si nec ipsa hora, qua percantata id fieri debeat, expectari potest, disponat abbas vel prior sicut melius possit, quia necessitas lege non tenetur', éd. D. Knowles (Corpus Consuetudinum monasticarum 3; Siegburg 1967) 98.28–30.

51. *Consuetudines canonicorum regularium Springirsbacenses-Rodenses* 43: 'Eadem ratio est de omnibus canonicis horis nullatenus exeundi, nec ab his, qui foris sunt, aliquem deintus evocandi, quod nec abbati licet, nisi incumbat necessitas, que lege caret', éd. CCL cont. med. 48.22.6–23.9. Sur la diffusion de ces coutumes: J. Simon, 'Springiersbach', LMA 7 (1995) 2142.

52. Stephanus de Liciaco, *Regula venerabilis Stephani Muretensis* 47: 'Silentium secundum loca et tempora

référant encore à l'exemple de David, prescrit qu'en cas de nécessité manifeste les frères pourront agir pour jouir des largesses du Seigneur en prélevant sur les aumônes ce qui est nécessaire à leur subsistance, 'car la nécessité n'a pas de loi'.[53]

Ce succès aussi précoce qu'important de la maxime *Necessitas non habet legem* ou de ses dérivés se confirme si l'on examine à présent la réception de l'adage en dehors du droit canonique.

III

Dès le XIIe siècle ou le début du XIIIe siècle, en effet, cinq branches au moins du savoir médiéval ont reçu le brocard. On le retrouve dans le droit civil, dans la liturgie, dans la théologie, dans la philosophie et même, par-delà les disciplines scolaires, dans la littérature narrative.

S'agissant d'abord du droit civil, la maxime paraît avoir été empruntée assez tôt aux canonistes par les légistes, dans la seconde moitié du XIIe siècle. Ainsi que l'a relevé Ennio Cortese, elle figure en effet dans une série de gloses au *Digestum vetus* découvertes en 1952 par Guido Rossi, sur le folio de garde d'un manuscrit du Décret de Gratien.[54] Les gloses en question commentent un fragment de Papinien qui permettait au proconsul de confier son pouvoir de juridiction à un mandant, avant même d'être parvenu au siège de celle-ci pour en prendre possession. Une telle possibilité existait, expliquait le jurisconsulte romain, lorsque le magistrat subissait un retard incontournable *(mora necessaria)* au cours de son voyage. S'attachant à ces derniers mots, une glose marginale anonyme, tracée par une main du début du XIIIe siècle mais s'inscrivant dans un apparat reportant un enseignement antérieur à Azon, justifie cette possibilité en affirmant que 'la nécessité n'a point de loi'.[55]

La chronologie de cette réception de l'adage dans le droit civil peut toutefois être

---

constituta custodiatur. In his autem locis, hoc est in ecclesia, in claustro, in refectorio, in dormitorio, nec non in his temporibus, id est a completorio usque mane finito capitulo, continuum silentium fratres observent, nisi magna necessitas quae legem non habet quandoque coegerit, sicut enim Isaias testatur: "Cultus justitiae, silentium et pax (Is.32.17)",' éd. CCL cont. med. 8.89.1–8. Sur cette règle: J. Becquet, 'Étienne de Muret', *Dictionnaire de spiritualité* 4 (1961) 1504.

53. Franciscus Assisiensis, *Regula non bullata* 9.16: 'Similiter etiam tempore manifestae necessitatis faciant omnes fratres de eorum necessariis, sicut eis Dominus gratiam largietur, quia necessitas non habet legem', éd. K. Esser, *Die opuscula des hl. Franziskus von Assisi. Neue textkritische Edition* (Spicilegium Bonaventurianum 13; Grottaferrata 1976) 386.

54. G. Rossi, 'Di alcune glosse preaccursiane rinvenute in un foglio di guardia del cod. XII A 5 della Biblioteca Nazionale di Napoli', dans: *Atti dell'Accademia dei Lincei. Rendiconti Classe di scienze morali, storiche e filosofiche* 8.7 (1952) 189–202; E. Cortese, *La norma giuridica. Spunti teorici nel diritto comune classico* I (Ius nostrum 6.1; Milano 1962) 265 n. 23.

55. *Glossa ad* Dig.1.16.10 pr. s.v. *necessariam moram:* 'Nota quod necessitas non habet legem', éd. G. Rossi, 'Di alcune glosse' 200.

précisée davantage, grâce à sa présence dans une célèbre collection de brocards, dite *Dolum per subsequentia purgari*, confectionnée en Angleterre vers 1160 qui a eu un certain succès dans le nord de l'Europe, au point d'être encore glosée au début du XIIIe siècle.[56] La vingt-quatrième rubrique de la collection, intitulée 'Quando necessitas vel paupertas non habet legem' ne coiffe pas moins de onze allégations renvoyant à différents *sedes materiae* du *Corpus Juris Civilis* relatifs à des questions liées à l'excuse de nécessité ou de pauvreté.[57] La maxime se retrouve encore, sous une forme légèrement différente, dans les *Brocarda Dunelmensia*, également composés en Angleterre, à la fin du XIIe siècle, qui proclament: 'La nécessité n'a pas de loi commune mais fait loi par exception'.[58] Elle passe ensuite dans les brocards d'Othon de Pavie, sous la rubrique 'De necessitate et paupertate', dont la collection *Dolum per subsequentia* semble avoir été une des sources.[59] La disposition adoptée dans l'œuvre d'Othon se retrouve ensuite textuellement dans la compilation d'Azon, qui en constitue un remaniement.[60] La collection d'Azon, par sa diffusion importante, allait assurer le succès de l'adage. Comme l'a relevé Detlev Liebs, celui-ci se retrouve aussi dans la glose ordinaire d'Accurse sur le Digeste vieux.[61] À la fin du Moyen Âge, il figure encore dans le fameux répertoire de Giovanni Bertachino, même si ce dernier ne mentionne plus, finalement, que trois *sedes materiae* dans le Digeste, ce qui laisse supposer que le succès de la maxime, dans la longue durée, ne fut peut-être pas aussi complet en droit civil qu'en droit canonique.[62]

L'adage est aussi très tôt présent dans les traités systématiques de liturgie. Dans sa *Summa de ecclesiasticis officiis*, élaborée vers 1160–1164, alors qu'il professait à Paris, et qui connut une diffusion importante, Jean Beleth explique ainsi que l'ensevelissement obéit à une règle stricte, qui exige que le défunt soit porté en terre par des semblables,

56. M. Schwaibold, *Brocardica 'Dolum per subsequentia purgari'. Eine englische Sammlung von Argumenten des römischen Rechts aus dem 12. Jahrhundert* (Ius commune, Sonderheft 25; Frankfurt/M. 1985).

57. On dénombre, plus précisément, 6 allégations au Digeste vieux, 2 au Digeste neuf, 2 au Code et 1 aux Institutes, qui ont toutes été identifiées et analysées dans le détail par M. Schwaibold, *Brocardica* 48, 115–17.

58. *Brocardica Dunelmensia* 54: 'Necessitas legem communem non habet set extra ordinem sibi legem facit', éd. H. van de Wouw, ZRG Rom. Abt. 108 (1991) 258; le texte n'est pas ici emprunté au *Liber pauperum* qui constitue pourtant par ailleurs la source principale de la collection.

59. Otto Papiensis, *Brocardica* 83 (Paris, BN lat. 4601, fol. 19ra). La rubrique s'y trouve divisée en trois sections: 'Quedam fiunt propter paupertatem que alias fieri prohibentur'; 'Quando necessitas vel paupertas non habet legem'; 'Necessitas excusatur'. Il s'agit là d'un ms. de la 2e recension de l'œuvre: M. Schwaibold, 'Wer sucht, der findet', *Rechtshistorisches Journal* 4 (1985) 212.

60. Azo, *Brocardica* 81 (Corpus Glossatorum Juris Civilis IV; Neapoli 1568, réimpr. Augustae Taurinorum 1967) fol. 165va–166ra; Paris BN lat. 4609, fol. 47ra. Il s'agit de la version remaniée par Cacciavillanus. Sur l'histoire de ces différentes collections de brocards, voir Schwaibold, 'Wer sucht'; et la présentation concise d'H. Lange, *Römisches Recht im Mittelalter* I: *Die Glossatoren* (München 1997) 144–46.

61. Accursius, *Glossa ordinaria, ad* Dig.1.10.1 s.v. *Expedire*, ed. *Corpus juris civilis* I (Lyon 1527, réimpr. Osnabrück 1965) col. 83.

62. Johannes Bertachinus de Firmo, *Repertorium*, s.v. *Necessitas* II (Lugduni 1499) fol. 305va.

de rang égal.[63] Un diacre doit donc l'être par des diacres, un prêtre par des prêtres, du moins, ajoute-t-il, s'il s'en trouve, car, dans le cas contraire, on peut se passer de cette formalité 'parce que la nécessité ne sert pas la loi'.[64] Cette explication se trouve reprise, à peu près mot pour mot, à la fin du XIIIᵉ siècle, dans le *Rationale divinorum officiorum* composé par Guillaume Durand, qui affirme, lui aussi, qu'en l'absence d'individus de semblable qualité, on procèdera autrement, 'car la nécessité n'est pas soumise à la loi'.[65] On sait le succès de l'œuvre liturgique du Spéculateur, dont on conserve plus de deux cents manuscrits et qui fut traduite, dès la fin du Moyen Âge, en français, en allemand, en espagnol ou en italien.[66]

Si l'on passe à présent à la théologie, les témoignages de la réception de la maxime, sous des formes diverses, deviennent innombrables et l'on ne peut donc s'en tenir ici qu'à quelques exemples, parmi les plus significatifs. À ce titre, il convient d'évoquer d'abord la lettre 28 de Pierre le Vénérable, adressée vers 1130 à Bernard de Clairvaux. Ce texte célèbre, qui constitue la missive la plus citée de la correspondance de l'abbé de Cluny, se présente en réalité comme un véritable traité. Placée au cœur de la controverse entre les clunisiens et les cisterciens, elle constitue une virulente défense des premiers face aux attaques des seconds, lesquels leur reprochaient une interprétation laxiste de la règle bénédictine.[67] Au nom de la nécessité, Pierre le Vénérable justifie ainsi la possibilité de modifier les règles monastiques. Sa démonstration se trouve appuyée sur une série de citations, toutes empruntées à la lettre de Jean VIII, précédemment mentionnée, à travers le Prologue d'Yves de Chartres, parmi lesquelles figure le fragment attribué à saint Léon qui proclamait: 'Ex necessitate fit mutatio legis'; cet empilement d'*auctoritates* vise naturellement à offrir la possibilité de modérer les prescriptions de la règle.[68]

---

63. On conserve quelque 180 manuscrits de l'ouvrage: F. Courth, 'Johannes Beleth', LMA 5 (1992) 557.

64. Johannes Beleth, *Summa de ecclesiasticis officiis* 161, éd. CCL cont. med. 41A.318.121–23: 'Et debet portari a consimilibus, ut si dyaconus est, a dyaconis, sacerdos a sacerdotibus, si sint ibi. Aliter vero non, quia necessitas non servat legem'. Le même auteur (*Summa* 120, éd. ibid. 224.30) utilise encore la maxime pour commenter un passage de Samuel (1 Reg.21.4) faisant, encore une fois, allusion à l'épisode de David et des pains de proposition.

65. Guillelmus Duranti, *Rationale divinorum officiorum* 7.35.37: 'Si sint ibi, aliter non est vis quia necessitas legi non subiacet', éd. CCL cont. med. 140B.98.396.

66. Cf. R. Reynolds, 'Guillaume Durand parmi les théologiens médiévaux de la liturgie', dans: *Guillaume Durand, évêque de Mende (v. 1230–1296), canoniste, liturgiste et homme politique. Actes de la table ronde du CNRS, Mende, 24–27 mai 1990*, éd. P.-M. Gy (Paris 1992) 155–68.

67. Cf. G. Knight, *The Correspondance Between Peter the Venerable and Bernard of Clairvaux. A Semantic and Structural Analysis* (Aldershot 2002) 28–51.

68. Petrus Venerabilis, *Epistolae* 28.1: 'Haec et multa his similia a quibusdam patribus statuta, ab aliis certa necessitate vel utilitate immutata persepe reperiuntur. Synodus Nicena, secundo capitulo dicit: "Frequenter sive ex necessitate sive alio quolibet modo transgredi contingit homines aecclesiasticos canones". Et sanctus papa Leo: "Ubi", inquit, "necessitas fuerit, ad utilitatem aecclesiae qui potestatem habet, ea dispenset. Ex necessitate enim fit mutatio legis". Et Felix papa: "Contemplari oportet", inquit, "quod ubi occurrit necessi-

La même série de citations, approximativement, se trouve dans le traité sur le précepte et la dispense rédigé vers 1142 par Bernard de Clairvaux, à la demande, semble-t-il, de deux bénédictins de Chartres qui, à l'insu de leur abbé, avaient sollicité son avis sur la règle de Benoît. Les différents extraits y sont placés au cœur d'un long développement sur la nécessité, dans lequel Bernard justifie, lui aussi, la possibilité de changer les règles monastiques, lorsque celles-ci apparaissent contraires à la charité.[69] Dans ses sermons sur le Cantique des Cantiques, prononcés entre 1139 et 1143, saint Bernard utilise par ailleurs la formule *necessitas non habet legem* pour justifier, cette fois-ci, la nécessité éventuelle pour un prêtre de se dispenser de certains devoirs du sacerdoce—y compris, le cas échéant, la célébration de la messe—, afin de ne pas négliger des tâches matérielles qui relèvent de son obligation de charité.[70] Le propos s'inscrit ici dans le commentaire du verset proclamant: 'Le roi m'a introduit dans la cave au vin, il a ordonné en moi la charité (Cant.2.4)', dans lequel la cave est vue par l'exégète comme le lieu de la Sagesse et le vin comme l'amour excessif qui enivre l'esprit. Commentant le même passage, Guillaume de Saint-Thierry († 1148/49) a lui aussi recours à la maxime pour expliquer qu'on puisse changer l'ordre dans lequel doivent s'exercer les différents types de charité—corporelle, spirituelle, divine—qu'il différencie. Il en vient de la sorte à opérer une distinction entre la 'loi de la charité' et la 'nécessité de la charité', cette dernière constituant à ses yeux la justification même de l'existence du brocard 'nécessité n'a point de loi'.[71] Un autre proche de Bernard, Ælred de Rievaulx († 1167), utilise

---

tas sepe constitutiones patrum transgredimur". Haec diximus istis vos expugnantibus exemplis et testimoniis cinximus, ut nullus jam evadendi vobis supersit locus. Cum enim audiatis necessitatis sive utilitatis gratia posse patres mandata moderari, negabitis hominem ad monachatum nisi post annum posse suscipi? Et que major necessitas aut utilitas, animarum salute potest inveniri?', éd. G. Constable, *The Letters of Peter the Venerable* I (Harvard Historical Studies 78; Cambridge, MA 1967) 61–62. L'éditeur commet ici une erreur en identifiant le dernier fragment avec la pseudo-décrétale de Félix IV telle qu'elle passe dans le Décret d'Yves (3.61) sous la forme du canon *Satius est*, alors qu'il s'agit ici d'une lettre de Félix III (JK 609).

69. Bernardus Claraevallensis, *Liber de praecepto et dispensatione* 5: 'Numquid autem hoc ego vel solus sentio, vel primus dico? Annon hoc ipsum et papa Gelasius sensit? Ait siquidem: "Ubi necessitas non est, inconvertibilia maneant sanctorum Patrum decreta". Leo quoque papa: "Ubi", inquit, "necessitas non est, nullo modo violentur sanctorum Patrum constituta". Et infert: "Ubi ergo necessitas fuerit, ad utilitatem ecclesiae, qui potestatem habet, ea dispenset, ex necessitate enim fit mutatio legis",' éd. et trad. F. Callerot, J. Miethke et Ch. Jaquinod (Sources chrétiennes 457; Paris 2000) 156.18–158.25.

70. Bernardus Claraevallensis, *Sermones super Cantica Canticorum* 50.5: 'Quoties pro administrandis terrenis justissime ipsis supersedemus celebrandis missarum solemniis! Ordo praeposterus; sed necessitas non habet legem. Agit ergo suum actualis caritas ordinem juxta patrisfamilias jussionem, "inscipiens a novissimis (Mt.8.20)", pia certe et justa, quae non sit acceptrix personarum, nec pretia consideret rerum, sed hominum necessitates', éd. et trad. P. Verdeyen et R. Fassetta (Sources chrétiennes 452; Paris 2000) 354.32–356.38.

71. Guillelmus de Sancto Theodorico, *Brevis commentatio* 33: 'Sed et in nobismetipsis debemus actum caritatis corporis praeponere actui caritatis animae; et actus caritatis animae, actui caritatis Dei, id est contemplationi. Haec tamen omnia, cum exigit necessitas, quae non habet legem. Est enim lex caritatis, est et necessitas caritatis. Lex caritatis praecipit actum caritatis Dei praeponere actui animae, et actum animae actui corporis.

aussi l'adage dans ses sermons, se référant au passage de l'évangile de Jean (11.5) qui proclame que Jésus aimait Marthe, Marie et Lazare, pour justifier le partage de l'amour 'excepté s'il survenait une nécessité, qui n'a pas de loi'.[72] On le retrouve enfin dans les Soliloques pseudo-augustiniens, lesquels furent probablement élaborés par Alcher de Clairvaux († 1153), élève de Bernard, et connurent un grand succès au second versant du Moyen Âge.[73]

La sentence *Necessitas non habet legem* semble ainsi devenir, dès la première moitié du XIIᵉ siècle, un véritable lieu commun chez les théologiens. Ainsi, commentant un passage du premier livre de Samuel (1 Sam.2.18) rapportant que celui-ci, enfant, accomplissait déjà le service du Seigneur, Abélard justifie cette possibilité en invoquant la maxime qu'il présente comme étant un véritable proverbe.[74] Celle-ci figure par ailleurs en bonne place dans l'*Histoire scolastique* de Pierre le Mangeur, qui fut composée entre 1168 et 1176 et dont le succès fut considérable, en particulier grâce à sa traduction en langue vernaculaire.[75] Le fragment de Bède proclamant 'Quod non licitum erat in lege, necessitate factum est licitum' passe de son côté dans la glose ordinaire de la Bible s'attachant au verset de l'évangile de Marc (2.27) à propos duquel l'avait formulé le théologien anglais, pour justifier, encore une fois, la rupture éventuelle du jeûne.[76] Et si le succès de cette dernière formule, moins percutante que la précédente, paraît moindre, on ne la retrouve pas moins chez un certain nombre d'auteurs commentant le même passage, comme, par exemple, Zacharie de Besançon.[77] En tout état de cause,

---

Necessitas caritatis omnia his contraria. Inde est quod multi dicunt, pauci intelligunt: "Necessitas non habet legem",' éd. CCL cont. med. 87.192.16–24.

72. Aelredus Rievallensis, *Sermones* 19.28: 'Quia autem ab unoquoque nostrum ambae hae partes exercendae sunt, sine dubio "certis temporibus" debemus ea agere quae sunt Marthae, "certis temporibus" ea quae sunt Mariae, nisi necessitas intercurrerit, quae legem non habet', éd. CCL cont. med. 2A.153.248–51. La construction stylistique 'certis temporibus' s'inspire d'un passage de la Règle de Benoît 48.1, éd. et trad. A. de Vogüé et J. Neufville (Sources chrétiennes 182; Paris 1972) 598.

73. Ps. Augustinus, *Soliloquia* 2 (PL 40.866): 'Parce mihi colloquenti tibi, ignosce servo qui praesumit loqui Domino. Legem non habet necessitas'. On conserve quelque 276 manuscrits de cette œuvre contre seulement 113 pour les Soliloques authentiques, E. Dekkers, 'Le succès étonnant des écrits pseudo-augustiniens au Moyen Âge', dans: *Fälschungen im Mittelalter. Internationaler Kongreß der MGH, München, 16–19 September 1986* (MGH Schriften 33.1–5; Hannover 1988) 5.362.

74. Petrus Abaelardus, *Problemata Heloissae* 35 (PL 178.717B): 'Denique quis improbet Samuelem, licet puerum, in officio levitarum pro necessitate ministrare, hoc etiam Heli jubente, cum nullus tunc in domo Heli reperiretur hoc officio dignus? Notum quippe proverbium est: Necessitas non habet legem'.

75. Petrus Comestor, *Historia scolastica* 1 Reg.20 (PL 198.1315B); il s'agit, encore une fois, de l'épisode de David et des pains de proposition. Sur le succès de cette œuvre, J. Longère, 'Pierre le Mangeur', *Dictionnaire des lettres françaises. Le Moyen Âge* (Paris 1992²) 1183–84.

76. *Glossa ordinaria, ad* Mc.2.27 s.v. *Homo propter Sabbatum:* 'Quod non est licitum in lege, necessitas licitum facit. Sic et hodie in jejuniis, si quis jejunium fregerit aegrotus, reus non tenetur', ed. *Biblia latina cum glossa ordinaria* IV (Strassburg 1480–81, réimpr. Turnhout 1992) 96.

77. Zacharias Chrysopolitanus, *In unum ex quatuor sive de concordia evangelistarum* 2.68 (PL 186.220B), qui reprend, à peu près mot pour mot, le commentaire de Bède.

l'ensemble des exemples qui précèdent montre la permanence, chez les théologiens de la scolastique naissante, de l'esprit dans lequel s'étaient répandues les différentes formes de la maxime durant le haut Moyen Âge, celle-ci traduisant généralement le souci pastoral de tempérer la rigueur de la règle canonique.

S'il l'on quitte à présent les domaines juridique et ecclésiastique, on peut observer que le proverbe *Necessitas non habet legem* est aussi reçu, au milieu du XIIIᵉ siècle, comme un *topos*, par la philosophie. L'adage apparaît en effet dans une œuvre célèbre, longtemps attribuée par les savants médiévaux à Aristote, le *Secretum secretorum*. Connu sous plusieurs formes, ce miroir des princes, dont l'origine remonte au Xᵉ siècle, mais dont l'auteur demeure inconnu, a été l'objet d'une très importante diffusion, en Occident, à la suite de la traduction d'une de ses versions en latin, élaborée vers 1220–1230 par Roger de Tripoli.[78] Commenté par Roger Bacon, il a fait l'objet de plusieurs traductions en langue vernaculaire, notamment en allemand, en anglais, en castillan, en français ou en italien.[79] Un passage de l'ouvrage, qui contient de longs chapitres relatifs à la médecine et l'hygiène, conseille à ceux qui sont contraints de changer l'heure et la fréquence de leurs repas 'par la nécessité qui n'a point de loi', de le faire avec discernement et sagesse, changeant seulement une habitude après l'autre.[80]

La diffusion de l'adage sous le nom d'Aristote ne pouvait manquer de lui attribuer davantage d'autorité. Au début du XIVᵉ siècle, la maxime est ainsi reprise dans les *Auctoritates Aristotelis*, lesquelles l'empruntent directement au 'Secret des secrets'.[81] Ce florilège fameux, probablement élaboré par Marsile de Padoue, allait être utilisé par tous les savants non-philosophes de la fin du Moyen Âge, en particulier par les juristes dont nombre de citations d'Aristote demeurent indirectes.[82]

78. M. Grignaschi, 'L'origine et les métamorphoses du "Sirr-al-'asrâr",' *Archives d'histoire doctrinale et littéraire du moyen âge* 43 (1976) 7–112, spéc. 87.

79. Cf. idem, 'La diffusion du "Secretum secretorum" (Sirr-al-'asrâr) dans l'Europe occidentale', *Archives d'histoire doctrinale et littéraire du moyen âge* 47 (1980) 7–70; pour les versions françaises, voir J. Monfrin, 'La place du *Secret des secrets* dans la littérature française médiévale', dans: *Pseudo-Aristotle, The Secret of Secrets. Sources and Influences*, éd. W. F. Ryan et Ch. B. Schmitt (Warburg Institute Surveys 9; London 1982) 73–113.

80. *Secretum secretorum* 2.8: 'Si igitur aliqua necessitas, que legem non habet, te compellit ad hoc, videlicet ut consuetudo comedi mutetur, hoc debet fieri discrete et sapienter, videlicet ut fiat mutacio consuetudinis paulatim una vice post aliam, et sic, Dei adjutorio, undique bene fiet', éd. R. Steele (Opera hactenus inedita Rogeri Baconi V; Oxonii 1920) 75.13–17. Cf. *Hilgart von Hürnheim, Mittelhochdeutsche Prosaübersetzung des 'Secretum secretorum'*, éd. R. Möller (Deutsche Texte des Mittelalters 56; Berlin 1963) 72, qui transcrit le texte latin en regard du texte en moyen haut allemand, d'après le MS Berlin, SB lat. 70/4, lequel présente une version proche de la traduction d'Hilgart, élaborée en 1282, qui, pour le proverbe, donne ici: 'Notturfft . . . , die er nit ee het'. La version anglaise dite 'Ashmole', élaborée après 1445, donne: 'Necessitee that hath no lawe', éd. M. A. Manzalaoui, *Secretum secretorum. Nine English Versions* I (Oxford 1977) 55.8.

81. *Auctoritates Aristotelis* 19.23, éd. J. Hamesse (Philosophes médiévaux 17; Louvain-Paris 1974) 272.22. La rub. 19 'De regimine principium' est tout entière extraite du *Secretum secretorum*.

82. Voir par ex. l'étude de N. Horn, 'Philosophie in der Jurisprudenz der Kommentatoren: Baldus Philosophus', *Ius commune* 1 (1967) 104–49 spéc. 128–33.

Pour finir, il convient de noter la réception, dès la seconde moitié du XIIe siècle, de la maxime dans la littérature narrative. Un des premiers exemples semble être fourni par Guillaume de Tyr, dans son *Histoire des croisades* rédigée vers 1180–1186. Celui-ci relate que le comte d'Édesse, ayant fomenté en 1138 des troubles pour exciter la population d'Antioche contre l'empereur byzantin qui comptait cantonner ses troupes dans la ville, vient se jeter hypocritement aux pieds de ce dernier au mépris des usages, justifiant cette attitude en expliquant que la nécessité n'a pas de loi et qu'étant poursuivi par le peuple en fureur, il n'a méconnu l'étiquette que pour échapper à la mort.[83] La culture juridique de Guillaume de Tyr, qui étudia le droit à Bologne, pourrait sans doute expliquer l'usage d'une telle formule.[84] D'autres exemples viennent cependant bientôt montrer que l'adage se répand rapidement dans la littérature, dans le courant du XIIIe siècle, tendant à devenir une véritable figure de style.[85]

Apparu dans la littérature exégétique du début du VIIIe siècle, sous une forme légèrement différente de ce qui allait devenir sa configuration la plus courante, le brocard 'Nécessité n'a point de loi', qui entre presque aussitôt dans la langue canonique, connaît ainsi, à partir de la fin du IXe siècle, une diffusion fulgurante. Son succès paraît en grande partie avoir été assuré par sa circulation dans d'innombrables collections canoniques, laquelle s'intensifie avec la multiplication de ces dernières, à la période grégorienne. À l'époque de la confection du Décret de Gratien, il fait déjà figure de lieu commun parmi les canonistes. Son triomphe est confirmé presque aussitôt avec son adoption par les civilistes qui, l'incluant dans leurs propres recueils de brocards, en ont ainsi involontairement dissimulé l'origine, conduisant souvent les modernes à lui attribuer à tort des racines romaines. Dans le même temps, les liens étroits unissant la théologie scolastique naissante au droit canonique ont aussi permis à la maxime de sortir très tôt du monde étroit des juristes. Par delà même un usage scolaire récurrent, attesté notamment par sa présence dans les florilèges pseudo-aristotéliciens, elle était vouée à devenir, dans le courant du XIIIe siècle, un véritable proverbe populaire.

---

83. Willelmus Tyrensis, *Chronicon* 15.4: 'Respondit necessitatem legem non habere seque populi furentis insectatione coactum, ut mortis evitaret discrimen, contra morum regulas advenisse', éd. CCL cont. med. 63A.678.10–12. Pour une traduction française de l'ensemble du passage, voir F. Guizot, *Collection de mémoires relatifs à l'histoire de France* XVII.2 (Paris 1823) 391–92.

84. R. B. C. Huygens, 'Guillaume de Tyr étudiant. Un chapitre (XIX, 12) de son "Histoire" retrouvé', *Latomus* 21 (1962) 811–29.

85. Ainsi: Saba Malaspina, *Chronicon* 6.8, éd. W. Koller et A. Nitschke (MGH Scriptores 35; Hannover 1999) 255.11–17, dont l'œuvre, qui décrit ici les agissements du roi Charles de Sicile, a été rédigée vers 1283–1285; ou encore Margareta Porete, *Speculum simplicium animarum* 119 = *Le Mirouer des simples ames* 119, éd. CCL cont. med. 69.332.8–335.9, dont l'œuvre fut rédigée avant 1306, chez qui l'adage devient presque une simple formule de politesse.

22

Innocent III, Huguccio de Ferrare et Hubert de Pirovano

Droit canonique, théologie et philosophie à Bologne dans les années 1180[1]

Charles de Miramon

❉

Il y a trente ans, le maître que nous honorons dans ce volume faisait paraître un article sur l'éducation juridique d'Innocent III. Il y montrait que rien dans les écrits du pape ne laisse transparaître une culture technique de canoniste ou de civiliste. La thèse proposée par Kenneth Pennington d'un Innocent, pur théologien, fut d'abord mal reçue. Son maître, Stephan Kuttner, continuait à penser que l'œuvre législatrice considérable d'Innocent III ne pouvait s'expliquer que par une formation juridique. Werner Maleczeck et Wilhelm Imkamp ont repris par la suite la thèse d'un Innocent juriste. Kenneth Pennington a répondu à leurs critiques en ajoutant des nouveaux éléments à sa thèse.[2]

Si Innocent III fut un grand pape législateur sans avoir de formation juridique, il fit pourtant, durant sa jeunesse, un séjour d'étude à Bologne, capitale de l'enseignement du droit savant. L'auteur des *Gesta* du pontife écrit en effet:[3]

1. Pour la préparation de cet article, le DAAD a financé un séjour de travail à Munich au *Stephan Kuttner Institute of Medieval Canon Law.* Lors de la rédaction, des médiévistes parisiens spécialistes d'histoire de la médecine ou des sciences ont répondu à mes (nombreuses) questions. Qu'ils soient remerciés et au premier chef, Maaike van der Lugt.

2. K. Pennington, 'The Legal Education of Pope Innocent III', BMCL 4 (1974) 70–77; cf. idem, 'Review of: Wilhelm Imkamp, Das Kirchenbild Innozenz' III.', ZRG Kan. Abt. 72 (1986) 417–28 = 'Further Thoughts on Pope Innocent III's Knowledge of Law', dans: idem, *Pope, Canonists and Texts, 1150–1550* (Aldershot 1993) no. I–II.

3. *Gesta* c.2 (PL 214.xvii–xviii).

Il poursuivit avec ardeur des études scolastiques d'abord à Rome, puis à Paris et enfin à Bologne et il surpassa ses contemporains comme le montrent les opuscules qu'il composa et édita à diverses époques de sa vie.

Le départ de Lothaire de la France date de 1186 ou 1187. Il fut créé cardinal-diacre entre l'été 1189 et janvier 1190. Les études à Bologne furent donc de courte durée, de deux ou trois ans et vraisemblablement entrecoupées de séjours à la curie pontificale itinérante en Lombardie entre mi-1184 et début 1188.[4] À Paris, le futur pape avait suivi un enseignement de théologie. On suppose traditionnellement, qu'à Bologne, il s'assit aux pieds des principaux enseignants de droit canonique et qu'il suivit les cours d'Huguccio de Ferrare dont la carrière professorale se termine en 1190.[5] Cependant Pennington a montré que la tradition qui faisait d'Huguccio de Ferrare le maître du jeune Lothaire de Segni était une légende dont la première trace se découvre chez Jean d'André.

Notre article essaiera d'aller plus loin encore dans la déconstruction de l'image d'Innocent canoniste. Nous montrerons, d'une part, qu'il existe des indices qui laisse penser que Bologne dans les 1180–1190 est un centre d'élaboration d'une théologie mâtinée de philosophie naturelle et que, d'autre part, Innocent III peut se replacer dans une mouvance de théologiens italiens dont le représentant le mieux connu est le maître Hubert de Pirovano, actif à Bologne à la fin du XIIe siècle.

Huguccio, Innocent et le flegme du Christ

La légende d'un Huguccio maître d'Innocent reste pleine d'attraits pour les historiens qui aiment que les grands personnages se rencontrent et s'apprécient. Pourtant, les faits sont têtus et montrent qu'Innocent, une fois pape, traita Huguccio avec indifférence, sinon avec froideur et animosité, alors qu'il fut très attentif à récompenser ses anciens professeurs. La carrière ecclésiastique de l'ancien maître bolonais ne connut aucune amélioration sous son pontificat. Huguccio est nommé en 1190 par Clément III sur le siège de Ferrare qui dépendait directement du Saint-Siège. Sous le pontificat de Célestin III, il n'obtient quasiment pas de missions de confiance en dehors de son diocèse.[6] Durant le pontificat d'Innocent, Huguccio croupit dans son petit épiscopat exigu, écarté des manœuvres politiques et religieuses dans la plaine du Pô dont le pape charge ses

4. J. Moore, 'Lotario dei Conti di Signi (Pope Innocent III) in the 1180s', AHP 29 (1991) 255–58.
5. W. Müller, *Huguccio. The Life, Works, and Thought of a Twelfth-Century Jurist* (Washington/DC 1994).
6. En 1197, Célestin III le charge de l'administration provisoire du monastère de Nonantola en crise financière: *Italia pontificia* 5.359 n. 109. Nous n'avons pas pu consulter G. Catalano, 'Contributo alla biografia di Uguccione da Pisa', *Il diritto ecclesiastico* 65 (1954) 3–67, qui enquête sur cet épisode.

fidèles afin de contenir le parti impérial, actif dans cette zone disputée.[7] Huguccio meurt en 1210, toujours évêque de Ferrare.

Innocent a adressé à Huguccio deux décrétales, *Quanto* en 1199 et, dix ans plus tard, *In quadam*. La première lettre fixe la casuistique sur les limites du 'privilège paulin' qui autorise dans certains cas la dissolution d'un mariage entre un chrétien et un infidèle ou un hérétique. À la demande de l'évêque de Ferrare, Innocent revient sur la position de ses prédécesseurs et adopte la solution avancée par Huguccio dans sa *Somme*. Dans l'*arenga* de la décrétale, le pape qualifie positivement Huguccio de *iuris peritus*.

Le ton de la deuxième décrétale *In quadam* est tout différent. *In quadam* forme le pendant d'une autre décrétale d'Innocent, *Cum Marthe* qui date de 1202. Jean de Bellesmains, ancien archevêque de Lyon, avait adressé au pape une série de questions sur la doctrine de la transsubstantiation eucharistique. Innocent lui répond dans une longue décrétale à caractère théologique. Nous ne rentrerons pas dans le détail de ces deux textes complexes et riches qui ont été analysés plusieurs fois et dernièrement dans un mémoire précis et documenté de Christoph Egger auquel nous renvoyons pour nous arrêter au seul conflit qui opposa Innocent et Huguccio.[8] Jean de Bellesmains s'interrogeait entre autres sur le devenir de l'eau mélangée au vin durant la messe dans le calice. Était-elle transformée en sang du Christ avec le vin?

Dans son *Traité sur les mystères de la messe*, Innocent abordait déjà cette question au chapitre 29 de son quatrième livre qui débute une petite série casuistique sur les aspects physiques des espèces consacrées.[9] Le chapitre 29 a pour titre: *L'eau mêlée au vin est-elle convertie en sang?;* le 30: *Est-ce que le Christ a récupéré le sang versé sur la croix en ressuscitant?;* 31: *Au sujet du vin mélangé après la consécration;* 32: *Le vin sans eau est-il consacré en sang?;* 33: *Le pain fermenté subit-il la transsubstantiation?*[10] Le lien entre les chapitres 29 et 30 peut sembler tenu. Il s'explique par l'autorité qui sert de point de départ au débat sur l'eau mélangée au vin, le célèbre passage de l'évangile de Jean (Jo.19.34) qui narre que du flanc blessé du Christ mort sur la croix jaillit du sang et de l'eau. Dans la

---

7. Sur le détail de la politique d'Innocent III envers les cités de la plaine du Pô, M. Alberzoni, 'Innocenzo III e la difesa della *libertas ecclesiastica* nei comuni dell'Italia settentrionale', dans: *Innocenzo III. Urbs et Orbis*, éd. A. Sommerlechner (2 vols; Rome 2003) 2.837–928. Huguccio est juge-délégué pour une affaire relativement mineure concernant le diocèse de Vérone en 1206–1207, ibid. 2.915.

8. C. Egger, 'Papst Innocenz III. als Theologe. Beiträge zur Kenntnis seines Denkens im Rahmen der Frühscholastik', AHP 30 (1992) 55–123.

9. La datation du *Traité sur les mystères de la messe*, édité sous le titre *De sacro altaris libri sex* (PL 217.773–916), n'est pas encore certaine. A-t-il été écrit durant les années de cardinalat?, cf. M. Maccarone, 'Innocenzo III teologo dell'eucarestia', dans: idem, *Studi su Innocenzo III* (Padoue 1972) 341–431 ici 345; modifié et mis à jour durant son pontificat?, cf. H. Tillmann, *Papst Innocenz III.* (Bonn 1954) 14 n. 89. Maccarone a remarqué la présence d'interpolations entre le texte de l'édition de PL et les manuscrits les plus anciens. Ceci appuierait l'idée qu'Innocent a révisé ce texte, le plus ambitieux de son œuvre littéraire.

10. PL 217.875–78.

décrétale *Cum Marthe,* Innocent reprend ce qu'il a écrit dans le *Traité sur les mystères de la messe:*[11]

Tu as demandé également si l'eau en même temps que le vin est changée en sang. À ce sujet les opinions varient parmi les scolastiques. Certains en effet pensent que, puisque du côté du Christ ont coulé les deux sacrements principaux, celui de la rédemption dans le sang et celui de la régénération dans l'eau, le vin et l'eau qui sont mêlés dans le calice sont changés dans ces deux-là par la vertu divine [. . .] D'autres en revanche tiennent que l'eau est transsubstantiée en sang avec le vin, puisque mêlée au vin, elle devient vin même si les physiciens avancent le contraire, c'est-à-dire que l'eau peut-être séparée artificiellement du vin [. . .] En outre, on peut dire que l'eau ne devient pas vin mais qu'elle reste entourée par les accidents du vin antérieur [. . .] Mais il est impie de penser ce que certains ont eu la présomption de penser, à savoir que l'eau est changée en flegme en avançant de manière fausse que du flanc du Christ n'est pas sorti de l'eau mais une humeur aqueuse [. . .] Cependant parmi les opinions mentionnées ci-dessus, celle-là est considérée comme la plus probable qui affirme que l'eau est changée en sang avec le vin.

Christoph Egger a observé que le statut du mélange de l'eau et du vin avait peu intéressé les théologiens parisiens de la fin du xiie siècle. Dans sa *Somme sur les sacrements,* Pierre le Chantre se déclare brièvement en faveur de l'idée que l'eau disparaît dans le vin en s'appuyant sur un texte de Boèce (*Opuscules* 5.6) qui explique que si l'on verse du vin dans la mer, il n'est pas mélangé dans la mer mais disparaît *(corruptum)* dans celle-ci. Innocent retient donc une solution identique à celle avancée par Pierre le Chantre. Néanmoins, Egger n'a pas remarqué qu'Innocent développe une théorie du mélange plus complexe qui puise sa source chez Aristote. Dans le *De generatione et corruptione* (327a30–328b22), le Stagyrite discute de la définition du mélange *(mixtio).* Aristote explique qu'un corps qui paraît mélangé n'est pas nécessairement un mélange mais un composé *(compositio)* si l'on peut séparer par la suite les deux composants. Et il donne l'exemple de grains d'orge mêlés à du froment. Si le mélange fait intervenir deux composants dont l'un est très majoritaire par rapport à l'autre alors il n'y a pas non plus mélange car le minoritaire est absorbé par le majoritaire. Aristote propose le même exemple que Boèce. Si l'on verse une petite quantité de vin dans beaucoup d'eau, le vin garde sa *species* mais est transmuté en eau. Pour Aristote, on parle véritablement de mélange quand on fait intervenir deux composants liquides dont la réunion provoque une transformation de chacun des éléments, nous dirions aujourd'hui une réaction chimique. Aristote donne l'exemple du bronze, alliage d'étain et de cuivre. Les deux métaux ne disparaissent pas dans le *mixtum* mais leurs propriétés sont irrémédiablement altérées.

---

11. X 3.41.6 = Reg.5.120, éd. O. Hageneder et al., *Die Register Innocenz' III.: 5. Pontifikatsjahr (1202–03)* (Vienne 1993).

Traduit par Burgundio de Pise dans les années 1150, le *De generatione et corruptione* a été peu utilisé au XIIe siècle sinon par les médecins salernitains à partir de Barthélémy de Salerne.[12] Le texte scolaire de base salernitain, l'*Isagogue* de Johannicius place ainsi dans son deuxième chapitre la liste des sept choses naturelles qui régissent l'homme: les éléments, les mélanges, les composés, les membres, les vertus ou forces naturelles, les opérations ou processus physiologiques et les esprits.[13] La physique salernitaine va se fonder sur les trois premiers éléments de cette liste pour produire une littérature physique sur la composition des corps utilisant le *De generatione et corruptione* et dont le chef d'œuvre est le *De commixtionibus elementorum* d'Urso de Salerne.

Innocent semble connaître certains textes salernitains. En effet, il y a de bonnes chances qu'il puise son savoir sur la physique du mélange chez Maure de Salerne. Maure († 1214) enseigne à Salerne vraisemblablement entre 1165 et 1200. Qualifié dans les sources d'*optimus physicus*, il est le maître dominant à Salerne avant d'être supplanté par Urso.[14] Dans son *Commentaire sur l'Isagogue*, Maure juxtapose trois définitions du mélange *(commixtio)*. À la suite du *Pantegni*, il explique que le mélange est l'union primitive des éléments dans un corps élémenté.[15] Puis, il résume les positions d'Aristote en reprenant en particulier l'exemple du vin mélangé à l'eau. Selon lui, il ne faut pas parler alors de mélange mais d'accroissement ou d'insertion *(insertio)*. Ce deuxième terme correspond peut-être à l'idée évoquée par Innocent d'une eau entourée de vin.[16] Il ajoute ici ce détail que l'on retrouve chez Innocent que l'on peut artificiellement séparer les deux

12. Les manuscrits de la *translatio vetus*, éd. J. Judycka (Aristoteles Latinus 9.1; Leyde 1986), du *De generatione et corruptione* ne porte pas mention du traducteur. R. Durling, 'The Anonymous Translation of Aristotle's *De generatione et corruptione (Translatio Vetus)*', *Traditio* 49 (1994) 320–30, a remarqué des correspondances stylistiques entre la *translatio vetus* et la traduction par Burgundio du *De interioribus*. Il est suivi par F. Bossier, 'L'élaboration du vocabulaire philosophique chez Burgundio de Pise', dans: *Aux Origines du lexique philosophique européen: L'influence de la 'latinitas'*, éd. J. Hamesse (Louvain-la-Neuve 1997) 81–116. Pour la chronologie de l'apparition de citations de la *translatio vetus* dans les commentaires salernitains, cf. D. Jacquart, 'Aristotelian Thought in Salerno', dans: *A History of Twelfth-Century Western Philosophy*, éd. P. Dronke (Cambridge 1988) 407–28.

13. Johannicius, *Isagogue ad Techne Galieni:* 'Res vero naturales sunt septem scilicet elementa, commixtiones, compositiones, membra, virtutes, operationes et spiritus (éd. G. Maurach, *Sudhoffs Archiv* 62 [1978] 148–74 ici 151)'. Les différents commentaires salernitains sur l'*Isagogue* sont présentés par M. D. Jordan, 'Medecine as Science in the Early Commentaries on *Johannitius*', *Traditio* 43 (1987) 121–45.

14. M. H. Saffron, *Maurus of Salerno. Twelfth-Century 'Optimus Physicus' with the Commentary on the 'Prognostics' of Hippocrates* (Transactions of the American Philosophical Society, n.s. 62.1; Philadelphie 1972).

15. Maurus Salernitanus, *In Isagoge:* 'Commixtio igitur, ut inquit Constantinus in Pantegni, est prima elementorum in unoque elementato corpore coniunctio (Paris, BN lat. 18499, fol. 8v)'. Texte transcrit et commenté par D. Jacquart, 'De *crasis* à *complexio*, note sur le vocabulaire du tempérament en latin médiéval', dans: *Mémoires V, textes médicaux latins antiques*, éd. G. Sabbah (Saint-Étienne 1984) 71–76 = D. Jacquart, *La science médicale occidentale entre deux renaissances (XIIe s.–XVe s.)* (Aldershot 1997) no. 6.

16. Cette théorie est, en tout cas, compatible avec les conceptions physico-humorales pour lesquelles dans un composé les éléments chauds et aérés (ici le vin) ont une force centrifuge et les éléments froids et humides une force centripète, chacun cherchant à rejoindre son lieu naturel.

composants d'un mélange d'eau et de vin.[17] Enfin, il distingue entre les mélanges égaux et inégaux. Un mélange est dit inégal, si, dans le cas le plus simple d'un assemblage de deux corps, l'un des corps est quatre fois plus important que l'autre par sa quantité ou sa qualité. La comparaison de *Cum Marthe* et du *Commentaire sur l'Isagogue* de Maure montre ainsi une correspondance étroite entre leurs théories du mélange. Néanmoins, le pape s'écarte de la physique salernitaine en adoptant une physique de la chose articulée entre essence et accidents. Cette approche, fondamentale pour expliquer la transsubstantiation, n'a pas d'importance dans le modèle salernitain.

Dans *Cum Marthe*, Innocent a des mots très durs pour l'opinion de ceux qui avancent que l'eau qui jaillit du flanc du Christ est en fait du flegme. Il la qualifie d'impie *(nefas)*. Comme les historiens l'ont montré depuis longtemps, le pape vise ici une personne spécifique: Huguccio de Ferrare. Huguccio dans son commentaire sur la deuxième distinction du *De consecratione* prend appui sur l'équivocité du mot sang dans la médecine gréco-arabe qui désigne à la fois le composé des quatre humeurs et l'une des quatre humeurs. Le sang consacré du calice peut donc correspondre au seul vin et en même temps être la conversion du mélange de l'eau et du vin; l'eau correspondant alors aux humeurs aqueuses du Christ. Huguccio explique de surcroît que le coup de lance fit jaillir du sang et des humeurs aqueuses et que le miracle ne tient pas à une création surnaturelle de liquide mais dans le fait que les humeurs coulèrent séparées alors qu'elles sont toujours mêlées dans le corps et qu'un cadavre ne saigne normalement pas.[18] Huguccio ajoute un

17. Maurus Salernitanus, *In Isagoge* (fol. 8v): 'Notandum quod non quelibet elementorum coniunctio dicitur commixtio. Terra enim coniungitur aque et eadem ab aqua separatur. Non quorumlibet liquidorum coniunctio dicitur commixtio inquantum enim constanter in prima <natura>. Et si vinum coniungatur aque eorum tamen coniunctio non dicitur commixtio nam utrumque in prima natura permanet. Talis igitur coniunctio dicitur simplex accessio. Vinum enim aque artificialiter coniungitur et ab ea artificialiter separatur. Est autem simplex coniunctio que dicitur insercio. Illa autem que proprie dicitur commixtio est in qua substantie et forme commixtorum in aliud esse sit transitus. Unde Arist. in Libro Generationis: "Commixtio est miscibilium per minima coniunctorum unio". Item Plato: "Commixta separare solius Dei est et nonne opus". Commixtionis vero alia est equalis et alia inequalis'. La citation d'Aristote déjà présente dans le *Commentaire* de Barthélémy de Salerne est un assemblage qui déforme sa pensée et réintroduit l'idée du mélange comme assemblage de particules élémentaires *(minima)*. Ces particules élémentaires se retrouveront dans la médecine scolastique postérieure, cf. D. Jacquart, *La médecine médiévale dans le cadre parisien* (Paris 1998) 346. Je n'ai pas réussi à retrouver chez Calcidius l'autorité attribuée à Platon. Laurent d'Espagne, *ad* 3 Comp.3.33.5: 'Licet phisici contrarium assererent (éd. B. McManus, *The Ecclesiology of Laurentius Hispanus* [Ph.D. diss.; Syracuse University 1991] 523–24)', reste incrédule devant l'idée que l'on puisse séparer le mélange de l'eau et du vin entre ses composants.

18. Huguccio, *Summa*, De cons. D.2 c.1 *quia utrumque* (éd. Egger, 'Papst Innozenz III.' 88 n. 204). On trouvera dans le mémoire de Egger le dossier des gloses d'Huguccio sur le sujet. Il faut y ajouter que la première apparition de la théorie humorale se trouve dans l'Apparat *Ordinaturus Magister*, De cons. D.2 c.4: 'Queritur an vinum et aqua transeant scilicet in sanguinem tantum vel in aqua tantum: Non, sed vinum in sanguinem et aqua in aquam id est naturalem humorem aquaticum. Sicut enim in humano corpore quatuor sunt humores, sic in corpore Christi. Unde sic expone: Hec tria sunt unum in uno Christo et hec tria sunt tria et tantum tria quia vinum in sanguinem, aqua in aquam, panis in corpus convertitur (Munich, BSB lat. 27337, fol. 193v)'; voir aussi ibid., De cons. D.2 c.1 *utrumque permixtum* (fol. 193r). Dans les deux cas, les gloses ne sont pas signées. Dans la

commentaire symbolique à son invention: le flegme est une humeur moins noble que le sang et dans le sacrement de l'eucharistie, il désigne des grâces mineures.

On peut se demander d'où Huguccio tire son savoir médical. La théorie des quatre humeurs est extrêmement répandue au Moyen Âge et elle ne peut servir de marqueur pour déterminer la source de ses connaissances. À la fin du *Décret* de Gratien, dans le *De consecratione* (De cons. D.5 c.29), on trouve un passage de Jérôme contre la gloutonnerie où il est fait mention de Galien et des *Aphorismes* d'Hippocrate. Huguccio glose le titre d'*Aphorismes* en lui donnant plusieurs définitions et ajoute qu'il existe un livre nommé *Physique* qui contient de nombreux aphorismes.[19] Peut-on déterminer à partir de cette glose si Huguccio connaissait les *Aphorismes* dans la tradition ancienne où le texte circule seul ou accompagné du *Commentaire* d'Oribase ou dans la nouvelle version qui voit les *Aphorismes* intégrés dans le recueil salernitain connu sous le nom d'*Articella*?[20] La première des définitions des *Aphorismes* proposées par Huguccio est très commune et semble présente tant dans la tradition pré-salernitaine que salernitaine.[21] Néanmoins, l'indication, du reste mystérieuse, d'un livre dénommé *In fisica* fait plutôt penser à Salerne.[22]

Huguccio a des connaissances médicales mais rien n'indique un savoir appro-

---

Somme *Omnis qui iuste iudicat,* la théorie est attribuée à 'G.', Egger, 'Papst Innozenz III.' 84–85. Il reste néanmoins douteux qu'il faut voir en Gandulphe son inventeur. Tout laisse penser que son auteur est Huguccio.

19. Huguccio, *Summa,* De cons. D.5 c.29 *aphorismis:* 'Aphorismus dicitur quasi aporismus scilicet sermo brevis sensum integrum rei proposite continens, sic dictus a poris que sunt aperationes scilicet parva et subtilia foramina corporis unde sudor emanat vel sic dicitur a foris id est foraminibus unde rheume [ms. remi] emittuntur. Et liber quidam sic dicitur *In fisica* ubi multi aforismi continentur (Paris, BN lat. 15397, fol. 150r)'.

20. Sur les *Aphorismes* au Haut Moyen Âge, A. Beccaria, 'Sulle trace di un antico canone latino di Ippocrate e di Galeno, I'; 'II. Gli aforismi di Ippocrate nella versione e nei commenti del primo medioevo'; 'III. Quattro opere di Galeno nei commenti della scuola di Ravenna all'inizio del medioevo', *Italia medioevale e umanistica* 2 (1959) 1–56; 4 (1961) 1–75; 14 (1971) 1–23.

21. La définition: *Quid est Aphorismus? Sermo brevis integrum sensum propositae rei describens,* se trouve à la fin de la préface au *Commentaire* d'Oribase aux *Aphorismes* (éd. Paris 1533). Cette préface est déjà présente dans les manuscrits médicaux du Haut Moyen Âge, cf. A. Beccaria, *I codici di medicina del periodo presalernitano (secoli IX, X e XI)* (Storia e Letteratura 53; Rome 1956), sous l'incipit: *Quia necesse est semper in omnibus codicibus.* La définition passe ensuite dans les textes salernitains comme le *Commentaire aux Aphorismes* de Maure, éd. S. de Renzi, *Collectio Salernitana* (Naples 1856) 4.515.

22. Dans la classification du savoir en cours à Salerne, la médecine se divise entre théorie et pratique, la théorie constituant une branche de la physique, cf. D. Jacquart et F. Micheau, *La médecine arabe et l'Occident médiéval* (Paris 1990) 124–27. On peut aussi noter que les deux définitions (pseudo-)étymologiques qu'Huguccio donne de l'"aphorisme" renvoient aux pores ou aux ouvertures du corps par lesquelles s'écoulent les sécrétions. L'*Isagogue* accorde une grande importance aux pores et aux sécrétions comme le note D. Jacquart, 'Aristotelian Thought' 421 n. 58. Enfin la description d'un livre qui contient beaucoup d'aphorismes peut faire penser à un exemplaire précoce de l'*Articella*. En effet, dans la première phase de sa constitution (Jordan, 'Medecine as Science' 126–28), l'*Articella* ne rassemble que cinq textes courts et formulaires à vocation mnémotechnique (*Isagogue* de Johannicius, *Aphorismes* et *Prognostics* d'Hippocrate, *Sur les urines* de Théophile, *Sur le pouls* de Philarète). Par la suite, on y ajouta des œuvres avec des formes littéraires différentes comme le *Tegni* de Galien.

fondi. En tout cas, l'innovation d'Huguccio sur la blessure du flanc du Christ n'est pas seulement rejetée par Innocent; elle était aussi contestée avec modération par Bazianus et Melendus, deux enseignants bolonais de droit canonique actifs dans les années 1180–90, comme nous l'apprend Jean le Teutonique.[23] Pourtant, la théorie d'Huguccio ne semble pas avoir été perçue comme particulièrement dangereuse par l'opinion théologique de l'époque. Certes, Prévôtin de Crémone la qualifie de ridicule.[24] Cependant, dans la lignée de Pierre le Chantre, Robert de Courson récupère la théorie d'Huguccio et l'amplifie pour l'appliquer au cas de l'hostie confectionnée à partir d'une farine impure. Il imagine que le grain d'orge mélangé au froment ou la particule de la meule qui se serait mêlée à la farine de l'hostie seront transformés dans le calice en les superfluités du Christ (cheveux, poils, sueur).[25] De même, l'explication naturaliste de la blessure du Christ aura une longue survie. On trouve aujourd'hui encore dans la *Traduction Œcuménique de la Bible* sur Jean 19.34 une note qui avance que l'écoulement de la blessure du Christ pourrait résulter d'un 'épanchement pleural'. On comprend dès lors l'étonnement d'Huguccio de voir sa position qualifiée d'impie dans la décrétale *Cum Marthe* et sa requête au pape de reconsidérer sa position.

Innocent répond pourtant très durement au canoniste devenu évêque par sa décrétale *In quadam*.[26] Il lui explique que 'même si des personnes fameuses et d'autorité ont accepté l'opinion que tu as suivie dans tes écrits et ton enseignement, tu seras obligé d'adhérer à notre solution car nous pensons le contraire'. Il donne ensuite une démonstration théologique qui s'articule en trois moments. Tant l'évangéliste que le commentaire de la *Glose* parlent d'eau et pas d'un autre liquide.[27] Il faut, par conséquent,

---

23. *Glossa Ordinaria*, De cons. D.2 c.1 *quia utrumque* (éd. Venise 1605 p. 1177b): 'Nomine sanguinis dicitur quilibet humor humani corporis. Hic non invenitur nisi large accipiatur nomen sanguinis unde vinum in sanguinem convertitur et aqua in alios humores, ita quod aqua dicitur profluxisse, id est alii humores, de latere Christi. Sed numquid vera aqua, aut humor aquae similis fluxit? Si vera aqua, quando fuit illa creata? Numquid in corpore, aut in egressu a corpore? Si humor fuit sine aqua, quod fuit ibi miraculum? Responsio secundum Hug.: Separatim et cum segregatione fluxerunt. Alii tamen dicunt ut Mel. et Baz. quod vera aqua et extra corpus illius fuit illa creata, sicut fuit cum fluxit aqua de petra educta'. Jean le Teutonique reprend ici Laurent d'Espagne, *Glossa Palatina* ad eod. loc. (Vatican, BAV Reg. lat. 977, fol. 279r).

24. Egger, 'Papst Innozenz III.' 75.

25. Robert de Courson, *Summa*, De eucharistia: 'Magister noster Cantor ita solet solvi quod adeo modicum de aqua debet cum vino apponi ut totum absorbeatur a vino et illud commixtum totum vinum iudicetur et tunc illud totum transit in sanguinem Christi. Sed si tantum aque apponatur quod non absorbeatur a vino illud manet inconfectum et sic dicendum est de farinula ordeacea; idem de pulviculo lapilli adiuncto farine triticee dicimus scilicet quod non transit in corpus Christi sed manet in sui natura et talia transeunt in fomitum corporale vel in humores. Alii asserunt quod non potest adeo parum de aqua apponi quin semper maneat aqua et ideo illa aqua non transsubstantiatur in corpus vel sanguinem sed transit in humores (Paris, BN lat. 14524, fol. 147r)'. Dans ce chapitre Robert de Courson utilise largement le commentaire d'Huguccio sur De cons. D.2 sans le citer explicitement.

26. X 3.41.8 = Reg. 12.7 (PL 216.16–18).

27. Pierre le Chantre, *In 1ᵃ epist. Iohan.* 5.6 s.v. *spiritus*: 'Humana anima quam in Passione emisit cum

lire de manière littérale le récit johannique. Le Christ est un homme véritable avec un corps véritablement humain. Jean rend compte de cette vérité de la nature humaine du Christ en expliquant que l'esprit vital s'est échappé de Jésus à sa mort et que du sang et de l'eau s'échappent de son corps.[28] Tout cela n'aurait pas été possible si le corps du Christ avait été un fantôme.[29] D'un corps véritable sourd une eau véritable. Innocent ne se prononce pas sur le caractère miraculeux ou naturel de cette eau. Cette eau a pu être créée par Dieu mais elle a pu aussi être produite naturellement à partir des composants corporels. Innocent explique ainsi qu'un corps est composé des quatre éléments (air, eau, feu, terre) et quant à ses fonctions vitales *(ad vegetationem)* des quatre humeurs. Il est ainsi possible de revenir naturellement des 'élémentés' du corps aux éléments primitifs, et donc en particulier à de l'eau.

Innocent utilise le terme technique d'élémenté *(elementatum)*. La physique du XIIe siècle explique que tous les corps sont le résultat d'un mélange d'éléments. Les éléments n'existent pas vraiment en tant que tel dans le monde. Avant la création, la matière n'existe qu'en puissance, en tant que quintessence. Au moment de la création, les éléments apparaissent mais se mélangent immédiatement pour donner naissance à des élémentés, c'est-à-dire à des corps majoritairement composés d'un élément. Par la suite, les élémentés se mêlent pour former les corps. Le terme d'élémenté se trouve dans l'école chartraine et en particulier chez Guillaume de Conches.[30] Néanmoins, il est plus logique de penser qu'Innocent le reprend du *Commentaire sur l'Isagogue* de Maure où l'on trouve des définitions des éléments utilisant le concept d'élémenté mais aussi la présentation du corps humain comme un mélange de composants résultant en une complexion particulière.[31] La démonstration naturaliste d'Innocent suit donc l'ordre de

---

centurio exclamabat dicens: "Vere filius Dei erat iste"; vel *caro* alia littera *aqua et sanguis* que in passione fluxerunt de latere eius quod non posset fieri nisi veram naturam carnis haberet. Quod de latere Christi iam mortui contra naturam aqua et sanguis vivaciter fluxerunt significat quod corpus Domini post mortem melius esset victurum et mors eius nobis vitam daret. Quod vero sudor eius in mente factus est sicut gutte sanguinis decurrentis in terram significat quod suo sanguine ecclesiam toto orbe lavaret (Paris, BN lat. 682, fol. 32v)'. Cette glose de Pierre le Chantre est reprise, légèrement résumée, dans la *Glose Ordinaire* sur la Première Épître de Jean (PL 114.702).

28. Innocent lit la glose de Pierre le Chantre avec un œil médical. Il comprend *spiritus:* 'humana anima quam in passione emisit' comme l'esprit vital *(spiritus vitalis)* reprenant un concept puisé, vraisemblablement, dans l'*Isagogue* (§ 12–17, éd. Maurach 153–55). L'esprit vital est le substrat matériel d'une des trois fonctions *(virtus)* du corps, la fonction spirituelle, responsable, en particulier, du battement du cœur.

29. Innocent parle de *corpus fantasticum*, allusion aux corps des démons et des anges fabriqués à partir d'air chaud et qui sont incapables de reproduire les processus physiologiques humains, cf. M. van der Lugt, *Le Ver, le Démon et la Vierge. Les théories médiévales de la génération extraordinaire* (Paris 2004) 230–43.

30. T. Silverstein, 'Elementatum: Its Appearance Among the Twelfth-Century Cosmogonists', *Mediaeval Studies* 16 (1954) 156–62; I. Caiazzo, 'Les quatre éléments chez Alain de Lille et Radulphe de Longo Campo', dans: *Actes du Colloque Alain de Lille, Paris, 23–25 octobre 2003* (à paraître).

31. D. Jacquart, 'De *crasis* à *complexio*'. Maure introduit le concept d'élémenté vers la fin de son commentaire sur le troisième paragraphe de l'Isagogue. Il pose en particulier la question: 'Restat inquirere utrum

l'*Isagoge* où s'articule une physique du corps humain fondée sur les quatre éléments (§ 3) puis une physiologie humorale (§ 5). L'originalité consiste à appliquer ce modèle au Christ.

La position d'Innocent ne change pas depuis son *Traité sur les mystères de la messe* et les décrétales postérieures *Cum Marthe* et *In quadam*. Il se situe à la confluence d'une double tradition. D'un côté, il reste fidèle à son enseignement parisien. Il donne une grande autorité à la récente *Glose ordinaire* sur la Bible qu'Huguccio ne semble pas connaître. Il reprend surtout le concept de vérité de la nature humaine, nœud du débat théologique sur l'aspect physiologique de l'humanité du Christ et qui fait l'objet d'un chapitre dans les *Sentences* de Pierre Lombard.[32] De l'autre côté, les chapitres sur la physique des espèces consacrées correspondent à la casuistique bolonaise sur De cons. D.2 qui se développe dans les années 1180.[33] Innocent a vraisemblablement assisté à ce débat lors de son séjour d'étude à Bologne. Il suit, semble-t-il, des positions souvent différentes de celles d'Huguccio.[34]

Les excursus sur le mélange et la composition des corps tirés de Maure de Salerne sont absents du *Traité sur les mystères de la messe* et apparaissent dans les décrétales postérieures. Est-ce que cela veut dire qu'Innocent ne connaissait pas ce texte lors de la rédaction de son traité? Nous ne le pensons pas. Dans son *Traité sur les mystères de la*

---

elementa remaneant in corporibus elementatis aut per generationem in aliud essentie transeant. Quod elementa in corporibus elementatis non permaneant et in aliud transeant nostra est opinio (fol. 8r)'. Pour Maure, l'élément est la qualité substantielle de l'élémenté. L'usage du terme élémenté par Maure avait déjà été indiqué par P. Morpurgo, 'I capitolo sugli elementi di Mauro Salernitano: elementa, elementata', dans: *Atti del Convegno sur Aristotelismo e Platonismo nel Mezzogiorno d'Italia* (Palerme 1989) 211–28. Dans ce même chapitre (fol. 6v) Maure expose les successifs emboîtements depuis l'élément simple jusqu'au corps complexe et vice-versa. Ce passage a vraisemblablement influencé Innocent.

32. La vérité de la nature humaine c'est pour les théologiens en premier lieu ce qui matériellement en nous est spécifiquement humain en sachant que le corps est le résultat de la digestion d'aliments et que le sperme est aussi compris comme un résidu de l'alimentation. La vérité de la nature humaine est débattue en premier lieu dans le cadre de la transmission du pêché originel puis devient une discussion christologique. Jusqu'à quel point le Christ a partagé les mécanismes physiologiques des autres hommes? Sur la vérité de la nature humaine, voir P. Reynolds, *Food and the Body. Some Peculiar Questions in High Medieval Theology* (Leyde 1999), et surtout la note d'A. Boureau, 'Humain, sur-humain, sous-humain: la théologie du xiiie siècle et la question de la vérité de la nature humaine' (http://forum.quipo.it/alchimia/detailf.asp?id=27).

33. La casuistique des chapitres 29–32 du quatrième livre du *Traité sur les mystères de la messe* correspond à de nombreuses gloses du De cons. D.2 où l'on se pose aussi la question de savoir si l'on peut utiliser à la place du vin, du vin nouveau *(mustum)* ou du vinaigre; de la validité de la consécration de vin sans eau, ou de pain avec levain.

34. Ainsi Innocent (PL 217.876) pense que si le prêtre n'utilise pas du vin mais du vinaigre, la consécration reste valide. Huguccio pense le contraire mais il laisse la porte ouverte au vin cuit ou parfumé aux herbes, *Summa*, De cons. D.2 c.5 *frumento*: 'Quid de aceto? Respondendum: Si acetum fiat et non de vino, non consecrabitur. [. . .] Quid de vino cocto? Potest offeri. Quid de vino ubi semina vel radices vel herbe vel species apponuntur? Distinguo. Si huiusmodi apposita trahunt vinum ad aliam speciem liquoris non consecrabitur. Aliter consecrari potest. Sed quia circa hoc non est omnino veritas aperta, illud teneamur pro certo quod nihil transit in corpus Christi preter panem frumenti et vinum uvarum cum aqua (Paris, BN lat. 15397, fol. 120v)'.

messe, Innocent écrit en tant que théologien reprenant le style pédagogique de l'école moralo-théologique parisienne de la fin du XIIe siècle et il s'abstient de citations savantes. Une fois pape, il a une plus grande liberté pour montrer un savoir original. De plus, on ne trouve pas dans les écrits d'Innocent d'autres passages où ce savoir soit utilisé. C'est le débat bolonais sur la nature de l'épanchement du flanc du Christ qui a certainement conduit les acteurs de ce conflit à rechercher les théories physiologiques les plus à jour. C'est durant son séjour à Bologne qu'Innocent a pris connaissance de l'*Isagogue* et du *Commentaire* de Maure.

La rebuffade d'Innocent envers Huguccio est finalement de deux ordres. Il lui montre qu'il n'est pas un véritable théologien car il ne maîtrise pas la culture commune théologique parisienne de la fin du XIIe siècle. Il ridiculise ensuite son utilisation d'un savoir naturaliste par le recours à une connaissance plus approfondie des concepts médicaux.

La philosophie au miroir du droit canonique bolonais des années 1180

Huguccio utilise la théorie humorale comme un savoir commun qui ne nécessite ni explications, ni justifications. Du reste, on trouve mention du système des quatre humeurs dans les écrits de droit civil bolonais de la même époque ce qui marque une certaine porosité entre sciences juridiques et naturaliste.[35] D'autre part, dans l'apparat *Ordinaturus magister* ainsi que dans la *Somme* d'Huguccio, on trouve des gloses qui s'appuient sur l'*Éthique à Nicomaque* traduite par Burgundio de Pise dans les années 1150 mais dont on n'avait pas de traces d'utilisation au XIIe siècle, sinon dans des textes salernitains.[36] Les œuvres des théologiens parisiens des années 1180 ne révèlent aucune trace de ce type de savoir médical ou philosophique. Est-ce une particularité bolonaise? Plus généralement, y-a-t-il eu un enseignement de philosophie ou de théologie à Bologne dans le dernier quart du XIIe siècle? Les historiens de l'université de Bologne au XIIe

---

35. Dans sa *materia* aux *Institutes*, Placentin remarque que les *Institutes* constituent un livre élémentaire et que le mot élément renvoie aux quatre éléments qui constituent le monde: 'Dicitur et elementorum per similitudinem IIII elementorum, sicut enim ex IIII elementis totus mundus confectus est, sic et in libro Institutionum, qui distinctus est per IIII libros, totius romani iuris scientia summotenus tangitur, breviter prelibatur (éd. H. Fitting, *Juristische Schriften des früheren Mittelalters* [1876; reprint Aalen 1976] 22)'. Dans la glose ordinaire d'Accurse, cette remarque est développée en une longue glose sur la théorie des éléments, Accurse, *Glossa ad Inst.*, Proem. *prima elementa*: 'Quia sicut ex quatuor elementis omnia corpora conficiuntur, ut terra et aqua et igne et aere, id est ex viribus horum quatuor elementorum totus mundus gubernatur, ita hic liber comprehendit omnia iura. Et nota quod terra est frigida et sicca, aqua frigida et humida, ignis calidus et siccus, aer calidus et humidus. Naturam prime habet melancolia; secunde, scilicet aque, flegma; ignis colera; sanguis respondet aeri. Ac. (éd. P. Torelli [Bologne 1939])'. Mes efforts pour dater la composition de cette glose ont été vains.

36. L'étude de ces gloses fera l'objet d'un prochain travail.

siècle se sont concentrés sur le droit romain et canonique. Il est certain que Bologne a constitué un centre mineur par rapport à Paris en ce qui concerne les arts libéraux et la théologie. Pour le dernier quart du XIIe siècle, nous avons peu ou pas de sources sur le sujet. Néanmoins, il est possible d'utiliser une méthode indirecte en partant de la littérature canonique, aujourd'hui bien cataloguée et bien datée, afin d'éclairer le reste du tableau. Il ne s'agit pas de faire la recherche des citations explicites de théologiens et de philosophes dans les gloses bolonaises comme a pu le faire pour Aristote et pour le droit romain Gerhard Otte.[37] Nous enquêterons en effet sur l'attitude générale par rapport aux sciences profanes telle qu'elle se manifeste dans les commentaires bolonais sur la Distinction 37.

Les commentaires sur la Distinction 37: l'ouverture bolonaise à la philosophie

À la fin du XIXe siècle, Heinrich Singer avait remarqué l'intérêt des commentaires des canonistes pour la Distinction 37 du *Décret* au cours de laquelle Gratien se demande si les clercs doivent connaître les sciences profanes.[38] Gratien classe ces autorités entre les *pro* et les *contra* et introduit une distinction: il est permis de lire ces auteurs pour son instruction *(eruditio)* mais pas pour son plaisir *(voluptas)*. Il rejoignait là l'opinion commune de l'Église depuis l'époque patristique selon laquelle les écrits des auteurs latins pré-chrétiens ne pouvaient être lus que dans la mesure où ils pouvaient contenir des vérités pouvant aider à la compréhension de la foi et à une meilleure lecture de la Bible.[39]

Les premiers décrétistes ne vont pas chercher à gommer l'approche frileuse de Gratien mais plutôt à la transcrire dans le cadre du renouvellement de l'enseignement au XIIe siècle. Ainsi, disent-ils, parmi les sciences profanes, celles du *trivium* sont utiles et doivent être enseignées dans les écoles cathédrales. Au contraire, les sciences du *quadrivium* sont inutiles. Enfin, certaines sciences ne sont pas simplement inutiles mais elles peuvent être dangereuses, c'est le cas de l'astronomie et de la nigromantie.[40] Si Étienne de Tournai propose une analyse relativement mesurée des sciences profanes,

---

37. G. Otte, 'Die Aristoteleszitate in der Glosse. Beobachtungen zur philosophischen Vorbildung der Glossatoren', ZRG Rom. Abt. 85 (1968) 368–93.

38. H. Singer, 'Beiträge zur Würdigung der Decretistenlitteratur II', AKKR 73 (1895) 3–124.

39. Une glose caractéristique est par exemple, Apparat *Ordinaturus magister*, D.37 c.7: 'Sicut ethicam scripturam utilem quam si neglexerimus scripturam divinam recte discere et intelligere non poterimus (Munich, BSB lat. 10244, fol. 19v)'. Sur le *topos* de la philosophie comme servante de la théologie dans les écoles parisiennes de la fin du XIIe siècle, cf. J. Baldwin, *Masters, Princes and Merchants. The Social Views of Peter the Chanter and His Circle* (2 vols; Princeton 1970) 1.78–79.

40. Rufin, *Summa*, D.37 c.9, éd. H. Singer (Paderborn 1902; repr. Aalen 1963) 89. La glose de Rufin sera synthétisée par Sicard de Crémone.

Rufin est beaucoup plus véhément et adopte une approche très négative, n'hésitant pas à forcer le trait.[41] Les commentaires des premiers décrétistes sont marqués par une attitude finalement hostile vis-à-vis des sciences profanes; elle témoigne du hiatus entre la culture conservatrice du *Studium* bolonais à cette époque et les expérimentations contemporaines audacieuses chartraines.

Une génération plus tard, l'Apparat *Ordinaturus magister* et la *Somme* d'Huguccio marquent une transformation. Il ne s'agit pas véritablement d'un retournement de position; tant l'Apparat *Ordinaturus magister* que la *Somme* d'Huguccio restent relativement méfiants face aux sciences profanes. Ce qui se modifie, c'est le statut de cette science. Il ne s'agit plus d'un savoir uniquement livresque que l'on découvre en feuilletant les livres d'une bibliothèque, une lecture tentante mais oiseuse, mais d'une matière enseignée et qui, mal comprise, peut conduire à des erreurs doctrinales. En un mot, la science profane rentre sur le devant de la scène universitaire locale.

Si Gratien et la première génération de décrétistes utilisaient le mot 'lecture' dans son sens actuel, cette deuxième génération de canonistes le comprend dans son nouveau sens pédagogique qui distingue la lecture privée et la lecture publique, c'est-à-dire l'enseignement en tant que le cours du professeur est une lecture commune devant les étudiants du texte commenté. Ainsi une glose schématisant un sermon de Pierre le Mangeur indique qu'il y a cinq finalités pour la lecture: on peut lire pour connaître; on peut lire (enseigner) pour être connu; on peut lire (étudier) pour s'enrichir; on peut lire pour être édifié et enfin on peut lire (enseigner) pour édifier. Les dernières finalités sont bien plus recommandables que les premières.[42] Cette distinction montre la réception à Bologne de la définition des prélats comme les docteurs et prédicateurs, définition fréquente dans l'éxégèse parisienne de la fin du XIIe siècle. Cette maîtrise du savoir et de la parole que l'on acquiert à l'université devient centrale à la justification de la fonction du prélat dans l'ecclésiologie de l'époque.

C'est ainsi qu'Huguccio articule de manière nouvelle pouvoir et science dans la figure du prélat qui doit être tant un savant qu'un gardien du dogme. Il développe une longue glose sur un court canon (D.37 c.1) provenant du quatrième concile de Carthage qui autorisait l'évêque à lire les livres des païens et des hérétiques *pro necessitate aut tempore.*

41. H. Kalb, *Studien zur Summa Stephans von Tournai* (Innsbruck 1983) 46–50.
42. Apparat *Ordinaturus magister,* ad D.37 Proem.: 'Quinque sunt fines quibus homines legunt: ut sciant, hic finis est superbia; ut sciatur, hic finis est vana gloria; ut lucretur, hic finis est avaritia; ut edificetur, hic finis est prudentia; ut edificet, hic finis est caritas (Munich, BSB lat. 27337, fol. 19r)'. Cette glose se trouve dans une œuvre contemporaine les *Notae Atrebatenses,* ad eod. loc., qui indique la source: 'secundum mag. Petrum Manducatorem (éd. J. van de Vouw [Thèse; Leyde 1969] 9)'; cf. *Sermo II in adventu Domini* (PL 198.1278). Pour R. Weigand, 'Die ersten Jahrzehnte der Schule von Bologna', Proc. Munich (MIC C.9; 1997) 445–55, ici 449, cette œuvre est issue de l'école anglo-normande et pas de l'école bolonaise comme le pensait Van de Vouw. Ceci ne change pas le fait que les *Notae Atrebatenses* compilent uniquement des opinions de maîtres bolonais.

Le canoniste distingue la lecture publique de ces livres—c'est-à-dire leur enseignement ou étude—qui est interdite aux évêques mais qui est permise à tous les autres clercs d'ordre mineur ou majeur.[43] L'évêque a seulement le droit de lire chez lui de manière privée les ouvrages païens ou hérétiques. La lecture des ouvrages hétérodoxes n'est plus simplement admissible dans certains cas, elle devient une obligation pour le prélat qui doit contrecarrer les erreurs doctrinales.[44] Ceci le conduit à s'opposer aux autodafés prescrits par le droit romain dont il restreint de beaucoup le champ d'application.[45] La connaissance doit être encouragée, même si elle provient de sources douteuses.

Qui sont ces hérétiques? On pourrait être tenté d'y deviner des cathares. Nous sommes à l'époque de la prise de conscience par les intellectuels du catharisme et Huguccio indique que la lecture des livres hérétiques est permise *pro tempore* 'lorsque de nombreux hérétiques pullulent dans l'Église de Dieu et la mettent en danger'.[46] Néanmoins, une étude plus approfondie des allégations et des gloses qui s'y rattachent pointe dans une toute autre direction. Ainsi, l'Apparat *Ordinaturus magister* s'attaque aux 'hommes qui abusent des arts et veulent tellement suivre l'ordre naturel *(cursum nature)* qu'ils en viennent à refuser d'admettre l'accouchement d'une vierge et les autres miracles accomplis de manière surnaturelle *(preter cursum nature)*'.[47] Cette glose s'accroche à un extrait

---

43. Robert de Courson adopte lors du Concile de Paris de 1213 une position plus dure. L'étude des sciences séculières à l'Université de Paris est interdite aux clercs ayant une charge d'âme, éd. H. Denifle et E. Chatelain, *Chartularium Universitatis Parisiensis* 1–4 (Paris 1889–97, réimpr. Bruxelles 1964) 1.77 no. 19.

44. On retrouve trente ans plus tard à Paris tant l'opposition entre lecture privée et publique d'ouvrages philosophiques que le rôle de l'évêque dans l'organisation d'autodafés lors des censures des *libri naturales* d'Aristote et la livraison au bûcher des *Quaternuli* de David de Dinant. Cf. en dernier lieu, L. Bianchi, *Censure et liberté intellectuelle à l'Université de Paris (XIIIᵉ–XIVᵉ siècles)* (Paris 1999) 89–116. Sur ce livre voir la note critique d'A. Boureau, 'La censure dans les universités médiévales', *Annales* 55 (2000) 313–23.

45. Huguccio, *Summa*, D.37 c.1 s.v. *Episcopus libros gentilium non legat:* 'Ad delectationem sed nec in scolis, etiam ad eruditionem. Si non in domo sua vult ibi quandoque legere ut revocaret ad memoriam aliquid utile ad expositionem sacre scripture vel ad revincendam paganorum vanitatem non prohibetur, ut infra eodem, Qui de mensa (D.37 c.11), Si quid (c.13). Relatum (c.14). De clericis in minoribus ordinibus constitutis dico quod etiam in scolis licite eos causa eruditionis legunt, idem credo de subdiaconis et diaconis et presbiteris si contingat eos esse promotos ita inscios et illiteratos [. . .]; *pro necessitate:* scilicet cum vult heresim impugnare quod ut sciat facere necesse est eum libros eorum legere. Aliter nesciret eis respondere vel eis obicere et eorum sectam impugnare. Vitium enim vitari non posset nisi cognitum; *pro tempore:* scilicet heresi emergente scilicet cum multi heretici pullulant contra ecclesiam Dei et eam molestant sed et libri gentilium ut dixi possunt legi etiam ab episcopo ad eorum vanitatem revincendam vel ad aliud utile ad memoriam revocandam [. . .] Hic dicitur quod libri hereticorum sunt legendi sed in lege precipiuntur comburi, ut C. De hereticis vel combusto, Si quis impia (Cod. 1.5.15?). Sed forte hoc dicitur de illis qui manifestam continent falsitatem qui possent nocere nisi comburerentur. Hic autem dicitur de aliis, scilicet qui aliquam utilitatem vel veritatem continent vel continent ad eorum sectam sciendam et convincendam (Paris, BN lat. 15396, fol. 41v)'. La D.37 c.1 est le lieu où les décrétistes traitent de la question de savoir si les clercs ont le droit d'étudier le droit romain, P. Legendre, *La pénétration du droit romain dans le droit canonique classique de Gratien à Innocent IV (1140–1254)* (Paris 1964) 48–49.

46. Voir le texte à la note précédente.

47. Apparat *Ordinaturus magister*, D.37 d.p.c.7 s.v. *mittunt in errorem:* 'Non quod scientia artium vel artes mittunt in errorem sed quia homines abutentes artibus mittuntur in errorem dum volentes tam sequi cursum

d'Ambroise (D.37 d.p.c.7 § 6) où l'astrologie et certaines autres sciences sont accusées 'd'être méprisables, de n'avoir aucune utilité pour le salut mais plutôt de conduire à l'erreur'. La glose non signée de l'Apparat *Ordinaturus magister* provient vraisemblablement de l'école d'Huguccio car on le trouve sous une autre forme dans sa *Somme*.[48]

Il montre la réception à Bologne de la nouvelle conception du miracle qui se forge dans la théologie de l'époque. Dans la tradition augustinienne, le miracle n'était pas véritablement distingué de la Nature. Toute la création était œuvre de Dieu et tout fait naturel pouvait être d'une certaine façon être considéré comme un miracle. Au contraire, la philosophie et la théologie à partir du xiie siècle va essayer de décrire un monde autonome régi par les causes naturelles. Le miracle se définit essentiellement comme une suspension temporaire de cet ordre.

La glose d'Huguccio mentionne des hommes qui nieraient la possibilité de l'Incarnation. Le thème des philosophes païens refusant d'admettre la génération du Christ car elle est impossible dans la nature est ancien.[49] Dès l'époque patristique, l'apologétique chrétienne pense qu'il peut être utile pour convaincre les païens qui refusent la génération virginale du Christ d'employer des analogies avec des cas naturels de génération sans semence (abeille, vautour, etc.). La première scolastique reprend l'argument des Pères et on trouve dans l'Abrégé de la *Somme* de Robert de Melun rédigé autour des années 1160 un paragraphe qui propose d'utiliser les exemples naturalistes pour convaincre le *philosophus mundi* de la réalité de l'Incarnation.[50] Ce philosophe est un adversaire imaginaire, tout comme le philosophe du *Dialogue* d'Abélard, un ennemi de parchemin qui ne raisonnerait qu'à l'aide de la loi naturelle et contre lequel le théologien bataille. Aucun philosophe médiéval n'a en effet nié la possibilité ou la réalité des miracles. Il est ainsi étonnant qu'Huguccio contextualise le mythique philosophe païen en un artien zélote.

En effet, les philosophes médiévaux les plus aventureux n'ont pas cherché à récuser les miracles mais plutôt à les expliquer au moyen d'arguments scientifiques. Cette approche naturaliste des miracles bibliques, principalement ceux de l'Ancien Testament, se découvre chez David de Dinant. Ce mystérieux personnage, contemporain d'Huguccio, pionnier dans la lecture et l'étude de la philosophie naturelle d'Aristote et

---

nature non admittunt partum virginis et huiusmodi que miraculose facta sunt preter cursum nature (Munich, BSB lat. 27337, fol. 19r)'.

48. Huguccio, *Summa*, D.37 d.p.c.7 *mittunt in errorem:* 'Non enim scientia artium vel artes mittunt in errorem sed homines abutentes artibus et invenientes ibi tantum ea que fiunt secundum cursum nature; mittuntur in errorem dum volentes tantum sequi cursum nature non admittunt partum virginis et huiusmodi que facta sunt preter cursum nature. Alio etiam modo dicuntur artes mittere in errorem quia dum homines illis intendunt que Dei sunt non curant (Paris, BN lat. 15396, fol. 42r)'.

49. M. van der Lugt, *Le Ver, le Démon et la Vierge* 475–504.

50. Ibid. 493–94. L'idée que les miracles vont contre l'ordre de la nature *(cursus naturalis)* est d'origine anselmienne, cf. ibid. 41.

dont les *Cahiers* furent livrés au bûcher à Paris explique le Déluge comme une marée d'une amplitude exceptionnelle, la destruction de Sodome et Gomorre comme le résultat d'un tremblement de terre; les sauterelles qui s'abattent sur l'Égypte sont nées de génération spontanée; la manne est une espèce de nuage condensé que l'on rencontre couramment en Arabie; l'étoile qui annonce le Christ est une comète; enfin la météorologie permet d'expliquer pourquoi les tremblements de terre ont souvent lieu lors des éclipses solaires comme au moment de la Passion.[51] Il faut noter que David de Dinant a été un familier d'Innocent III qui en a fait son chapelain et qu'une chronique malveillante accuse Innocent de s'intéresser avec passion à ces questions subtiles, c'est-à-dire aux doctrines dangereuses de David.[52]

De surcroît, la lecture d'Avicenne et de certains textes magiques dont la diffusion débute à la fin du xiie siècle conduisait à étendre la sphère des phénomènes naturels. On pouvait, en effet, s'inspirer du philosophe persan pour imaginer que certains êtres humains puissent bénéficier de pouvoirs surhumains, mais non surnaturels, de par un charisme particulier ou un savoir très développé. On trouve trace à Bologne de cet attrait pour le gonflement des capacités de la Nature. Ainsi, Roland de Crémone écrit dans sa *Somme* à propos de la génération du Christ 'qu'il y a encore aujourd'hui des philosophes insensés *(stulti naturales)* qui croient qu'une vierge peut naturellement enfanter par elle même, opinion hérétique tant en théologie qu'en science'.[53] Roland de Crémone, l'un des premiers maîtres dominicains, écrit sa *Somme* à la fin de sa vie mais, avant d'entrer dans l'ordre des prêcheurs en 1219, il a tenu une place importante dans l'enseignement de la philosophie à Bologne. On ne sait rien de la chronologie de son activité à Bologne et on ne conserve aucun écrit de cette période mais la très grande richesse des sources philosophiques discutées dans ses œuvres théologiques témoigne de la vitalité et de l'originalité de la culture philosophique bolonaise au début du xiiie siècle.[54] L'attaque contre les philosophes insensés vise ici, peut-être, les lecteurs du *De diluviis*, un chapitre des *Météréologiques* d'Avicenne traduit au début du xiiie siècle dans lequel le philosophe persan explique qu'en cas de cataclysme aboutissant dans l'annihilation de l'espèce humaine, celle-ci réapparaîtrait par génération spontanée.[55] Avicenne donne ainsi une

---

51. David de Dinant, *Quaternuli*, éd. M. Kurdzialek (Varsovie 1963) 57, 64, 59, 93, 60, 51, 63.

52. *Chronique anonyme de Laon:* 'Magister vero David, alter hereticus de Dinant, huius novitatis inventor, circa papam Innocentium conversabatur, eo quod idem papa subtilibus studiose incumbebat (éd. *Recueil des Historiens des Gaules et de la France* 18.715)'. Sur ce personnage voir E. Maccagnolo, 'David of Dinant and the Beginnings of Aristotelianism in Paris', in: *Twelfth-Century Western Philosophy* 429–42.

53. Roland de Crémone, *Summa* 3.20: 'Adhuc sunt aliqui stulti naturales qui putant quod virgo naturaliter posset de se ipsa concipere; quod hereticum est in theologia et in phisica disciplina', éd. A. Cortesi (Bergame 1962) 70. Sur le contexte, Van der Lugt, *Le Ver, le Démon et la Vierge* 404–07.

54. E. Filthaut, *Roland von Cremona O. P. und die Anfänge der Scholastik im Predigerorden* (Vechta 1936).

55. Van der Lugt, *Le Ver, le Démon et la Vierge* 166–70, avec un extrait (ibid. 170 n. 186) du *Commentaire sur Job* de Roland de Crémone qui semble montrer qu'il connaît le *De diluviis*.

base scientifique à la possibilité d'une génération spontanée de l'homme et donc d'une naturalisation de l'Incarnation.

La glose d'Huguccio contre les dangers de la philosophie reste en fin de compte difficile à contextualiser. Elle s'inscrit en premier lieu dans une tradition rhétorique d'origine patristique qui consiste à accuser les philosophes d'un excès de rationalisme qui les empêche d'accepter la foi chrétienne. Cet argument se retrouve dans la littérature apologétique du XIIᵉ siècle et a sa place dans un commentaire sur la D.37 qui charrie tous les lieux communs anti-philosophiques de la patristique. Néanmoins, il est difficile de voir dans cette glose un simple exemple d'écriture automatique. Le fragment d'Ambroise commenté appelait plutôt une critique plus générale de l'inutilité des sciences du *quadrivium* comme on en trouve chez Rufin.[56] La glose ne vise pourtant pas les figures indéterminées du philosophe, païen ou infidèle mais le personnage concret de l'étudiant en Arts qui dans la conception pédagogique conservatrice d'Huguccio devrait se contenter d'apprendre la grammaire et la logique.[57] Faut-il comprendre donc cette glose comme une réaction inquiète à la diffusion d'une philosophie naturelle? Comme nous l'avons vu, le nouveau savoir gréco-arabe au tournant du XIIᵉ et du XIIIᵉ siècle n'est pas tant utilisé pour nier le miracle que pour le naturaliser. Les dangers de cette approche ont été bien perçus par Roland de Crémone qui se donne pour tâche dans la préface de sa *Somme* théologique de montrer que la science naturaliste ne peut pas être en contradiction avec la foi. Il explique ainsi que l'astronomie nous apprend qu'une éclipse ne pouvait avoir lieu à l'heure de la Passion et que celle que rapporte l'évangéliste est donc surnaturelle.[58] Huguccio a une attitude beaucoup plus conservatrice. Comme il le dit dans sa *Somme* à l'occasion d'une glose sur la digestion de l'hostie consacrée: 'Les arguments doivent cesser là où cesse la Nature. Le miracle ne suit pas la Nature'.[59] Le théologien doit faire taire le scientifique. Huguccio ne semble pas avoir seulement proclamé cette maxime; il l'a aussi mise en pratique.

56. *Supra*, n. 40.

57. Comme il l'indique dans son introduction à la D.37, Huguccio, *Summa*, D.37 d.a.c.1 *Sed quare:* 'Hic intitulatur xxxvii di. in qua Gratianus interserit incidentem questionem, scilicet utrum ordinandus debeat esse eruditus secularibus litteris et respondetur quod sic. Gratianus tamen sic procedit. Primo ostendit quod libros gentilium et secularium artium clerici legere non debent. Postea ostendit quod licite eos possunt legere. Postea huius contrarietatis subiicit solutionem et dicit quod quidam legunt talia ad delectationem et voluptatem, hoc prohibetur; alii legunt ad eruditionem scilicet ut instruantur accentuare et dictiones construere, verum a falso discernere et huiusmodi, hoc permittitur. Unde, sicut postea subdit Gratianus, precipitur ut per singula loca doctores liberalium artium constituantur (Admont, Stiftsbibliothek 7, fol. 53r)'.

58. G. Cremascoli, 'La *Summa* di Rolando da Cremona. Il testo del prologo', *Studi medievali* 16 (1975) 825–76 ici 874.

59. Huguccio, *Summa*, De cons. D.2 c.72: 'Cessent ergo argumenta ubi cessat natura. Que miraculose fiunt naturam non sequuntur (Paris, BN lat. 15397, fol. 128r)'.

Huguccio et les prophètes

Dans les années 1180, des lettres circulèrent en France, en Angleterre annonçant une grande catastrophe planétaire pour septembre 1186.[60] En effet, le 15 septembre eut lieu une conjonction exceptionnelle des planètes du système solaire dans la constellation de la Balance. Les astrologues juifs, musulmans et chrétiens prédirent une Grande Année, un cataclysme marquant la fin d'un cycle historique qui serait provoqué par les astres et qui anéantirait les civilisations et les peuples. On vit apparaître la missive d'un certain Corumphiza, astrologue de son état, qui détaillait les fléaux météorologiques qui allaient s'abattre sur les pays arabes et les conduire à la ruine. Les chroniqueurs recopient aussi le courrier d'un deuxième personnage fictif, Pharamella, se présentant comme un savant arabe qui utiliserait les armes de l'astrologie savante pour ridiculiser les prédictions de Corumphiza. La grande peur de 1186 participe aux nombreuses éruptions millénaristes médiévales. L'archevêque de Cantorbéry, à la réception de ces courriers, ordonna ainsi la tenue d'un jeûne purificateur de trois jours dans son diocèse. Néanmoins, il s'agit d'un millénarisme savant et nourri de la lecture d'Albumasar, principal vecteur de la renaissance astrologique du XIIᵉ siècle. Il fait peu de doute que l'étudiant Lothaire de Segni a entendu parler de l'une de ces lettres lors de son séjour parisien.

L'opinion savante est à l'époque généralement favorable à l'astrologie tant qu'elle ne verse pas dans une astrologie judiciaire divinatoire qui nierait le libre arbitre et l'omnipotence divine.[61] L'astrologie est ainsi incluse dans les sciences naturelles. Cependant, pour rendre la lecture des traités astrologiques acceptables, il fallait arriver, tout comme pour les textes antiques, à les relier au christianisme et donc laisser la porte ouverte à une prophétie astrologique et scientifique compatible avec la Révélation. Parmi les autorités rassemblées dans la D.37 pour prouver l'utilité des sources païennes se trouve un passage d'Augustin (c.13) qui explique que l'on peut utiliser les textes prophétiques païens de la Sibylle et d'Orphée pour convertir les gentils.[62] Ce rapprochement qui peut sembler étrange aujourd'hui entre philosophie païenne et prophétie correspond en fait à l'air du temps. Abélard pensait que les textes philosophiques païens recelaient des éléments préfigurant la Révélation et pouvaient ainsi être placés sur le même plan que les

---

60. D. Weltecke, 'Die Konjunktion der Planeten im September 1186. Zum Ursprung einer globalen Katastrophenangst', *Saeculum* 54 (2003) 179–212, avec une annexe listant l'ensemble complexe des textes du dossier qu'il n'est pas possible, dans l'état actuel de la recherche, de dater et de hiérarchiser; G. Callataÿ, 'La grande conjonction de 1186', dans: *Occident et Proche-Orient. Contacts scientifiques au temps des croisades*, éd. I. Draelants, A. Tihon et B. van den Abeele (Turnhout 2000) 369–95.

61. J. Tester, *A History of Western Astrology* (Woodbridge 1987) 142–50.

62. Ce canon est absent de la première version du *Décret*, A. Winroth, *The Making of Gratian's Decretum* (Cambridge 2000) 200.

prophéties de l'Ancien Testament.[63] La littérature antique ne constituait pas une simple boite à outils pour l'intellectuel du xiie siècle; elle pouvait être le support d'une lecture herméneutique. Les médiévaux interprétaient ainsi certains vers de Virgile et d'Ovide comme des prémonitions de l'Incarnation.

L'ambivalence de la culture occidentale vis-à-vis de la prophétie est bien connue. Au xiie siècle, elle se manifeste par une tension dans le champ intellectuel entre une narration historique extrêmement réceptive au récit prophétique et une théologie qui met en avant la connaissance de Dieu par la raison et réduit les possibilités théoriques de l'inspiration et de la prescience. Dans le dernier quart du xiie siècle, le balancier se trouve plutôt dans le premier de ces deux camps. Le théologien le plus influent de son époque, Pierre le Mangeur, n'est ainsi pas hostile à la prophétie païenne. Il inclut dans son *Histoire scolastique* (1169–73) une référence positive à la Sibylle; il accueille dans son commentaire des schémas chronologiques tirés de sources sibyllines; enfin sa réécriture de deux passages clefs du Nouveau Testament—les rois mages astrologues de la naissance du Christ et les philosophes athéniens est—favorable à des correspondances entre astrologie, philosophie et Révélation.[64] Les mages sont des savants sabéens qui auraient tracé l'horoscope du Christ accomplissant la prophétie de Balaam; ils seraient l'équivalent perse des philosophes grecs.[65] Connaisseur de la théorie de la grande année, Pierre le Mangeur donne une généalogie prestigieuse à l'astronomie inventée selon lui par les patriarches Japhet et Jonithus, un personnage issu de la tradition du pseudo-Méthode. Jonithus aurait de surcroît énoncé des prédictions sur la succession des royaumes.[66] Pour le cas de l'étoile de Bethléem, le théologien parisien ne se déclare pas en faveur de l'astrologie judiciaire mais, plus subtilement, il avance que Dieu a envoyé un signe adapté aux Orientaux dont la civilisation aimait faire correspondre les évènements ici-bas et les mouvements des corps sidéraux.[67] Pour les gréco-romains, les signes sont des *mirabilia*.[68] Pour les juifs, le signe a été donné lors de l'épisode de la piscine probatique (Jo. 5). Pierre le Mangeur brode aussi autour de l'anecdote de Paul devant l'Aréopage (Act. 17.23–24) émerveillé de sa découverte d'un autel qui portait l'inscription 'au dieu inconnu' dans lequel il voit une prémonition du Christ. L'Aréopage devient sous la plume de l'exégète parisien le Quartier latin d'Athènes et Denys l'un des

63. T. Gregory, 'The Platonic Inheritance', dans: *Twelfth-Century Western Philosophy* 54–80.
64. Sur les schémas chronologiques, PL 198.1540.
65. PL 198.1089, 1454, 1541–42.
66. PL 198.1088; Pseudo-Méthode 3, éd. E. Sackur, *Sibyllinische Texte und Forschungen* (Halle 1898; repr. Turin 1963) 63–64.
67. Pierre le Mangeur, *Sermo primus in adventu Domini* (PL 198.1722–23).
68. Il s'agit de l'effondrement du temple de la Paix à Rome, légende transmise par les *Mirabilia*, cf. M. Th. d'Alverny, 'Humbertus de Balesma', *Archives d'histoire doctrinale et littéraire du moyen âge* 59 (1984) 168 n. 59.

maîtres des écoles de philosophie de l'époque. Les Athéniens ont ainsi édifié cet autel sous l'injonction des enseignants qui s'étaient révélés incapables d'expliquer par des causes naturelles les ténèbres qui suivirent la mort du Christ.[69]

Dans l'un de ses sermons, Innocent III reprend avec quelques transformations la présentation de Pierre le Mangeur des mages comme des philosophes qui ont bien analysé le signe envoyé par Dieu.[70] Le motif des trois types de signes divins est repris de manière plus originale par un certain maître Hubert. En 1192 ou en 1193, à Paris, il prêche devant une assemblée choisie de maîtres et d'élèves sur la prophétie d'Isaïe 'Ecce virgo concipiet'.[71] Son sermon s'attache presque uniquement à l'exposition des prédictions des païens sur la naissance du Christ. Il cite Platon, la Sibylle, Ovide et fait montre d'un goût et d'une large connaissance en astrologie. Hubert utilise les œuvres de l'astrologue arabe du IXe siècle Albumasar traduites au XIIe siècle. Ainsi, dans son *Introductorium maius in astronomiam*, Albumasar décrit les *paranatellonta*, c'est-à-dire des constellations qui montent à l'horizon après le coucher du soleil et qui sont associées à un signe du zodiaque. Pour le signe de la Vierge, la figure dessine une vierge à l'enfant. Les deux traducteurs d'Albumasar, Jean de Séville et bien plus encore Hermann de Carinthie dans son *De essentiis* terminé en 1143 ont interprété cette figure comme une représentation de la Vierge Marie et de Jésus. L'utilisation d'Albumasar comme prophète du Christ est cependant rare dans la deuxième moitié du XIIe siècle sinon chez quelques originaux dont l'œuvre a été peu lue ce qui rend son usage par maître Hubert significative. L'agrégation d'Albumasar au noyau des annonciateurs de la Révélation ouvre en effet un verrou. L'autorité de la Sibylle comme prophète du Christ crédibilise les oracles politiques sibyllins ou pseudo-sibyllins. De même, la 'christianisation' d'Albumasar permet à maître Hubert d'ouvrir la porte à la prédiction astrologique. Le Christ a vécu sous l'Ère de la Vierge mais Hubert explique à son auditoire qu'il se trouve dans le onzième degré de l'Ère de la Balance qui s'écoule entre 1166/67 et 1200. Onze est un chiffre particulièrement funeste qui annonce de grands malheurs. Hubert ne fait pas d'allusion explicite à la Grande Année de 1186 mais ses élucubrations semblent bien un effort pour redonner souffle à la défunte prophétie en transformant la terrible année charnière en une prévision plus floue d'une période temporelle néfaste.

Le sermon de maître Hubert montre ainsi une virtualité de l'exégèse de Pierre le Mangeur. Huguccio connaît l'*Historia scolastica* qu'il utilise dans sa *Somme*. Il ne reprend pourtant pas l'exégèse du Mangeur sur le séjour de Paul à Athènes. Rufin faisait

---

69. PL 198.1702. La légende des philosophes grecs perplexes devant l'éclipse de la Passion trouve sa source dans la septième lettre du Pseudo-Denys (PG 3.1079).

70. PL 217.485.

71. Édité par d'Alverny, 'Humbertus', 158–80.

allusion à l'inscription sur l'autel au dieu inconnu en notant qu'elle avait été écrite par 'des poètes ou des philosophes'.[72] Huguccio récupère, en l'allongeant quelque peu, la glose de Rufin mais il indique que l'inscription a été écrite par 'des poètes ou des prophètes'.[73] Les philosophes disparaissent. Ces philosophes-prophètes se retrouvent dans la glose d'Huguccio sur D.37 c.4. Ce canon relativement obscur qui avait été laissé de côté par les autres commentateurs est tiré du commentaire de Jérôme sur le vingt-huitième chapitre d'Isaïe où le prophète accuse d'ivrognerie les prêtres et les prophètes de Samarie. Jérôme comprend le vin comme la parole de Dieu et explique que ceux qui s'enivrent de vin comprennent de travers et pervertissent l'écriture sainte, ceux qui s'enivrent de *sicera* (une espèce de boisson alcoolisée) sont abusés par les sciences profanes et doivent être compris tropologiquement comme les pseudo-prophètes dont parle Isaïe. Enfin, ceux qui mangent des raisins verts sont ceux qui comprennent l'écriture de manière erronée. Huguccio explique que beaucoup de ceux qui enseignent la théologie mangent du raisin vert. Plus grave, d'aucuns s'enivrent de vin en prédisant des choses futures alors que les seuls évènements dont nous pouvons être certains de l'avènement sont ceux annoncés par l'Écriture comme l'Antéchrist, le Jugement dernier et les signes qui le précéderont et la résurrection des morts.[74]

Huguccio ne rejette pas l'utilité des prophéties christiques de la Sibylle et d'Orphée pour convertir les gentils comme il est expliqué D.37 c.5 mais il dévalorise fortement leur autorité. Il donne dans son commentaire un premier argument juridique en renvoyant à D.16 c.1, texte dans lequel il est expliqué que les canons des hérétiques même s'ils contiennent des choses utiles doivent être classés parmi les apocryphes. Dans sa glose sur ce canon, Huguccio, revenant à l'étymologie grecque, avance que l'apocryphe ne peut avoir valeur d'autorité car on ne peut tracer son origine et qu'il n'a pas été reçu par l'Église.[75] C'est une bonne définition de la norme canonique qui doit être ancienne, avoir une origine certaine et être sanctionnée par le pouvoir. Les prophéties, tout comme les apocryphes, ne passent pas au crible pour devenir ce qu'il nomme un *autenticum*. Le deuxième argument anti-prophétique est d'ordre théologique. Huguccio rapproche les prophéties païennes des prémonitions des démons. Les démons

---

72. Rufin, *Summa*, D.37 c.8 (éd. Singer 89).

73. Huguccio, *Summa*, D.37 c.8 (Paris, BN lat. 15396, fol. 42r).

74. Huguccio, *Summa*, D.37 c.5: 'In multis illi qui docent theologiam comedunt acerbam. Sed utique nullus inebrietur vino divino. Sunt illi qui preter auctoritatem divine scripture predicant futura'; ibid. *absque quorum:* 'Hoc ideo dicit quia sunt quedam futura que de auctoritate sacre scripture possumus dicere, immo tenentur ea dicere et docere ut est adventus Antichristi, dies iudicii, signa circa diem iudicii, resurrectio mortuorum et huiusmodi (Paris, BN lat. 15396, fol. 41v)'.

75. Huguccio, *Summa*, D.16 c.1: 'Apocrifum dicitur occultum et secretum; ab "apo" quod est de et "crifi" quod est secretum. Inde liber dicitur apocrifus, id est occultus et secretus scilicet cuius auctor ignoratur vel si non ignoratur ab Ecclesia tamen non recipitur sed reprobatur quod non in Ecclesia sed secrete et remote (Paris, BN lat. 15396, fol. 14v)'. Sur l'utilisation de l'étymologie par Huguccio, voir Müller, *Huguccio* 61–64.

ne savaient pas avant la résurrection que Jésus était le fils de Dieu; ils pouvaient le supposer en le voyant accomplir des miracles même si la condition humaine du Christ les
induisait en erreur. Les prophéties des démons ne sont pas autre chose que des *educated
guesses*. Les vaticinations de la Sibylle et d'Orphée sont du même ordre.[76] Huguccio est
donc un exégète traditionnel et frileux. Il explique—contre la pratique parisienne de
son temps—qu'en cas de doute sur l'interprétation d'un verset, il ne faut pas revenir
aux originaux grecs ou hébreux. Depuis la traduction de Jérôme, la traduction latine est
parfaite alors que les exemplaires grecs et hébreux sont aujourd'hui corrompus.[77] Dans
la D.37, Gratien avait inclus une lettre de Clément Ier qui justifie l'apprentissage des
arts libéraux afin de lire correctement la Bible et de corriger les faux sens que certains
faisaient. Huguccio prend le contre-pied de Gratien pour lire dans ce canon *Relatum*
une attaque des mauvaises lectures du texte sacré. Certains tordent le texte de la Bible
comme une prostituée que l'on pourrait plier à son gré et proposent des interprétations
subtiles et personnelles qui vont à l'encontre de l'intention de l'auteur ou qui sont tirées
des textes philosophiques ou païens.[78] Dans l'interprétation de la Bible, il faut toujours suivre les Pères catholiques.[79] Puis dans une brusque incise, le canoniste ajoute
que quelqu'un ne doit pas enseigner s'il n'est pas docteur et il allègue deux canons dans
lequel il est écrit que l'on ne peut être maître si l'on n'a pas été d'abord disciple et un
troisième qui traite des conditions selon lesquelles on peut accepter le témoignage d'un
enfant.[80] Sur l'un des canons allégués par Huguccio, on trouve une nouvelle glose du
canoniste expliquant que le disciple non seulement ne pourrait pas enseigner 'mais
qu'il ne devrait pas le faire car s'il présumait de son savoir il serait en fait le maître de
l'erreur.'[81] Huguccio termine sa glose en renvoyant à *Relatum*. Le deuxième canon al-

---

76. Huguccio, *Summa*, D.37 c.13 *sacrilegio*: 'Id est infidelium et gentilium ut Platonis, Orfei, Sibille, Virgilis
et aliorum quod quamvis aliquid veri dixerint de Deo non tamen ideo est autenticum quia illi et alii hoc dixerunt. Sicut nec illud quod demones de Christo dixerunt ideo est autenticum quia ipsi hoc dixerunt (Paris, BN
lat. 15396, fol. 42v)'.

77. Huguccio, *Summa*, D.9 c.6 (Paris, BN lat. 15396, fol. 17v).

78. Huguccio, *Summa*, D.37 c.14: 'In hoc capitulo reprehenduntur illi qui sacram scripturam interpretan-
tur secundum suum intellectum et sensum [. . .]. Transferunt *ex his que legere* in Sacra Scriptura *verisimilitudi-
nes* et verisimiles rationes et probabiles intellectus quia sensus ille quem in aliquibus locis scripture habent
non multum longe est a ratione et satis videtur probabilis sed mentem auctoris non sequitur vel potius ex his
que legunt in secularibus artibus et in libris gentilium [. . .]; *ad eum sensum:* littera enim meretrix est et con-
vertibilis et ad sensum cuiusque inclinatur. Quod in divina pagina valde est periculosum (Paris, BN lat. 15396,
fol. 42v)'.

79. Ibidem: 'In concilio etiam Meldensi habetur quod in exponendis sacris scripturis non debet quis sequi
suum sensum sed catholicorum et probatissimorum patrum ut B[urchardus] lib. i ca. Novum (*Decretum* 1.61
[PL 140.564])'.

80. Ibid. *ab eo:* 'Non enim debet quis docere nisi primo habeat doctorem et instruatur ut Di. lviiii Ordina-
tos (c.4) et xvi q.i Si clericatus (c.27) in pueritia; ar. quem posse testificari de his qui in pueritia vidit, ar. De con.
di.iiii Placuit (c.111)'.

81. Huguccio, *Summa*, D.59 c.4: 'Scilicet ut primo sit discipulus quam doctor et primo discat quam doceat;

légué dans le commentaire est analysé comme une interdiction des 'maîtres éclairs.[82] À la manière d'un juriste savant, c'est-à-dire dans l'écheveau des allégations et des renvois glose à glose, Huguccio critique durement de jeunes clercs qui auraient tenu un enseignement biblique mâtiné de philosophie particulièrement répréhensible. Pourrait-il s'agit du maître Hubert ou de quelqu'un de son cercle?

Hubert de Pirovano: théologien bolonais naturaliste

Le rapprochement entre le maître Hubert qui prononce un sermon astrologique en 1192–93 et Huguccio de Ferrare n'est pas purement gratuit. Dans l'unique manuscrit où se trouve ce texte, il est attribué à un *magister Humbertus de Balesma* que Marie-Thérèse d'Alverny a rapproché du *magister Humbertus* auteur de la somme théologique *Colligite fragmenta* conservée en un seul exemplaire et encore peu étudiée.[83] Grâce aux notices des chroniqueurs, on peut identifier ce personnage à Hubert II de Pirovano, archevêque de Milan entre 1206 à 1211.[84] Balesma pourrait être une déformation du copiste renvoyant à Balesmo, une petite localité à côté de Monza. Rejeton d'une famille féodale liée à l'archevêque de Milan, les Pirovano, Hubert apparaît dans la documentation en 1194 comme chanoine de Monza. Entre 1199 et 1201, des indications tirées du registre d'Innocent III indiquent sa présence à Bologne. Il est à l'époque vraisemblablement enseignant en théologie. En effet, il est qualifié dans deux lettres de *magister* et dans une autre de *theologus*.[85] Innocent III nomme Hubert en 1201 *subdiaconus noster* puis en 1206 l'élèvera au cardinalat.[86] Il ne restera cardinal qu'une très courte période car il est élu archevêque de Milan en 1206 ou en 1207, un poste stratégique dans l'affrontement entre la papauté et l'empire. Il accomplira jusqu'à sa mort en 1211 de nombreuses missions de confiance pour le pape.[87] Hubert de Pirovano est donc très proche d'Innocent III. Au début de son pontificat, il est son point de contact à Bologne. Il fait ensuite partie du

---

non poterat: id est non debebit sed si presumat erit magister erroris, ut Di. xxxvii Relatum (c.14) et ii q.vii Nos si (c.41) et xxiiii q.iiii Quidam (c.18) (Paris, BN lat. 15396, fol. 66r)'.

82. Huguccio, *Summa*, C.16 q.1 c.26–27 *multo tempore disce:* 'Argumentum contra momentaneos magistros et generaliter contra illos qui ascendunt ad aliquod officium quod non debet conferri nisi longo tempore exercitatis (Paris, BN lat. 15397, fol. 13v)'.

83. Cf. Alverny, 'Humbertus' 154–58; R. Heinzmann, *Die Summe "Colligite Fragmenta" des Magister Hubertus (Clm 28799). Ein Beitrag zur theologischen Systembildung in der Scholastik* (Veröffentlichungen des Grabmann-Institutes 24; Paderborn 1974).

84. Il ne faut pas le confondre avec son oncle homonyme qui fut, lui aussi, archevêque de Milan.

85. Notice biographique récente par M. P. Alberzoni, 'Hubert de Pirovano', *Dictionnaire d'histoire et de géographie ecclésiastiques* 25 (1995) 14–18, qui ignore néanmoins Alverny, 'Humbertus'.

86. W. Maleczek, 'Zwischen lokaler Verankerung und universalem Horizont. Das Kardinalscollegium unter Innocenz III.', dans: *Innocenzo III. Urbs et Orbis* 1.102–74 ici 124–25.

87. Alberzoni, 'Innocenzo III' *passim*.

petit groupe de cardinaux italiens non romains créés par le pontife. Enfin, durant son archiépiscopat, il n'est pas uniquement un allié politique du pape mais il agit en son nom pour les aspects religieux plus novateurs du pontificat comme la négociation d'un statut pour les Humiliés.

Il serait tentant de faire remonter cette familiarité entre les deux hommes à un compagnonnage d'étude. Comme le jeune Lothaire, Hubert a fréquenté Paris et Bologne et a suivi un cursus de théologien. Le sermon de 1192 montrait sa connaissance des œuvres d'Albumasar. Dans la somme inédite *Colligite fragmenta*, il manifeste encore son goût pour les sciences dangereuses. Il y pose la question originale: est-ce que Dieu connaît les arts magiques? Il répond que oui et explique qu'une branche de la magie est naturelle (l'exemple qu'il propose de ce type de magie sont les images astrologiques) et qu'il s'agit donc d'une science et d'un art naturel dont l'usage peut même être parfois licite.[88] On a voulu voir dans *Colligite fragmenta* une somme parisienne. Néanmoins, plusieurs indices pointent vers Bologne. Un premier argument tient au fait que la Somme est conservée dans un manuscrit unique et que l'on ne trouve pas de citations d'un maître Hubert dans les œuvres théologiques du premier quart du XIIIᵉ siècle. Ceci laisse penser que le travail fut composé loin de Paris. Un deuxième argument est l'utilisation de l'éthique aristotélicienne de la vertu comme médiété, théorie en circulation dans le *Studium* italien. Si *Colligite fragmenta* cite un grand nombre d'auteurs parisiens, elle renvoie aussi à un décrétaliste bolonais Richard l'Anglais actif à Bologne durant les années où Hubert s'y trouvait.[89] Enfin, on trouve trace d'un débat sur la licité de la magie chez Huguccio. Dans sa *Somme*, le canoniste pose la proposition de base que toute science provient de Dieu et donc que tout savoir est bon en soi. Néanmoins, certains savoirs, comme la magie, conduisent presque immanquablement au mal, il est préférable alors de les ig-

---

88. Hubertus de Pirovano, Summa *Colligite fragmenta:* 'De arte maleficandi sive magica, questio est utrum sit scientia vel error, et placet quampluribus quod sit error, eo quod semper errat, quod sic operatur. Aliis autem videtur quod sit scientia vel ars naturalis; sed eius usus non est bonus, quia pro malo et in illicitis rebus exercetur. Forte tamen posset eius etiam usus esse bonus, puta ut cum dicitur quia Moyses fecit anulum oblivionis quem dedit Egiptie. Sed si etiam hic sit error, potest tamen concedi quod Deus artem illam novit, vel illum errorem, quia et errores hominum et cogitationes que varie sunt novit Deus (éd. Alverny, 'Humbertus' 158)'. Sur l'originalité de la position d'Hubert, cf. Alverny, 'Humbertus', et sur le débat théologique autour des images astrologiques, N. Weill-Parot, *Les 'images astrologiques' au Moyen Âge et à la Renaissance. Spéculations intellectuelles et pratiques magiques (XIIᵉ–XVᵉ siècle)* (Paris 2002).

89. Richard l'Anglais a vraisemblablement étudié à Paris vers 1186–1187 et y a écrit une *Summa questionum*, cf. S. Kuttner et E. Rathbone, 'Anglo-Norman Canonists of the Twelfth Century', *Traditio* 7 (1949–51) 331 = S. Kuttner, *Gratian and the Schools of Law 1140–1234* (Londres 1983) no. 8. Les canonistes de l'école anglo-normande ne sont pas cités par les théologiens parisiens. Il y a clairement une réception de l'enseignement d'Huguccio par Pierre le Chantre et son cercle, mais les théologiens parisiens de la génération suivante semblent ignorer les nouveautés de la science canonique et en particulier les décrétalistes bolonais, voir C. de Miramon, 'La place d'Hugues de Saint-Cher dans les débats sur la pluralités des bénéfices', dans: *Hugues de Saint-Cher († 1253), bibliste et théologien*, éd. L. J. Bataillon o.p., G. Dahan et P. M. Gy (Turnhout 2004) 341–86.

norer en suivant l'autorité d'Augustin. Revenant un peu plus loin sur le sujet, il oppose quelques arguments à sa position. Si l'on veut combattre les erreurs des mauvais, il faut les connaître. Les arts prohibés sont spécialement dangereux pour les gens peu savants pour qui leur lecture serait comme mettre un glaive entre les mains d'un fou furieux.[90] La *Glose Palatine* postérieure laissera la porte ouverte à une attitude plus permissive. Elle expliquera qu'il est prohibé de *lire* la nigromancie.[91] Comme nous l'avons vu plus haut, le verbe 'lire' est équivoque et le lecteur de cette glose pouvait comprendre que la lecture publique est interdite mais que la lecture privée ne l'est pas. L'opinion bolonaise sur la magie n'est certes pas aussi favorable que Hubert mais tend à avancer que les prélats savants peuvent et même doivent lire ces dangereux ouvrages afin de mieux combattre les hérétiques. Huguccio, du reste, ne semble pas être ignorant des arts magiques de son temps. Il emploie le lexique patristique des divinations superstitieuses (nigromantie, pyromantie, etc.) que les décrétistes pouvaient lire dans les canons de la C.26 q.5 qui traite des superstitions. Cependant, il décrit aussi le magicien comme le faiseur d'*experimenta,* un terme qui renvoie aux textes magiques gréco-arabes qui apparaissent en Occident à partir du XIIᵉ siècle.[92] Plus tard, Roland de Crémone, grand lecteur de magie, avance une opinion sur cet art occulte comparable aux positions d'Huguccio.[93]

90. Huggucio, *Summa*, D.37 d.p.c.7 *est in eo:* 'Id est ab eo scilicet Deo. Per hoc efficaciter probatur quod nigromantia et piromantia et quelibet alia sciencia est a Deo; ergo quelibet sciencia bona est vel bonum et nulla est peccatum quod verum est enim ar. infra eo. Qui de mensa (c.11). Prohibentur tamen quedam scientie non propter se, sed propter sequelam quia occasionem prestant ad malum ut xxvi q.v, fere per totum (Paris, BN lat. 15396, fol. 42r)'; ibid., D.38 c.11: 'Dictum est quod ignorantia est nociva et periculosa sacerdotibus; ne ergo quis crederet hoc esse verum de ignorantia quarumlibet rerum subditur auctoritate Augustini quod quedam sunt quorum ignorantia non est nociva sed utilis et expediens ut ignorantia illius sciencie que licet bona sit in se prestat tamen actionem mali ut est sciencia nigromantie et piromantie et huiusmodi [. . .]; *noxia:* ut vitia et peccata et ars divinandi vel faciendi experimenta et acquirendi divitias et huiusmodi. Tales artes vel scientie dicuntur noxie et male licet rei veritate sint bone quia sunt occasio mali [. . .] Hinc nec mala scire peccatum est quia mala vitari vel reprobari non possunt nisi cognita ut supra Di.xxxvii Qui de Mensa (c.11), Si quid (c.13). Dicitur tamen sciencia malorum mala et scire mala esse malum quia est occasio mali; nam ex parva sciencia facile quis labitur ad delictum sicut ergo furioso vel irato malus est gladius quia est ei materia mali, ut xxii q.ii Ne quis (c.14) et xxiii q.v Qui vitiis (c.38). Sic et illicite rei sciencia et propter talem occasionem quedam scientie prohibite sunt et sunt dicte ut nigromantia, piromantia et generaliter sciencia divinandi et incantandi et experimenta faciendi (fol. 43v)'.

91. *Glossa Palatina*, D.37 c.7 *ratio:* 'Ex hoc patet quod omnis sciencia ut geometria (sic pour "geomancia") et nigromancia a Deo est et in se ipsa bona est. Prohibetur tamen legi propter sequelam sicut iurare, ut xxii q.i c.i (BAV Pal. lat. 658, fol. 9v; BAV Reg. lat. 977, fol. 26r)'.

92. J. Agrimi et C. Crisciani, 'Per una ricerca su "experimentum-experimenta". Riflessione epistemologica e tradizione medica (secoli XIII–XV)', dans: *Presenza del lessico greco e latino nelle lingue contemporanee*, éd. P. Janni et I. Mazzini (Macerata 1990) 9–49.

93. Roland de Crémone, *In Job:* 'Dicit Ptolemeus quod quidam sunt nigromantici qui occulta et secreta quedam sciunt per que faciunt mortuos loqui, spiritus malignos de loco ad locum transire, cuiusmodi scientiam dicit se Eliphaz habuisse . . . Fateor me vidisse librum illum et ibi legisse. Verba ibi sunt obscura, sed multa mala ibi dicuntur que possunt fieri ex illa sciencia, et similiter multa bona . . . Nec malum est scire quamvis malum sit operari secundum illam. Scire quidem malum non est malum et tamen facere malum est

On peut donc replacer le chapitre de *Colligite fragmenta* dans un débat bolonais qui n'a pas d'équivalent parisien avant Guillaume d'Auvergne.[94]

Conclusion

Les différents indices que nous avons rassemblés tentent de donner corps à la thèse suivante. À partir du milieu des années 1180, on trouve la trace d'une réception à Bologne de textes de philosophie naturelle en provenance de Salerne ou faisant partie du corpus des traductions de textes gréco-arabes. Ce nouveau savoir est mis en œuvre dans des débats théologiques. Huguccio, principal canoniste bolonais de cette époque, a été très frileux face à ces nouvelles autorités qu'il comprenait vraisemblablement mal et il s'est opposé à ses propagateurs. Il a pourtant utilisé un raisonnement médical pour nourrir sa propre inventivité théologique.[95] Dans le camp des naturalistes, il faut ranger de jeunes clercs italiens formés entre Paris et Bologne dont Lothaire de Segni et Hubert de Pirovano. Ces jeunes clercs n'ont pas uniquement nourri ces idées mais les ont peut-être professées tirant parti de l'absence d'enseignant de théologie en chaire à l'époque, poussant leur audace jusqu'à l'inclusion de prévisions astrologiques hasardeuses qui pour le canoniste fleuraient l'hérésie. Cet enseignement correspondait au climat de l'époque. Le 12 octobre 1187, Albert de Morra Bénévent est élu pape à Ferrare et prend le nom de Grégoire VIII. Quatre jours plus tard, il apprend la chute de Jérusalem. Il rédige une encyclique de déploration, d'exhortation à la croisade mais aussi enjoignant à la pénitence publique.[96] Il n'est pas improbable que flottait à la curie pontificale—alors résidente en Émilie-Romagne—un parfum de fin des temps propice au bourgeonnement prophétique. Nous ne savons pas comment se termina le conflit entre le canoniste expérimenté féru de théologie et les jeunes turcs à la pointe du progrès mais il laissa des aigreurs. Lothaire, devenu pape, prendra le canoniste conservateur à son propre piège en lui montrant la fausseté de son raisonnement médical, en l'obligeant à revenir à la lettre du texte biblique et en ridiculisant ses prétentions de théologien. C'est dans ce courant naturaliste bolonais que le jeune Roland de Crémone se formera et acquerra son encyclopédisme si particulier. Bologne pourrait se comparer

(éd. A. Dondaine, 'Un commentaire scripturaire de Roland de Crémone: le livre de Job', *Archivum fratrum praedicatorum* 11 (1941) 109–37 ici 129)'. Je dois cette référence à Maaike van der Lugt.

94. La Somme *Colligite fragmenta* ne comporte malheureusement pas—partie perdue ou jamais écrite— de traité sur les sacrements qui aurait permis de comparer les opinions d'Hubert sur l'eucharistie avec celles d'Innocent III et d'Huguccio.

95. Sur Huguccio comme théologien voir l'article ancien mais riche en textes de A. Landgraf, 'Diritto canonico e teologia nel secolo dodicesimo', SG 1 (1953) 373–407.

96. Mansi 22.527–30. Sur le caractère étrange des décrétales de Grégoire VIII, W. Holtzmann, 'Die Dekretalen Gregors VIII.', MIÖG 58 (1950) 113–23.

ainsi à un autre centre secondaire de la connaissance à la fin du XIIe siècle, Hereford, où l'on trouve aussi un va-et-vient des intellectuels entre Paris et le centre local, une diffusion précoce du nouveau savoir naturaliste et une grande liberté dans l'enquête sur les savoirs douteux astrologiques ou magiques, insouciance qui s'explique sans doute par la faible institutionnalisation de la théologie.

Cette thèse est séduisante. Il faut pourtant insister sur les points faibles de notre argumentation. Nous n'avons aucune preuve de la présence d'Hubert de Pirovano à Bologne durant l'enseignement d'Huguccio. Comme nous l'avons vu, nous n'avons aucun document sur Hubert avant 1194 et aucun texte philosophique ou théologique bolonais que l'on peut dater des années 1180. La méthode que nous avons suivie dans ces pages consiste à établir un dialogue entre la *Somme* d'Huguccio et des textes contemporains pour reconstruire des factions contradictoires.[97] Cette méthode suppose que les attaques voilées que l'on trouve au détour d'une page d'un manuscrit renvoient la plupart du temps à des adversaires réels. L'analyse des gloses sur la D.37 d'Huguccio comme une réaction à chaud contre les philosophes de son temps garde pourtant sa part d'acrobatie. Notre fréquentation depuis plusieurs années de la *Somme* d'Huguccio nous a appris que son commentaire s'appuie sur les gloses antérieures mais est aussi influencé par les canons qui entourent celui qu'il glose. Il reste toujours délicat de juger si Huguccio contextualise le canon qu'il commente à la situation présente ou s'il tisse à partir des canons disparates une narration continue dans laquelle chacune des autorités trouverait sa place. L'historien a pour réflexe professionnel de faire correspondre à un texte son époque et son contexte de rédaction. Cependant, un commentateur médiéval compose avant tout un méta-texte qui tente de donner une logique aux incohérences et au foisonnement initial. Le texte et son commentaire forme ainsi souvent un monde clos avec sa chronologie interne dans lequel le présent transparaît lors d'incises, sous le mode de l'*exemplum*. Ainsi, les civilistes médiévaux quand ils expliquent dans leurs commentaires que *hodie* la règle est de telle sorte, ne renvoient souvent pas à leurs pratiques mais à Justinien, l'empereur qui a actualisé le droit romain. En un mot, Huguccio a-t-il rêvé de combattre comme un nouvel Ambroise les mauvais philosophes qui nient les miracles ou les a-t-il rencontrés? Une enquête sur les textes inédits comme la *Somme* d'Hubert de Pirovano permettrait peut-être de résoudre cette énigme.

97. Pour une application de cette méthode pour un cas postérieur, de Miramon, 'Hugues de Saint-Cher'.

23

Considerazioni sulla pervasività della religione nella società e negli ambienti di studio universitari in età tardo-medievale

Manlio Bellomo

❀

In un suo classico libro su 'La cultura della città', pubblicato nel lontano 1938, l'urbanista e architetto americano Mumford scolpiva con poche parole uno dei tratti fisionomici della società europea del medioevo: 'L'individuo isolato, durante il medio-evo, si trova ad avere per destino o l'esilio o la morte'.[1]

Sono parole che mi tornano in mente nel momento in cui comincio a riflettere su un tema che tocca direttamente la vita degli studenti convergenti verso le città dotte, e verso Bologna e Parigi prima che altrove e più che altrove.

Alcuni giovani non giungono isolatamente. Conoscono i rischi del viaggio e perciò solo in gruppo 'si fanno pellegrini per l'amore della scienza', per adoperare le belle parole della famosa *Constitutio* 'Habita' di Federico Barbarossa.[2] Stanno in un gruppo che raccoglie solamente giovani votati allo studio, studenti o prossimi a diventare tali, oppure in un gruppo che accomuna studenti, mercanti, viandanti per affari o per am-bascerie, pellegrini e penitenti per ragione di fede.[3]

---

1. L. Mumford, *La cultura della città* (tradotto dall'edizione in inglese del 1938; Milano 1954) 20. Sul brano vedi M. Bellomo, *Società e diritto nell'Italia medievale e moderna* (I Libri di Erice 30; Roma 2003²) 148.

2. Constitutio 'Habita', ed. W. Stelzer, 'Zum Scholarenprivileg Friedrich Barbarossas (Authentica "Habi-ta")', DA 34 (1978) 165, che propone Bologna 1155 come luogo e anno della promulgazione. Di diversa opinione K. Zeillinger, 'Das erste roncaglische Lehensgesetz Friedrich Barbarossas, das Scholarenprivileg (Authentica Habita) und Gottfried von Viterbo', *Römische Historische Mitteilungen* 26 (1984) 191–217, che propone Goffredo da Viterbo come autore e Roncaglia 1154 come luogo e anno della promulgazione.

3. Per un quadro d'insieme vedi M. Bellomo, 'Il medioevo e l'origine dell'Università', in: *L'Università e la sua storia*, ed. L. Stracca. (Torino 1979–80) 13–25, ora anche in M. Bellomo, *Medioevo edito e inedito*. I. *Scholae, Universitates, Studia* (I Libri di Erice 20; Roma 1998²) 13–30. Per i rapporti degli studenti con i mercanti è specifico M. Bellomo, 'Studenti e "populus" nelle città universitarie italiane dal secolo XII al XIV', in: *Università e società*

Già prima di raggiungere la meta desiderata, la città degli studi, e poi ancora di più in questa, sono 'in esilio'. Si trovano in una condizione che sembra preludere al destino più tragico, a quello della morte: e nel fatto, come testimoniano con dettagli alcune fonti, tutti stanno sulla soglia della morte, e per molti la morte arriverà.[4]

Mi riesce difficile immaginare, mi riesce difficile credere, che quei giovani ardenti e speranzosi, sprezzanti del pericolo e abbacinati dalla visione di città che i predicatori presentano come eletti ricettacoli di vizi e di perdizione, mi riesce difficile pensare che nessuno di loro non abbia messo in conto la probabilità della propria morte e non abbia mai avuto il dubbio e il timore di perdere l'anima nell'inferno minacciato da confessori e da parroci. Una preghiera l'hanno recitata. È certo, è documentato, che fra i primi atti del nuovo arrivato vi sono la visita in chiesa, la preghiera, l'affidamento al santo protettore. La descrizione la dobbiamo a Nigellus Wireker: come ogni viandante, lo studente, dopo avere scorciato la zazzera e vestita la sua tunica migliore, 'va . . . in chiesa: ringrazia Iddio, prega e fa voti'.[5]

Nella città l'incontro, o lo scontro, con i goliardi, forse desiderato, forse temuto, dà un diverso segnale: innanzi agli occhi dei nuovi arrivati si concretizzano, plasticamente, le fantasie sognate di una vita tutta terrena, condotta nell'ozio, nelle ore dell'amore, nel disordine materiale e morale della taverna e del postribolo, fuori da ogni regola, fuori da ogni impegno: 'il tempo viene, e io non ho fatto niente / il tempo ritorna, e io non ho fatto niente', recita un adagio corrente: non ho fatto niente di serio, si capisce.[6]

Sul filo dell'ironia Piacentino dà una voce colta alle tempeste emotive degli studenti diventati bolognesi: la giurisprudenza è donna avida, rapace, ha un viso esangue e denti affilati, mentre all'opposto la vita ordinata e operosa ha il viso lieto e sereno di donna che canta nei campi, specchio di fiducia e di affidabilità.[7]

Si può fare dell'ironia, ma la chiesa incombe. E ora può sorgere il dubbio che Piacen-

nei secoli XII–XVI (Atti del Nono Convegno Internazionale del Centro Italiano di Studi di Storia e d'Arte, Pistoia 20–25 settembre 1979; Pistoia 1982) 61–78, ora anche in Bellomo, *Medioevo edito e inedito* I. 31–49.

4. A Bologna vi è addirittura una rubrica degli Statuti universitari del 1317/1432 dedicata alle esequie degli studenti morti. La rubr. 82, *De exequiis et suffragiis mortuorum*, ed. H. Denifle, 'Die Statuten der Juristen-Universität Bologna von 1317–1347 und deren Verhältniss zu jener Paduas, Perugias, Florenz', *Archiv für Litteratur und Kirchengeschichte des Mittelalters* 3 (1887) 363–65 (specialmente 364), dispone che tutti gli studenti assistano a una messa annuale obbligatoria celebrata in suffragio delle anime dei compagni morti.

5. Sono i versi della testimonianza, percorsa da una venatura di ironia, di Nigellus Wireker, *Speculum stultorum*, ed. T. Wright, *The Anglo-Latin Satirical Poets and Epigrammatists of the Twelfth Century* (2 voll.; London 1872) 1.63.

6. Sul punto vedi M. Bellomo, *Saggio sull'Università nell'età del diritto comune* (Catania 1979¹; I Libri di Erice 4; Roma 1999² e ³) specialmente 35–37, e la letteratura ivi citata; anche in lingua spagnola, *La Universidad en la época del derecho común*, trad. E. Montanos Ferrín (I Libri di Erice 28; Roma 2001) 30–32.

7. Piacentino, *Sermo de legibus*: ms. Basel, UB C.I.7, ed. H. Kantorowicz, 'The Poetical Sermon of a Mediaeval Jurist. Placentinus and His "Sermo de legibus",' *Journal of the Warburg Institute* 2 (1938) 22–41, anche in H. Kantorowicz, *Rechtshistorische Schriften*, ed. H. Coing e G. Immel (Karlsruhe 1970) 111–35.

tino un prezzo lo abbia pagato per quel suo sorriso sulla fragilità umana attirata dal denaro e dal potere più che da un'arte pia, sacra, rispettosa della morale e dei buoni costumi: non saprei dire se proprio per pagare quel prezzo sia dovuto emigrare a Montpellier.

Come che sia andata la vicenda per il giurista di Piacenza, credo che non possiamo sottovalutare la frequenza con la quale compaiono segnali di fede e di pratiche religiose. E più tardi ne avremo copiosa testimonianza in numerosi brani di Odofredo e negli statuti universitari.

Odofredo sa e racconta, sorridendo, insinuando, che gli studenti vanno dai padri predicatori non per ascoltare il verbo divino, ma per mirare e ammirare le donne, forse con occhi invitanti e amorosi: 'Quidam sunt scolares in civitate ista . . . , qui tota die ibant spaciatum ut [ed. 'et'] viderent dominas et ibant ad predicatores ut viderent dominas, non ut adiscerent theologiam'.[8]

Gli statuti delle *universitates* e delle *nationes* prescrivono l'obbligo delle pratiche religiose: gli studenti vadano la domenica e le feste comandate in chiesa ad ascoltare messe e prediche; siano presenti ai riti funebri per i compagni morti nel tempo dello studio; tengano il loro posto nella fila delle processioni, col cero in mano, e che i ceri siano eguali per tutti, come per esprimere e rendere evidente che, nell'insieme, gli studenti costituiscono una vera comunità dominata dalla fede, dalla convinzione che tutte le anime sono eguali, e non divisa all'interno da distinzioni di ceto o di ricchezza.[9]

In breve: credo che si cominci a comprendere come non siano da sottovalutare, da considerare marginali, episodi e convinzioni ampiamente documentati nelle fonti. Però ora, fra parentesi, per evitare di essere frainteso, desidero dire, a chiare lettere, che sto riflettendo e sto cercando di rappresentare un mondo popolato di credenti e di peccatori con l'occhio di un laico: senza enfasi, senza condivisione, senza avere alcuna intenzione di esaltare e neppure, al contempo, senza volere condannare, ma—come si conviene, credo, allo storico—con la coscienza che vada riscoperta e valorizzata una dimensione della vita universitaria finora rimasta troppo in ombra, tanto che il quadro d'insieme forse ne è risultato falsato.

Su questa linea vorrei continuare a riflettere, coordinando fatti che sono noti, o notissimi, ma che finora sono rimasti dispersi, o sono stati considerati accidentali. Né posso escludere che si tratti davvero di fatti accidentali e casuali: non posso escluderlo,

8. Odofredo, *Lectura in* Cod. 2.4.21, *de transactionibus*, l. *cum ea* (Lugduni 1552; ristampa Bologna 1967–69, fol. 75va). Il testo continua irridendo allo studente che 'de nocte semper studebat sine lumine', con un accento che darà colore alle novelle di Boccaccio, in un contesto narrativo in cui affiorerà costantemente il senso religioso del rimorso.

9. Vedi per esempio Bologna, Statuti universitari del 1317/1432, rubr. 95: *De festivitatibus per universitatem processionaliter cum cereis honorandis*, ed. Denifle, 'Die Statuten' 375–77. Degli stessi Statuti vedi anche la rubr. 82 (sopra, nota 4).

perché le mie indagini sono incomplete su questo filo del discorso, e perciò mi parrebbe azzardato dire che queste considerazioni possano costituire un risultato acquisito.

Torno al punto dal quale sono partito. Se l'individuo isolato, lo studente nel nostro caso, che è già in esilio, corre rischio di morte, o ha certezza di morte imminente e violenta, deve sembrare cosa ovvia che ciascuno cerchi la propria compagnia. Mumford ci guida ancora. Osserva infatti che quando l'individuo non trova di meglio, può bastare anche una banda di briganti.[10] Così lo studente, se non trova di meglio, può associarsi ai goliardi, che propriamente briganti non sono, ma che come tali sono sempre rappresentati: setta di maldicenti senza fissa dimora, 'pauperes, vagi', 'discurrentes et scurriles, maledicti et blasphemi', oziosi, furfanti.[11]

Vi è di meglio, però. Anzi: si collabora e ci si riunisce per costruire qualcosa di meglio. Vi è la chiesa, la singola, specifica chiesa, e questa è e diventa sempre più un punto di riferimento obbligato, non solo per essere accolti, con la fiducia nella preghiera e nel conforto della fede, nel momento dell'arrivo nella città ignota e pericolosa, ma anche per essere assistiti nelle innumerevoli necessità della vita quotidiana: a volte anche con un'ospitalità non temporanea nella parrocchia e nei locali contigui, come accade e come è documentato. Polacchi e ungheresi si concentrano nel convento dei Frati del Sacco, per gli studenti siciliani è rifugio consueto un *hospitium* della chiesa di San Cristoforo da Saragoza, due tedeschi nel 1286 fanno capo alla Chiesa dei SS. Filippo e Giacomo.[12]

Si può aggiungere un altro episodio, minimo se si vuole, eppure esemplare. Riguarda Andrea Barbazza. Giunto da Messina a Bologna, si ritrova a corto di denaro e di candele. Per studiare nelle ore del buio risolve in chiesa il suo problema, perché è nella chiesa che si avvale della luce delle candele poste sull'altare: se pur fioca, questa tuttavia gli consente di leggere e di scrivere.[13]

Vi sono scenari più sontuosi. Stanno al loro centro gli ordini dei domenicani e dei

---

10. Vedi sopra, nota 1.

11. I brani riportati nel testo sono di Raimondo di Rocosel, *De certamine anime. Invectio contra goliardos,* ed. J. Werner, 'Nachtrag zum *Certamen animae* des Raymundus de Rocosello', NA 36 (1911) 550–56. Un frammento della *Invectio,* con traduzione francese, è edito da O. Dobiache-Rojedestvensky, *Les poesies des goliards* (Paris 1931) 183–85. Fra le fonti più significative sono da vedere anche i versi dei *Carmina burana* e alcuni coloriti brani di Odofredo: per esempi presenti in entrambe le fonti vedi Bellomo, *Saggio sull'Università* 36–37 (idem, *La Universidad* 30–32).

12. Vedi G. Zaccagnini, *La vita dei maestri e degli scolari nello Studio di Bologna nei secoli XIII e XIV* (Ginevra 1926) 73.

13. L'episodio è narrato da A. Ghiselli, *Memorie antiche manoscritte di Bologna* 8.86 (Bologna, BU ms. 770): 'Hic Barbatia in adolescentia homo pauperrimus, qua re lectiones suas a preceptoribus audivisset, Bononie in templis repetere solebat, quod ibi sacrorum luminum usu iuvaret et ipse tantum non haberet ut candelas comparare sibi posset'. Il brano è edito da A. L. Trombetti Budriesi, 'Andrea Barbazza tra mondo bolognese e Mezzogiorno d'Italia', in: *Scuole, diritto e società nel Mezzogiorno medievale d'Italia,* ed. M. Bellomo (2 voll.; Studi e Ricerche dei "Quaderni Catanesi" 7; Catania 1985) 2.306.

francescani e il ruolo che i due ordini hanno nello sviluppo delle scuole universitarie. Per i giuristi sono predominanti gli spazi e il favore offerti dai primi. Il caso di Padova, tra il 1226 e il 1229, è significativo, per il sostegno che i domenicani offrono agli studenti emigrati da Bologna.[14] I medici e gli artisti, in parallelo, sono legati ai francescani.

In nessun caso si tratta di eccezioni. Da alcuni anni gli studenti cercano spazi adeguati alle cresciute esigenze didattiche e organizzative, e le città offrono chiese allo scopo. Nel 1204 questo accade a Vicenza, dove l'arcidiacono e il vescovo donano la chiesa di San Vito a un gruppo di studenti emigrati da Bologna.[15] Fra il 1226 e il 1229 i domenicani costruiscono a Padova un loro convento e vi ospitano le prime scuole universitarie della città.[16]

A Bologna vi è dapprima la vecchia chiesa di San Procolo, ospitale e adatta ad accogliere assemblee studentesche. Poi, verso la metà del secolo XIII, si attivano i nuovi conventi di San Domenico e di San Francesco, il primo attento soprattutto alle esigenze dei legisti e dei canonisti, il secondo dei medici e degli artisti.[17] Nel 1252 si radunano le *universitates* dei giuristi 'tanto degli ultramontani quanto dei citramontani *in ecclesia sancti Dominici*', affinché si abbia un luogo sufficiente per l'assemblea che vota il primo statuto (forse di notevole ampiezza) per le due *universitates* riunite.[18]

Fuori d'Italia posso ricordare almeno due esempi. Il primo, noto per gli studi di Domenico Maffei e per qualche mia aggiunta, ci porta a Orleans, 'in domo fratrum predicatorum'. Alla prima lettura della *quaestio* che fu dibattuta nel convento domenicano di Orleans sembrava che si trattasse di un caso isolato, curioso, da registrare e da lasciare da parte, se non da dimenticare.[19] Ora credo che abbia un preciso significato.

14. Per Padova è specifico G. Arnaldi, 'Le origini dello Studio di Padova. Dalla migrazione universitaria del 1222 alla fine del periodo ezzeliniano', *La Cultura* 15 (1977) 388–431.

15. Sull'episodio G. Arnaldi, 'Scuole nella Marca Trevigiana e a Venezia nel secolo XIII', in: *Storia della cultura veneta. Dalle origini al Trecento* (2 voll.; Venezia 1977) 1.377–84.

16. Vedi Arnaldi, 'Scuole nella Marca Trevigiana' 355, che giudica il convento padovano 'uno dei più importanti e popolati dell'intera provincia di Lombardia' (che, come è noto, comprendeva la gran parte dell'Italia settentrionale). Cfr. anche Arnaldi, 'Le origini dello Studio' 405–31.

17. Vedi F. Cavazza, *Le scuole dell'antico Studio bolognese* (Milano 1896) 211–15.

18. Bologna, Statuti universitari del 1252, rubr. I: *Nota quod doctores et magistri non possunt facere collectam nisi post festum sancti Andree*, ed. D. Maffei, 'Un trattato di Bonaccorso degli Elisei e i più antichi statuti dello Studio di Bologna nel manoscritto 22 della Robbins Collection', BMCL 5 (1975) 93.

19. Per l'edizione del testo D. Maffei, 'Il giudice testimone e una *quaestio* di Jacques de Revigny (Ms. Bon. Coll. Hisp. 82)', TRG 35 (1967) 74–75. Per la segnalazione di altro testimone e per considerazioni sulla natura del testo M. Bellomo, 'Legere, repetere, disputare. Introduzione ad una ricerca sulle "quaestiones" civilistiche', in: M. Bellomo, *Aspetti dell'insegnamento giuridico nelle Università medievali*, I. *Le 'quaestiones disputatae'. Saggi* (Reggio Calabria 1974), ora anche in M. Bellomo, *Medioevo edito e inedito* I.72 nota 63, I.92 nota 122. Il problema di merito riguarda la qualificazione della *quaestio*: sebbene nel ms. utilizzato da Maffei sembra trattarsi di una *quaestio* disputata, in altro testimone da me individuato (Vaticano, BAV Pal. lat.733, fol. 27va–b) una mano ignota, scrivendo sul margine del frammento del *Digestum Vetus* contenuto in quel codice, ha qualificato il testo come *repetitio*. A Orleans, dunque, sembra che l'attività didattica in un luogo religioso non si sia limitata alla

Il secondo caso ci porta a Palencia. Il re Ferdinando dispone che la *fabrica* della cattedrale cittadina e l'insegnamento del diritto che vi si tiene debbano essere finanziati, *pro parte*, da ciascuna chiesa officiata nella città. Nel 1220, e in anni successivi, Onorio III darà una esplicita conferma a sostegno della disposizione regia.[20]

Del resto, già che stiamo nominando un papa, perché non valutare, come coerenti alla linea interpretativa che sto proponendo, i ripetuti interessamenti pontifici per Bologna e per i suoi studenti? Penso, prima di tutto, a Innocenzo III, che nel 1210 invia alle scuole bolognesi la sua raccolta *extravagans*, affinché il testo ne sia conosciuto e utilizzato nelle scuole e nel foro.[21] In tal modo inaugura una prassi che sarà poi seguita da altri grandi legislatori della chiesa universale.[22] E penso poi alle lettere, non poche, inviate da Onorio III a sostegno della *libertas* studentesca negli anni in cui regge la città felsinea il podestà Guglielmo da Pusterla, nella seconda decade del '200.[23]

Onorio III: è sua la decretale 'Super specula' del 1219, da ricordare non solo per l'importanza in sé, ma anche per l'ambiguità del testo.[24] Scatenerà dissapori e dissidi fino al noto scontro che nel 1270 vedrà fronteggiarsi nella cattedrale, con scambio di insulti e di atti violenti, alcuni dei professori, da una parte, e il clero della cattedrale, dall'altra parte, per come l'episodio è descritto a proposito della zuffa che i professori scatenano 'nella chiesa del beato Pietro di Bologna e nella canonica e nelle stesse navate della chiesa e nei confronti del vescovo di Bologna (Ottaviano Ubaldini) e dell'arcidiacono (Ruggero Ubaldini, fratello del vescovo) e contro i loro servitori e i canonici della stessa chiesa, anche turbando il divino ufficio che si celebrava in quel momento all'interno della chiesa'.[25]

Onorio III merita altra attenzione, per un filone di immagini che da lui sembrano prendere vigore, se non propriamente le mosse. Nella bolla 'Super specula', in un immaginifico parallelismo, Onorio vede i professori 'come stelle destinate a durare in una perpetua eternità'.[26] Poco più tardi, nel 1245, Innocenzo IV ricorderà che le avversità

---

disputa di qualche *quaestio*, ma si sia articolata nella consueta forma tripartita della *lectura*, della *repetitio* e della *quaestio*. Sono incompatibili con le testimonianze delle fonti e con i fondati dubbi della storiografia le osservazioni di C. H. Bezemer, *Les répétitions de Jacques de Revigny. Recherches sur la répétition comme forme d'enseignement juridique et comme genre littéraire, suivies d'un inventaire des textes* (Leiden 1987) 24–25. Sul problema, in generale, vedi ora M. Bellomo, *I fatti e il diritto tra le certezze e i dubbi dei giuristi medievali (secoli XIII–XIV)* (I Libri di Erice 27; Roma 2000) 421–22.

20. Documentazione in H. Denifle, *Die Entstehung der Universitäten des Mittelalters bis 1400* (2 voll.; Berlin 1885; ristampa Graz 1956) 1.475–78.

21. Innocenzo III, 3 Comp., ed. 105.

22. Onorio III, 5 Comp., ed. 151.

23. Vedi Bellomo, *Saggio sull'Università* 77–78, 85–86 (idem, *La Universidad* 79–80, 83–84).

24. Onorio III, Const. *Super specula*, ed. Sarti-Fattorini 2.15, doc. 4; anche *Chartularium Universitatis Parisiensis*, ed. H. Denifle e E. Chatelain (3 voll.; Paris 1889; ristampa Bruxelles 1964) 1.90–93, doc. 32.

25. L'episodio è documentato in Sarti-Fattorini 2.56–57, doc. 34.

26. Onorio III, Const. *Super specula*, ed. *Chartularium Universitatis Parisiensis* 1.91 = X.5.5.5.

della vita non possono offuscare la luce che si irradia sui professori, 'come la notte non spegne le stelle del cielo'.[27] E ancora Alessandro IV vedrà i *doctores* 'come assunti in una perpetua eternità, a somiglianza delle stelle'.[28]

A riguardare i fatti che sto recuperando alla memoria e sto allineando per provocare benefiche reazioni del pensiero storiografico ho come l'impressione di trovarmi innanzi a un gioco degli specchi.

Da una parte vi sono giovani audaci, cattolici osservanti che proprio per essere frequentatori di chiese e di parroci ascoltano discorsi che eccitano la fantasia e spingono all'azione, anche impudica: sono i discorsi che condannano le città dotte, e le presentano come le sentine del malcostume e di tutti i peccati: 'Parigi è la saetta dell'inferno'.[29] Accanto alle scuole i lupanari tentano la gioventù votata allo studio.[30] Le meretrici stanno sull'angolo delle strade.[31] La taverna induce all'ozio, al vino e al gioco.[32]

Dall'altra parte vi è la chiesa che continua ad attirare quanti non si fanno devoti di Golia, e a suscitare il rimorso che si accompagna al peccato; vi è la chiesa che muovendo dall'alto del magistero pontificio e passando per le gerarchie costituite e per gli ordini domenicano e francescano si insinua nel mondo giovanile, lo attraversa, lo attira, lo plasma (o tenta di plasmarlo), dà un ordine a ciò che appare scomposto e disarticolato, fissa norme atte a legittimare ciò che nasce spontaneamente per le necessità di una vita che nell'esilio esige d'essere vita di comunità contro il pericolo dell'isolamento e della morte.

27. Innocenzo IV, Lettera da Lione, 4 settembre 1245, ed. *Chartularium Universitatis Parisiensis* 1.183, doc. 146.

28. Alessandro IV, Lettera da Anagni, 11 luglio 1259, ed. *Chartularium Universitatis Parisiensis* 1.392, doc. 343.

29. L'espressione è di Pietro Cellense, *Epistolae* 73 (PL 202.519); sta in un contesto che merita di essere ricordato: 'O Parigi, quanto sei pronta a prendere e a distruggere le anime! In te le trame e le reti dei vizi, in te il barbaglio del male, in te la costellazione dell'inferno trafiggono i cuori degli stolti!'

30. Jacques de Vitry, *Historia Occidentalis* 7: *De statu Parisiensis civitatis*, ed. J. Hinnenbusch (Spicilegium Friburgense 17; Fribourg 1972) 91: 'Nella stessa casa vi erano le scuole al piano superiore, i postriboli al piano inferiore. Sopra i maestri davano lezione, sotto le meretrici esercitavano i loro vergognosi uffici. Da una parte le meretrici litigavano tra loro e con i loro lenoni, dall'altra gli scolari vociavano mentre disputavano o contrapponevano le loro ragioni'.

31. Ibid.: 'La città di Parigi, come molte altre, vagava nelle tenebre, avviluppata in crimini vari e deturpata da abiezioni innumerevoli. . . . La semplice fornicazione non si reputava per nulla un peccato. Dovunque, pubblicamente, accanto ai loro lupanari, le meretrici attiravano con inviti spudorati e irridenti gli studenti che passavano per le vie e per le piazze della città. E se ve n'erano che rifiutavano di entrare, esse a voce alta li chiamavano, dietro le spalle, sodomiti'.

32. *Carmina Burana*, canto 196: *In taberna quando sumus*, ed. A. Hilka e O. Schumann (2 voll.; Heidelberg 1970) I.3.35–37. Vedi anche gli insistenti e ironici rimproveri di Odofredo, *Lectura in* Dig. 24.3.22.1, *Soluto matrimonio*, l. *Si cum dotem*, § *Si post* (Lugduni 1552, fol. 9ra): 'Filius qui tota die vel tota nocte vult esse in caupona vel lupanario'; idem, *Lectura in* Dig. 41.4.8, *Pro emptore*, l. *Si quis* (ibidem, fol. 73vb): 'Qui tota die vult esse in taberna vel lupanar(i)o et ita faciunt multi tota die'; (ibidem, fol. 74ra): 'Nam quidam sunt scholares qui putantur diligentes et non sunt: in nocte ludunt ad hazardum, ut faciunt scholares'.

Si profila una doppia faccia del mondo giovanile, studentesco, e anche del mondo dei *doctores*. Nel cuore di ognuno convivono opposti sentimenti: vi è il fascino del vizio che non si cura del peccato, ma vi è all'opposto il tormento del rimorso e l'aspirazione alla redenzione. Nella realtà complessiva vi è da una parte una linea di laicità tutta terrena, e vi è all'opposto un costante tentativo della chiesa di imbrigliare questa linea in un ordine che è costruito ed è da costruire nel nome della religiosità e nel rispetto dei comandamenti cristiani.

Si spiegano così altri episodi. Fra tanti almeno due mi pare che esprimano i differenti punti di vista.

Il primo episodio. Gerardo de Fracheto narra che Giordano di Sassonia, secondo maestro generale dell'ordine domenicano, andava per le predicazioni quaresimali un anno a Parigi e l'anno appresso a Bologna, alternativamente; che portava con sé tuniche già confezionate e denari; che convertiva tanti studenti che spesso le tuniche non bastavano per vestirli e i denari per pagarne i debiti. Aggiunge anche, con una testimonianza preziosa per altro ordine di problemi, che Giordano aveva maggiore successo nelle scuole di arti e minore successo in quelle di leggi: perché le prime erano frequentate soprattutto da *rustici*, giovani di campagna, più facili ad essere ubbriacati dalle prediche, come col vino che non erano avvezzi a bere, e perché le scuole di leggi erano invece frequentate da nobili di campagna e da cittadini, che come resistevano al vino, ch'era per loro d'uso comune, così resistevano alle prediche e alle esortazioni a vestire l'abito ecclesiastico.[33]

L'episodio mostra, così penso, quanto penetrante fosse nel mondo studentesco l'iniziativa della chiesa, in questo caso l'iniziativa dei padri predicatori. Mostra, al di là del preciso e avvertito interesse del momento, quanto programmato fosse ogni intervento che mirava a pervadere la società cittadina e prima di tutto quegli ambienti di studio tendenzialmente più critici e più irrequieti e più difficili da assoggettare all'ordine voluto dalla chiesa universale.

Passo ora al secondo episodio. Sta sul filo del doppio versante della nostra storia il testo di una lettera databile fra il 1325 e il 1333. La lettera è inedita.[34] È scritta da frate Iohannes de Persico, giurista e teologo, su richiesta del vescovo di Brescia, Tiberio Torriani, ed è a questi indirizzata. Il vescovo ha chiesto e vuole sapere 'utrum credere papam Iohannem non habere utriusque iurisdictionem, spiritualem scilicet et temporalem, et de temporalibus non debere se intromittere, sit hereticum'.[35] Qui i problemi

---

33. L'episodio è raccontato e documentato da Arnaldi, 'Scuole nella Marca Trevigiana' 355 e nota 18; vedi anche G. Arnaldi, 'Discorso inaugurale', in: *Le scuole degli ordini mendicanti (secoli XIII–XIV)* (Atti del XVII Convegno Internazionale del Centro di Studi sulla Spiritualità Medievale, Todi 11–14 ottobre 1976; Todi 1978) 25.

34. È tràdita dal ms. Vaticano, BAV Chigi E.VIII.245, fol. 97vb–99rb.

35. Il brano è edito in Bellomo, *I fatti e il diritto* 445–46.

si presentano in modo complesso, e stanno tutti dentro la trama di una nota tradizione dottrinaria e di una realtà contraria e diffusa, come già si intravede dal tenore stesso della domanda che il vescovo rivolge a frate Giovanni Persico.

Per quanto riguarda la tradizione, vi è un pensiero che affiora, almeno, nella *Glossa* accursiana. Ad Accursio sembra evidente che 'nec papa in temporalibus nec imperator in spiritualibus se debeant immiscere'. Il punto è che Accursio può non solo pensare in questi termini, ma può pensarlo senza timore di censura, o di condanna. La realtà nega la netta distinzione e divisione dei poteri: perciò Cino da Pistoia può deplorare che 'dominus papa ratione peccati intromittit se de omnibus'.[36] Vi è di più: se in una taverna qualcuno osa mettere in dubbio o addirittura negare che il papa abbia poteri temporali oltre che spirituali, scattano per il malcapitato il giudizio e la condanna per eresia, se diamo credito a una testimonianza di Alberico da Rosciate.

Si fronteggiano due articolazioni della medesima realtà: ciò che è consentito ad Accursio e a Cino e ad altri dottori di leggi, non è consentito agli abituali frequentatori di bettole e locande; vi è nelle scuole di diritto una *libertas* che sembra negata al di fuori di esse; per una parte non vi è eresia, per l'altra parte vi è eresia.

Si capisce che il buon vescovo Tiberio Torriani, 'ex nobili prosapia oriundus', forse in gioventù poco propenso a frequentare le scuole e in età matura il mondo, abbia dei dubbi e questi suoi dubbi voglia farseli sciogliere da frate Giovanni Persico. Ma il frate ha la sua furbizia. Sa di essere spinto su un terreno minato e nella lettera di risposta, che lettera è e lettera resta, si rifugia perciò nel genere della *quaestio* disputata, forma tipica che assicura e garantisce una sorta di immunità accademica, tipica di tale esercizio didattico, perché consente di elencare le ragioni a favore di due posizioni contrapposte e non richiede necessariamente che in una lettera vi sia una *solutio*, una scelta che potrebbe essere fin troppo impegnativa.

Ora sono alla conclusione. Nella letteratura sulla storia dell'Università, e nei miei stessi lavori sul tema, si è stati propensi a pensare che le *comitivae*, le *nationes*, le *universitates*, i collegi per gli studenti e quelli dei *doctores*, in breve tutte le associazioni studentesche e dottorali, siano nate e si siano sviluppate e affermate come espressione di una società fondamentalmente laica, impegnata solo a vivere e a risolvere i rapporti fra individui, fra gruppi, consorterie, corporazioni, da una parte, e il potere politico della città o del pontefice o dell'imperatore, dall'altra parte. Una visione tutta terrena, nella quale non hanno trovato posto le considerazioni sulla pervasività della religione e tanto meno sulle censure esterne e sulle autocensure che a quella pervasività erano intrinseche. Non hanno trovato posto neppure quanto si è rappresentata l'importanza della

---

36. Per i due brani citati nel testo vedi F. Calasso, *Medioevo del diritto* (Milano 1954) 486.

bolla 'Super specula' di Onorio III, neppure quando si è spiegato che a reggere le sorti di uno *studium* vi era a Bologna l'arcidiacono e altrove un vescovo o un arcivescovo, e neppure quando si è parlato dei canonisti, delle loro scuole, delle loro opere, e neppure quando si è constatato che i professori delle grandi scuole giuridiche di Bologna o di Padova inauguravano i dibattiti scolastici invocando il nome di Dio e della beata vergine Maria e della Santa Croce e dell'intera corte celeste, o del Padre, del Figlio e dello Spirito Santo, o dei santi eletti a personali protettori, come Sant'Agostino, San Nicola, Santa Caterina, gli apostoli Pietro e Paolo, San Giovanni evangelista, San Giacomo, l'arcangelo Michele.[37]

Ridotti i problemi della coscienza e dell'agire sul piano intravisto da Graziano e affrontati quei problemi su un piano giuridico che riguarda e può e deve riguardare solo le relazioni interpersonali e collettive di una società tutta terrena si è come perso di vista un filo rosso che nella realtà impegnava ogni cuore e ogni mente a non immaginare e neppure a pensare fratture insanabili fra peccato e reato, fra peccato e azione capace di provocare un danno a cose o a persone.

Non so se ora valga la pena di ripensare la vita dei nostri antenati, studenti e professori, come vita desiderosa di una protezione divina, bisognosa dello sguardo amorevole della madonna e dei santi, come vita percorsa da una religiosità intima e imperante, da un modo di essere e di agire che poteva scadere quotidianamente nel peccato, ma che quotidianamente si riscattava col rimorso e col pentimento. Boccaccio insegni. I suoi personaggi peccano—e quanto peccano!—, ma nel momento dell'azione il loro occhio è sempre rivolto al Padreterno e all'aldilà, nel timore della punizione e però anche nell'attesa e nella speranza del perdono.

Si può avere il sospetto che fino ad oggi ci siamo lasciati condizionare da Giosué Carducci?[38]

37. Gli esempi sono ricordati in Bellomo, *I fatti e il diritto* 365–66.

38. È noto che Giosuè Carducci, bolognese, professore di letteratura italiana, nume tutelare della poesia italiana del tardo Ottocento e poeta egli stesso, ha inventato un inesistente anno iniziale dell'Università di Bologna, il 1088, e per conseguenza ha celebrato nel 1888 un fantasioso ottavo centenario dalla fondazione. È altrettanto nota la marcata collocazione laica e massonica del professore e poeta bolognese, fortemente ispiratrice del *Discorso* che inaugurò quelle celebrazioni: G. Carducci, 'Lo Studio di Bologna. Discorso tenuto nell'Archiginnasio di Bologna il dì XII giugno MDCCCLXXXVIII alla presenza di Umberto I Re d'Italia', in: G. Carducci, *Discorsi letterari e storici* (Bologna 1889) 1–26. Finora, però, si è poco considerata l'enorme influenza che ha avuto nella storiografia contemporanea la visione carducciana del problema, letteraria e celebrativa più che storiografica (il *Discorso* è, oltre tutto, privo di qualsiasi nota e per ciò stesso non ha basi documentarie neppure riferimenti storiografici). Qualche novità, tuttavia, è cominciata a circolare a proposito di Irnerio, del cui stato laicale si dubita ora fortemente: vedi i due importanti e documentati saggi di G. Mazzanti, 'Irnerio: contributo a una biografia', RIDC 11 (2000) 117–82; E. Spagnesi, 'Irnerio teologo, una riscoperta necessaria', *Studi Medievali* 42 (2001) 325–79, nonché qualche spunto storiografico ivi citato.

24

Il diritto canonico, fonte della giurisprudenza occidentale nell'Ungheria e nella Polonia del medioevo

Péter Erdö

✳

Il sistema dello *Ius commune* cristallizzatosi nelle università e nella prassi dell'Italia medievale ebbe il suo influsso in tutto il continente europeo. Tale influsso però era diverso a seconda le varie regioni. Nella parte orientale dell'Europa centrale, in presenza di regni talmente gelosi della propria indipendenza dall'Impero Romano-Germanico come la Polonia e l'Ungheria, il diritto dei cesari non poteva essere direttamente recipito. Era invece valido, e non soltanto come *ratio scripta* ma anche praticamente nella vita quotidiana, l'ordinamento universale della Chiesa, cioè il diritto canonico. Esso era infatti il canale principale dell'influsso della cultura giuridica occidentale, soprattutto italiana in quella regione. Le ricerche si riferiscono a quella antica storia del funzionamento dello *Ius commune* come rappresentante di una certa unità giuridica europea, e in questo contesto esaminiamo il ruolo del diritto canonico nella formazione di tale unità, un ruolo unico ed insostituibile in Europa centro-orientale, che acquista una nuova attualità nei nostri giorni, quando i popoli di questo territorio compiono degli sforzi enormi per essere partecipi all'unità anche giuridica del continente.[1]

Per poter parlare del ruolo del diritto canonico nella formazione della cultura giuridica specificamente 'europea' in quella regione che fino a poco tempo fa era chiamata l'Est europeo, bisogna precisare i limiti storici e geografici dell'argomento. La cortina di ferro fino al 1989 ha diviso l'Europa in due parti. Dopo quell'anno di profondi cam-

---

1. Del diritto canonico come diritto comune vedi per esempio M. Bellomo, *L'Europa del diritto comune* (I Libri di Erice 1; Roma 1994[7]) 67–89; cf. P. Koschaker, *Europa und das römische Recht* (Monaco e Berlino 1958[3]); F. Calasso, *Medio Evo del diritto*. I. *Le fonti* (Milano 1954).

biamenti è riemersa l'antica differenza culturale che persisteva anche prima, all'interno della parte politicamente orientale del continente, cioè la differenza fra i paesi e regioni di cultura latina e quelli di cultura bizantina. I paesi di tradizione latina, culturalmente, facevano e fanno parte dell'Occidente e ad esso sono legati anche con innumerevoli vincoli propri della cultura giuridica.

Per vedere il ruolo del diritto canonico nella formazione del lato giuridico della realtà culturale europea bisogna tener presente i diversi livelli del suo influsso. Tali sono: le nozioni e la terminologia, gli studi e le teorie, e le istituzioni, con particolare riguardo a quelle di diritto processuale. Una funzione speciale del ricambio giuridico culturale avevano i sinodi particolari e i libri sinodali con essi collegati.

L'attività giudiziaria autonoma della Chiesa nei paesi della parte orientale dell'Europa centrale si è consolidata gradualmente dalla cristianizzazione fino alla seconda metà del XIII secolo. Nelle due formazioni di stato che erano determinanti nella regione, cioè nella Polonia e nell'Ungheria, il cammino di questo sviluppo era diverso. L'istituzione che sin dal XIII secolo diventava quella più tipica nella giurisdizione ecclesiastica e cioè l'officialato *(officialatus)*, è nata sotto altro nome in un modo ben diverso e si è diffusa anche diversamente in questi due paesi. Eppure, alla fine del medioevo possiamo assistere ad una convergenza notevolissima.

Se è vero che l'autonoma giurisdizione ecclesiastica fu possibile farla valere prima in Ungheria e poi in Polonia, con riguardo all'introduzione degli officialati come una delle istituzioni più importanti dell'attività giudiziaria della Chiesa è pur vero che la Polonia precedette l'Ungheria.

In Polonia i tribunali degli officiali dei vescovi, cioè gli officialati, si sono diffusi assai presto e molto rapidamente. La figura dell'officiale viene menzionata per la prima volta dal legato pontificio Giacomo (arcidiacono di Liegi, più tardi papa Urbano IV) nei suoi statuti emanati nel concilio provinciale della chiesa polacca celebrato a Wroclaw nel 1248. Il testo originale di questi statuti è sconosciuto. Ma essi, dietro la richiesta di un nuovo legato, sono stati rinnovati nel 1262 e 1263 da papa Urbano IV per le province di Riga, Gniezno e Salisburgo, nonchè per il territorio della Boemia e della Moravia.[2]

Tale disposizione però venne rinnovata da un nuovo legato, il Cardinale Guido, nel 1267. Dopo il 1267 l'officiale divenne abbastanza presto un funzionario stabile dell'organizzazione giudiziaria ecclesiale.[3] Ambedue i legati pontifici, sia Giacomo che Guido, erano francesi. Essi trasmisero l'esperienza delle regioni di cultura francese. Secondo Adam Vetulani l'imitazione della forma francese di questa istituzione si manifesta nei seguenti fenomeni: nella definizione della competenza degli officiali (il vescovo,

---

2. A. Vetulani, 'Die Einführung der Offizialate in Polen. Ein Beitrag zur Verbreitungsgeschichte des bischöflichen Offizialats im Mittelalter', *Collectanea Theologica* 15 (1934) 285.

3. Cf. ibid. 306.

infatti, conserva il diritto di riservarsi le cause maggiori); nelle disposizioni riguardanti la stesura degli atti; nel possesso e nel carattere del sigillo; e infine nella determinazione dei fori di appello. Il fatto che l'officiale venisse nominato ogni anno di nuovo, dovendo perciò rinnovare ogni anno il proprio giuramento prestato, può considerarsi come imitazione di una prassi esistente in certi luoghi nella Francia.[4]

Per quanto riguarda la formazione del personale, soprattutto dei giudici dei tribunali ecclesiastici polacchi, bisogna riconoscere che essi avevano una buona preparazione giuridico-canonica. Nei documenti, accanto ai loro nomi, troviamo spesso l'appellativo di *magister* o *doctor decretorum*.[5] Gli officiali—anche quelli foranei—hanno applicato i principi del processo romano-canonico con la dovuta competenza.[6]

Il più antico diploma da noi conosciuto proveniente da un *officialis* polacco risale all'anno 1286.[7]

Quanto alla formazione degli 'officialati' ungheresi, bisogna fare una osservazione preliminare. Il nome *officialis* in Ungheria significava (come termine tecnico) l'amministratore dei beni temporali e veniva usato soltanto raramente e piuttosto a mo' di formula per indicare un giudice ungherese del foro spirituale (ecclesiale), ma anche ciò si riscontra soprattutto nei documenti pontifici.[8] Tuttavia questo modo di esprimersi costituisce un segno del fatto che la Santa Sede considerava i tribunali diocesani ungheresi (guidati regolarmente dal vicario generale) e gli officialati europei come la stessa identica istituzione. Tale identificazione era fondata anche nella letteratura canonistica.[9] Il tribunale del vicario generale in Ungheria, infatti, e quello dell'officiale generale o principale in Polonia (specialmente nel secolo XV) erano delle istituzioni piuttosto prossime all'identità.

La diffusione del procedimento romano-canonico era nell'anno 1279 ormai un fatto compiuto in Ungheria.[10] I tribunali dei vicari generali (praticamente: gli officialati) diventarono però organi tipici della giurisdizione ecclesiastica soltanto nella prima metà

4. Cf. ibid. 293–95.

5. Cf. ibid. 310–11; secondo l'autore, le disposizioni sulla formazione giuridica degli arcidiaconi sono state promulgate per la Polonia e per l'Ungheria negli statuti del sinodo del legato pontificio, Filippo da Fermo, celebrato nel 1279, piuttosto a motivo della situazione ungherese.

6. Cf. P. Hemperek, 'Sprawy malzenskie w oficjalacie okregowym w Lublinie w XV w.', *Roczniki Teologiczno-Kanoniczne* 17/5 (1970) 27–44; cf. Vetulani, 'Einführung' 311.

7. Ibid. 306.

8. Per esempio, A. Theiner, *Vetera monumenta historica Hungariam sacram illustrantia* (2 voll.; Romae 1859–60) 2.36 (a. 1358); *Monumenta Vaticana historiam Hungariae illustrantia* (Series I.1–6; Budapest 1885–1891) 1.3, 1.37, 1.62–63 (a. 1389–90); cf. G. Bónis, 'Die Entwicklung der geistlichen Gerichtsbarkeit in Ungarn vor 1526', ZRG Kan. Abt. 49 (1963) 203.

9. Per esempio, Federicus Petruccius Senensis, *Consilia sive responsa, quaestiones et placita* (Venetiis 1570) cons. 127 n. 4; cf. W. Trusen, 'Die gelehrte Gerichtsbarkeit der Kirche', in: Coing, *Handbuch* 1.481.

10. Concilium Budense (a. 1279), can. 24, 39, 58, ed. C. Péterffy, *Sacra Concilia Ecclesiae Romano-Catholicae in Regno Hungariae celebrata* (2 voll.; Posonii et Viennae 1741–1742) I.2.111, 114, 120–21.

del secolo XIV. Per questo sviluppo (e probabilmente anche per la formazione della terminologia riguardo alla giurisdizione ecclesiale) l'attività del legato pontificio Gentilis (1308–1311) dava un impulso importante. Questi emanò una serie di norme giuridiche—sempre per l'Ungheria e per la Polonia allo stesso tempo—e diede inizio anche ad una larga attività giudiziaria in base alla giurisdizione delegata. I collaboratori (uditori, notai pontifici che stendevano i protocolli o rappresentavano le parti, cursori e avvocati) erano generalmente canonisti italiani ben formati.[11] Questo fatto può essere una delle cause determinanti di questi tribunali ungheresi concepiti e richiamati conformemente agli usi italiani.[12] Del resto accadeva molto spesso che anche nei secoli successivi canonisti italiani lavorassero come vicari generali di vescovi ungheresi. Tra il 1380 e l'inizio del secolo XVI, ad esempio, nella città di Esztergom (sede del Primate) è documentata l'attività di ben nove vicari generali italiani. La situazione era simile anche nelle altre diocesi del paese. La legislazione statale cercò di escludere i giuristi italiani ed anche gli altri stranieri della funzione di vicario generale. La Dieta ungherese varò diverse leggi in questo senso (così ad esempio l'Articolo 32 del 1495 e l'Articolo 35 del 1500).

Tuttavia sarebbe esagerato vedere nella configurazione istituzionale dei tribunali dei vicari generali ungheresi e nella rispettiva terminologia adottata soltanto una conseguenza dell'influsso italiano. Non possiamo dire che le forme italiane fossero introdotte puntualmente ed integralmente. Il ruolo del giudice diocesano fu rivestito dal vicario generale anche nella penisola iberica. Così anche in quella regione si può parlare piuttosto di tribunali vicariali invece di officialati.[13] Anzichè affermare la completa identità istituzionale dei tribunali dei vicari ungheresi con quelli italiani è sufficiente precisare che questi tribunali ungheresi appartenevano al 'tipo meridionale' dei tribunali diocesani.[14] Si noti però che abbiamo degli esempi anche in altri paesi europei di affidamento dell'ufficio del vicario generale e di quello dell'officiale alla medesima persona.[15] Tale collegamento è diventato regola generale per esempio in Polonia.

---

11. *Monumenta Vaticana* 2.43, 2.100–12, 2.126–50, 2.154–77, 2.188–267, 2.298–99, 2.356–62; cf. Bónis, 'Entwicklung' 198, 202.

12. Cf. Trusen, 'Gelehrte Gerichtsbarkeit' 481–82; idem, 'Gericht, Gerichtsbarkeit. III. Kanonisches Recht', *LMA* 4 (1989) 1325–26.

13. Il giudice episcopale viene chiamato vicario per esempio anche in diversi documenti sinodali dei paesi iberici: Sínodo de Pedro Vaz Gaviao, can. 69, ed. A. Garcia y Garcia, *Synodicon Hispanum* 2 (Madrid 1982) 261; Sínodo de Justo Baldino, can. 1, ed. ibid. 2.449 ('nosso vigairo hou officiall'); Gonzalo de Alba, 'Liber synodalis' 73, ed. ibid. 4 (Madrid 1987) 164–65; cf. A. Garcia y Garcia, 'Las constituciones del Concilio legatino de Valladolid (1322)', in: *Ecclesia Militans. Studien zur Konzilien- und Reformationsgeschichte. Remigius Bäumer zum 70. Geburtstag gewidmet* (2 voll.; Paderborn 1988) 1.111–127.

14. Cf. P. Erdö, 'Az esztergomi vikáriusi bíróság könyvkultúrája legrégebbi "protocolluma" tükrében', in: *Doctor et apostol. Szent István tanulmányok*, ed. J. Török (Studia Theologica Budapestinensia 10; Budapest 1994) 274.

15. Cf. Trusen, 'Gelehrte Gerichtsbarkeit' 475, 482. Per simili esempi nella Svizzera vedi A. Meyer, 'Die Schweiz', in: Donahue, *Records* 1.196–97, 205–6.

I vicari, anche in Ungheria, erano dei canonisti ben formati, quasi senza eccezione portavano il titolo di *doctor decretorum*.[16] Tutti avevano però dovuto studiare all'estero, dato che nell'Ungheria medievale, malgrado le diverse fondazioni, nessuna università potè avere vita lunga.[17]

I protocolli dei tribunali ecclesiastici medievali ungheresi generalmente non sono pervenuti a noi. Sorge quindi l'interrogativo se questa mancanza non sia una conseguenza del fatto che i vicari generali avevano svolto allo stesso tempo delle attività amministrative e giudiziarie così forse non registrando in libri separati gli atti relativi ai due tipi di attività. Libri di imbreviature di tipo italiani, però, che contengono indistintamente le registrazioni di ambedue i generi, provenienti dall'Ungheria medievale, non sono conosciuti.[18] Recentemente è stato descritto il più antico libro di protocollo conservato, proveniente da un tribunale ecclesiastico ungherese (Esztergom, primi decenni del secolo XVI).[19] In base a questo documento possiamo affermare che alla fine del medioevo il linguaggio e le forme usate nei protocolli in Ungheria rassomigliavano notevolmente alla prassi seguita dai notai della Rota Romana.[20]

Se applichiamo le nozioni principali dei generi letterari, chiarite nella ricerca occidentale degli ultimi decenni, ai libri sinodali diocesani e provinciali di Europa centro-orientale, gli influssi italiani e l'intercambio continentale a livello normativo risultano particolarmente chiari. L'influsso del famoso libro sinodale di Pietro da Sampsona, professore bolognese, che fu promulgato prima per la diocesi di Nîmes, era notevole anche in diverse diocesi dell'Europa centro-orientale.[21] La circolazione dei libri sinodali all'interno di questa regione era poi così forte che il libro sinodale di Cracovia per esempio, nella sua forma che risaliva agli anni Settanta del 1300, attraverso l'analogo libro

---

16. Cf. Bónis, 'Entwicklung' 220–21.

17. Vedi per esempio P. Erdö, *Introductio in historiam scientiae canonicae. Praenotanda ad Codicem* (Roma 1990) 83 n. 190: 'Studentes ex Transylvania provenientes similiter ac alii ex Europa orientali maxime studia iuris canonici frequentabant'; per una edizione aggiornata di questo lavoro vedi idem, *Storia della scienza del diritto canonico. Una introduzione* (Roma 1999); cf. S. Tonk, *Erdélyiek egyetemjárása a középkorban* (Bucarest 1979) 99–100. In Ungheria, negli ultimi decenni del secolo XIII, i canonisti formati in Italia conquistarono quasi ogni posizione principale nelle cancellerie del re e degli aristocratici, nonché i benefici episcopali e gli altri più importanti; cf. G. Bónis, *A jogtudó értelmiség a Mohács elötti Magyarországon* (Budapest 1971) 23–25.

18. Cf. per esempio G. Dolezalek, *Das Imbreviaturbuch des erzbischöflichen Gerichtsnotars Hubaldus aus Pisa. Mai bis August 1230* (Forschungen zur neueren Privatrechtsgeschichte 13; Colonia e Vienna 1969); idem, 'Une nouvelle source pour l'étude de la pratique judiciaire au treizième siècle: les livres d'imbréviatures des notaires de cour', in: *Confluence des droits savants et des pratiques juridiques. Actes du colloque de Montpellier (1977)* (Milano 1979) 223–41.

19. P. Erdö, 'Das älteste Protokollbuch des Vikariatsgerichtes von Esztergom (Ungarn)', in: *De Iure Canonico Medii Aevi. Festschrift für Rudolf Weigand*, ed. P. Landau e M. Petzolt (SG 27; Roma 1996) 71–84.

20. Cf. H. Hoberg, 'Die Protokollbücher der Rotanotare von 1464 bis 1517', ZRG Kan. Abt. 70 (1953) 177–227.

21. Cf. per esempio P. Erdö, 'Libri sinodali tardo-medievali in Ungheria. Il libro sinodale di Esztergom', REDC 135 (1993) 607–22.

di Esztergom ha determinato il contenuto di quasi tutti i libri sinodali dell'Ungheria tardo-medievale.[22]

Nella creazione dei grandi libri sinodali organicamente redatti delle singole province ecclesiastiche della medesima regione era spesso decisivo l'influsso dei legati pontifici che avevano normalmente una competenza pure regionale dall'Ungheria fino alla Polonia.[23] E' significativo che l'autorità pontificia centrale e la tradizione giuridica regionale che riuscì a sopravvivere lunghi secoli, a volte persino la riforma tridentina, sembra che siano state in rapporto dialettico. Quanto più risalì un libro sinodale provinciale alla legislazione dei legati pontifici o ad un'atto pontificio, tanto più divenne fondamento di una disciplina locale stabile e fortemente speciale. Fenomeno questo che dovrebbe essere esaminato più profondamente per la sua attualità anche nel contesto di un Europa in via verso l'unità in cui le regioni riacquistano sempre di più la loro propria fisionomia anche giuridica.

Già a proposito dei libri sinodali emerge un fenomeno significativo: la presenza delle glosse nei più importanti libri sinodali provinciali soprattutto in Polonia. Nel XV secolo i diversi manoscritti e poi le antiche stampe del grande *Sinodale* della Provincia di Gniezno contengono molte glosse marginali con somiglianze significative nei diversi esemplari senza costituire però un vero apparato di glosse. La maggioranza di queste glosse riproduce i generi elementari delle glosse al Decreto di Graziano, risalenti al XII secolo. Sembra che questo fondamentale libro provinciale—malgrado l'affermazione tradizionale generalmente diffusa nella storiografia giuridica secondo cui soltanto le collezioni del diritto universale costituivano la base dell'insegnamento—sia stato usato per scopi didattici nelle scuole capitolari polacche.[24]

Delle scuole capitolari ungheresi invece abbiamo un libro manoscritto proveniente dall'inizio del 1500 che sembra di esser stato il testo base dell'insegnamento del diritto canonico. Questo volume non è altro che una abbreviazione speciale del grande commentario del Panormitano alle Decretali.[25] Il canonico maestro ungherese ha trascritto i sommari dei singoli capitoli che precedono la spiegazione esegetica nel Panormitano offrendo così un corso più elementare ai suoi alunni.

Per quanto riguarda poi gli studi di un livello più alto, giova notare che la maggio-

---

22. Cf. P. Erdö, 'Polnische Quellen des großen Synodalbuchs von Esztergom (1382)', ZRG Kan. Abt. 83 (1997) 377–91; idem, *Die Quellen des Kirchenrechts. Eine geschichtliche Einführung* (Adnotationes in ius canonicum 23; Frankfurt/M. 2002).

23. Cf. per esempio P. Erdö, 'Synodalbücher der Kirchenprovinzen von Gnesen, Prag und Salzburg. Zu den Erscheinungsformen einer spätmittelalterlichen literarischen Gattung', RIDC 10 (1999) 9–36.

24. Cf. P. Erdö, 'Die Glossen in der Handschrift MS 3 der Robbins Collection in Berkeley. Ein Beitrag zur Frage der wissenschaftlichen Bearbeitung des Partikularkirchenrechts im Mittelalter', AKKR 164 (1995) 390–414.

25. Cf. P. Erdö, 'Nágocsi Gáspár kodexe és a középkori veszprémi jogtanítás', *Magyar Könyvszemle* 112 (1995) 119–30.

ranza degli studenti ungheresi che frequentavano nel medioevo le università straniere studiava diritto, soprattutto quello canonico. Gli studenti ungheresi frequentavano prima di tutto le università italiane. Già all'inizio del XIII secolo era significativa a Bologna la presenza dei ungheresi, tra i quali alcuni, come Damaso e Paolo Ungaro sono diventati professori di diritto canonico alla medesima università. Alla fine dello stesso secolo invece i canonisti formati in Italia hanno persino occupato quasi tutti i posti importanti del governo civile dell'Ungheria.[26] Nella seconda metà del XIV secolo, sotto il regno di Lodovico il Grande, angoino di Napoli, è stata fondata in Ungheria la prima università nella città di Pécs (1367), dove si insegnava soprattutto il diritto. Tra i professori vi erano dei famosi italiani, come Galvano Bettini, particolarmente ben pagati.[27]

Le ricerche degli ultimi decenni hanno dimostrato che tra i codici manoscritti e loro frammenti usati in Ungheria nel medioevo hanno un peso statisticamente molto rilevante le opere giuridiche soprattutto canoniche di provenienza italiana. A volte le annotazioni marginali attestano che diversi esemplari sono stati usati da futuri canonici e vescovi ungheresi durante i loro studi a Padova o in altre università italiane.[28] Altre volte protocolli tardo-medievali conservano delle osservazioni circa i libri usati dai giudici ecclesiastici ungheresi. Si tratta delle opere dei più famosi canonisti italiani dell'epoca da Giovanni d'Andrea fino a Nicolò de' Tudeschi.[29] La stessa prevalenza italiana si rispecchia anche nei cataloghi delle biblioteche e nei testamenti degli ecclesiastici. L'interesse di alcuni intellettuali e membri dell'alto clero ungherese si estendeva anche alle fonti e commenti principali del diritto romano, e a volte persino al diritto delle città italiane come dimostra un bel frammento degli statuti glossati di Venezia conservato nella biblioteca capitolare di Esztergom.[30]

Dopo tutto questo sembra naturale che il famoso *Tripartitum* di István Werbőczy,

26. Cf. Tonk, *Erdélyiek egyetemjárása a középkorban* 99–100; Bónis, *A jogtudó értelmiség a Mohács előtti Magyarországon* 23–25; Erdö, *Storia della scienza del diritto canonico* 88–89.

27. Cf. *Régi magyar egyetemek emlékezete. Memoria universitatum et scholarum maiorum Regni Hungariae 1367–1777*, ed. L. Szögi (Budapest 1995) 9.

28. Vedi per esempio *Fragmenta latina codicum in Bibliotheca Universitatis Budapestinensis*, rec. L. Mezey et P. Erdö (Fragmenta codicum in Bibliothecis Hungariae I/1; Budapest 1983); *Fragmenta latina codicum in Bibliotheca Seminarii Cleri Hungariae Centralis*, rec. L. Mezey et P. Erdö (Fragmenta codicum in bibliothecis Hungariae I/2; Budapest 1988); P. Erdö, 'Codici manoscritti di diritto canonico e loro frammenti in Ungheria', *Apollinaris* 61 (1988) 341–54; cf. S. Kuttner, 'Manuscripts of Canon Law in Hungary: An Index to Peter Erdö's Article in Apollinaris', BMCL 18 (1988) 64–68; *Mittelalterliche lateinische Handschriftenfragmente in Esztergom*, ed. A. Vizkelety e P. Erdö (Fragmenta et codices in bibliothecis Hungariae II; Budapest 1993); P. Erdö, 'Mittelalterliche lateinische Handschriftenfragmente in Esztergom, Hrsg. Vizkelety, A.' (recensione), *Folia Theologica* 4 (1993) 159–62; idem, 'Partikulare Kirchenrechtsquellen in Ungarn', in: Proc. Munich (MIC C.10; 1997) 757–70; *Mittelalterliche lateinische Handschriftenfragmente in Györ*, ed. A. Vizkelety e P. Erdö (Fragmenta et codices in bibliothecis Hungariae III; Budapest 1998).

29. Cf. Erdö, 'Das älteste Protokollbuch' 81.

30. P. Erdö, 'Statuti civili veneziani di Jacopo Tiepolo nella Bibliotheca del Capitolo di Esztergom (Ungheria)', *Glossae* 4 (1992) 247–55.

grandioso riassunto del diritto 'consuetudinario' ungherese alla fine del medioevo, è pieno di elementi, nozioni, riferimenti provenienti dal diritto romano, dallo *ius commune*, specialmente attraverso il diritto canonico.[31] In tal modo l'eredità della cultura del diritto comune che penetrava il ceto dirigente dell'Ungheria medievale continuava ad esercitare il suo organico influsso fino alla seconda guerra mondiale.

Il ritorno attuale della cultura giuridica ungherese e polacca in Europa occidentale significa anche la riscoperta di questo patrimonio del diritto romano e l'attualità della ricerca e dell'insegnamento di questa disciplina nelle nostre università.

31. Cf. J. Félehgyházy, *Werböczy hármaskönyve és a kánonjog* (Budapest 1942).

25

Hohfeld on Ockham

A Canonistic Text in the *Opus nonaginta dierum*

Brian Tierney

❉

Of course Wesley Hohfeld did not write about William of Ockham; but he could have done.[1] Since Hohfeld originally published his fourfold classification of the meanings of the word 'right' in English law, his work has proved applicable in various other fields of study. Judith Thomson pointed out that Hohfeld's argument could be useful in considering problems of moral and political philosophy. She noted that Hobbes's concept of a right corresponded to Hohfeld's 'privilege' or 'liberty'. More importantly in the present context, Charles Reid has shown how Hohfeld's analysis can be applied to medieval canonistic texts; he was able to present a full-scale Hohfeldian account of the various meanings of *ius* in thirteenth-century canon law.[2] The purpose of the present inquiry is to ask whether Hohfeld might help us to understand an apparent anomaly in Ockham's handling of a canonistic text in the *Opus nonaginta dierum* (henceforth OND).

The text in question is the decree *Exiit*, promulgated by Pope Nicholas III in 1279 and included in the *Liber Sextus* of Boniface VIII (VI 5.7.3). The anomaly in Ockham's work can be stated briefly at the outset. At one point in the OND, Ockham wrote that the Franciscans could sometimes use things by virtue of a natural right but that they did not have this right 'except only at a time of extreme necessity' *(illud ius non habent nisi tantummodo pro tempore necessitatis extremae)* and that outside the case of extreme necessity they did not have any right whatsoever. But a little further on he wrote that

---

1. W. N. Hohfeld, *Fundamental Legal Conceptions* (New Haven, CT 1923). The chapter on rights discussed below is a revised version of an article originally published in the *Yale Law Review* 23 (1913).

2. J. J. Thomson, *The Realm of Rights* (Cambridge, MA 1990) 49–50; C. Reid, 'The Canonistic Contribution to the Western Rights Tradition: An Historical Inquiry', *Boston College Law Review* 33 (1991) 37–92.

the friars could use by natural right 'however much they are outside a situation of extreme necessity' *(quantumcumque sint extra articulum necessitatis extremae).*[3]

The two statements were both expressed emphatically but they seem flatly to contradict one another. In the following discussion I want first to consider Ockham's argument in order to explain how the two apparently conflicting texts came to appear in his work, then to discuss Hohfeld's classification of rights and its possible application to Ockham's texts.

Ockham and Natural Right

Nicholas III's decree *Exiit* presented a definition of Franciscan poverty that provided a starting point for the later controversies in which William of Ockham became involved. The pope first distinguished between 'property, possession, usufruct, right of use, and simple factual use'; then he asserted that the friars had retained for themselves only this simple factual use and had renounced every other kind of relationship to temporal goods, including right of use *(ius utendi).* The pope explained that this factual use without a right came into play when the friars used anything by permission or license of another person. He also noted that the friars did not tempt providence by seeking to live in this fashion because by a 'right of heaven' *(ius poli),* available to everyone, they could take what they needed to sustain life in case of extreme necessity.[4] These were all positions that Ockham would undertake to defend.

The last point, about a right in extreme necessity, requires a little more explanation here since it became an important element in Ockham's later argument. The issue had arisen in the canonistic works of the twelfth century because an ancient maxim, taken into Gratian's *Decretum,* declared that by natural law all things were common. The decretists therefore had to explain how the existing system of private property, established by human law, could be justified. One solution, presented by the influential canonist Huguccio (c. 1190), argued that natural law did not actually prohibit the institution of private possessions, but required that they be shared with the poor in time of necessity.[5] In the next few years the canonists developed from this position a further argument that a starving person who took food from a rich owner without his permis-

---

3. *Opus nonaginta dierum,* in: *Guillelmi de Ockham opera politica,* ed. H. S. Offler (2 vols; Manchester 1974) 2.561, 578.

4. For these texts of *Exiit,* see VI 5.7.3. The phrase *ius poli* was taken from a text of Augustine included in the *Decretum* at C.17 q.4 c.43. Since Nicholas used this expression instead of the more common *ius naturale,* it often occurred in later discussions of Franciscan poverty.

5. This topic is discussed most fully with many relevant canonistic texts in J. Couvreur, *Les pauvres: Ont-ils des droits?* (Paris 1961). For Huguccio, see ibid. 141–49. On the canonists' idea of a permissive natural law, see B. Tierney, 'Permissive Natural Law and Property: Gratian to Kant', *Journal of the History of Ideas* 62 (2001) 381–99.

sion was not guilty of an act of theft. Instead, as one of them wrote, 'It was as if he used his own right and his own thing'.[6] The canonistic teaching came to be widely accepted in thirteenth-century thought and it persisted down to the time of Locke.[7] According to this argument a person in extreme need had a right in the sense that he had a rightful claim to the surplus property of others, a right that he could assert for himself. But it was a natural right, not a positive civil right for which he could sue in court.[8]

Exiit had defined evangelical poverty in a fashion wholly acceptable to the Franciscan Order; but during the 1320s Pope John XXII launched a series of vigorous criticisms of the teaching that his predecessor had asserted. The pope's arguments proved to be utterly unacceptable to Ockham and his faction of dissident Franciscans. In the passages of Ockham that we shall consider, the Franciscan was arguing, against John XXII, that the friars had renounced not only all property but also all rights to property, including the right of use. Specifically, he was responding to two of Pope John's assertions. The pope maintained that, when the friars used goods by permission or license of another, they did indeed acquire a right of use and further that, in principle, there could be no just use without a right of using. Ockham's responses in his OND were very diffuse and repetitive but they depended on three basic distinctions—between a natural right and a positive right, between a revocable license and an irrevocable license, and between use in case of necessity and use by license of another.[9]

In considering the first distinction Ockham was especially concerned to argue that the right the friars had renounced was every kind of positive legal right, any right derived from civil law for which one could sue in court, and, moreover, that this was what Nicholas III had intended to assert in *Exiit*. Accordingly, Ockham wrote, 'Every right of using is either a natural right *(ius naturale)* or a positive right *(ius positivum)*'. But Nicholas clearly attributed to the Franciscans a natural right when he wrote that they could avail themselves of a *ius poli* in case of necessity; therefore the right that the friars had renounced must have been a positive right according to the pope. Here and throughout the subsequent argument Ockham equated the terms *ius poli* and *ius naturale*.[10]

6. Couvreur, *Les pauvres* 102, citing Laurentius Hispanus.

7. On the history of the doctrine, see S. Swanson, 'The Medieval Foundations of John Locke's Theory of Natural Rights: Rights of Subsistence and the Principle of Extreme Necessity', *History of Political Thought* 18 (1997) 399–459.

8. At best he could appeal to the bishop to intervene; see Couvreur, *Les pauvres* 108–11.

9. The OND was a word-by-word reply to John XXII's bull *Quia vir reprobus* (1329). The passages discussed in the text above are from chapters 60–65, 554–80. Modern commentators have sometimes discussed Ockham's argument here but without any treatment of the particular problem we are considering; see e.g. M. Damiata, *Guglielmo d'Ockham: povertà e potere* (2 vols; Florence 1978–79) 1.429–34; J. Miethke, *Ockhams Weg zur Sozialphilosophie* (Berlin 1969) 487–95; A. S. Brett, *Liberty, Right and Nature* (Cambridge 1997) 50–68; B. Tierney, *The Idea of Natural Rights: Studies on Natural Rights, Natural Law and Church Law, 1150–1625* (Atlanta 1997) 120–30.

10. OND 2.556: 'Omne enim ius utendi aut est ius naturale aut ius positivum. Sed Nicholaus non accepit ius

The distinction between an irrevocable license and a revocable one formed another part of Ockham's argument about the Franciscans' renunciation of all positive legal rights. Ockham acknowledged that an irrevocable license, a permanent alienation of some right by its owner, did confer a positive right for which the recipient could sue in court if necessary. But a revocable license that could be terminated at any time at the discretion of the granter—the kind of license that the friars claimed to use in their day-to-day life—did not convey any such right.[11]

The complications that led on to the apparent anomaly in Ockham's argument arose from his handling of the third distinction, between use in case of necessity and use by license. In a first approach to the issue, Ockham distinguished again between a positive right and a natural right and developed further both definitions. A positive right was a licit power over a temporal thing such that one could not be deprived of it unwillingly without fault or reasonable cause, and persons who were so deprived could sue in court. A natural right on the other hand was held from nature, not from any statute, and it was common to all people.[12] According to Ockham, this was the only kind of right that pertained to the friars. 'The Friars Minor . . . do not have any positive right, but they do have a right, namely a natural right'.[13] Ockham further asserted here that this natural right existed only in time of need. 'They do not have this right except only in time of extreme necessity'.[14] The argument so far was enough to establish that there could on occasion be use by natural right that did not imply any positive right. At this point, however, the anomaly that we are trying to explain began to appear, for Ockham went on at once to deploy his argument about natural right and extreme necessity in considering the situation of the friars who used goods by license of another in their normal everyday way of life. Ockham's principal concern here was to refute Pope John XXII's assertion that persons who used by license necessarily had a *ius utendi*, a right of using. To counter the pope's argument, Ockham had to show that having a license was

utendi pro iure naturali. . . . Secundum eum habent ius utendi naturale, cum dicat *ipsis iure poli ad providen-dum sustentationi naturae viam non esse praeclusam;* ergo non accepit ius utendi pro iure naturale. Sumit ergo ius utendi pro iure positivo'.

11. Ibid. 2.560, 571: 'Quando enim obtenta licentia non potest ad libitum revocari, ius quoddam acquiritur; quando vero potest ad libitum revocari, nec virtute licentiae potest habens eam in iudicio litigare, nullum ius acquiritur'.

12. Ibid. 2.559: 'Ius utendi naturale commune est omnibus hominibus, quia ex natura, non aliqua constitutione superveniente, habetur. . . . Aliud est ius utendi positivum, quod ex constitutione aliqua vel humana pactione habetur. . . . Unde istud ius utendi non est aliud quam quaedam licita potestas exercendi actum aliquem circa rem temporalem extrinsicam, qua quis sine culpa et absque causa rationabili privari non debet invitus, et si privatus fuerit, privantem iniuste poterit in iudicio convenire'.

13. Ibid. 2.561: 'Fratres Minores . . . non habent aliquod ius positivum, habent tamen aliquod ius in eis scilicet ius naturale'.

14. Ibid.: 'Sed illud ius non habent nisi tantummodo pro tempore necessitatis extremae'.

not the same as having a right. He maintained, therefore, that the friars who used by license in their day-to-day lives did not have any right, not even a natural right, and this precisely because their natural right came into play only in extreme need. 'The Friars Minor have a license of using things at other times than a time of extreme necessity; but they do not have any right whatsoever except at a time of extreme necessity; therefore a license is not a right'.[15]

So far, so good. However, when Ockham came to consider in detail, in a later discussion, the position of the Franciscans using by license of an owner, he argued in a different fashion and apparently to a contrary conclusion. At this point in his argument Ockham was commenting directly on John XXII's assertion that any just use required a right of using. In response, the Franciscan now argued that when the friars used by license they used justly because they used by virtue of a natural right or 'right of heaven'. Referring again to the teaching of Nicholas III, Ockham wrote that, although the pope had conceded to the friars a right of use in extreme necessity, he had not denied that they might have this 'right of heaven' in other circumstances.[16] But earlier Ockham had written, 'They do not have that right except only at a time of extreme necessity'. Ockham's subsequent argument ran like this. The natural right of common use derived from natural law could not be renounced and it could not be wholly abolished by human positive laws; but the exercise of the right could be restricted by such laws and it had been so restricted by the laws instituting private property. The existence of private possessions restricted the natural right of use; the ownership of property by one person was an impediment to its use by another. It followed then that, if an owner granted to another a license or permission to use some property, the impediment to its use was removed. The license did not confer any new right; it merely allowed the exercise of a preexisting natural right. And so, the argument concludes, the friars who had been granted a license could use by natural right 'however much they are outside a situation of extreme necessity'.[17] The argument seems reasonably persuasive if we grant Ockham's premises; but the conclusion precisely contradicts Ockham's previous assertion that the Franciscans had no natural right except only at a time of extreme need. Moreover, this earlier argument had been used to explain that, when the friars used by license, they did not have 'any right whatsoever'.

---

15. Ibid.: 'Fratres habent licentiam utendi rebus pro alio tempore quam pro tempore necessitatis extremae; sed non habent quodcumque ius nisi pro tempore necessitatis extremae; ergo licentia utendi non est ius utendi'.

16. Ibid. 2.577: 'Nicholaus . . . non tamen negat aliquos posse in aliis casibus uti rebus iure poli'.

17. Ibid. 2.578: 'Tunc tamen primo, quando est licentiatus seu permissus, utitur licite iure poli tali re, et non prius; quia modo est amotum prohibens ius naturale ne exiret in actum utendi quod ante amotum minime fuit. Et ex hoc patet quod Fratres Minores . . . iure poli et non iure fori utuntur, quantumcumque sint extra articulum necessitatis extremae'.

Ockham was a master logician and passionately concerned to vindicate his own version of Franciscan poverty. How then could he have come to defend his case by deploying two such apparently contradictory arguments? Perhaps an answer can be found in a remark of one of the canonists who first shaped the doctrine of extreme need in the years around 1200. Ricardus Anglicus observed that no incoherence was involved if *ius naturale* taken in one sense of the term was opposed to *ius naturale* taken in another sense.[18]

Hohfeld and Ockham

Hohfeld used the expression 'chameleon-hued words' when he discussed the varied meanings of the English word 'right'. His phrase is equally applicable to the Latin *ius*. Twelfth-century decretists commonly presented six or more meanings of the term *ius naturale* and, in the fourteenth century, Johannes Monachus found more than twenty meanings of the word *ius* itself in Roman and canon law (and the list was still not exhaustive). In modern scholarship the distinction most emphasized has been between *ius* as meaning a right (as in *ius testandi*) and *ius* as meaning law or a body of law (as in *ius civile, ius canonicum*). But Annabel Brett has pointed out that, in medieval discourse, we can also find different meanings among the subjective usages of *ius*.[19] Hohfeld addressed a similar issue when he complained about 'the very broad and indiscriminate use of the term "right"' in the ordinary legal discourse of his own day.

To clarify matters, Hohfeld presented a four-fold classification. A right could be either a legal claim, a privilege (or liberty), a power, or an immunity. It is the first two meanings that will concern us. According to Hohfeld, a right 'in its strictest sense' was a legal claim against another that the law would recognize. The essence of such a claim right of X against Y was that Y had a correlative duty or obligation toward X.[20] A privilege was more complicated. Hohfeld was not using the word in its normal everyday sense as meaning 'a special or peculiar legal advantage' but as referring to conduct that was legally permissible.[21] The holder of a privilege was at liberty to act in the relevant sphere and Hohfeld noted that 'the closest synonym of legal "privilege" seems to be legal "liberty".'[22] Most later writers have therefore preferred to use the term 'liberty right' as expressing Hohfeld's meaning more clearly.

An essential characteristic of a privilege understood in Hohfeld's sense was that it

---

18. Couvreur, *Les pauvres* 289.
19. Johannes Monachus, *Glossa aurea* (Paris 1535), *ad* VI 1.6.16, fol. xci^r; *Liberty, Right and Nature* 2–3.
20. Hohfeld, *Fundamental Legal Conceptions* 36–38.
21. Ibid. 44.
22. Ibid. 47.

did not imply any correlative duty on the part of others. It meant only that the privilege holder had no duty not to act in the way specified by the privilege. Hohfeld understood that the two rights would commonly coexist in a given legal situation. Thus, he explained that a property owner had a right, a claim, against others that they stay off his land, but he also had a privilege of entering upon the land himself, that is to say he had no duty to stay off his own land. Hohfeld thought that it was important to keep the conceptions of a claim right and of a privilege or liberty distinct from one another in order to avoid confusion in legal thinking.

However, it is not intuitively self evident that the two different kinds of right exist in the single act of owning something, and many juridical texts cited by Hohfeld failed to distinguish between them. To explain his position further, therefore, Hohfeld cited the hypothetical case of a man who bought a shrimp salad. He would have a right to eat the salad (a privilege) and he would also have a claim right against others, that they not interfere with his doing so. To show that there really were two conceptually different rights, Hohfeld then offered a little thought experiment. The owners of a salad, A, B, C, and D, might say to X, 'Eat the salad if you can; you have our license to do so, but we don't agree not to interfere with you'.[23] X would then have a privilege of eating the salad but he would have no claim that he could assert against the owners.

It will perhaps be evident at this point that Hohfeld was envisaging a situation similar to that described by Ockham when he discussed the position of a friar using by virtue of a revocable license. The friar could licitly use the goods in question but he had no claim against the owner. Earlier discussions on Franciscan poverty had not referred specifically to shrimp salads but they had often considered the possibility of a right of use in consumable goods like foodstuffs. Hervaeus Natalis, a supporter of John XXII writing a few years before Ockham, wrote that, on the face of it, it would be ridiculous for anyone to concede to another a right to eat a loaf of bread while retaining for himself a right to snatch it away from his teeth. But Ockham envisaged just such a situation when the Franciscans used by virtue of a revocable license.[24] The position of the friars in such a case could be defined precisely by a phrase quoted by Hohfeld. 'A license is merely a *permission* to do an act which *without such permission* would amount to a trespass'.[25] The natural right of the friars using by license was a permissive right; the Franciscans did not commit any offense or trespass by exercising their right. But their right was not a claim right; the granter had no duty correlative to the friars' right; he could revoke the right at will. That was Ockham's whole point in insisting that the

23. Ibid. 41.

24. J. G. Sikes (ed.), 'Hervaeus Natalis: De paupertate Christi et apostolorum', *Archives d'histoire doctrinale et littéraire du moyen âge* 12–13 (1937–38) 209–97, 242.

25. Hohfeld, *Fundamental Legal Concepts* 50 (italics in original).

license was revocable. In Hohfeld's language the right that the friars enjoyed was a privilege or liberty right.

But, on the other hand, the right of the friars in extreme need was a claim right in the sense defined by Hohfeld, a right of one person associated with a correlative duty of another. The duty of the rich to share their surplus wealth with the poor was a common theme in patristic writings and several relevant texts were included in the *Decretum*.[26] The contribution of the canonists of around 1200 was to insist on the correlative right of the poor. This was the kind of natural right that Ockham invoked when he considered the case of extreme need. But when he discussed the friars' use of things by license the meaning of the term *ius naturale* had shifted. The friars had no duty not to use the things conceded to them but they had no claim that they could assert against the owners.

It might seem inappropriate to apply a modern kind of legal analysis in explicating Ockham's medieval argument. But the varied meanings of *ius* that we can discern in Ockham's work can all be found in the legal discourse of his own day. They are not peculiar to modern legal systems. The point of applying Hohfeld's modern analysis to Ockham's medieval text is that Hohfeld makes explicit what was only implicit in the medieval sources. In Hohfeld's language, then, when Ockham wrote that the friars had no right outside the case of extreme necessity he meant that they had no claim right, no right against others; when he wrote that they had a right outside the case of extreme necessity he meant that they had a privilege, a liberty to act. Both meanings can be discerned in Ockham's definition of ownership, *dominium*, at the beginning of the OND, '*Dominium* is a principal human power of laying claim to a temporal thing in court and of treating it in any way not forbidden by natural law'.[27] The first part of the definition refers to a claim right, the second to a liberty right. Hohfeld of course was not arguing that the jurists of his own day were consciously equivocating in their use of the word 'right'; his point was rather that they created unnecessary problems by shifting from one meaning of the word to another unreflectively, without noticing the equivocation or alerting their readers to it. It was the same, I think, with Ockham's use of the term *ius naturale*. Ockham himself was aware of the problem at least in theory. In his *Summa logicae* he wrote, 'There is scarcely a term which is not employed equivocally in different places in the writings of philosophers . . . Those who want to take a term univocally . . . frequently make mistakes about the intentions of authors'.[28]

Ockham's own way of equivocating in his use of the term *ius naturale* is especially

26. See Couvreur, *Les pauvres* 80–85.
27. OND 1.308.
28. M. J. Loux (trans.), *Ockham's Theory of Terms: Part I of the Summa logicae* (Notre Dame, IN 1974) 220.

evident in another of his usages of the word *ius*—as meaning either law or subjective right. Ockham would move from one meaning to the other in the course of a single sentence. Thus, he wrote *quilibet . . . habet ius utendi ex iure naturali,* which we should normally translate as, 'Everyone . . . has a right of using from natural law'.[29] In the sections of the OND that we have considered, Ockham nearly always used *ius* to mean a natural right, but at one point he defined it as natural equity or natural law, and without any explanation to the reader that he was departing from his previous usage.[30] It is the same with the shift in the meaning of *ius naturale* from a claim right to a privilege.[31] Ockham was not seeking to mislead his readers by conscious equivocation. It was just that for him, as for his contemporaries, the word *ius* had a variety of connotations and he deployed one or the other meaning unreflectively as the course of his argument required (just as we can use the word 'right' without explaining on each occasion which of its many meanings is intended). Normally the meaning is clear from the context, but occasionally there can be an appearance of confusion.

If Ockham had been exceedingly scrupulous, he could have avoided even this appearance. In place of the passages quoted above he could have written something like this: 'The Franciscans have no positive right of using but they do have a natural right. This is a natural claim right against others that exists only in time of extreme necessity. Outside the case of extreme necessity they have no claim right whatsoever'. Then he could have explained that another kind of natural right came into play when the friars used by license. To understand why Ockham was not so exceedingly scrupulous we must remember that the OND was after all a 'Work of Ninety Days'. Ockham was writing impetuously, at a furious pace. He produced this long involuted work—it runs to over five hundred pages in a modern printed edition—in the space of three months. In such a work one might expect to find a certain untidiness around the edges of the argument.

In analyzing his legal texts, Hohfeld complained that 'chameleon-hued words are a peril both to clear thought and to lucid expression'.[32] In Ockham's case there is a lack

---

29. OND 2.562.

30. Ibid. 2.574: 'Ius autem poli vocatur aequitas naturalis . . . consona rationi rectae . . . hoc ius aliquando vocatur ius naturale'. In the much-discussed passage of the *Dialogus* (3.2.3.6.) where Ockham gave three meanings of *ius naturale,* the term was again used equivocally to mean either natural law or a natural right. On these usages in Ockham, see Tierney, *Idea of Natural Rights* 118–30, 175–82.

31. Ockham often used the common medieval phrase *iura et libertates* and in one context, unusually, he distinguished between the two words. In the *Breviloquium* (2.17), Ockham wrote that the pope's power was limited 'not only by the rights . . . but also by the liberties conceded to mortals by God and nature'. The liberties that Ockham had in mind here concerned works of supererogation—to fast or not to fast, to enter a religious order or not to do so. In Hohfeld's terminology they would be called privileges or liberty rights.

32. Hohfeld, *Fundamental Legal Concepts* 35.

of lucidity in the language but not an underlying confusion of thought. As Ricardus Anglicus had explained, there was no necessary incoherence if one meaning of *ius naturale* conflicted with another meaning. A close examination of Ockham's uses of the term can help us to discern a coherent thread of argument running through some apparently conflicting texts. We might even apply to Ockham the conclusion that Hohfeld reached about his legal sources: 'In short, the deeper the analysis, the greater becomes one's impression of fundamental unity and harmony'.[33]

33. Ibid. 64.

26

Thomas More and the Canon Law

R. H. Helmholz

✿

Introduction

How much did English common lawyers know of the Roman and canon laws? What use did they make of what they knew? These are questions of perennial inter- est to legal historians.[1] This paper makes a small contribution to the subject, taking a famous lawyer as its focus. I hope it will interest the honoree of this volume. It might. The interaction between canon law and secular law has been among the many subjects his own work has illuminated.[2] In this hope, the paper appraises the role of the canon law in the life and work of Thomas More (1478–1535), the famous humanist, common lawyer, Chancellor to King Henry VIII, and canonized martyr for the Catholic cause in Tudor England.

The paper has three objectives. The first is to discover how much of the law of the church More knew; that is, to make a reasonable estimate of how familiar he was with the vast ocean of the medieval *ius commune*. The second is to uncover any possibilities to suggest a means by which More, a common lawyer by training and profession, learned

---

1. See, e.g., J. H. Baker, 'Roman Law at the Third University of England', *Current Legal Problems* 55 (2002) 123– 50; A. Lewis, 'What Marcellus Says Is Against You: Roman Law and Common Law', in: *The Roman Legal Tradi- tion*, ed. A. D. E. Lewis and D. J. Ibbetson (Cambridge 1994) 199–208; D. Seipp, 'The Reception of Canon Law and Civil Law in English Common Law Courts before 1600', *Oxford Journal of Legal Studies* 13 (1993) 388–420; D. R. Coquillette, 'Legal Ideology and Incorporation IV: The Nature of Civilian Influence on Modern Anglo-American Commercial Law', *Boston University Law Review* 67 (1987) 877–970; P. Stein, *Roman Law and English Jurisprudence Yesterday and Today* (Cambridge 1969); P. Vinogradoff, *Roman Law in Medieval Europe* (Cambridge 1929, repr. 1968) 97–118; T. E. Scrutton, *The Influence of Roman Law on the Law of England* (Cambridge 1885).

2. See, e.g., K. Pennington, *The Prince and the Law, 1200–1600: Sovereignty and Rights in the Western Legal Tradition* (Berkeley and Los Angeles 1993); idem, 'Innocent until Proven Guilty: The Origins of a Legal Maxim', in: *A Ennio Cortese* (3 vols.; Rome 2003) 3.59–73; idem, 'The *ius commune*, Suretyship and Magna Carta', RIDC 11 (2001) 255–74.

what he did know about the canon law. The third is to describe his attitude towards the canon law, making some judgment about what, if any, influence Christian humanism had upon his attitude towards the law of the medieval church.

Before turning directly to these topics, however, a remark about the *status quaestionis* is in order. It can be brief. Not much has been written on this subject. Most of the few scholars who have dealt with it at all have done so only in passing. They have assumed that More's familiarity with the *ius commune* was very slight, if indeed it existed at all.[3] There is certainly evidence to support this negative conclusion. His career and education were in the English common law, not the canon or Roman laws, and gaining a familiarity with the medieval *ius commune* requires spending more than the odd free hour. It requires books and time. It seems unlikely that he had enough of either to turn himself into a civilian. Moreover, More himself wrote, 'I neither understand the doctors of the law nor well can turn their book'.[4] His disavowal appears to bring the inquiry to a close.

However, it does not. Two scholars have taken the trouble to go further, and they both have concluded that more can be said. On the basis of the available evidence, J. D. M. Derrett concluded that More 'almost certainly had more than a smattering of legal knowledge on the Roman side', but that he had 'no intimate knowledge' of the canon law half of the *ius commune*.[5] By contrast, R. J. Schoeck reached a conclusion close to the reverse of Derrett's.[6] He described More as 'more than ordinarily interested and competent in the canon law' even though he was not an actual canonist.[7] Their conclusions invite a closer look.

One more introductory word: The question is more complicated than it may seem. It is a mistake to equate the canon law with defense of the medieval church against the rise of Protestantism. The position men took on religious and theological issues did not necessarily track their views of law. It is certainly true that canon law *could* be used in

---

3. L. Baldwin Smith, *Tudor Prelates and Politics 1536–1558* (Princeton 1953) 49: More 'was trained in the common law and was ignorant of the ecclesiastical code'.

4. See *The Correspondence of Sir Thomas More*, ed. E. Rogers (Princeton 1947) 536.

5. J. D. M. Derrett, 'Withernam: A Legal Practical Joke of Sir Thomas More', *The Catholic Lawyer* 7 (1961) 221.

6. E.g., the question of whether More was admitted to Doctors' Commons: compare J. D. M. Derrett, 'Was Sir Thomas More a Roman Lawyer?', *Notes and Queries* 194 (1949) 203, concluding that he was not a competent civilian, with R. J. Schoeck, 'Canon Law in England on the Eve of the Reformation', *Mediaeval Studies* 25 (1963) 141, concluding that he probably was. See also F. D. Logan, 'Doctors' Commons in the Early Sixteenth Century: A Society of Many Talents', *Historical Research* 61 (1988) 151–65; P. Hogrefe, 'Sir Thomas More and Doctors' Commons', *Moreana* 14–15 (1967) 15–21, concluding, at 20, that More's 'knowledge of canon and of Roman law remains a topic for further research'.

7. Schoeck, 'Canon Law in England' 146. See also idem, 'Common Law and Canon Law in their Relation to Thomas More', in: *St. Thomas More: Action and Contemplation*, ed. R. S. Sylvester (New Haven, CT 1972) 48, describing More as 'skilled in much of the lore and technique of the civil and canon laws'.

defense of the medieval church's position. Sometimes it was. However, in most of the controversial literature, defenders of the Catholic position relied on other witnesses. In fact the canon law was sometimes used by the Reformers themselves—positively as well as negatively—in making arguments for the Protestant position.

Moreover, it is essential to remember that the Reformation did not sweep away the canon law from English law and life. Stripped of its specifically papal aspects, the canon law remained an important source of law and practice in the English ecclesiastical courts and in some of the prerogative courts, as it did in many Protestant lands on the Continent.[8] It is equally important to recall that many European regimes that remained committed to the papacy did not necessarily admit the validity of the canon law on jurisdictional matters that had long been points of contention between the courts of church and state. It is therefore a mistake to inject the question of the worth of the canon law into most controversies between Catholic and Protestant, or even into early disputes, like the Hunne affair, between the clergy and the laity.[9] This is an area where, if we are to judge aright, we are obliged to address, and indeed to stick to, technical questions of law. One cannot assume that attachment to the old religion necessarily carried with it an admiration for the contents of the canon law. Nor can one assume that attachment to the new always carried with it a rejection of the canon law.

More's Knowledge of Canon Law

The first question requires estimating how much More knew of the canon law. We can only judge by his writings, but the splendid modern edition of *The Complete Works of St. Thomas More* permits a fuller exploration than was previously possible.[10] In one's first steps, however, it can be the source of consternation. Chapter 40 of *The Apology* in the *Complete Works* contains a reference to 'Extravagant. de hereticis ca. Ad abolendam'.[11] This is almost the only reference to a specific canon to be found in *The Apology*, and it is obviously a reference to the decree of Pope Lucius III defining procedures to be used against suspected heretics and requiring lay rulers to assist in implementing the

---

8. Evidence in support of this point is presented in R. H. Helmholz, *Roman Canon Law in Reformation England* (Cambridge 1990) and in U. Walter, 'Die Fortgeltung des kanonischen Rechts und die Haltung der protestantischen Juristen zum kanonischen Recht in Deutschland bis in die Mitte des 18. Jahrhunderts', in: *Canon Law in Protestant Lands*, ed. R. H. Helmholz (Berlin 1992) 13–47.

9. On this famous incident, see Richard J. Schoeck, 'Common Law and Canon Law in the Writings of Thomas More: The Affair of Richard Hunne', Proc. Strasbourg (MIC C.4; 1971) 237–54; and S. F. C. Milsom, 'Richard Hunne's Praemunire', *English Historical Review* 76 (1961) 80–82.

10. The *Yale Edition of the Complete Works of St. Thomas More* (New Haven, CT 1963–) (abbreviated below as CW).

11. CW IX: 131.

procedures. The difficulty is that the quoted passage in *The Complete Works* identifies it as coming from the *Extravagantes*, the final book of the *Corpus iuris canonici*, which contained decrees of popes and councils after the Clementines were issued in 1318.[12] This is a mistake. *Ad abolendam* is the ninth chapter of the seventh title of the fifth book of the *Decretales Gregorii IX*. It is not from the *Extravagantes* at all. No author familiar with the canon law would have made this mistake. The 1557 edition, however, also contains the same error.[13] It suggests, therefore, a lack of familiarity with the canonical sources on More's part.

It may be, however, that the error was not actually More's. The common way of referring to the Decretals of Gregory IX at the time was *'Ext'* or *'Ex'*. This stood for *Liber extra*, meaning originally that it stood outside the *Decretum Gratiani*, the earlier and first half of the classical canon law. This abbreviation long continued to be used and was the most common form of citation in the sixteenth century. It is quite possible, indeed likely, that More's printer extended this abbreviation wrongly, and that the Yale edition has perpetuated the error. Similar mistakes are not repeated in most of the references to canonical texts in the places they appear in other of More's works. They get the citation form right. Why a mistake here, but not there? There is unfortunately no original manuscript of *The Apology* to yield a definitive answer, and a few minor mistakes in citation found in More's controversial works make one hesitate.[14] However, overall the balance of probabilities stands in favor of More's first having used the correct form.

Certainly that is the conclusion that best fits with examination of the other relevant works. At several places in them, More made effective and professional use of Gratian's *Decretum*, including the *Glossa ordinaria* that was all but necessary to understand the text's contemporary meaning.[15] He cited texts from the Gregorian Decretals and the *Liber sextus* with accuracy and also entirely consistently with the habits of the civilians of the time.[16] He took note of the *Summa Rosella*, of which his opponent, Christopher St. German, had also made use.[17] More seems at least to have examined carefully the contents of some of its pages, although he professed to find the *Summa* 'hard to un-

---

12. The textual tradition of this collection, or rather collections, is not straightforward; see J. Brown, 'The *Extravagantes communes* and Its Medieval Predecessors', in: *A Distinct Voice: Medieval Studies in Honor of Leonard E. Boyle, O.P.* (Notre Dame, IN 1997) 373–436.

13. *The Workes of Sir Thomas More, Knyght, Sometyme Lorde Chancellour of England, Written by Him in the Englysh Tonge* (London 1557) 908.

14. E.g., *Dialogue Concerning Heresies*, CW VI: 1.431. He cited a text from the *Decretum* as coming from C.22 q.5, when C.24 q.3 would be right.

15. *Confutation of Tyndale's Answer*, CW VIII: 2.917, a reference to C.24 q.1 c.9, and the *Glossa ordinaria* accompanying it. Another example: *The Answer to a Poisoned Book*, CW XI: 117, a reference to De cons. D.2 c.53.

16. E.g., *Debellation*, CW X: 146, a reference to VI 5.2.8 §3; ibid. 117, a reference to X 5.7.13.

17. *Debellation*, CW X: 83.

derstand'.[18] He made reference to the fifteenth-century canonist William Lyndwood, author of the *Provinciale*, the authoritative work on the English provincial constitutions.[19] He even made a joke—a pretty good joke—in his letter to Dorp by referring to an imaginary *Directorium concubinariorum*, or a 'Directory for keepers of concubines'.[20] This indicates at least a nodding familiarity with the literature of the *ius commune*.

More's work gives other evidence of his familiarity with substantive provisions of the canon law. He gave, for instance, an accurate and approving account of a papal decretal that treated a person suspected of heresy as worthy of condemnation for the crime if he had remained excommunicate for more than one year.[21] He had a good understanding of the nature and uses of canonical purgation, the method of testing the innocence of persons publicly suspected of having committed a crime.[22] And he made use at several points of language that seems to have been lifted from the *ius commune*—for instance, *adminicula probationis*, full proof, and the like.[23]

That More had some knowledge of the canon law is also demonstrated by one of his Latin letters composed in 1519.[24] His correspondent had asserted that Latin texts were generally more reliable than Greek texts, citing St. Jerome for the proposition. More wrote, 'I began to recall, as if through a fog, that I had once read something of the sort in the book of pontifical decrees. I took up the book, hoping to find that you were mistaken'. He found the passage all right, but on consulting it, More found that its words and the accompanying gloss actually confirmed his correspondent's view. Only when he looked for and found the original of Jerome's writing was his own view—that Jerome could never have written such foolishness—fully vindicated. The occasion does not show that More admired the work of canonists. If anything, it shows the reverse. But it does prove that he had read in the canon law already before 1519, that he remembered what he had read, and that he could use the texts and ordinary gloss with tolerable skill when he had the occasion.

Somewhat similar in character, if not in result, is one of his most effective sallies in More's *Dialogue Concerning Heresies*. It depended upon knowledge of the canon law.

---

18. *The Apology*, CW IX: 146.

19. *Dialogue Concerning Heresies*, CW VI: 1.316; *Dialogue Concerning Tyndale*, in: *The English Works of Sir Thomas More* 2, ed. W. E. Campbell and A. W. Reed (London 1931) 231.

20. *Letter to Dorp*, CW XV: 52–53.

21. X 5.7.13 §3; *Debellation*, CW X: 118.

22. *Debellation*, CW X: 112–13.

23. *Debellation*, CW X: 108; *Dialogue Concerning Heresies*, CW VI: 1.327.

24. *Letter to a Monk*, CW XV: 254–57; the editors have translated 'in codice decretorum pontificiorum' as 'in the book of pontifical decretals'. I think, as the notes to the volume show the editors themselves do (ibid. 582–83), that the reference must refer to the *Decretum* by Gratian (D.9 c.6), not the Decretals of Pope Gregory IX and have therefore changed the translation slightly.

His opponent had cited a canon in Gratian's *Decretum*, taken originally from the work of Gregory the Great, which apparently prohibited the veneration of images (De cons. D.3 c.27). More replied that no lawyer would look at this text in isolation. He must have regard for the gloss to the text and also for the next following canons in the *Decretum*.[25] They would show clearly that the church had not forbidden the veneration of images; it merely showed that one must not worship them as if they were God. Images served the legitimate purpose of reminding us of the saints who had gone before. In other words, More showed that a fuller understanding of the canon law undermined a conclusion drawn from a superficial reading of one of its texts. Of course, he also went on (as in the case just mentioned) to take down from the shelf the full text of Gregory the Great in order to cement the point. But it is the citation to the *Glossa ordinaria* that gives his account its bite. More knew, as did all canonists of the time, that one should not draw conclusions from a text from the *Decretum* or the Decretals without consulting the Ordinary gloss.

On the other hand, More's use of the canon law was relatively infrequent, at least compared to the number of times he *could* have made use of it, and it was also relatively shallow. His opponent and fellow common lawyer, Christopher St. German, referred to the canonical texts and also to the *Summa Rosella* and the *Summa Angelica* with greater regularity than did More. However, neither man went much beyond the texts, the *Glossa ordinaria*, and these two relatively elementary manuals of the canon law. My search uncovered no references to the works of the canonists and civilians whose treatises were the real foundation for learning in the *ius commune*. Hostiensis, Innocent IV, Panormitanus, Bartolus, Joannes Andreae, Antonius de Butrio do not figure in the controversial works of either man, or indeed elsewhere in More's writings. Recall that More himself said that he had not turned the pages of the works of the doctors of the law. A survey suggests that he was telling the truth. He made no systematic use of these sophisticated treatises, although he had become familiar enough with the basic law of the *Corpus iuris canonici* so that he could cite it and use it in formulating his own arguments.

There is just one more point to report; it is relevant because of Professor Derrett's assessment that More knew little about canon law but relatively more about Roman law. I did not find this to be true in the controversial writings or other works by More. There were points where the Roman law would have been relevant to his arguments, although somewhat fewer than the canon law. However, More did not refer to civilian sources at these points. For example, in endorsing the punishment of religious dissent,

25. CW VI: 1.356–58.

he took no notice of the Roman law, though it contained many relevant texts, and his attacks on scholasticism made no mention of the civilian commentators, though they would have been a good target for him.[26] Why he chose not to take the opportunity is not altogether easy to say, but it nonetheless seems to be the fact that in his written works More used the canon law to a greater extent than he did the Roman law.

Sources of More's Knowledge of the Canon Law

The second topic is the source of More's knowledge. How did he, a common lawyer, learn anything about the canon law? This can be the briefest section of this paper. Indeed there is virtually nothing to be said that is not guesswork. We simply do not know where he acquired the knowledge he had. Nonetheless, for two reasons the question should not be left in silence. The first is that there were in fact numerous ways in which More could have picked up some canon law, and it is worth knowing this. Considering them makes believable the fact of his knowledge. Second, More was not untypical of common lawyers as a class in having found a way to learn something about the *ius commune*. Training in English common law did not exclude some familiarity with the Roman and canon laws. More's kind of knowledge is a good example of a broader phenomenon among English lawyers.

A review of the course of his life reveals several opportunities where he might have come into contact with the canon law, quite apart from the familiarity available to most English men and women arising from the ubiquity of the church's tribunals. As a boy, More served in the household of Thomas Morton, archbishop of Canterbury. Morton was himself a civilian, and More might well have heard something about the church's laws during that time. He was a student at Oxford, where both Roman and canon law were taught, and although he does not seem to have been involved with the law faculty, he might have learned its rudiments while a student. He also took part in official visits to the Continent, stopping at the Universities of Paris and Louvain, where he turned out to have more leisure than had been expected. It is certainly possible that during these interludes he read himself into the subject. In 1514 More became a member of Doctors' Commons, the center of the study of the *ius commune* in London, and this too would have been an appropriate venue for acquiring some familiarity with the canon law.[27]

It is difficult to see any way to choose from among these possibilities for learning.

---

26. *Debellation*, CW X: 23–27; *Letter to Dorp*, CW XV: 2–127.

27. But see K. R. Massingham, 'Thomas More, "Laicus" gent', *Moreana* 87–88 (1985) 29–35, concluding that the most probable reason for More to have entered Doctors' Commons was his desire to enter royal service; see also Hogrefe, 'Sir Thomas More'.

Beyond telling us in the *Debellation* that he himself knew many of the judges in the ecclesiastical courts, More himself wrote nothing about the question.[28] Why should he? It was a becomingly modest act to minimize the extent of his learning, and he was not wrong to do so. His familiarity was not great, and it was, moreover, not exceptional. Many English common lawyers knew something about the *ius commune*—not normally very much, but something.[29] An educated lawyer like More, interested in ecclesiastical matters and (if R. W. Chambers is right) accustomed to sleeping only four hours a night, was likely to have acquired some familiarity with the canon law.[30] This informal style of learning would have given him all the more reason for not claiming any real expertise.

More's Attitude to the Canon Law

The third question is More's attitude towards the canon law. The picture is not altogether simple. It contains what look like internal contradictions. Only a three-faceted depiction does justice to the complexity of More's view of the canon law.

His Defense of the Canon Law

In one sense, More was a vigorous defender of the existing canon law. He wielded a sword against critics of the church's laws, and he applauded the canon law's part in putting Protestant martyrs to death. Defenses of the canon law appear at various places in More's writing. The canon law was not the subject of any sustained treatment in his works, but the point is made evident enough by its recurrence. In the *Responsio ad Lutherum*, for example, he reproved the madness of the German reformer in casting the papal lawbooks into the fire.[31] In the *Apology*, he spoke approvingly of the canon law as characterized by 'charity with justice' and as constituting the 'common laws of all Christ's Catholic Church'.[32] Against Christopher St. German, he defended at length the canon law's *ex officio* oath and the procedures accompanying it, procedures he rightly discussed as typical of, and indeed essential to, the ordinary course of procedure in the ecclesiastical courts.[33]

Some of More's defenses of canonical rules will strike modern readers as little

---

28. CW X: 77.

29. See above note 1.

30. Cf. R. W. Chambers, *Thomas More* (London 1935, repr. 1967) 85.

31. *Responsio ad Lutherum* 1.10, CW V: 1.170; see also *A Supplication of Souls*, CW VII: 158–59.

32. CW IX: 92.

33. *Debellation*, CW X: 72–149. On the place of this controversy in More's life, see J. Guy, 'Thomas More and Christopher St German: The Battle of the Books', ed. A. Fox and J. Guy, *Reassessing the Henrician Age: Humanism, Politics and Reform 1500–1550* (Oxford 1986) 95–120.

more than debating points. For instance, St. German had said that open indictment of heretics would be better than the secret canonical procedure in which the accused did not know the names of the witnesses against him. More countered, saying that public indictment would be *better* does not prove that the canonical procedure is necessarily *bad*.[34] Perhaps this sally was a trifle too logical. On the other hand, More made several points about the canon law forcefully and effectively. His disposal of St. German's argument that the law of the church would be made more popular, and thereby stronger, if it was first weakened, is particularly telling.[35]

A good deal of the defense of the canon law found in the later controversial works does resemble the position characteristic of a man growing older in times that had changed from his youth. 'No change. No change whatever' was More's theme. Innovation inevitably meant taking a turn for the worse. Better to defend what exists than to follow the call for change into something that will almost certainly be no improvement. Indeed, at one point More himself admitted that he might not defend everything in the existing law of the church were the times less evil.[36] But, in his view, they were evil. Heretics would 'swarm in the streets' if given half a chance, and this spectre drove him to defending some of the worst features of the medieval canon law. He granted that the law sometimes punished innocent men.[37] But he wanted little change. Abandoning it because of its faults seemed a serious mistake to More.

However, More was decidedly not a defender of *all* the law found in the Decretals. For example, St. German noticed that, according to the canon law, in cases of defect of justice in the temporal courts, the courts of the church were permitted to intervene to set things right. St. German regarded this part of the canon law as a threat to the ordinary course of justice in England, as indeed it was, and he thundered against it on that account. More's response was short and effective. He would have agreed with his opponent, he wrote, but in fact he had never seen this part of the canon law implemented.[38] In England, it was pure theory. More did not make a case for its adoption.

This workaday approach, found in a number of places in More's writing, stands as a warning against making him into too much of an advocate for the independence of

34. *Debellation*, CW X: 136: '[A]ll these dyfferences and dyversyties . . . prove yet nothing that the suyte ex offico is not good, but onely at the very uttermost, that the ordre not to procede wythoute an open presentement were better'.

35. This difference of opinion is old and fundamental; see, e.g., the description of the clergy after the martyrdom of Thomas Becket written by Archbishop Baldwin of Canterbury (d. 1190) described in B. Smalley, *The Becket Conflict and the Schools* (Oxford 1973) 216–20.

36. *The Apology*, CW IX: 96, where More wrote, '[A]lbe it that in place and tyme convenyent I wolde gyve myne advyce and counsayle to the chaunge, yet to put out bookes in wrytynge abrode amonge the people agaynste them, that wold I neyther do my selfe, nor in the so doynge commende any man that doth'.

37. *Debellation*, CW X: 228–29.

38. *Debellation*, CW X: 209–10. Another example: *The Supplication of Souls*, CW VII: 130–32.

the church and its law.[39] More was an experienced lawyer. He knew that the English Parliament and the common law courts had never admitted canonical jurisdiction to operate with the independence some of the canonical texts claimed for it. He did not advocate any change in this situation. The English Statutes of *Praemunire* were threats to the freedom of the church, punishing anyone who invoked papal jurisdiction to upset the decisions of the royal courts, but these statutes had been passed in the fourteenth century. They were old. They were an accepted part of the legal landscape by the time of More's controversial works, and he accepted their validity.[40] Similarly, the exercise of jurisdiction over clerics in civil cases was a clear violation of the canonical *privilegium fori*. However, it had a long history by the 1530s, and More noted confidently that it was an everyday occurrence for clerics to be parties to litigation in the royal courts.[41] His writings contain no suggestion that this long-tolerated situation in English law should be overturned because it was unlawful under the canon law. Indeed More asserted that the English clergy had acquiesced in the situation. That itself was a measure of its rightness.

His Ready Reference to the Canon Law

More's attitude towards the canon law was shaped by the character of his knowledge of its basic tenets. He was familiar with Gratian's *Decretum* and the other principal books of the canon law—the Decretals and the *Liber sextus* in particular. He knew enough about them to call upon them when they served his purposes. At the same time, he made much less frequent use of other literature from the *ius commune*. More rarely, he incorporated contemporary manuals or treatises on the *ius commune* into his own works.

The range of subjects covered by the canonical texts was impressively wide, and More had a general familiarity with their coverage. He looked to the texts from time to time. For instance, his discussion of the role of custom in mitigating the strictness of the laws at least appears to have been influenced by the canon law. In discussing some of the laws about religious observance, he noted, 'the custom of the country may either to the bond or to the discharge and interpretation of the laws . . . do much'.[42] This was standard fare for the canonists, and More chided St. German for not recognizing

---

39. E.g., J. A. Guy, *The Public Career of Sir Thomas More* (Brighton 1980) 154: 'More could not have stomached . . . that Parliament had the power to correct clerical abuses and prune canon law in the interests of national unity'; R. J. Schoeck, 'Common Law and Canon Law in their Relation to Thomas More', in: *St. Thomas More: Action and Contemplation* 48: 'More's death resulted directly from his belief that no lay ruler could have jurisdiction over the church of Christ'.

40. E.g., *The Supplication of Souls*, CW VII: 132–34. See also *Debellation*, CW X: 187.

41. *Debellation*, CW X: 195.

42. *The Apology*, CW IX: 106.

this feature of the canonical system. Most prominently, More learned about the legal treatment of heresy from the study of canon law, not simply from the Parliamentary statutes on the subject, and he incorporated the former into his writing. Speaking for myself, I must say that I find his comparison of the procedures used by the church with those of the English common law more interesting than his citations from canonical sources, because the former were more original. But there is little doubt that he used both. More's persistent effort was to show that persons accused of heresy were treated no worse than murderers and rapists were under the common law.[43]

Two other points, probably more speculative and certainly more attractive, at which he may have made use of what he knew of the canon law come from an earlier period in his life. One arises in the *History of Richard III* and deals with the contemporary law of sanctuary. After her eldest son had been spirited away from her, the Queen fled to Westminster Abbey with the rest of her family out of fear for their safety. In the course of discussing what to do, the Duke of Buckingham delivers a peroration about the origins and the abuses that had come to characterize the law of sanctuary. The content of his speech suggests the possibility of canonical influence.

At the beginning of the sixteenth century, the law of sanctuary, which allowed persons to escape justice by taking refuge inside a church, stood badly in need of reform. Although most modern historians have treated the church as the bitterest opponent of change, in fact the law of the church was considerably more balanced on the subject than was the English common law.[44] The canon law held that asylum should not be eliminated, but that it should be confined to those most in need. For example, deliberate murders were excluded; those who had killed inadvertently were admitted. Those who used sanctuaries to sally forth, commit crimes, and then return to church were likewise excluded under the canon law; those who had committed a crime without intent to flee to sanctuary were admitted. We cannot enter into the legal complexities that attended development of the subject, but it is worth saying that many of the remarks that More put into Buckingham's mouth express the canonical position of the law of asylum. For instance, Buckingham remarks that stolen property taken into sanctuary should always be returned to the person from whom it had been taken.[45] This was the *communis opinio* among the canonists, although it was not the common law's position. What Buckingham says about thieves taking sanctuary only to plan their next crimes, stealing forth at night and returning with their ill-gotten gains—i.e. that they should in no case be able to claim the protection of the church—could also have been taken directly from a

---

43. E.g., *Debellation*, CW X: 114–22 (additional action required of defendants after successful purgation no different than some of the steps required of persons accused of crimes at common law).

44. See R. H. Helmholz, *The Ius commune in England* (Oxford and New York 2001) 16–81.

45. *History of Richard III*, CW XV: 374–75.

treatise of the *ius commune* at the time.[46] More gave no source for Buckingham's words. That would have been quite out of place in the *Historia*. But it would not be wholly surprising if the author had drawn some of Buckingham's ideas from the canon law itself.

The other example comes from the *Utopia*. In an oft-cited passage, the traveller reports that the Utopian clergy who committed crimes suffered no temporal punishment but were instead left to God and their own consciences.[47] This was read by R. W. Chambers as an endorsement of the principle of clerical immunity, stripped however of its abuses by restricting the size of the clerical order sufficiently to guarantee its quality.[48] This argument is plausible, although the canon law itself did not envision that clerical criminals should suffer no punishment whatsoever. An even better example is More's statement that the high priest in Utopia was elected by the people, and that the choice was made by secret ballot to avoid party splits.[49] It is an entirely legitimate speculation to ask whether the author might have been influenced in this by the canon law. The means of voting, and its purpose, might have been taken directly from the canon law. That is how an election *per scrutinium* was to be conducted. Moreover, as found in the ancient texts in the *Decretum*, the election of bishops was to be done *per clerum et populum*. The people had a voice. By the time the *Utopia* was composed, this ancient system had been reduced to a hollow shell by the growth of the system of papal provisions. Under the newer system, the selection of the church's leaders was removed from both the people and the clergy entitled to elect under the classical canon law, typically the cathedral chapter. If More had looked into the canon law itself, however, he would have found the older system stated as the norm. Perhaps he did. It would not have been heretical to advocate restoration of the older system, and it would have suited the position of a Christian humanist. Of course, this would make him somewhat less of a spokesman for clerical privileges than he has been portrayed in recent literature. But it would not contradict any of the specific points raised in the later controversial works.

His Indifference towards the Canon Law

Although More regarded the canon law as useful, indeed necessary for Christian society, and although he made use of it on occasion, he seems not to have been truly interested in it. One must of course make some allowance for the haste with which More's polemical literature was written. Even so, it contains few signs that the subject appealed to him. Except occasionally, and then not very deeply, he had no desire to explore the

---

46. E.g., Prosper Farinacius, *De immunitate ecclesiarum et confugientibus ad eas* (Lyons 1621) c. 16, containing a discussion of these issues. The exception was based upon a decretal of Pope Gregory IX (X 3.49.10).

47. *Utopia*, CW IV: 228–29.

48. See R. W. Chambers, *Thomas More* (Ann Arbor, MI 1958) 133–34.

49. *Utopia*, CW IV: 226–27.

resources of the European *ius commune*. He could use it, at least on a basic level, but it did not intrigue him enough to look much further. Indeed, in some respects it appears that he was not particularly interested in English common law either, although it was the source of his professional career and he obviously knew a great deal about it.[50] Even with the common law, he rarely devoted the attention to detail or evinced an interest in unresolved or difficult problems that is the mark of an ardent lawyer. It was his profession, not a source of his enthusiasm. A general aversion among humanists to the fruits of scholasticism, of which the canon law and treatises from the *ius commune* are a notable example, must have been one part of More's attitude towards it.[51]

There are several strong and specific indications in his writing of a lack of real interest in the subject. First, he says so himself. The *Summa Rosella*, for instance, he described as 'so strange a book to find and so hard to understand that few men have meddled with it before'.[52] He also remarked that he had not himself turned over any of the books of the Continental jurists. Second, when he cited the canon law, he did not go much beyond the texts and the *Glossa ordinaria* of the canon law, though it would not have been difficult for him to do so. The works of the most familiar canonists were organized to follow the texts of the Decretals; they are relatively easy to consult and use once one becomes familiar with the organization of the basic work. If any reader of the texts wants to achieve a real understanding of the canon law, those commentaries beckon. But More did not wish to follow. Third, often he did not use the canon law even when its use would have been entirely appropriate. This is most obvious in his answer to St. German, who had raised a number of interesting points about ecclesiastical jurisdiction. With few exceptions, More declined the challenge to debate these points, except as to the canon law relating to heresy. About the *ex officio* oath, More wrote, 'I will no further speak at this time than concerning the crime of heresy'.[53] Use of the *ex officio* oath in contemporary practice raised important legal points of law and policy, many of which were discussed at length by the canonists. Prosecutions for many offenses, many involving sexual relations, were quite frequent occurrences in Tudor England. They raised relevant points of conflict and contrast with the common law. They would become matters of legal controversy. However, More chose not to explore the subject himself.

---

50. See M. Hastings, 'Sir Thomas More: Maker of English Law?', in: *Essential Articles for the Study of Thomas More*, ed. R. S. Sylvester and G. P. Marc'hadour (Hamden 1977) 104–18, finding the attempt to describe his accomplishments as a lawyer to be 'elusive'. This also seems to have been the view of Sir Geoffrey Elton; see his 'Thomas More, Councillor', in: *St. Thomas More: Action and Contemplation* 87–122. There is much useful information about More's work as a judge in J. A. Guy, *The Public Career*.

51. See C. Thompson, 'The Humanism of More Reappraised', *Thought* 52 (1977) 231–48; see also *Letter to Dorp*, CW XV: 22–35, for an example of More's attitude towards scholasticism.

52. *The Apology*, CW IX: 146.   53. *The Apology*, CW IX: 130.

What did interest More was heresy—the extirpation of heresy. A very large part of the references to the canon law found in his work relate to the canon law on this subject. About the Protestant John Frith, More suggested the likelihood that 'Christ will kindle a fire of faggots for him . . . and send his soul for ever into the fire of Hell'.[54] To me at least, it seems blasphemous to suppose that Jesus Christ would himself light the fire in which such a man as Frith was meant to die. But this is not an opinion More shared. And it is undeniable that the canon law of the time was closer to More's opinion than to mine.

The subject of heresy was, it seems, the sole regular occasion for More's excursions into the canon law. Exceptions exist, it is true. At places in More's work, he makes other use of the law of the church, almost always with accuracy, and there is little doubt that he wished to see the canon law continued in force as a general matter. But beyond his special interest in the canon law as the proper instrument for repressing heresy, it was not a subject that engaged his enthusiasm, or even much of his attention.

Conclusion

More's attitude towards the canon law thus includes more than a single point of view. He knew something about it, and he made use of what he knew. Yet at the same time he had neither real affection for it nor any sustained interest in its details. His attitude was that of a humanist, impatient with the scholastic method and the intricacies of the *ius commune*. One cannot go very far with the canon law without some patience with, if not indeed a liking for, the distinctions and arguments characteristic of scholasticism. That is true today, and it was true in 1500. On this reading, More did not have either that patience or that liking. Perhaps there is some contradiction in this conclusion, since More was a defender of the canon law. But many people have less than harmonious opinions about things that matter, and in the early sixteenth century, the canon law was one of the things that mattered.

54. *The Apology*, CW IX: 122. See also ibid. 113, discussing three 'apostates', Hytton, Blomfeld, and Bayfield, who were in his opinion 'well and worthely burned in Smythfeld'.

Bibliography of Kenneth Pennington's
Published Works

❋

1970   'Bartolomé de Las Casas and the Tradition of Medieval Law', *Church History* 39, 149–61.

      'A "Consilium" of Johannes Teutonicus', *Traditio* 26, 435–40.

1971   '*Summae* on Raymond de Pennafort's *Summa de casibus* in the Bayerische Staatsbibliothek, Munich', *Traditio* 27, 471–80.

1973   'The *Libellus* of Telesphorus and the Decretals of Gregory IX', *Courier of the Syracuse University Library* 11, 17–26.

1974   'The Rite for Taking the Cross in the Twelfth Century', *Traditio* 30, 429–35.

      'The Legal Education of Pope Innocent III', BMCL 4, 70–77.

      'The Manuscripts of Johannes Teutonicus' Apparatus to *Compilatio tertia*: Some Considerations on the Stemma', BMCL 4, 17–31.

1975   'The French Recension of *Compilatio tertia*', BMCL 5, 53–71.

1976   'Pluralism and the Canonists in the Thirteenth Century', *Speculum* 51, 35–48.

      Review of: Monaco, M. *Il De officio collectoris in regno Angliae*, in: *Speculum* 51, 338–40.

      Review of: Russell, J. *The Just War in the Middle Ages*, in: *Canadian Journal of History* 11, 367–70.

1977   Edited with R. Somerville: *Law, Church and Society: Essays in Honor of Stephan Kuttner* (The Middle Ages; Philadelphia, PA).

      'A Note to Decameron 6.7: The Wit of Madonna Filippa', *Speculum* 52, 902–5.

      'Pope Innocent III's Views on Church and State: A Gloss to *Per venerabilem*', in: *Law, Church and Society* 49–67.

      '*Cum causam que:* A Decretal of Innocent III', BMCL 7, 100–103.

      Review of: Ullmann, W. *Law and Politics in the Middle Ages*, in: *Speculum* 52, 752.

      Review of: Boockmann, H. *Johannes Falkenberg, der Deutsche Orden und die polnische Politik*, in: *Speculum* 52, 925–26.

1978   '*Pro peccatis patrum puniri:* A Moral and Legal Problem of the Inquisition', *Church History* 47, 137–54.

1979   Review of: Beumann, H. *Sigebert von Gembloux und der Traktat De investitura episcoporum,* in: *Speculum* 54, 545–46.

1980   Edited with S. Kuttner: *Proceedings of the Fifth International Congress of Medieval Canon Law, Salamanca 1976* (MIC C.6; Vatican City).

'The Making of a Decretal Collection: The Genesis of *Compilatio tertia',* in: Proc. Salamanca (MIC C.6; Vatican City) 67–92.

Review of: Schubert, E. *König und Reich,* in: *American Historical Review* 85, 1185–86.

1981   Edited: *Johannis Teutonici Apparatus glossarum in Compilationem tertiam* (MIC A.3.1; Vatican City).
    Reviewed by: R. Weigand, in: *Historische Zeitschrift* 236 (1983) 437–38; J. Tarrant, in: *Speculum* 60 (1985) 985–87; C. Donahue, Jr., in: *American Journal of Legal History* 30 (1986) 79–85.

'Bischof', LMA 2, 228–33.

'Bistum', LMA 2, 251–53.

Review of: Marcus, M. *An Allegory of Form,* in: *Speculum* 56, 890.

1982   Review of: Muldoon, J. *Popes, Lawyers, and Infidels,* in: *Catholic Historical Review* 68, 300–302.

Review of: Horst, U. *Die Kanonensammlung des Polycarpus,* in: *Speculum* 57, 190.

Review of: *Authority and Power,* ed. B. Tierney and P. Linehan, in: ZRG Kan. Abt. 68, 483–87.

1983   'Johannes Teutonicus and Papal Legates', AHP 21, 183–94.

'The Epitaph of Johannes Teutonicus', BMCL 13, 61–62.

'Codex Theodosianus', *Dictionary of the Middle Ages* 3, 475.

'Corpus iuris civilis', *Dictionary of the Middle Ages* 3, 608–10.

Review of: Laufs, A. *Politik und Recht,* in: ZRG Kan. Abt. 69, 409–12.

1984   *Pope and Bishops: The Papal Monarchy in the Twelfth and Thirteenth Centuries* (The Middle Ages; Philadelphia, PA).
    Reviewed by: R. Helmholz, in: *Speculum* 60 (1985) 1011–13; J. Canning, in: *Journal of Ecclesiastical History* 36 (1985) 123–25; C. Morris, in: *Journal of Theological Studies* 36 (1985) 516–20; R. Weigand, in: AKKR 154 (1985) 391–95; L. Schmugge, in: *Historische Zeitschrift* 242 (1986) 678–81; J. Sayers, in: ZRG Kan. Abt. 72 (1986) 428–34; A. García y García, in: REDC 43 (1986) 298–300; J. Watt, in: *Catholic Historical Review* 73 (1987) 305–6.

Review of: Hilpert, H. *Kaiser- und Papstbriefe in den Chronica majora des Matthaeus Paris,* in: *Speculum* 59, 159–60.

1985   Edited with S. Kuttner: *Proceedings of the Sixth International Congress of Medieval Canon Law, Berkeley 1980* (MIC C.7; Vatican City).

'Gratian', *Dictionary of the Middle Ages* 5, 656–58.

'Huguccio', *Dictionary of the Middle Ages* 6, 327–28.

Review of: Wettengel, M. *Der Streit um die Vogtei Kelkheim, 1275–1276*, in: *Speculum* 58 (1983) 856–57.

Review of: Berman, H. *Law and Revolution*, in: *American Journal of Comparative Law* 33, 546–48.

Review of: Imkamp, W. *Das Kirchenbild Innocenz' III.*, in: *Journal of Ecclesiastical History* 36, 653–55.

Review of: Kuttner, S. *Gratian and the Schools of Law (1140–1234)*, in: *American Journal of Legal History* 29, 271–72.

Review of: Ziese, J. *Wibert von Ravenna*, in: *American Historical Review* 90, 1175–76.

1986 '*Epistolae Alexandrinae:* A Collection of Pope Alexander III's Letters', in: *Miscellanea Rolando Bandinelli, Papa Alessandro III*, ed. F. Liotta (Accademia senese degli Intronati; Siena) 337–53.

'A "Quaestio" of Henricus de Segusio and the Textual Tradition of His "Summa super decretalibus",' BMCL 16, 91–96.

'Johannes Teutonicus', *Dictionary of the Middle Ages* 7, 121–22.

'Laurentius Hispanus', *Dictionary of the Middle Ages* 7, 385–86.

'Law Codes: 1000–1500', *Dictionary of the Middle Ages* 7, 425–31.

'Law, Procedure of: 1000–1500', *Dictionary of the Middle Ages* 7, 502–6.

Review of: Imkamp, W. *Das Kirchenbild Innocenz' III.*, in: ZRG Kan. Abt. 72, 417–28.

Review of: Landi, A. *Il papa deposto, Pisa 1409*, in: *American Historical Review* 91, 1181–82.

Review of: Black, A. *Guilds and Civil Society in European Political Thought from the Twelfth Century to the Present*, in: DA 42, 707–8.

Review of: Oakley, F. *Omnipotence, Covenant, and Order*, in: DA 42, 737–38.

Review of: Davis, C. *Dante's Italy, and Other Essays*, in: DA 42, 741–42.

1987 'An Earlier Recension of Hostiensis's *Lectura* on the Decretals', BMCL 17, 77–90.

'Innocent III', *The Encyclopedia of Religion* 7, 248–50.

'Maxims, Legal', *Dictionary of the Middle Ages* 8, 231–32.

'Petri Exceptiones', *Dictionary of the Middle Ages* 9, 544.

Review of: Sayers, J. *Pope Honorius III and England*, in: *Catholic Historical Review* 73, 317–18.

Review of: Laudage, J. *Priesterbild und Reformpapsttum im 11. Jahrhundert*, in: *Speculum* 62, 695–96.

Review of: Mordek, H. *Aus Kirche und Reich*, in: ZRG Kan. Abt. 73, 363–69.

Review of: Maleczek, W. *Papst und Kardinalskolleg von 1191–1216*, in: ZRG Kan. Abt. 73, 381–84.

Review of: Sturm-Maddox, S. *Petrarch's Metamorphoses*, in: *Speculum* 62, 996–98.

Review of: Ferruolo, S. *The Origins of the University*, in: DA 43, 342–43.

1988 'Law, Legislative Authority, and Theories of Government, 1150–1300', in: *The Cambridge History of Medieval Political Thought c.350–c.1450*, ed. J. Burns (Cambridge)

424–53; trans. J. Ménard, *Histoire de la pensée politique médiévale 350–1450* (Paris 1993) 428–49.

'Johannes Andreae's *Additiones* to the Decretals of Gregory IX', ZRG Kan. Abt. 74, 328–47.

'The *Consilia* of Baldus de Ubaldis', TRG 56, 85–92.

'Panormitanus's *Lectura* on the Decretals of Gregory IX', in: *Fälschungen im Mittelalter: Internationaler Kongreß der Monumenta Germaniae Historica München, 16.–19. September 1986: Gefälschte Rechtstexte: Der bestrafte Fälscher* (MGH Schriften 33.2; Hannover) 363–73.

'Vincentius Hispanus', *Dictionary of the Middle Ages* 12, 455–56.

Review of: Vodola, E. *Excommunication in the Middle Ages*, in: *Speculum* 63, 242–44.

Review of: Migliorino, F. *Fama e infamia*, in: *American Historical Review* 93, 131.

Review of: Bartlett, R. *Trial by Fire and Water*, in: *Journal of Ecclesiastical History* 39, 263–66.

Review of: *Akten des 26. Deutschen Rechtshistorikertages*, ed. D. Simon, in: DA 44, 657.

1989   'Gregory IX, Emperor Frederick II, and the Constitutions of Melfi', in: *Popes, Teachers and Canon Law in the Middle Ages: Festschrift for Brian Tierney*, ed. S. Chodorow and J. Sweeney (Ithaca, NY, and London) 53–61.

Review of: Opll, F. *Stadt und Reich im 12. Jahrhundert (1125–1190)*, in: *American Historical Review* 94, 113–114.

Review of: Stürner, W. *Peccatum und Potestas*, in: *American Historical Review* 94, 737.

Review of: Strömholm, S. *A Short History of Legal Thinking in the West*, in: DA 45, 282.

Review of: Quaritsch, H. *Souveränität*, in: DA 45, 283–84.

Review of: Canning, J. *The Political Thought of Baldus de Ubaldis*, in: DA 45, 289.

1990   'Lotharius of Cremona', BMCL 20, 43–50; reprinted in: *Miscellanea Domenico Maffei dedicata: Historia—Ius—Studium*, ed. A. García y García and P. Weimar (Goldbach) 1, 231–38.

Review of: Bellomo, M. *Scuole, diritto e società*, in: *American Historical Review* 95, 480–81.

Review of: *Proceedings of the Seventh International Congress of Medieval Canon Law, Cambridge 1984*, ed. P. Linehan, in: *Journal of Ecclesiastical History* 41, 297–99.

Review of: Blumenthal, U. *The Investiture Controversy*, in: *Catholic Historical Review* 76, 342.

Review of: Heft, J. *John XXII and Papal Teaching Authority*, in: DA 46, 268.

Review of: Godding, P. *Le droit privé dans les Pays-Bas méridionaux*, in: DA 46, 674.

1991   'Il diritto dell'accusato: L'origine medievale del regolare procedimento legale', in: *La parola all'accusato*, ed. J.-C. Vigueur and A. Paravicini Bagliani (Palermo) 33–41.

Review of: Bellomo, M. *L'Europa del diritto comune*, in: *American Historical Review* 96, 1189.

Review of: Meduna, B. *Studien zum Formular der päpstlichen Justizbriefe*, in: *Catholic Historical Review* 77, 678–79.

1992   'Henry VII and Robert of Naples', in: *Das Publikum politischer Theorie im 14. Jahrhundert*, ed. J. Miethke and A. Bühler (Schriften des Historischen Kollegs, Kolloquien 21; München) 81–92.

'The Authority of the Prince in a *Consilium* of Baldus de Ubaldis', in: *Studia in honorem Eminentissimi Cardinalis Alfonsi M. Stickler*, ed. R. I. Card. Castillo Lara (Studia et Textus Historiae Iuris Canonici 7; Roma) 483–515.

'Medieval Law', in: *Medieval Studies: An Introduction*, ed. J. Powell (2nd ed.; Syracuse, NY) 333–52.

Review of: Melloni, A. *Innocenzo IV*, in: *Journal of Ecclesiastical History* 43, 147.

Review of: Borgolte, M. *Petrusnachfolge und Kaiserimitation*. in: *American Historical Review* 97, 823.

Review of: Belloni, A. *Le questioni civilistiche del secolo XII*, in: *Speculum* 67, 931–33.

1993   *The Prince and the Law, 1200–1600: Sovereignty and Rights in the Western Legal Tradition* (Berkeley, Los Angeles, and London).
     Reviewed by: B. Lyon, in: *Manuscripta* 37 (1993) 208–10; G. Leff, in: *The Times Literary Supplement*, January 14 (1994) 24; C. Reid, in: *Michigan Law Review* 92 (1994) 1646–74; J. Burns, in: *Journal of Ecclesiastical History* 45 (1994) 499–500; R. Warnicke, in: *Renaissance Quarterly* 47 (1994) 390–91; J. Lynch, in: *Medievalia et Humanistica* 21 (1994) 194–96; R. Figueira, in: *Speculum* 70 (1995) 667–71; F. Oakley, in: *American Historical Review* 100 (1995) 886; K. Nörr, in: ZRG Kan. Abt. 81 (1995) 464–68: M. Keen, in: EHR 111 (1996) 441–43; R. van Answaarden, in: *Journal of Modern History* 69 (1997) 812–13; J. Miethke, in: DA 53 (1997) 735–36.

Popes, Canonists, and Texts 1150–1550 (Collected Studies Series 412; Aldershot).
     Reviewed by: J. Gaudemet, in: RHDFE 72 (1994) 65–66; A. García y García, in: REDC 51 (1994) 886–87.

'Stephan Kuttner', in: *Der Einfluss deutscher Emigranten auf die Rechtsentwicklung in den USA und in Deutschland: Vorträge und Referate des Bonner Symposions im September 1991*, ed. M. Lutter, E. Stiefel, and M. Hoeflich (Tübingen) 361–64.

'Enrico da Susa, detto l'Ostiense (Hostiensis, Henricus de Segusio o Segusia)', DBI 42, 758–63; English version, 'Henricus de Segusio (Hostiensis)', in: idem, *Popes, Canonists, and Texts*, article XVI.

Review of: Fell, A. *Origins of Legislative Sovereignty and the Legislative State* 4, in: *American Historical Review* 98, 153–54.

Review of: Georgi, W. *Friedrich Barbarossa und die auswärtigen Mächte*, in: *International History Review* 15, 144–45.

Review of: *The Church and Sovereignty, c. 590–1918*, ed. D. Wood, in: *Catholic Historical Review* 79, 719–20.

Review of: Danusso, C. *Ricerche sulla Lectura feudorum di Baldo degli Ubaldi*, in: DA 49, 348.

1994   'Learned Law, Droit Savant, Gelehrtes Recht: The Tyranny of a Concept', RIDC 5, 197–209; reprinted in: *Syracuse Journal of International Law and Commerce* 20, 205–15.

'The Pazzi Conspiracy and the Jurists', in: *Cristianità ed Europa: Miscellanea di studi in onore di Luigi Prosdocimi*, ed. C. Alzati (Roma, Freiburg, and Wien) 1.2, 635–48.

The World Book Encyclopedia (Chicago, IL): Biographies of Popes Adrian IV, Alexander III, Boniface VIII, Clement VII, Eugene III, Gregory VII, Gregory IX, Gregory X, Honorius III, Innocent III, Innocent IV, John XXII, John XXIII, Leo IX, Martin V, Urban VI.

Review of: Schmidt, T. *Der Bonifaz-Prozeß*, in: *Historische Zeitschrift* 258, 167–68.

Review of: Landau, P. *Officium und Libertas christiana*, in: *Journal of Ecclesiastical History* 45, 170–71.

Review of: Scholz, S. *Transmigration und Translation*, in: *Journal of Ecclesiastical History* 45, 486–89.

Review of: Glöckner, H. *Cogitationis poenam nemo patitur*, in: *Cristianesimo nella storia* 15, 689–92.

Review of: *Diritto canonico e comparazione*, ed. A. Bertolino et al., in: DA 50, 737.

1995   *The American Historical Association's Guide to Historical Literature* (3rd ed.; New York and Oxford): entries for Section 20, 'Medieval Europe: Church and Intellectual History'.

Review of: *Histoire du christianisme des origines à nos jours*, 5, ed. A. Vauchez et al., in: *Speculum* 70, 439–42.

Review of: Gaudemet, J. *La doctrine canonique médiévale*, in: *Catholic Historical Review* 71, 417–19.

Review of: *William of Ockham, A Short Discourse on the Tyrannical Government*, ed. A. McGrade and J. Kilcullen, in: *Parergon* 13, 186–89.

Review of: *Bartolomé de las Casas: The Only Way*, ed. H. Parish and F. Sullivan, in: *Journal of Church and State* 37, 907–08.

1996   'Interpretation of Privileges: Raoul of Chennevières's Repetition to *Volentes* (VI 5.7.1)', in: *De iure canonico medii aevi: Festschrift für Rudolf Weigand* (SG 27; Roma) 465–80.

'Roman and Secular Law', in: *Medieval Latin: An Introduction and Bibliographical Guide*, ed. F. Mantello and A. Rigg (Washington, DC) 254–66.

Review of: *Summa Elegantius in iure diuino seu Coloniensis* 4, ed. G. Fransen, in: *Journal of Ecclesiastical History* 47, 151.

Review of: Cohen, E. *The Crossroads of Justice*, in: *The Historian* 59, 182–83.

Review of: Migliorino, F. *In terris ecclesiae*, in: ZRG Kan. Abt. 82, 424–26.

1997   'The Spirit of Legal History', *University of Chicago Law Review* 64, 1097–1116.

'Baldus de Ubaldis', RIDC 8, 35–61.

'Allegationes, Solutiones, and Dubitationes: Baldus de Ubaldis' Revisions of his *Consilia*', in: *Die Kunst der Disputation: Probleme der Rechtsauslegung und Rechtsanwendung im 13. und 14. Jahrhundert*, ed. M. Bellomo (Schriften des Historischen Kollegs, Kolloquien 38; München) 29–72.

Review of: *Origins of Modern Freedom*, ed. R. Davis, in: EHR 112, 1031–32.

Review of: *From Personal Duties towards Personal Rights*, ed. P. Monahan, in: *Law and History Review* 15, 356–57.

1998   'The History of Rights in Western Thought', *Emory Law Journal* 47, 237–52.

'Due Process, Community, and the Prince in the Evolution of the *Ordo iudiciarius*', RIDC 9, 9–47.

Review of: Brown, P. *The Rise of Western Christendom*, in: *Speculum* 73, 816–18.

Review of: Brundage, J. *Medieval Canon Law*, in: *Journal of Ecclesiastical History* 49, 339–41.

Review of: Somerville, R. *Pope Urban II, the Collectio Britannica, and the Council of Melfi (1089)*, in: *Catholic Historical Review* 84, 735–37.

Review of: Löfstedt, B. *Gratiani Decretum: La traduction en ancien français du Décret de Gratien 3*, in: *Speculum* 74, 171–72.

1999   Review of: Fornasari, G. *Medioevo riformato del secolo XI*, in: *Speculum* 74, 164–65.

Review of: Paravicini Bagliani, A. *Il trono di Pietro*, in: *Speculum* 74, 238–40.

Review of: *Die Register Innocenz' III.: 7./8. Pontifikatsjahr (1204–05/1205–06)*, ed. O. Hageneder et al., in: ZRG Kan. Abt. 85, 577–84.

2000   'Nicholaus de Tudeschis (Panormitanus)', in: *Niccolò Tedeschi (Abbas Panormitanus) e i suoi Commentaria in Decretales*, ed. O. Condorelli (Roma) 9–36; also on CD Rom: *Nicholaus de Tudeschis (Abbas Panormitanus) Commentaria in Decretales Gregorii IX et in Clementinas Epistolas* (Edizioni Informatiche; Roma).

'Innocent III and the *Ius commune*', in: *Grundlagen des Rechts: Festschrift für Peter Landau zum 65. Geburtstag*, ed. R. Helmholz, P. Mikat, J. Müller, and M. Stolleis (Rechts- und Staatswissenschaftliche Veröffentlichungen der Görres-Gesellschaft, NF 91; Paderborn) 349–66.

'The *Ius commune*, Suretyship, and *Magna carta*', RIDC 11, 255–74.

Review of: Müller, H. *Päpstliche Delegationsgerichtsbarkeit in der Normandie*, in: *Historische Zeitschrift* 270, 746–47.

Review of: Somerville, R., and B. Brasington. *Prefaces to Canon Law Books*, in: *Journal of Ecclesiastical History* 51, 378–79.

Review of: Stroll, M. *The Medieval Abbey of Farfa*, in: *American Historical Review* 105, 262–63.

2001   Edited with S. Chodorow and K. Kendall: *Proceedings of the Tenth International Congress of Medieval Canon Law, Syracuse 1996* (MIC C.11; Vatican City).

'Innocente fino a prova contraria: Le origini di una massima giuridica', in: *A Ennio Cortese* (Roma) 3.59–73; revised English version, 'Innocent Until Proven Guilty: The Origins of a Legal Maxim', *The Jurist* 63 (2003) 106–24 (reprinted in: *The Penal Process and the Protection of Rights in Canon Law*, ed. P. M. Dugan [Montreal 2005] 45–66).

'Library of St. Gall', in: *International Dictionary of Library Histories*, ed. D. Stam (Chicago, IL) 2, 684–85.

Review of: Rosenwein, B. *Negotiating Space*, in: *American Historical Review* 106, 1435–36.

Review of: Drossbach, G. *Die 'Yconomica' des Konrad von Megenberg*, in: *Speculum* 76, 720–21.

Review of: Shepard, L. *Courting Power*, in: *The International History Review* 23, 638–39.

2002   'Pope Alexander III', *The Great Popes through History: An Encyclopedia* 1, 113–22.

'Bishops and Their Dioceses', *Folia canonica* 5, 7–17; also in: *Territorialità e personalità nel diritto canonico ed ecclesiastico: Il diritto canonico di fronte al terzo millennio: Atti dell'XI Congresso Internazionale di Diritto Canonico e del XV Congresso Internazionale della Società per il Diritto delle Chiese Orientali*, ed. P. Erdö and P. Szabó (Budapest) 123–35.

'Innocent IV, Pope', *New Catholic Encyclopedia* 7, 473–76.

'Frederick II, Emperor', *New Catholic Encyclopedia* 5, 926–28.

'Holy Roman Empire', *New Catholic Encyclopedia* 7, 42–44.

Review of: Bellamy, J. *The Criminal Trial in Later Medieval England*, in: *University of Toronto Quarterly* 71, 200–02.

Review of: Briggs, C. *Giles of Rome's De Regimine Principum*, in: *Manuscripta* 45/46, 169–71.

Review of: Tubbs, J. *The Common Law Mind*, in: *Speculum* 77, 1007–9.

Review of: Winroth, A. *The Making of Gratian's Decretum*, in: *The Historian* 65, 775–77.

2003   'Panormitanus' *Additiones* to *Novit ille* [X 2.1.13] in His Commentary on the *Decretales*', in: *'Ins Wasser geworfen und Ozeane durchquert': Festschrift für Knut Wolfgang Nörr*, ed. M. Ascheri et al. (Köln, Weimar, and Wien) 697–707; also in: RIDC 13 (2002) 39–51.

'Sovereignty and Rights in Medieval and Early Modern Jurisprudence: Law and Norms without a State', in: *Rethinking the State in the Age of Globalisation: Catholic Thought and Contemporary Political Theory*, ed. H. Justenhoven and J. Turner (Politik, Forschung und Wissenschaft 10; Münster) 117–41; also in: *Roman Law Formative of Modern Legal Systems: Studies in Honour of Wiesław Litewski*, ed. J. Sondel et al. (Kraków) 2, 25–36.

'Gratian, Causa 19, and the Birth of Canonical Jurisprudence', in: *La cultura giuridico-canonica medioevale: Premesse per un dialogo ecumenico*, ed. E. de Léon et al. (Roma) 215–36; expanded version in: *'Panta rei': Studi dedicati a Manlio Bellomo*, ed. O. Condorelli (Roma 2004) 4.339–55.

Review of: Winroth, A. *The Making of Gratian's Decretum*, in: *Speculum* 78, 293–97.

Review of: *The Papacy: An Encyclopedia*, ed. P. Levillain, in: *Speculum* 78, 943–46.

Review of: *Law and Theology in the Middle Ages*, ed. G. Evans, in: *Journal of Ecclesiastical History* 54, 339–40.

Review of: Gallagher, C. *Church Law and Church Order in Medieval Byzantium*, in: *The Jurist* 63, 431–32.

2004   'Was Baldus an Absolutist? The Evidence of His *Consilia*', in: *Politische Reflexion in der Welt des späten Mittelalters: Political Thought in the Age of Scholasticism: Essays in Honour of Jürgen Miethke*, ed. M. Kaufhold (Studies in Medieval and Reformation Thought 103; Leiden) 305–19.

'The Birth of the Modern Nation State in the Work of Helene Wieruszowski', in: *A Medievalist's Odyssey: Helene Wieruszowski, Scholar* (Uomini e dottrine 41; Roma) 17–23.

'Representation in Medieval Canon Law', *The Jurist* 64, 361–83.

'Albericus de Rosate', *Dictionary of the Middle Ages: Supplement* 1, 7.

'Gratian', *Dictionary of the Middle Ages: Supplement* 1, 246–47.

'Johannes Bassianus', *Dictionary of the Middle Ages: Supplement* 1, 295–96.

'Law, Feudal', *Dictionary of the Middle Ages: Supplement* 1, 320–23.

'Law, Criminal Procedure', *Dictionary of the Middle Ages: Supplement* 1, 309–20.

'Natural Law', *Dictionary of the Middle Ages: Supplement* 1, 417–20.

'Oldradus da Ponte', *Dictionary of the Middle Ages: Supplement* 1, 433.

'Rolandinus de Passageriis', *Dictionary of the Middle Ages: Supplement* 1, 540–41.

'The Formation of the Jurisprudence of the Feudal Oath of Fealty', in: RIDC 15, 57–76.

'Justice in the *Ius commune*', in: *Cristianesimo nella storia* 25, 897–902.

Review of: *Illuminating the Law*, ed. S. L'Engle and R. Gibbs, in: *Studies in Iconography* 25, 304–6.

Review of: Piazzoni, A. *Storia delle elezioni pontificie*, in: *Catholic Historical Review* 90, 730–32.

2005   'The Church from Pope Innocent III to Pope Gregory IX', in: *Domenico di Caleruega e la nascita dell'ordine dei frati predicatori, Todi, 10–12 ottobre 2004* (Spoleto) 25–37.

Review of: *Die Register Innocenz' III.: 8. Pontifikatsjahr, 1205/1206. Texte und Indices*, ed. O. Hageneder et al., in: ZRG Kan. Abt. 91, 813–17.

Review of: Lepsius, S. *Der Richter und die Zeugen*, in: *Speculum* 80, 263–65.

Review of: Meyer, C. *Die Distinktionstechnik in der Kanonistik des 12. Jahrhunderts*, in: *Speculum* 80, 282–84.

Review of: Nold, P. *Pope John XXII and His Franciscan Cardinal*, in: *American Historical Review* 110, 1239–40.

Contributors

Mario Ascheri, *Università di Roma III, Rome (Italy)*

Greta Austin, *University of Puget Sound, Tacoma, WA (USA)*

Manlio Bellomo, *Università di Catania, Catania (Italy)*

James A. Brundage, *University of Kansas, Lawrence, KS (USA)*

Orazio Condorelli, *Università di Catania, Catania (Italy)*

Charles Donahue, Jr., *Harvard University, Cambridge, MA (USA)*

Péter Erdö, *Pázmány Péter Katolikus Egyetem, Budapest (Hungary)*

Wilfried Hartmann, *Universität Tübingen, Tübingen (Germany)*

R. H. Helmholz, *University of Chicago, Chicago, IL (USA)*

Keith H. Kendall, *Northern Michigan University, Marquette, MI (USA)*

Lotte Kéry, *Universität Bonn, Bonn (Germany)*

Ludger Körntgen, *Universität Tübingen, Tübingen (Germany)*

Peter Landau, *Universität München, Munich (Germany)*

Carlos Larrainzar, *Universidad de La Laguna, Santa Cruz de Tenerife (Spain)*

Titus Lenherr, *Bistum Chur, Chur (Switzerland)*

Susanne Lepsius, *Universität Frankfurt, Frankfurt/M. (Germany)*

Charles de Miramon, *Centre National de Recherches Scientifiques, Paris (France)*

Jörg Müller, *Universität München, Munich (Germany)*

Wolfgang P. Müller, *Fordham University, New York City, NY (USA)*

Franck Roumy, *Université de Paris XI, Paris (France)*

Rudolf Schieffer, *Monumenta Germaniae Historica, Munich (Germany)*

Gerhard Schmitz, *Monumenta Germaniae Historica, Munich (Germany)*

List of Contributors

LUDWIG SCHMUGGE, *Universität Zürich, Zurich (Switzerland)*

ROBERT SOMERVILLE, *Columbia University, New York City, NY (USA)*

MARY E. SOMMAR, *Stephan Kuttner Institute of Medieval Canon Law, Munich (Germany)*

BRIAN TIERNEY, *Cornell University, Ithaca, NY (USA)*

ANDERS WINROTH, *Yale University, New Haven, CT (USA)*

Index

Medieval Church Law and the Origins of the Western Legal Tradition: A Tribute to Kenneth Pennington
was designed and typeset in Stoneprint by Kachergis Book Design of Pittsboro, North Carolina.

www.ingramcontent.com/pod-product-compliance
Lightning Source LLC
Chambersburg PA
CBHW021025210326
41598CB00016B/915